2020
RUGBY
ALMANACK

2020
RUGBY
ALMANACK

Edited by Clive Akers, Adrian Hill
& Campbell Burnes

Cover Photograph
Front: New Zealand Player of the Year, Ardie Savea. *Getty*

A catalogue record for this book is available from the National Library of New Zealand.

A Mower Book
Published in 2020 by Upstart Press Ltd
BDO Tower, Level 6/19 Como Street, Takapuna 0622
Auckland, New Zealand

ISBN 978-1-988516-82-0
© 2020 Text C.A. Akers, A.D. Hill and C.M. Burnes
The moral rights of the authors have been asserted.
© 2020 Upstart Press Ltd

Typesetting and design by CVD Limited (www.cvdgraphics.nz)
Printed by Printlink Ltd, Wellington

The editors welcome notification of any errors or omissions.

Please correspond directly with the editors:

Clive Akers
Opiki
RD4
Palmerston North 4474
Phone: 06 329 1822
email: akers@xtra.co.nz

Campbell Burnes
2/37 Grotto Street
Onehunga
Auckland 1061
Phone: 021 717 150
email: cmburnes@hotmail.com

Adrian Hill
1/212 Grove Road
Hastings 4122
email: adhill@xtra.co.nz

ACKNOWLEDGEMENTS

The publishers and editors acknowledge the assistance of the New Zealand Rugby Union and appreciate their co-operation and the co-operation of the 26 rugby unions in compiling the *2020 Rugby Almanack*.

KEY

In team record charts

RS	Ranfurly Shield
LC	Sir Brian Lochore Cup
MC	Sir Colin Meads Cup
P	Mitre 10 Cup Premiership
C	Mitre 10 Cup Championship
cr	Mitre 10 Cup crossover match
H	Mitre 10 Heartland Championship

In individual appearance charts

15	fullback
14	right wing
13	centre
12	second five-eighth
11	left wing
10	first five-eighth
9	halfback
8	number eight
7	open-side flanker
6	blind-side flanker
5	right lock
4	left lock
3	right (tighthead) prop
2	hooker
1	left (loosehead) prop
*	retired injured or substituted
s	substitute
t	includes penalty try

CONTENTS

EDITORIAL

Another bumper year in the New Zealand game culminated in the ninth Rugby World Cup, but the All Blacks fell, for the fourth time, at the semi-final stage.

While that disappointment tended to overshadow some of the good that happened in rugby through 2019, and was exacerbated by the All Blacks losing their No 1 world ranking for the first time since 2009, after no less than 509 weeks, the Black Ferns stayed atop the women's international game.

The Black Ferns Sevens provided the most consistent, compelling rugby of all the national teams, extending their winning streak in all matches to nigh on 50 before losing in April. They deservedly won the team of the year at the Halberg Awards, rare recognition for rugby at that event.

The All Blacks won eight of their 11 test matches but, as in 2017–18, they were often inconsistent, and in fact were poor in no less than four outings, highly unusual for this team. They did successfully blood four rookies, and still have enviable depth in most positions, barring No 8.

We were told not to panic after they placed a lowly third in the Investec Rugby Championship, their lowest finish since 1998. The 36–0 blanking of Australia to tie up the Bledisloe Cup for a 16th season proved a false dawn.

The World Cup campaign was mostly solid, disrupted as it was with the cancellation of the All Blacks' final pool match due to Typhoon Hagibis. The manner in which they dispatched Ireland with such style in the quarter-final meant widespread shock at the decisive defeat to England in the semi-final seven days later. While most pundits avoided the mud-slinging of past World Cups, we hope that the harsh lessons of that match are used to good effect in 2020 and onwards.

While the All Blacks' attack was not always in sync during 2019, we must tip our hat to the work of defence coach Scott McLeod. The team was as hard to score against as ever, notwithstanding the heavy loss in Perth.

Most of the discussion in the six weeks after the World Cup surrounded who would succeed Steve Hansen after an unparalleled eight years of success as head coach and 16 seasons with the All Blacks. While 26 individuals were "shoulder-tapped" to apply, it did seem strange that the contest swiftly morphed into a two-horse race. New Zealand Rugby opted for Ian Foster, the 2012–19 assistant, ahead of three-time Super Rugby winning-coach Scott Robertson. It was a vote for continuity, as has been the case since 2007.

Hansen was duly knighted in the New Year's honours, fair reward for a marvellous tenure. Also recognised in the honours, as an Officer of the New Zealand Order of Merit, was outgoing Chief Executive Steve Tew, who has put in a notable 12-year shift in the role. He has overseen times of great change in the game but has proven an able administrator and was able to help to secure important new revenue streams to fund the game and its top players.

Many breathed a sigh of relief when Sky TV won the broadcast rights to screen New Zealand rugby from 2021 to 2025. That followed high emotion during the World Cup when many fans did not have good viewing experiences with rights holders Spark Sport. It seemed strange that a company would pay big bucks, quoted by one source to be as high as $13 million, and then not be able to guarantee a seamless service. More work is needed before New Zealanders will be fully convinced about live streaming of their favourite sport.

The Black Ferns played six test matches and had one hiccup against France in the Super Series in San Diego. They look on track for their 2021 Rugby World Cup defence in this country. They will have access then to some of their top talent currently involved in the Black Ferns Sevens. This team goes from strength to strength and we applaud the decision by World Rugby to finally run an official women's tournament alongside the men in the New Zealand Sevens in Hamilton. Both this team and the All Blacks Sevens look in good shape heading into an Olympics year.

The Maori All Blacks and New Zealand Under 20s, conversely, need work. The Maori played poorly against Fiji in Suva but did hit back to take the international in Rotorua. We would like to see this team involved in both the July and November windows.

The Under 20s placed seventh at the World Rugby championship, their worst placing ever. They still perform one of their core aims of preparing young talent for the transition to professionalism, but to have three defeats in eight games (in all) does raise questions around selection and talent ID in an age grade where New Zealand has traditionally been very strong. The annual Jock Hobbs Memorial National Under 19 Tournament is still, however, a worthy and vital part of the calendar.

The Nations League proposal by World Rugby might have proven a revenue spinner from 2022, but much of the detail was never nailed down, and it did appear to again shut the Pacific nations out of the top tier, arousing strong emotions from prominent tier one players. The idea was shelved, especially as the idea of promotion/relegation left the likes of Scotland and Italy cold.

Media coverage of the game is now a major problem, though not for the All Blacks, who receive the lion's share. But with the squeeze on local, regional and national newspapers, we now have a dearth of coverage on all bar two levels of the game. Some papers, such as the *Otago Daily Times* and *Oamaru Mail*, still valiantly fly the local flag, but all too often the club and Heartland Championship scenes are now neglected or even ignored.

Furthermore, coverage of the Mitre 10 Cup has sharply declined in recent years. The nation's largest daily, which from 2014–16, at least, covered several areas of the game, now has eyes only for the All Blacks and Investec Super Rugby, doing a major disservice to the supporters of no less than three provincial unions in a region which houses a third of the country's population.

The internet may have changed the way rugby news is consumed, but there is a still thirst for good information and journalism. Even in these times of great flux in the media industry, all it needs is some enlightened management to redress the balance and make better use of admittedly thinner resources.

Happily, *Rugby News* magazine has taken up the cudgels in recent times and shines the light on the lower levels of the game and the many untold stories out of provincial, schools and club rugby.

The main interest for New Zealand Investec Super Rugby fans continues to centre on the local clashes. Once again four Kiwi teams reached the playoffs, and the Crusaders, though not as dominant as in 2018, won when it mattered, annexing a 10th championship.

This year's 25th edition of Investec Super Rugby will happily be the last in the current format. From 2021, it will revert to a 14-team round-robin competition, which is more equitable. This removes the problematic Sunwolves, but what of future expansion?

The Mitre 10 Cup continues to provide a vital third tier to our men's game. It is challenging for marketing departments in the provincial unions and still fails to attract large crowds, but the abolition of Wednesday fixtures was a step forward. Some unions are still struggling to balance the books, so perhaps the salary cap needs some further tightening.

The rugby itself, though competing with the World Cup for the last month, was always interesting, and is a proven ground for talent ID.

Tasman fully deserved its first Premiership title, uncorking the first unbeaten season since Auckland's class of 2007, while Bay of Plenty won promotion off the back of a compelling Championship season. Otago produced a stirring run of Ranfurly Shield defences with a depleted squad, and Canterbury did well to usurp its southern neighbour before edging North Harbour to lock away the Log O' Wood for the summer.

The Farah Palmer Cup added the Northland Kauri to the numbers, meaning Southland remains the sole Mitre 10 Cup union to not have a senior women's rep team. This competition received more television exposure than ever and is unearthing raw young talent, but needs careful nurturing and marketing.

It is disappointing that some Heartland Championship unions are still failing to ensure their paperwork when it comes to registering players, but the rugby itself still evokes local pride and passion. North Otago clinched the Meads Cup, and South Canterbury the Lochore Cup, a poignant moment after the passing of one of the great men of New Zealand rugby, Sir Brian Lochore.

Earlier in 2019, New Zealand Rugby released its commissioned review into secondary schools rugby. It is another area of the game that needs close attention. The flagship First XV competitions, which garner plenty of TV coverage, still produce good coaches, players and rugby. But lower grades need TLC and we hope to see the benefits of this in the coming seasons.

The abolition of the iconic Roller Mills northern region tournament for intermediate school children, after nearly a century, was a sad day for supporters and former players. There is much discussion among rugby people and on social media around how unions integrate young talent into junior rep rugby, but it seems most unions have now abolished rep teams lower than Under 16s.

Our heartfelt thanks go to New Zealand Rugby and the team managers of the national sides, franchises and provincial unions for assisting us with team sheets and information. The accuracy of this information is the foundation upon which the *Almanack* is built.

Individuals contributed vital information and copy, in particular Geoff Miller, Chris Jansen (referees), John Lea (overseas players), Rikki Swannell (women's rugby), Lindsay Knight, Brent Drabble, Matt Shaw and Kelly Plummer.

We look forward to the 150th jubilee, in May 2020, of the genesis of rugby in New Zealand.

Clive Akers, Adrian Hill, Campbell Burnes
January 2020

Geoff Miller had been co-editor of the Almanack since 1998 and through the 21 editions in which he was involved had produced some remarkable statistics to enhance the publication.

His passion for lists, statistics and milestones is well known and for many decades he has been regarded as the "stats man" of New Zealand rugby. Geoff's attention to detail and accuracy is extraordinary and every conversation one has with Geoff he always makes mention of a player's, or team's, milestone or unusual achievement "just as a matter of interest".

It is with some sadness that Geoff has chosen to retire as co-editor and we wish him well to enjoy watching rugby without the pressure of compiling another edition of the Almanack.

Campbell Burnes has kindly accepted the invitation to join the Almanack in place of Geoff. Campbell brings with him a wealth of rugby experience, a former first-class player, and journalist who early in 2019 became editor of *Rugby News*. We welcome Campbell to the publication as we endeavour to accurately record all the important events of the rugby year, played in New Zealand and by teams of New Zealanders overseas.

UNION DIRECTORY

New Zealand Rugby Union
Auckland office:
 4A, 125 The Strand, Parnell, Auckland
Postal: PO Box 2453, Shortland Street,
 Auckland 1140
Telephone: 09 300 4995
Wellington office:
 New Zealand Rugby House, Level 4,
 100 Molesworth Street, Wellington
Postal: PO Box 2172, Wellington 6140
Telephone: 04 499 4995
Fax: 04 499 4224
email: info@nzrugby.co.nz
Websites: www.allblacks.com
 www.nzrugby.co.nz

Auckland RU
Office: Eden Park, Walters Rd, Auckland
Postal: PO Box 56-152, Dominion Rd,
 Auckland 1446
Telephone: 09 815 4850
Fax: 09 849 5300
email: info@aucklandrugby.co.nz
Website: www.aucklandrugby.co.nz

Bay of Plenty RFU
Office: University of Waikato HP Centre,
 Blake Park, 52 Miro Street, Mt Manganui
Postal: PO Box 4058, Mt Maunganui South 3149
Telephone: 07 574 2037
Fax: 07 574 2046
email: reception@boprugby.co.nz
Website: www.boprugby.co.nz

Buller RFU
Office: Craddock Park, Domett Street
Postal: PO Box 361, Westport 7866
Telephone: 03 789 8330
Fax: 03 789 8330
email: andrew@bullerrugby.co.nz
Website: www.bullerrugby.co.nz

Canterbury RFU
Office: Rugby Park, Cnr Malvern and Rutland
 Streets, Christchurch
Postal: PO Box 755, Christchurch 8140
Telephone: 03 379 8300
Fax: 03 365 3565
email: info@crfu.co.nz
Website: www.crfu.co.nz

Counties Manukau RFU
Office: Navigation Homes Stadium,
 Stadium Drive, Pukekohe
Postal: PO Box 175, Pukekohe 2340
Telephone: 09 237 0033
Fax: 0800 478429
email: admin@steelers.co.nz
Website: www.steelers.co.nz

Hawke's Bay RFU
Office: 3 Orotu Drive, Poraiti, Napier
Postal: PO Box 201, Napier 4140
Telephone: 06 835 7617
Fax: 06 835 4630
email: admin@hbrugby.co.nz
Website: www.hbmagpies.co.nz

Horowhenua Kapiti RFU
Office: 15-19 Bristol Street, Levin
Postal: PO Box 503, Levin 5540
Telephone: 06 367 8059
email: office@hkrfu.co.nz
Website: www.hkrfu.co.nz

King Country RFU
Office: Cotter St, Te Kuiti
Postal: PO Box 159, Te Kuiti
Telephone: 07 878 7545
email: generalmanager@kingcountryrugby.co.nz

Manawatu RU
Office: Central Energy Trust Arena,
 61 Pascal Street, Palmerston North
Postal: PO Box 1729, Palmerston North 4440
Telephone: 06 357 2633
Fax: 06 354 1670
email: pamh@manawaturugby.co.nz
Website: www.manawaturugby.co.nz

Mid Canterbury RU
Office: A&P Showgrounds, Brucefield Avenue,
 Ashburton
Postal: PO Box 98, Ashburton 7740
Telephone: 03 308 8718
Fax: 03 308 0103
email: admin@midcanterburyrugby.co.nz
Website: www.midcanterburyrugby.co.nz

Ngati Porou East Coast RFU
Office: Whakarua Park, Ruatoria
Postal: PO Box 106, Ruatoria 4032
Telephone: 06 864 8812
Fax: 06 864 8813
email: admin@npec.co.nz
Website: www.npec.co.nz

North Harbour RU
Office: QBE Stadium, Stadium Drive, Albany
Postal: PO Box 300 492, Albany 0752
Telephone: 09 447 2100
Fax: 09 447 2101
email: harbour@harbourrugby.co.nz
Website: www.harbourrugby.co.nz

North Otago RFU
Office: Shop 6a, Thames Arcade,
 203 Thames Street, Oamaru
Postal: PO Box 102, Oamaru 9444
Telephone: 03 434 2053   *Fax:* 03 434 2054
email: admin@northotagorugby.co.nz
Website: www.northotagorugby.co.nz

Northland RU
Office: 50 Kioreroa Rd, Whangarei
Postal: PO Box 584, Whangarei 0140
Telephone: 09 438 4743
Fax: 09 438 9185
email: reception@northlandrugby.co.nz
Website: www.taniwha.co.nz

Otago RFU
Office: Forsyth Barr Stadium, Anzac Avenue,
Dunedin
Postal: PO Box 691, Dunedin 9054
Telephone: 03 477 0928
email: orfu@orfu.co.nz
Website: www.orfu.co.nz

Poverty Bay RFU
Office: River Oak Mews
74 Grey St, Gisborne
Postal: PO Box 520, Gisborne 4040
Telephone: 06 868 9968
Fax: 06 868 9954
email: karen@povertybayrugby.co.nz
Website: www.povertybayrugby.co.nz

Rugby Southland
Office: Surrey Park, Surrey Park Road,
Invercargill
Postal: PO Box 291, Invercargill 9840
Telephone: 03 216 8694
Fax: 03 216 8695
email: reception@rugbysouthland.co.nz
Website: www.rugbysouthland.co.nz

South Canterbury RFU
Office: Alpine Energy Stadium,
Church Street, Timaru
Postal: PO Box 787, Timaru 7910
Telephone: 03 688 8653
Fax: 03 688 6179
email: tracy@scrfu.co.nz
Website: www.scrfu.co.nz

Taranaki RFU
Office: Pukekura Raceway, Rogan Street,
New Plymouth
Postal: PO Box 5004, New Plymouth 4343
Telephone: 06 759 0167
email: rachael@trfu.co.nz
Website: www.trfu.co.nz

Tasman RU
Office: Hathaway Terrace, Nelson
Postal: PO Box 7157, Nelson 7042
Telephone: 03 548 7030
Fax: 03 548 8282
email: info@tasmanrugby.co.nz
Website: www.makos.co.nz

Thames Valley RFU
Office: 140a Normanby Rd, Paeroa
Postal: PO Box 245, Paeroa 3600
Telephone: 07 862 6352
Fax: 07 862 7577
email: swampfoxes@xtra.co.nz
Website: www.thamesvalleyswampfoxes.co.nz

Waikato RU
Office: FMG Stadium,
128 Seddon Road, Hamilton
Postal: PO Box 9507, Hamilton 3240
Telephone: 07 839 5675
Fax: 07 838 1713
email: admin@mooloo.co.nz
Website: www.mooloo.co.nz

Wairarapa Bush RFU
Office: 149 Dixon St, Masterton
Postal: PO Box 372, Masterton 5840
Telephone: 06 378 8369
Fax: 06 387 0012
email: info@waibush.co.nz
Website: www.waibush.co.nz

Wanganui RFU
Office: 40 Maria Place Extn, Wanganui
Postal: PO Box 4213, Wanganui 4541
Telephone: 06 349 2313
Fax: 06 347 8006
email: info@wanganuirugby.co.nz
Website: *www.*wanganuirugby.co.nz

Wellington RFU
Office: 191 Thorndon Quay, Wellington
Postal: PO Box 7201, Wellington South 6242
Telephone: 04 389 0020
Fax: 04 389 0889
email: mail@wrfu.co.nz
Website: www.wrfu.co.nz

West Coast RFU
Office: 123 Main South Rd, Greymouth
Postal: PO Box 31, Greymouth 7840
Telephone: 03 768 7822
email: wcrugby@netaccess.co.nz
Website: www.westcoastrfu.co.nz

New Zealand Rugby Museum
326 Main St, Palmerston North
Postal: PO Box 36, Palmerston North 4440
Telephone: 06 358 6947
Fax: 06 358 6947
email: info@rugbymuseum.co.nz
Website: www.rugbymuseum.co.nz

NEW ZEALAND RUGBY UNION

OFFICE BEARERS
2019–2020

Patron
Sir Brian Lochore ONZ, KNZM, OBE*

President
W.M. Osborne (*Tauranga*)

Vice-president
M.G. Spence (*Nelson*)

Chairman
B.G. Impey

Board

Elected members:	A.J. Golightly (*Northland*), J.S. Mitchell (*Canterbury*), S.R. Nixon (*North Harbour*), M.P. Robinson (*Taranaki*), Sir Michael Jones KNZM, MNZM (*Auckland*).
Appointed members:	R.P. Dellabarca (*Auckland*), B.G. Impey (*Auckland*), P.N. Kean (*Auckland*).
Maori representative:	Dr F.R. Palmer ONZM (*Manawatu*).

Chief Executive Officer
S.J. Tew

Life Members
R.A. Guy ONZM; E.J. Tonks CBE; R.A. Fisher ONZM;
J.A Sturgeon ONZM, MBE; Sir Brian Lochore ONZ, KNZM, OBE*;
A.R. Leslie MNZM; Sir Graham Henry KNZM; R.J. Littlejohn.

NZRU Team Coaches, Selectors

New Zealand:	S.W. Hansen (*coach*), I.D. Foster M. Cron, S.J. McLeod (*assistants*), G.J. Fox (*selector*).
New Zealand Under 20:	C.A. Philpott (*coach*), D. Hill (*assistant*), W.T.C. Rickards (*assistant*).
New Zealand Maori:	C.R. McMillan (*coach*), J.S. Maddock (*assistant*), R.Q. Randle (*assistant*).
New Zealand Heartland:	M.P. Rutene (*coach, Wairarapa Bush*), N.P. Walsh (*assistant, South Canterbury*), E.W. Kirton (*selector*).
New Zealand Sevens:	C. Laidlaw (*coach*), T. Cama (*assistant*).
New Zealand Secondary Schools:	M.G. Hammett (*coach*), S. Rasch, K. Harding (*assistants*).
New Zealand Women:	G.M. Moore (*coach*), W. Clarke (*assistant*), J. Haggart (*assistant*).
New Zealand Women's Sevens:	A.M. Bunting (*coach*).

*Died in office.

2019 HONOURS
THE ALMANACK NEW ZEALAND XV

Beauden Barrett
Hurricanes

Sevu Reece	Anton Lienert-Brown	George Bridge
Crusaders	*Chiefs*	*Crusaders*

Ngani Laumape
Hurricanes

Richie Mo'unga
Crusaders

Aaron Smith
Highlanderss

Kieran Read (capt)
Crusaders

Sam Cane	Samuel Whitelock	Scott Barrett	Ardie Savea
Chiefs	*Crusaders*	*Crusaders*	*Hurricanes*

Nepo Laulala	Codie Taylor	Joe Moody
Chiefs	*Crusaders*	*Crusaders*

Reserves –

Dane Coles (*Hurricanes*), Atu Moli (*Chiefs*), Tyrel Lomax (*Highlanders*), Brodie Retallick (*Chiefs*), Shannon Frizell (*Highlanders*), TJ Perenara (*Hurricanes*), Ryan Crotty (*Crusaders*), David Havili (*Crusaders*).

COMMENTS

The following comment on leading players is on those who appeared in Super Rugby, being the basis of selection for the All Blacks.

Fullback: Damian McKenzie appeared for the Chiefs initially at first five-eighth, continuing where he left off in 2018. A shift back to fullback made him more influential for the team, a circumstance that did, however, coincide with improved performances by the Chiefs forward pack. There is not much doubt he would have been All Blacks fullback in 2019 if it wasn't for his season-ending injury in April.

With their commitment to dual playmakers in the 10 and 15 jerseys, the All Blacks selectors then predictably placed Beauden Barrett at fullback even though he played all his 2019 rugby at first five-eighth for the Hurricanes. While he had played test rugby previously at the back it had never been for a full 80 minutes in a match. He showed he could defend well and still position himself as an optional first receiver. With his pace he was able to threaten from the back in the extra space available and was the official man of the match in the victories over South Africa and Ireland at the World Cup. The transition would have to be termed a successful one.

Ben Smith was his usual efficient self for the Highlanders and again placed on the wing by the All Blacks selectors. He ultimately found himself outside the first-choice All Blacks 23 after the loss to Australia in Perth. A hamstring injury against the Chiefs at Dunedin caused him to miss matches and on his return he was unable to reproduce his Highlanders form for the All Blacks.

The Crusaders' David Havili was the best performing New Zealand fullback in Super Rugby and entitled to feel disappointed at missing All Blacks selection, with the selectors again preferring the incumbent utility value offered by Jordie Barrett. Both the Hurricanes and the All Blacks used Barrett in four different positions, and for both teams his best displays came at fullback. His effort against the Chiefs at Wellington was probably the best individual fullback display of the year.

Melani Nanai benefitted from an injury to Michael Collins to play every game for the Blues, an opportunity that allowed him to produce his best ever form for the club.

A foot injury and the sublime form of David Havili restricted Will Jordan to only nine appearances for the Crusaders. Nevertheless, that was still enough games for this exciting talent to score eight tries. The Chiefs' Solomon Alaimalo was shifted to fullback after McKenzie's injury and was a little disappointing after an impressive season last year.

Wing three-quarters: Sevu Reece had a sensational debut season in Super Rugby. He only joined the Crusaders fulltime after round two due to the season-ending injury to Manasa Mataele, and proceeded to score the competition high 15 tries in 14 games. His All Blacks selection became automatic. On the left wing our choice is his Crusaders and All Blacks teammate George Bridge, who has probably the best all-round game of current New Zealand wings. He was always a threat out wide, was able to kick well defensively and his work rate was high, it not being unusual in the course of a match to see him appear in the midfield or even on the opposite wing in an attacking or defensive position.

After a handful of appearances off the bench last year Braydon Ennor gave some impressive exhibitions in a full season for the Crusaders including the scoring of 10 tries, second only to Reece. This led to a test debut against Argentina. He looked equally good at centre on the few occasions he played there, a position he has played first-class rugby in for Canterbury and New Zealand Under 20. For the Crusaders to get the full advantage from this trio a shift to centre would seem a logical move for next year (with Jack Goodhue to second five-eighth) as Ryan Crotty will be overseas.

Rieko Ioane played some very good rugby at times for the Blues, particularly in the first half of their season, and was their top try-scorer, but his form towards the end of Super Rugby and for the All Blacks did not approach this level. He was another to find himself outside the All Blacks first choice 23 after the loss to Australia at Perth.

The Highlanders' Waisake Naholo had a disappointing season, although a contributory factor was missing half the matches due to injury. In his debut season for the Chiefs 19-year-old Etene Nanai-Seturo showed glimpses of why NZR secured his services from rugby league last year with his five tries.

The Hurricanes pairing of Ben Lam and Wes Goosen was a threatening duo, although Lam did not hit the heights of last year and his defence was found wanting at times. Sadly, Nehe Milner-Skudder did not appear at all for the Hurricanes, enduring a shoulder injury.

Centre three-quarter: Like the All Blacks selectors, we found selecting both midfield positions to be a tough choice due to having to leave someone out rather than having to find someone to put in. Although he played most of his rugby at second five-eighth we have picked Anton Lienert-Brown as our centre. His brilliant form throughout the year just simply made him the best midfield back in the country. In the All Blacks three best performances of 2019 Lienert-Brown was at centre for two of them — the wins over Australia and South Africa.

Jack Goodhue played to a consistently high level all year for the champion Crusaders but did not show up to the same extent in the tests.

The Hurricanes' Matt Proctor was a reliable defender but was not as prominent on attack. For the Chiefs Tumua Manu had a steady debut season after four matches on the wing for the Blues last year.

Rob Thompson only regularly appeared for the Highlanders in the second half of their season and ran into form the further he went along. He never gives less than 100 per cent and remains an underrated player. TJ Faiane had his first full season for the Blues and was certainly an improved player at the end of it.

Second five-eighth: For the second year in a row due to injuries, Sonny Bill Williams hardly featured for the Blues, while at the World Cup his role in the three big games was as a second-half sub off the bench which were solid but not influential.

The leading performers in this position in Super Rugby were Anton Lienert-Brown, Ngani Laumape and Ryan Crotty. One of them was always destined to miss World Cup selection, and it turned out to be Ngani Laumape.

Crotty's defensive ability was superb throughout the year — a 93 per cent tackle rate in Super Rugby — and while selected for the World Cup his main contributions there were starting in the opening and bronze medal matches. Laumape's 13 tries for the Hurricanes was the second highest in the competition, then proved to be a huge asset for Manawatu in the Mitre 10 Cup as you would expect a test player to be. Having picked Lienert-Brown as our centre, our selection for second five-eighth is Laumape.

Ma'a Nonu was something of a surprise signing by the Blues, and although the 37-year-old was never likely to regain All Black honours, his experience proved to be a valuable commodity for the young backline around him.

First five-eighth: In a repeat of last year Richie Mo'unga had a brilliant season for the Crusaders as they won their tenth title. In the test arena he started off nervously against South Africa at Wellington but in the next two tests against Australia he played with authority, despite the contrasting scorelines, to dispel any doubts about his selection.

With Mo'unga proving his worth, the All Blacks selectors were able to confidently move Beauden Barrett to fullback in Damian McKenzie's absence. For the Hurricanes Barrett was again a key player and his shift to the Blues will leave a large gap for the capital team to fill.

Barrett and Mo'unga are the best players in this position in the country by a large distance currently. Josh Ioane benefited from a first full season for the Highlanders to earn a call-up to the All Blacks: unused against Argentina and 40 minutes against Tonga.

Halfback: The two established All Blacks maintained their position as the best in the country. For the fast-paced tempo the All Blacks choose to play, the speed and accuracy of pass Aaron Smith gets away upon his swift arrival to the breakdown was all there. His kicking game against Australia at Eden Park was superb and he had a strong World Cup tournament.

Having the captaincy for the majority of the Hurricanes season, when Dane Coles was injured, did not inhibit TJ Perenara at all. If anything, it spurred him on even more. He is a combative player defensively, aggressive for turnovers at the breakdown and involved in a lot of support play running, all of which adds something different to the All Blacks.

Brad Weber's form for the Chiefs was irresistible to the All Blacks selectors and he was deservedly picked as their third halfback. There were numerous inspiring runs carried by his speed, and his passing and kicking was accurate too. As a consequence, last year's All Black Te Toiroa Tahuriorangi found himself reduced to a bit-part role of just 17 per cent playing time with the Chiefs and overtaken in the All Blacks rankings.

At the Crusaders, Bryn Hall played some good games, again being preferred starter ahead of last year's All Black Mitchell Drummond.

Number eight: For the first time in three years Kieran Read had a season uninterrupted by injury, although he did have a contracted delayed start to his Crusaders campaign. His performances in the two tests against Australia answered his critics, and the form continued at the World Cup. In his third season for the Crusaders Whetu Douglas started at number eight in Read's absence, and he looks to have booked the position for next year. After a prominent season for the Hurricanes in 2018, this year Gareth Evans had one that was blighted by a calf injury. Luke Whitelock served the Highlanders well in his final year.

Canadian international Tyler Ardron played mainly in this position for the Chiefs and proved his value with a consistently high work rate around the field. He was moved into lock for the final month and Pita Gus Sowakula took over with excellent late-season form.

Akira Ioane continues to be an enigma. Despite the undoubted ability he has, his form was erratic over the season, including within games. He was in the All Blacks foundation camps held during Super Rugby, and played every game for the Blues, but the All Blacks coach fully explained his non-selection, citing their concern over lack of required fitness.

Flankers: This was another position where there were more contenders than available spots in national selection. Ardie Savea was the best player in the country this year regardless of playing position.

After the serious neck injury sustained against South Africa in October last year, Sam Cane returned for the Chiefs' final five games. By the end of them he was demonstrating his hoped for, expected form. The selection of these two openside flankers as dual starters for the All Blacks did not surprise anyone. Cane's selection on the bench for the lost World Cup semi-final was subsequently labelled by the All Blacks coach as a tactical error.

In his final season, Matt Todd had another good year. He made his test debut in 2013 and was certainly good enough to play more than the 25 tests he did play, it just being unfortunate for him his career coincided with a number of extremely talented players in the same hotly contested position.

With Sam Cane's unavailability for the first three months Lachlan Boshier had an opportunity for an extended run for the Chiefs and responded with his best season to date. He co-topped the try-scoring for the club (five) and topped their tackles made (169) at a success rate of 93 per cent.

Liam Squire had an unfortunate season. If things had gone to plan, as the incumbent he would likely have been the first-choice blindside flanker in the All Blacks, instead injury prevented him from playing all but the last three matches for the Highlanders. He ruled himself out of All Blacks selection as not being ready in an honest conversation with the All Blacks coach.

There were a number of candidates in contention for Squire's position in the All Blacks. Shannon Frizell (Highlanders), Luke Jacobson (Chiefs) and Dalton Papali'i (Blues) all served their clubs well with the selectors' choice falling on Jacobson for the World Cup. It was a disappointment the 22-year-old then had to withdraw just four days after the team's arrival in Japan due to the ongoing effects of concussion, with Frizell taking his place.

Tom Robinson had a highly promising debut season for the Blues that tailed off towards the end due to an ACL injury. After an excellent 2018, in which he only missed out on an All Blacks debut in the series against France because of injury, Jordan Taufua played every game for the Crusaders this year but national honours could very well now elude him as did not catch the selectors' eyes. The Hurricanes' Vaea Fifita is another who could find an All Blacks recall a tough proposition. His Super Rugby form was down compared to other candidates and his outing against Argentina was a poor one.

Locks: Scott Barrett had an immense season for the champion Crusaders and played impressively at the World Cup. Sam Whitelock was his usual consistent self throughout the year.

Brodie Retallick's season was unfortunately one of injuries. He missed half the Chiefs' season due to a wrist injury then against South Africa at Wellington he suffered a dislocated shoulder when cleaned out at a ruck. Although he played at the World Cup, he was clearly still working his way back to full match fitness.

The Blues season would have been a lot worse if Patrick Tuipulotu had not been in the tremendous form he was in, leading by example with his co-captaincy in the forwards' toils. An excellent performance against Australia at Auckland clinched his World Cup spot in a last chance, as he had not distinguished himself in the earlier tests he had appeared in.

Jackson Hemopo exhibited a number of fine performances with aggression and determination for the Highlanders, and he would seem to have missed World Cup selection in a straight choice between him and Patrick Tuipulotu. Tom Franklin had a delayed start for the Highlanders after returning from a season in Japan, but by the end of the campaign the locking partnership of him and Jackson Hemopo was the second best one in New Zealand Super Rugby.

After a solitary appearance last year Isaia Walker-Leaware looked very promising for the Hurricanes and has enormous potential.

Props: At the start of the year the All Blacks selectors put all props on notice that they wanted to see more work rate around the field from them, not just set-piece performances. They certainly meant it as Owen Franks, despite being the All Blacks' first-choice tighthead since 2010 and with 108 caps, missed World Cup selection.

Nepo Laulala (Chiefs), Angus Ta'avao (Chiefs) and Ofa Tu'ungafasi (Blues) all played to a similar level at tighthead for their respective clubs with Laulala getting the starts at the World Cup and Ta'avao coming off the bench. Both played well without setting the world alight. Ofa Tu'ungafasi was used by the All Blacks at loosehead off the bench, with the ability to cover both sides.

We see a long All Blacks career coming shortly for Tyrel Lomax who was the best New Zealand performer at tighthead in Super Rugby, his scrummaging and work around the field being of great value to the Highlanders. He has signed for the Hurricanes in 2020.

Joe Moody remains the best loosehead prop in the country. It was pleasing to see Atu Moli return to the Chiefs in April after 14 months out of the game when his career could have ended due to the haematoma on his left leg that subsequently required four operations. He produced the form the All Blacks selectors were after and against Canada at the World Cup played the whole 80 minutes, a rarity for a prop these days.

Karl Tu'inukuafe was unable to replicate last year's stellar form but still turned in some solid games for the Blues as did his teammate Alex Hodgman, the two men being in something of an alternating pattern at loosehead for the club.

Debuting for the Highlanders, Ayden Johnstone looked an interesting prospect, while for the second year in a row Kane Hames played no rugby at all for the Chiefs due to the ongoing effects of concussion.

Hooker: This position almost required a toss of the coin for us. Codie Taylor's form throughout the year was not the same high standard of recent years and Dane Coles has not played a full season in three years, so a return to his 2016 eminence was something of a long shot. As the incumbent and preferred starter in the key World Cup quarter-final and semi-final matches Taylor is our choice. Nevertheless, despite neither of them at peak form they are still clearly the top two hookers in the country.

Liam Coltman enjoyed a superb season at the Highlanders, his best ever. His work at the breakdown, ball carrying, and core roles in the scrum and throwing into the lineout were all of a high standard. He was the form New Zealand hooker in Super Rugby and his selection for the All Blacks was well merited.

Nathan Harris (Chiefs) and Ricky Riccitelli both failed to match their efforts of last year. From being third All Blacks hooker in 2018 Harris was not one of the four hookers picked when the 39-man All Blacks squad was announced in July, while Riccitelli could not make the match day 23 in the final month of the Hurricanes season.

FIVE PLAYERS OF THE YEAR

Scott Kevin Barrett (Crusaders/Taranaki) was a dominant figure for the Crusaders throughout their triumphant year of a third consecutive Super Rugby title. The lock played in 15 of their 18 games but missed the final due to a fractured finger sustained in the semi-final.

The injury caused him to miss the first two tests of the year and returned for the Australian test at Perth where he received a debatable red card (certainly yellow) just before halftime for connecting with Michael Hooper's head when tackling the falling player. He made up for it with big performances in the two important wins over South Africa and Ireland at the World Cup. He will take over the Crusaders' captaincy in 2020.

Scott Barrett was an Almanack Promising Player of the Year for 2014 and an Almanack Player of the Year last year.

David Keatau Havili (Crusaders/Tasman) was unlucky to miss All Blacks selection in 2019. He was the form New Zealand fullback in Super Rugby and even with his ability to cover midfield could not earn a spot as a utility back. However, this gave him the opportunity to captain Tasman to their maiden Mitre 10 Cup title, achieving it rather emphatically with the rare distinction of winning all 12 games. His second year of captaincy showed a growing influence on the team.

Born at Nelson on December 23, 1994 David was educated at Motueka High School 2008–11 and Nelson College in 2012. He played for the Motueka First XV in 2011, while at Nelson he spent the majority of 2012 in the Second XV, but did appear three times for the First XV.

Leaving school in 2013 he took up a builder's apprenticeship and joined the Nelson Club who went on to win the Tasman championship that year. There were also appearances for the Nelson Bays sub-union, Tasman Under 20 and Tasman Sevens rep teams.

David's first-class debut occurred in 2014 when he joined the New Zealand Under 20 team as an injury replacement during the World Championship in Auckland. He made his first appearances for Tasman, appearing in 10 matches as they finished runner up in the ITM Cup. The Almanack noted, "David Havili is a versatile back with a great future".

Signed by the Crusaders for 2015 he made 11 appearances in his first season for them. Two years later he only missed one of the Crusaders' 19 games, significantly retaining the fullback position in the final stages of their season with the return from injury of All Black Israel Dagg who was placed on the wing. This led to his All Blacks test debut off the bench against Argentina in Buenos Aires and further tests against South Africa in Cape Town and Australia in Brisbane. He concluded 2017 with All Blacks selection for their end of year northern tour where he played in the two non-test matches. To date, these remain his only five appearances for New Zealand.

His father Bill played 61 games for Nelson Bays 1993–98, scoring 19 tries.

The choice for the All Blacks midfeld positions at the World Cup was always going to end up with one of the five leading contenders missing selection. **Anton Russell Lienert-Brown** (Chiefs/Waikato) displayed compelling form with the Chiefs that at the halfway point of the Super Rugby season his selection for the World Cup already seemed a certainty. And so it was.

With the rush defence now the usual tactic employed against the All Blacks backline, Lienert-Brown always seemed the most likely to break through the opposition which he demonstrated in the important wins over South Africa and Ireland at the World Cup. His defence was top notch too.

Born at Christchurch on April 15, 1995 he was educated at Christchurch Boys High School and was in the First XV in his final two years of 2011–12. In 2012 Christchurch won the Press Cup as Crusaders Secondary School champions to play Otago Boys High School in the South Island playoff to determine which school would advance to the National Top Four. Lienert-Brown scored two tries in the first half, but in scoring the second he dislocated his shoulder. Christchurch lost the game and any possibility of Anton's selection in the NZ Secondary Schools team ended with that season-ending injury.

But there was a silver lining. The Chiefs were aware of his performances and enticed him north to Hamilton. He joined the Waikato University club for 2013, but did not play a game all year due to the shoulder still not being right, while undertaking a Sports and Leisure diploma.

In 2014 Anton made his first-class debut when appearing for the Chiefs against the Bulls at Pretoria. He is one of a small number of players whose NZ first-class debut has been made when playing for a Super Rugby team. It was the first of three Super Rugby appearances this year, and was followed by four matches for the New Zealand Under 20 team at the World Championship in New Zealand and nine appearances for Waikato in the ITM Cup. There were appearances for all three teams again in 2015.

2016 was the breakthrough year, establishing himself as a regular player in his third season for the Chiefs with 15 appearances in their 16 matches, which then led to the start of his All Blacks career where he played in nine of the 14 tests.

Elder brother Daniel plays for Canterbury and the Highlanders.

Koinonia Halafungani 'Ngani' Laumape (Manawatu) was in outstanding form scoring 13 tries for the Hurricanes and finishing the season with 19 tries, a tally equalled only by Sevu Reece. However, the strong-running second five-eighth was given little opportunity to exhibit his power for the All Blacks, scoring a try in his full game against Argentina but in the two tests against Australia, both as a substitute, he was given only 75 minutes of game-time.

He was considered a surprise omission from the Rugby World Cup squad but turned that disappointment into producing extraordinary displays for Manawatu. Seldom does one player have such an influence on lifting team performance.

Following four losses the arrival of Laumape saw Manawatu win its next three games, including a shock defeat of Canterbury. In his five games Manawatu won four, their only successes of the season. Laumape not only scored four tries, he was involved in several other team tries and his confident play lifted the form of those about him. His outstanding form in the Mitre 10 Cup had fans wondering, "Why is he not in Japan?" He was the saviour of Manawatu's season and it was commonly believed that the Turbos would have been winless without Laumape's presence.

Born at Palmerston North on April 22 1993, Ngani Laumape attended Central Normal Primary School and Palmerston North Boys' High School. In the First XV he formed a formidable midfield partnership with Jason Emery and the pair were chosen for the 2011 NZ Schools team.

League scouts hunted down the schoolboy and, disappointed in not being chosen for the Hurricanes Schools team, he accepted an offer from the Warriors. Laumape was in the junior team 2012 and the next year appeared for the Junior Kiwis and was promoted to the Warriors senior side. He played 30 games for the Warriors until suffering a season-ending injury in 2015 and he then chose a return to union.

Returning from league Laumape was immediately in the Hurricanes 2016 squad and his form in 2017, scoring 16 tries in 18 games, saw him promoted to the All Blacks, but he has been in the shadow of Williams and Crotty. He has now played 61 games for the Hurricanes, scoring 38 tries. All Blacks commitments have restricted his appearances for Manawatu to 19 games, scoring 14 tries. For New Zealand he has played 15 games (13 tests) and scored 10 tries. The still developing 26-year-old looks to be a destructive force in teams in coming seasons. He is contracted through to end of 2021.

Ardie Suemalo Savea (Hurricanes/Wellington) had another outstanding season in 2019 with numerous inspired performances in both the Hurricanes' and All Blacks' campaigns. Such was the form he displayed for the Hurricanes that the openside flanker just had to be in the All Blacks loose forward mix somewhere, being placed at blindside flanker for the majority of the tests in tandem with first choice openside flanker Sam Cane and captain Kieran Read.

At the World Cup it was almost commonplace for Savea to pack at number eight for the scrums in which New Zealand had the put in, regularly making ground with his strong leg drive running off the back. He was the All Blacks' best player in the semi-final loss to England, which followed near similar performances against South Africa and Ireland.

He seems set to miss the majority of the 2020 Super Rugby season, having undergone surgery in December on a knee injured in the World Cup semi-final.

Ardie Savea was an Almanack Promising Player of the Year for 2012 and an Almanack Player of the Year last year.

PROMISING PLAYERS
OF THE YEAR

*Qualification for consideration is usually players in their debut season
at first-class level or first full season.*

Leicester Ofa Ki Wales Twickenham Faingaanuku (Tasman) co-topped the try-scoring list for the Mitre 10 Cup champions with seven tries. The 107kg 1.88m left winger was fast and elusive, his size and power making him a hard man to bring to ground. He had started the season with his Crusaders debut off the bench against the Brumbies and five appearances for the New Zealand Under 20 team at the World Championship.

Born at Auckland on October 11, 1999 Leicester was schooled at Victory Primary school in Nelson, on to Nelson Intermediate and finished with five years at Nelson College 2013–17.

In 2014 he played for the Tasman Titans U15 rugby league team that was runner-up at the South Island tournament, earning the tournament's MVP award. The following year he debuted for the Nelson College rugby first XV and also played for the Tasman Titans U17 rugby league team at the South Island tournament, attracting interest from the Parramatta Eels NRL club. He ended 2015 making a commitment to rugby by signing a two-year development contract with the Tasman Mako.

In his three years in the First XV Nelson College won the Moascar Cup in 2016, then in 2017, despite Nelson College being eliminated in the semi-finals of the Crusaders Secondary Schools championship, and Leicester won the Phillip McDonald Memorial Medal for tournament MVP. In his last two years at Nelson College he was selected in the Tasman Under 18 and New Zealand Secondary Schools teams both years, and made First XV captain in 2017, emulating elder brother Tima of two years earlier.

Leicester joined Nelson club in 2018, his first year out of school, and made his first-class debut for the New Zealand Under 20 team at both the Oceania and World Championship tournaments. There was also representation for Tasman at the National Under 19 tournament as well as two appearances for Tasman in the Mitre 10 Cup, ending the year signing a three-year contract with the Crusaders for Super Rugby.

His father Malakai "Tau" played 12 tests at prop for Tonga 1999–2001, including three at the 1999 World Cup as well as representing Marlborough 2001–02 and Counties Manukau 2003–04. Brother Lotima "Tima" preceded Leicester into the Tasman, New Zealand Under 20 and Crusaders teams.

Dallas Alexander McLeod (Canterbury) had a season of great promise in 2019. Playing at second five-eighth he appeared in seven of the New Zealand Under 20's eight matches, his entire career to this point being in either five-eighth position. Picked in his first Mitre 10 Cup season he made nine appearances for Canterbury in the very unfamiliar position of right wing, adapting very well to score four tries and gain the Canterbury Rookie of the Year award. He finished the year with a Super Rugby contract for 2020 with the Crusaders.

Dallas was born at Christchurch on April 30, 1999 and was educated at Our Lady of the Snows School in Methven 2004–11, joining the Methven rugby club at the age of six. His secondary schooling was at Mount Hutt College in Methven for four years and one year (2016) at Christ's College in Christchurch. He made the

Ashburton Combined College's First XV in 2014 and 2015 and the Christ's College First XV in 2016.

In all four years at Mount Hutt College he was selected in Mid Canterbury age grade teams, with two years in the Under 14s (2012–13) and two years in the Under 16s (2014–15), being player of the year of the 2013–15 rep teams.

He enrolled at Canterbury University in 2017 to undertake a Bachelor of Sports Coaching majoring in Sport Science. Linking up with the Christchurch club he was straight into the Division One side and selected in the Canterbury Under 19 team for the 2017 and 2018 National Jock Hobbs tournaments.

At the 2016 Canterbury Secondary Schools Athletic Championship Dallas placed second in the senior boy's discus and third in the senior boy's shot put then at the South Island Secondary Schools event he finished third in the senior boy's discus.

Paternal grandfather Alan played 56 games for Mid Canterbury at lock and for the combined Hanan Shield Unions teams against the 1955 Wallabies and 1956 Springboks, maternal grandfather Nigel Marcon represented South Canterbury in 1969 on four occasions and uncle Murray McLeod, a first five-eighth, played 74 games for Mid Canterbury 1978–89 and South Island 1986.

Emoni Rokomoce Narawa (Bay of Plenty) was a standout for Bay of Plenty as they won promotion to the Premiership for 2020. Part of an outstanding back three that scored a number of spectacular tries, Emoni's nine tries made him the team's top try scorer and Opta Statistics recorded him making the most clean breaks (36) and carrying the ball the most metres (1027) in the Mitre 10 Cup competition.

Born at Suva, Fiji, on July 13, 1999 he attended Christian Mission Fellowship Primary School and Marist Brothers Primary School before enrolling at Queen Victoria High School in 2014. In 2016 he was part of the First XV that won the Deans Cup as Fiji national secondary schools champions.

A scholarship brought Emoni to Hamilton Boys High School in 2017 and was part of the First XV that finished runner-up to Hastings Boys High School in the national schools final. A shift to Bay of Plenty in 2018 followed, joining the Tauranga Sports club and appearing for the senior club side. He was selected in the Bay of Plenty Under 19 team that won the National Jock Hobbs tournament and went on to make his first-class debut for Bay of Plenty in their final Mitre 10 Cup match of 2018 against Northland. On the right wing he scored a try in the 29th minute with a step and a fend but 26 minutes later his rugby year ended abruptly with a broken ankle.

Oliver Matthew Norris (Waikato) took the opportunity presented when he appeared in his debut season for Waikato in the Mitre 10 Cup. The 19-year-old 1.94m 120kg loosehead prop played in all ten games, scrummaging well against the invariably more experienced tightheads he opposed and got himself involved around the field too. Earlier in the year he was first choice loosehead prop for the New Zealand Under 20 team at the Oceania and World Championships.

Born at Sydney on December 11, 1999 he attended Tauranga Primary School and Tauranga Intermediate then commenced secondary schooling at St Peters, Cambridge in 2013. In all three years in the First XV (2015–2017) his position was number eight but his selection in the Chiefs Under 18 team in 2017 saw a transition to prop.

Leaving school in 2018 he joined the Hautapu Club and was called into the New Zealand Under 20 team at the World Championship in France as an injury replacement for the final match. Selection into the Waikato Under 19 team for the National Jock Hobbs tournament and the Chiefs Under 20 team followed later in the year.

His brother Jacob is a current flanker for the Tasman Mako.

Ethan Joseph Roots (North Harbour) displayed very good form throughout 2019. His consistent displays for his club East Coast Bays were ultimately rewarded with the North Harbour premier club player of the year award, and it was this form that gained the 21-year-old 1.89m 112kg blindside flanker due selection for the first time into the North Harbour Mitre 10 Cup squad. He not only played all ten games for North Harbour, he played 797 of the 800 minutes. To play every minute of a Mitre 10 Cup season is a rare feat in modern day rugby, and even more particularly for a debutant. The only three minutes he missed were the final three minutes of the Tasman match due to front rower Ropate Rinakama receiving a yellow card (and therefore having to be replaced by Sione Mafileo for scrum safety) with Ethan being the player designated to go off to reduce North Harbour to the required 14 men.

To cap his year, he was picked up by the Crusaders for the 2020 Super Rugby season.

Ethan was born at North Shore on November 10, 1997 and attended St Johns School, Mairangi Bay before going to Rosmini College for both his intermediate and secondary schooling. The only year he played rugby at Rosmini was his final year (2015) when he captained the Second XV. Prior to that final year his rugby career consisted of just four years of junior rugby for the East Coast Bays club as a hooker.

Leaving school in 2016 he played for the East Coast Bays under 21 team for two years, gaining selection into the North Harbour Under 19 team in 2016 and the North Harbour Maori and Sevens teams in 2017. In 2018 he played for his club's premier team for the first time, and made the North Harbour B team.

Ethan had success in 2014 in Brazilian Jiu Jitsu. At the Pan Pacific Championship, Blue Belt 17 years old division, he won a gold medal for no GI and silver medal for GI. In the open no GI division he won a silver medal. He was NZ Grappler Intermediate champion for Blue Belt no GI.

Younger brother Jimmy played for the North Harbour Under 19 team at both the 2018 and 2019 Jock Hobbs Memorial National Under 19 tournament and debuted in the Mitre 10 Cup in 2019, playing alongside Ethan twice.

NEW ZEALAND REPRESENTATIVES 2019

Of the 39 All Blacks used in the 11 test matches of 2019, just four were making their debuts, while Atu Moli made his Test debut after appearing in a non-test match in 2017.

Details of the four new All Blacks are:

ENNOR, Braydon Maurice *born Auckland, July 16, 1997*
All Blacks #1184   New Zealand Under 20 2017 (5), Canterbury 2017 (10) 2018 (9), 2019 (5), Crusaders 2018 (8), 2019 (17), New Zealand 2019 (1)

IOANE, Joshua *born Auckland, July 11, 1995*
All Blacks #1185   Otago 2017 (11), 2018 (10), 2019 (8), Highlanders 2018 (9), 2019 (14), New Zealand Maori 2018 (3), New Zealand 2019 (1)

JACOBSON, Luke Brittain *born Cambridge, April 20, 1997*
All Blacks #1183   New Zealand Under 20 2016 (7), 2017 (8), Waikato 2017 (10), 2019 (1), Chiefs 2018 (13), 2019 (8), New Zealand 2019 (2)

REECE, Sevuloni Lasei *born Nadi (Fiji), February 13, 1997*
All Blacks #1182   Waikato 2016 (12), 2017 (10), 2018 (11), NZ Barbarians Provincial XV 2017 (1), Crusaders 2019 (14), New Zealand 2019 (7)

ALL BLACKS MANAGEMENT 2019

Head Coach:	Steve Hansen
Assistant Coach (Selector):	Ian Foster
Assistant Coach (Forwards):	Mike Cron
Assistant Coach (Defence):	Scott McLeod
Selector:	Grant Fox
Manager (Business):	Darren Shand
Manager (Leadership):	Gilbert Enoka
Coach (Strength and Conditioning):	Dr Nic Gill
Assistant Coach (Strength and conditioning):	Kim Simperingham
Player Development Manager:	Mike Anthony
Performance Analyst:	Jamie Hamilton
Assistant Performance Analyst:	Hayden Chapman
Doctor:	Dr Tony Page
Physiotherapist:	Peter Gallagher
Manual Therapist:	George Duncan
Nutritionist:	Katrina Darry
Team Services Manager:	Bianca Thiel
Media Manager:	Joe Locke
Logistics Manager:	James Iversen

TEST MATCH RECORDS OF 2019
NEW ZEALAND REPRESENTATIVES
ALL BLACKS CAREER RECORDS TO JANUARY 1, 2020

	Debut	Tests	Starts	Wins	Winning %	Tries	Conversions	Penalty Goals	Dropped Goals	Points
Beauden Barrett	2012	83	53	72	86.8	36	149	55	2	649
Jordie Barrett	2017	17	10	14	82.3	11	9	–	–	73
Scott Barrett	2016	36	18	28	77.8	5	–	–	–	25
George Bridge	2018	9	6	6	66.7	9	–	–	–	45
Sam Cane	2012	68	48	59	86.7	13	–	–	–	65
Dane Coles	2012	69	49	59	85.6	11	–	–	–	55
Liam Coltman	2016	8	1	7	87.5	–	–	–	–	0
Ryan Crotty	2013	48	35	42	87.5	12	–	–	–	60
Braydon Ennor	2019	1	–	1	100	–	–	–	–	0
Vaea Fifita	2017	11	7	10	90.9	2	–	–	–	10
Owen Franks	2009	108	98	91	84.2	–	–	–	–	0
Shannon Frizell	2018	9	8	8	88.9	2	–	–	–	10
Jack Goodhue	2018	13	12	8	61.5	3	–	–	–	15
Jackson Hemopo	2018	5	1	5	100	–	–	–	–	0
Josh Ioane	2019	1	–	1	100	–	4	–	–	8
Rieko Ioane	2016	29	25	23	79.3	24	–	–	–	120
Luke Jacobson	2019	2	–	2	100	–	–	–	–	0
Nepo Laulala	2015	26	17	22	84.6	–	–	–	–	0
Ngani Laumape	2017	13	6	10	76.9	8	–	–	–	40
Anton Lienert-Brown	2016	43	24	35	81.3	9	–	–	–	45
Atu Moli	2019	4	1	3	75	–	–	–	–	0
Joe Moody	2014	46	39	38	82.6	5	–	–	–	25
Richie Mo'unga	2018	17	10	13	76.4	3	45	9	–	132
Dalton Papali'i	2018	3	1	2	66.7	–	–	–	–	0
TJ Perenara	2014	64	16	54	84.3	13	–	–	–	65
Kieran Read	2008	127	120	107	84.2	26	–	–	–	130
Sevu Reece	2019	7	7	6	85.7	4	–	–	–	20
Brodie Retallick	2012	81	67	72	88.9	5	–	–	–	25
Ardie Savea	2016	44	19	36	81.8	9	–	–	–	45
Aaron Smith	2012	92	84	78	84.8	19	1	–	–	97
Ben Smith	2009	84	72	74	88.1	39	–	–	–	195
Angus Ta'avao	2018	14	3	11	78.6	1	–	–	–	5
Codie Taylor	2015	50	27	40	80	11	–	–	–	55
Matt Todd	2013	25	7	22	88	3	–	–	–	15
Patrick Tuipulotu	2014	30	11	25	83.3	3	–	–	–	15
Ofa Tuungafasi	2016	35	4	29	82.9	1	–	–	–	5
Brad Weber	2015	5	–	5	100	2	–	–	–	10
Sam Whitelock	2010	117	97	101	86.3	6	–	–	–	30
Sonny Bill Williams	2010	58	42	52	89.7	13	–	–	–	65

INVESTEC RUGBY CHAMPIONSHIP, BLEDISLOE CUP AND TONGA IN NZ

	Franchise	Date of Birth	Height	Weight	Tests at 1/1/19
B.J. (Beauden) Barrett	Hurricanes	27-05-91	1.87	91	73
J.M. (Jordie) Barrett	Hurricanes	17-02-97	1.96	101	9
S.K. (Scott) Barrett	Crusaders	20-11-93	1.97	111	29
G.C. (George) Bridge	Crusaders	01-04-95	1.85	96	1
S.J. (Sam) Cane	Chiefs	13-01-92	1.89	106	60
D.S. (Dane) Coles	Hurricanes	10-12-86	1.84	110	60
L.J. (Liam) Coltman	Highlanders	25-01-90	1.86	110	4
R.S. (Ryan) Crotty	Crusaders	23-09-88	1.81	94	44
B.M. (Braydon) Ennor	Crusaders	16-07-97	1.87	93	-
V.T.L. (Vaea) Fifita	Hurricanes	17-06-92	1.96	112	9
O.T. (Owen) Franks	Crusaders	23-12-87	1.85	122	106
S.M. (Shannon) Frizell	Highlanders	11-02-94	1.95	108	4
E.J. (Jack) Goodhue	Crusaders	13-06-95	1.87	98	7
J.N. (Jackson) Hemopo	Highlanders	14-11-93	1.94	113	3
J.R. (Josh) Ioane	Highlanders	11-07-95	1.76	85	-
R.E. (Rieko) Ioane	Blues	18-03-97	1.89	103	24
L.B. (Luke) Jacobson	Chiefs	20-04-97	1.91	107	-
N.E. (Nepo) Laulala	Chiefs	06-11-91	1.84	116	17
K.H. (Ngani) Laumape	Hurricanes	24-04-93	1.77	103	10
A.R. (Anton) Lienert-Brown	Chiefs	15-04-95	1.85	96	33
A. (Atu) Moli	Chiefs	12-06-95	1.89	125	-
J.P.T. (Joe) Moody	Crusaders	18-09-88	1.88	120	37
R. (Richie) Mo'unga	Crusaders	25-05-94	1.76	88	9
D.R. (Dalton) Papali'I	Blues	11-10-97	1.9	105	2
T.T.R. (TJ) Perenara	Hurricanes	23-01-92	1.84	90	55
K.J. (Kieran) Read	Crusaders	26-10-85	1.93	111	118
S.L. (Sevu) Reece	Crusaders	13-02-97	1.78	92	-
B.A. (Brodie) Retallick	Chiefs	31-05-91	2.04	123	75
A.S. (Ardie) Savea	Hurricanes	14-10-93	1.88	100	35
A.L. (Aaron) Smith	Highlanders	21-11-88	1.71	83	82
B.R. (Ben) Smith	Highlanders	01-06-88	1.86	94	76
C.J.D. (Codie) Taylor	Crusaders	31-03-91	1.83	106	41
A.W.F.(Angus) Ta'avao-Matau	Chiefs	22-03-90	1.94	128	3
M.B. (Matt) Todd	Crusaders	24-03-88	1.85	103	17
P.T. (Patrick) Tuipulotu	Blues	23-01-93	1.98	120	21
A.O.H.M. (Ofa) Tuungafasi	Blues	19-04-92	1.95	122	26
B.M. (Brad) Weber	Chiefs	17-01-91	1.75	75	1
S.L. (Samuel) Whitelock	Crusaders	12-10-88	2.02	122	108
S. (Sonny Bill) Williams	Blues	03-08-85	1.91	111	51

INVESTEC RUGBY CHAMPIONSHIP, BLEDISLOE CUP AND TONGA IN NEW ZEALAND 2019 ALL BLACKS APPEARANCES

ALL BLACKS 2019	Argentina	South Africa	Australia 1	Australia 2	Tonga	Totals
J. Barrett	11*	–	–	s	s	3
B. Barrett	10	15	15	15	10	5
B. Smith	15	14	14*	–	15*	4
Reece	14	–	–	14	14	3
Bridge	–	s	s	11	11	4
R. Ioane	–	11*	11	–	–	2
Ennor	s	–	–	–	–	1
Goodhue	–	13	13*	–	–	2
Lienert-Brown	13	s	12	13	13	5
Crotty	–	–	–	–	12	1
Laumape	12	–	s	s	–	3
Williams	–	12*	–	12*	–	2
Mo'unga	–	10	10	10*	–	3
J. Ioane	–	–	–	–	s	1
Perenara	–	9*	s	s	9*	4
A. Smith	9*	s	9*	9*	s	5
Weber	s	–	–	–	–	1
Read (capt)	–	8	8	8	8	4
Savea	8	–	6	6	6	4
Cane	7	–	7*	7*	–	3
Todd	–	7	s	s	7*	4
Papali'i	–	s	–	–	–	1
Jacobson	s	–	–	–	s	2
Frizell	–	6*	–	–	–	1
Fifita	6*	s	–	–	–	2
Hemopo	s	–	–	s	–	2
S. Barrett	–	–	4	–	s	2
Tuipulotu	5*	–	s	4*	4	4
Whitelock	–	5	5*	5	5*	4
Retallick	4	4*	–	–	–	2
Laulala	s	–	–	3*	3*	3
Franks	–	3*	3*	–	–	2
Ta'avao	3*	s	s	s	s	5
Moli	s	–	s	–	–	2
Tuungafasi	1*	s	–	s	s	4
Moody	–	1*	1*	1*	1*	4
Coles	2*	s	2*	2*	–	4
Taylor	-	2*	s	s	2*	4
Coltman	s	-	-	-	s	2

INDIVIDUAL SCORING

	Tries	Con	PG	DG	Points
B. Barrett	1	11	3	–	36
Mo'unga	1	6	3	–	26
Bridge	5	–	–	–	25
Crotty	2	–	–	–	10
Laumape	2	–	–	–	10
Reece	2	–	–	–	10
B. Smith	2	–	–	–	10
J. Ioane	–	4	–	–	8
Goodhue	1	–	–	–	5
R. Ioane	1	–	–	–	5
Lienert-Brown	1	–	–	–	5
Perenara	1	–	–	–	5
Read	1	–	–	–	5
Retallick	1	–	–	–	5
Savea	1	–	–	–	5
A. Smith	1	–	–	–	5
Taylor	1	–	–	–	5
Todd	1	–	–	–	5
Williams	1	–	–	–	5
Total	**26**	**21**	**6**	**0**	**190**
Opposition scored	9	7	9	0	86

INVESTEC RUGBY CHAMPIONSHIP, BLEDISLOE CUP AND TONGA IN NEW ZEALAND SCORING RECORD 2019

Played 5   Won 3   Drew 1   Lost 1   Points for 190   Points against 86

Date	Opponent	Location	Score	Tries	Con	PG	DG	Referee
Jul-20	Argentina (RC)	Buenos Aires	20–16	Laumape, Retallick	B. Barrett (2)	B. Barrett (2)		A. Gardner *(Australia)*
July 27	South Africa (RC)	Wellington	16–16	Goodhue	B. Barrett	Mo'unga (2), B. Barrett		N. Berry *(Australia)*
August 10	Australia (RC, BC)	Perth	26–47	R. Ioane, Lienert-Brown, Laumape, B. Barrett	Mo'unga (3)			J. Garces *(France)*
August 17	Australia (BC)	Auckland	36–0	Mo'unga, A. Smith, Williams, Reece, Bridge	Mo'unga (3), B. Barrett	Mo'unga		J. Peyper *(South Africa)*
September 7	Tonga	Hamilton	92–7	Bridge (4), B. Smith (2), Crotty (2), Reece, Taylor, Read, Perenara, Todd, Savea	B. Barrett (7), J. Ioane (4)			A. Gardner *(Australia)*

NEW ZEALAND v ARGENTINA

Test #581 Estadio Jose Amalfitani, Buenos Aires July 20, 2019

Won by New Zealand 20-16

NEW ZEALAND

Ben Smith

Sevu Reece	Anton Lienert-Brown	Jordie Barrett

Ngani Laumape

Beauden Barrett

Aaron Smith

Ardie Savea

Sam Cane (capt)	Patrick Tuipulotu	Brodie Retallick	Vaea Fifita
Angus Ta'avao		Dane Coles	Ofa Tuungafasi

Nahuel Tetaz Chaparro	Agustin Creevy	Juan Figallo
Marcos Kremer	Guido Petti	Tomas Lavanini	Pablo Matera (capt)

Javier Ortega Desio

Tomas Cubelli

Nicolas Sanchez

Jeronimo de la Fuente

Ramiro Moyano	Matias Orlando	Matias Moroni

Emiliano Boffelli

ARGENTINA

Reserves: New Zealand – Luke Jacobson (sub Fifita 57m), Jackson Hemopo (sub Tuipulotu 57m), Atu Moli (sub Tuungafasi 60m), Nepo Laulala (sub Ta'avao 60m), Liam Coltman (sub Coles 65m), Brad Weber (sub A. Smith 68m), Braydon Ennor (sub J. Barrett 68m); Josh Ioane unused

Argentina – Santiago Medrano (sub Figallo 48m), Julian Montoya (sub Creevy 48m), Mayco Vivaz (sub Chaparro 57m), Joaquin Tuculet (sub Boffelli 60m), Tomaz Lezana (sub Lavanini 64m), Matias Alemanno (sub Kremer 71m), Felipe Ezcurra (sub Cubelli 72m), Joaquin Diaz Bonilla (sub Sanchez 77m)

Referee: Angus Gardner (*Australia*)
Assistant referees: Andrew Brace (*Ireland*)
Alexandre Ruiz (*France*)
TMO: Graham Hughes (*England*)

Kickoff: 3.05pm
Attendance: 32,000
Conditions: Excellent

Scorers: New Zealand:
  Tries: Laumape, Retallick
  Conversions: B. Barrett (2)
  Penalties: B. Barrett (2)

Argentina:
  Try: Boffelli
  Conversion: Sanchez
  Penalties: Sanchez (2), Boffelli

Scoring: First half: 2m Sanchez penalty goal 0-3, 7m Boffelli penalty goal 0-6, 18m Laumape try, B. Barrett conversion 7-6, 21m Sanchez penalty goal 7-9, 23m B. Barrett penalty goal 10-9, 37m B. Barrett penalty goal 13-9, 39m Retallick try, B. Barrett conversion 20-9

Second half: 47m Boffelli try, Sanchez conversion 20-16

All Blacks Test debuts: Sevu Reece, Luke Jacobson, Atu Moli, Braydon Ennor

This was the All Blacks' 450th international win in 581 Tests.

NEW ZEALAND v SOUTH AFRICA

Test #582   Westpac Stadium, Wellington   July 27, 2019

Drawn 16-16

NEW ZEALAND

Beauden Barrett

Ben Smith   Jack Goodhue   Rieko Ioane

Sonny Bill Williams

Richie Mo'unga

TJ Perenara

Kieran Read (capt)

Matt Todd   Sam Whitelock   Brodie Retallick   Shannon Frizell

Owen Franks   Codie Taylor   Joe Moody

Steven Kitshoff   Malcolm Marx   Frans Malherbe

Pieter-Steph du Toit   Eben Etzebeth   Franco Mostert   Kwagga Smith

Duane Vermeulen (capt)

Faf de Klerk

Handre Pollard

Damian de Allende

Makazole Mapimpi   Lukhanyo Am   Cheslin Kolbe

Willie Le Roux

SOUTH AFRICA

Reserves: New Zealand – Ofa Tuungafasi (sub Moody 45m), Angus Ta'avao (sub Franks 45m), Anton Lienert-Brown (sub Williams 58m), Aaron Smith (sub Perenara 58m), George Bridge (sub Ioane 61m), Vaea Fifita (sub Retallick 61m), Dane Coles (sub Taylor 61m), Dalton Papali'i (sub Frizell 77m)

South Africa – Herschel Jantjies (sub de Klerk 45m), RG Snyman (sub Etzebeth 51m), Jesse Kriel (sub Am 51m), Francois Steyn (sub de Allende 56m), Trevor Nyakane (sub Malherbe 56m), Tendai Mtawarira (sub Kitshoff 59m), Francois Louw (sub K. Smith 68m), Bongi Mbonambi (sub Marx 70m)

Referee: Nic Berry (*Australia*)   Kickoff: 7.35pm
Assistant referees: Angus Gardner (*Australia*)   *Attendance:* 35,213
                 Shuhei Kubo (*Japan*)   *Conditions:* Fine, chilly
TMO: Rowan Kitt (*England*)

Scorers: New Zealand: *South Africa:*
   Try: Goodhue   *Try:* H. Jantjies
   Conversion: B. Barrett   *Conversion:* Pollard
   Penalties: Mo'unga (2), B. Barrett   *Penalties:* Pollard (3)

Scoring: First half: 3m Pollard penalty goal 0-3, 10m Pollard penalty goal 0-6, 37m Goodhue try, B. Barrett conversion 7-6

Second half: 49m Barrett penalty goal 10-6, 61m Pollard penalty goal 10-9, 67m Mo'unga penalty goal 13-9, 75m Mo'unga penalty goal 16-9, 79m Jantjies try, Pollard conversion 16-16

The All Blacks became the first team to pass 16,000 points in internationals.

NEW ZEALAND v AUSTRALIA
Bledisloe Cup

Test #583	Optus Stadium, Perth	August 10, 2019

Won by Australia 47-26

NEW ZEALAND

Beauden Barrett

Ben Smith	Jack Goodhue	Rieko Ioane

Anton Lienert-Brown

Richie Mo'unga

Aaron Smith

Kieran Read (capt)

Sam Cane	Sam Whitelock	Scott Barrett	Ardie Savea
Owen Franks	Dane Coles		Joe Moody

Scott Sio	Tolu Latu	Allan Alaalatoa
Lukhan Salakaia-Loto	Izack Rodda	Rory Arnold	Michael Hooper (capt)

Isi Naisarani

Nic White

Christian Lealiifano

Samu Kerevi

Marika Koroibete	James O'Connor	Reece Hodge

Kurtley Beale

AUSTRALIA

Reserves: New Zealand – Ngani Laumape (sub Goodhue 19m), Angus Ta'avao (sub Franks 50m), Patrick Tuipulotu (sub Cane 50m), Atu Moli (sub Moody 50m), Codie Taylor (sub Coles 56m), TJ Perenara (sub A. Smith 62m), George Bridge (sub B. Smith 64m), Matt Todd (sub Whitelock 71m)

Australia – Adam Coleman (sub Arnold 56m), Taniela Tupou (sub Alaalatoa 56m), Folau Fainga'a (sub Latu 64m), James Slipper (sub Sio 64m), Matt Toomua (sub Lealiifano 64m), Will Genia (sub White 69m), Tom Banks (sub Kerevi 71m), Luke Jones (sub Rodda 76m)

Referee: Jerome Garces (*France*)
Assistant referees: Jaco Peyper (*South Africa*)
Shuhei Kubo (*Japan*)
TMO: Marius Jonker (*South Africa*)

Kickoff: 5.45pm
Attendance: 61,241
Conditions: Fine

Scorers: New Zealand:
Tries: Ioane, Lienert-Brown, B. Barrett, Laumape
Conversions: Mo'unga (3)

Australia:
Tries: Hodge (2), Salakaia-Loto, White, Koroibete, Beale
Conversions: Lealiifano (2), Toomua (2)
Penalties: Lealiifano (3)

Scoring: First half: 7m Lealiifano penalty goal 0-3, 10m Hodge try, Lealiifano conversion 0-10, 13m Lienert-Brown try, Mo'unga conversion 7-10, 17m Ioane try 12-10, 28m Lealiifano penalty goal 12-13, 40m Lealiifano penalty goal 12-16

Second half: 46m Salakaia-Loto try 12-21, 49m White try 12-26, 55m B. Barrett try, Mo'unga conversion 19-26, 62m Koroibete try, Lealiifano conversion 19-33, 69m Hodge try, Toomua conversion 19-40, 71m Laumape try, Mo'unga con 26-40, 79m Beale try, Toomua conversion 26-47

This was the All Blacks' heaviest Test defeat and most points conceded in an international.

Red card to S. Barrett 40m.

NEW ZEALAND v AUSTRALIA
Bledisloe Cup
Eden Park, Auckland
Won by New Zealand 36-0

Test #584

August 17, 2019

NEW ZEALAND

Beauden Barrett

Sevu Reece

Anton Lienert-Brown

George Bridge

Sonny Bill Williams

Richie Mo'unga

Aaron Smith

Kieran Read (capt)

Sam Cane	Sam Whitelock	Patrick Tuipulotu	Ardie Savea
Nepo Laulala		Dane Coles	Joe Moody
Scott Sio		Tolu Latu	Allan Alaalatoa
Lukhan Salakaia-Loto	Izack Rodda	Adam Coleman	Michael Hooper (capt)

Isi Naisarani

Nic White

Christian Lealiifano

Samu Kerevi

Marika Koroibete

James O'Connor

Reece Hodge

Kurtley Beale

AUSTRALIA

Reserves: New Zealand – TJ Perenara (sub Smith 51m), Ofa Tuungafasi (sub Moody 52m), Codie Taylor (sub Coles 55m), Jordie Barrett (sub Mo'unga 58m), Angus Ta'avao (sub Laulala 63m), Matt Todd (sub Cane 65m), Ngani Laumape (sub Williams 65m), Jackson Hemopo (sub Tuipulotu 68m)

Australia – James Slipper (sub Sio 46m), Matt Toomua (sub Lealiifano 46m), Taniela Tupou (sub Alaalatoa 48m), Will Genia (sub White 51m), Folau Fainga'a (sub Latu 55m), Rob Simmons (sub Coleman 55m), Liam Wright (sub Salakaia-Loto 59m), Adam Ashley-Cooper (sub O'Connor 68m)

Referee: Jaco Peyper (*South Africa*) Kickoff: 7.35pm
Assistant referees: Matthew Carley (*England*) **Attendance:** 48,339
Shuhei Kubo (*Japan*) **Conditions:** Drizzle
TMO: Marius Jonker (*South Africa*)

Scorers: New Zealand:
Tries: Mo'unga, Smith, Williams, Reece, Bridge
Conversions: Mo'unga (3), B. Barrett
Penalty: Mo'unga

Scoring: First half: 3m Mo'unga penalty goal 3-0, 28m Mo'unga try, conversion 10-0, 32m Smith try, Mo'unga conversion 17-0

Second half: 45m Williams try, Mo'unga conversion 24-0, 66m Reece try, B. Barrett conversion 31-0, 76m Bridge try 36-0

This was the 16th straight season the All Blacks have held the Bledisloe Cup.

Yellow card to Dane Coles 36m.

NEW ZEALAND v TONGA

Test #585 FMG Stadium Waikato, Hamilton September 7, 2019

Won by New Zealand 92-7

NEW ZEALAND

Ben Smith

Sevu Reece Anton Lienert-Brown George Bridge

Ryan Crotty

Beauden Barrett

TJ Perenara

Kieran Read (capt)

Matt Todd Sam Whitelock Patrick Tuipulotu Ardie Savea

Nepo Laulala Codie Taylor Joe Moody

Siegfried Fisi'ihoi Siua Maile Siua Halanukonuka

Sione Kalamafoni Sam Lousi Leva Fifita Fotu Lokotui

Maama Vaipulu

Tane Takalua

Kurt Morath

Siale Piutau (capt)

Viliami Lolohea Mali Hingano Cooper Vuna

David Halaifonua

TONGA

Reserves: New Zealand – Josh Ioane (sub B. Barrett 40m), Scott Barrett (sub Whitelock 49m), Liam Coltman (sub Taylor 53m), Jordie Barrett (sub B. Smith 53m), Ofa Tuungafasi (sub Moody 53m), Angus Ta'avao (sub Laulala 54m), Luke Jacobson (sub Todd 54m), Aaron Smith (sub Perenara 60m)

NB. Crotty left the field but was not replaced at 65m

Tonga – Ma'afu Fia (sub Halanukonuka 40m), Afa Pakalani (sub Halaifonua 40m), Zane Kapeli (sub Lokotui 49m), James Faiva (sub Lolohea 54m), Vunipola Fifita (sub Fisi'ihoi 60m), Sione Anga'aelangi (sub Maile 62m), Leon Fukofuka (sub Hingano 62m), Dan Faleafa (sub L Fifita 64m)

Referee: Angus Gardner (*Australia*) Kickoff: 2.35pm
Assistant referees: Jordan Way (*Australia*) *Attendance:* 23,443
Damon Murphy (*Australia*) **Conditions:** Fine, windy
TMO: James Leckie (*Australia*)

Scorers: New Zealand:
Tries: Bridge (4), B.Smith (2), Crotty (2), Reece, Taylor, Read, Perenara, Todd, Savea
Conversions: B. Barrett (7), Ioane (4)

Tonga
Try: Piutau
Conversion: Takalua

Scoring: First half: 8m Reece try, B Barrett conversion 7-0, 16m B. Smith try, B. Barrett conversion 14-0, 19m Taylor try, B. Barrett conversion 21-0, 27m Bridge try 26-0, 33m Read try, B. Barrett conversion 33-0, 35m Perenara try, B. Barrett conversion 40-0, 38m B. Smith try, B. Barrett conversion 47-0, 40m Crotty try, B. Barrett conversion 54-0

Second half: 41m Bridge try 59-0, 45m Todd try 64-0, 47m Savea try, Ioane conversion 71-0, 52m Bridge try, Ioane conversion 78-0, 56m Bridge try, Ioane conversion 85-0, 64m Crotty try, Ioane conversion 92-0, 76m Piutau try, Takalua conversion 92-7

Yellow card to Sam Lousi 60m.

INVESTEC RUGBY CHAMPIONSHIP

Results

July 20	South Africa	35	Australia	17	Johannesburg
July 20	New Zealand	20	Argentina	16	Buenos Aires
July 27	New Zealand	16	South Africa	16	Wellington
July 27	Australia	16	Argentina	10	Brisbane
August 10	Australia	47	New Zealand	26	Perth
August 10	South Africa	46	Argentina	13	Salta

Final standings

Team	P	W	D	L	For	Against	Bonus	Total
South Africa	3	2	1	–	97	46	2	12
Australia	3	2	–	1	80	71	–	8
New Zealand	3	1	1	1	62	79	–	6
Argentina	3	–	–	3	39	82	2	2

Scoring distribution

Team	FOR					AGAINST				
	T	C	PG	DG	Pts	T	C	PG	DG	Pts
South Africa	11	9	8	–	97	4	4	6	–	46
Australia	9	7	7	–	80	10	9	1	–	71
New Zealand	7	6	5	–	62	8	6	9	–	79
Argentina	3	3	6	–	39	8	6	10	–	82
TOTALS	**30**	**25**	**26**	**0**	**278**	**30**	**25**	**26**	**0**	**278**

NEW ZEALAND AT RUGBY WORLD CUP 2019

	Union	Date of Birth	Height	Weight	Tests at 20/9/19
B.J. (Beauden) Barrett	Hurricanes	27-05-91	1.87	91	78
J.M. (Jordie) Barrett	Hurricanes	17-02-97	1.96	101	12
S.K. (Scott) Barrett	Crusaders	20-11-93	1.97	111	31
G.C. (George) Bridge	Crusaders	01-04-95	1.85	96	5
S.J. (Sam) Cane	Chiefs	13-01-92	1.89	106	63
D.S. (Dane) Coles	Hurricanes	10-12-86	1.84	110	64
L.J. (Liam) Coltman	Highlanders	25-01-90	1.86	110	6
R.S. (Ryan) Crotty	Crusaders	23-09-88	1.81	94	45
S.M. (Shannon) Frizell*	Highlanders	11-02-94	1.95	108	5
E.J. (Jack) Goodhue	Crusaders	13-06-95	1.87	98	9
R.E. (Rieko) Ioane	Blues	18-03-97	1.89	103	26
L.B. (Luke) Jacobson*	Chiefs	20-04-97	1.91	107	2
N.E. (Nepo) Laulala	Chiefs	06-11-91	1.84	116	20
A.R. (Anton) Lienert-Brown	Chiefs	15-04-95	1.85	96	38
A. (Atu) Moli	Chiefs	12-06-95	1.89	125	2
J.P.T. (Joe) Moody	Crusaders	18-09-88	1.88	120	41
R. (Richie) Mo'unga	Crusaders	25-05-94	1.76	88	12
T.T.R. (TJ) Perenara	Hurricanes	23-01-92	1.84	90	59
K.J. (Kieran) Read	Crusaders	26-10-85	1.93	111	122
S.L. (Sevu) Reece	Crusaders	13-02-97	1.78	92	3
B.A. (Brodie) Retallick	Chiefs	31-05-91	2.04	123	77
A.S. (Ardie) Savea	Hurricanes	14-10-93	1.88	100	39
A.L. (Aaron) Smith	Highlanders	21-11-88	1.71	83	87
B.R. (Ben) Smith	Highlanders	01-06-88	1.86	94	80
C.J.D. (Codie) Taylor	Crusaders	31-03-91	1.83	106	45
A.W.F.(Angus) Ta'avao-Matau	Chiefs	22-03-90	1.94	128	8
M.B. (Matt) Todd	Crusaders	24-03-88	1.85	103	21
P.T. (Patrick) Tuipulotu	Blues	23-01-93	1.98	120	25
A.O.H.M. (Ofa) Tuungafasi	Blues	19-04-92	1.95	122	30
B.M. (Brad) Weber	Chiefs	17-01-91	1.75	75	2
S.L. (Samuel) Whitelock	Crusaders	12-10-88	2.02	122	112
S. (Sonny Bill) Williams	Blues	03-08-85	1.91	111	53

*Luke Jacobson was replaced, due to concussion symptoms, by Shannon Frizell before the tournament.

NEW ZEALAND AT RUGBY WORLD CUP 2019

	South Africa	Canada	Namibia	Ireland	England	Wales	Totals
J. Barrett	–	14	10	s	s	s	5
B. Barrett	15	15	–	15	15	15	5
B. Smith	s	s	15	–	–	14	4
Reece	14	–	14*	14*	14	–	4
Bridge	11	–	11	11	11*	–	4
R. Ioane	–	11	s	–	–	11	3
Goodhue	–	13*	13*	13*	13*	–	4
Lienert-Brown	13	–	12	12	12	s	5
Crotty	12*	s	–	–	–	13*	3
Williams	s	12*	–	s	s	12*	5
Mo'unga	10*	10	–	10	10	10	5
Perenara	s	9*	s	s	s	–	5
A. Smith	9*	–	9*	9*	9*	9*	5
Weber	–	s	s	–	–	s	3
Read (capt)	8	8	–	8	8	8	5
Savea	6	s	8*	6	7	–	5
Cane	7*	–	7*	7*	s	7	5
Todd	–	7*	s	s	–	s	4
Frizell	s	6	6	–	–	6*	4
S. Barrett	5*	4*	–	s	6*	5*	5
Tuipulotu	s	5	s	–	s	s	5
Whitelock	4	s	5	5	5*	–	5
Retallick	–	–	4*	4*	4	4	4
Laulala	3*	s*	3	3*	3*	3*	6
Ta'avao	s	3*	s	s	s	s	6
Moli	–	1	–	–	–	s	2
Tuungafasi	s	s	s	s	s	–	5
Moody	1*	–	1*	1*	1*	1*	5
Coles	2*	–	s	s	s	2*	5
Taylor	s	s	2*	2*	2*	–	5
Coltman	–	2*	–	–	–	s	2

INDIVIDUAL SCORING

	Tries	Con	PG	DG	Points
Mo'unga	1	20	3	–	54
J. Barrett	3	8	–	–	31
B. Smith	4	–	–	–	20
B. Barrett	3	–	1	–	18
S. Barrett	2	–	–	–	10
Bridge	2	–	–	–	10
Lienert-Brown	2	–	–	–	10
Moody	2	–	–	–	10
Reece	2	–	–	–	10
A. Smith	2	–	–	–	10
Weber	2	–	–	–	10
Crotty	1	–	–	–	5
Frizell	1	–	–	–	5

	Tries	Con	PG	DG	Points
R. Ioane	1	–	–	–	5
Perenara	1	–	–	–	5
Savea	1	–	–	–	5
Ta'avao	1	–	–	–	5
Taylor	1	–	–	–	5
Todd	1	–	–	–	5
Whitelock	1	–	–	–	5
Williams	1	–	–	–	5
Totals	**36***	**28**	**4**	**0**	**250**
Opposition scored	6#	5	9	1	72

*Total includes one penalty try (worth 7 points)   #Total includes one penalty try (worth 7 points)

NEW ZEALAND AT THE RUGBY WORLD CUP 2019

Played 6   Won 5   Lost 1   Points for 250   Points against 72

Date	Opponent	Location	Score	Tries	Con	PG	DG	Referee
September 21	South Africa	Yokohama	23–13	S. Barrett, Bridge	Mo'unga (2)	Mo'unga (2), B. Barrett		J. Garces (France)
October 2	Canada	Oita	63–0	Weber (2), J. Barrett, B. Barrett, S. Barrett, Williams, Ioane, Frizell, penalty try	Mo'unga (8)			R. Poite (France)
October 6	Namibia	Tokyo	71–9	Reece (2), Lienert-Brown (2), B. Smith (2), Ta'avao, Moody, Whitelock, J. Barrett, Perenara	J. Barrett (8)			P. Gauzere (France)
October 19	Ireland (quarter-final)	Tokyo	46–14	A. Smith (2), B. Barrett, Taylor, Todd, Bridge, J. Barrett	Mo'unga (4)	Mo'unga		N. Owens (Wales)
October 26	England (semifinal)	Yokohama	7–19	Savea	Mo'unga			N. Owens (Wales)
November 1	Wales (bronze final)	Tokyo	40–17	B. Smith (2), B. Barrett, Crotty, Moody, Mo'unga	Mo'unga (5)			W. Barnes (England)

RUGBY WORLD CUP SCORING

POOL A

	P	W	D	L	TF	PF	PA	BP	Pts
Japan	4	4	–	–	13	115	62	3	19
Ireland	4	3	–	1	18	121	27	4	16
Scotland	4	2	–	2	16	119	55	3	11
Samoa	4	1	–	3	8	58	128	1	5
Russia	4	–	–	4	1	19	160	–	0

Date	Winner		Loser		Venue	Referee
September 20	Japan	30	Russia	10	Tokyo	N. Owens (Wales)
September 22	Ireland	27	Scotland	3	Yokohama	W. Barnes (England)
September 24	Samoa	34	Russia	9	Kumagaya	R. Poite (France)
September 28	Japan	19	Ireland	12	Shizuoka	A. Gardner (Australia)
September 30	Scotland	34	Samoa	0	Kobe	P. Gauzere (France)
October 3	Ireland	35	Russia	0	Kobe	J. Garces (France)
October 5	Japan	38	Samoa	19	Toyota	J. Peyper (South Africa)
October 9	Scotland	61	Russia	0	Shizuoka	W. Barnes (England)
October 12	Ireland	47	Samoa	5	Fukuoka	N. Berry (Australia)
October 13	Japan	28	Scotland	21	Yokohama	B. O'Keeffe (New Zealand)

POOL B

	P	W	D	L	TF	PF	PA	BP	Pts
New Zealand	3	3	–	–	22	157	22	2	16
South Africa	4	3	–	1	27	185	36	3	15
Italy	3	2	–	1	14	98	78	2	12
Namibia	3	–	–	3	3	34	175	–	2
Canada	3	–	–	3	2	14	177	–	2

Date	Winner		Loser		Venue	Referee
September 21	New Zealand	23	South Africa	13	Yokohama	J. Garces (France)
September 22	Italy	47	Namibia	22	Osaka	N. Berry (Australia)
September 26	Italy	48	Canada	7	Fukuoka	N. Owens (Wales)
September 28	South Africa	57	Namibia	3	Toyota	M. Raynal (France)
October 2	New Zealand	63	Canada	0	Oita	R. Poite (France)
October 4	South Africa	49	Italy	3	Shizuoka	W. Barnes (England)
October 6	New Zealand	71	Namibia	9	Tokyo	P. Gauzere (France)
October 8	South Africa	66	Canada	7	Kobe	L. Pearce (England)

*The New Zealand v Italy (scheduled for October 12 in Toyota) and Namibia v Canada (scheduled for October 13 in Kamaishi) matches were cancelled due to Typhoon Hagibis, each side being awarded two competition points

POOL C

	P	W	D	L	TF	PF	PA	BP	Pts
England	3	3	–	–	17	119	20	3	17
France	3	3	–	–	9	79	51	1	15
Argentina	4	2	–	2	14	106	91	3	11
Tonga	4	1	–	3	9	67	105	2	6
USA	4	–	–	4	7	52	156	–	0

Date	Winner		Loser		Venue	Referee
September 21	France	23	Argentina	21	Tokyo	A. Gardner (Australia)
September 22	England	35	Tonga	3	Sapporo	P. Williams (New Zealand)
September 26	England	45	USA	7	Kobe	N. Berry (Australia)
September 28	Argentina	28	Tonga	12	Osaka	J. Peyper (South Africa)
October 2	France	33	USA	9	Fukuoka	B. O'Keeffe (New Zealand)
October 5	England	39	Argentina	10	Tokyo	N. Owens (Wales)
October 6	France	23	Tonga	21	Kumamoto	N. Berry (Australia)
October 9	Argentina	47	USA	17	Kumagaya	P. Williams (New Zealand)
October 13	Tonga	31	USA	19	Osaka	N. Owens (Wales)

*The England v France match (scheduled for October 12 in Yokohama) was cancelled due to Typhoon Hagibis, each side being awarded two competition points

POOL D

	P	W	D	L	TF	PF	PA	BP	Pts
Wales	4	4	–	–	17	136	69	3	19
Australia	4	3	–	1	20	136	68	4	16
Fiji	4	1	–	3	17	110	108	3	7
Georgia	4	1	–	3	9	65	122	1	5
Uruguay	4	1	–	3	6	60	140	–	4

Date	Winner		Loser		Venue	Referee
September 21	Australia	39	Fiji	21	Sapporo	B. O'Keeffe (New Zealand)
September 23	Wales	43	Georgia	14	Toyota	L. Pearce (England)
September 25	Uruguay	30	Fiji	27	Kamaishi	P. Gauzere (France)
September 29	Georgia	33	Uruguay	7	Kumagaya	W. Barnes (England)
September 29	Wales	29	Australia	25	Tokyo	R. Poite (France)
October 3	Fiji	45	Georgia	10	Osaka	P. Williams (New Zealand)
October 5	Australia	45	Uruguay	10	Oita	M. Raynal (France)
October 9	Wales	29	Fiji	17	Oita	J. Garces (France)
October 11	Australia	27	Georgia	8	Shizuoka	P. Gauzere (France)
October 13	Wales	35	Uruguay	13	Kumamoto	A. Gardner (Australia)

PLAYOFFS

QUARTER-FINALS

October 19, Oita Stadium, Oita, 4.15pm
England 40 (May 2, Sinckler, Watson tries; Farrell 4 conversions, 4 penalty goals) defeated
Australia 16 (Koroibete try; Lealiifano conversions, 3 penalties)
Referee: Jerome Garces (France)

October 19, Tokyo Stadium, Tokyo, 7.15pm
New Zealand 46 (A. Smith 2, B. Barrett, Taylor, Todd, Bridge, J. Barrett tries; Mo'unga 4
conversions, penalty goal) defeated **Ireland 14** (Henshaw try, penalty try; Carbery conversion)
Referee: Nigel Owens (Wales)

October 20, Oita Stadium, Oita, 4.15pm
Wales 20 (Wainwright, Moriarty tries; Biggar 2 conversions, 2 penalty goals) defeated
France 19 (Vahaamahina, Ollivon, Vakatawa tries; Ntamack 2 conversions)
Referee: Jaco Peyper (South Africa)

October 20, Tokyo Stadium, Tokyo, 7.15pm
South Africa 26 (Mapimpi 2, de Klerk tries; Pollard conversion, 3 penalty goals) defeated
Japan 3 (Tamura penalty goal)
Referee: Wayne Barnes (England)

SEMIFINALS

October 26, International Stadium, Yokohama, 5pm
England 19 (Tuilagi try; Farrell conversion; Ford 4 penalty goals) defeated **New Zealand 7**
(Savea try; Mo'unga conversion)
Referee: Nigel Owens (Wales)

October 27, International Stadium, Yokohama, 6pm
South Africa 19 (De Allende try; Pollard conversion, 4 penalty goals) defeated **Wales 16** (Adams
try; Halfpenny conversion; Biggar 3 penalty goals)
Referee: Jerome Garces (France)

BRONZE FINAL

November 1, Tokyo Stadium, Tokyo, 6pm
New Zealand 40 (B. Smith 2, Moody, B. Barrett, Crotty, Mo'unga tries; Mo'unga 5 conversions)
defeated **Wales 17** (Amos, Adams tries; Patchell conversion, Biggar conversion)
Referee: Wayne Barnes (England)

FINAL

November 2, International Stadium, Yokohama, 6pm
South Africa 32 (Mapimpi, Kolbe tries; Pollard 2 conversions, 6 penalty goals) defeated
England 12 (Farrell 4 penalty goals)
Referee: Jerome Garces (France)

TEAMS FOR FINAL:

South Africa: Willie Le Roux (replaced by Frans Steyn), Cheslin Kolbe, Lukhanyo Am, Damian de Allende, Makazole Mapimpi, Handre Pollard, Faf de Klerk (Herschel Jantjies), Duane Vermeulen, Pieter-Steph du Toit, Siya Kolisi (capt) (Francois Louw), Lood de Jager (Franco Mostert), Eben Etzebeth (RG Snyman), Frans Malherbe (Vincent Koch), Bongi Mbonambi (Malcolm Marx), Tendai Mtawarira (Steven Kitshoff)

England: Elliot Daly, Anthony Watson, Manu Tuilagi, Owen Farrell (capt), Jonny May (Jonathan Joseph), George Ford (Henry Slade), Ben Youngs (Ben Spencer), Billy Vunipola, Sam Underhill (Mark Wilson), Tom Curry, Courtney Lawes (George Kruis), Maro Itoje, Kyle Sinckler (Dan Cole), Jamie George (Luke Cowan-Dickie), Mako Vunipola (Joe Marler)

RUGBY WORLD CUP

NEW ZEALAND v SOUTH AFRICA

Test #586

International Stadium, Yokohama September 21, 2019

New Zealand won by 23-13

NEW ZEALAND

Beauden Barrett

Sevu Reece   Anton Lienert-Brown   George Bridge

Ryan Crotty

Richie Mo'unga

Aaron Smith

Kieran Read (capt)

| Sam Cane | Scott Barrett | Sam Whitelock | Ardie Savea |
| Nepo Laulala | | Dane Coles | Joe Moody |

Steven Kitshoff   Malcolm Marx   Frans Malherbe

Pieter-Steph du Toit   Eben Etzebeth   Franco Mostert   Siya Kolisi (capt)

Duane Vermeulen

Faf de Klerk

Handre Pollard

Damian de Allende

Makazole Mapimpi   Lukhanyo Am   Cheslin Kolbe

Willie Le Roux

SOUTH AFRICA

Reserves: New Zealand – Patrick Tuipulotu (sub Cane 40m), Codie Taylor (sub Coles 40m), Ofa Tuungafasi (sub Moody 50m), Angus Ta'avao (sub Laulala 50m), Sonny Bill Williams (sub Crotty 50m), TJ Perenara (sub A. Smith 61m), Ben Smith (sub Mo'unga 66m), Shannon Frizell (sub S. Barrett 75m)

South Africa – Francois Louw (sub Kolisi 50m), Trevor Nyakane (sub Malherbe 54m), Jesse Kriel (sub Am 56m), Bongi Mbonambi (sub Marx 61m), Tendai Mtawarira (sub Kitshoff 67m), RG Snyman (sub Etzebeth 69m), Herschel Jantjies (sub de Klerk 71m), Malherbe (sub Nyakane 75m)

Referee: Jerome Garces (*France*)
Assistant referees: Romain Poite (*France*)
Karl Dickson (*England*)
TMO: Graham Hughes (*England*)

Kickoff: 6.45pm
Attendance: 63,649
Conditions: Fine

Scorers: New Zealand:
Tries: S. Barrett, Bridge
Conversions: Mo'unga (2)
Penalties: Mo'unga (2), B. Barrett

South Africa:
Try: Du Toit
Conversion: Pollard
Penalty: Pollard
DG: Pollard

Scoring: First half: 2m Pollard penalty goal 0-3, 22m Mo'unga penalty goal 3-3, 23m Bridge try, Mo'unga conversion 10-3, 27m S Barrett try, Mo'unga conversion 17-3

Second half: 47m du Toit try, Pollard conversion 17-10, 59m Pollard drop goal 17-13, 66m Mo'unga penalty goal 20-13, 72m B. Barrett penalty goal 23-13

The All Blacks recorded their 15th straight RWC victory and remain undefeated in pool play at Rugby World Cups.

RUGBY WORLD CUP

NEW ZEALAND v CANADA

Test #587 Oita Stadium, Oita October 2, 2019

Won by New Zealand 63-0

NEW ZEALAND

Beauden Barrett

Jordie Barrett Jack Goodhue Rieko Ioane

Sonny Bill Williams

Richie Mo'unga

TJ Perenara

Kieran Read (capt)

Matt Todd Patrick Tuipulotu Scott Barrett Shannon Frizell

Angus Ta'avao Liam Coltman Atu Moli

Djustice Sears-Duru Eric Howard Cole Keith

Lucas Rumball Evan Olmstead Conor Keys Matt Heaton

Tyler Ardron (capt)

Gordon McRorie

Peter Nelson

Ciaran Hearn

DTH van der Merwe Conor Trainor Jeff Hassler

Patrick Parfrey

CANADA

Reserves: New Zealand – Nepo Laulala (sub Ta'avao 25m), Brad Weber (sub Perenara 40m), Ryan Crotty (sub Goodhue 40m), Ben Smith (sub Williams 50m), Ofa Tuungafasi (sub Laulala 50m), Sam Whitelock (sub S. Barrett 70m), Ardie Savea (sub Todd 70m), Codie Taylor (sub Coltman 70m)

Canada – Andrew Quattrin (sub Howard 40m), Josh Larsen (sub Olmstead 45m), Jake Ilnicki (sub Keith 48m), Andrew Coe (sub Parfrey 51m), Mike Sheppard (sub Keys 60m), Phil Mack (sub McRorie 65m), Hubert Buydens (sub Sears-Duru 68m), Taylor Paris (sub van der Merwe 72m)

Referee: Romaine Poite (*France*) Kickoff: 7.15pm
Assistant referees: Pascal Gauzere (*France*) *Attendance:* 34,411
  Alexandre Ruiz (*France*) *Conditions:* Humid, under roof
TMO: Marius Jonker (*South Africa*)

Scorers: New Zealand:
  Tries: Weber (2), J. Barrett, B. Barrett,
  S. Barrett, Williams, Ioane, Frizell, penalty try
  Conversions: Mo'unga (8)

Scoring: First half: 4m penalty try 7-0, 8m J. Barrett try, Mo'unga conversion 14-0, 16m Williams try, Mo'unga conversion 21-0, 36m B. Barrett try, Mo'unga conversion 28-0

Second half: 41m Ioane try, Mo'unga conversion 35-0, 44m S. Barrett try, Mo'unga conversion 42-0, 47m Frizell try, Mo'unga conversion 49-0, 50m Weber try, Mo'unga conversion 56-0, 56m Weber try, Mo'unga conversion 63-0

The Barretts became the first trio of siblings to start a match together for New Zealand.

RUGBY WORLD CUP

NEW ZEALAND v NAMIBIA

Test #588
Tokyo Stadium, Tokyo
October 6, 2019

Won by New Zealand 71-9

NEW ZEALAND

Ben Smith

Sevu Reece | Jack Goodhue | George Bridge

Anton Lienert-Brown

Jordie Barrett

Aaron Smith

Ardie Savea

Sam Cane | Sam Whitelock (capt) | Brodie Retallick | Shannon Frizell

Nepo Laulala | Codie Taylor | Joe Moody

Andre Rademeyer | Torsten van Jaarsveld | AJ de Klerk

Prince Gaoseb | PJ van Lill | Tjiuee Uanivi | Thomasau Forbes

Janco Venter

Damian Stevens

Helarius Kisting

Johan Deysel (capt)

JC Greyling | Justin Newman | . Lesley Kim

Johan Tromp

NAMIBIA

Reserves: New Zealand – Patrick Tuipulotu (sub Retallick 30m), Angus Ta'avao (sub Cane 40m), Brad Weber (sub A. Smith 50m), Dane Coles (sub Taylor 50m), Ofa Tuungafasi (sub Moody 53m), Matt Todd (sub Savea 60m), Rieko Ioane (sub Goodhue 60m), TJ Perenara (sub Reece 66m)

Namibia – Johan Retief (sub van Lill 16m), Johan Coetzee (sub de Klerk 40m), Janry du Toit (sub Greyling 50m), Darryl de la Harpe (sub Deysel 56m), Adriaan Booysen (sub Forbes 61m), Obert Nortje (sub van Jaarsveld 66m), Eugene Jantjies (sub Stevens 66m), Nelius Theron (sub Rademeyer 75m)

Referee: Pascal Gauzere (*France*) | Kickoff: 1.45pm
Assistant referees: Luke Pearce (*England*) | *Attendance:* 48,354
Shuhei Kubo (*Japan*) | *Conditions:* Fine
TMO: Rowan Kitt (*England*)

Scorers: New Zealand: | *Namibia:*
Tries: Reece (2), Lienert-Brown (2), | Penalties: Stevens (3)
B. Smith (2), Ta'avao, Moody, Whitelock
J. Barrett, Perenara
Conversions: J. Barrett (8)

Scoring: First half: 3m Stevens penalty goal 3-0, 6m Reece try 5-3, 20m Lienert-Brown try 10-3, 26m Stevens penalty goal 10-6, 29m Stevens penalty goal 10-9, 35m Ta'avao try, J. Barrett conversion 17-9, B. Smith try, J. Barrett conversion 24-9

Second half: 42m Moody try, J. Barrett conversion 31-9, 46m Lienert-Brown try, J. Barrett conversion 38-9, 51m Reece try, J. Barrett conversion 45-9, 55m Whitelock try, J. Barrett conversion 52-9, 67m B. Smith try, J. Barrett conversion 59-9, 76m J. Barrett try, conversion 66-9, 78m Perenara try, 71-9

Yellow cards to Laulala 30m, and Tuungafasi 72m.

This was Sam Whitelock's 100th Test match victory in 115 Tests.

RUGBY WORLD CUP – Quarter-final

NEW ZEALAND v IRELAND

Test #589   Tokyo Stadium, Tokyo   October 19, 2019

Won by New Zealand 46-14

NEW ZEALAND

	Beauden Barrett	
Sevu Reece	Jack Goodhue	George Bridge
	Anton Lienert-Brown	
	Richie Mo'unga	
	Aaron Smith	
	Kieran Read (capt)	
Sam Cane	Sam Whitelock (capt) Brodie Retallick	Ardie Savea
Nepo Laulala	Codie Taylor	Joe Moody
Cian Healy	Rory Best (capt)	Tadhg Furlong
Peter O'Mahony	Iain Henderson James Ryan	Josh van der Flier
	CJ Stander	
	Conor Murray	
	Johnny Sexton	
	Robbie Henshaw	
Jacob Stockdale	Garry Ringrose	Keith Earls
	Rob Kearney	

IRELAND

Reserves: New Zealand – Scott Barrett (sub Cane 40m), Angus Ta'avao (sub Laulala 48m), Ofa Tuungafasi (sub Moody 48m), Sonny Bill Williams (sub Goodhue 52m), Matt Todd (sub Retallick 56m), TJ Perenara (sub A. Smith 60m), Dane Coles (sub Taylor 60m), Jordie Barrett (sub Reece 62m)

Ireland – Dave Kilcoyne (sub Healy 48m), Tadhg Beirne (sub Henderson 48m), Jordan Larmour (sub Kearney 52m), Rhys Ruddock (sub O'Mahony 56m), Andrew Porter (sub Furlong 60m), Niall Scannell (sub Best 62m), Joey Carbery (sub Sexton 62m), Luke McGrath (sub Murray 73m)

Referee: Nigel Owens (*Wales*)   Kickoff: 7.15pm
Assistant referees: Pascal Gauzere (*France*)   *Attendance:* 48,656
                    Angus Gardner (*Australia*)   *Conditions:* Fine
TMO: Graham Hughes (*England*)

Scorers: New Zealand: *Ireland:*
    Tries: A. Smith (2), B. Barrett, Taylor,   *Tries:* Henshaw, penalty
    Todd, Bridge, J. Barrett   Con: Carbery
    Conversions: Mo'unga (4)
    Penalty: Mo'unga

Scoring: First half: 6m Mo'unga penalty goal 3-0, 13m A. Smith try, Mo'unga conversion 10-0, 19m A. Smith try, Mo'unga conversion 17-0, 32m B. Barrett try 22-0

Second half: 48m Taylor try, Mo'unga conversion 29-0, 61m Todd try 34-0, 68m Henshaw try, Carbery conversion 34-7, 72m Bridge try, Mo'unga conversion 41-7, 76m penalty try 41-14, 78m J. Barrett try

This was the first RWC meeting between the two sides since 1995.

Yellow card to Todd 76m.

RUGBY WORLD CUP – Semi-final

NEW ZEALAND v ENGLAND

Test #590

International Stadium, Yokohama

October 26, 2019

Won by England 19-7

NEW ZEALAND

Beauden Barrett

Sevu Reece   Jack Goodhue   George Bridge

Anton Lienert-Brown

Richie Mo'unga

Aaron Smith

Kieran Read (capt)

Ardie Savea	Sam Whitelock	Brodie Retallick	Scott Barrett
Nepo Laulala		Codie Taylor	Joe Moody
Mako Vunipola		Jamie George	Kyle Sinckler
Tom Curry	Maro Itoje	Courtney Lawes	Sam Underhill

Billy Vunipola

Ben Youngs

George Ford

Owen Farrell (capt)

Jonny May   Manu Tuilagi   Anthony Watson

Elliot Daly

ENGLAND

Reserves: New Zealand – Sam Cane (sub S. Barrett 40m), Dane Coles (sub Taylor 50m), Jordie Barrett (sub Bridge 50m), TJ Perenara (sub A. Smith 54m), Angus Ta'avao (sub Laulala 54m), Sonny Bill Williams (sub Goodhue 54m), Ofa Tuungafasi (sub Moody 63m), Patrick Tuipulotu (sub Whitelock 67m)

England – Henry Slade (sub May 45m), Dan Cole (sub Sinckler 47m), George Kruis (sub Lawes 55m), Willi Heinz (sub Youngs 63m), Luke Cowan-Dickie (sub George 70m), Joe Marler (sub M. Vunipola 70m), Mark Wilson (sub Underhill 70m), Jonathan Joseph (sub Tuilagi 74m)

Referee: Nigel Owens (*Wales*)   Kickoff: 5pm
Assistant referees: Pascal Gauzere (*France*)   *Attendance:* 68,843
          Romain Poite (*France*)   *Conditions:* Fine
TMO: Marius Jonker (*South Africa*)

Scorers: New Zealand: England:
     Try: Savea   *Try:* Tuilagi
     Conversion: Mo'unga   Con: Farrell
          Penalties: Ford (4)

Scoring: First half: 2m Tuilagi try, Farrell conversion 0-7, 40m Ford penalty goal 0-10

Second half: 49m Ford penalty goal 0-13, 56m Savea try, Mo'unga conversion 7-13, 62m Ford penalty goal 7-16, 69m Ford penalty goal 7-19

This was the 50th Test match for Codie Taylor.

This was England's first win over the All Blacks at a Rugby World Cup.

It was also the All Blacks' first RWC defeat since the 2007 quarter-final against France, 18 straight victories.

RUGBY WORLD CUP – Bronze final

NEW ZEALAND v WALES

Test #591   Tokyo Stadium, Tokyo   November 1, 2019

Won by New Zealand 40-17

NEW ZEALAND

Beauden Barrett

Ben Smith   Ryan Crotty   Rieko Ioane

Sonny Bill Williams

Richie Mo'unga

Aaron Smith

Kieran Read (capt)

Sam Cane	Scott Barrett	Brodie Retallick	Shannon Frizell
Nepo Laulala		Dane Coles	Joe Moody

Nicky Smith	Ken Owens		Dillon Lewis
Justin Tipuric	Adam Beard	Alun Wyn Jones (capt)	James Davies

Ross Moriarty

Tomos Williams

Rhys Patchell

Owen Watkin

Josh Adams   Jonathan Davies   Owen Lane

Hallam Amos

WALES

Reserves: New Zealand – Liam Coltman (sub Coles 25m), Atu Moli (sub Moody 56m), Angus Ta'avao (sub Laulala 57m), Anton Lienert-Brown (sub Crotty 57m), Jordie Barrett (sub Williams 57m), Brad Weber (sub A. Smith 57m), Patrick Tuipulotu (sub S. Barrett 61m), Matt Todd (sub Frizell 61m)

Wales – Elliott Dee (sub Owens 44m), Rhys Carre (sub Smith 44m), Aaron Shingler (sub Moriarty 47m), Gareth Davies (sub Williams 47m), Dan Biggar (sub Patchell 47m), Jake Ball (sub AW Jones 57m), Hadleigh Parkes (sub Watkin 62m), Wyn Jones (sub Lewis 78m)

Referee: Wayne Barnes (*England*)   Kickoff: 6pm
Assistant referees: Pascal Gauzere (*France*)   *Attendance:* 48,842
         Jaco Peyper (*South Africa*)   *Conditions:* Fine, windy
TMO: Marius Jonker (*South Africa*)

Scorers: New Zealand: *Wales:*
     Tries: B. Smith (2), B. Barrett, Crotty,   *Tries:* Amos, Adams
     Moody, Mo'unga   *Conversions:* Patchell, Biggar
     Conversions: Mo'unga (5)   *Penalty:* Patchell

Scoring: First half: 5m Moody try, Mo'unga conversion 7-0, 13m B. Barrett try, Mo'unga conversion 14-0, 19m Amos try, Patchell conversion 14-7, 26m Patchell penalty goal 14-10, 32m B. Smith try, Mo'unga conversion 21-10, 40m B. Smith try, Mo'unga conversion 28-10

Second half: 42m Crotty try, Mo'unga conversion 35-10, 59m Adams try, Biggar conversion 35-17, 75m Mo'unga try 40-17

This was the final Test match for both Steve Hansen and Warren Gatland as head coaches of the respective sides.

U.K. BARBARIANS

Fiji was the 2019 opponent for the Barbarians in the club's annual Killik Cup match. Four days later the club played its first ever match against Brazil.

Five New Zealanders made first-class appearances for the team. Former All Black coach John Mitchell coached the Barbarians v Brazil; Warren Gatland coached the Barbarians against Wales.

Former Canterbury and Crusaders outside back Johnny McNicholl made his debut for Wales, having qualified through residence.

U.K. BARBARIANS 2019

		Fiji	Brazil	Wales	TOTAL
D.K. Havili	Tasman	15	15	–	2
A. Makalio	Tasman	s	2	–	2
S.T. Stevenson	North Harbour	–	–	15	1
B.D. Hall	North Harbour	–	–	9	1
M.D. Duffie	North Harbour	–	–	s	1

Date	Opponent	Location	Score	Tries	Con	PG	Referee
November 16	Fiji	Twickenham, London	31–33				T. Foley (England)
November 20	Brazil	Sao Paulo	47–22	Havili (2)			F. Anselmi (Argentina)
November 30	Wales	Cardiff	33–43	Stevenson			N. Owens (Wales)

NEW ZEALAND UNDER 20
WORLD RUGBY U20 CHAMPIONSHIP

It was not a season to remember, results-wise, for the New Zealand Under 20s, falling to their worst ever placing — seventh — in 12 years of the Junior World Championship.

Winning the tournament is, of course, one of two major goals of this team, the other being to develop players to move higher into the professional ranks and ultimately the All Blacks.

Worrying signs started in the Oceania tournament, losing 24–0 to Australia, which was eventual runner-up in Argentina. New Zealand was denied a late bonus point against South Africa in JWC pool play which would have secured passage to the semi-finals.

France won its second straight world title.

Pool A

June 4	Wales	30	Argentina	25	Rosario
	France	36	Fiji	20	Rosario
June 8	France	32	Wales	13	Rosario
	Argentina	41	Fiji	14	Santa Fe
June 12	Argentina	47	France	26	Rosario
	Wales	44	Fiji	28	Santa Fe

Pool B

June 4	Australia	36	Italy	12	Santa Fe
	Ireland	42	England	26	Santa Fe
June 8	Australia	45	Ireland	17	Santa Fe
	England	24	Italy	23	Santa Fe
June 12	Ireland	38	Italy	14	Santa Fe
	England	56	Australia	33	Santa Fe

Pool C

June 4	South Africa	43	Scotland	19	Rosario
	New Zealand	45	Georgia	13	Santa Fe
June 8	South Africa	48	Georgia	20	Rosario
	New Zealand	52	Scotland	33	Rosario
June 12	Georgia	17	Scotland	12	Rosario
	South Africa	25	New Zealand	17	Rosario

9th place semi-final

June 17	Italy	26	Scotland	19	Rosario
	Georgia	12	Fiji	8	Rosario

5th place semi-final

June 17	Wales	8	New Zealand	7	Rosario
	England	30	Ireland	23	Rosario

Semi-finals

June 17	Australia	34	Argentina	13	Rosario
	France	20	South Africa	7	Rosario

11th place playoff

June 22	Fiji	59	Scotland	34	Rosario

9th place playoff

June 22	Italy	29	Georgia	17	Rosario

7th place playoff

June 22	New Zealand	40	Ireland	17	Rosario

5th place playoff

June 22	England	45	Wales	26	Rosario

3rd place playoff

June 22	South Africa	41	Argentina	16	Rosario

Final

June 22	France	24	Australia	23	Rosario

In finishing 12th, Scotland was relegated to the Under 20 Trophy for 2020. In July Japan won the eight-team Under 20 Trophy tournament in Brazil and earned promotion to the 2020 World Championship in Italy.

NEW ZEALAND UNDER 20, 2019

Player	Union	DOB	Height	Weight	Games	Points
N.S. (Naitoa) Ah Kuoi	Wellington	07/10/1999	1.94	106	1	–
K.L. (Kaylum) Boshier	Taranaki	09/04/1999	1.87	100	6	5
F.W. (Ferg) Burke	Canterbury	03/09/1999	1.89	85	6	26
L.B. (Leroy) Carter	Bay of Plenty	24/02/1999	1.76	86	7	5
R.L. (Rob) Cobb	Auckland	08/04/1999	1.89	117	6	–
G.E. (George) Dyer	Waikato	22/10/1999	1.87	114	7	5
L.O.K.W.T. (Leicester) Faingaanuku	Tasman	11/10/1999	1.88	104	9	35
L.C.V (Chay) Fihaki	Canterbury	03/01/2001	1.87	97	1	5
S.U. (Samipeni) Finau	Waikato	10/05/1999	1.93	109	6	5
D.J. (Devan) Flanders	Hawke's Bay	20/07/1999	1.90	98	11	5
C. (Cole) Forbes	Bay of Plenty	10/08/1999	1.80	91	5	5
S.T. (Taufa) Funaki	Auckland	29/07/2000	1.72	91	7	5
S.J. (Sam) Gilbert	Canterbury	23/01/1999	1.89	94	1	5
C.J. (Cullen) Grace	Canterbury	20/12/1999	1.90	106	7	–
S.J. (Scott) Gregory	Northland	07/01/1999	1.88	106	11	10
K.J. (Kohan) Herbert	Bay of Plenty	19/10/1999	1.79	102	7	20
K.R. (Kianu) Kereru-Symes (c)	Hawke's Bay	28/02/1999	1.77	108	7	–
S.I. (Shilo) Klein	Canterbury	04/05/1999	1.76	106	8	10
L. (Lalomilo) Lalomilo	Bay of Plenty	12/02/1999	1.73	99	6	30
D.A.M (Dallas) McLeod	Canterbury	30/04/1999	1.88	99	7	10
E.J. (Jeriah) Mua	Bay of Plenty	11/10/1999	1.86	104	6	5
E.W.P.S. (Etene) Nanai-Seturo	Counties Man	20/08/1999	1.83	92	5	10
F.D. (Fletcher) Newell	Canterbury	01/03/2000	1.86	112	5	–
O.M (Ollie) Norris	Waikato	11/12/1999	1.92	122	8	10
S.C. (Simon) Parker	Waikato	06/05/2000	1.93	109	7	–
T. (Taine) Plumtree	Wellington	09/03/2000	1.95	108	7	10
B.D. (Billy) Proctor	Wellington	14/05/1999	1.87	96	12	10
I.A. (Isaiah) Punivai	Canterbury	01/12/2000	1.82	96	1	–
R.W.M. (Rivez) Reihana	Waikato	25/05/2000	1.89	94	7	53
J.M.P. (James) Thompson	Waikato	13/07/1999	1.91	106	1	–
D.S. (Danny) Toala	Hawke's Bay	23/03/1999	1.76	95	2	–
Q.P.C. (Quinn) Tupaea	Waikato	10/05/2000	1.86	97	7	20
K. (Pasi) Uluilakepa	Wellington	18/01/1999	1.90	135	14	5
T.P.O (Tupou) Vaa'i	Taranaki	27/01/2000	1.97	118	6	10
T.P.T. (Tamaiti) Williams	Canterbury	10/08/2000	1.92	134	5	15

Manager: Martyn Vercoe **Head coach:** Craig Philpott
Assistant coaches: Aaron Good, David Hill, Derren Witcombe, Tom Donnelly (Oceania only)

Leicester Fainga'anuku (injury) and Etene Nanai-Seturo (recalled by the Chiefs) were original selections for the Oceania Championship who withdrew before assembly and replaced by Isaiah Punivai and Chay Fihaki.

James Thompson joined the team at the Oceania Championship as a replacement for Naitoa Ah Kuoi who was injured in the opening match and returned home. Thompson did not take the field.

Rob Cobb, Chay Fihaki and James Thompson joined the team at the World Championship for the last match as injury replacements

NEW ZEALAND UNDER 20 AT WORLD RUGBY CHAMPIONSHIP 2019

	Georgia	Scotland	South Africa	Wales	Ireland	TOTALS
Forbes	15	–	15	–	15	3
Gregory	–	15	s	15	–	3
Nanai-Seturo	14	11	14	s	14	5
Lalomilo	–	14	s	14	–	3
Tupaea	13	12	–	13	12	4
McLeod	12	–	12	12	s	4
Proctor	s	13	13	s	13	5
Faingaanuku	11	s	11	11	11	5
Reihana	10	s	–	s	10	4
Burke	–	10	10	10	s	4
Carter	9	s	9	–	s	4
Funaki	s	9	–	9	9	4
Flanders	8	–	8	8	–	3
Parker	s	8	s	–	8	4
Herbert	7	s	7	7	–	4
Mua	s	7	–	–	7	3
Boshier	–	6	s	6	6	4
Finau	6	–	6	s	–	3
Vaa'i	–	5	5	5	5	4
Thompson	–	–	–	–	s	1
Plumtree	5	4	s	4	s	5
Grace	4	s	4	–	4	4
Newell	3	–	3	–	3	3
Williams	–	s	–	3	s	3
Uluilakepa	s	3	–	s	s	4
Kereru-Symes	2	s	2	2	–	4
Klein	s	2	s	s	2	5
Norris	1	s	1	1	1	5
Dyer	s	1	s	s	–	4
Cobb	–	–	–	–	s	1

INDIVIDUAL SCORING AT WORLD U20 TOURNAMENT

	Tries	Con	PG	DG	Points
Reihana	–	10	–	–	20
Burke	–	8	1	–	19
Lalomilo	3	–	–	–	15
Nanai-Seturo	2	–	–	–	10
Tupaea	2	–	–	–	10
Faingaanuku	2	–	–	–	10
Plumtree	2	–	–	–	10
Norris	2	–	–	–	10
Williams	2	–	–	–	10
Penalty try	1	–	–	–	7

	Tries	Con	PG	DG	Points
Dyer	1	–	–	–	5
Herbert	1	–	–	–	5
McLeod	1	–	–	–	5
Mua	1	–	–	–	5
Uluilakepa	1	–	–	–	5
Gregory	1	–	–	–	5
Totals	**24**	**18**	**1**	**0**	**161**
Opposition scored	13	5	7	0	68

NEW ZEALAND UNDER 20 AT OCEANIA TOURNAMENT 2019

	Fiji	Japan	Australia	TOTALS
Toala	15	–	s	2
Forbes	–	15	15	2
Lalomilo	14	13	14	3
Fihaki	–	14	–	1
Tupaea	13	s	13	3
McLeod	12	12	12	3
Gilbert	11	–	–	1
Gregory	–	11	11	2
Punivai	–	s	–	1
Burke	10	–	10	2
Reihana	s	10	s	3
Carter	9	s	9	3
Funaki	s	9	s	3
Flanders	8	–	–	1
Parker	s	8	s	3
Mua	7	s	s	3
Herbert	s	7	7	3
Finau	6	s	6	3
Boshier	–	6	8	2
Va'ai	5	–	5	2
Plumtree	–	5	s	2
Ah Kuoi	4	–	–	1
Grace	s	4	4	3
Uluilakepa	3	s	s	3
Newell	s	3	–	2
Williams	–	s	3	2
Klein	s	2	s	3
Kereru-Symes	2	s	2	3
Norris	1	–	1	2
Dyer	s	1	s	3

INDIVIDUAL SCORING AT OCEANIA TOURNAMENT

	Tries	Con	PG	DG	Points		Tries	Con	PG	DG	Points
Reihana	1	14	–	–	33	Funaki	1	–	–	–	5
Herbert	3	–	–	–	15	Gregory	1	–	–	–	5
Lalomilo	3	–	–	–	15	McLeod	1	–	–	–	5
Tupaea	2	–	–	–	10	Fihaki	1	–	–	–	5
Burke	–	2	1	–	7	Forbes	1	–	–	–	5
Gilbert	1	–	–	–	5	Williams	1	–	–	–	5
Finau	1	–	–	–	5						
Carter	1	–	–	–	5	**Totals**	**21**	**16**	**1**	**0**	**140**
Klein	1	–	–	–	5						
Vaa'i	1	–	–	–	5	Opposition scored*	5	2	4	0	43
Boshier	1	–	–	–	5						

Includes penalty try, worth seven points

NEW ZEALAND UNDER 20 TEAM RECORD 2019

Played 8   Won 5   Lost 3   Points for 301   Points against 139

Date	Opponent	Location	Score	Tries	Con	PG	DG	Referee
April 26	Fiji (O20)	Gold Coast	53–7	Tupaea (2), Gilbert, Finau, Carter, Lalomilo, Klein, Vaa'i	Reihana (3), Burke (2)	Burke		D. Tonks (Australia)
April 30	Japan (O20)	Gold Coast	87–12	Herbert (3), Lalomilo (2), Boshier, Funaki, Gregory, McLeod, Fihaki, Forbes, Reihana, Williams	Reihana (11)			K. Talemaivalagi (Fiji)
May 4	Australia (O20)	Gold Coast	0–24					J. Way (Australia)
June 4	Georgia (W20)	Santa Fe	45–13	Fainga'anuku, Tupaea, Dyer, Herbert, McLeod, Plumtree, Mua	Reihana (5)			A. Piardi (Italy)
June 8	Scotland (W20)	Rosario	52–33	Lalomilo (2), Uluilakepa, Gregory, Norris, Tupaea, Williams, Plumtree	Burke (6)			N. Amashukeli (Georgia)
June 12	South Africa (W20)	Rosario	17–25	Lalomilo, Penalty Try	Burke	Burke		D. Murphy (Australia)
June 17	Wales (W20)	Rosario	7–8	Vaa'i	Burke			C. Ridley (England)
June 22	Ireland (W20)	Rosario	40–17	Nanai-Seturo (2), Fainga'anuku, Norris, Klein, Williams	Reihana (5)			A. Piardi (Italy)

MAORI ALL BLACKS 2019

The Maori All Blacks had a two-match programme in July, a home and away series against Fiji who held a world ranking of ninth. Fiji's comprehensive win in Suva was their first win against the Maori All Blacks since 1957.

	Province	Date of Birth	Height	Weight	Games to 1/1/20
O.W. (Otere) Black	Manawatu	04/05/95	1.84	86	9
A.L. (Ash) Dixon (capt)	Hawke's Bay	01/09/88	1.80	103	16
W.H. (Whetu) Douglas	Canterbury	18/04/91	1.90	107	4
T.S.G. (Tom) Franklin	Bay of Plenty	13/08/90	2.00	110	9
J.K. (Jackson) Garden-Bachop *	Wellington	03/10/94	1.83	99	2
B.D. (Bryn) Hall	North Harbour	03/02/92	1.83	93	5
W.K. (Billy) Harmon *	Canterbury	23/12/94	1.87	104	3
N.P. (Nathan) Harris	Bay of Plenty	08/03/92	1.86	110	2
H.B.G. (Haereiti) Hetet	Waikato	10/07/97	1.84	128	1
J.S.C. (Jordan) Hyland	Northland	03/10/89	1.88	102	2
A.L. (Akira) Ioane	Auckland	16/06/95	1.94	113	13
M.R. (Mitch) Karpik	Bay of Plenty	02/06/95	1.86	103	5
T.S. (Tyrel) Lomax	Tasman	01/06/96	1.92	127	6
A.P. (Alex) Nankivell	Tasman	25/10/96	1.88	98	2
P.P.M. (Pari Pari) Parkinson	Tasman	12/09/96	2.04	119	5
R.J. (Reed) Prinsep	Canterbury	17/02/93	1.92	109	7
P.G. (Pouri) Rakete-Stones	Hawke's Bay	17/06/97	1.82	115	1
M.T. (Marcel) Renata	Auckland	24/02/94	1.89	118	12
J.L. (Jonathan) Ruru *	Auckland	02/02/93	1.84	94	3
F.H. (Fletcher) Smith	Waikato	01/03/95	1.80	88	2
S.T. (Shaun) Stevenson	North Harbour	14/11/96	1.92	96	7
T.T.H. (Te Toiroa) Tahuriorangi	Taranaki	31/03/95	1.74	85	3
R. (Rob) Thompson	Manawatu	02/08/91	1.84	103	8
S.T. (Sean) Wainui	Taranaki	23/10/95	1.91	102	7
T.T. (Tei) Walden	Taranaki	25/05/97	1.82	94	6
I.E.T. (Isaia) Walker-Leawere	Hawke's Bay	16/04/97	1.97	119	5
R.G. (Ross) Wright	Northland	25/08/86	1.80	113	6

*Did not take the field

When the squad was announced there was still one prop to be added. Elliot Dixon (Southland) and Ben May (Hawke's Bay) both withdrew injured after original selection, with Billy Harmon replacing Dixon, and May's withdrawal allowed both Haereiti Hetet and Pouri Rakete-Stones to join the squad.

Coach: Clayton McMillan
Assistant Coaches: Joe Maddock, Roger Randle
Manager: Tony Ward

INDIVIDUAL SCORING

	Tries	Con	PG	DG	Points
Wainui	3	–	–	–	15
Black	–	3	–	–	6
Thompson	1	–	–	–	5
Nankivell	1	–	–	–	5
Walker-Leawere	1	–	–	–	5
Totals	**6**	**3**	**–**	**–**	**36**
Opposition scored	6	4	2	–	44

MAORI ALL BLACKS 2019

	Fiji	Fiji	Totals
Smith	15*	s	2
Stevenson	14	15	2
Wainui	11	11	2
Hyland	s	14	2
Thompson	13	13*	2
Walden	12*	s	2
Nankivell	s	12	2
Black	10	10*	2
Tahuriorangi	9*	s	2
Hall	s	9*	2
Ioane	8*	s	2
Douglas	s	8	2
Karpik	7	7*	2
Prinsep	6	6	2
Franklin	5	4	2
Walker-Leawere	4*	s	2
Parkinson	s	5*	2
Lomax	3*	3*	2
Renata	s	s	2
Wright	1*	1*	2
Hetet	s	–	1
Rakete-Stones	–	s	1
Dixon (capt.)	2*	2*	2
Harris	s	s	2

*replaced during match

MAORI ALL BLACKS 2019

PLAYED 2   WON 1   LOST 1   POINTS FOR 36   POINTS AGAINST 44

Date	Opponent	Location	Score	Tries	Con	PG	DG	Referee
July 13	Fiji	Suva	10–27	Wainui (2)				D. Murphy *(Australia)*
July 20	Fiji	Rotorua	26–17	Wainui, Thompson, Nankivell, Walker-Leawere	Black (3)			N. Berry *(Australia)*

NEW ZEALAND UNIVERSITIES
v KANSAI UNIVERSITIES

University Oval, Dunedin   April 6, 2019

Won by NZU 32-29

NEW ZEALAND UNIVERSITIES

Caleb Makene
Lincoln

Taylor Haugh	Hamish Northcott	Te Rangatira Waitokia
Otago	*Massey*	*Massey*

Rameka Poihipi
Lincoln

Tyler Campbell
Waikato

Luke Donaldson
Lincoln

Kirk Tufuga (capt)
Massey

Hauwai McGahan	Joshua Hill	Antonio Shalfoon	Doug Juszczyk
Marist (NH)	*Otago*	*Lincoln*	*Massey*
Stanley Paese	Nic Souchon		Kilipati Lea
Waikato	*Lincoln*		*Otago*

Yuichiro Taniguchi	Mataena Ieremia	Yura Kokaji
Hisanobu Okayama	Syohei Ito Kenshi Yamamoto	Naoki Horibe
(capt)		

Asipeli Moala

Shinobu Fujiwara

Takuro Matsunaga

Siosaia Fifita

Haruto Kida	Viliame Tuidraki	Kosuke Naka

Nicholas Hohua

KANSAI UNIVERSITIES

Reserves: New Zealand Universities – Connor McLeod (*Otago*) sub Donaldson 45m, George Stratton (*Lincoln*) sub Poihipi 56m, Codi Rogers (*Waikato*) sub McGahan 56m, Kalin Felise (Marist, North Harbour) sub Shalfoon 56m, Frazer Harrison (*Auckland*) sub Kilipati-Lea 56m, Te Ariki Te Puni (*Auckland*) sub Souchon 56m, Maile Koloto (*Auckland*) sub Makene, 60m, Mamea Taimalie (*Otago*) sub Paese, 77m

Kansai Universities – Hisomitsu Shimada (sub Yamamoto 36m), Yota Kamimori (sub Taniguchi 72m), Syun Terawaki (sub Kokaji 72m), Keitaro Hitora (sub Fujiwara 75m)

Referee: Michael Woodhouse (*Otago*)

Scorers: New Zealand Universities:	*Kansai Universities:*
Tries: Haugh (2), Juszczyk, Donaldson, Waitokia	*Tries:* Kida (2), Ieremia, Moala, Naka
Conversions: Makene, McLeod	*Conversions:* Matsunaga (2)
Penalty: McLeod	

Yellow card to Felise 58m

Before the NZU team assembled, original selection Trent Lawn (Canterbury) withdrew due to injury and was replaced by Te Ariki Te Puni (Auckland).

Another original selection, prop Angus Williams (Otago) was called up by the Highlanders Bravehearts, who played Japan A the night before the NZU fixture. He was replaced by Mamea Taimalie (Otago).

The match, the first played by NZU in Dunedin since 1992, formed part of the University of Otago 150th jubilee celebrations. It needed a last-minute penalty goal by local lad and replacement halfback Connor McLeod to seal the NZU victory.

Kansai Universities were defeated 54-39 by Otago University on April 2 in Dunedin.

Manager: P.R. (Peter) Magson (*Lincoln*)
Coach: B.P. (Brendon) Timmins (*Otago*)
Assistant Coach: S.J. (Simon) Forrest (*Otago*)
Doctor: S.J. (Stephen) Williams (*Otago*)
Physio: J.D. (Jonathon) Moyle (*Auckland*)

NEW ZEALAND HEARTLAND

The New Zealand Heartland team assembled twice in 2019. Firstly for a one-off match against Samoa in August, and then for a three-match programme in November which contained the annual match v NZ Marist and two matches in Fiji.

Samoa held a world ranking of 16th at the time of the match.

The Fiji Vanua XV was selected from players in the Vodafone Vanua Championship, the Fiji B division provincial competition.

Of the 39 players used, Campbell Hart was the only player to play the maximum 320 minutes. James Lash increased his record points tally for the NZ Heartland team to 99. The only union not represented was Poverty Bay

	Union	Date of Birth	Height	Weight	Games*	Points*
S.A. (Scott) Cameron	Horowhenua Kapiti	02/08/1987	1.83	120	7	10
C.W. (Carl) Carmichael	King Country	16/03/1985	1.85	112	9	0
C.D. (Craig) Clare	Wanganui	19/08/1984	1.84	93	4	20
J.A. (Josh) Clark	North Otago	15/09/1986	1.92	105	4	0
R.K. (Ralph) Darling	North Otago	21/08/1986	1.78	115	18	10
A.W. (Anthony) Ellis	Buller	22/04/1991	1.81	123	3	0
T.R. (Tristan) Flutey	Wairarapa Bush	03/07/1998	1.77	86	1	0
J.W.P.R. (James) Goodger	Wairarapa Bush	27/05/1988	1.92	93	6	0
Hone Haerewa	Ngati Porou East Coast	29/05/1996	1.87	102	3	5
C.J. (Campbell) Hart	Wanganui	11/10/1991	1.94	107	6	5
H.T.W.K. (Himiona) Henare	Horowhenua Kapiti	24/09/1996	1.78	82	3	2
S.F. (Sione) Holani	West Coast	18/04/1986	1.75	102	6	10
L.D. (Lindsay) Horrocks	Wanganui	13/02/1990	1.78	87	7	0
T.J. (Tyler) Kearns	West Coast		1.88	112	3	0
N.J. (Nathan) Kendrick	Horowhenua Kapiti	13/11/1993	1.83	96	4	0
Meli Kolinisau	North Otago	20/03/1995	1.76	128	7	0
S.S. (Seta) Koroitamana	Mid Canterbury	01/06/1995	1.84	100	6	0
H.K. (Harry) Lafituanai	Thames Valley	13/10/992	1.90	90	1	0
A.D. (Aaron) Lahmert	Horowhenua Kapiti	17/02/1991	1.82	100	3	0
J.J. (James) Lash	Buller	16/01/1990	1.70	78	9	99
K.V. (Kalavini) Leatigaga	South Canterbury	01/11/1992	1.67	82	1	0
P.J. (Jeff) Lepa	Buller	10/09/1991	1.93	113	9	0
S.P. (Sam) Liebezeit	West Coast				3	0
Chulainn Mabbett-Sowerby	King Country	26/07/1994	1.90	109	2	0
L.J.M. (Lachie) McFadzean	Wairarapa Bush	14/02/1989	1.95	101	3	0
G.F. (Glen) McIntyre	Thames Valley	30/10/1990	1.83	112	3	5
M.W. (Miles) Medlicott	South Canterbury	12/06/1991	1.78	94	2	2
P.B. (Peni) Nabainivalu	Wanganui	06/03/1987	1.82	97	8	20
W.E. (Willie) Paia'aua	Horowhenua Kapiti	24/12/1992	1.73	90	10	25
Patrick Pati	North Otago	20/05/1999	1.75	86	3	5
T.C. (Tim) Priest	Wairarapa Bush	13/10/1987	1.71	75	7	24
B.D. (Brett) Ranga (capt.)	Thames Valley	19/01/1991	1.91	107	6	0
T.S. (Timoci) Seruwalu	Horowhenua Kapiti	09/01/1992	1.86	117	1	0

R.L. (Robbie) Smith	North Otago	24/05/1989	1.78	84	3	2
N.J.C. (Nick) Strachan	South Canterbury	04/12/1985	1.75	98	2	0
J.F. (Jaxon) Tagavaitau	Horowhenua Kapiti	10/08/1986	1.84	106	3	10
T.K. (Troy) Tauwhare	West Coast	12/01/1990	1.85	108	7	0
A.M. (Alex) Thrupp	King Country	15/08/1996	1.87	98	3	5
W.A. (Willie) Wright	South Canterbury	30/04/1992	1.75	87	7	22

*As at November 30, 2019

For the match v Samoa, original selections Mark Atkins and Adrian Wyrill (both Poverty Bay) withdrew after selection and replaced by Jeff Lepa and Aaron Lahmert respectively.

For the end of year tour, original selections Josh Clark (North Otago) and Reegan O'Gorman (South Canterbury) withdrew after selection and replaced by Sam Liebezeit and Lachie McFadzean.

Coach: M.P. (Mark) Rutene (*Horowhenua Kapiti*)
Assistant coach: N.G. (Nigel) Walsh (*South Canterbury*)
Manager: G.I. (Gavin) Hodder (*Wairarapa Bush*)
Physiotherapist: P.J. (Philippa) Masoe (*North Otago*)
Doctor: P.J. (Patrick) McHugh (*Poverty Bay*)

INDIVIDUAL SCORING

	Tries	Con	PG	DG	Points
Wright	2	1	–	–	12
Tagavaitau	2	–	–	–	10
Holani	1	–	–	–	5
Paia'aua	1	–	–	–	5
Pati	1	–	–	–	5
Haerewa	1	–	–	–	5
Thrupp	1	–	–	–	5
Lash	–	2	–	–	4
Smith	–	1	–	–	2
Medlicott	–	1	–	–	2
Henare	–	1	–	–	2
TOTALS	**9**	**6**	**0**	**0**	**57**
Opposition scored	14	7	1	0	87

NEW ZEALAND HEARTLAND, 2019

	Samoa	NZ Marist	Vanua XV	Vanua XV	TOTALS
C. Clare	15	–	–	–	1
P. Pati	–	15	s	11	3
H. Henare	–	s	15	15	3
H. Lafituanai	14*	–	–	–	1
W. Paia'aua	11	11	11	14*	4
K. Leatigaga	s	–	–	–	1
A. Thrupp	–	14*	–	s	2
T. Flutey	–	–	14*	–	1
P. Nabainivalu	13*	–	13	13*	3
T. Seruwalu	s	–	–	–	1
J. Tagavaitau	–	13	12*	s	3
S. Holani	12	12	s	12	4
J. Lash	10	–	–	–	1
T. Priest	–	10*	–	10*	2
M. Medlicott	–	s	10*	–	2
W. Wright	9*	s	9	s	4
L. Horrocks	s	–	–	–	1
R. Smith	–	9*	s	9	3
J. Lepa	8	–	–	–	1
C. Mabbett-Sowerby	–	8*	–	s	2
S. Koroitamana	7*	–	s	s	3
B. Ranga (capt)	6	6	8*	8*	4
A. Lahmert	s	–	–	–	1
N. Strachan	–	7*	–	–	1
N. Kendrick	–	s	7	7	3
H. Haerewa	–	s	6	6*	3
C. Hart	5	4	4	4	4
J. Clark	4*	–	–	–	1
J. Goodger	s	–	–	–	1
S. Liebezeit	–	5*	s	5	3
L. McFadzean	–	s	5*	–	2
S. Cameron	3*	–	–	–	1
C. Carmichael	1*	1	s	s	4
M. Kolinisau	s	3*	s	s	4
R. Darling	s	s	1*	1*	4
T. Kearns	–	s	3*	3*	3
T. Tauwhare	2*	–	2	s	3
G. McIntyre	s	–	–	–	1
A. Ellis	–	2*	–	2*	2

* replaced during match

NEW ZEALAND HEARTLAND, 2019

PLAYED 4 WON 1 LOST 3 POINTS FOR 57 POINTS AGAINST 87

Date	Opponent	Location	Score	Tries	Con	PG	Referee
August 31	Samoa	Auckland	19-36	Wright, Holani, Paia'aua	Lash (2)		P. Williams
November 2	NZ Marist (MacRae Cup)	Te Aroha	19–29	Pati, Wright, Tagavaitau	Smith, Wright		R. Mahoney
November 6	Vanua XV	Lautoka	12–7	Haerewa, Tagavaitau	Medlicott		S. Loga (Fiji)
November 9	Vanua XV	Sigatoka	7–15	Thrupp	Henare		A. Drekeni (Fiji)

Photo by Bruce Jarvis Photographic Services Ltd

ALL BLACKS 2019 INVESTEC RUGBY CHAMPIONSHIP AND BLEDISLOE CUP

BACK ROW: G. Enoka (*Manager — Leadership*), G. Duncan (*Muscle Therapist*), A. Page (*Doctor*), C. Taylor, A. Ta'avao-Matau, J. Hemopo, J. Barrett, V. Fifita, P. Tuipulotu, O. Tu'ungafasi, D. Papali'i, M. Cron (*Asst Coach*), S. McLeod (*Asst Coach*), N. Gill (*S&C Coach*). *THIRD ROW:* J. Hamilton (*Analyst*) J. Ioane, R. Mo'unga, M. Todd, N. Laulala, B. Ennor, L. Coltman, R. Ioane, S. Frizell, L. Jacobson, J. Goodhue, A. Aumua, J. Locke (*Media Manager*), K. Simperingham (*Asst S&C Coach*). *SECOND ROW:* I Foster (*Asst Head Coach*), B. Thiel (*Team Services Manager*), N. Laumape, S. Reece, J. Moody, K. Tu'inukuafe, A. Savea, A. Lienert-Brown, G. Bridge, A. Moli, B. Webber, G. Fox (*Selector*), P. Gallagher (*Physio*). *FRONT ROW:* S. Williams, D. Coles, B. Barrett, O. Franks, B. Smith, K. Read (*Captain*), S. Hansen (*Head Coach*), S. Whitelock, B. Retallick, S. Cane, T. Perenara, A. Smith. *INSETS:* S. Barrett, J. Iversen (*Logistics Manager*), D. Shand (*Manager — Business & Operations*), K. Darry (*Nutritionist*), H. Chapman (*Asst Performance Analyst*).

Photo by Bruce Jarvis Photographic Services Ltd

ALL BLACKS 2019 RUGBY WORLD CUP

BACK ROW: A. Page (*Doctor*), G. Enoka (*Manager — Leadership*), J. Moody, A. Moli, A. Ta'avao-Matau, J. Barrett, S. Barrett, P. Tuipulotu, O. Tu'ungafasi, S. McLeod (*Asst Coach*), N. Gill (*S&C Coach*), K. Simperingham (*Asst S&C Coach*). **THIRD ROW**: J. Hamilton (*Performance Analyst*), K. Darry (*Nutritionist*), J. Iversen (*Logistics Manager*), N. Laulala, C. Taylor, L. Coltman, R. Ioane, L. Jacobson, J. Goodhue, M. Cron (*Asst Coach*), D. Shand (*Manager — Business & Operations*), J. Locke (*Media Manager*), J. Malcolm (*Asst Media Manager*). **SECOND ROW**: I. Foster (*Asst Head Coach*), B. Thiel (*Team Services Manager*), B. McLean (*Opposition Analyst*), S. Reece, R. Mo'unga, A. Lienert-Brown, A. Savea, G. Bridge, M. Todd, B. Weber, H. Chapman (*Asst Performance Analyst*), G. Fox (*Selector*), P. Gallagher (*Physio*), G. Duncan (*Muscle Therapist*). **FRONT ROW**: T. Perenara, D. Coles, R. Crotty, B. Barrett, B. Smith, K. Read (*Captain*), S. Hansen (*Head Coach*), S. Whitelock, B. Retallick, S. Cane, S. Williams, A. Smith. **INSET**: S. Frizell.

Photo by Bruce Jarvis Photographic Services Ltd

BLACK FERNS 2019

International Series —v Canada, USA, France, England & Australia

BACK ROW: J. Haggart (*Asst Coach*), A-P. Nelson, K. Faneva, C. Alley, O. Ward-Duin, C. Smith, P. Tapsell, J. Ngan-Woo, J. Patea-Fereti, J. Tout (*S&C Coach*). **THIRD ROW:** K. Cottrell, A. Marino-Tauhinu, K. Moata'ane, T. Natua, Te K. Ngata-Aerengamate, F. Burkin, N. Moors, S. Smith (*Doctor*), J. Gavala (*Mental Skills Coach*). **SECOND ROW:** L. Cournane (*Manager*), A. Hodge (*Analyst*), M. Keys (*Media Manager*), L. Perese, G. Brooker, L. Connor, R. Demant, K. Simon, A. Leti-I'iga, W. Clarke (*Asst Coach*), G. Milne (*Physio*). **FRONT ROW:** R. Wickliffe, C. Hohepa, K. Cocksedge, G. Moore (*Head Coach*), L. Elder (*Captain*), S. Winiata, E. Blackwell, C. McMenamin. **INSETS:** P. Love, T. Fitzpatrick, K. Brazier, A. Saili, M. Parkes.

Photo by Tulloch Photography

MĀORI ALL BLACKS

BACK ROW: F. Smith, H. Hetet, T. Walden, R. Wright, J. Ruru, N. Harris, B. Harmon, B. Hall, M. Karpik, J. Garden-Bachop, P. Rakete-Stones, S. Thomas (*S&C Coach*). *SECOND ROW:* C. Shaw (*Asst Physio*), J. Ross (*Analyst*), A. Letts (*Physio*), R. Durie (*Doctor*), J. Hyland, T. Lomax, I. Walker-Leaware, P. Parkinson, S. Stevenson, W. Douglas, A. Nankivell, R. Randle (*Asst Coach*), E. Iupeli (*Team Administrator*), M. Sexton (*Campaign Manager*), J. Clausen (*Media Manager*). *FRONT ROW:* J. Maddock (*Asst Coach*), Te T. Tahuriorangi, S. Wainui, O. Black, A. Ioane, C. McMillan (*Head Coach*), A. Dixon (*Captain*), L. Crawford (*Kaumatua*), T. Franklin, R. Thompson, M. Renata, R. Prinsen, T. Ward (*Manager*).

BLACK FERNS SEVENS

Winners of the 2019 Dubai Sevens

FROM LEFT: G. Broughton, S. Kaka, N. Williams, K. Brazier, H. Harding, S. Waaka, T. Nathan-Wong (*Captain*), T. Fitzgerald, R. Tui, M. Tairakena, R. Pouri-Lane, T. Willison, A. Saili.

Photo by Tulloch Photography

ALL BLACKS SEVENS

BACK ROW: V. Koroi, N. McGarvey-Black, T. Joass, T. McMaster (*Asst S&C Coach*), A. Rokolisoa, S. Fenemor (*Performance Support*), T. Ng Shiu, A. Knewstubb, J. Nareki. *SECOND ROW:* T. Cama (*Asst Coach*), B. Mills (*S&C Coach*), D. Banks (*Physio*), N. Jones, S. Gregory, L. Masirewa, A. Nicole, J. Ravouvou, L. Barry (*Asst Coach*), T. Martin (*Analyst*), K. Neiderer (*Asst Physio*). *FRONT ROW:* C. Laidlaw (*Coach*), D. Collier, J. Webber, K. Baker, T. Mikkelson (*Co-captain*), S. Curry (*Co-captain*), S. Dickson, S. Molia, R. Ware, R. Everiss (*Manager*). *INSETS:* E. Nanai-Seturo, T. Haugh, Te P. Stephens.

NEW ZEALAND UNDER 20

BACK ROW: D. Neilson (*Analyst*), J. Bishop (*Doctor*), S. Klein, T. Funaki, E. Nanai-Seturo, J. Mua, L. Carter, K. Herbert, L. Lalomilo, F. Newell, A. Good (*Asst Coach*), K. Houltham (*Physio*). **SECOND ROW:** T. Hurst (*S&C Coach*), D. Witcombe (*Set Piece Coach*), R. Reihana, G. Dyer, S. Parker, S. Finau, T. Vaa'i, T. Plumtree, T. Williams, C. Grace, F. Burke, C. Forbes, D. Hill (*Asst Coach*). **FRONT ROW:** M. Vercoe (*Manager*), Q. Tupaea, D. Flanders, K. Uluilakepa, D. McLeod, K. Kereru-Symes (*Captain*), K. Boshier, B. Proctor, L. Faingaanuku, O. Norris, C. Philpott (*Head Coach*). **INSETS:** S. Gregory, R. Cobb, J. Thompson, C. Fihaki.

NEW ZEALAND SECONDARY SCHOOLS

BACK ROW: B. Strang, M. Dobbyn, W. Gualter, C. Church, J. Sexton, Te R. Reuben, M. Grindlay, V. Ekuasi, S. Calder, R. Love, R. Solo. **THIRD ROW:** N. Reid (*Manager*), E. Iupeli (*National Team Administrator*), R. Marsden (*Physio*), D. Neilson (*Analyst*), C. Kellow, A. Craig, D. Gardiner, M. Hammett (*Head Coach*), S. Rasch (*Asst Coach*), K. Harding (*Asst Coach*), M. Sexton (*Campaign Manager*), S. van Gruting (*S&C*). **FRONT ROW:** B. Lopas, M. Paea, M. Hughes, G. Wrampling, A. Segner, Z. Gallagher (*Captain*), T. Tauakipulu, J. Ratumaitavuki-Kneepkens, B. Murray, O. Lewis, A. Morgan.

Photo by Farrelly Photos

BLUES

BACK ROW: M. Duffie, S. Scrafton, T. Robinson, J. Goodhue, J. Pierce, S. Williams. **FIFTH ROW:** J. Craig (*S&C Intern*), B. Afeaki (*Scrum Coach*), A. Hodgman, H. Sotutu, D. Papalii, J. Tupou, T. Tele'a, T. Phillipson-Puna (*S&C Intern*), K. Ogura (*Analyst Intern*). **FOURTH ROW:** M. Collins, H. Plummer, E. Lindenmuth, J. Brown, M. Moulds, C. Clarke, M. Renata, L. Aumua, H. McCrae (*Massage Therapist*). **THIRD ROW:** Josh Yarnton (*Asst Analyst*), J. Smethurst (*Physio*), S. Perofeta, W. Havili, J. Ruru, M. Matich, J. Stratton, J. Trainor, L. Li, O. Black, J. McGarvey (*Doctor*), P. Healey (*Head S&C Coach*). **SECOND ROW:** J. Ryan (*Asst S&C*), T. Webber (*Analyst*), T. Umaga (*Asst Coach*), TJ Faiane, S. Mafileo, L. Apisai, M. Nonu, A. Pulu, S. Nock, D. Halangahu (*Asst Coach*), S. Pinford (*Asst S&C*), A. Draper (*Physio*). **FRONT ROW:** R. Fry (*Manager*), R. Ioane, A. Ioane, O. Tu'ungafasi, B. Gibson (*Co-captain*), L. MacDonald (*Head Coach*), P. Tuipulotu (*Co-captain*), J. Parsons, M. Nanai, G. Cowley-Tuioti, T. Coventry (*Asst Coach*). **ABSENT:** H. Sasagi, K. Tu'inukuafe.

Photo by Richard Spranger Photography

CHIEFS

BACK ROW: T. Mafileo, O. Leger, B. Slater, A. Moeakiola, R. Coxon, T. Campbell, A. Teece *(PhD)*. **FOURTH ROW:** T. Banfield *(S&C Coach)*, L. Elisara *(PDM)*, Te T. Tahuriorangi; T. Falcon, R. O'Neill, M. Jacobson, S. Taukei'aho, S. McNicol, J. Taumateine, A. Hay *(S&C Coach)*, R. Johns *(Nutritionist)*. **THIRD ROW:** D. Galbraith *(Sports Psychologist)*, R. Hall *(Head Analyst)*, S. Kautai, T. Manu, A. Ross, S. Wainui, J. Debreczeni, M. Karpik, M. McKenzie, A. Nankivell, L. Polwart, T. Te Tamaki *(Physio)*, Z. Khouri *(Doctor)*. **SECOND ROW:** N. Hall *(Manager)*, N. White *(Asst Coach)*, K. Rottier *(Head Physio)*, L. Jacobson, P-G. Sowakula, M. Brown, T. Ardron, L. McWhannell, F. Hoeata, D. Leasuasu, J. Parete, A. Ta'avao, C. Argus *(Head S&C)*, M. Collins *(CEO)*, T. Cawood *(Chair)*. **FRONT ROW:** C. Cooper *(Head Coach)*, N. Barnes *(Asst Coach)*, B. Weber, D. McKenzie, D. Sweeney, L. Boshier, A. Moli, T. Matson *(Asst Coach)*, R. Randle *(Asst Coach)*. S. Cane *(Co-captain)*, B. Retallick *(Co-captain)*, B. Weber, D. McKenzie, D. Sweeney, L. Boshier, A. Moli, T. Matson *(Asst Coach)*, R. Randle *(Asst Coach)*. **ABSENT:** A. Carroll, S. Donald, K. Hames, N. Laulala, E. Nanai-Seturo, T. Seu, B. Sullivan.

Photo by Mark Tantrum Photography

HURRICANES

BACK ROW: J. Dickie (*S&C Coach*), A. Aumua, N. Milner-Skudder, W. Goosen, V. Aso, D. Kirifi, R. Judd, D. Toala, X. Numia, S. Henwood, F. Christie, J. Lowe, D. Wildash (*Lead S&C Coach*). **THIRD ROW:** A. David-Perrot (*PDM*), P. Minehan (*Baggageman/Masseur*), T. Smith, P. Umaga-Jensen, A. Fidow, J. Garden-Bachop, R. Geldenhuys, R. Prinsep, G. Evans, F. Smith, C. Tiatia, C. Shaw (*Head Physio*), D. Gray (*Head of Physical Performance*). **SECOND ROW:** R. Runciman (*Analyst*), D. Larsen (*R&D Manager*), L. Santos (*Physio*), H. Bedwell-Curtis, B. Lam, S. Rayasi, L. Mitchell, J. Barrett, I. Walker-Leawere, K. Le'aupepe, G. Cridge, J. Blackwell, F. Armstrong, S. Tafua (*Analyst*), J. Ross (*Head Analyst*), R. Goodes (*Analyst*). **FRONT ROW:** T. Ward (*Operations Manager*), R. Watt (*Coach*), A. Savea, C. Eves, V. Fifita, B. Barrett, J. Holland (*Asst Coach*), T. Perenara, D. Coles, (*Captain*), J. Plumtree (*Head Coach*), B. May, Jeff Toomaga-Allen, M. Proctor, R. Riccitelli, J. Marshall, D. Cron (*Scrum Coach*), C. Spencer (*Coach*). **ABSENT:** T. Dorfing (*Doctor*), N. Hogg (*Mental Skills*).

Photo by Ken Baker Photography

CRUSADERS

Winners of the 2019 Investec Super Rugby Championship

BACK ROW: M. Alaalatoa, J. Moody, W. Jordan, W. Douglas, M. Dunshea, Q. Strange, S. Barrett, O. Jager, E. Blackadder, N. Punivai. **FIFTH ROW:** J. Roach (*Lead Physio*), S. Thomas (*Lead Physical Performance*), S. Owen (*Sports Science*), B. Ennor, G. Bridge, T. Sanders, J. Goodhue, D. Havili, J. Taufua, J. Gardner (*Lead Analyst*), M. Swan (*Doctor*). **FOURTH ROW:** V. Peterson (*Analyst*), G. Duder (*Physical Performance*), C. Taylor, I. Tu'ungafasi, T. Perry, G. Bower, H. Allan, V. Le Bas (*PDM*), C. Goodhew (*Dietician*), N. Tucker (*Physio*). **THIRD ROW:** J. Miles (*Logistics Manager*), C. Te Haara (*Communications*), S. Reece, B. McAlister, T. Christie, B. Harmon, M. Mataele, B. Hall, J. Spowart, R. Archibald (*Administrator*), S. Fletcher (*Manager*). **SECOND ROW:** R. O'Gara (*Coach*), J. Ryan (*Coach*), M. Hunt, B. Cameron, A. Makalio, M. Drummond, E. Enari, R. Mo'unga, B. Mooar (*Coach*), Andrew Goodman (*Coach*), P. Bowden (*Analyst*). **FRONT ROW:** I. Dagg, L. Romano, K. Read, R. Crotty (*Vice-captain*), S. Robertson (*Head Coach*), S. Whitelock (*Captain*), M. Todd (*Vice-captain*), O. Franks, B. Funnell, T. Bateman. **INSET:** L. Faingaanuku.

Photo by McRobie Studios, Dunedin

HIGHLANDERS

BACK ROW: W. Naholo, T. Nabura, L. Squire, J. Whetton, P.P. Parkinson, J. Dickson, T. Lomax, J. Hemopo, S. Frizell. *FIFTH ROW:* H. Hyndman *(Baggage Master)*, P. Osborne, M. Banks, J. Lentjes, I. Iosefa-Scott, M. Mikaele-Tu'u, D. Hunt, J. Hyland, R. Buckman, M. Ranby *(PDM)*. *FOURTH ROW:* F. Simpson *(Dietician)*, G. Delaney *(Asst Coach)*, C. Dermody *(Scrum Coach)*, R. Thompson, T. Umaga-Jensen, S. Fa'agase, D. Hollinshead, P. Tomkinson, R. Flutey *(Skills Coach)*, A. Watts *(Analyst)*. *THIRD ROW:* I. Blake *(Asst S&C Coach)*, A. Beardmore *(S&C Coach)*, T. Li, A. Seiuli, M. Faddes, A. Johnstone, J. Ioane, A. Letts *(Physio)*, J. Montgomery *(Asst Physio)*, H. Chapman *(Asst Analyst)*. *SECOND ROW:* G. O'Brien *(GM Rugby)*, R. Clark *(CEO)*, F. Fakatava, R. Niuia. T. Walden, J. McKay, R. Jackson, S. Tokolahi, K. Hammington, A. Singh *(Doctor)*, P. McLaughlan *(Manager)*. *FRONT ROW:* A. Mauger *(Head Coach)*, D. Lienert-Brown, T. Franklin, E. Dixon, L. Whitelock *(Co-captain)*, B. Smith *(Co-captain)*, A. Dixon, A. Smith, L. Coltman, M. Hammett *(Asst Coach)*. *ABSENT:* B. Gatland, K. Tuiloma.

NEW ZEALAND HEARTLAND XV

BACK ROW: M. Medlicott, A. Thrupp, T. Tauwhare, S. Holani, P. Nabainivalu, M. Kolinisau, A. Ellis, T. Flutey, P. Pati. **SECOND ROW:** M. Rutene (*Head Coach*), P. Masoe (*Physio*), T. Kearns, N. Strachan, L. McFadzean, S. Liebezeit, C. Mabbett-Sowerby, H. Haerewa, J. Tagavaitau, N. Walsh (*Asst Coach*), G. Hodder (*Manager*). **FRONT ROW:** N. Kendrick, R. Smith, C. Carmichael, C. Hart, B. Ranga (*Captain*), W. Paia'aua, W. Wright, R. Darling, T. Priest, H. Henare. **ABSENT:** S. Koroitamana, P. McHugh (*Doctor*).

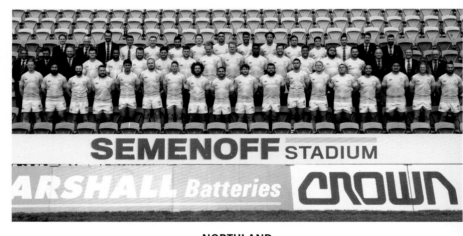

NORTHLAND

BACK ROW: M. Carpinter (*Analyst*), C. Locke (*Doctor*), J. Smethurst (*Physio*), E. Bellas (*Manager*), C. Taylor, H. Levien, W. Grant, J. Cherrington, P. Leilua, R. Roberts-Te Nana, N. Hyde, T. Smith, I. Martin-Lopez (*Asst S&C*), H. Slobbe (*Head S&C*), B. Parkes (*Asst S&C*). **SECOND ROW:** A. Balasingham (*Chairman*), B. Te Haara (*Asst Coach*), C. Goodhue (*Asst Coach*), K. Jacobson, S. Uluinakauvadra, B. Wiggins, M. Johnson, J. Byrne, T. Robinson, S. Caird, T. Mayanavanua, S. Sweetman, F. Funaki, C. Te Whata-Colley, J. Rae, G. Konia (*Asst Coach*), D. Witcombe (*Head Coach*), A. McGinn (*CEO*). **FRONT ROW:** S. McNamara, J. Straker, D. Hawkins, P. Atkins, T. Tua, J. Goodhue, J. Hyland, R. Ranger, S. Nock (*Vice-captain*), J. Olsen (*Captain*), R. Wright, J. Debreczeni, M. Matich, J. Matiu, B. Hohaia, I. Tu'ungafasi, S. Gregory, A. Stokes.

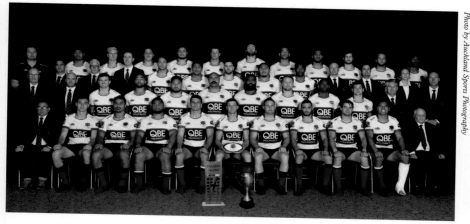

NORTH HARBOUR

BACK ROW: J. Pretorius (*Physio*), L. Inisi, J. Heighton, J. Roots, E. Roots, T. Evans, J. Pierce, N. Nee-Nee, X. Cowley-Tuioti, B. McNaughton, J. Little, M. Telea. **THIRD ROW:** D. Gibson (*General Manager*), P. White (*Manager*), A. King (*S&C*), H. Groundwater, F. Inisi, J. Page, L. Tolai, A. Tikoirotuma, M. Wenham (*Physio*), A. Beeton (*Analyst*), C. Winstanley (*Doctor*). **SECOND ROW:** J. McKittrick (*President*), S. Ward (*Asst Coach*), B. Gatland, T. Aoake, D. Meki, K. Tu'inukuafe, R. Rinakama, N. Mayhew, O. Qamasea, L. Gjaltema, B. Craies (*Skills Coach*), G. Howarth (*Chairman*). **FRONT ROW:** K. Keane (*Coach*), S. Stevenson, G. Cowley-Tuioti, S. Mafileo, D. Hunt (*Vice-captain*), M. Duffie (*Co-captain*), J. Parsons (*Co-captain*), B. Hall, M. McGahan, M. Taramai, C. Kelly (*Asst Manager*). **ABSENT:** L. Li, G. Preston.

NORTH HARBOUR HIBISCUS

BACK ROW: D. McGrory (*Head Coach*), A. Nathan, C. Sio, J. Taylor, S. Fisher, P. Tapsell, A. Berry, N. Brown. **THIRD ROW:** A. Robertshaw, D. Haigh, T. Nanjan, R. Adams, K. Williams, A. Gray, T. Fletcher, C. Quedley. **SECOND ROW:** N. Doyle (*Physio*), W. Walker (*Asst Coach*), M. Brooke, M. Robinson, N. Abel, S. Small, J. Harris (*Manager*), K. Cribb (*Trainer*). **FRONT ROW:** C. Cox, R. Wharawhara, T. Dallow, O. Ward-Duin (*Captain*), J. Vizirgianakis (*Vice-captain*), K. Hilton, I. Timani, H. Beale.

AUCKLAND

BACK ROW: M. Lea, T. Tele'a, E. Lindenmuth, S. Rayasi, K. Heatherley, S. Scrafton, J. Lane,
D. Papali'i. *FOURTH ROW:* A. Dabek, H. Sotutu, C. Suafoa, L. Dunshea, P-C. Tagaloa,
W. Riedlinger-Kapa, P. Tufuga, J. Ruru, A. Hodgman. *THIRD ROW:* A. Thomas (*PDM*), P. Downes
(*S&C Coach*), I. Jacobs (*Doctor*), J. Adams, J. Trainor, C. Clarke, A. Lam, A. Choat, D. Leuila,
H. McCrae (*Muscular Therapist/Asst Manager*), J. Yarnton (*Lead Analyst*). *SECOND ROW:* M. Plummer
(*Physio*), J. Bear (*CEO*), D. Kirkpatrick, T. Koroi, M. Sosene-Feagai, M. Fepulea'i, R. Abel, T. Manu,
L. Apisai, D. Tusitala, S. Mather (*Chairman*), K. Ogura (*Asst Analyst*). *FRONT ROW:* M. Casey
(*Scrum Coach*), M. Renata, F. Tiatia (*Asst Coach*), J. Whetton, B. Gibson (*Co-captain*), A. Ieremia
(*Head Coach*), TJ Faiane (*Co-captain*), A. Ioane, T. Lavea (*Asst Coach*), H. Plummer, M. McHattie
(*Manager*). *ABSENT:* R. Ioane, D. Liaina, A. Ta'avao, P. Tuipulotu, O. Tu'ungafasi, Sir Graham Henry
(*Technical Advisor*).

AUCKLAND STORM

BACK ROW: A. Itunu, K. Demant, J. Naime-Purcell, M. Roos, A-P. Nelson, J. Fanene, A. Toia-
Tigafau, L. Tufuga. *THIRD ROW:* S. Halafihi, S. Abraham, L. Thompson, G. Freeman, D. Nankivell,
M. Hokianga, L. Sa'u, K. Die-Besten (*Physio*). *SECOND ROW:* M. Robinson (*Manager*), I. Norman-
Bell, C. Tofa, C. Viliko, M. Cook, A. Roache, P. Elliot, J. Young (*S&C Coach*). *FRONT ROW:* R. Walker
(*Head Coach*), N. Moors, P. Maliepo, R. Demant, L. Itunu (*Captain*), E. Blackwell, C. McMenamin,
L. Mafi, A. Richards (*Asst Coach*). *INSETS:* R. Cox, C. Smith, V. Moimoi. *ABSENT:* L. Lefale, T. Lafaele,
M. Tu'inukuafe, A. Lenssen, G. Milne (*Physio*), M. Fownes-Walpole (*S&C Coach*), C. Hall (*Asst Coach*).

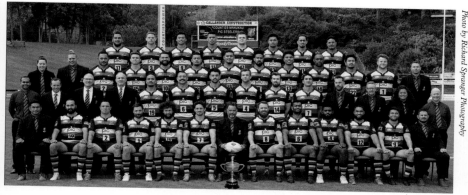

COUNTIES MANUKAU STEELERS

BACK ROW: M. Royal, T. Metcher, L. Daniela, E. Nanai-Seturo, L. Hughes, J. Gray, K. Hala, S. Nginingini. **THIRD ROW:** J. Souchon (*Head Analyst*), B. Tarapa (*Masseur*), D. Maka, A. Kellaway, R. Hohepa, N. Apa, S. Asomua, M. Ilaua, N. Foliaki, K. Kuridrani, L. Laulala, C. O'Donnell, P. Shaw (*Asst Trainer*). **SECOND ROW:** A. Kumar (*Doctor*), B. Hoggard (*CEO*), G. Wright (*President*), C. Carter (*Chairman*), S. Ropati, S. Slade, D. Leasuasu, M. Woolliams, L. Fitzsimons, J. Kawau, T. Ralph (*Physio*), J. Knox (*Sport Science Manager*), M. Leilua (*Manager*), R. Graham (*Mental Skills*). **FRONT ROW:** S. Sititi (*Asst Coach*), M. Martin, J. Royal, S. Bagshaw, O. Leger, S. Henwood (*Captain*), D. Suasua (*Coach*), D. Hyatt, S. Nabou, V. Rarasea, C. Vaega, J. Taumateine, G. Henson (*Asst Coach*). **ABSENT:** S. Furniss, T. Nabura, S. Williams, N. Laulala, K. Read, R. Tongotea, S. Withers (*Intern*), J. Hattori (*Intern*), A. Sharples (*Nutritionist*).

COUNTIES MANUKAU POWER HEAT

BACK ROW: L. Vaka, S. Woodman, V. Meki, J. Auva'a, G. Gago, W. Flesher. **THIRD ROW:** O. Tierney, J. Aiono, G. Aiono, A. Mamea, I. Molia, B. Munro-Smith, L. Veainu, A. Brider, L. Lima. **SECOND ROW:** H. Lemon (*Physio*), D. Suasua (*Asst Coach*), J. Craig (*Trainer*), R. Burch, T. Mataroa, A. Matau, J. Wong, L. Perese, C. Shepherd (*Head Coach*), H. Kapsin-Ali (*Manager*). **FRONT ROW:** L. Stead, M. Eli, L. Tauhalaliku, J. Lavea (*Vice-captain*), A. Marino-Tauhinu (*Captain*), H. Tubic, U. Antonio, S. Thompson, E. Kitson. **ABSENT:** Y. Ono, Z. Leaupepe, H. Te Irirangi, P. Shaw (*Trainer*).

THAMES VALLEY SWAMP FOXES

BACK ROW: R. Ibanez (*Asst Coach*), N. Aandewiel, J. Laurich, M. Axtens, K. Lewis, R. Leopold, H. Lafituanai, S. To'a, W. Newbold, P. Pawley (*Chaplin*). **THIRD ROW:** M. Rolleston (*Asst Coach*), C. Bishop (*Asst Manager*), C. Berridge, L. McIntyre, L. Neels, F. Kei Fotofili, L. Mitchell, G. McIntyre, M. Bartleet (*Coach*), L. McIver (*Manager*). **SECOND ROW:** K. Plummer (*President*), T. Evanson (*Physio*), J. Murray (*Asst Coach*), B. Toia, L. Mau, S. De La Fuente, S. Tupou, L. Easton, B. Motuliki, C. Doak (*H20*), G. Dickey (*Chairman*), D. Harrison (*Asst Coach*). **FRONT ROW:** R. Crosland, S. McMahon, M. Fisher, C. Muir, B. Bonnar, C. McVerry, R. Boughton, K. Ramage, K. Lee. **ABSENT:** B. Ranga III, D. Kayes, M. Abraham, Z. Clark, C. Wisnewski (*Chef*), J. Bennett (*Sport Psychiatrist*), M. Holmes (*Trainer*).

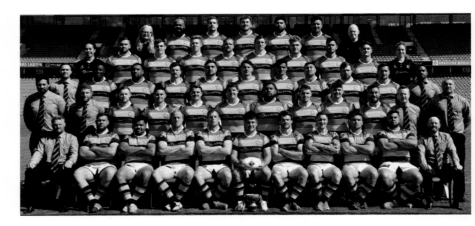

WAIKATO

BACK ROW: R. Stephenson (*PDM*), A. Naikatini, A. Shalfoon, L. McWhannell, T. Seu, S. Finau, D. McClunie (*Masseur*). **FOURTH ROW:** E. Pene (*Physio*), R. Cobb, H. Burr, J. Thompson, T. Bond, S. Parker, O. Norris, S. Alaimalo, Q. Tupaea, T. Te Tamaki (*Physio*). **THIRD ROW:** J. Christy (*Analyst*), B. Mudzekenyedzi, M. Veitayaki, J. Stratton, J. Brown, R. Reihana, B. Sullivan, S. Lopeti-Moli, A. Johnstone, L. Rogers, L. Vasu (*Asst Trainer*). **SECOND ROW:** R. Filipo (*Asst Coach*), T. Hurst (*Head Trainer*), R. Takarangi, C. Price, T. Campbell, S. Cooper, H. Hetet, F. Smith, V. Te Whare, N. Tudreu, M. Crawford (*Manager*), R. Randle (*Asst Coach*). **FRONT ROW:** N. White (*Asst Coach*), J. Iosefa-Scott, S. Taukei'aho, J. Tucker, T. Smith, D. Sweeney (*Captain*), M. Jacobson, D. O'Donnell, M. Iti, S. Kautai, A. Strawbridge (*Head Coach*). **ABSENT:** A. Lienert-Brown, D. McKenzie, S. Reece, H. Nankivell, B. Foote (*CEO*), Z. Khouri (*Doctor*), P. Kennedy (*Doctor*), G. Currie (*Doctor*), K. Abbott (*Nutritionist*).

Photo by PhotoLife Studios

WAIKATO FPC

BACK ROW: C. Ruruku, J. Ngare, T. Begbie, K. Nolan, K. Tahau, R. Anderson-Pitman. **THIRD ROW:** C. Bradey (*S&C Coach*), K. Macey, R. Holmes, K. Simon, J. Coates, R. Paraone, A. Tangen-Wainohu, S. Millar, K. Turvey (*Physio*). **SECOND ROW:** J Nayacakalou (*Asst Coach*), A. Bayler (*Asst Manager*), E. Tilo-Faiaoga, M. Hyde, F. Hansen, L. Kloppers, T. Kalounivale, S. Lualua, R. Stephenson (*PDM*), N. Kewish (*Manager*). **FRONT ROW:** C. Tane (*Asst Coach*), L. Mitchell, D. Reynolds, C. Hohepa, C. Alley (*Captain*), A. Gaby-Sutherland (*Vice-captain*), T. Gaby-Sutherland, L. Ngalu-Lavemai, W. Maxwell (*Head Coach*). **ABSENT:** W. Hodges (*Asst Coach*), A. Yama, E-L. Heta, H. Fraser, R. Hayes, T. Natua, A. Josephs (*S&C Manager*).

Photo by Stephen Jones Photography

POVERTY BAY

BACK ROW: S. McKinley, K. Love, A. Wyrill, W. Bolingford, J. Holmes, R. Terekia, B. Waaka. **THIRD ROW:** M. Reedy, M. McGuire, S. Akana, A. Tauatevalu, Q. Tapsell, N. Carrizo, M. Raleigh. **SECOND ROW:** G. MacDonald (*Physio*), M, Jefferson (*Asst Coach*), J. Swift (*Trainer*), T. Cairns (*Head Coach*), G. Te Kani, Jody Allen, Juston Allen, S. Smith (*Asst Manager*), B. Amai (*Manager*), M. Nikora (*Asst Coach*). **FRONT ROW:** J. Willoughby (*CEO*), K. Smith, W. Grogan, T. Hill, K. Houkamau (*Captain*), C. Chrisp, E. Reeves, M. Counsell, H. Swann (*Chairman*). **ABSENT:** J. Leaf, H. Mokomoko, N. Rangihuna, M. Tawa, J. Cook, T. McGuire, J. McFarlane, L. Dickson.

Photo by Shannon Gray

BAY OF PLENTY

Winners of the Mitre 10 Cup Championship

BACK ROW: F. Sella (*Asst S&C Coach*), K. Kinoshita (*Analyst*), Te A. Toma, L. Lalomilo, K. Trask, L. Polwart, J. Robertson, S. Kiyohara, A. Tai Kie (*Doctor*), C. McNeill (*Asst S&C Coach/Analyst*). **THIRD ROW:** S. Joblin (*Asst S&C Coach*), K. Eklund, J. Webber, D. Robinson-Bartlett, J. Johnston, T. Mafileo, C. McMillan (*Head Coach*), E. Narawa, P. Collier, L. Carter, C. Forbes, F. Fuatai, B. Olsen (*Physio*). **SECOND ROW:** T. Stebbing (*Head S&C Coach*), N. Vella, J. Ravouvou, H. Matenga, A. Ainley A. Carroll, B. Wardlaw, S. van den Hoven, T. Franklin, A. Papali'i, R. Geldenhuys, C. Eves, M. Rogers (*Asst Coach*), B. Drabble (*Statistics*). **FRONT ROW:** M. Delany (*Asst Coach*), W. Brill (*Manager*), R. Judd, L. Campbell, H. Blake, J. Thwaites, A. Ross (*Captain*), D. Hollinshead, C. Tiatia, M. Karpik, N. Harris, A. Aaifou-Olive (*PDM*), M. Bourke (*Asst Coach*). **ABSENT:** T. McHugh, M. Skipwith-Garland, A. Mua, D. Barnett, S. Cane, P. Cameron (*Physio*).

KING COUNTRY

BACK ROW: D. Clapcott, J. Balme, C. Dunster, B. Armstrong. **THIRD ROW:** S. Luoni (*Technical Adviser*), D. Baxter, B. Jeffries, T. Tupaea, K. Dunster, J. Pinkerton, G. Williams (*Trainer*). **SECOND ROW:** C. Hubbard (*Asst Coach*), N. Clarke (*Manager*), D. Ross, C. Robinson, S. Cullen, M. Owens, A. Tapili, N. Barnes, J. Reid (*Physio*), C. Jeffries (*Head Coach*). **FRONT ROW:** E. Reihana, R. Vosaki, A. Thrupp, Z. Tipping, C. Carmichael (*Captain*), L. Rowlands, C. Mabbett-Sowerby, S. Turner, W. Cunningham. **ABSENT:** C. Henare.

WANGANUI

BACK ROW: K. Latu, W. Cottrell, G. Hakaraia, D. Gallien, R. Tikoisolomone, A. Pogia, C. Clare, K. Pascoe, R. Salu, P. Nabainivalu, A. Middleton. **SECOND ROW:** P. O'Shaughnessy (*Analyst*), E. Robinson, T. Brown, C. Breuer, S. Kubunavanua, N. Harding, J. Lane, S. Madams, J. Rokotakala, J. Hodges, E. Meleisea, D. Whale, V. Tikoisolomone, D. Robinson (*Manager*). **FRONT ROW:** M. McGrath (*Selector*), S. Wiperi, R. Tutauha, C. Davies, P. Rowe (*Technical Adviser*), J. Caskey (*Head Coach*), C. Hart (*Captain*), T. Kilgariff (*President*), J. Hamlin (*Asst Coach*), J. Edwards, L. Horrocks, T. Rogers-Holden, H. Fitzgerald (*Physio*). **ABSENT:** P-T. Hay-Horton, J. Myers, K. Stembridge (*Physio*), L. Nimarota (*Physio*).

TARANAKI BULLS

BACK ROW: V. Peterson (*Analyst*), D. Brighouse, S. Mellow, R. Verney, M. McKenzie, J. Potroz, B. Northcott-Hill, L. Halls, K. Naholo, B. Wylde (*Psychologist*). *FOURTH ROW:* P. Veric (*Interim CEO*), R. Shepherd (*Asst S&C Coach*), S. Ritchie (*Head S&C Coach*), T. Florence, C. Gawler, A. Sorovaki, J. Proffit, B. Slater, J. Faletagoa'i-Malase, D. Ormond (*Manager*), N. Coombes (*Asst Physio*). *THIRD ROW:* L. Thomson (*Chairman*), C. Clarke (*Asst Coach*), H. Bedwell-Curtis, J. Parete, F. Hoeata, J. Lord, T. Vaa'i, L. Price. P. Sowakula, K. Boshier, P. Riley (*Doctor*). *SECOND ROW:* L. Corlett (*Scrum Coach*), M. Radich (*Nutritionist*), X. Roe, L. Blyde, D. Waite, K. Stewart, S. Perofeta, L. Milo-Harris, R. Riccitelli, L. Holland (*PDM*), A. Larkin (*Head Physio*). *FRONT ROW:* T. Stuck (*Asst Coach*), Te T. Tahuriorangi, S. Wainui, J. Ormond, M. Brown (*Captain*), T. Walden (*Vice-captain*), L. Boshier, W. Naholo, R. O'Neill, W. Rickards (*Head Coach*).

TARANAKI WHIO

BACK ROW: M. Callaghan, S. Brown, K-R. Kahui, J. Lampe, C. Fowler. *THIRD ROW:* M. Stone (*Head Coach*), A. Williams, L. Appert, L. Nauga-Grey, B. Gibbs, B. Neilson, A. Bynon-Powell (*Physio*). *SECOND ROW:* R. Corry (*Co-manager*), N. Hintz, N. Haupapa, D. King, A. Cole, K. Parkinson, B. Peterson (*Asst Coach*). *FRONT ROW:* N. Chamberlain (*Co-manager*), I. Hohaia L. Barnard, J. Smith (*Co-captain*), B. Sim (*Co-captain*), V. McCullough, S. Winter, T. Maltman (*Doctor*). *ABSENT:* E. Andrews, C. Austin, D. Brooks, (*Asst Coach*), E. Johns, A. Kingi, M. Karalus, T. Taylor, C. Tulloch, P. Zwart.

HAWKE'S BAY MAGPIES

BACK ROW: B. Jenkinson (*Asst Manager*), H. Scaloni (*S&C Intern*), J. Mills (*Physio*), S. van der Peet (*Analyst*), L. McClutchie, F. Fakatava, S. Ili, C. Makene, D. Toala, N. Fomai, Z. Donaldson, J. Hintz, L. Stephenson (*Head S&C*), F. Deformes (*Scrum Coach*), J. Syms (*Asst Coach*), J. Pinfold (*Asst S&C*). **SECOND ROW:** M. Ozich (*Head Coach*), K. Kereru-Symes, T. Vaiusu, S. McNicol, H. Brighouse, J. Kaifa, D. Flanders, I. Walker-Leawere, O. Sapsford, S. Funaki, N. Waa, J. Tavita-Metcalf, J. Devery, M. Smith (*Manager*). **FRONT ROW:** T. Falcon, M. Emerson, J. Lowe, M. Mikaele-Tu'u, G. Cridge, B. O'Connor (*Vice-captain*), A. Dixon (*Captain*), G. Evans (*Vice-captain*), M. Allardice, B. May, T. Parsons, J. Long, P. Rakete-Stones. **ABSENT:** T. Farrell, B. Weber, J. Shoemark (*Technical Advisor*), I. Taylor (*Doctor*).

HAWKE'S BAY TUI

BACK ROW: B. Pohio (*Trainer*), W. Olsen, K. Huata, T. Iosefo, M. Palu, R. Hurae, L. Mikaele-Tu'u, N. Adamsom, N. Jefferson, H. Macdonald, S. Young (*Videographer*). **THIRD ROW:** S. Bell (*Backs Coach*), J. Simati, W. Mareikura, K. Brown, Te A. Papanui-Hunt, T. Feleu, C. Te Pou, I. Fa'avae, Te M. MacGregor, A. McKenzie, S. Woods (*Head Coach*). **FRONT ROW:** E. Oldham, E. Jensen, S. Bockman, S. Tipiwai, J. Taueki, H. Brough (*Co-captain*), G. Woods (*Co-captain*), T. Meyer, F. Powdrell, F. Burkin, K. Cottrell, M-J. Durkin (*Manager*). **ABSENT:** C. Atkin.

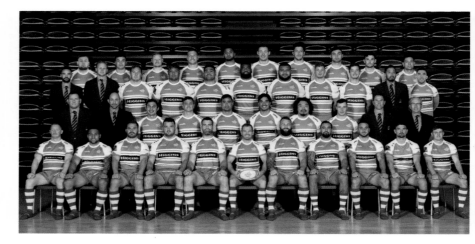

MANAWATU TURBOS

BACK ROW: S. Wasley, B. Iose, R. Pedersen, J. Galloway, S. Tu'ipulotu, T. Hughes, L. Mitchell, T. Laubscher, A. Boult, R. Thompson. **THIRD ROW:** T. Fitzgerald (*Physio*), B. Brugman (*Trainer*), S. Stewart, F. Sione, P. Leleisiuao, S. Tawake, S. Asi, B. Werthmuller, G. Culver, I. Tuputala (*Analyst*), N. Milner-Skudder. **SECOND ROW:** G. Fleming (*Asst Coach*), P. Russell (*Coach*), A. Henare, S. Cruden, J. Tofa, J. Maraku, S. Takizawa, B. Wyness, A. Good (*Asst Coach*), A. Berry (*Manager*). **FRONT ROW:** H. Northcott, N. Laumape, N. Grogan, F. Armstrong, N. Crosswell, J. Booth (*Captain*), F. Stone, J. Hemopo, A. Taylor, O. Black, S. Malcolm. **ABSENT:** S. Lombard (*Doctor*), G. Syminton, Te R. Waitokia, D. Wild.

MANAWATU CYCLONES

BACK ROW: M. Polson, S. Hemingway, J. Fagan-Pease, K. Sturmey, N. Kuiti. **THIRD ROW:** S. Olsen, L. Balsillie, K. Takitimu-Cook, K. Olsen-Baker, N. Tavake, M. Leota, S. Tipene. **SECOND ROW:** K. Murphy (*Trainer*), C. Agwen-Jones (*Asst Coach*), F. Feaunati (*Head Coach*), W. Stent (*Manager*), C. Gillespie (*Physio*), R. Rakatau (*Asst Manager*). **FRONT ROW:** J. Vaughan, S. Solomon, S. Talawadua (*Co-captain*), S. Winiata (*Co-captain*), J. Nuku, K. Tipene, L. Brown. **ABSENT:** L. Sae, R. Sturmey, Y. Sue, C. Dallinger, L. Claridge, T. Davison, A. Knight, M. Live, C. Mayes, C. Windle, K. Sue.

WAIRARAPA BUSH

BACK ROW: L. Hebenton-Prendeville, J. Pakoti, S. Shaw, A. Smith, D. Pickering, B. Kauika-Petersen, B. Price. **FOURTH ROW:** A. Priest, L. Bush, T. Flutey, S. Tufuga, M. Tufuga, J. Tako, M. Falaniko. **THIRD ROW:** B. Weatherstone (*President*), J. Carruthers (*Chairman*), S. Cottier (*Trainer*), L. Flutey, U. Tufuga, D. Castorina (*Physio*), J. Nuku (*Trainer*), S. Wright (*Scrum Coach*). **SECOND ROW:** S. O'Gorman (*Manager*), D. van Deventer (*Asst Coach*), J. Harwood (*Head Coach*), B. Arnold, I. Katia, R. Petersen, W. Reiri (*Strapper*), B. Hansen (*Strapper*), O Browne (*Physio*). **FRONT ROW:** L. McFadzean, A. McLean, B. Campbell, S. Gammie, R. Anderson, K. Tufuga (*Captain*), J. Goodger, J. van Vliet, T. Haira, T. Priest. **ABSENT:** J. Cameron, C. Hayton, R. Knell, T. Tekii, B. Wilson.

HOROWHENUA KAPITI

BACK ROW: K. Tamou, S. Gray, T. Zimmerman, H. Henare, E. Reti, P. Turia, C. Hemi, D. Ropata, D. Taylor, J. Ihaka, S. Pape, T. Barnsley (*Physio*). **SECOND ROW:** N. Taylor (*Asst Manager*), D. Jackson (*Strapper*), M. Rutene (*Asst Coach*), P. Marshall, L. Broughton, I. Ulutoa, S. Woodmass, T. Katoa, J. Tupai-Ui, K. Kuruyabaki, C. Wilton (*Coach*), R. Wright (*Manager*). **FRONT ROW:** J. Mowbray (*Chairman*), T. Woodmass, D. McErlean, S. Cameron, A. Lahmert (*Captain*), R. Praat, W. Paia'aua, N. Kendrick, C. Kennett (*CEO*). **ABSENT:** S. Arthur, T. Brown, N. Erasmus, A. Henare, J. Laloifi, M. Laursen, M. Pakau-Wallace, R. Paleaae, T. Paringatai, T. Reti, T. Seruwalu, J. Tagavaitau, C. Tahiwi-MacMillan, H. Thomas, J. White (*Analyst*), J. Winterburn.

WELLINGTON LIONS

BACK ROW: W. Goosen, S. Fa'agase, V. Aso, T. Umaga-Jensen, K. Uluilakepa, C. Collins. **THIRD ROW:** P. Paraone, L. Filipo, C. Woodmass, C. Garden-Bachop, M. Poi, P. Umaga-Jensen, A. Fidow, J. Furno, B. Lam, B. Proctor, T. Ben-Nicholas, X. Numia, S. Paongo, P. Patafilo. **SECOND ROW:** M. Poutoa (*Manager*), J. Dickie (*Head S&C*), K. Shigeeda (*S&C Intern*), N. Hogg (*Mental Skills*), R. MacNaughton (*S&C Intern*), M. Higgins (*Nutrition*), B. Treanor (*Physio*), L. Tau'alupe, N. Ah Kuoi, G. Stanbridge (*Gear*), M. Healey (*Analyst Intern*), V. Serangeli (*Head Analyst*), H. Otumuli (*Physio*), C. Jane (*Asst Coach*), A. Narayan (*Doctor*), R. Runciman (*Analyst*). **FRONT ROW:** K. Hauiti-Parapara, T. Renata, A. Aumua, J. Blackwell, J. Garden-Bachop, L. Crowley (*Asst Coach*), G. Halford (*Scrum Coach*), M. Proctor (*Co-captain*), D. Kirifi (*Co-captain*), C. Gibbes (*Head Coach*), M. Blandford (*President*), M. Evans (*CEO*), J. O'Reilly, M. Kafatolu, G. Taufale, V. Fifita. **ABSENT:** D. Coles, A. Savea, T. Perenara, S. Tafua (*Analyst*).

WELLINGTON PRIDE

BACK ROW: N. Foaese, P. Auimatagi, S. Mose-Samau, R. Uluinayau, S. Tabua, M. Heslop, A-M. Afuie. **FOURTH ROW:** E. Dalley, J. Bryce, A. Uila, A. Soper, M. Takano, R. Stirling. K. Lomani, K. MacDonald. **THIRD ROW:** B. Taumoli, S. To'oala-Ryder, M. Kupa-Cummings, A. Rasch, M. Solia, F. Makisi, E. Taito, A. Print. **SECOND ROW:** J. Taumoli, A. Jones (*Backs Coach*), B. Reidy (*Forwards Coach*), M. Conley (*Manager*), M. Higgins (*Trainer*), R. Bond (*Head Coach*), B. Joyes (*Physio*), L. Faleafaga. **FRONT ROW:** Te A. Ngata-Aerengamate, L. Hopoi, J. Ngan-Woo, B. Robertson, J. Patea-Fereti, S. Levave, M-L. Sa'u, E. Hopoi, R. Lolo. **ABSENT:** A. Leti-Iiga, T. Newton, B. Mockett (*Analyst*).

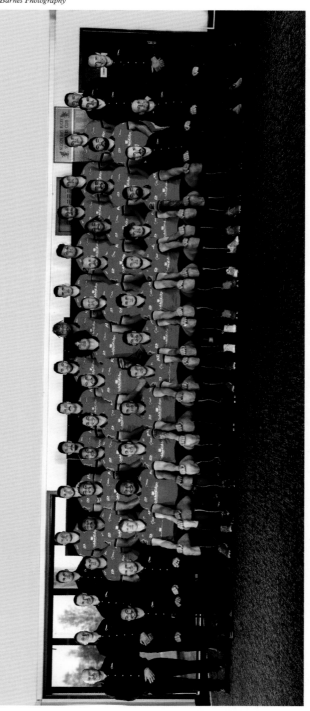

TASMAN MAKO

Winners of the Mitre 10 Cup Premiership

BACK ROW: K. Harrington (*Physio*), H. Roach, D. Smith, U. Keisuke, R. Coxon, T. O'Malley, Te A. Cirikidaveta, W. Jordan, L. Aumua, S. Havili, I. Salmon, B. Stewart, N. Price (*Analyst*). **SECOND ROW:** M. Vercoe (*Manager*), J. Holden (*Trainer*), N. Whitfield (*Trainer Intern*), J. Spowart, S. Moli, T. Faingaanuku, F. Paea, J. Norris, T. Lomax, P. Parkinson, W. Crockett, S. Prattley, L. Faingaanuku, S. Matenga, B. Prinsep, N. Dewar (*Doctor*), R. Marsden (*Asst Physio*). **FRONT ROW:** S. Christie (*Defence Coach*), C. Dermody (*Co-Head Coach*), F. Christie, A. Makalio, L. Squire, T. Perry, M. Hunt (*Vice-Captain*), D. Havili (*Captain*), Q. Strange (*Vice-captain*), A. Nankivell, E. Blackadder, J. Taufua, A. Goodman (*Co-Head Coach*), G. Cornelius (*Asst Coach*).

TASMAN MAKO FPC

BACK ROW: D. Salton, H. Hutana, A. Dempster, J. Thomson, G. Dixson, J. Harvie, R. Kersten. **SECOND ROW:** N. Marquet (*S&C Coach*), H. Davidsen (*Physio*), S. Mitchell, A. Bradley, P. Andrews, S. Wilkins, K. Grason (*Manager*), C. Binns (*Head Coach*). **FRONT ROW:** P. Hart, J. Drummond, M. Newman, W. Greig (*Vice-captain*), J. Foster-Lawrence (*Captain*), H. Gillespie, A. Schultz, J. Paenga.

BULLER

BACK ROW: P. Foote, J. Mackay, C. Aldridge, K. Parata, K. Te Tai, T. Samuels, I. Ravudra. **THIRD ROW:** A. Paterson, Z. Walsh, G. Simmiss, I. Lewaqai, G. de Kock, J. Best, M. Briant. **FRONT ROW:** C. Aldridge (*Manager*), G. Martyn (*Coach*), A. Stephens (*Co-captain*), H. McMillan (*Chairman*), W. Scott (*Co-captain*), S. Carey (*Physio*), A. Duncan (*CEO*). **ABSENT:** J. Lash, R. Malneek, T. Manawatu, P. Saukuru, D. Hytongue, J. Lepa, A. Ellis, M. Kaloudigibeci, B. Finau, M. Wells, L. Devery, B. Stewart, O. Fuataga.

WEST COAST

BACK ROW: B. Pearson (*Coach*), D. Davis, T. Kearns, L. Takura, P. Te Rakau, O. Varley, S. Soper, S. McClure, K. Tamatea, S. Shepherd (*Physio*), J. Costello (*Physio*). **SECOND ROW:** K. Parker (*Coach*), S. Cuttance (*Coach*), J. Tomlinson, B. Tauwhare, A. Lean, D. Foord, S. Liebezeit, T. Tu'ulua, A. Tukana, J. van Vliet, E. Munro, M. Connors (*Trainer*). **FRONT ROW:** K. Koch (*Physio*), M. Costello (*Manager*), T. Lawn, J. Ferguson, J. Coleman, J. Pitman-Joass (*Vice-captain*), T. Tauwhare (*Captain*), S. Holani, N. Thomson, N. Muir J. Mitchell, L. McNeish (*Manager*). **ABSENT:** J. MacRae, B. van Bruchem, L. Tukana, S. McLeod, E. Long, T. Struthers, M. Mudu, B. Eder.

CANTERBURY

2019 Ranfurly Shield Holders

BACK ROW: C. Grace, M. Dunshea, W. Tucker, J. Ratuva. **FIFTH ROW:** S. Owens (*Sports Science*), R. Poihipi, S. Gilbert, N. Punivai, O. Jager, D. McLeod, W. Douglas, T. Sanders, P. Bowden (*Lead Analyst*). **FOURTH ROW:** J. Roche (*Physio*), S. Dobson (*Analyst*), T. Christie, P. Osborne, F. Burke, B. Ennor, T. Murata, B. Harmon, C. Goodhew (*Dietician*), S. Hunter (*Asst Logistics*). **THIRD ROW:** N. Tucker (*Lead Physio*), C. Te Haara (*Content & Media Manager*), S. Siataga, H. Allan, B. McAlister, . McKay, S. Klein, R. Archibald (*Administrator*), M. Bowden (*PDM*). **SECOND ROW:** R. Thorne (*Coach*), M. Brown (*Coach*), T. Williamson (*Manager*), I. Finau, C. McManus, E. Enari, B. Cameron, G. Duder (*S&C*), J. Miles (*Logistics*), N. Mauger (*Coach*). **FRONT ROW:** S. Tokolahi, O. Franks, L. Romano, M. Drummond (*Vice-captain*), J. Maddock (*Head Coach*), L. Whitelock (*Captain*), R. Prinsep, D. Lienert-Brown, T. Bateman. **ABSENT:** G. Bridge, S. Whitelock, C. Taylor, R. Mo'unga, R. Crotty, J. Moody, M. Todd, M. Alaalatoa, H. Courtney, A. Tiplady (*Doctor*), M. Swan (*Doctor*).

Photo by Ken Baker Photography

CANTERBURY FPC

Winners of the Farah Palmer Cup Premiership

BACK ROW: G. Ponsonby, A. Bremner, N. Poletti, C. Bremner, C. Nelles, L. Anderson. **THIRD ROW:** C. Greenslade, R. Todd, P. Love, O. McGoverne, C. Siataga, A. Sisifa, E. Uren. **SECOND ROW:** N. Wong (*Manager*), G. O'Rourke, L. Jenkins, A. Rule, S. Curtis, M. Lolohea, M. Williams (*Physio*), J. Jowsey (*Coach*) **FRONT ROW:** K. Kite (*Coach*), M. Puckett, B. Davidson, S. Te Ohaere-Fox, O. Bernadel-Huey, Te R. Gapper, M. Ruscoe (*Coach*). **INSETS:** K. Cocksedge, G. Brooker, M. Yapper (*Trainer*), T. Aldridge, I. McArthur, K. Toга, B. Crowe.

MID CANTERBURY

BACK ROW: T. Lawn, J. Sutton, N. Caucau, J. McAtamney, T. Heywood, A. Lindsay, T. Ula, T. Blackburn, J. Donlan, S. Koroitamana. **SECOND ROW:** T. Harrison (*Manager*), J. Hodgins (*Physio*), R. Salton (*Trainer*), S. Sovea, K. Nordqvist, M. Bari, A. Langilangi, M. Bentley, E. Duff, T. Blyth, J. Leo, J. Rickard (*Asst Coach*), D. Palmer (*Coach*). **FRONT ROW:** J. Ross (*President*), C. Sinclair, T. Nabakeke, M. McAtamney, C. McKay, J. Dampney, T. Savaiinaea, I. Tonga, W. Mackenzie, A. Williamson, G. Rushton (*Chairman*). **ABSENT:** R. Catherwood, M. Groom, S. Madden, G. Frew (*Technical Advisor*).

SOUTH CANTERBURY
Winners of the Lochore Cup

BACK ROW: C. Hucker, R. McNab, B. Hewitson, J. Smith, S. Kakala, R. Cormack, A. Taelaga. **THIRD ROW:** G. Casey, T. Fakatava, M. Stewart, A. Amato, R. O'Gorman, K. Coll, S. Anderson, C. Moli. **SECOND ROW:** S. Breen (*Asst Coach*), Z. Saunders, J. Trevathan, W. Wright, C. Russell, T. Davidson, G. Thompson (*Physio*), N. Twaddell (*President*). **FRONT ROW:** K. Walsh (*Technical Advisor*), J. Wilson-Bishop, K. Leatigaga, C. Gard (*Asst Coach*), N. Strachan (*Captain*), N. Walsh (*Coach*), M. Medlicott, D. Suter, G. Brosnan (*Manager*). **ABSENT:** S. Wills (*Technical Advisor*), S. Lavaka, M. Fetu.

Photo By Phil Janssen

NORTH OTAGO

Winners of the Meads Cup

BACK ROW: B. Matthews *(Technical Advisor)*, P. Pati, M. Taiti, M. Williams, M. Vocea, M. Balchin, H. Tisdall, A. Johnson, D. Kingan *(Manager)*. **SECOND ROW:** D. Douglas *(President)*, W. Prescott *(Chairman)*, L. Kingan, K. Funaki, C. Elton, W. Kirkwood, M. Mata'afa, M. Kolinisau, J. Greenslade, T. Tamou, A. Harding *(Manager)*. **FRONT ROW:** C. Jackson *(CEO)*, J. Forrest *(Co-coach)*, J. Clark, S. Sturges *(Captain)*, R. Darling *(Captain)*, L. Masoe, R. Smith, J. Coghlan, N. Anderson *(Co-coach)*. **ABSENT:** S. Tatupu, J. Hayward, H. Packman, C. Gasca, A. Arty, M. Duff, S. Robins *(Physio)*, G. Sturgess *(Trainer)*, G. Witana, B. Templeton.

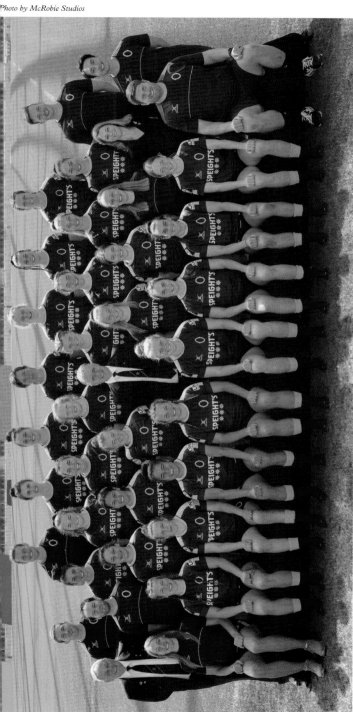

OTAGO SPIRIT

Winners of the Farah Palmer Cup Championship

BACK ROW: L. Cordell-Hull (*Asst S&C Coach*), K. Smith, S. Norris, H. Stolba, E. Doyle, J. Kendall, J. Gorinski. ***THIRD ROW:*** J. Angus (*Asst Coach*), S. Hume, I. Pringle, C. Hobbs, M. Henderson, C. Cunningham, R. Buchanan-Brown, A. du Plessis, K. Wetera, S. Wilson (*S&C Coach*). ***SECOND ROW:*** D. Smith (*President*), M. Ferguson (*Manager*), H. Watene, K. Moata'ane, G. Millar, R. Kinlay (*General Manager*), T. Hopcroft, M. Breen, Z. Whatarau (*Asst Manager*), R. Davenport (*Chairperson*), J. Kieu (*Physio*). ***FRONT ROW:*** A. Sutorius (*Asst Coach*), T. Ferguson, G. Mason, J. Tereu, P. Church, G. Muir, T. Hollows (*Captain*), R. Kelly, B. Thomas, S. Manson (*Head Coach*).

OTAGO

BACK ROW: M. Whaanga, S. Ma'u, J. Latta, L. Conradie, J. Hill, H. Boyle, S. Misiloi,
D. Nel. **FOURTH ROW:** R. Kinley (*GM*), A. Wilson (*Physio*), J. Ioane, R. Jackson, M. Mafi, H. Purdy,
K. Lea, J. Aoina, G. Bower, S. McDowall, T. Grant (*Asst Manager*). **THIRD ROW:** E. Brumwell
(*S&C Trainer*), R. Martin (*Asst Coach*), A. Williams, A. Morris-Lome, S. Misa, N. Souchon, J. Timu,
M. Scott, K. Hammer, L. Allan (*Asst Coach*), K. Bloxham (*Head S&C Trainer*). **SECOND ROW:**
S. O'Connor (*Manager*), J. Arscott, J. Nareki, T. Haugh, R. Davenport (*Chairperson*), R. Gouws,
C. McLeod, K. Hammington, D. Smith (*President*). **FRONT ROW:** T. Donnelly (*Asst Coach*), V. Koroi,
P. Tomkinson, A. Seiuli, M. Collins (*Captain*), J. Lentjes (*Vice-captain*), J. Dickson, A. Thomson,
H. Sasagi, B. Herring (*Head Coach*). **ABSENT:** S. Pole, B. Miller, B. Millar, W. Ngatai, H. Tatekawa,
H. Todd, M. Faddes, A. Frood, L. Halaleva, J. Ikani, J. Koroi, A. Moeke, B. Morris, L. Coltman.

SOUTHLAND STAGS

BACK ROW: R. Carter, T. Te Whata, J. Renton, I. Te Tamaki, C. Apoua, R. van Vugt, G. Pleasants-
Tate, M. James, M. Taylor, J. Fa'amoe-Ioane, M. Faletolu, R. Nu'u, L. Crowley. **SECOND ROW:**
B. Hopley (*General Manager*), S. Curry (*S&C Coach*), A. Mackintosh (*Physio*), J. Moorby, L. Tosi,
E. de Groot, B. Paulin, B. Fotheringham, C. Smith, C. Alaimalo, R. Tatafu, S. Wileman, H. Sililoto,
R. Bennett (*Analyst*), R. Fahey (*Asst Manager*), J. Hayes (*Asst S&C Coach*), R. Smith (*Manager*). **FRONT
ROW:** K. McDowall (*President*), D. Hewett (*Head Coach*), L. Ormond, P. Halder, M. Mitchell,
S. Stodart, M. McKenzie (*Vice-captain*), B. Mitchell (*Captain*), F. Thomas (*Captain*), S. Eade (*Vice-
captain*), B. Fukofuka, J. Walsh, M. McKee, J. Kawau (*Asst Coach*), D. MacLeod (*Asst Coach*),
B. McKone (*Chairman*). **ABSENT:** C. Stewart (*Doctor*), E. Dixon, L. Taliauli, N. Costa-Lindow,
M. Selby-Rickit, J. McKenzie (*PDM*), A. Hall (*Nutritionist*).

NEW ZEALAND MARIST

NZ Marist had their first win since 2011 in their annual encounter with the NZ Heartland team. They also took possession of the MacRae Cup for the first time since its inauguration in 2013.

v NEW ZEALAND HEARTLAND

Boyd Park, Te Aroha **2 November, 2019**

WON 29-19

Ben Werthmuller
OB Marist, Palm. Nth

Nash Fiso-Vaelei	Shayne Anderson	Josaia Bogileka
Hutt OB Marist	*Marist Albion, Chch*	*Marist, Wanganui*

Chase Tiatia (capt)
Rangataua

Sam Briggs
Marist, Nelson

Connor Collins
Hutt OB Marist

James Tuia
Marist St Pats, Wgtn

Rhys Pedersen	Josh Balme	Stan Van Den Hoven	Ricky Hayes
OB Marist, Palm. Nth	*Marist, Hamilton*	*Marist, Greerton*	*Napier OB Marist*
Josiah Tavita-Metcalfe	Jacob Devery		Leopino Maupese
Hastings RS	*Hastings RS*		*Marist, Nelson*

Reserves: Isefo Sokimi-Vulu *Marist St Michaels, Rotorua* (for Maupese 30 min), Garrett Casey *Celtic, Timaru* (for Tavita-Metcalfe 30 min), Brian Lima jnr, *Marist, Hamilton* (for Fiso-Vaelei 33min), Leopino Maupese *Marist, Nelson* (for Sokimi-Vulu 51 min), Josiah Tavita-Metcalfe *Hastings RS* (for Casey 56 min), Jack Nelson-Murray *Napier OB Marist* (for Devery 67 min), Jake Holmes *Gisborne OB Marist* (for Werthmuller 67 min), Quade Tapsell *Marist, Hamilton* (for Pedersen 69 min), Patrick Gluck *Marist, Masterton* (for Bogileka 70 min), Jordan Cox *Marist, Hamilton* (for Hayes 70 min)

Scorers:
Tries: Werthmuller (2), Tuia, Lima, Collins
Conversions: Briggs (2)

Referee: Rebecca Mahoney

Co-Coaches: Shaun Breen (*Timaru*), Dion Waller (Wellington)
Manager: Chris Back (*Wanganui*)
Assistant Manager: Mike Donoghue (*Wanganui*)
Physio: Sophie Martin (*Hawke's Bay*)

INVESTEC SUPER RUGBY 2019

The 24th edition of Super Rugby went the way of nine previous incarnations, with the Crusaders emerging as champions.

Once again, four New Zealand sides made the playoffs, while Australia had to content itself with the Brumbies, and their deadly rolling maul, as the sole Australian conference qualifiers.

The Jaguares followed up their 2018 quarter-final qualification by going all the way to the final for the first time, with their accurate yet expansive play. After making three straight finals, the Lions just missed the playoffs despite winning more games (8) than the Sharks (7), Chiefs (7) and Highlanders (6).

The Rebels were the early flag-flyers for the Australian conference but faded badly. The Sunwolves again propped up the table, despite recording a creditable win in Hamilton over the Chiefs.

The Waratahs' Israel Folau had just enough to time to post his record 60th try at this level before his controversial Twitter outburst ruined his rugby career.

SANZAAR has decided on a revamp of Super Rugby from 2021, when the next broadcast deal kicks in. The Sunwolves will drop out after the 2020 season, and the competition will revert to a 14-team, full round-robin format, which makes sense after four seasons of a competition table that often lacked integrity.

BLUES

The Blues were tougher to beat in 2019, but that did not translate into many more wins and that elusive playoffs berth.

Once again, they had to settle for last position in the tough New Zealand conference, but they did move up the overall table from 14th to 12th and were in contention for the playoffs until the penultimate game.

The pre-season coaching reshuffle saw Leon MacDonald move into the head coach role, while Tom Coventry took over the forwards, who proved more than competitive in most games. Deposed head coach Tana Umaga took the defence portfolio and did a good job. There were no more blowouts (33 was the most points conceded), but the attack lacked fluency.

Rieko Ioane was the leading tryscorer, with nine on the left wing, including a franchise-equalling four against the Sunwolves, but his output, like his brother Akira, who started every game, faded later in the season.

The sharpest back was Melani Nanai, mainly from fullback. He started every game, scored five tries, featured in the top 10 categories in several stats, and carried for a competition-high 1240 metres. His departure for the UK is a hammer blow.

Several of the backs had injury-plagued seasons, including Sonny Bill Williams. Ma'a Nonu performed far better than anticipated and formed a useful midfield combination with TJ Faiane. But the Blues had issues at 9 and 10, unable to settle on an effective halves duo. Otere Black was the better goalkicker, while Harry Plummer had issues off the tee. Jonathan Ruru had most chances in the No 9 jersey, but often overplayed his hand.

Tom Robinson was arguably Super Rugby's rookie of the year at blindside flanker, where his all-action style and lineout ability won plenty of new fans. Blake Gibson and Dalton Papali'i both had their moments in the loose.

Prop Karl Tu'inukuafe scrummaged well, but fell off the All Blacks' radar, and then dropped out with illness. The old warhorse James Parsons raised 100 Super Rugby outings for this team.

The Blues started with three losses, then bounced back with four straight victories. Thereafter their sole victory was a 23–8 home win over the Chiefs, possibly their best of the season.

But, like the Ioanes, they ran out of puff at the business end and fell to disappointing defeats in Brisbane and Wellington.

It is hoped that a change at the top, with new chief executive Andrew Hore now at the helm, and the signing of Beauden Barrett for 2020, will help deliver that long-awaited first playoffs qualification since 2011.

CHIEFS

The Chiefs had a topsy-turvy season but, on balance, they did very well to reach the playoffs with some gritty, competitive rugby in the latter stages of the regular season.

They endured an horrific start, losing their first four on the bounce, and not recording their first victory until round six in Pretoria. There were premature calls for the head of coach Colin Cooper. With their playoffs lives hanging by a thread, the Chiefs uncorked an astonishing 40–27 comeback win over the Crusaders in Suva and followed that with a decisive defeat of the Rebels to confirm their playoffs berth in seventh position. But their rails run came to an abrupt end in disappointing fashion in Buenos Aires.

Once more, the Chiefs had more than their share of injury problems. Sam Cane was a late starter after rehab on his neck operation, Brodie Retallick missed half the season, and Damian McKenzie did not play after April 13.

Up stepped the likes of Canadian international Tyler Ardron, who missed just one match and appeared in three positions. His versatility was gold under tough circumstances.

Atu Moli missed the first eight matches but thereafter established himself as one of the best New Zealand loosehead props.

Brad Weber's star again shone brightly, playing himself back into an All Blacks' jersey with his five tries and sparky play. The mercurial Marty McKenzie often played very well in the No 10 jersey, replacing his crocked brother.

Shaun Stevenson started badly at fullback but ended the campaign well on the right wing. Left wing Etene Nanai-Seturo made an encouraging start to his Super Rugby career, scoring five tries, but the best back and the best Chief of 2019 was Anton Lienert-Brown, whose work both with and without the ball and in either the 12 or 13 jersey was of the highest order. He often held the backline together.

Lachlan Boshier was the big mover in the pack, scoring five tries, keeping Cane's jersey warm and superseding Mitch Karpik in the pecking order with his tenacious breakdown work.

The trio of Angus Ta'avao, Mitch Brown and Jesse Parete all had strong, industrious seasons.

Coach Cooper's two-season tenure did come to an end, as Warren Gatland's return home to be head coach was the biggest signing for 2020.

HURRICANES

It will be little consolation to the Hurricanes that they were once again the second-best side in the New Zealand conference.

Nor will they take solace in the fact that their 12 wins were the most in the regular season, outstripping even the Crusaders, who picked up eight bonus points.

Their problem was inconsistency, losing three times to the Crusaders, struggling in games where they should have won in a canter, and dropping the clash to the Jaguares in Wellington. At times, they were irrepressible, such as the 43–13 win over the Brumbies in Palmerston North and 47–19 over the Chiefs in Wellington. They did push the Crusaders to the limit in their semi-final, only to come up short.

They possessed serious firepower in the backs, where Ngani Laumape chalked up his third straight compelling Super Rugby campaign — with 13 tries, while Ben Lam (9), Wes Goosen (8), TJ Perenara (6) and the brothers Barrett (sharing eight) were all dangerous much of the time.

Chase Tiatia turned heads with his sharp play in 11 games, mainly at fullback. Jordie Barrett was versatile and effervescent, appearing in four positions, while Beauden Barrett mostly played very well, and goalkicked accurately, but struggled against the Crusaders.

Ardie Savea was the pick of the pack, operating either off the back of the scrum or in his familiar No 7 jersey. His try against the Chiefs in Wellington is fit to rank as one of the best five-pointers of the season.

Du'Plessis Kirifi would be close to New Zealand's Super Rugby rookie of the year for his tigerish displays in the loose. A constant menace at the breakdown, he complemented Savea's work here and offered plenty in defence and carrying.

Vaea Fifita played well in the No 6 jersey but not well enough to make a cast-iron case for him to be the front-runner for the All Blacks' blindside berth.

James Blackwell was the unheralded workhorse of the pack. There were concerns about whether he had the requisite height to cope at this level, but they were allayed with his 17 starts and high work-rate. Liam Mitchell rolled his sleeves up alongside him, while Kane Le'aupepe showed real promise later in the season.

Prop Alex Fidow had another injury-plagued campaign, but veteran Ben May shunted a lot of work. The trio of Dane Coles, Ricky Riccitelli and Asafo Aumua all shared the hooking duties.

In 2020, the big question will be how the Hurricanes cope without Beauden Barrett after nine seasons.

CRUSADERS

The Crusaders were not as dominant as they were for much of 2017–18, but they were still good enough when it mattered and still scored no less than 82 tries as they annexed their 10th championship.

Working off a sound set-piece, allied to some real X-factor in the backs, and with Richie Mo'unga again conducting proceedings with aplomb, the Crusaders always took some beating.

Warming into their work, they had to deal with the mosque shootings tragedy in their city, which forced the cancellation of their March 16 clash with the Highlanders, and subsequent calls for manifestations of their culture, such as the pre-match horses and swordsmen, to be revisited.

The Crusaders were visibly off-colour in their loss to the Waratahs, and looked off the pace in a handful of other matches, notably the second stanza in Suva. But they had the Hurricanes' and Highlanders' numbers, while strangely struggling to repel the Blues.

Mo'unga was again imperious, his 182 points infused with seven tries, and he was one of the top players in the competition.

He had help. Sevu Reece was a late injury replacement, but then displayed quite brilliant form, scoring 15 tries in 14 outings to light up the Crusaders' attack. Braydon Ennor was not far behind, scoring 10 tries from either centre or wing and playing himself into the All Blacks. David Havili regained his 2017 touch, scoring seven tries from the back. Will Jordan scored eight tries and looked the goods. George Bridge was Mr Consistency once more.

The Ryan Crotty-Jack Goodhue combination was solid as a rock, especially on defence.

Halfback Bryn Hall job-shared with Mitch Drummond, but won the lion's share of starts.

Kieran Read appeared from round six, and was industrious and defensively sound but not as active on attack. It didn't matter, because Jordan Taufua and the much-improved Whetu Douglas were sharp all season. Matt Todd was his usual undemonstrative self, and was the best player on the field in the final. Scott Barrett and captain Sam Whitelock were without peer as a locking combination. Luke Romano and Quinten Strange offered solid support.

Owen Franks missed much of the campaign with injury, but Michael Alaalatoa stepped into the breach admirably. Joe Moody and Codie Taylor, aided by Andrew Makalio, had good seasons.

The Crusaders are losing a clutch of veterans, so will do it tough in their quest for an unprecedented fourth consecutive Super Rugby championship.

HIGHLANDERS

The bare facts show that the Highlanders won just four games after February 22, but they did so with a crippling injury toll, especially in the backline.

So to reach the playoffs again, albeit in eighth position, was a decent effort, before the Crusaders undid them in the quarter-final. The forwards always competed strongly in the set-pieces and the collisions.

The key moment came on May 4, when Ben Smith went down against the Chiefs, with what looked to be a serious leg injury. Until that moment, the fullback had been in prime form for the Highlanders. He missed the next five games and probably returned too early for the quarter-final against the Crusaders. Waisake Naholo missed eight games and that hurt the team's ability to finish teams off. The notable exception was the 49–12 victory over the Waratahs in Invercargill, which sealed their playoffs qualification.

Shannon Frizell and Sio Tomkinson were the leading tryscorers, with six apiece, while wing Tevita Li only hinted at his real promise, despite scoring four tries. Josh McKay was underutilised. Matt Faddes, in his last Highlanders campaign for some time, scored four tries from the wing, showing his skill and finishing ability.

Tei Walden and Rob Thompson, aided by Tomkinson, were once more a pair of defensively sound midfielders.

First-five Josh Ioane came of age at this level, posting 114 points in 14 matches and offsetting the injury to Bryn Gatland.

Aaron Smith's play continued to excel, while Kayne Hammington and Folau Fakatava both added value to the franchise's No 9 stocks.

Luke Whitelock was solidity personified at No 8, while James Lentjes usurped Dillon Hunt for the No 7 jersey with some committed performances. Liam Squire only played three games due to injury and unavailability.

Jackson Hemopo was a consistent second-rower, either at No 4 or 6, while Pari Pari Parkinson made more progress in his burgeoning career. Tyrel Lomax was again to the fore at tighthead prop, and was rarely bettered in the scrums. Ayden Johnstone was strong on the other side of the scrum.

Liam Coltman had his best season at hooker and, as ever, had Ash Dixon pushing him off the bench.

SUPER RUGBY STANDINGS

Final standings after round robin:

Team	P	W	D	L	F	A	TF	TA	BP	Pts
*Crusaders	16	11	3	2	497	257	73	31	8	58
*Jaguares	16	11	-	5	461	352	60	38	7	51
*Brumbies	16	10	-	6	430	366	65	49	8	48
Hurricanes	16	12	1	3	449	362	60	46	3	53
Bulls	16	8	2	6	410	369	42	50	5	41
Sharks	16	7	1	8	343	335	40	39	7	37
Chiefs	16	7	2	7	451	465	63	59	4	36
Highlanders	16	6	3	7	441	392	60	53	6	36
Lions	16	8	-	8	401	478	53	64	3	35
Stormers	16	7	1	8	344	366	34	46	5	35
Rebels	16	7	-	9	393	465	56	61	6	34
Blues	16	5	1	10	347	369	45	47	8	30
Waratahs	16	6	-	10	367	415	46	54	6	30
Reds	16	6	-	10	385	438	50	59	4	28
Sunwolves	16	2	-	14	294	584	34	85	4	12
TOTALS					**6013**	**6013**	**781**	**781**		

*Conference winners

NB. The Highlanders v Crusaders round-robin match, scheduled for 16 March, was declared a 0-0 draw when cancelled by SANZAAR due to the 15 March mosque shootings.

Points: 4 for a win
2 for a draw
Bonus points were for: a loss by seven points or fewer and/or for scoring three tries more than opponent

PREVIOUS WINNERS

1996	Auckland Blues	**2008**	Crusaders
1997	Auckland Blues	**2009**	Bulls
1998	Crusaders	**2010**	Bulls
1999	Crusaders	**2011**	Reds
2000	Crusaders	**2012**	Chiefs
2001	Brumbies	**2013**	Chiefs
2002	Crusaders	**2014**	Waratahs
2003	Blues	**2015**	Highlanders
2004	Brumbies	**2016**	Hurricanes
2005	Crusaders	**2017**	Crusaders
2006	Crusaders	**2018**	Crusaders
2007	Bulls	**2019**	Crusaders

SUPER RUGBY RECORDS

(S12 and S14 records have been rolled forward)

BY THE TEAMS

	BEST IN 2019	**RECORD**
Season totals		
Points	584 Crusaders	691 Crusaders *2018*
Tries	82 Crusaders	97 Hurricanes 2017
Conversions	57 Crusaders	75 Crusaders *2018*
Penalty goals	45 Bulls	76 Sharks *2014*
Dropped goals	2 Lions	11 Bulls *2009*
Match totals		
Points	66 Crusaders v Rebels	96 by Crusaders v Waratahs *2002*
Tries	10 Crusaders v Rebels	14 by Crusaders v Waratahs *2002*
		by Cheetahs v Sunwolves *2016*
		by Lions v Sunwolves 2017
Conversions	8 Crusaders v Rebels	13 by Crusaders v Waratahs *2002*
Penalty goals	6 Bulls v Lions	9 by Hurricanes v Blues *2010*
Dropped goals	1 on four occasions	4 by Bulls v Crusaders *2009*

BY THE PLAYERS

	BEST IN 2019	**RECORD**
Season totals		
Points	194 H. Pollard (Bulls)	263 M. Steyn (Bulls) *2010*
Tries	15 S.L. Reece (Crusaders)	16 M.B. Lam (Hurricanes) *2018*
Match totals		
Points	23 R. Mo'unga	50 G.E. Lawless (Natal v Highlanders) *1997*
	(Crusaders v Highlanders)	
Tries	4 R.E. Ioane	4 on 18 occasions
	(Blues v Sunwolves)	
Conversions	7 R. Mo'unga	13 A.P. Mehrtens
	(Crusaders v Rebels)	(Crusaders v Waratahs) *2002*
Penalty goals	6 H.L. Pollard (Bulls v Lions)	9 E.T. Jantjies
		(Lions v Cheetahs) *2012*
Dropped goals	1 on four occasions	4 M. Steyn (Bulls v Crusaders) *2009*
Career records		
Points	1708 D.W. Carter (Crusaders 2003-15)	
Tries	60 I. Folau (Waratahs 2013-19)	
Games	202 W.W.V. Crockett (Crusaders 2006-18)	

MOST GAMES

Games	Player	Teams
202	W.W.V. Crockett	Crusaders
178	L.J. Messam	Chiefs
177	S.T. Moore	Reds/Brumbies
175	K.F. Mealamu	Blues/Chiefs
174	M.A. Nonu	Hurricanes/Highlanders/Blues
164	G.B. Smith	Brumbies/Reds
162	N.C. Sharpe	Reds/Force
157	T. Mtawarira	Sharks
157	S.U.T. Polota-Nau	Waratahs/Force
156	J.A. Strauss	Cheetahs/Bulls
153	A.M. Ellis	Crusaders
150	C.R. Flynn	Crusaders
150	R.J. Crotty	Crusaders

MOST POINTS

Points	Player	Team	Games	Tries	Conv	PG	DG
1708	D.W. Carter	Crusaders	141	36	287	307	11
1449	M. Steyn	Bulls	123	13	242	275	25
1238	B.J. Barrett	Hurricanes	125	34	249	187	1
1098	E.T. Jantjies	Lions/Stormers	133	11	262	169	4
1092	B.T. Foley	Waratahs	119	29	244	153	–
1036	S.A. Mortlock	Brumbies	138	56	162	144	–

MOST TRIES

Tries	Player	Teams
60	I. Folau	Waratahs
59	D.C. Howlett	Blues/Hurricanes/Highlanders
58	C.S. Ralph	Chiefs/Crusaders
57	J.W.C. Roff	Brumbies
56	C.M. Cullen	Hurricanes
56	M.A. Nonu	Hurricanes/Blues/Highlanders
56	B.G. Habana	Bulls/Stormers
56	S.A. Mortlock	Brumbies
54	T.J. Perenara	Hurricanes
52	S.J. Savea	Hurricanes

SUPER RUGBY 2019 RESULTS

Date	Winning Team				Venue
February					
15	Highlanders	30	Chiefs	27	Hamilton
15	Rebels	34	Brumbies	27	Canberra
16	Crusaders	24	Blues	22	Auckland
16	Hurricanes	20	Waratahs	19	Sydney
16	Sharks	45	Sunwolves	10	Singapore
16	Bulls	40	Stormers	3	Pretoria
16	Lions	25	Jaguares	16	Buenos Aires
22	Highlanders	36	Reds	31	Dunedin
23	Waratahs	31	Sunwolves	30	Tokyo
23	Crusaders	38	Hurricanes	22	Christchurch
23	Brumbies	54	Chiefs	17	Canberra
23	Sharks	26	Blues	7	Durban
23	Stormers	19	Lions	17	Cape Town
23	Jaguares	27	Bulls	12	Buenos Aires
March					
1	Hurricanes	43	Brumbies	13	Palmerston North
1	Rebels	24	Highlanders	19	Melbourne
2	Sunwolves	30	Chiefs	15	Hamilton
2	Crusaders	22	Reds	12	Brisbane
2	Bulls	30	Lions	12	Johannesburg
2	Stormers	16	Sharks	11	Durban
2	Jaguares	23	Blues	19	Buenos Aires
8	Hurricanes	25	Highlanders	22	Wellington
8	Rebels	29	Brumbies	26	Melbourne
9	Crusaders	57	Chiefs	28	Christchurch
9	Blues	28	Sunwolves	20	Albany
9	Waratahs	28	Reds	17	Sydney
9	Lions	47	Jaguares	39	Johannesburg
9	Bulls	37	Sharks	14	Pretoria
15	Chiefs	23	Hurricanes	23	Hamilton
15	Brumbies	19	Waratahs	13	Canberra
16	Highlanders v Crusaders in Dunedin was cancelled: 0-0 draw				
16	Reds	34	Sunwolves	31	Tokyo
16	Stormers	35	Jaguares	8	Cape Town
16	Lions	36	Rebels	33	Johannesburg

22	Blues	33	Highlanders	26	Auckland
23	Hurricanes	34	Stormers	28	Wellington
23	Waratahs	20	Crusaders	12	Sydney
23	Lions	37	Sunwolves	24	Singapore
23	Chiefs	56	Bulls	20	Pretoria
23	Sharks	28	Rebels	14	Durban
24	Reds	36	Brumbies	14	Brisbane
29	Crusaders	32	Hurricanes	8	Wellington
29	Sunwolves	31	Waratahs	29	Sydney
30	Blues	24	Stormers	9	Auckland
30	Rebels	32	Reds	13	Brisbane
30	Bulls	19	Sharks	16	Durban
30	Chiefs	30	Jaguares	27	Buenos Aires
April					
5	Hurricanes	31	Highlanders	28	Dunedin
5	Reds	24	Stormers	12	Brisbane
5	Sharks	42	Lions	5	Johannesburg
6	Crusaders	36	Brumbies	14	Christchurch
6	Blues	32	Waratahs	29	Auckland
6	Rebels	42	Sunwolves	15	Melbourne
6	Jaguares	22	Bulls	20	Pretoria
12	Crusaders	43	Highlanders	17	Christchurch
12	Stormers	41	Rebels	24	Melbourne
13	Chiefs	33	Blues	29	Hamilton
13	Brumbies	31	Lions	20	Canberra
13	Jaguares	51	Sharks	17	Durban
13	Bulls	32	Reds	17	Pretoria
19	Lions	23	Chiefs	17	Hamilton
19	Hurricanes	29	Sunwolves	23	Tokyo
19	Reds	21	Sharks	14	Durban
20	Highlanders	24	Blues	12	Dunedin
20	Waratahs	23	Rebels	20	Sydney
20	Brumbies	19	Stormers	17	Cape Town
26	Crusaders	36	Lions	10	Christchurch
26	Highlanders	52	Sunwolves	0	Tokyo
27	Hurricanes	47	Chiefs	19	Wellington
27	Sharks	23	Waratahs	15	Sydney
27	Stormers	24	Bulls	23	Cape Town
27	Jaguares	20	Brumbies	15	Buenos Aires

May

3	Crusaders	21	Sharks	21	Christchurch
3	Reds	32	Sunwolves	26	Brisbane
4	Hurricanes	29	Rebels	19	Wellington
4	Highlanders	31	Chiefs	31	Dunedin
4	Brumbies	26	Blues	21	Canberra
4	Bulls	28	Waratahs	21	Pretoria
4	Jaguares	30	Stormers	25	Buenos Aires
10	Hurricanes	22	Blues	12	Auckland
10	Rebels	30	Reds	24	Melbourne
10	Crusaders	45	Bulls	13	Pretoria
11	Highlanders	32	Jaguares	27	Dunedin
11	Chiefs	29	Sharks	23	Hamilton
11	Lions	29	Waratahs	28	Johannesburg
12	Brumbies	33	Sunwolves	0	Canberra
17	Jaguares	28	Hurricanes	17	Wellington
17	Bulls	32	Rebels	17	Melbourne
18	Blues	23	Chiefs	8	Auckland
18	Waratahs	40	Reds	32	Brisbane
18	Lions	38	Highlanders	29	Johannesburg
18	Stormers	19	Crusaders	19	Cape Town
24	Chiefs	19	Reds	13	Hamilton
24	Brumbies	22	Bulls	10	Canberra
25	Rebels	52	Sunwolves	7	Tokyo
25	Crusaders	19	Blues	11	Christchurch
25	Jaguares	23	Waratahs	15	Sydney
25	Stormers	34	Highlanders	22	Cape Town
25	Sharks	27	Lions	17	Durban
31	Blues	22	Bulls	22	Auckland
31	Waratahs	20	Rebels	15	Melbourne

June

1	Brumbies	42	Sunwolves	19	Tokyo
1	Chiefs	40	Crusaders	27	Suva
1	Jaguares	34	Reds	23	Brisbane
1	Hurricanes	30	Sharks	17	Durban
1	Lions	41	Stormers	22	Johannesburg
7	Highlanders	24	Bulls	24	Dunedin
7	Reds	29	Blues	28	Brisbane

8	Crusaders	66	Rebels	0	Christchurch
8	Brumbies	34	Waratahs	24	Sydney
8	Hurricanes	37	Lions	17	Johannesburg
8	Stormers	31	Sunwolves	18	Cape Town
8	Jaguares	34	Sharks	7	Buenos Aires
14	Highlanders	49	Waratahs	12	Invercargill
14	Chiefs	59	Rebels	8	Melbourne
14	Jaguares	52	Sunwolves	10	Buenos Aires
15	Hurricanes	29	Blues	24	Wellington
15	Brumbies	40	Reds	27	Canberra
15	Sharks	12	Stormers	9	Cape Town
15	Bulls	48	Lions	27	Pretoria

Quarter-finals

21	Crusaders	38	Highlanders	14	Christchurch
21	Jaguares	21	Chiefs	16	Buenos Aires
22	Hurricanes	35	Bulls	28	Wellington
22	Brumbies	38	Sharks	13	Canberra

Semi-finals

| 28 | Jaguares | 39 | Brumbies | 7 | Buenos Aires |
| 29 | Crusaders | 30 | Hurricanes | 26 | Christchurch |

Final

July

| 6 | Crusaders | 19 | Jaguares | 3 | Christchurch |

QUARTER-FINALS

June 21, Christchurch

Crusaders 38 (Mo'unga 2, Havili, Douglas, Alaalatoa tries; Mo'unga 5 conversions, penalty goal) defeated **Highlanders 14** (Tomkinson, Walden tries; Ioane 2 conversions).
Referee: J. Peyper (South Africa)

June 21, Buenos Aires

Jaguares 21 (Matera, Moroni tries; Diaz Bonilla conversion, 3 penalty goals) defeated **Chiefs 16** (Boshier try; Debreczeni conversion, 2 penalty goals, M. McKenzie penalty goal).
Referee: G. Jackson (New Zealand)

June 22, Wellington

Hurricanes 35 (Rayasi 2, Perenara, Lam tries; B. Barrett 3 conversions, penalty goal; J. Barrett 2 penalty goals) defeated **Bulls 28** (Hendricks 2, Gelant tries, penalty try; Pollard 3 conversions).
Referee: N. Berry (Australia)

June 22, Canberra

Brumbies 38 (Samu 2, Speight, Powell, Lucas tries; Lealiifano 5 conversions, penalty goal) defeated **Sharks 13** (Esterhuizen try; Bosch conversion, 2 penalty goals).
Referee: M. Fraser (New Zealand)

SEMI-FINALS

June 28, Buenos Aires

Jaguares 39 (Orlando 2, Cubelli, Lavanini, Boffelli tries; Diaz Bonilla 4 conversions, 2 penalty goals) defeated **Brumbies 7** (Fainga'a try; Lealiifano conversion).
Referee: M. Fraser (New Zealand)

June 29, Christchurch

Crusaders 30 (Reece 2, Mo'unga tries; Mo'unga 3 conversions, 3 penalty goals) defeated **Hurricanes 26** (Laumape 2, Lam, Perenara tries; B. Barrett 3 conversions).
Referee: N. Berry (Australia)

FINAL

July 6, Christchurch

Crusaders 19 (Taylor try; Mo'unga conversion, 4 penalty goals) defeated **Jaguares 3** (Diaz Bonilla penalty goal).
Referee: J. Peyper (South Africa)

BLUES

Postal address: Box 77 012 Mt Albert,
Auckland 1350
Telephone: (09) 846 5425
Email: info@theblues.co.nz
Home venues: Eden Park, Auckland; North Harbour Stadium, Albany
Colours: Royal and navy blue

Played 329, Won 167, Lost 155, Drew 7

	Tries	Conv	Pen	DG	Points
For	1044	703	673	11	8680
Against	907	629	738	26	8095

RECORDS — TEAM

Most points in a game	74	*v Stormers, 1998*
Most points in a season	513	*1997*
Biggest winning margin	53	*60–7 v Hurricanes, 2002*
Most tries in a game	11	*v Stormers, 1998*
Most tries in a season	70	*1996*

RECORDS — INDIVIDUAL

Most points in a game	29	*G.W. Anscombe v Bulls, 2012*
Most points in a season	180	*A.R. Cashmore, 1998*
Most points in a career	619	*A.R. Cashmore, 1996-2000*
Most tries in a game	4	*J. Vidiri v Bulls, 2000;*
		D.C. Howlett v Hurricanes 2002;
		J.M. Muliaina v Bulls, 2002
		R.E. Ioane v Sunwolves, 2019
Most tries in a season	12	*D.C. Howlett, 2003*
Most tries in a career	55	*D.C. Howlett, 1999-2007*
Most conversions in a game	7	*A.R. Cashmore v Stormers, 1998;*
		A.R. Cashmore v Bulls, 2000;
		C.J. Spencer v Bulls, 2002
Most conversions in a season	34	*A.R. Cashmore, 1998*
Most conversions in a career	120	*C.J. Spencer*
Most penalty goals in a game	6	*A.R. Cashmore v Chiefs, 1998;*
		A.R. Cashmore v Hurricanes, 1999;
		J.A. Arlidge v Bulls, 2001;
		S.A. Brett v Bulls, 2010;
		C.M. Noakes v Stormers, 2013
Most penalty goals in a season	34	*A.R. Cashmore, 1999*
Most penalty goals in a career	114	*A.R. Cashmore*
Most dropped goals in a game	1	*on 11 occasions*
Most dropped goals in a season	2	*O. Ai'i, 2000*
Most dropped goals in a career	3	*C.J. Spencer*
Most games	164	*K.F. Mealamu, 2000-2015*

Player	Union	Date of birth	Height	Weight	Blues Games	Blues Points
L.C.A. (Leni) Apisai	Auckland	08-03-96	1.81	108	16	–
L.J.T (Levi) Aumua	Tasman	09-10-94	1.83	118	4	–
O.W.T.P (Otere) Black	Manawatu	04-05-95	1.85	86	15	84
J.C. (Jed) Brown	Tasman	12-03-91	1.86	105	3	–
C.D. (Caleb) Clarke	Auckland	29-03-99	1.87	103	13	20
M.W.V. (Michael) Collins	Otago	03-06-93	1.86	99	29	25
G.E. (Gerard) Cowley-Tuioti	North Harbour	16-06-92	1.96	110	44	20
M.D. (Matt) Duffie	North Harbour	16-08-90	1.92	95	41	50
T.J. (Tinoai) Faiane	Auckland	24-10-95	1.84	93	31	10
B.T. (Blake) Gibson (co-captain)	Auckland	19-04-95	1.86	102	41	15
J.K. (Josh) Goodhue	Northland	13-06-95	1.99	115	18	–
A.T.O.A. (Alex) Hodgman	Auckland	16-07-93	1.9	119	25	–
A.L. (Akira) Ioane	Auckland	16-06-95	1.94	113	65	75
R.E. (Rieko) Ioane	Auckland	18-03-97	1.88	103	49	160
L. (Luatangi) Li	North Harbour	11-05-91	1.8	120	4	–
E.V. (Ezekiel) Lindenmuth	Auckland	14-07-97	1.87	116	2	–
S.T. (Sione) Mafileo	North Harbour	14-04-93	1.78	128	42	–
M.E.S (Matt) Matich	Northland	10-07-91	1.85	105	3	–
M.G. (Matt) Moulds	Northland	15-05-91	1.88	108	31	10
M.H. (Melani) Nanai	Auckland	03-08-93	1.92	95	64	105
S.J. (Sam) Nock	Northland	18-06-96	1.78	85	23	5
M. A. (Ma'a) Nonu	N/A	21-05-82	1.82	105	39	35
D.R. (Dalton) Papali'i	Auckland	11-10-97	1.9	105	21	15
J.W. (James) Parsons	North Harbour	27-11-86	1.85	108	106	45
S. (Stephen) Perofeta	Taranaki	12-03-97	1.81	85	17	108
J.W.L. (Jacob) Pierce	North Harbour	10-09-97	2.02	112	2	–
H.R.J. (Harry) Plummer	Auckland	19-06-98	1.84	94	16	48
A.W. (Augustine) Pulu	Counties Manukau	04-01-90	1.8	90	37	20
M.T. (Marcel) Renata	Auckland	24-02-94	1.87	121	6	–
T.N. (Tom) Robinson	Northland	10-11-94	1.98	110	15	10
J.L. (Jonathan) Ruru	Auckland	02-03-93	1.83	94	26	5
Y. (Hisa) Sasagi	Otago	29-06-87	1.86	121	1	–
S.N. (Scott) Scrafton	Auckland	18-04-93	2	114	23	20
H.C.R (Hoskins) Sotutu	Auckland	12-07-98	1.92	106	1	–
T.R. (Tanielu) Tele'a	Auckland	16-06-98	1.87	107	9	20
J.V. (Jordan) Trainor	Auckland	31-01-96	1.87	86	2	–
G. K. (Karl) Tu'inukuafe	North Harbour	21-02-93	1.86	135	10	–
P.T. (Patrick) Tuipulotu (co-captain)	Auckland	23-01-93	1.98	120	67	45
S.J. (Jimmy) Tupou	Counties Manukau	08-08-92	1.96	109	16	5
A.O.H.M. (Ofa) Tuungafasi	Auckland	19-04-92	1.95	129	83	20
S.B. (Sonny Bill) Williams	Counties Manukau	03-08-85	1.91	108	18	5

*Pierce, Perofeta, Trainor and Tupou did not appear in 2019.

Manager: Richard Fry
Coach: Leon MacDonald
Assistant coaches: Tom Coventry, Tana Umaga, Daniel Halangahu, Ben Afeaki

BLUES 2019

	Crusaders	Sharks	Jaguares	Sunwolves	Highlanders	Stormers	Waratahs	Chiefs	Highlanders	Brumbies	Hurricanes	Chiefs	Crusaders	Bulls	Reds	Hurricanes	TOTALS
Collins	15	15	–	–	–	–	s	–	–	–	–	–	–	–	–	–	**3**
Nanai	14	14	15	15	15	15	15	15	15	15	15	15	15	15	15	15	**16**
Tele'a	–	s	14	14	14	14	–	–	–	–	14	–	–	s	11	13	**9**
Clarke	–	–	–	–	–	–	14	14	14	11	–	14	14	14	–	11	**8**
Duffie	–	–	–	–	–	–	–	–	s	14	s	s	–	–	14	–	**5**
R. Ioane	11	11	11	11	11	11	11	11	11	–	11	11	11	11	–	14	**14**
Faiane	12	13	13	13	13	13	13	13	13	13	13	13	13	13	13	–	**15**
Nonu	13	–	12	–	12	12	12	12	12	12	12	12	12	12	12	s	**14**
Williams	s	12	s	12	–	s	–	–	–	–	–	–	–	–	–	12	**6**
Aumua	–	–	–	s	–	–	–	–	–	s	–	–	s	–	s	–	**4**
Black	10	10	10	s	s	10	10	10	10	10	s	–	s	s	10	10	**15**
Plummer	s	s	s	10	10	s	s	s	s	s	10	10	10	10	s	s	**16**
Ruru	9	9	s	–	9	9	9	9	9	–	–	9	9	9	s	s	**13**
Pulu	s	s	9	9	s	s	–	–	–	s	s	s	s	s	9	9	**13**
Nock	–	–	–	s	–	–	s	s	s	9	9	–	–	–	–	–	**6**
A. Ioane	8	8	8	8	8	8	8	8	8	8	8	8	8	8	8	8	**16**
Papali'i	7	7	7	s	s	s	s	7	7	s	6	6	–	–	6	6	**14**
Gibson	–	–	–	7	7	7	7	s	s	–	7	7	7	7	7	7	**11**
Brown	–	–	–	–	–	–	s	s	–	s	–	–	–	–	–	–	**3**
Sotutu	–	–	–	–	–	–	–	–	–	–	–	–	s	–	–	–	**1**
Robinson	6	6	6	6	6	6	6	6	6	6	–	s	6	6	s	s	**15**
Matich	s	s	s	–	–	–	–	–	–	–	–	–	–	–	–	–	**3**
Goodhue	5	5	5	5	5	–	5	s	s	5	5	–	–	–	s	s	**12**
Tuipulotu	4	4	4	–	s	4	4	4	4	s	4	4	4	4	–	4	**14**
Cowley-Tuioti	s	s	s	4	4	5	s	5	5	4	–	s	s	s	4	–	**14**
Scrafton	–	–	–	s	–	–	s	–	–	–	s	5	5	5	5	5	**8**
Mafileo	3	s	s	3	3	3	3	s	3	–	–	–	–	–	–	–	**9**
Tuungafasi	s	3	3	–	s	s	s	3	s	3	3	3	3	3	3	–	**14**
Hodgman	1	s	1	–	1	1	1	s	s	1	–	1	1	1	1	–	**13**
Tu'inukuafe	s	1	s	1	s	s	–	1	1	s	1	–	–	–	–	–	**10**
Renata	–	–	–	s	–	–	s	–	–	s	s	–	–	s	–	3	**6**
Li	–	–	–	s	–	–	–	–	–	–	–	–	s	–	s	s	**4**
Sasagi	–	–	–	–	–	–	–	–	–	–	–	–	–	–	–	s	**1**
Lindenmuth	–	–	–	–	–	–	–	–	–	–	s	–	–	–	–	1	**2**
Parsons	2	2	2	2	2	2	2	2	2	s	2	–	s	2	2	2	**15**
Moulds	s	s	s	–	–	s	s	s	–	–	–	2	–	–	–	–	**7**
Apisai	–	–	–	–	s	–	–	–	s	2	s	s	2	s	s	s	**9**

BLUES INDIVIDUAL SCORING

	Tries	Con	PG	DG	Points
Black	1	20	13	–	84
Plummer	1	8	9	–	48
R. Ioane	9	–	–	–	45
Nanai	5	–	–	–	25
Tele'a	4	–	–	–	20
Clarke	3	–	–	–	15
Nonu	3	–	–	–	15
Pulu	3	–	–	–	15
Tuungafasi	3	–	–	–	15
Faiane	2	–	–	–	10
A. Ioane	2	–	–	–	10

	Tries	Con	PG	DG	Points
Papali'i	2	–	–	–	10
Robinson	2	–	–	–	10
Cowley-Tuioti	1	–	–	–	5
Gibson	1	–	–	–	5
Nock	1	–	–	–	5
Scrafton	1	–	–	–	5
Tuipulotu	1	–	–	–	5
Totals	**45**	**28**	**22**	**0**	**347**
*Opposition scored**	*47*	*31*	*22*	*0*	*369*

*Includes three penalty tries, worth 21 points

Played 16 Won 5 Lost 10 Drew 1 Points for 541 Points against 369

Date	Opponent	Location	Score	Tries	Con	PG	DG	Referee
February 16	Crusaders	Auckland	22–24	A. Ioane, Tuungafasi, Pulu	Black, Plummer	Black		N. Briant
February 23	Sharks	Durban	7–26	Tele'a	Black			P. Williams
March 2	Jaguares	Buenos Aires	19–23	Papali'i	Black	Black (4)		R. Rasivhenge (South Africa)
March 9	Sunwolves	Albany	28–20	R. Ioane (4)	Plummer	Black, Plummer		M. Fraser
March 22	Highlanders	Auckland	33–26	R. Ioane (2), Nanai, Tuipulotu	Plummer, Black	Plummer (2), Black		M. van der Westhuizen (South Africa)
March 30	Stormers	Auckland	24–9	Black, R. Ioane, Tele'a	Black (3)	Black		N. Briant
April 6	Waratahs	Auckland	32–29	Robinson, Nonu, Faiane, Clarke	Black (3)	Black (2)		F. Anselmi (Argentina)
April 13	Chiefs	Hamilton	29–33	Nonu (2), R. Ioane, Nanai	Black (2), Plummer	Black		A. Gardner (Australia)
April 20	Highlanders	Dunedin	12–24	Robinson, Nanai	Plummer			P. Williams
May 4	Brumbies	Canberra	21–26	Clarke, Faiane	Black	Plummer (2), Black		D. Murphy (Australia)
May 10	Hurricanes	Auckland	12–22	Papali'i, Nock	Plummer			N. Briant
May 18	Chiefs	Auckland	23–8	Tuungafasi, Plummer, Nanai, Cowley-Tuioti		Plummer		G. Jackson
May 25	Crusaders	Christchurch	11–19	R. Ioane		Plummer (2)		M. Fraser
May 31	Bulls	Auckland	22–22	Tuungafasi, Scrafton, A. Ioane	Plummer (2)	Plummer		M. Fraser
June 7	Reds	Brisbane	28–29	A. Pulu (2), Gibson, Tele'a	Black (4)			B. Pickerill
June 15	Hurricanes	Wellington	24–29	Clarke, Tele'a, Nanai	Black (3)	Black		G. Jackson

CHIEFS

Postal address: Box 4292, Hamilton East 3247
Telephone: (07) 853 0231
Email: admin@chiefs.co.nz
Home venues: FMG Stadium Waikato, Hamilton;
    International Stadium, Rotorua
Colours: Black base with yellow and red. Black shorts

Played 333, Won 178, Lost 145, Drew 10

	Tries	Conv	Pen	DG	Points
For	1009	733	720	8	8705
Against	915	655	763	24	8252

RECORDS — TEAM

Most points in a game	72	*v Lions, 2010*
Most points in a season	560	*2016*
Biggest winning margin	51	*(61-10) v Sunwolves 2018*
Most tries in a game	9	*v Force, 2007*
	9	*v Blues, 2009*
	9	*v Lions, 2010*
	9	*v Force 2016*
	9	*v Sunwolves 2018*
Most tries in a season	76	*2016*

RECORDS — INDIVIDUAL

Most points in a game	32	*S.R. Donald v Lions, 2010*
Most points in a season	251	*A.W. Cruden, 2012*
Most points in a career	878	*S.R. Donald, 2005-2019*
Most tries in a game	4	*S.W. Sivivatu v Blues, 2009*
	4	*A.T. Tikoirotuma v Blues 2012*
	4	*C.J. Ngatai v Force 2016*
Most tries in a season	12	*R.Q. Randle, 2002*
Most tries in a career	42	*S.W. Sivivatu, 2003-2011*
Most conversions in a game	9	*S.R. Donald v Lions, 2010*
Most conversions in a season	43	*A.W. Cruden, 2012*
	43	*D.S. McKenzie 2016*
Most conversions in a career	151	*S.R. Donald*
Most penalty goals in a game	6	*G.W. Jackson v Reds, 2001*
	6	*S.R. Donald v Crusaders, 2007*
Most penalty goals in a season	50	*A.W. Cruden, 2012*
Most penalty goals in a career	153	*S.R. Donald*
Most dropped goals in a game	1	*on eight occasions*
Most dropped goals in a season	2	*I.D. Foster, 1996*
Most dropped goals in a career	2	*I.D. Foster*
	2	*G.W. Jackson*
Most games	178	*L.J. Messam, 2006-2018*

Player	Union	Date of birth	Height	Weight	Chiefs Games	Chiefs Points
S. (Solomon) Alaimalo	Waikato	27–12–95	1.95	99	38	65
M.G. (Michael) Allardice	Hawke's Bay	19–10–91	2	115	42	–
T.J. (Tyler) Ardron	Bay of Plenty	16–10–91	1.94	110	26	25
L.S. (Lachlan) Boshier	Taranaki	16–11–94	1.91	106	44	50
M.M. (Mitchell) Brown	Taranaki	15–08–93	1.94	110	33	15
S.J. (Sam) Cane (co-capt)	Bay of Plenty	13–01–92	1.89	105	111	75
R.C. (Ryan) Coxon	Tasman	30–09–97	1.83	118	4	–
J.M. (Jack) Debreczeni	Northland	06–06–93	1.92	100	7	42
S.R. (Stephen) Donald	Counties Manukau	03–12–83	1.86	96	106	878
T.J. (Tiaan) Falcon	Hawke's Bay	19–06–97	1.81	90	3	–
K.S. (Kane) Hames	Tasman	28–08–88	1.8	113	25	10
N.P. (Nathan) Harris	Bay of Plenty	08–03–92	1.86	110	58	35
F.W.S.P (Fin) Hoeata	Taranaki	28–12–96	1.97	105	–	–
L.B. (Luke) Jacobson	Waikato	20–04–97	1.91	107	21	25
M.L. (Mitch) Jacobson	Waikato	13–01–96	1.9	105	3	–
M.R. (Mitch) Karpik	Bay of Plenty	02–06–95	1.86	103	20	15
S.S.V. (Sefo) Kautai	Waikato	16–08–96	1.89	133	11	–
N.E. (Nepo) Laulala	Counties Manukau	06–11–91	1.84	116	32	5
D.A. (Daymon) Leasuasu	Counties Manukau	20–01–93	1.99	118	2	–
O.N.T. (Orbyn) Leger	Counties Manukau	13–03–97	1.84	90	2	–
A.R. (Anton) Lienert-Brown	Waikato	15–04–95	1.87	103	68	35
T.T.P. (Tevita) Mafileo	Bay of Plenty	04–02–98	1.87	118	7	–
T. (Tumua) Manu	Auckland	18–04–93	1.83	97	16	15
D.S. (Damian) McKenzie	Waikato	20–04–95	1.75	81	72	638
M.R. (Marty) McKenzie	Southland	14–08–92	1.83	85	31	86
L.E. (Laghlan) McWhannell	Waikato	20–10–98	1.98	114	–	–
A. (Ataata) Moeakiola	N/A	02–06–96	1.85	107	9	15
A. (Atu) Moli	Waikato	12–06–95	1.89	125	38	15
E.W.P.S (Etene) Nanai-Seturo	Counties Manukau	20–08–99	1.83	92	11	25
A.P. (Alex) Nankivell	Tasman	25–10–96	1.88	98	21	15
R.G. (Reuben) O'Neill	Taranaki	17–02–95	1.83	117	–	–
J.W.Z. (Jesse) Parete	Taranaki	20–04–93	1.96	110	24	15
L.J. (Liam) Polwart	Bay of Plenty	02–04–95	1.85	107	25	10
B.A. (Brodie) Retallick (co-capt)	Hawke's Bay	31–05–91	2.04	121	107	80
A.(Aidan) Ross	Bay of Plenty	25–10–95	1.89	111	25	–
T.J.A. (Taleni) Seu	Waikato	26–12–93	1.98	110	45	20
B.A (Bradley) Slater	Taranaki	23–09–98	1.81	112	2	–
P-G.N. (Pita-Gus) Sowakula	Taranaki	10–10–94	1.95	110	15	5
S.T. (Shaun) Stevenson	North Harbour	14–11–96	1.93	95	44	50
B.W.M. (Bailyn) Sullivan	Waikato	03–09–98	1.87	93	4	–
A.(Angus) Ta'avao	Auckland	22–03–90	1.94	124	32	15
H.J.T.T. (Te Toiroa) Tahuriorangi	Taranaki	31–03–95	1.73	84	32	10
S.F. (Samisoni) Taukei'aho	Waikato	08–08–97	1.83	115	22	15
J.A. (Jonathan) Taumateine	Counties Manukau	28–09–96	1.77	82	10	–
S.T. (Sean) Wainui	Taranaki	23–10–95	1.92	104	26	40
B.M. (Brad) Weber	Hawke's Bay	17–01–91	1.75	75	71	79

N.B. Falcon, Hames, Hoeata, McWhannell and O'Neill did not appear in 2019.

Manager: Nikita Hall
Coach: Colin Cooper
Assistant coaches: Andrew Strawbridge, Neil Barnes, Tabai Matson, Nick White, Roger Randle

CHIEFS 2019

	Highlanders	Brumbies	Sunwolves	Crusaders	Hurricanes	Bulls	Jaguares	Blues	Lions	Hurricanes	Highlanders	Sharks	Blues	Reds	Crusaders	Rebels	Jaguares	TOTALS
Stevenson	15	15	15	–	–	–	–	–	s	–	s	s	14	14	14	14	14	11
Alaimalo	–	–	–	15	–	11	11	11	–	15	15	15	15	15	15	15	15	12
D. McKenzie	–	10	10	10	15	15	15	15	–	–	–	–	–	–	–	–	–	7
Debreczeni	–	–	–	s	–	10	–	–	15	–	–	–	–	s	10	10	10	7
Sullivan	14	s	–	–	–	–	–	–	–	–	s	–	–	–	–	–	–	3
Moeakiola	s	14	s	–	11	s	–	s	11	14	–	–	s	–	–	–	–	9
Wainui	–	–	14	14	14	14	14	14	14	–	14	14	–	–	11	11	11	12
Nanai-Seturo	11	11	11	11	s	–	s	–	–	11	11	11	11	11	–	–	–	11
Manu	13	13	–	13	13	13	13	13	s	13	13	13	13	13	s	s	13	16
Lienert-Brown	12	12	–	12	12	–	12	12	13	12	12	12	12	–	13	13	12	14
Nankivell	–	–	13	s	–	12	–	s	12	s	–	s	s	12	12	12	s	12
Leger	10	–	12	–	–	–	–	–	–	–	–	–	–	–	–	–	–	2
Donald	s	–	–	–	–	–	–	–	–	s	–	–	–	–	–	–	–	2
M. McKenzie	–	–	–	–	10	s	10	10	10	10	10	10	10	10	s	s	s	13
Weber	9	–	9	9	9	9	9	9	9	–	9	9	9	9	9	9	9	15
Tahuriorangi	s	9	s	s	s	s	s	s	–	9	s	–	s	s	s	s	s	15
Taumateine	–	s	–	–	–	–	–	–	–	s	–	–	–	–	–	–	–	2
Ardron	8	8	–	5	8	8	8	5	4	8	8	4	8	5	5	5	5	16
Parete	s	–	s	s	–	s	s	s	s	s	s	6	4	4	4	s	s	15
Boshier	7	7	s	7	–	7	7	7	7	7	7	–	–	6	6	6	6	14
Karpik	–	s	7	s	7	–	–	–	–	–	–	7	7	s	–	–	–	7
Cane	–	–	–	–	–	–	–	–	–	–	–	–	s	7	7	7	7	5
M. Jacobson	–	–	–	–	–	–	–	–	–	–	–	–	s	–	s	s	–	3
Seu	s	s	8	8	s	–	s	8	8	s	s	s	–	–	–	–	–	11
Brown	6	6	6	6	6	5	5	–	5	5	5	5	5	–	–	–	–	12
L. Jacobson	–	–	–	–	s	6	6	6	6	6	6	8	–	–	–	–	–	8
Sowakula	–	–	–	–	–	–	–	s	s	–	–	s	6	8	8	8	8	8
Allardice	5	5	5	–	5	s	4	–	–	4	4	–	–	–	–	–	–	8
Retallick	4	4	4	4	4	4	–	4	–	–	–	–	–	–	–	4	4	9
Leasuasu	–	–	–	–	–	–	–	–	–	–	–	–	–	s	s	–	–	2
Laulala	s	3	–	3	3	s	3	3	3	–	3	3	s	3	3	s	s	15
Ta'avao	3	–	3	s	s	3	s	1	1	3	s	s	3	–	s	3	3	15
Moli	–	–	–	–	–	–	–	–	s	1	1	1	1	1	1	1	1	9
Coxon	–	–	–	–	s	–	–	s	–	–	s	s	–	–	–	–	–	4
Ross	1	1	1	1	1	1	1	–	–	–	–	–	–	s	s	s	s	12
Mafileo	s	s	s	–	s	s	s	–	–	s	–	–	–	–	–	–	–	7
Kautai	–	s	s	–	–	–	s	s	s	–	–	–	s	–	–	–	–	6
Harris	2	2	–	2	2	2	2	2	–	2	2	2	2	2	–	2	2	14
Taukeiaho	s	s	2	s	s	s	s	s	s	–	–	–	–	s	2	s	s	13
Polwart	–	–	–	–	–	–	–	–	2	s	s	s	s	–	–	–	–	5
Slater	–	–	s	–	–	–	–	–	–	–	–	–	–	–	s	–	–	2

CHIEFS INDIVIDUAL SCORING

	Tries	Con	PG	DG	Points
D. McKenzie	2	19	11	–	81
Debreczeni	2	13	2	–	42
M. McKenzie	1	14	3	–	42
Weber	5	2	–	–	29
Boshier	5	–	–	–	25
Nanai-Seturo	5	–	–	–	25
Stevenson	4	–	–	–	20
Alaimalo	3	–	–	–	15
Lienert-Brown	3	–	–	–	15
Manu	3	–	–	–	15
Moeakiola	3	–	–	–	15
Nankivell	3	–	–	–	15
Ta'avao	3	–	–	–	15
Ardron	2	–	–	–	10
L. Jacobson	2	–	–	–	10
Karpik	2	–	–	–	10

	Tries	Con	PG	DG	Points
Parete	2	–	–	–	10
Retallick	2	–			10
Tahuriorangi	2	–	–	–	10
Taukeiaho	2	–	–	–	10
Wainui	2	–	–	–	10
Brown	1	–	–	–	5
Cane	1	–	–	–	5
Laulala	1	–	–	–	5
Moli	1	–	–	–	5
Seu	1	–	–	–	5
Sowakula	1	–	–	–	5
Donald	–	–	1	–	3
Totals	**64**	**48**	**17**	**0**	**467**
Opposition scored	61	47	28	1	486

CHIEFS TEAM RECORD 2019

Played 17 Won 7 Lost 8 Drew 2 Points for 467 Points against 486

Date	Opponent	Location	Score	Tries	Con	PG	DG	Referee
February 15	Highlanders	Hamilton	27–30	Nanai Seturo (2), Ardron, Ta'avao	Weber (2)	Donald		G. Jackson
February 23	Brumbies	Canberra	17–54	Moeakiola, Taukeiaho	D. McKenzie (2)	D. McKenzie		A. Gardner *(Australia)*
March 2	Sunwolves	Hamilton	15–30	Nanai Seturo, Nankivell	D. McKenzie	D. McKenzie		F. Anselmi *(Argentina)*
March 9	Crusaders	Christchurch	28–57	Brown, Seu, Nanai Seturo, Debreczeni	D. McKenzie (3), Debreczeni			B. Pickerill
March 15	Hurricanes	Hamilton	23–23	Lienert Brown, D. McKenzie	D. McKenzie (2)	D. McKenzie (3)		M. Fraser
March 23	Bulls	Pretoria	56–20	Retallick (2), Alaimalo (2), Nankivell (2), Tahuriorangi	D. McKenzie (6)	D. McKenzie (3)		AJ Jacobs *(South Africa)*
March 30	Jaguares	Buenos Aires	30–27	Manu, D. McKenzie, Tahuriorangi	D. McKenzie (3)	D. McKenzie (3)		A. Gardner *(Australia)*
April 13	Blues	Hamilton	33–29	Boshier (2), Weber, Parete, Moeakiola	D. McKenzie (2), M. McKenzie (2)			A. Gardner *(Australia)*
April 19	Lions	Hamilton	17–23	Laulala, Wainui, Manu	M. McKenzie			B. Pickerill
April 27	Hurricanes	Wellington	19–47	L. Jacobson, Boshier, Moeakiola	M. McKenzie (2)			R. Rasivhenge *(South Africa)*
May 4	Highlanders	Dunedin	31–31	Ta'avao (2), L. Jacobson, Ardron, Weber	M. McKenzie (3)			M. Fraser
May 11	Sharks	Hamilton	29–23	Weber (2), Karpik, Lienert Brown	M. McKenzie (3)	M. McKenzie		N. Berry *(Australia)*
May 18	Blues	Auckland	8–23	Karpik		M. McKenzie		G. Jackson
May 24	Reds	Hamilton	19–13	Moli, Sowakula, Nanai Seturo	M. McKenzie (2)			A. Gardner *(Australia)*
June 1	Crusaders	Suva	40–27	Taukeiaho, Parete, Weber, Stevenson, Alaimalo, Manu	Debreczeni (5)			B. O'Keeffe
June 14	Rebels	Melbourne	59–8	Stevenson (3), Boshier, Cane, Debreczeni, Wainui, M. McKenzie, Lienert Brown	Debreczeni (6), M. McKenzie			A. Gardner *(Australia)*
June 21	Jaguares (QF)	Buenos Aires	16–21	Boshier	Debreczeni	Debreczeni (2), M. McKenzie		G. Jackson

HURRICANES

Postal address: Box 7201, Wellington
Telephone: (04) 389 0020
Email: mail@hurricanes.co.nz
Home venues: Westpac Stadium, Wellington; McLean Park,
Napier; FMG Stadium, Palmerston North
Colours: Yellow and black.

Played 335, Won 190, Lost 138, Drew 7

	Tries	Conv	Pen	DG	Points
For	1023	719	656	5	8536
Against	837	577	730	24	7601

RECORDS — TEAM

Most points in a game	83	*v Sunwolves 2017*
Most points in a season	691	*2017*
Biggest winning margin	66	*83-17 v Sunwolves 2017*
Most tries in a game	13	*v Sunwolves 2017*
Most tries in a season	101	*2017*

RECORDS — INDIVIDUAL

Most points in a game	30	*D.E. Holwell v Highlanders, 2001*
Most points in a season	223	*B.J. Barrett, 2016*
Most points in a career	1238	*B.J. Barrett, 2011-2019*
Most tries in a game	4	*M.B. Lam v Rebels, 2018*
	4	*K.H. Laumape v Blues, 2018*
Most tries in a season	16	*K.H. Laumape, 2017*
	16	*M.B. Lam, 2018*
Most tries in a career	56	*C.M. Cullen, 1996-2003*
Most conversions in a game	9	*B.J. Barrett v Rebels, 2012*
		O.W. Black v Sunwolves, 2017
Most conversions in a season	50	*B.J. Barrett, 2016*
Most conversions in a career	249	*B.J. Barrett*
Most penalty goals in a game	7	*J.B. Cameron v Blues, 1996*
	7	*D.E. Holwell v Highlanders, 2001*
Most penalty goals in a season	40	*B.J. Barrett, 2014*
Most penalty goals in a career	178	*B. J. Barrett*
Most dropped goals in a game	1	*by five players*
Most dropped goals in a season	1	*by five players*
Most dropped goals in a career	1	*by five players*
Most games	127	*T.T.R. Perenara, 2012-2019*

Player	Union	Date of birth	Height	Weight	Hurricanes Games	Hurricanes Points
F.P. (Fraser) Armstrong	Manawatu	18–04–92	1.93	127	22	–
V.T. (Vince) Aso	Auckland	05–01–95	1.86	98	45	105
A.J. (Asafo) Aumua	Wellington	05–05–97	1.77	108	15	–
B.J. (Beauden) Barrett	Taranaki	27–05–91	1.86	92	125	1238
J.M. (Jordie) Barrett	Taranaki	17–02–97	1.96	96	49	272
H.K. (Heiden) Bedwell-Curtis	Taranaki	25–06–91	1.94	108	2	–
J. (James) Blackwell	Wellington	01–04–95	1.9	107	23	5
F.T. (Finlay) Christie	Tasman	19–09–95	1.77	84	14	5
D.S. (Dane) Coles (capt)	Wellington	10–12–86	1.84	110	110	90
G.O. (Geoff) Cridge	Wellington	06–02–95	2	114	1	–
G.O. (Gareth) Evans	Hawke's Bay	05–08–91	1.9	107	23	10
C.I. (Chris) Eves	North Harbour	11–12–87	1.87	123	86	10
A.F. (Alex) Fidow	Wellington	19–08–97	1.87	137	4	–
V.T.L. (Vaea) Fifita	Wellington	17–06–92	1.96	112	58	45
J.K. (Jackson) Garden-Bachop	Wellington	03–10–94	1.83	99	7	14
R. (Ross) Geldenhuys	Bay of Plenty	19–04–83	1.89	118	5	–
W.T. (Wes) Goosen	Wellington	20–10–95	1.78 ·	92	38	100
S.T. (Sam) Henwood	Counties Manukau	28–03–91	1.86	109	10	–
R.P. (Richard) Judd	Bay of Plenty	18–05–92	1.8	88	9	–
D.A. (Du'Plessis) Kirifi	Wellington	03–03–97	1.8	101	15	5
M.B. (Ben) Lam	Wellington	09–06–91	1.94	106	38	130
K.H. (Ngani) Laumape	Manawatu	22–04–93	1.77	103	61	210
K.T.V. (Kane) Le'aupepe	Bay of Plenty	03–12–92	2.01	119	10	10
S.T. (Sam) Lousi	Wellington	20–07–91	1.97	122	28	10
J.H. (Jonah) Lowe	Hawke's Bay	09–05–96	1.84	92	3	–
J.R. (James) Marshall	Taranaki	07–12–88	1.83	93	53	87
B. (Ben) May	Hawke's Bay	13–10–82	1.94	119	90	20
N.R. (Nehe) Milner-Skudder	Manawatu	15–12–90	1.82	90	36	40
L.F. (Liam) Mitchell	Manawatu	10–10–95	1.99	110	12	–
X.J.S (Xavier) Numia	Wellington	29–11–98	1.89	111	9	–
T.T.R. (TJ) Perenara	Wellington	23–01–92	1.84	94	127	270
R.J. (Reed) Prinsep	Canterbury	17–02–93	1.92	108	45	15
B.D. (Billy) Proctor	Wellington	14–05–99	1.87	96	1	–
M.P. (Matt) Proctor	Wellington	26–10–92	1.8	90	66	60
S.T.M (Salesi) Rayasi	Auckland	25–09–96	1.93	105	5	15
J.R. (Ricky) Riccitelli	Taranaki	03–02–95	1.92	110	57	15
A.S. (Ardie) Savea	Wellington	14–10–93	1.88	100	91	105
F.H. (Fletcher) Smith	Waikato	01–03–95	1.8	88	6	14
T.J. (Toby) Smith	Waikato	10–10–88	1.9	112	21	–
C.J. (Chase) Tiatia	Bay of Plenty	14–10–95	1.81	93	11	5
D.S. (Danny) Toala	Hawke's Bay	23–03–99	1.76	95	2	–
J.L. (Jeff) To'omaga-Allen	Wellington	19–11–90	1.92	125	118	25
P. (Peter) Umaga-Jensen	Wellington	31–12–97	1.87	95	5	10
I.E.T. (Isaia) Walker-Leaware	Wellington	16–04–97	1.87	127	18	5

NB. Cridge, Lousi and Milner-Skudder did not appear in 2019.

Manager: Tony Ward
Coach: John Plumtree
Assistant coaches: Jason Holland, Richard Watt, Dan Cron, Carlos Spencer

HURRICANES 2019

	Waratahs	Crusaders	Brumbies	Highlanders	Chiefs	Stormers	Crusaders	Highlanders	Sunwolves	Chiefs	Rebels	Blues	Jaguares	Sharks	Lions	Blues	Bulls	Crusaders	TOTALS
J. Barrett	15	15	–	14	14	12	14	13	–	15	15	15	15	15	15	–	15	15	**15**
Tiatia	–	–	15	15	15	15	15	15	15	11	11	s	–	–	11	–	–	–	**11**
Goosen	14	14	s	–	11	14	s	14	14	14	14	14	14	14	–	–	14	–	**14**
Lam	11	11	11	11	–	11	11	11	11	–	–	11	11	11	14	14	11	11	**15**
Rayasi	–	–	–	–	–	–	–	–	–	s	–	–	s	–	s	11	s	–	**5**
Lowe	–	–	–	–	–	–	–	–	–	–	–	–	–	–	–	s	–	14	**2**
Aso	13	12	14	s	–	–	–	–	–	–	–	–	–	–	–	–	–	–	**4**
Umaga-Jensen	–	–	–	–	–	–	–	–	–	–	–	–	–	–	13	13	13	s	**4**
Toala	–	–	–	–	–	–	–	–	–	–	–	–	–	–	s	12	–	–	**2**
B. Proctor	s	–	–	–	–	–	–	–	–	–	–	–	–	–	–	–	–	–	**1**
M. Proctor	–	13	13	13	13	13	13	s	13	13	13	13	13	13	–	–	–	13	**14**
Laumape	12	s	12	12	12	–	12	12	12	12	12	12	12	12	12	–	12	12	**16**
F. Smith	10	10	–	–	–	–	–	10	–	–	–	–	s	–	–	s	s	–	**6**
Marshall	s	–	–	–	–	–	–	–	s	s	s	–	10	s	10	15	–	s	**9**
Garden-Bachop	–	s	s	–	–	–	–	–	–	–	–	–	–	–	–	–	10	–	**3**
B. Barrett	–	–	10	10	10	10	10	10	–	10	10	10	–	10	–	–	10	10	**12**
Perenara	9	s	9	9	9	–	9	9	9	9	–	9	9	9	9	s	9	9	**16**
Christie	s	9	–	–	–	s	–	s	–	s	s	s	–	–	9	–	–	–	**8**
Judd	–	–	s	–	–	9	s	–	s	9	–	–	s	–	–	–	–	–	**6**
Evans	8	8	–	–	–	–	–	–	–	–	–	–	–	s	8	8	8	8	**7**
Savea	7	–	8	8	8	7	7	7	–	7	7	7	8	7	s	s	7	7	**16**
Prinsep	6	6	s	s	6	8	8	8	8	8	8	8	8	–	8	6	6	6	**17**
Kirifi	s	7	7	7	7	–	s	s	7	–	s	s	7	s	7	7	s	–	**15**
Henwood	–	s	–	–	–	s	–	–	s	s	s	–	–	–	–	–	–	–	**4**
Fifita	–	–	6	6	5	6	6	6	6	6	6	6	6	6	–	–	–	s	**13**
Bedwell-Curtis	–	–	–	–	s	–	–	–	–	–	–	s	–	–	–	–	–	–	**2**
Mitchell	5	5	5	5	5	5	5	s	5	–	s	–	–	–	s	s	–	–	**12**
Blackwell	4	4	4	4	4	4	4	4	4	4	4	4	4	4	4	–	4	4	**17**
Walker-Leawere	s	s	s	s	–	s	s	s	s	s	5	5	5	5	5	5	5	5	**17**
Le'aupepe	–	–	–	–	–	–	s	5	–	5	s	s	s	s	–	4	s	s	**10**
To'omaga-Allen	3	3	s	3	–	s	s	s	s	s	3	3	3	3	3	–	3	3	**16**
May	s	s	3	–	3	3	3	3	3	3	–	–	–	–	–	–	s	s	**11**
Eves	1	1	1	1	–	–	s	–	–	–	s	–	s	–	–	–	–	–	**7**
Numia	s	s	s	–	–	–	s	–	s	s	s	–	–	–	–	–	s	–	s	**9**
Fidow	–	–	–	s	s	–	–	–	–	–	–	–	–	–	–	–	s	–	**3**
Armstrong	–	–	–	s	s	1	1	1	1	1	1	s	–	s	s	1	s	–	**13**
T. Smith	–	–	–	–	1	–	–	–	–	–	s	1	1	1	1	–	1	1	**8**
Geldenhuys	–	–	–	–	–	–	–	–	–	–	–	s	s	s	s	3	–	–	**5**
Riccitelli	2	s	s	–	–	2	2	2	2	s	s	s	s	–	2	–	–	–	**12**
Coles	s	2	2	2	2	–	–	–	–	–	–	–	–	s	s	2	2	2	**10**
Aumua	–	–	–	–	s	–	s	s	s	2	2	2	2	2	–	s	s	–	**11**

HURRICANES INDIVIDUAL SCORING

	Tries	Con	PG	DG	Points		Tries	Con	PG	DG	Points
B. Barrett	3	35	11	–	118	Le'aupepe	2	–	–	–	10
J. Barrett	5	7	11	–	72	Umaga-Jensen	2	–	–	–	10
Laumape	13	–	–	–	65	Blackwell	1	–	–	–	5
Lam	9	–	–	–	45	Kirifi	1	–	–	–	5
Goosen	8	–	–	–	40	May	1	–	–	–	5
Perenara	6	–	–	–	30	M. Proctor	1	–	–	–	5
Coles	4	–	–	–	20	Tiatia	1	–	–	–	5
Savea	4	–	–	–	20	Walker-Leawere	1	–	–	–	5
Rayasi	3	–	–	–	15						
F. Smith	1	3	1	–	14	**Totals**	**68**	**49**	**24**	**0**	**510**
Garden-Bachop	–	4	1	–	11						
Fifita	2	–	–	–	10	*Opposition scored**	*53*	*41*	*23*	*0*	*420*

*Includes two penalty tries

HURRICANES TEAM RECORD 2019

Played 18   Won 13   Drew 1   Lost 4   Points for 510   Points against 420

Date	Opponent	Location	Score	Tries	Con	PG	DG	Referee
February 16	Waratahs	Sydney	20–19	Savea, Kirifi	J. Barrett (2)	J. Barrett (2)		A. Gardner (Australia)
February 23	Crusaders	Christchurch	22–38	Lam (2), Goosen, Perenara	J. Barrett			B. O'Keeffe
March 1	Brumbies	Palmerston North	43–13	Laumape (3); Coles (2), Blackwell	B. Barrett (4), Garden-Bachop	B. Barrett		N. Briant
March 8	Highlanders	Wellington	25–22	Laumape (2), Lam	B. Barrett (2)	B. Barrett (2)		D. Murphy (Australia)
March 15	Chiefs	Hamilton	23–23	Goosen, M. Proctor	B. Barrett (2)	B. Barrett (2), J. Barrett		M. Fraser
March 23	Stormers	Wellington	34–28	Goosen (2), May, B. Barrett, J. Barrett	B. Barrett (3)	B. Barrett		G. Jackson
March 29	Crusaders	Wellington	8–32	Laumape		J. Barrett		B. O'Keeffe
April 5	Highlanders	Dunedin	31–28	Savea (2), Perenara, Laumape	B. Barrett (4)	B. Barrett		G. Jackson
April 19	Sunwolves	Tokyo	29–23	Perenara, Lam, Goosen, Tiatia	F. Smith (3)	F. Smith		A. Gardner (Australia)
April 27	Chiefs	Wellington	47–19	J. Barrett (2), Le'aupepe, Savea, Perenara, Goosen, Rayasi	B. Barrett (6)			R. Rasivhenge (South Africa)
May 4	Rebels	Wellington	29–19	Fifita, B. Barrett, Laumape, Goosen	B. Barrett (3)	J. Barrett		N. Berry (Australia)
May 10	Blues	Auckland	22–12	B. Barrett, Lam, J. Barrett	B. Barrett (2)	J. Barrett		N. Briant
May 17	Jaguares	Wellington	20–28	Fifita, Laumape, Le'aupepe	J. Barrett	J. Barrett		B. Pickerill
June 1	Sharks	Durban	30–17	Laumape, Goosen, J. Barrett	B. Barrett (3)	B. Barrett (3)		N. Berry (Australia)
June 8	Lions	Johannesburg	37–17	Lam (2), Coles (2), Laumape	J. Barrett (3)	J. Barrett (2)		J. Peyper (South Africa)
June 15	Blues	Wellington	29–24	Umaga-Jensen (2), Walker-Leawere, F. Smith	Garden-Bachop (3)	Garden-Bachop		G. Jackson
June 22	Bulls (QF)	Wellington	35–28	Rayasi (2), Perenara, Lam	B. Barrett (3)	J. Barrett (2), B. Barrett		N. Berry (Australia)
June 29	Crusaders (SF)	Christchurch	26–30	Laumape (2), Lam, Perenara	B. Barrett (3)			N. Berry (Australia)

CRUSADERS

CRUSADERS™

Postal address: Box 755, Christchurch
Telephone: (03) 379 8300
Email: info@crfu.co.nz
Home venue: Orangetheory Stadium, Christchurch
Colours: Red and black.

Played 357, Won 249, Lost 100, Drew 8

	Tries	Conv	Pen	DG	Points
For	1250	876	883	46	10,804
Against	830	588	713	28	7551

RECORDS — TEAM

Most points in a game	96	*v Waratahs, 2002*
Most points in a season	691	*2018*
Biggest winning margin	77	*96–19 v Waratahs, 2002*
Most tries in a game	14	*v Waratahs, 2002*
Most tries in a season	96	*2018*

RECORDS — INDIVIDUAL

Most points in a game	31	*T.J. Taylor v Stormers, 2012*
Most points in a season	221	*D.W. Carter, 2006*
Most points in a career	1708	*D.W. Carter, 2003-2015*
Most tries in a game	4	*C.S. Ralph v Waratahs, 2002*
	4	*S.D. Maitland v Brumbies, 2011*
Most tries in a season	15	*R.L. Gear, 2005*
	15	*G.C. Bridge 2018*
	15	*S.L. Reece, 2019*
Most tries in a career	52	*C.S. Ralph, 1999-2008*
Most conversions in a game	13	*A.P. Mehrtens v Waratahs, 2002*
Most conversions in a season	38	*D.W. Carter, 2006*
	38	*R. Mo'unga 2018*
Most conversions in a career	287	*D.W. Carter*
Most penalty goals in a game	8	*T.J. Taylor v Stormers, 2012*
Most penalty goals in a season	46	*C.R. Slade, 2014*
Most penalty goals in a career	307	*D.W. Carter*
Most dropped goals in a game	3	*A.P. Mehrtens v Highlanders, 1998*
Most dropped goals in a season	4	*A.P. Mehrtens, 1998, 1999, 2002*
Most dropped goals in a career	17	*A.P. Mehrtens*
Most games	203	*W.W.V. Crockett, 2006-2018*

Player	Union	Date of birth	Height	Weight	Crusaders Games	Crusaders Points
M.S. (Michael) Alaalatoa	Canterbury	28–08–91	1.9	136	71	25
H.M. (Harry) Allan	Canterbury	07–05–97	1.83	110	12	–
S.K. (Scott) Barrett	Taranaki	20–11–93	1.98	116	68	65
T.E.S. (Tim) Bateman	Canterbury	03–06–87	1.82	91	51	40
E.J. (Ethan) Blackadder	Tasman	22–03–95	1.91	107	8	–
G.G. (George) Bower	Otago	28–05–92	1.86	120	10	–
G.C. (George) Bridge	Canterbury	01–04–95	1.85	96	50	135
B.D. (Brett) Cameron	Canterbury	04–10–96	1.71	83	6	9
R.S. (Ryan) Crotty	Canterbury	23–09–88	1.81	96	152	122
I.J.A. (Israel) Dagg	Hawke's Bay	06–06–88	1.86	96	89	140
W.H. (Whetu) Douglas	Canterbury	18–04–94	1.9	109	21	25
M.D. (Mitch) Drummond	Canterbury	15–12–94	1.8	86	80	80
M.T.W. (Mitch) Dunshea	Canterbury	18–11–95	1.96	114	10	5
E.C. (Ere) Enari	Canterbury	30–05–97	1.78	84	5	–
B.M. (Braydon) Ennor	Canterbury	16–07–97	1.87	93	25	65
L.O.K.W.T. (Leicester) Faingaanuku	Tasman	11–10–99	1.88	103	1	–
O.T. (Owen) Franks	Canterbury	23–01–87	1.85	121	153	10
B.C.J. (Ben) Funnell	Canterbury	06–06–90	1.8	109	91	35
E.J. (Jack) Goodhue	Northland	13–06–95	1.86	98	45	50
B.D. (Bryn) Hall	North Harbour	03–02–92	1.83	89	53	65
W.K. (Billy) Harmon	Canterbury	23–12–94	1.87	104	9	5
D.K. (David) Havili	Tasman	23–12–94	1.84	95	76	117
M.J. (Mitch) Hunt	Tasman	19–06–95	1.79	88	49	149
O.G.J.T. (Oli) Jager	Canterbury	05–07–95	1.92	120	16	–
W.T. (Will) Jordan	Tasman	24–02–98	1.88	91	9	40
B.L. (Brodie) McAlister	Canterbury	17–06–97	1.84	109	1	–
A. (Andrew) Makalio	Tasman	22–01–92	1.82	122	34	20
M.M.B.T. (Manasa) Mataele	Taranaki	27–11–96	1.85	100	23	80
J.P.T. (Joe) Moody	Canterbury	16–09–88	1.88	120	82	10
R. (Richie) Mo'unga	Canterbury	25–05–94	1.76	86	58	647
T.G. (Tim) Perry	Tasman	01–08–88	1.88	122	25	5
N.G.J (Ngane) Punivai	Canterbury	30–08–98	1.91	100	2	–
K.J. (Kieran) Read	Counties Manukau	26–10–85	1.93	110	157	135
S.L. (Sevu) Reece	Waikato	13–02–97	1.78	92	14	75
L. (Luke) Romano	Canterbury	16–02–86	1.59	120	125	40
T.B. (Tom) Sanders	Canterbury	05–02–94	1.91	109	8	–
Q.J. (Quinten) Strange	Tasman	21–08–96	1.99	112	27	5
J. (Jordan) Taufua	Tasman	29–01–92	1.85	110	100	70
C.J. (Codie) Taylor	Canterbury	31–03–91	1.83	111	78	75
M.B. (Matt) Todd	Canterbury	24–03–88	1.85	105	140	135
I.J. (Isi) Tuungafasi	Northland	10–01–95	1.87	122	4	–
S.L. (Sam) Whitelock (captain)	Canterbury	12–10–88	2.03	120	144	40

NB. Dagg did not appear in 2019.

Manager: Shane Fletcher
Coach: Scott Robertson
Assistant coaches: Brad Mooar, Jason Ryan, Ronan O'Gara

CRUSADERS 2019

	Blues	Hurricanes	Reds	Chiefs	Waratahs	Hurricanes	Brumbies	Highlanders	Lions	Sharks	Bulls	Stormers	Blues	Chiefs	Rebels	Highlanders	Hurricanes	Jaguares	TOTALS
Havili	15	15	s	s	15	15	15	15	15	–	15	15	15	15	15	15	15	15	17
Jordan	s	–	15	15	s	14	14	s	–	15	–	–	–	–	–	–	–	s	9
Mataele	14	14	–	–	–	–	–	–	–	–	–	–	–	–	–	–	–	–	2
Bridge	11	11	11	–	11	–	–	–	11	11	11	11	11	s	–	11	11	11	13
Ennor	13	s	14	11	14	11	–	11	13	13	s	s	s	11	11	s	s	13	17
Reece	–	–	–	14	–	s	11	14	14	14	14	14	14	14	14	14	14	14	14
Faingaanuku	–	–	–	–	–	–	s	–	–	–	–	–	–	–	–	–	–	–	1
Punivai	–	–	–	–	–	–	–	–	s	–	–	–	–	–	s	–	–	–	2
Bateman	–	–	12	–	–	–	13	–	–	s	–	–	–	–	–	–	–	–	3
Goodhue	–	13	13	13	13	13	–	13	–	12	13	13	13	13	13	13	13	12	15
Crotty	12	12	–	12	12	12	12	12	12	–	12	12	12	12	12	12	12	–	15
Hunt	–	s	s	–	s	–	–	s	s	10	s	–	–	–	s	–	–	s	10
Mo'unga	10	10	10	10	–	10	10	10	10	–	10	10	10	10	10	10	10	10	16
Cameron	–	–	–	s	10	s	s	–	–	–	–	–	–	–	s	–	–	–	5
Enari	–	–	–	9	s	–	–	–	s	–	–	–	–	–	s	–	–	–	4
Hall	9	9	s	s	9	9	s	9	–	9	9	9	9	s	9	9	9	9	17
Drummond	s	s	9	–	–	s	9	–	9	s	s	s	s	9	–	s	s	s	14
Read	–	–	–	–	–	8	8	8	8	8	8	–	8	8	8	8	8	8	12
Douglas	8	8	8	8	8	6	–	6	6	–	s	–	–	6	6	6	6	6	14
Sanders	s	s	6	–	s	–	–	–	–	–	–	–	–	–	–	–	–	–	4
Todd	7	7	7	–	7	7	7	7	–	7	7	7	7	–	7	7	7	7	15
Harmon	–	–	–	7	–	–	–	–	7	s	–	–	7	–	–	–	–	–	4
Taufua	6	6	s	6	6	s	s	s	s	6	6	8	6	s	s	s	s	s	18
Blackadder	–	–	–	s	–	–	6	–	–	–	–	6	s	–	–	–	–	–	4
Barrett	4	4	4	5	–	4	4	4	–	5	5	4	4	4	4	4	4	–	15
Whitelock	–	–	–	–	5	5	s	5	5	–	–	5	5	5	5	5	5	5	12
Dunshea	–	–	–	4	–	–	–	–	s	4	4	–	–	–	s	–	–	4	6
Strange	5	5	5	–	4	s	5	s	4	–	–	–	–	–	–	–	–	–	8
Romano	s	s	s	s	–	–	–	–	s	s	s	s	–	s	s	s	s	s	13
Franks	3	3	3	–	–	–	3	–	–	–	–	–	–	–	–	3	3	3	7
Alaalatoa	s	s	s	3	3	3	s	3	3	3	3	3	3	3	3	s	s	s	18
Jager	–	–	–	–	–	s	–	s	s	s	s	s	–	–	–	–	–	–	6
Allan	–	s	s	s	1	1	s	s	s	–	s	s	–	–	–	–	–	–	10
Moody	1	1	1	1	–	–	1	1	1	1	1	–	1	1	1	1	1	1	15
Perry	s	–	–	–	–	–	–	–	–	–	–	–	–	–	s	–	–	–	2
Bower	–	–	–	s	s	s	–	–	–	–	–	1	s	s	s	s	s	s	10
Tuungafasi	–	–	–	–	s	–	–	–	–	s	–	–	s	s	–	–	–	–	4
Makalio	2	2	2	2	s	s	s	2	–	–	s	s	2	2	2	s	s	s	16
Funnell	s	s	s	–	–	–	2	s	s	s	–	–	–	s	s	–	–	–	9
Taylor	–	–	–	s	2	2	–	–	2	2	2	2	–	–	–	2	2	2	10
McAlister	–	–	–	–	–	–	–	–	–	–	–	–	s	–	–	–	–	–	1

CRUSADERS INDIVIDUAL SCORING

	Tries	Con	PG	DG	Points		Tries	Con	PG	DG	Points
Mo'unga	7	48	17	–	182	Douglas	2	–	–	–	10
Reece	15	–	–	–	75	Drummond	2	–	–	–	10
Ennor	10	–	–	–	50	Mataele	2	–	–	–	10
Jordan	8	–	–	–	40	Cameron	–	3	1	–	9
Havili	7	–	–	–	35	Crotty	1	1	–	–	7
Penalty tries	3	–	–	–	21	Dunshea	1	–	–	–	5
Barrett	4	–	–	–	20	Goodhue	1	–	–	–	5
Bridge	4	–	–	–	20	Makalio	1	–	–	–	5
Taylor	4	–	–	–	20	Todd	1	–	–	–	5
Hall	3	–	–	–	15						
Hunt	1	5	–	–	15	**Totals**	**82**	**57**	**18**	**0**	**584**
Taufua	3	–	–	–	15						
Alaalatoa	2	–	–	–	10	Opposition scored	37	26	21	0	300

CRUSADERS TEAM RECORD 2019

Date	Opponent	Location	Played 18 Score	Won 14 Tries	Lost 2	Drew 2 Con	Points for 584 PG	DG	Points against 300 Referee
February 16	Blues	Auckland	24–22	Mataele (2), Penalty tries (2)					N. Briant
February 23	Hurricanes	Christchurch	38–22	Barrett (2), Mo'unga (2), Taufua, Bridge		Mo'unga (3), Hunt			B. O'Keeffe
March 2	Reds	Brisbane	22–12	Douglas, Ennor, Jordan, Taufua		Mo'unga			M. van der Westhuizen (South Africa)
March 9	Chiefs	Christchurch	57–28	Jordan (2), Taylor (2), Makalio, Alaalatoa, Ennor, Reece, Hall		Mo'unga (5), Cameron			B. Pickerill
March 23	Waratahs	Sydney	12–20	Bridge, Jordan		Cameron			J. Peyper (South Africa)
March 29	Hurricanes	Wellington	32–8	Havili (2), Ennor, Jordan		Mo'unga (3)	Mo'unga (2)		B. O'Keeffe
April 6	Brumbies	Christchurch	36–14	Reece (2), Jordan (2), Taufua		Mo'unga (3), Cameron	Cameron		J. Peyper (South Africa)
April 12	Highlanders	Christchurch	43–17	Ennor, Reece, Havili, Drummond, Jordan, penalty try		Mo'unga (3), Hunt	Mo'unga		B. O'Keeffe
April 26	Lions	Christchurch	36–10	Bridge (2), Reece (2), Ennor		Mo'unga (4)	Mo'unga		P. Williams
May 3	Sharks	Christchurch	21–21	Taylor, Hunt, Goodhue		Hunt (3)			B. Pickerill
May 10	Bulls	Pretoria	45–13	Reece (3), Mo'unga (2), Dunshea, Barrett		Mo'unga (5)			R. Rasiwhenge (South Africa)
May 18	Stormers	Cape Town	19–19	Todd, Havili, Ennor		Mo'unga (2)			N. Berry (Australia)
May 25	Blues	Christchurch	19–11	Hall		Mo'unga (2)	Mo'unga (4)		M. Fraser
June 1	Chiefs	Suva	27–40	Barrett, Drummond, Ennor, Reece		Mo'unga (2)	Mo'unga		B. O'Keefe
June 8	Rebels	Christchurch	66–0	Ennor (3), Reece (3), Havili (2), Hall, Crotty		Mo'unga (7), Crotty			G. Jackson
June 21	Highlanders (QF)	Christchurch	38–14	Mo'unga (2), Douglas, Havili, Alaalatoa		Mo'unga (5)	Mo'unga		J. Peyper (South Africa)
June 28	Hurricanes (SF)	Christchurch	30–26	Reece (2), Mo'unga		Mo'unga (3)	Mo'unga (3)		N. Berry (Australia)
July 6	Jaguares (F)	Christchurch	19–3	Taylor		Mo'unga	Mo'unga (4)		J. Peyper (South Africa)

HIGHLANDERS

Postal address: Box 6070, Dunedin 9059
Telephone: (03) 479 9280
Email: contactus@highlanders.net.nz
Home venues: Forsyth Barr Stadium, Dunedin;
          Rugby Park Stadium, Invercargill
Colours: Blue with gold and maroon.

Played 332, Won 165, Lost 163, Drew 4

	Tries	Conv	Pen	DG	Points
For	932	649	749	27	8,292
Against	959	693	677	15	8263

RECORDS — TEAM

Most points in a game	65	v Bulls, 1999
Most points in a season	530	2015
Biggest winning margin	49	55-6 v Force, 2017
Most tries in a game	9	v Bulls, 1999
Most tries in a season	64	2017

RECORDS — INDIVIDUAL

Most points in a game	28	B.A. Blair v Sharks, 2005
Most points in a season	191	L.Z. Sopoaga, 2015
Most points in a career	892	L.Z. Sopoaga, 2011-2018
Most tries in a game	3	on 11 occasions
Most tries in a season	13	W.R. Naholo, 2015
Most tries in a career	41	W.R. Naholo, 2015-2019
Most conversions in a game	7	T.E. Brown v Bulls, 1999
Most conversions in a season	41	L.Z. Sopoaga 2018
Most conversions in a career	163	L.Z. Sopoaga
Most penalty goals in a game	8	W.C. Walker v Chiefs, 2003
Most penalty goals in a season	34	T.E. Brown, 2000
Most penalty goals in a career	180	T.E. Brown
Most dropped goals in a game	1	on 27 occasions
Most dropped goals in a season	3	L.Z. Sopoaga, 2015
Most dropped goals in a career	6	T.E. Brown
Most games	153	B.R. Smith, 2009-2019

Player	Union	Date of birth	Height	Weight	Highlanders Games	Highlanders Points
M. (Marty) Banks	Tasman	19–09–89	1.9	90	40	200
R.J. (Richard) Buckman	Kobe Steelers (Japan)	27–05–89	1.84	95	50	55
L.J. (Liam) Coltman	Otago	25–01–90	1.85	112	102	35
J.M. (Josh) Dickson	Otago	02–01–94	2	109	19	–
A.L. (Ash) Dixon (co-capt)	Hawke's Bay	01–09–88	1.82	105	73	15
E.C. (Elliot) Dixon	Southland	04–09–89	1.93	110	105	62
S.K. (Sef) Fa'agase	Canterbury	05–03–91	1.85	113	3	–
M.A. (Matt) Faddes	Otago	06–11–91	1.85	94	46	100
F.M.L.N. (Folau) Fakatava	Hawke's Bay	16–12–99	1.77	80	3	–
T.S.G. (Tom) Franklin	Bay of Plenty	11–08–90	2	113	85	25
S.M. (Shannon) Frizell	Tasman	11–02–94	1.95	108	27	55
B.E.C. (Bryn) Gatland	North Harbour	05–10–95	1.78	88	4	6
K.W. (Kayne) Hammington	Manawatu	24–09–90	1.7	75	39	20
J.N. (Jackson) Hemopo	Manawatu	14–11–93	1.94	113	39	5
D.C. (Dan) Hollinshead	Bay of Plenty	07–06–95	1.86	92	2	4
D. (Dillon) Hunt	North Harbour	23–02–95	1.89	103	32	25
J.S.C. (Jordan) Hyland	Northland	03–10–89	1.88	101	4	5
J.R. (Josh) Ioane	Otago	11–07–95	1.76	85	23	116
J.Z.A. (Josh) Iosefa-Scott	Waikato	16–07–96	1.93	133	1	–
R.D. (Ricky) Jackson	Otago	02–08–98	1.8	100	1	–
C.A. (Ayden) Johnstone	Waikato	24–10–96	1.84	120	15	–
J.A.R. (James) Lentjes	Otago	16–01–91	1.88	104	37	25
D.P. (Daniel) Lienert-Brown	Canterbury	09–02–93	1.84	112	73	15
T. (Tevita) Li	North Harbour	23–03–95	1.82	95	38	60
T.S. (Tyrel) Lomax	Tasman	01–06–96	1.92	127	31	15
J.A. (Josh) McKay	Canterbury	10–10–97	1.83	92	7	20
M.E.R. (Marino) Mikaele-Tu'u	Hawke's Bay	06–11–97	1.93	114	8	–
T. (Tevita) Nabura	Counties Manukau	28–06–92	1.92	107	3	–
W.R. (Waisake) Naholo	Taranaki	08–05–91	1.86	96	62	225
R.F. (Ray) Niuia	Tasman	19–06–91	1.74	118	1	–
P.P.M. (Paripari) Parkinson	Tasman	12–09–96	2.04	119	8	5
A. (Aki) Seiuli	Otago	22–12–92	1.84	116	40	15
A.L. (Aaron) Smith	Manawatu	21–10–88	1.71	83	137	130
B.R. (Ben) Smith (co-capt)	Otago	01–06–86	1.86	94	153	200
L.I.J. (Liam) Squire	Tasman	20–03–91	1.95	113	33	35
R. (Robert) Thompson	Manawatu	29–08–91	1.84	103	49	70
S.F. (Siate) Tokolahi	Canterbury	16–03–92	1.84	116	41	15
P.F. (Sio) Tomkinson	Otago	27–05–96	1.82	94	21	40
T.N.M. (Thomas) Umaga-Jensen	Wellington	31–12–97	1.87	95	8	–
T.T. (Tei) Walden	Taranaki	25–05–93	1.82	94	35	50
J.C. (Jack) Whetton	Auckland	24–05–95	1.96	114	3	–
L.C. (Luke) Whitelock	Canterbury	29–01–91	1.94	112	53	20

NB. Nabura and Seiuli did not appear in 2019.

Manager: Paul McLaughlan
Coach: Aaron Mauger
Assistant coaches: Mark Hammett, Glen Delaney, Clarke Dermody

HIGHLANDERS 2019

	Chiefs	Reds	Rebels	Hurricanes	Blues	Hurricanes	Crusaders	Blues	Sunwolves	Chiefs	Jaguares	Lions	Stormers	Bulls	Waratahs	Crusaders	TOTALS
B. Smith	15	15	–	15	15	15	15	15	–	15	–	–	–	–	–	15	9
Faddes	14	s	–	–	–	14	14	14	15	14	15	15	15	–	–	–	10
McKay	–	–	11	–	–	–	–	–	–	s	–	–	–	15	15	–	4
Naholo	–	14	14	s	14	–	–	–	–	–	–	–	14	14	14	14	8
Li	11	11	–	11	11	11	11	11	11	11	11	–	–	11	11	–	12
Buckman	–	–	–	14	s	13	–	–	–	–	–	–	–	–	–	–	3
Hyland	–	–	–	–	–	–	–	s	–	–	14	11	11	–	–	–	4
Tomkinson	s	–	s	13	13	–	s	13	14	s	12	14	12	12	–	11	13
Thompson	13	13	–	–	–	s	13	–	13	13	13	13	13	13	13	13	12
Umaga-Jensen	12	–	13	12	12	–	–	–	–	–	–	s	–	s	–	–	6
Walden	–	12	12	–	–	12	12	12	12	12	–	12	–	–	12	12	10
Ioane	10	10	15	10	s	–	10	10	10	10	10	10	–	10	10	10	14
Banks	–	s	s	s	10	10	–	–	–	–	–	–	10	–	s	s	8
Gatland	–	–	10	–	–	–	s	s	s	–	–	–	–	–	–	–	4
Hollinshead	–	–	–	–	–	–	–	–	–	–	–	s	s	–	–	–	2
A. Smith	s	9	–	9	9	–	–	s	9	9	9	9	9	9	9	9	13
Hammington	9	s	9	s	–	9	9	9	s	s	–	–	s	–	s	s	12
Fakatava	–	–	s	–	–	s	s	–	–	–	–	–	–	–	–	–	3
Whitelock	8	8	–	8	8	8	–	s	6	6	6	6	6	8	8	8	14
Mikaele-Tu'u	–	s	–	–	–	–	–	–	–	–	–	s	–	–	–	–	2
Lentjes	7	–	7	7	–	7	7	7	7	7	7	s	7	7	7	7	14
Hunt	s	7	–	–	7	–	–	–	s	–	–	7	–	–	–	s	6
Frizell	s	6	6	–	6	6	6	6	s	s	–	8	s	s	s	–	13
Hemopo	6	4	4	6	s	s	s	4	4	4	–	–	–	4	4	4	13
E. Dixon	–	–	8	s	–	s	8	8	8	8	8	s	8	–	s	s	12
Squire	–	–	–	–	–	–	–	–	–	–	–	–	–	6	6	6	3
Dickson	5	5	–	4	s	4	s	s	s	s	4	4	s	s	s	s	14
Parkinson	4	–	5	5	4	–	4	–	–	–	–	–	4	–	–	–	6
Franklin	–	–	s	s	5	5	5	5	5	5	5	5	5	5	5	5	14
Whetton	–	s	–	–	–	–	–	–	–	–	–	s	s	–	–	–	3
Lomax	3	3	–	3	3	3	3	3	3	3	–	3	3	3	3	3	15
Tokolahi	s	s	3	–	s	s	s	s	s	s	3	s	s	s	s	s	15
Johnstone	1	1	s	1	1	1	s	s	–	s	1	1	s	1	1	s	15
Lienert-Brown	s	s	1	s	s	s	1	1	1	1	–	s	1	–	s	1	14
Iosefa-Scott	–	–	s	–	–	–	–	–	–	–	–	–	–	–	–	–	1
Fa'agase	–	–	–	–	–	–	–	s	–	s	–	–	s	–	–	–	3
Coltman	2	2	–	2	2	2	2	2	2	2	2	2	2	2	2	2	15
A. Dixon	s	s	2	s	–	s	s	s	s	s	s	s	s	s	s	s	15
Jackson	–	–	s	–	–	–	–	–	–	–	–	–	–	–	–	–	1
Niuia	–	–	–	–	s	–	–	–	–	–	–	–	–	–	–	–	1

HIGHLANDERS INDIVIDUAL SCORING

	Tries	Con	PG	DG	Points		Tries	Con	PG	DG	Points
Ioane	4	32	10	–	114	Walden	2	–	–	–	10
Banks	–	10	5	–	35	Gatland	–	3	–	–	6
Frizell	6	–	–	–	30	A. Dixon	1	–	–	–	5
Tomkinson	6	–	–	–	30	Hammington	1	–	–	–	5
Penalty tries	3	–	–	–	21	Hemopo	1	–	–	–	5
Faddes	4	–	–	–	20	Hunt	1	–	–	–	5
Li	4	–	–	–	20	Hyland	1	–	–	–	5
Naholo	4	–	–	–	20	Lomax	1	–	–	–	5
Coltman	3	–	–	–	15	Parkinson	1	–	–	–	5
Franklin	3	–	–	–	15	Whitelock	1	–	–	–	5
Lentjes	3	–	–	–	15	Hollinshead	–	2	–	–	4
McKay	3	–	–	–	15	E. Dixon	–	1	–	–	2
B. Smith	3	–	–	–	15						
Thompson	3	–	–	–	15	**Totals**	**62**	**48**	**15**	**0**	**455**
A. Smith	2	–	–	–	10						
Tokolahi	2	–	–	–	10	Opposition scored*	58	45	16	0	430

*Includes one penalty try

HIGHLANDERS TEAM RECORD 2019

Played 16   Won 6   Lost 8   Drew 2   Points for 455   Points against 430

Date	Opponent	Location	Score	Tries	Con	PG	DG	Referee
February 15	Chiefs	Hamilton	30–27	Parkinson, Frizell, A. Smith	Ioane (3)	Ioane (3)		G. Jackson
February 22	Reds	Dunedin	36–31	Frizell (2), Hunt, Thompson, B. Smith	Ioane (4)	Ioane		F. Anselmi (Argentina)
March 1	Rebels	Melbourne	19–24	Tokolahi, Frizell, Hemopo	Gatland, Banks			AJ Jacobs (South Africa)
March 8	Hurricanes	Wellington	22–25	Coltman, A. Smith, Tomkinson	Banks (2)	Ioane		D. Murphy (Australia)
March 22	Blues	Auckland	26–33	Whitelock, Li	Banks (2)	Banks (4)		M. van der Westhuizen (South Africa)
April 5	Hurricanes	Dunedin	28–31	Frizell, Lentjes, Hammington, A. Dixon	Banks (4)			G. Jackson
April 12	Crusaders	Christchurch	17–43	B. Smith, Ioane	Ioane, Gatland	Ioane		B. O'Keeffe
April 20	Blues	Dunedin	24–12	Frizell, Faddes, penalty try	Ioane (2)	Ioane		P. Williams
April 26	Sunwolves	Tokyo	52–0	Li (2), Coltman, Lomax, Franklin, Ioane, Thompson, Tomkinson	Ioane (5), Gatland			B. O'Keeffe
May 4	Chiefs	Dunedin	31–31	Lentjes, Ioane, Faddes, B. Smith	Ioane (4)	Ioane		M. Fraser
May 11	Jaguares	Dunedin	32–27	Coltman, Lentjes, Tomkinson, Faddes	Ioane (3)	Ioane (2)		B.O'Keeffe
May 18	Lions	Johannesburg	29–38	Franklin, Ioane, Hyland, Tomkinson, Faddes	Ioane, Hollinshead			R. Rasivhenge (South Africa)
May 25	Stormers	Cape Town	22–34	Tomkinson, Naholo, Tokolahi	Banks, Hollinshead	Banks		N. Berry (Australia)
June 7	Bulls	Dunedin	24–24	Naholo (2), McKay (2)	Ioane (2)			A. Gardner (Australia)
June 14	Waratahs	Invercargill	49–12	Franklin, Li, Walden, Thompson, Naholo, McKay, penalty try	Ioane (5), E. Dixon			M. Fraser
June 21	Crusaders (QF)	Christchurch	14–38	Tomkinson, Walden	Ioane (2)			J. Peyper (South Africa)

RESULTS FROM 2019
FIRST-CLASS SEASON

Key:	WC	World Cup
	RC	SANZAAR Rugby Championship
	W20	World Rugby Under 20 Championship
	OJC	Oceania Rugby Junior Championship
	S15	SANZAAR Super 15
	RS	Ranfurly Shield
	P	Mitre 10 Cup Premiership
	. C	Mitre 10 Cup Championship
	cr	Mitre 10 Cup Crossover match between teams from Premiership and Championship divisions.
	H	Heartland Championship
	MC	Meads Cup
	LC	Lochore Cup
	qf	Quarter-final
	sf	Semi-final
	f	Final
	*	not first-class
	aet	after extra time

Winning team listed first

JANUARY

Sat-Sun 26-27	*	Round Three 2018-2019 World Rugby Sevens Series				Hamilton, New Zealand

FEBRUARY

Sat-Sun 2-3	*	Round Four 2018-2019 World Rugby Sevens Series				Sydney, Australia
Fri	15	S15	Highlanders	30	Chiefs	27	Hamilton
Sat	16	S15	Crusaders	24	Blues	22	Auckland
	16	S15	Hurricanes	20	Waratahs	19	Sydney
Fri	22	S15	Highlanders	36	Reds	31	Dunedin
Sat	23	S15	Crusaders	38	Hurricanes	22	Christchurch
	23	S15	Brumbies	54	Chiefs	17	Canberra
	23	S15	Sharks	26	Blues	7	Durban

MARCH

Fri	1	S15	Hurricanes	43	Brumbies	13	Palmerston North
	1	S15	Rebels	24	Highlanders	19	Melbourne
Fri-Sun 1-3	*	Round Five 2018-2019 World Rugby Sevens Series				Las Vegas, USA
Sat	2	S15	Sunwolves	30	Chiefs	15	Hamilton
	2	S15	Crusaders	22	Reds	12	Brisbane
	2	S15	Jaguares	23	Blues	19	Buenos Aires
Fri	8	S15	Hurricanes	25	Highlanders	22	Wellington
Sat	9	S15	Crusaders	57	Chiefs	28	Christchurch
	9	S15	Blues	28	Sunwolves	20	Albany
Sat-Sun 9-10	*	Round Six 2018-2019 World Rugby Sevens Series				Vancouver, Canada
Fri	15	S15	Chiefs	23	Hurricanes	23	Hamilton
Fri	22	S15	Blues	33	Highlanders	26	Auckland

Day	Date	Comp	Home	Score	Away	Score	Venue
Sat	23	S15	Hurricanes	34	Stormers	28	Wellington
	23	S15	Waratahs	20	Crusaders	12	Sydney
	23	S15	Chiefs	56	Bulls	20	Pretoria
Fri	29	S15	Crusaders	32	Hurricanes	8	Wellington
Sat	30	S15	Blues	24	Stormers	9	Auckland
	30	S15	Chiefs	30	Jaguares	27	Buenos Aires

APRIL

Day	Date	Comp	Home	Score	Away	Score	Venue
Fri	5	S15	Hurricanes	31	Highlanders	28	Dunedin
Fri-Sun	5-7	*	Round Seven 2018-2019 World Rugby Sevens Series				Causeway Bay, Hong Kong
Sat	6		New Zealand Universities	32	Kansai Universities	29	Dunedin
	6	S15	Crusaders	36	Brumbies	14	Christchurch
	6	S15	Blues	32	Waratahs	29	Auckland
Fri	12	S15	Crusaders	43	Highlanders	17	Christchurch
Sat-Sun	13-14	*	Round Eight 2018-2019 World Rugby Sevens Series				Kallang, Singapore
Sat	13	S15	Chiefs	33	Blues	29	Hamilton
Fri	19	S15	Lions	23	Chiefs	17	Hamilton
	19	S15	Hurricanes	29	Sunwolves	23	Tokyo
Sat	20	S15	Highlanders	24	Blues	12	Dunedin
Fri	26	O20	New Zealand Under 20	53	Fiji Under 20	7	Gold Coast
	26	S15	Crusaders	36	Lions	10	Christchurch
	26	S15	Highlanders	52	Sunwolves	0	Tokyo
Sat	27	S15	Hurricanes	47	Chiefs	19	Wellington
Tues	30	O20	New Zealand Under 20	87	Japan Under 20	12	Gold Coast

MAY

Day	Date	Comp	Home	Score	Away	Score	Venue
Fri	3	S15	Crusaders	21	Sharks	21	Christchurch
Sat	4	S15	Hurricanes	29	Rebels	19	Wellington
	4	S15	Highlanders	31	Chiefs	31	Dunedin
	4	O20	Australia Under 20	24	New Zealand Under 20	0	Gold Coast
	4	S15	Brumbies	26	Blues	21	Canberra
Fri	10	S15	Hurricanes	22	Blues	12	Auckland
	10	S15	Crusaders	45	Bulls	13	Pretoria
Sat	11	S15	Highlanders	32	Jaguares	27	Dunedin
	11	S15	Chiefs	29	Sharks	23	Hamilton
Fri	17	S15	Jaguares	28	Hurricanes	20	Wellington
Sat	18	S15	Blues	23	Chiefs	8	Auckland
	18	S15	Lions	38	Highlanders	29	Johannesburg
	18	S15	Stormers	19	Crusaders	19	Cape Town
Fri	24	S15	Chiefs	19	Reds	13	Hamilton
Sat	25	S15	Crusaders	19	Blues	11	Christchurch
	25	S15	Stormers	34	Highlanders	22	Cape Town
Sat-Sun	25-26	*	Round Nine 2018-2019 World Rugby Sevens Series				London, England
Fri	31	S15	Blues	22	Bulls	22	Auckland

JUNE

Day	Date	Comp	Home	Score	Away	Score	Venue
Sat	1	S15	Chiefs	40	Crusaders	27	Suva
	1	S15	Hurricanes	30	Sharks	17	Durban
Sat-Sun	1-2	*	Round Ten 2018-2019 World Rugby Sevens Series				Paris, France

Tues	4	W20	New Zealand Under 20	45	Georgia Under 20	13	Santa Fe
Fri	7	S15	Highlanders	24	Bulls	24	Dunedin
	7	S15	Reds	29	Blues	28	Brisbane
Sat	8	S15	Crusaders	66	Rebels	0	Christchurch
	8	S15	Hurricanes	37	Lions	17	Johannesburg
	8	W20	New Zealand Under 20	52	Scotland Under 20	33	Rosario
Wed	12	W20	South Africa Under 20	25	New Zealand Under 20	17	Rosario
Fri	14	S15	Highlanders	49	Waratahs	12	Invercargill
	14	S15	Chiefs	59	Rebels	8	Melbourne
Sat	15	S15	Hurricanes	29	Blues	24	Wellington
Mon	17	W20 5th-6th	Wales Under 20	8	New Zealand Under 20	7	Rosario
Fri	21	S15 qf	Crusaders	38	Highlanders	14	Christchurch
	21	S15 qf	Jaguares	21	Chiefs	16	Buenos Aires
Sat	22	S15 qf	Hurricanes	35	Bulls	28	Wellington
	22	W20 7th-8th	New Zealand Under 20	40	Ireland Under 20	17	Rosario
Sat	29	S15 sf	Crusaders	30	Hurricanes	26	Christchurch
JULY							
Sat	6	S15 f	Crusaders	19	Jaguares	3	Christchurch
Sat	13	RS	Otago	41	Thames Valley	21	Wanaka
	13		Fiji	27	New Zealand Maori	10	Suva
Sat	20		New Zealand Maori	26	Fiji	17	Rotorua
	20	RC	New Zealand	20	Argentina	16	Buenos Aires
Fri	26	RS	Otago	49	North Otago	14	Oamaru
Sat	27	RC	New Zealand	16	South Africa	16	Wellington
AUGUST							
Thurs	8	C	Northland	27	Southland	17	Invercargill
Fri	9	P	Auckland	28	North Harbour	28	Auckland
Sat	10	P	Tasman	45	Wellington	8	Blenheim
	10	cr	Taranaki	34	Counties Manukau	29	Pukekohe
	10	P	Waikato	31	Canterbury	28	Hamilton
	10	RC	Australia	47	New Zealand	26	Perth
Sun	11	C	Bay of Plenty	50	Otago	7	Tauranga
	11	C	Hawke's Bay	31	Manawatu	13	Palmerston North
Thurs	15	cr	Auckland	43	Northland	10	Whangarei
Fri	16	P	Counties Manukau	39	North Harbour	25	Albany
	16	cr	Hawke's Bay	27	Wellington	27	Napier
Sat	17	C	Taranaki	13	Manawatu	10	Palmerston North
	17	C RS	Otago	41	Southland	22	Dunedin
	17		New Zealand	36	Australia	0	Auckland
Sun	18	P	Tasman	23	Canterbury	8	Christchurch
	18	cr	Bay of Plenty	40	Waikato	14	Rotorua
Thurs	22	C	Hawke's Bay	29	Otago	21	Napier
Fri	23	P	Wellington	23	Canterbury	22	Wellington
Sat	24	H	Poverty Bay	17	Thames Valley	15	Paeroa
	24	H	Buller	54	Ngati Porou East Coast	19	Westport
	24	H	Horowhenua Kapiti	17	Mid Canterbury	10	Ashburton
	24	H	North Otago	26	South Canterbury	20	Timaru
	24	H	Wairarapa Bush	28	Wanganui	18	Masterton

	24	H	West Coast	56	King Country	27	Greymouth
	24	cr	Tasman	64	Manawatu	3	Blenheim
	24	cr	Auckland	19	Bay of Plenty	13	Auckland
	24	P	Waikato	31	Counties Manukau	26	Pukekohe
Sun	25	C	Taranaki	52	Northland	19	New Plymouth
	25	cr	North Harbour	33	Southland	12	Invercargill
Thurs	29	P	Wellington	29	Counties Manukau	22	Wellington
Fri	30	H	North Otago	25	Wairarapa Bush	11	Dunedin
	30	H	King Country	34	Buller	12	Taupo
	30	C RS	Otago	37	Manawatu	20	Dunedin
Sat	31		Samoa	36	NZ Heartland	19	Auckland
	31	H	Mid Canterbury	22	Ngati Porou East Coast	15	Ruatoria
	31	H	West Coast	27	Horowhenua Kapiti	21	Levin
	31	H	South Canterbury	40	Poverty Bay	29	Gisborne
	31	H	Thames Valley	36	Wanganui	30	Wanganui
	31	cr	Canterbury	80	Southland	0	Christchurch
	31	C	Hawke's Bay	43	Northland	28	Whangarei
	31	P	Waikato	20	Auckland	20	Hamilton
September							
Sun	1	cr	Bay of Plenty	27	North Harbour	19	Albany
	1	cr	Tasman	28	Taranaki	18	New Plymouth
Thurs	5	C	Manawatu	31	Northland	25	Palmerston North
Fri	6	C	Hawke's Bay	41	Southland	23	Napier
	6	P	Tasman	36	Counties Manukau	0	Pukekohe
Sat	7	H	Thames Valley	43	Ngati Porou East Coast	15	Paeroa
	7	H	North Otago	34	Poverty Bay	30	Gisborne
	7	H	South Canterbury	57	Horowhenua Kapiti	7	Timaru
	7	H	Buller	22	Wanganui	21	Westport
	7	H	Wairarapa Bush	37	King Country	31	Masterton
	7	H	West Coast	43	Mid Canterbury	41	Greymouth
	7		New Zealand	92	Tonga	7	Hamilton
	7	P	North Harbour	38	Waikato	36	Albany
	7	cr	Wellington	16	Bay of Plenty	15	Rotorua
Sun	8	P	Canterbury	32	Auckland	22	Auckland
	8	C RS	Otago	35	Taranaki	27	Dunedin
Thurs	12	cr	Hawke's Bay	27	Waikato	24	Hamilton
Fri	13	cr	Canterbury	42	Northland	12	Whangarei
Sat	14	H	King Country	27	Ngati Porou East Coast	12	Tokomaru Bay
	14	H	Buller	46	Horowhenua Kapiti	31	Levin
	14	H	Mid Canterbury	13	South Canterbury	13	Ashburton
	14	H	North Otago	22	Thames Valley	21	Oamaru
	14	H	Wairarapa Bush	36	Poverty Bay	31	Masterton
	14	H	Wanganui	36	West Coast	18	Wanganui
	14	C	Bay of Plenty	31	Taranaki	17	New Plymouth
	14	C	Manawatu	31	Southland	26	Invercargill
	14	P	Auckland	28	Counties Manukau	13	Pukekohe
Sun	15	cr	Wellington	54	Otago	24	Wellington
	15	P	Tasman	21	North Harbour	17	Nelson
Thurs	19	cr	Manawatu	32	Canterbury	29	Christchurch
Fri	20	C	Hawke's Bay	35	Taranaki	17	Napier

Sat	21	H	Thames Valley	29	Wairarapa Bush	23	Paeroa
	21	H	West Coast	18	North Otago	17	Greymouth
	21	H	Horowhenua Kapiti	35	King Country	19	Te Kuiti
	21	H	Poverty Bay	52	Mid Canterbury	38	Gisborne
	21	H	South Canterbury	38	Buller	27	Timaru
	21	H	Wanganui	67	Ngati Porou East Coast	24	Wanganui
	21	P	Tasman	35	Waikato	26	Hamilton
	21	cr	Southland	42	Counties Manukau	14	Invercargill
	21	cr	Otago	21	North Harbour	15	Albany
	21	WC	New Zealand	23	South Africa	13	Yokahama
Sun	22	P	Wellington	34	Auckland	15	Auckland
	22	C	Bay of Plenty	46	Northland	22	Whangarei
Thurs	26	C	Taranaki	19	Southland	0	New Plymouth
Fri	27	P	Tasman	40	Auckland	0	Nelson
Sat	28	H	Wairarapa Bush	20	Buller	17	Westport
	28	H	West Coast	21	Ngati Porou East Coast	19	Ruatoria
	28	H	Horowhenua Kapiti	38	Poverty Bay	28	Waikanae
	28	H	South Canterbury	21	King Country	19	Taupo
	28	H	Thames Valley	31	Mid Canterbury	17	Ashburton
	28	H	Wanganui	27	North Otago	22	Oamaru
	28	C	Bay of Plenty	51	Hawke's Bay	24	Tauranga
	28	cr	Wellington	57	Northland	36	Wellington
	28	P	Canterbury	38	Counties Manukau	5	Christchurch
Sun	29	cr RS	Otago	45	Waikato	35	Dunedin
	29	cr	North Harbour	29	Manawatu	16	Palmerston North

October

Wed	2	WC	New Zealand	63	Canada	0	Oita
Thurs	3	cr	Hawke's Bay	22	Counties Manukau	10	Pukekohe
Fri	4	P	North Harbour	42	Wellington	34	Albany
Sat	5	H	Thames Valley	28	South Canterbury	24	Paeroa
	5	H	North Otago	34	Mid Canterbury	10	Oamaru
	5	H	Poverty Bay	24	Ngati Porou East Coast	20	Gisborne
	5	H	Wairarapa Bush	25	Horowhenua Kapiti	20	Masterton
	5	H	Wanganui	57	King Country	19	Wanganui
	5	H	Buller	47	West Coast	7	Greymouth
	5	C	Bay of Plenty	46	Manawatu	10	Tauranga
	5	cr	Auckland	64	Southland	7	Auckland
	5	cr RS	Canterbury	35	Otago	25	Dunedin
Sun	6	cr	Tasman	52	Northland	6	Nelson
	6	cr	Waikato	38	Taranaki	19	Hamilton
	6	WC	New Zealand	71	Namibia	9	Tokyo
Thurs	10	C	Bay of Plenty	22	Southland	12	Invercargill
Fri	11	cr	Auckland	35	Taranaki	11	New Plymouth
Sat	12	H	Wairarapa Bush	31	Mid Canterbury	10	Ashburton
	12	H	Buller	36	Poverty Bay	26	Westport
	12	H	North Otago	61	Ngati Porou East Coast	29	Ruatoria
	12	H	Wanganui	38	Horowhenua Kapiti	15	Levin
	12	H	Thames Valley	37	King Country	15	Te Kuiti
	12	H	West Coast	27	South Canterbury	24	Timaru
	12	cr	Tasman	47	Hawke's Bay	28	Napier

	12	cr	Manawatu	33	Counties Manukau	17	Palmerston North
	12	P	Wellington	39	Waikato	21	Wellington
Sun	13	C	Northland	40	Otago	10	Whangarei
	13	P RS	Canterbury	31	North Harbour	25	Christchurch
Fri	18	C sf	Bay of Plenty	64	Manawatu	3	Rotorua
Sat	19	MC sf	Wanganui	20	Thames Valley	15	Paeroa
	19	LC sf	West Coast	41	Poverty Bay	35	Greymouth
	19	P sf	Tasman	18	Auckland	9	Blenheim
	19	LC sf	South Canterbury	56	Buller	24	Westport
	19	MC sf	North Otago	27	Wairarapa Bush	25	Oamaru
	19	C sf	Hawke's Bay	44	Otago	39	Napier
				aet		aet	
	19	P sf	Wellington	30	Canterbury	19	Wellington
	19	WC qf	New Zealand	46	Ireland	14	Tokyo
Fri	25	C f	Bay of Plenty	12	Hawke's Bay	7	Rotorua
Sat	26	MC f	North Otago	33	Wanganui	19	Oamaru
	26	P f	Tasman	31	Wellington	14	Nelson
	26	WC sf	England	19	New Zealand	7	Yokohama
Sun	27	LC f	South Canterbury	23	West Coast	19	Greymouth
November							
Fri	1	WC 3-4	New Zealand	40	Wales	17	Tokyo
Sat	2		NZ Marist	29	NZ Heartland	19	Te Aroha
Wed	6		NZ Heartland	12	Vanua XV	7	Lautoka
Thurs-Sat	7-9	*	Oceania Sevens				Suva
Sat	9		Vanua XV	15	NZ Heartland	7	Sigatoka
Sat	16		Fiji	33	UK Barbarians	31	London
Wed	20		UK Barbarians	47	Brazil	22	Sao Paulo
Sat	30		Wales	43	UK Barbarians	33	Cardiff
December							
Thurs-Sat	5-7	*	Round One 2019-2020 World Rugby Sevens				Dubai
Fri-Sun	13-15	*	Round Two 2019-2020 World Rugby Sevens				Cape Town
Sat-Sun	14-15	*	National Sevens				Tauranga

225 first-class matches

NATIONAL PROVINCIAL CHAMPIONSHIP WINNERS

	First Division	Second Division (North)	Second Division (South)
1976	Bay of Plenty	Taranaki	South Canterbury
1977	Canterbury	North Auckland	South Canterbury
1978	Wellington	Bay of Plenty	Marlborough
1979	Counties	Hawke's Bay	Marlborough
1980	Manawatu	Waikato	Mid Canterbury
1981	Wellington	Wairarapa Bush	South Canterbury
1982	Auckland	Taranaki	Southland
1983	Canterbury	Taranaki	Mid Canterbury
1984	Auckland	Taranaki	Southland

	First Division	Second Division	Third Division
1985	Auckland	Taranaki	North Harbour
1986	Wellington	Waikato	South Canterbury
1987	Auckland	North Harbour	Poverty Bay
1988	Auckland	Hawke's Bay	Thames Valley
1989	Auckland	Southland	Wanganui
1990	Auckland	Hawke's Bay	Thames Valley
1991	Otago	King Country	South Canterbury
1992	Waikato	Taranaki	Nelson Bays
1993	Auckland	Counties	Horowhenua
1994	Auckland	Southland	Mid Canterbury
1995	Auckland	Taranaki	Thames Valley
1996	Auckland	Southland	Wanganui
1997	Canterbury	Northland	Marlborough
1998	Otago	Central Vikings	Mid Canterbury
1999	Auckland	Nelson Bays	East Coast
2000	Wellington	Bay of Plenty	East Coast
2001	Canterbury	Hawke's Bay	South Canterbury
2002	Auckland	Hawke's Bay	North Otago
2003	Auckland	Hawke's Bay	Wanganui
2004	Canterbury	Nelson Bays	Poverty Bay
2005	Auckland	Hawke's Bay	Wairarapa Bush

	Air New Zealand Cup	Meads Cup	Lochore Cup
2006	Waikato	Wairarapa Bush	Poverty Bay
2007	Auckland	North Otago	Poverty Bay
2008	Canterbury	Wanganui	Poverty Bay
2009	Canterbury	Wanganui	North Otago

	ITM Cup	Meads Cup	Lochore Cup
2010	Canterbury	North Otago	Wairarapa Bush

	ITM Premiership	ITM Championship	Meads Cup	Lochore Cup
2011	Canterbury	Hawke's Bay	Wanganui	Poverty Bay
2012	Canterbury	Counties Manukau	East Coast	Buller

	ITM Cup Premiership	Championship	PINK BATTS HEARTLAND CHAMPIONSHIP Meads Cup	Lochore Cup
2013	Canterbury	Tasman	Mid Canterbury	South Canterbury
2014	Taranaki	Manawatu	Mid Canterbury	Wanganui
2015	Canterbury	Hawke's Bay	Wanganui	King Country

	MITRE 10 CUP Premiership	Championship	MITRE 10 HEARTLAND CHAMPIONSHIP Meads Cup	Lochore Cup
2016	Canterbury	North Harbour	Wanganui	North Otago
2017	Canterbury	Wellington	Wanganui	Mid-Canterbury
2018	Auckland	Waikato	Thames Valley	Horowhenua Kapiti
2019	Tasman	Bay of Plenty	North Otago	South Canterbury

MITRE 10 CUP

Tasman won their maiden national championship and did it in style with a perfect 12 wins from 12 games. In the 44 years of the national championship, it is only the eighth time the first division/Mitre 10 Cup title has been won with a perfect record, the last team being Auckland in 2007.

The 14 tries Tasman conceded were the fewest a team had conceded since Canterbury (13) in 2008 while the 137 points Tasman conceded were the fewest points a team had conceded since both Otago (119) and Auckland (130) in 1991.

After a spell of seven years in the Premiership Counties Manukau were relegated to the Championship for 2020 while Bay of Plenty earned promotion to next year's Premiership, where they last competed in 2013.

ROUND ROBIN

Each team played all six other teams in their division plus crossover matches against four teams in the other division for a total of ten matches.

	P	W	D	L	B⁴	B⁷	Pts	T	C	PG	DG	Total	T	C	PG	DG	Total
										FOR					AGAINST		
PREMIERSHIP DIVISION																	
Tasman	10	10	0	0	8	0	**48**	57¹	40	8	0	391	13¹	7	11	0	114
Wellington	10	7	1	2	7	0	**37**	43	32	14	0	321	40	24	7	0	269
Canterbury	10	6	0	4	8	3	**35**	49	35	10	0	345	27	15	11	0	198
Auckland	10	5	2	3	5	0	**29**	38¹	29	8	0	274	26	21	12	0	208
North Harbour	10	4	1	5	7	3	**28**	41¹	23	6	0	271	36³	26	9	0	265
Waikato	10	3	1	6	6	2	**22**	38¹	30	8	0	276	43	30	14	0	317
Counties Manukau	10	1	0	9	4	3	**11**	26¹	14	5	0	175	45¹	32	9	0	318
CHAMPIONSHIP DIVISION																	
Bay of Plenty	10	8	0	2	7	2	**41**	50	29	11	0	341	22	16	6	0	160
Hawke's Bay	10	7	1	2	9	0	**39**	47¹	29	4	0	307	36	24	11	0	261
Otago	10	5	0	5	5	0	**25**	37	24	11	0	266	45¹	35	10	0	327
Manawatu	10	4	0	6	4	1	**21**	25	19	12	0	199	48¹	27	7	0	317
Taranaki	10	4	0	6	2	0	**18**	30²	20	11	0	227	37¹	23	9	0	260
Northland	10	2	0	8	2	1	**11**	29	22	12	0	225	59	40	6	0	393
Southland	10	1	0	9	2	1	**7**	23	14	6	0	161	56	40	4	0	372
TOTALS								533	360	126	0	3779	533	360	126	0	3779

B⁴ bonus points for four or more tries in a match.
B⁷ bonus points for loss by seven or fewer points.
¹ includes one penalty try (7 points)
² includes two penalty tries (14 points)
³ includes three penalty tries (21points)

PLAYOFF SUMMARY

In the semi-finals, the top qualifier was home to the fourth-placed qualifier and the second-placed qualifier was home to the third-place qualifier. In the final, the highest qualifier of the two participants played at home.

PREMIERSHIP

Semi-finals: Tasman **18** (2t, c, 2pg) v Auckland **9** (3pg), at Blenheim
Wellington **30** (3t, 3c,2 pg, dg) v Canterbury **19** (3t, 2c), at Wellington

Final: Tasman **31** (3t, 2c, 4pg) v Wellington **14** (t, 3pg), at Nelson

CHAMPIONSHIP

Semi-finals: Bay of Plenty **64** (10t, 7c) v Manawatu **3** (pg), at Rotorua
Hawke's Bay **44** aet (5t, 5c, 3pg) v Otago **39** aet (5t, 4c, 2pg),
at Napier (31–31 after 80 minutes)

Final: Bay of Plenty **12** (4pg) v Hawke's Bay **7** (t, c), at Rotorua

ALMANACK NEW ZEALAND MITRE 10 CUP XV

Josh McKay
Canterbury

Will Jordan   Quinn Tupaea   Emoni Narawa
Tasman   *Waikato*   *Bay of Plenty*

Ngani Laumape
Manawatu

Mitch Hunt
Tasman

Richard Judd
Bay of Plenty

Gareth Evans
Hawke's Bay

Du'Plessis Kirifi   Pari Pari Parkinson   James Blackwell   Ethan Blackadder
Wellington   *Tasman*   *Wellington*   *Tasman*

Alex Fidow   Andrew Makalio   Karl Tu'inukuafe
Wellington   *Tasman*   *North Harbour*

Reserves: Ash Dixon (*Hawke's Bay*), Aidan Ross (*Bay of Plenty*), Owen Franks (*Canterbury*), Josh Dickson (*Otago*), Mitch Karpik (*Bay of Plenty*), Jamie Booth (*Manawatu*), Vilimoni Koroi (*Otago*), Chase Tiatia (*Bay of Plenty*) .

RECORDS

BY THE TEAMS

BEST PERFORMANCES 2019

In a Season

Most points	440	Tasman	521	Otago, 1998
Most tries	62	Tasman	74	Wellington, 2017
Most conversions	43	Tasman	57	Canterbury, 2017
Most penalty goals	19	Wellington	45	Otago, 2012
Most dropped goals	1	Wellington	12	Bay of Plenty, 1985

In a Match

Highest Score	80	Canterbury v Southland	97	Auckland v King Country, 1993
Biggest winning margin	80	Canterbury v Southland (80–0)	94	Auckland v King Country, 1993 (97–3)
Most tries	12	Canterbury v Southland	15	Auckland v King Country, 1993
Most conversions	10	Canterbury v Southland	12	Canterbury v Southland, 2012
Most penalty goals	4	Bay of Plenty v Hawke's Bay, 25 October	9	Taranaki v Bay of Plenty, 2011
		Tasman v Wellington, 26 October		
Most dropped goals	1	Wellington v Canterbury, 19 October	4	Bay of Plenty v Waikato, 1985

BY THE PLAYERS

RECORD 1976–2019

First Division 1976–2005, Air New Zealand Cup 2006–2009,
ITM Cup 2010–2015, Mitre 10 Cup 2016-

BEST PERFORMANCES 2019

In a Season

Most points	116	J.K. Garden-Bachop (Wellington)	196	T.E. Brown (Otago), 1998
Most tries	11	J.A. McKay (Canterbury)	15	T.J. Wright (Auckland), 1984
				B.J. Laney (Otago), 1998

In a Match

Most points	20	V.T. Koroi (Otago) v Taranaki	37	B.A. Blair (Canterbury) v Counties Manukau, 1999
Most tries	3	J.W. Spowart (Tasman) v Manawatu	5	T.J. Wright (Auckland) v Manawatu, 1984
		V.T. Koroi (Otago) v Manawatu		W.R. Gordon (Waikato) v Southland, 1990
		N. Fomai (Hawke's Bay) v Northland		C.J. Spencer (Auckland) v Otago, 1996
		W.T. Goosen (Wellington) v Otago		M.P. Robinson (Taranaki) v Southland, 1997
		C.J. Tiatia (Bay of Plenty) v Hawke's Bay, 28 September		J. Maddock (Canterbury) v North Harbour, 2002
		J. Ravouvou (Bay of Plenty) v Manawatu, 5 October		S.W. Sivivatu (Waikato) v Auckland, 2004
		E.R. Narawa (Bay of Plenty) v Manawatu, 18 October		T. Li (North Harbour) v Taranaki, 2017
Most conversions	7	T.W.K. Renata (Wellington) v Otago	12	T.J. Taylor (Canterbury) v Southland, 2012
		J.K. Garden-Bachop (Wellington) v Northland		
		H.R.J. Plummer (Auckland) v Southland		
Most penalty goals	4	D.C. Hollinshead (Bay of Plenty) v Hawke's Bay, 25 October	9	B.J. Barrett (Taranaki) v Bay of Plenty, 2011
		M.J. Hunt (Tasman) v Wellington, 26 October		
Most dropped goals	1	J.K. Garden-Bachop (Wellington) v Canterbury, 19 October	4	R.J. Preston (Bay of Plenty) v Waikato, 1985

Leading point-scorers in the Mitre 10 Cup:

J.K. Garden-Bachop	Wellington	116
M.J. Hunt	Tasman	102
B.D. Cameron	Canterbury	99
J.M. Debreczeni	Northland	86
F.H. Smith	Waikato	83

Leading Try scorers in the Mitre 10 Cup:

J.A. McKay	Canterbury	11
E.R. Narawa	Bay of Plenty	9
J.M. Nareki	Otago	8
J. Ravouvou	Bay of Plenty	8

MITRE 10 HEARTLAND CHAMPIONSHIP

North Otago claimed the Meads Cup to become Heartland Champion for the third time. Only Wanganui has won more, with six.

North Otago's three Meads Cup winning finals have all been won against the same opponent — Wanganui: 25–8 in 2007, 39–18 in 2010 and now 33–19 in 2019.

Prop Ralph Darling's drop goal for North Otago in the final was the second time a forward has kicked a dropped goal in a Heartland Championship match. The first forward to do so was Puri Hauiti, also a prop, for East Coast against Wairarapa Bush in 2010.

West Coast's six wins in the round robin is the most wins in the competition's history achieved by a team while still failing to make the top four.

South Canterbury won the Lochore Cup for the second time.

Going into the last round of the round-robin, eight teams had a chance of making the top four, and the eventual 11 points spread between the first and eighth placed finishers is the smallest points spread between the top eight since the current format started in 2011.

ROUND ROBIN SUMMARY

	P	W	D	L	B⁴	B⁷	Pts	FOR					AGAINST				
								T	C	PG	DG	Total	T	C	PG	DG	Total
Thames Valley	8	6	0	2	4	2	**30**	31	20	15	0	240	20¹	11	13	0	163
North Otago	8	6	0	2	3	2	**29**	31	22	14	0	241	22¹	12	10	0	166
Wairarapa Bush	8	6	0	2	4	1	**29**	28	16	13	0	211	24	17	8	1	181
Wanganui	8	5	0	3	6	2	**28**	44	28	5	1	294	22	13	16	0	184
West Coast	8	6	0	2	3	0	**27**	31¹	18	7	1	217	34	22	6	0	232
Buller	8	5	0	3	5	1	**26**	39	24	6	0	261	28	22	4	0	196
South Canterbury	8	4	1	3	4	3	**25**	34¹	22	7	0	237	24¹	12	10	0	176
Poverty Bay	8	3	0	5	6	2	**20**	34³	23	5	0	237	37¹	23	8	0	257
Horowhenua Kapiti	8	3	0	5	3	2	**17**	25	19	7	0	184	37²	23	4	1	250
King Country	8	2	0	6	3	2	**13**	28¹	17	5	0	191	39¹	23	8	0	267
Mid Canterbury	8	1	1	6	2	2	**10**	21¹	15	8	0	161	35	23	5	0	236
Ngati Porou East Coast	8	0	0	8	1	3	**4**	24¹	11	3	0	153	48¹	34	3	0	319
TOTALS								362	235	95	2	2627	362	235	95	2	2627

B⁴ bonus point for scoring four or more tries in a match.   B⁷ bonus point for a loss by seven points or less.
¹ includes one penalty try (7 points)   ² includes two penalty tries (14 points)   ³ includes three penalty tries (21 points)

North Otago and Wairarapa Bush both finished on 29 points. North Otago had the higher rank due to winning their individual match.

PLAYOFF SUMMARY

The top four teams played off for the Meads Cup, and the teams finishing fifth to eighth played off for the Lochore Cup. In the semi-finals, the top qualifier was home to the fourth-placed qualifier and the second-placed qualifier was home to the third-place qualifier. In the final, the highest qualifier of the two participants played at home..

MEADS CUP (1st–4th)

Semi-finals: Wanganui **20** (2t, 2c, 2pg) v Thames Valley **15** (5pg), at Paeroa
North Otago **27** (4t, 2c, pg) v Wairarapa Bush **25** (3t, 2c, 2pg), at Oamaru

Final: North Otago **33** (4t, 2c, 2pg, dg) v Wanganui **19** (3t, 2c), at Oamaru

LOCHORE CUP (5th–8th)

Semi-finals: West Coast **41** (7t, 3c) v Poverty Bay **35** (5t, 5c), at Greymouth
South Canterbury **56** (8t, 5c, 2pg) v Buller **24** (3t, 3c, pg), at Westport

Final: South Canterbury **23** (2t, 2c, 3pg) v West Coast **19** (3t, 2c), at Greymouth

HEARTLAND CHAMPIONSHIP RECORDS

BY THE TEAMS

	BEST PERFORMANCE 2019	RECORD 2006–2019
In a Season		
Most points	333 Wanganui	440 Wanganui, 2016
Most tries	49 Wanganui	63 Wanganui, 2008
Most conversions	32 Wanganui	45 Wanganui, 2008
Most penalty goals	20 Thames Valley	30 Wairarapa Bush, 2012
Most dropped goals	1 Wanganui, West Coast, North Otago	2 on ten occasions (eight teams)
In a Match		
Most points	67 Wanganui v Ngati Porou East Coast	116 North Otago v East Coast, 2010
Biggest winning margin	50 South Canterbury v Horowhenua Kapiti (57–7)	113 North Otago v East Coast, 2010 (116–3)
Most tries	11 Wanganui v Ngati Porou East Coast	17 North Otago v East Coast, 2010
Most conversions	8 North Otago v Ngati Porou East Coast	14 North Otago v East Coast, 2010
Most penalty goals	7 Thames Valley v Wanganui	7 Thames Valley v Mid Canterbury, 2009 Thames Valley v East Coast, 2011 Poverty Bay v Buller, 2013 Thames Valley v Wanganui, 2019
Most dropped goals	1 Wanganui v Wairarapa Bush West Coast v Horowhenua Kapiti North Otago v Wanganui, October 26	1 57 occasions

BY THE PLAYERS

	BEST PERFORMANCE 2019	RECORD 2006–2019
In a Season		
Most points	109 R.L. Smith (North Otago)	147 J.J. Lash (Buller), 2017
Most tries	13 V.W. Tikoisolomone (Wanganui)	14 P. Fetuai (Wanganui), 2006
In a Match		
Most points	27 J.J. Lash (Buller) v West Coast	35 S.C. Leighton (Poverty Bay) v Thames Valley, 2007
Most tries	4 T.T.H. Rogers-Holden (Wanganui) v Ngati Porou East Coast	5 L.M. Herden (North Otago) v East Coast, 2010; S. Malatai (Wairarapa Bush) v Buller, 2018
Most conversions	7 J.J. Lash (Buller) v Ngati Porou East Coast; R.L. Smith (North Otago) v Ngati Porou East Coast	9 R.F. Aloe (Horowhenua Kapiti) v East Coast, 2008; B. Patston (North Otago) v East Coast, 2010
Most penalty goals	7 R.D. Crosland (Thames Valley) v Wanganui	7 D.P. Harrison (Thames Valley) v Mid Canterbury, 2009; J.R. Reynolds (Thames Valley) v East Coast, 2011; S.P. Parkes (Poverty Bay) v Buller, 2013; R.D. Crosland (Thames Valley) v Wanganui, 2019
Most dropped goals	1 C.D. Clare (Wanganui) v Wairarapa Bush; J. Pitman-Joass (West Coast) v Horowhenua Kapiti; R.K. Darling (North Otago) v Wanganui, October 26	1 on 57 occasions (41 players)

Leading Points-scorers in the Championship:

R.L. Smith	North Otago	109
R. Boughton	Thames Valley	86
J.J. Lash	Buller	82
W.A. Wright	South Canterbury	82
A.H. Tauatevalu	Poverty Bay	66

Leading Try scorers in the Championship:

V.W. Tikoisolomone	Wanganui	13
T.R. Flutey	Wairarapa Bush	7
H.K. Lafituanai	Thames Valley	7
A.H. Tauatevalu	Poverty Bay	6
H.T.W.K. Henare	Horowhenua Kapiti	6
E. Lotawa	Ngati Porou East Coast	6
R.K. Darling	North Otago	6
S.I.F. Kakala	South Canterbury	6
B.R.T. Waaka	Poverty Bay	6

AUCKLAND

2019 Status: Mitre 10 Cup Premiership
Founded 1883. Original member 1892
President: E. (Eroni) Clarke
Chairman: S.M. (Stuart) Mather
Chief executive officer: J.M. (Jarrod) Bear
Coach: A. (Alama) Ieremia
Assistant coaches: F.I. (Filo) Tiatia, T.R. (Tai) Lavea
Main ground: Eden Park, Auckland
Capacity: 47,000
Colours: Blue and white

RECORDS

Most appearances	196	*'Snow' White, 1949–63*
Most points	2746	*Grant Fox, 1982–93*
Most tries	112	*Terry Wright, 1984–93*
Most points in a season	322	*Grant Fox, 1990*
Most tries in a season	19	*Terry Wright, 1984*
Most conversions in a season	77	*Grant Fox, 1990*
Most penalty goals in a season	48	*Grant Fox, 1989, 1990*
Most dropped goals in a season	8	*Grant Fox, 1990*
Most points in a match	43	*Adrian Cashmore v Mid Canterbury, 1995*
Most tries in a match	8	*John Kirwan v North Otago, 1993*
Most conversions in a match	12	*Grant Fox v Marlborough, 1984*
		Brett Craies v Horowhenua, 1986
		Grant Fox v Nelson Bays, 1991
		Lachie Munro v North Otago, 2008
Most penalty goals in a match	7	*Grant Fox v Canterbury, 1990*
		Grant Fox v Waikato, 1992
Highest team score	139	*v North Otago, 1993*
Record victory (points ahead)	134	*139–5 v North Otago, 1993*
Highest score conceded	59	*v Waikato, 2004*
Record defeat (points behind)	48	*11–59 v Waikato, 2004*

Auckland looked a shadow of the team that swept almost all before it in 2018.

While the defending Premership champions defended well, for the most part, they could not get their attacking game going, lacking fluency and cohesion in the backline. They scored 23 fewer tries in 2019. Sir Graham Henry took a step back from the coaching staff, which may not have helped.

Yet, for all that, were it not for one questionable TMO decision in the Blenheim semi-final, they could well have contested the decider again.

There were early glimpses of Auckland's best, such as in the opening 20 minutes of the Battle of the Bridge clash, the win over Northland in Whangarei and patches of the draw in Hamilton. Auckland did not actually lose a game until round five against Canterbury, which kickstarted a patchy mid-season period in which it was humiliated 40–0 in Nelson by the Mako. Convincing wins over Southland and Taranaki hauled Auckland back into playoffs contention and then the team had to do the unthinkable: cheer for Canterbury to beat North Harbour in the final regular season clash.

That done, a trip to Blenheim for the semi looked a step too far, but the pack, often inconsistent in 2019, rolled its sleeves up and gave one of its best displays of the season, pushing the unbeaten

Mako to the limit.

Auckland saw nothing of Patrick Tuipulotu due to All Blacks duty, while new signing Angus Ta'avao also had a higher calling. Rieko Ioane did score a try in his sole outing, his first for Auckland since 2016.

Auckland's squad was not hugely different to that of 2018. There were 5–6 front-liners missing, including Vince Aso (Wellington), Michael Fatialofa (UK), Leon Fukofuka (Tonga RWC), Fa'atiga Lemalu and Melani Nanai (UK), and Evan Olmstead (Canada, RWC). The biggest losses were Nanai and Olmstead, the latter bringing real starch to the pack.

Alex Hodgman signed from Canterbury and did a solid job at loosehead prop, but questions have to be asked as to why Auckland had two loan players, hooker Leni Apisai (Wellington) and Kurt Heatherley (Waikato), who comes from an Australian Rules background. Apisai was industrious enough, but why does a province of Auckland's size need to hire loan players, a rare occurrence indeed?

Fullback Jordan Trainor only came right from a long-term injury late in the season. Salesi Rayasi was the star back, scoring six tries, setting up several others and saving some with his defence. Caleb Clarke had his best season for Auckland, scoring five tries and finally looking fully comfortable at this level.

Tanielu Tele'a was solid enough in the midfield, but co-captain TJ Faiane looked tired after a heavy Super Rugby season and was not the player of 2018.

Harry Plummer took two steps backwards from his 2018 form, struggling at times to impose himself on games and still inconsistent off the tee. Veteran Daniel Kirkpatrick kicked some important goals.

Halfback Jonathan Ruru was good, but not as good as in 2018. Danny Tusitala was a transplanted outside back who did well on occasion as the replacement No 9.

Hoskins Sotutu looked to have built on his promise until a mid-season injury. Akira Ioane was a pale shadow of the brilliant player of 2018 or even earlier in 2019 for the Blues. He was apparently crestfallen at his All Blacks rejection and looked cumbersome and off the pace. Blake Gibson and Dalton Papali'i both had injury problems, so it was Waimana Riedlinger-Kapa who made the most inroads in his loose forward game. Adrian Choat was a good man to bring in on the openside, and he must have been unlucky to miss a Super Rugby deal, but did sign with Bristol.

Jack Whetton and Jamie Lane took most of the locking duties, performing well without often dominating. Lane won his place through a sterling tour with the 'Auckland Contenders' to Australia in March.

Marcel Renata and Hodgman were a reliable pair of props, and the scrum was only defeated by Tasman. Hooker Robbie Abel, like many of the players, was not quite able to reproduce his 2018 form.

Higher honours went to:

New Zealand:	R. Ioane, D. Papali'i, A. Ta'avao, P. Tuipulotu, O. Tu'ungafasi
New Zealand Maori:	A. Ioane, J. Ruru, M. Renata
New Zealand Under 20:	R. Cobb, T. Funaki
NZ Universities:	F. Harrison, M. Koloto, T-A. Te Puni

AUCKLAND REPRESENTATIVES 2019

	Club	Games for Union	Points for Union
Robbie Abel	College Rifles	18	15
Jarred Adams	Suburbs	17	0
Leni Apisai	Northern United (1)	11	10
Adrian Choat	Waitemata	12	10
Caleb Clarke	Suburbs	20	35
Aleks Dabek	Ponsonby	1	0
Lyndon Dunshea	University	5	0
TJ Faiane	Pakuranga	39	45
Marco Fepulea'i	Ponsonby	19	5
Blake Gibson	Ponsonby	31	25
Kurt Heatherley	Hautapu (2)	6	0
Alex Hodgman	Suburbs	11	0
Akira Ioane	Ponsonby	47	60
Rieko Ioane	Ponsonby	16	65
Daniel Kirkpatrick	University	11	19
Taniela Koroi	Marist	5	0
AJ Lam	Grammar TEC	5	5
Jamie Lane	Ponsonby	16	5
Michael Lea	Marist	1	0

	Club	Games for Union	Points for Union
D'Angelo Leuila	Papatoetoe	5	20
Ezekiel Lindenmuth	Suburbs	8	0
Tumua Manu	College Rifles	23	35
Dalton Papali'i	Pakuranga	18	20
Harry Plummer	Grammar TEC	23	180
Salesi Rayasi	Marist	22	75
Marcel Renata	University	43	10
Waimana Riedlinger-Kapa	Ponsonby	12	5
Jonathan Ruru	University	22	25
Scott Scrafton	Grammar TEC	28	5
Mike Sosene-Feagai	Mt Wellington	14	15
Hoskins Sotutu	Marist	15	10
Cameron Suafoa	College Rifles	1	0
Peter-Chanel Tagaloa	Marist	4	0
Tanielu Tele'a	Marist	13	10
Jordan Trainor	Ponsonby	24	42
Presley Tufuga	Ponsonby	1	0
Danny Tusitala	Ponsonby	11	10
Jack Whetton	Grammar TEC	36	15

1 Loaned from Wellington   *2 Loaned from Waikato*

INDIVIDUAL SCORING

	Tries	Con	PG	DG	Points
Plummer	1	17	8	–	63
Rayasi	6	–	–	–	30
Clarke	5	–	–	–	25
Leuila	–	7	2	–	20
Papali'i	3	–	–	–	15
Kirkpatrick	–	5	1	–	13
Apisai	2	–	–	–	10
Faiane	2	–	–	–	10
Gibson	2	–	–	–	10
Ruru	2	–	–	–	10
Sotutu	2	–	–	–	10
Tele'a	2	–	–	–	10
Tusitala	2	–	–	–	10

	Tries	Con	PG	DG	Points
Penalty try	1	–	–	–	7
Choat	1	–	–	–	5
A. Ioane	1	–	–	–	5
R. Ioane	1	–	–	–	5
Lam	1	–	–	–	5
Lane	1	–	–	–	5
Riedlinger-Kapa	1	–	–	–	5
Trainor	1	–	–	–	5
Whetton	1	–	–	–	5
Totals	**38**	**29**	**11**	**0**	**283**
Opposition scored	*28*	*22*	*14*	*0*	*226*

AUCKLAND 2019

	North Harbour	Northland	Bay of Plenty	Waikato	Canterbury	Counties Manukau	Wellington	Tasman	Southland	Taranaki	Tasman (P, SF)	Totals
J.V. Trainor	–	–	–	–	–	–	15	15	15	15	15	**5**
S.T.M. Rayasi	15	15	15	15	11	11	11	s	11	11	11	**11**
K.J. Heatherley	–	s	s	s	15	15	–	–	–	s	–	**6**
A.J. Lam	14	14	–	14	–	–	–	–	–	14	s	**5**
C.D. Clarke	11	11	14	11	14	14	14	11	14	–	14	**10**
R.E. Ioane	–	–	11	–	–	–	–	–	–	–	–	**1**
T.R. Tele'a	13	13	13	13	s	s	s	14	13	–	–	**9**
T.P. Manu	–	–	–	–	13	13	13	13	s	13	13	**7**
T.J. Faiane (capt)	12	12	12	12	12	12	12	12	12	12	12	**11**
A.D. Leuila	s	10	10	10	–	–	s	–	–	–	–	**5**
D.J.P. Kirkpatrick	–	s	s	s	s	s	–	s	s	s	s	**9**
H.R.J. Plummer	10	–	–	–	10	10	10	10	10	10	10	**8**
J.L. Ruru	–	9	9	9	9	s	9	s	9	9	9	**10**
D.J.K. Tusitala	9	s	s	s	s	9	s	9	s	s	s	**11**
A.L. Ioane	–	–	–	s	8	8	8	8	s	s	s	**8**
H.C.R. Sotutu	8	8	8	8	6	–	–	–	–	–	–	**5**
P. Tufuga	–	–	–	–	–	–	–	s	–	–	–	**1**
A.J.F. Dabek	–	–	–	–	–	–	–	s	–	–	–	**1**
A.J. Choat	s	7	–	–	s	s	6	7	7	7	7	**9**
B.T. Gibson (capt)	7	–	7	7	7	7	7	–	–	–	–	**6**
D.R. Papali'i	–	s	6	–	–	–	–	–	6	6	6	**5**
W. Riedlinger-Kapa	6	6	s	6	–	–	s	6	8	8	8	**9**
C.J.T.S. Suafoa	–	–	–	–	–	6	–	–	–	–	–	**1**
L.J. Dunshea	s	–	–	–	–	–	–	–	–	s	s	**3**
J.C. Whetton	4	5	5	5	5	5	5	5	5	–	–	**9**
J.H. Lane	5	4	4	4	s	s	s	4	s	4	4	**11**
S.N. Scrafton	–	–	–	–	–	–	4	–	4	5	5	**4**
M.P-C. Tagaloa	–	s	–	s	4	4	–	–	–	–	–	**4**
M.C. Renata	3	3	3	3	3	3	3	3	3	3	3	**11**
M.L. Fepulea'i	s	s	–	–	–	s	s	s	s	s	s	**8**
T.T. Koroi	–	–	s	s	s	–	–	–	–	–	–	**3**
A.T.O.A. Hodgman	1	1	1	1	1	s	1	1	1	1	1	**11**
E.V. Lindenmuth	s	s	–	–	–	–	s	–	–	–	–	**3**
J.J. Adams	–	–	s	s	s	1	–	s	s	s	s	**8**
L.C.A. Apisai	s	2	s	s	2	2	2	2	2	2	2	**11**
M.H. Lea	–	s	–	–	–	–	–	–	–	–	–	**1**
R.J. Abel	2	–	2	2	s	–	–	s	s	s	s	**8**
M.A. Sosene-Feagai	–	–	–	–	–	s	s	–	–	–	–	**2**

AUCKLAND TEAM RECORD, 2019

Played 11 Won 5 Drew 2 Lost 4 Points for 283 Points against 226

Date	Opponent	Location	Score	Tries	Con	PG	DG	Referee
August 9	North Harbour (P)	Auckland	28–28	Sotutu (2), Tele'a, penalty try	Plummer (3)			P.M. Williams
August 15	Northland (cr)	Whangarei	43–10	Faiane, Whetton, Clarke, Lane, Lam, Tele'a	Leuila (4), Kirkpatrick	Leuila		M.I. Fraser
August 24	Bay of Plenty (cr)	Auckland	19–13	Rayasi (2), R. Ioane	Leuila (2)			B.E. Pickerill
August 31	Waikato (P)	Hamilton	20–20	Clarke, Apisai	Leuila, Kirkpatrick	Leuila, Kirkpatrick		R.P. Kelly
September 8	Canterbury (P)	Auckland	22–32	A. Ioane, Gibson, Rayasi	Plummer (2)	Plummer		N.E.R. Hogan
September 14	Counties Manukau (P)	Pukekohe	28–13	Gibson, Clarke, Plummer, Rayasi	Plummer (3), Kirkpatrick			T.N. Griffiths
September 22	Wellington (P)	Auckland	15–34	Apisai, Ruru	Plummer	Plummer		J.J. Doleman
September 27	Tasman (P)	Nelson	0–40					J.D. Munro
October 5	Southland (cr)	Auckland	64–7	Clarke (2), Tusitala (2), Papali'i (2), Riedlinger-Kapa, Rayasi, Faiane, Ruru	Plummer (7)			T.N. Griffiths
October 11	Taranaki (cr)	New Plymouth	35–11	Papali'i, Choat, Rayasi, Trainor	Kirkpatrick (2), Plummer	Plummer (3)		G.W. Jackson
October 19	Tasman (P, sf)	Blenheim	9–18			Plummer (3)		J.J. Doleman

BAY OF PLENTY

2019 Status: Mitre 10 Cup Championship
Founded 1911. Affiliated 1911
President: K.J. (Kevin) Hennessy
Chairman: P.L. (Paul) Owen
Chief executive officer: M.W. (Mike) Rogers
Coach: C.R. (Clayton) McMillan
Assistant coaches: M.J. (Marty) Bourke, M.P. (Mike) Delany,
             M.J.K. (Mike) Rogers
Main ground: Rotorua International Stadium
Capacity: 20,000
Colours: Blue and gold.

RECORDS

Most appearances	161	*Greg Rowlands, 1969–82*
Most points	1008	*Greg Rowlands, 1969–82*
Most tries	62	*Graeme Moore, 1967–80*
Most points in a season	245	*Andrew Miller, 1996*
Most tries in a season	14	*Damon Kaui, 1995*
Most conversions in a season	53	*Andrew Miller, 1996*
Most penalty goals in a season	48	*Eion Crossan, 1991*
Most dropped goals in a season	13	*Ron Preston, 1985*
Most points in a match	36	*Adrian Cashmore v Thames Valley, 1993*
Most tries in a match	5	*Ian Backhouse v North Otago, 1965*
		Damon Kaui v Thames Valley, 1995
Most conversions in a match	9	*Eion Crossan v Poverty Bay, 1991*
Most penalty goals in a match	6	*Ron Preston v Poverty Bay, 1982*
		Eion Crossan v North Harbour, 1990
		Eion Crossan v Fiji President's XV, 1991
		Eion Crossan v Western Samoa, 1991
		Erin Cossey v Hawke's Bay, 1994
		Andrew Miller v Counties, 1995
		Andrew Miller v King Country, 1996
		Glen Jackson v Northland, 2001
		Glen Jackson v Otago, 2004
		Mike Delany v Waikato, 2009
Highest team score	88	*v East Coast, 1972*
Record victory (points ahead)	79	*88–9 v East Coast, 1972*
		82–3 v Thames Valley, 1995
Highest score conceded	93	*v New Zealand XV, 1993*
Record defeat (points behind)	88	*5–93 v New Zealand XV, 1993*

After a mediocre 2018 season, Bay of Plenty's fortunes changed dramatically in 2019 to win the Mitre 10 Cup Championship and earn promotion to the Premiership. Coach Clayton McMillan had retained his position but his three assistants from last year were all replaced, with two of the new assistants being Mike Rogers and Marty Bourke who had guided last year's champion Under 19 team to win the Jock Hobbs tournament.

The Steamers started with a big win over Otago and their next four games were all against Premiership opposition. There were deserving wins against Waikato and North Harbour, while the conceding of an intercept try to Auckland and poor goalkicking against Wellington resulted in two narrow losses in matches the Bay had real chances of winning. After this, Bay of Plenty went on the rampage scoring some lovely tries and big scores all the way through to the semi-final.

This set up a home final with Hawke's Bay, and in contrast to the free flowing 51–24 win in the round robin match, superb defence, particularly in the final ten minutes, produced a 12–7 victory with Dan Hollinshead landing four penalty goals from five attempts.

Starting at fullback and finishing at second five-eighth when injuries struck, Chase Tiatia had an outstanding season. A man with many talents in all facets of play, he led by example and at season's end deservedly collected the player of the year award at the Union's annual awards night.

Bay of Plenty had a lot of firepower on the wing. Emoni Narawa was exceptional, scoring nine tries. His ability to create try scoring opportunities was wonderful to watch and he has been snapped up by the Blues for the 2020 season. Joe Ravouvou was a crowd favourite and he also scored some great tries, especially his first one against Waikato. Fa'asiu Fuatai was solid on defence and deceptive on attack and Pryor Collier proved to be a dependable utility. Joe Webber was available for the first half of the season, and played an outstanding game against North Harbour, before rejoining the New Zealand sevens team.

After two seasons of sporadic appearances Matt Skipwith-Garland at last got his opportunity at centre, playing in all the games except one. An excellent ball distributor, he was able to create opportunities for his outsides. At first five-eighth Dan Hollinshead was back after a three-year stint overseas. Reliable in general play, his goalkicking was below par on occasions, particularly against Wellington. Kaleb Trask continues to improve but his season came to an early end when he broke his jaw tackling Ngani Laumape in the first game against Manawatu. Jason Robertson was a more than able backup being quick, deceptive and a reliable goalkicker when the chances came his way.

Richard Judd was again a sound halfback. His understudy Luke Campbell was injured in the opening match which allowed New Zealand Under 20 rep Leroy Carter to debut at this level.

The scrum and lineout were of a high standard, and served the team well throughout the season. At number eight, A.J. Lafaele-Mua was into everything with his fine all-round play until injury curtailed his season. Hoani Matenga performed well there and Abraham Papali'i, after a career in rugby league, had some good moments. Mitchell Karpik had another stellar season at flanker with some great performances that resulted in him winning the BOPRU forward of the year award. Hugh Blake had his best season in the Bay jersey and Tom Franklin, after a season overseas, returned in the second half of the campaign to make a firm presence.

Aaron Carroll and Baden Wardlaw were a locking pair with high work rates, and the arrival of the wily Alex Ainley brought a huge amount of experience into the forward pack. He didn't disappoint. The props all received plenty of game time by rotation. Captain Aidan Ross, Jeff Thwaites, Ross Geldenhuys and Tevita Mafileo were all mobile and set a great scrum which had many opposition packs back pedalling. Tom McHugh again had injury curtail his season prematurely, while Chris Eves' greater experience was injected at the end of the season.

Not wanted by the All Blacks selectors, hooker Nathan Harris was quickly into the groove until he broke his leg against Auckland. Nathan Vella was promoted to start, displaying all-round soundness while Kurt Eklund was in tremendous form despite most of his game time coming off the bench.

New arrivals Pryor Collier, Joe Ravouvou, Kurt Eklund (all Auckland), Nathan Vella (Auckland, Canterbury), Alex Ainley (Tasman) and Chris Eves (Manawatu, North Harbour) all had previous provincial first-class experience, and Declan Barnett had been loaned to King Country last year.

Absent after the previous season were Tyler Ardron (Canada), Zane Kapeli (Tonga), Kane Leaupepe and James Lay (Samoa) who were all involved with their respective countries at the World Cup, while Tanerau Latimer and Mike Delany had retired and Terrence Hepetema was playing in England. Bailey Simonsson was another to have departed, returning to rugby league where he played for the Canberra Raiders in the 2019 NRL Grand Final, and Liam Steel was playing in North America.

Higher honours went to:

New Zealand:	S. Cane
New Zealand Under 20:	L. Carter, C. Forbes, K. Herbert, L. Lalomilo, J. Mua
New Zealand Maori:	T. Franklin, N. Harris, M. Karpik
New Zealand Sevens:	S. Curry, N. McGarvey-Black, R. Ware, J. Webber

BAY OF PLENTY 2019

	Otago	Waikato	Auckland	North Harbour	Wellington	Taranaki	Northland	Hawke's Bay	Manawatu	Southland	Manawatu (sf)	Hawke's Bay (f)	Totals
C.J. Tiatia	15	15	15	15	15	15	12	12	12	12	12	12	12
C.D. Forbes	–	–	–	–	–	–	15	–	–	–	–	–	1
E.R. Narawa	14	s	14	14	14	14	14	14	14	14	15	15	12
F. Fuatai	11	11	–	11	11	11	11	–	–	–	14	14	8
P.G. Collier	s	–	11	–	–	–	–	15	15	11	s	s	7
J. Ravouvou	–	14	s	s	–	s	s	11	11	–	11	11	9
D.D. Robinson-Bartlett	–	–	–	–	–	–	–	s	–	s	–	–	2
D.G. Barnett	–	–	–	–	–	–	–	–	–	s	–	–	1
T.J. Webber	13	13	–	13	13	–	–	–	–	–	–	–	4
M.D. Skipwith-Garland	12	12	13	–	s	13	13	13	13	13	13	13	11
L. Lalomilo	–	–	s	12	–	–	–	–	–	–	–	–	2
D.C. Hollinshead	10	10	12	10	12	12	–	–	–	10	10	10	9
J.R. Robertson	s	s	10	–	–	s	s	s	s	15	s	–	9
K.R. Trask	–	–	–	s	10	10	10	10	10	10	–	–	6
R.P. Judd	9	9	9	9	9	9	9	9	9	–	9	9	11
L.A. Campbell	s	–	–	–	–	–	–	–	–	–	–	–	1
L.B. Carter	–	s	s	s	s	s	s	s	s	9	s	s	11
T.A.T.M.L.A. Toma	–	–	–	–	–	–	–	–	–	s	–	–	1
A.L. Papali'i	8	–	8	–	s	–	–	–	s	8	–	–	5
H.M. Matenga	s	8	–	s	s	s	8	8	8	–	8	8	10
A.J. Lafaele-Mua	s	s	s	8	8	8	7	–	–	–	–	–	7
M.R. Karpik	7	7	7	7	7	7	s	7	–	7	7	7	11
H.P. Blake	6	6	6	6	6	6	6	s	7	6	s	s	12
T.S.G. Franklin	–	–	–	–	–	–	s	6	–	s	6	6	5
J.F.I. Johnston	–	–	–	–	–	–	–	–	s	–	–	–	1
B.M. Wardlaw	5	s	s	5	5	4	5	4	4	5	4	4	12
A.P. Carroll	4	4	4	s	4	s	4	s	6	4	s	s	12
A.N. Ainley	–	5	5	4	–	5	–	5	5	–	5	5	8
S. Van Den Hoven	–	–	–	–	–	–	–	–	s	s	–	–	2
J.R. Thwaites	3	s	3	s	s	s	s	3	–	3	s	s	11
A. Ross (capt)	1	1	1	1	1	1	1	1	1	1	1	1	12
T.J. McHugh	s	s	s	–	–	–	–	–	–	–	–	–	3
T.T.P. Mafileo	s	–	s	s	s	s	s	s	s	s	–	–	9
R. Geldenhuys	–	3	–	3	3	3	3	s	3	–	3	3	9
C.I. Eves	–	–	–	–	–	–	–	–	s	s	s	s	4
N.P. Harris	2	2	2	–	–	–	–	–	–	–	–	–	3
K.A. Eklund	s	s	s	2	s	s	s	s	2	s	s	s	12
N.B. Vella	–	–	–	s	2	2	2	2	s	2	2	2	9

BAY OF PLENTY REPRESENTATIVES 2019

	Club	Games for Union	Points for Union		Club	Games for Union	Points for Union
Alex Ainley	Rangiuru	8	5	Lalomilo Lalomilo	Te Puke Sports	3	0
Declan Barnett	Te Puke Sports	1	0	Tevita Mafileo	Tauranga Sports	9	5
Hugh Blake	Mt Maunganui	36	25	Hoani Matenga	Rangiuru	19	5
Luke Campbell	Te Puke Sports	27	43	Tom McHugh	Whakarewarewa	3	0
Aaron Carroll	Mt Maunganui	21	15	Emoni Narawa	Tauranga Sports	13	50
Leroy Carter	Tauranga Sports	11	0	Abraham Papali'i	Greerton Marist	5	5
Pryor Collier	Mt Maunganui	7	5	Joseva Ravouvou	Tauranga Sports	9	40
Kurt Eklund	Mt Maunganui	12	5	Jason Robertson	Te Puke Sports	14	34
Chris Eves	Rangataua	4	0	Dennon Robinson-Bartlett	Whakarewarewa	2	0
Cole Forbes	Te Puke Sports	2	5	Aidan Ross	Te Puke Sports	36	20
Tom Franklin	Opotiki	16	15	Mathew Skipwith-Garland	Whakarewarewa	19	10
Fa'asiu Fuatai	Rangataua	18	30	Jeff Thwaites	Te Puna	42	5
Ross Geldenhuys	Rangiuru	19	5	Chase Tiatia	Rangataua	47	90
Nathan Harris	Te Puke Sports	32	5	Te Aihe Toma	Te Puna	37	37
Dan Hollinshead	Te Puke Sports	36	243	Kaleb Trask	Tauranga Sports	13	60
Joe Johnston	Te Puke Sports	1	0	Stan Van Den Hoven	Greerton Marist	2	0
Richard Judd	Mt Maunganui	28	40	Nathan Vella	Rangataua	9	5
Mitchell Karpik	Rangataua	27	30	Baden Wardlaw	Whakarewarewa	20	0
Aileone "AJ" Lafaele-Mua	Tauranga Sports	12	0	Joe Webber	Rangiuru	15	50

INDIVIDUAL SCORING

	Tries	Con	PG	DG	Points		Tries	Con	PG	DG	Points
Hollinshead	1	15	12	–	71	Geldenhuys	1	–	–	–	5
Narawa	9	–	–	–	45	Ainley	1	–	–	–	5
Ravouvou	8	–	–	–	40	Blake	1	–	–	–	5
Tiatia	6	5	–	–	40	Forbes	1	–	–	–	5
Trask	1	9	3	–	32	Mafileo	1	–	–	–	5
Robertson	3	6	–	–	27	Eklund	1	–	–	–	5
Karpik	5	–	–	–	25	Franklin	1	–	–	–	5
Fuatai	4	–	–	–	20	Vella	1	–	–	–	5
Judd	4	–	–	–	20	Matenga	1	–	–	–	5
Ross	2	–	–	–	10	Collier	1	–	–	–	5
Webber	2	–	–	–	10						
Skipwith-Garland	2	–	–	–	10	**Totals**	**60**	**36**	**15**	**0**	**417**
Toma	1	1	–	–	7						
Papali'i	1	–	–	–	5	Opposition scored	23	17	7	0	170
Campbell	1	–	–	–	5						

BAY OF PLENTY TEAM RECORD, 2019

Played 12   Won 10   Lost 2   Points for 417   Points against 170

Date	Opponent	Location	Score	Tries	Con	PG	DG	Referee
August 11	Otago (C)	Tauranga	50–7	Fuatai (2), Papali'i, Karpik, Ross, Webber, Campbell, Robertson	Hollinshead (5)			F. Murphy (Ireland)
August 18	Waikato (cr)	Rotorua	40–14	Judd, Geldenhuys, Ravouvou, Narawa, Tiatia	Hollinshead (3)	Hollinshead (3)		D. Waenga
August 24	Auckland (cr)	Auckland	13–19	Karpik	Hollinshead	Hollinshead (2)		B. Pickerill
September 1	North Harbour (cr)	Albany	27–19	Karpik, Webber, Ainley	Hollinshead (3)	Hollinshead (2)		N. Hogan
September 7	Wellington (cr)	Rotorua	15–16	Judd, Narawa	Hollinshead	Hollinshead		T. Griffiths
September 14	Taranaki (C)	New Plymouth	31–17	Tiatia, Narawa, Hollinshead, Fuatai, Ravouvou	Hollinshead (2), Robertson			J. Doleman
September 22	Northland (C)	Whangarei	46–22	Skipwith-Garland (2), Blake, Fuatai, Forbes, Tiatia, Narawa	Trask (4)	Trask		C. Stone
September 28	Hawke's Bay (C)	Tauranga	51–24	Tiatia (3), Ravouvou (2), Trask, Karpik, Mafileo	Trask (4)	Trask		J. Doleman
October 5	Manawatu (C)	Tauranga	46–10	Ravouvou (3), Eklund, Narawa, Judd, Robertson	Robertson (3), Trask	Trask		D. Waenga
October 10	Southland (C)	Invercargill	22–12	Karpik, Narawa, Toma, Franklin	Toma			M. Winter
October 18	Manawatu (C sf)	Rotorua	64–3	Narawa (3), Ravouvou, Vella, Matenga, Judd, Ross, Collier, Robertson	Tiatia (5), Robertson (2)			R. Kelly
October 25	Hawke's Bay (C f)	Rotorua	12–7			Hollinshead (4)		R. Kelly

BULLER

2019 Status: Heartland Championship
Founded 1894. Affiliated 1894
Chairman: H.W. (Hugh) McMillan
Rugby Manager: A.C. (Andrew) Duncan
Coach: Justin "Gus" Martyn
Assistant coach: Sam Gibbens
Main ground: Victoria Square, Westport
Capacity: 5000
Colours: Cardinal and blue

RECORDS

Highest attendance	5000	*West Coast-Buller v South Africa, 1956*
Most appearances	174	*L.G. Brownlee, 1999-2018*
Most points	575	*D.J. Baird, 1981–91*
Most tries	44	*T.J. Stuart, 1984–99*
Most points in a season	147	*J.J. Lash, 2017*
Most tries in a season	11	*I. Ravudra, 2014*
Most conversions in a season	32	*J.J. Lash, 2016*
Most penalty goals in a season	27	*D.J. Baird, 1985*
Most dropped goals in a season	7	*D.J. Baird, 1984*
Most points in a match	27	*J.J. Lash v West Coast, 2019*
Most tries in a match	4	*J. Easton v Wellington Colts, 1935*
		T.J. Stuart v West Coast, 1992
		M. Taylor v East Coast, 2007
		I. Ravudra v Wairarapa Bush, 2014
		S.T. Sauqaqa v Thames Valley, 2015
Most conversions in a match	7	*J.J. Lash v Wairarapa Bush, 2014*
		J.J. Lash v East Coast, 2017
		J.J. Lash v Ngati Porou East Coast, 2019
Most penalty goals in a match	6	*D.J. Baird v East Coast, 1987*
		C.J. Hart v East Coast, 1999
		S.N. Jack, v Wairarapa Bush, 2002
		A.P. Stephens v Horowhenua Kapiti, 2010
Highest team score	67	*v East Coast, 2014*
Record victory (points ahead)	61	*67–6 v East Coast, 2014*
Highest score conceded	81	*v Wanganui, 1994*
Record defeat (points behind)	73	*0–73 v Horowhenua Kapiti, 1999*

With five wins and three defeats, Buller finished the round robin in sixth place for a home Lochore Cup semi-final. Despite the 24–56 defeat in the semi-final to South Canterbury, the season was an improvement on last year when the side achieved just two wins and failed to make the top eight playoffs.

There was a tight one-point win over Wanganui after trailing 0–14, a good win over Poverty Bay where, down 3–14 at halftime, they completely overcame their opponent with 33 points in the last 28 minutes of the second half. But the best performance of the season was the 47–7 win over neighbour, and top of the table at the time, West Coast at Greymouth which secured the Rundle Cup. Conversely, the match lost to Wairarapa Bush was a match Buller ought to have won.

Halfback Andrew Stephens announced his retirement after the final match, having played 109 games for Buller in an exemplary representative career dating back to 2007. At the age of 38 he still served his team well. James Lash again was the influential figure with his general play and goalkicking, and it was a blow injury prevented him from playing in the semi-final. His 27 points against West Coast was a new individual record for the union.

Second five-eighth Louis Devery was a handful for the opposition with his strong running and centre Iliesa Ravudra and wing Mitieli Kaloudigibeci both had the pace and finishing ability to top the try-scoring with five tries apiece. After a single game in 2017, diminutive winger Alex Paterson had a good first full season. The experienced Robbie Malneek was a steady and safe fullback who was always willing to attack.

The big mobile forward pack was a settled unit. Flanker Petrus De Kock was the outstanding forward who performed extremely well throughout the season. His loose forward colleagues Daniel Hytongue and Willis Scott also were prominent, both with the ball and with their defensive work, together they formed a very effective trio. Lock Isei Iewaqai was a great source of lineout ball and had a good turn of pace around the field, while locking partner Jeff Lepa, converted from number eight, regularly breached the advantage line with his robust ball carrying.

Loosehead prop Jack Best, in his second season, started every game and his work rate around the field was impressive, and his fellow props Anthony Ellis and Jareth MacKay were also hard-working tight forwards. The only non-injury change the coach made in the forward pack during the season was the switching of tighthead prop Ellis to starting hooker after the Wairarapa Bush match.

Tim Manawatu (in 2000), now working for the Buller RU as a development officer, Tokohau Samuels (2004), Gene Simmiss (2013) and Mitieli Kaloudigibeci (2015) all reappeared after lengthy absence.

Of last year's local regulars, Robbie Bonisch, Maifea Feso and Anthony Tailua were all in Canterbury, and centurion Logan Mundy had retired. For the first time since 2005 neither Craig Neill nor Craig Scanlon were involved in the coaching of the side.

Higher honours went to:
New Zealand Heartland: A. Ellis, J. Lash, J. Lepa

BULLER REPRESENTATIVES 2019

	Club	Games for Union	Points for Union		Club	Games for Union	Points for Union
Jack Best	Westport	17	15	Jareth MacKay	Old Boys	22	10
Mason Briant	Ngakawau-Karamea	9	0	Robbie Malneek	Old Boys	15	45
Petrus "Gabba" De Kock	White Star	8	10	Tim Manawatu	Old Boys	18	37
Louis Devery	Ngakawau-Karamea	5	10	Kahu Parata	Westport	21	10
Anthony Ellis	Ngakawau-Karamea	39	20	Alex Paterson	White Star	9	20
Ben Finau	Moutere [2]	3	0	Iliesa Ravudra	White Star	52	167
Peter Foote	Westport	5	0	Tokohau Samuels	Westport	14	0
Olve Fuatuga	White Star	2	0	Petaia Saukuru	Westport	29	25
Will Hamilton	Wanderers [2]	1	0	Willis Scott	Ngakawau-Karamea	9	0
Joel Hands	Nelson [2]	5	10	Gene Simmiss [1]	Central [2]	21	0
Daniel Hytongue	Waimea Old Boys [2]	20	28	Andrew Stephens	Ngakawau-Karamea	109	270
Corey Jenkins	Westport	10	0	Bailey Stewart	Old Boys	2	0
Mitieli Kaloudigibeci	Westport	43	105	Kyle Te Tai	Westport	4	0
James Lash	Waimea Old Boys [2]	43	530	Zach Walsh	Westport	16	0
Jeff Lepa	White Star	25	10	Michael Wells	White Star	10	61
Isei Lewaqai	Stoke [2]	34	25				

1 Player of Origin   *2 Tasman RU*

INDIVIDUAL SCORING

	Tries	Con	PG	DG	Points
Lash	4	22	6	–	82
Ravudra	5	1	–	–	27
Kaloudigibeci	5	–	–	–	25
Malneek	4	–	–	–	20
Paterson	4	–	–	–	20
Saukuru	4	–	–	–	20
Manawatu	2	1	–	–	12
Best	2	–	–	–	10
Kock	2	–	–	–	10
Hytongue	2	–	–	–	10
Mackay	2	–	–	–	10

	Tries	Con	PG	DG	Points
Devery	2	–	–	–	10
Stephens	–	3	1	–	9
Lepa	1	–	–	–	5
Wells	1	–	–	–	5
Lewaqai	1	–	–	–	5
Ellis	1	–	–	–	5
Totals	**42**	**27**	**7**	**0**	**285**
Opposition scored	36	27	6	0	252

BULLER 2019	Ngati Porou East Coast	King Country	Wanganui	Horowhenua Kapiti	South Canterbury	Wairarapa Bush	West Coast	Poverty Bay	South Canterbury (sf)	Totals
R.T. Malneek	10	15	–	15	15	15	15	15	15	8
M. Kaloudigibeci	15	13	15	14	14	14	14	14	14	9
A.M.J. Paterson	14	11	14	s	–	11	11	11	11	8
P.T. Saukuru	11	14	11	11	11	s	s	s	s	9
C.W. Jenkins	s	s	–	s	–	–	–	–	–	3
O.A. Fuatuga	–	s	–	–	–	–	–	s	–	2
J.G. Hands	–	–	–	–	s	–	–	–	–	1
I. Ravudra	13	12	12	12	s	13	13	13	13	9
T.R. Samuels	–	s	13	s	13	s	s	–	s	7
M.O. Wells	–	–	–	13	12	–	–	–	–	2
L.J.S. Devery	12	–	–	–	–	12	12	12	12	5
J.J. Lash	9	–	10	10	10	10	10	10	–	7
T.J. Manawatu	s	10	–	–	s	–	s	s	–	5
B.J. Finau	s	9	–	–	–	–	–	–	10	3
A.P. Stephens (co capt)	–	–	9	9	9	9	9	9	9	7
D.W.L. Hytongue	8	8	8	8	8	8	8	8	8	9
K.G. Parata	7	6	–	–	s	s	s	7	s	7
P.J. De Kock	6	4	7	7	7	7	7	–	7	8
K.J.S. Te Tai	s	–	–	–	–	s	–	s	s	4
W.J. Hamilton	–	7	–	–	–	–	–	–	–	1
W.T. Scott (co capt)	–	–	s	6	6	6	6	6	6	7
Z.L. Walsh	5	5	5	s	s	s	s	–	s	8
P.J. Lepa	4	–	4	4	4	4	4	4	4	8
G.K. Simmiss	s	s	s	s	–	s	s	s	s	7
I.N.T. Lewaqai	–	–	6	5	5	5	5	5	5	7
A.W. Ellis	3	3	3	3	s	–	2	2	2	8
J.W. Best	1	1	1	1	1	1	1	1	1	9
J.J.I. Mackay	s	s	s	s	3	3	3	3	3	7
B.R. Stewart	s	s	–	–	–	–	–	–	–	2
M.A. Briant	2	2	2	2	2	2	s	s	s	9
P.G. Foote	–	s	–	s	–	–	–	s	–	3

Daniel Hytongue captained the first two matches and was co-captain with Stephens in the third match.

BULLER TEAM RECORD, 2019

Date	Opponent	Location	Score (Played 9)	Tries (Won 5)	Con (Lost 4)	PG (Points for 285)	DG	Referee (Points against 252)
August 24	Ngati Porou East Coast (H)	Westport	54–19	Lash (2), Manawatu (2), Malneek, Paterson, Best, Saukuru	Lash (7)			T. Griffiths
August 30	King Country (H)	Taupo	12–34	De Kock (2)	Manawatu			H. Reed
September 7	Wanganui (H)	Westport	22–21	Paterson, Saukuru, Ravudra	Lash (2)	Lash		N. Webster
September 14	Horowhenua Kapiti (H)	Levin	46–31	Ravudra (2), Hytongue, Malneek, Saukuru, Kaloudigibeci, Lepa	Lash (4)	Lash		N. Hogan
September 21	South Canterbury (H)	Timaru	27–38	Wells, Kaloudigibeci, Malneek, Mackay, Saukuru	Lash			R. Mahoney
September 28	Wairarapa Bush (H)	Westport	17–20	Paterson, Devery, Kaloudigibeci	Lash			S. Curran
October 5	West Coast (H)	Greymouth	47–7	Lash (2), Mackay, Paterson, Lewaqai, Malneek	Lash (4)	Lash (3)		M. Playle
October 12	Poverty Bay (H)	Westport	36–26	Best, Devery, Ellis, Kaloudigibeci, Ravudra	Lash (3), Stephens	Lash		J. Bredin
October 19	South Canterbury (LC sf)	Westport	24–56	Ravudra, Kaloudigibeci, Hytongue	Stephens (2), Ravudra	Stephens		N. Webster

CANTERBURY

2019 Status: Mitre 10 Cup Premiership
Founded 1879. Affiliated 1894
President: J.E.A. (Julie) Patterson
Chairman: P.A. (Peter) Winchester
Chief executive officer: T.P. (Tony) Smail
Coach: J.S. (Joe) Maddock
Assistant coaches: N.K. (Nathan) Mauger,
R.D. (Reuben) Thorne,
M.B. (Mark) Brown
Main ground: Orangetheory Stadium, Christchurch
Capacity: 20,000
Colours: Red and black

RECORDS

Most appearances	220	*Fergie McCormick, 1958–75*
Most points	1625	*Robbie Deans, 1979–90*
Most tries	94	*Paula Bale, 1989–96*
Most points in a season	279	*Robbie Deans, 1989*
Most tries in a season	24	*Paula Bale, 1989*
Most conversions in a season	52	*Greg Coffey, 1991*
		Ben Blair, 2001
Most penalty goals in a season	50	*Robbie Deans, 1989*
Most dropped goals in a season	10	*Andrew Mehrtens, 1994*
Most points in a match	44	*Jon Preston v West Coast, 1992*
Most tries in a match	7	*Bruce McPhail v Combined Services, 1959*
Most conversions in a match	20	*Jon Preston v West Coast, 1992*
Most penalty goals in a match	7	*Robbie Deans v Counties, 1984*
		Andrew Mehrtens v Fiji, 2003
		Cameron McIntyre v Wellington, 2003
Highest team score	128	*v West Coast, 1992*
Record victory (points ahead)	128	*128–0 v West Coast, 1992*
Highest score conceded	60	*v Wellington, 2017*
Record defeat (points behind)	46	*14–60 v Wellington, 2017*

Canterbury will not be satisfied with the losing Premership semi-finalist tag.

But it could have been a worse after an 0–3 start which had the rugby nation scratching its head. One should not, however, be ready to write off Canterbury in 2020, not with no less than nine players from the province making the New Zealand Under 20s in 2019.

The Ranfurly Shield came back to Christchurch for the 16th occasion, which was the seventh (of eight) games in which the tryscoring bonus point was secured. There was a sound reliance on set-piece, after which there was enough X-factor provided by a backline that included Josh McKay and Braydon Ennor, two fearless young threequarters.

Stunned in the opening round by Waikato, Canterbury looked toothless in the defeats to Tasman and Wellington, but came right in emphatic fashion by putting 80 points on Southland. Clinical wins over Auckland and Northland were followed by a shock 32–29 crossover defeat to Manawatu in Christchurch, before normal service was resumed with sound victories over Counties Manukau, Otago and North Harbour. The latter was the first and last Shield defence of the season and might have gone Harbour's way were it not for better goalkicking and coolness in the clutch by the home team.

In the semi-final in the capital, Wellington hit the visitors early and, despite a courageous comeback, led by rookie hooker Shiloh Klein, Canterbury left its run too late.

Canterbury gained several players back from injury plus Michael Alaalatoa (Manawatu) and the veteran midfielder Tim Bateman (Japan). There were several losses, especially in the front row, but the union could still parade plenty of depth that paid dividends.

McKay, shifting from the wing to fullback, was full of running, scoring 11 tries and clearly Canterbury's best player, officially and unofficially. He was an intuitive counter-attacker with his pace and elusiveness and knew how to finish. Hence his standing as the top tryscorer in the Mitre 10 Cup.

Sam Gilbert scored five tries and showed his range of wares. Dallas McLeod, fresh from an NZ Under 20s campaign as a midfielder, thrived on the right wing, four tries underlining his immense promise. The tries didn't come for Ngane Punivai, but he consistently showed his quality. Ennor did not see a lot of action due to injury, but he looks a likely centre. Bateman raised the 50-games milestone and showed all his rugby nous. Ryan Crotty scored a brace in his first appearance for Canterbury since 2016.

Cameron kicked on after a mediocre Super Rugby season to stave off the challenge of Ferg Burke for the pivot position. Cameron kicked well again and racked up 99 points.

Co-captain Mitch Drummond, who again scored five tries, job-shared with Ere Enari. Both offered plenty of skill and leadership.

Whetu Douglas was again industrious, but often off the bench, while co-captain Luke Whitelock bowed out of domestic rugby with another consistent campaign, and three tries.

Billy Harmon and Tom Christie were a fine pair of No 7s, in the Matt Todd mould, but it was Christie who needed more patience as Harmon won more starts.

Reed Prinsep hit 50 and was as indefatigable as ever, even after a tiring Hurricanes campaign. Mitch Dunshea and Luke Romano were the mainstays of the second row, the latter raising his half-century in the semi-final. While not as dominant as in 2018 as the Duane Monkley Medal winner, the former All Black was still invaluable to his young side. Cullen Grace showed promise as the third lock.

Alaalatoa's early injury was offset by the unexpected return, after nine years, of rejected All Blacks tighthead prop Owen Franks, who ensured a stable scrum platform and won his first Shield match. Harry Allan and Daniel Lienert-Brown did the job on the loosehead.

Brodie McAlister was the preferred hooker to Seb Siataga and then Klein.

Higher honours went to:

New Zealand:	G. Bridge, R. Crotty, B. Ennor, O. Franks, J. Moody, R. Mo'unga, C. Taylor, M. Todd, S. Whitelock
New Zealand Maori:	W. Douglas, R. Prinsep
New Zealand Under 20:	F. Burke, C. Fihaki, S. Gilbert, C. Grace, S. Klein, D. McLeod, F. Newell, I. Punivai, T. Williams
New Zealand Sevens:	S. Dickson, A. Nicole
NZ Universities:	L. Donaldson, R. Poihipi, N. Souchon, G. Stratton

CANTERBURY REPRESENTATIVES 2019

	Club	Games for Union	Points for Union
Michael Alaalatoa	Linwood	1	0
Harry Allan	Sydenham	14	10
Tim Bateman	Christchurch	58	120
Fergus Burke	Canterbury University	11	20
Brett Cameron	Lincoln University	34	300
Tom Christie	Christchurch	23	10
Harrison Courtney	Lincoln University	1	0
Ryan Crotty	New Brighton	68	85
Whetu Douglas	Canterbury University	15	5
Mitch Drummond	HSOB	58	99
Mitch Dunshea	Springston	44	35
Ere Enari	Lincoln University	31	5
Braydon Ennor	Canterbury University	24	85
Inga Finau	Linwood	23	10
Owen Franks	Linwood	24	5
Sam Gilbert	Lincoln University	6	25
Cullen Grace	Lincoln University	4	5

	Club	Games for Union	Points for Union
Billy Harmon	New Brighton	35	30
Oli Jager	New Brighton	25	0
Shiloh Klein	HSOB	2	10
Daniel Lienert-Brown	HSOB	39	15
Brodie McAlister	Sydenham	16	15
Dallas McLeod	Christchurch	9	20
Josh McKay	Lincoln University	33	111
Patrick Osborne	Green Island [1]	43	70
Rameka Poihipi	Lincoln University	5	0
Reed Prinsep	HSOB	57	30
Ngane Punivai	Lincoln University	23	5
Luke Romano	Hurunui	50	35
Seb Siataga	New Brighton	12	10
Will Tucker	Christchurch	4	0
Siate Tokolahi	Sydenham	54	0
Luke Whitelock	Canterbury University	76	60

1 Loaned from Otago

INDIVIDUAL SCORING

	Tries	Con	PG	DG	Points
Cameron	1	32	10	–	99
McKay	11	–	–	–	55
Drummond	5	–	–	–	25
Gilbert	5	–	–	–	25
Burke	2	5	–	–	20
McLeod	4	–	–	–	20
Whitelock	3	–	–	–	15
Allan	2	–	–	–	10
Crotty	2	–	–	–	10
Dunshea	2	–	–	–	10
Harmon	2	–	–	–	10
Klein	2	–	–	–	10
McAlister	2	–	–	–	10

	Tries	Con	PG	DG	Points
Romano	2	–	–	–	10
Bateman	1	–	–	–	5
Christie	1	–	–	–	5
Douglas	1	–	–	–	5
Enari	1	–	–	–	5
Ennor	1	–	–	–	5
Grace	1	–	–	–	5
Siataga	1	–	–	–	5
Totals	**52**	**37**	**10**	**0**	**364**
Opposition scored	30	18	13	1	228

CANTERBURY 2019

	Waikato	Tasman	Wellington	Southland	Auckland	Northland	Manawatu	Counties Manukau	Otago	North Harbour	Wellington (SF)	Totals
J.A. McKay	15	15	15	15	15	15	15	15	15	15	15	11
S.J. Gilbert	11	11	–	–	–	14	–	s	11	–	11	6
D.A.M. McLeod	–	–	s	14	14	s	14	14	14	14	14	9
P.J.J. Osborne	–	–	–	11	–	–	–	–	–	–	–	1
N.G.J. Punivai	14	14	14	s	11	11	11	11	13	11	–	10
B.M. Ennor	–	–	11	–	13	13	–	–	–	13	13	5
T.E.S. Bateman	13	13	13	13	12	–	13	13	12	12	–	9
R.S. Crotty	–	–	–	12	–	–	–	–	–	–	–	1
R.H. Poihipi	12	12	–	–	–	–	12	–	s	–	s	5
K.F. Finau	s	s	12	–	s	12	s	12	–	s	12	9
F.W. Burke	s	s	s	10	s	s	10	s	s	s	s	11
B.D. Cameron	10	10	10	s	10	10	s	10	10	10	10	11
E.C.S. Enari	s	9	9	s	s	9	s	s	s	s	s	11
M.D. Drummond (co-capt)	9	–	–	9	9	s	9	9	9	9	9	9
W.H. Douglas	s	6	6	–	–	s	8	8	s	s	s	9
L.C. Whitelock (co-capt)	8	8	8	8	8	8	–	–	8	8	8	9
W.K. Harmon	7	7	7	s	7	–	7	7	7	7	7	10
T.M. Christie	s	s	s	7	s	7	s	s	s	s	s	11
R.J. Prinsep	6	5	s	6	6	6	6	6	6	6	6	11
W.A. Tucker	–	s	–	5	–	s	–	–	–	–	–	3
M.T.W. Dunshea	–	–	5	s	5	5	5	5	5	5	5	9
L. Romano	4	4	4	4	4	–	4	4	4	4	4	10
C.J. Grace	5	–	–	–	s	4	–	s	–	–	–	4
O.G.J.T. Jager	s	–	s	3	3	–	–	–	–	–	s	5
S.F. Tokolahi	3	3	3	s	s	s	s	3	s	s	1	11
O.T. Franks	–	–	–	–	–	3	3	s	3	3	3	6
M.S. Alaalatoa	–	s	–	–	–	–	–	–	–	–	–	1
H.M. Allan	1	s	s	1	s	s	1	s	s	s	–	10
H.J. Courtney	–	–	–	–	–	–	–	–	–	–	s	1
D.P. Lienert-Brown	s	1	1	s	1	1	1	1	1	1	–	10
B.L. McAlister	2	2	2	s	2	2	–	2	2	2	–	9
S.P. Siataga	s	s	s	2	s	s	2	s	s	s	–	10
S.I. Klein	–	–	–	–	–	–	s	–	–	–	2	2

CANTERBURY TEAM RECORD, 2019

Played 11   Won 6   Lost 5   Points for 364   Points against 228

Date	Opponent	Location	Score	Tries	Con	PG	DG	Referee
August 10	Waikato (P)	Hamilton	28–31	McKay (2), Whitelock, Gilbert	Cameron (4)			D. Jones (Wales)
August 18	Tasman (P)	Christchurch	8–23	McKay		Cameron		N.P. Briant
August 23	Wellington (P)	Wellington	22–23	McKay, Dunshea, Allan	Cameron (2)	Cameron		B.D. O'Keeffe
August 30	Southland (cr)	Christchurch	80–0	Crotty (2), McKay (2), Drummond (2), Christie, Romano, Burke, Dunshea, McLeod, Whitelock	Cameron (6), Burke (4)			D.J. Waenga
September 8	Auckland (P)	Auckland	32–22	Harmon (2), McLeod, Enari	Cameron (2), Burke	Cameron (2)		N.E.R. Hogan
September 13	Northland (cr)	Whangarei	42–12	Gilbert, McAlister, McKay, Douglas, Burke, Grace	Cameron (3)	Cameron (2)		T.T.N. Cottrell
September 19	Manawatu (cr)	Christchurch	29–32	McLeod, Romano, McKay, Siataga, Cameron	Cameron (2)			R.P. Kelly
September 28	Counties Manukau (P)	Christchurch	38–5	Drummond (2), Gilbert (2), McAlister, McLeod	Cameron (4)			N.E.R. Hogan
October 5	Otago (RS, cr)	Dunedin	35–25	McKay, Drummond, Gilbert, Bateman	Cameron (3)	Cameron (3)		G.W. Jackson
October 13	North Harbour (P)	Christchurch	31–25	McKay (2), Ennor, Allan	Cameron (4)	Cameron		J.J. Doleman
October 19	Wellington (P, sf)	Wellington	19–30	Klein (2), Whitelock	Cameron (2)			G.W. Jackson

COUNTIES MANUKAU

2019 Status: Mitre 10 Cup Premiership
Founded 1926 as South Auckland and affiliated to Auckland.
Granted full union status as South Auckland Counties in 1955.
Name changed to Counties 1956, to Counties Manukau 1996.
President: G.B. (Gary) Wright
Chairman: C.W. (Craig) Carter
Chief executive officer: B.A. (Barton) Hoggard
Coach: D.B. (Darryl) Suasua
Assistant coaches: G.W. (Grant) Henson, S. (Semo) Sititi
Main ground: Navigation Homes Stadium, Pukekohe
Capacity: 18,000
Colours: Red, white and black

RECORDS

Most appearances	201	*Alan Dawson, 1976–89*
Most points	698	*Danny Love, 1993–96*
Most tries	59	*Alan Dawson, 1976–89*
Most points in a season	208	*Danny Love, 1995*
Most tries in a season	22	*Luke Erenavula, 1993*
Most conversions in a season	52	*Danny Love, 1993*
Most penalty goals in a season	47	*Stu Hollier, 1989*
Most dropped goals in a season	4	*Bob Lendrum, 1976*
		Joe Harvey, 1983
Most points in a match	37	*Jim Graham v East Coast, 1972*
Most tries in a match	5	*Koiatu Koiatu v King Country, 2004*
Most conversions in a match	14	*Jim Graham v East Coast, 1972*
Most penalty goals in a match	6	*Stu Hollier v France, 1989*
		Stu Hollier v Thames Valley, 1989
		Danny Love v Manawatu, 1994
		James Semple v Manawatu, 2011
		Baden Kerr v Auckland 2012
Highest team score	108	*v Horowhenua, 1994*
Record victory (points ahead)	103	*103–0 v Poverty Bay, 1993*
Highest score conceded	100	*v Auckland, 2004*
Record defeat (points behind)	85	*15–100 v Auckland, 2004*

Counties Manukau's ultimately disappointing Premiership season can be divided into two distinct parts.

In each of the first four games, despite a 1–3 record, the Steelers scored at least four tries, presented a stable scrum, and played with flair in the backs and combativeness in the forwards.

Thereafter injuries took their toll, a faltering lineout imploded and on just one occasion were three tries scored in a match.

Coach Darryl Suasua, whose four-year tenure came to an end, was up against it from the start due to injuries, Rugby World Cup defections and then the Steelers' propensity for untimely errors, both with and without the ball.

All four crossover games were lost and the Steelers now have the unenviable record of having dropped their last 10 home games in Pukekohe.

It did, however, start in promising enough fashion, a narrow loss to Taranaki on a day when a crowd of around 5000 streamed through the gates and the 1979 NPC winners were honoured. A creditable win in Albany over North Harbour followed for the Lion Red Challenge Trophy. Narrow defeats to Waikato and Wellington might have hinted at better things to come, but instead came six reality checks to seal relegation. The Steelers will play in the Championship in 2020 for the first time since 2012.

There was no sign of All Blacks Kieran Read and Nepo Laulala, but Sonny Bill Williams played a rousing hand in his solitary appearance against Taranaki, making several offloads and signing many more autographs.

Among those missing from 2018 were Latiume Fosita and Fotu Lokotui (Tonga RWC), Nigel Ah Wong (Japan), Matt Vaa'i (France), Toni Pulu (Australia), Gafatasi Sua (Australia), Coree Te Whata-Colley (Northland) and a clutch of long-term injured such as Luteru Laulala, Tevita Nabura and Kalolo Tuiloma.

New signings were Andrew Kellaway (formerly Waratahs), Nathaniel Apa (Waikato), Nikolai Foliaki (Auckland), Kris Kuridrani (Japan), Samuel Slade (Auckland via Manawatu) and props Tim Metcher (USA) and Conan O'Donnell (Japan).

Kellaway found a home at fullback, but his later form did not match his first few games, where he proved dangerous on attack. Kuridrani, who also started every match, on the right wing, was adept at offloading and finished four tries to lead the team. He was also on the field for every minute of the 10 games.

Etene Nanai-Seturo was unfortunately not sighted after the first match. Apa never really got going, but Kali Hala scored three tries and looked good with the ball. Cardiff Vaega struck up a useful midfield partnership with Foliaki, but that did not stop opponents making metres through their channels.

Orbyn Leger tried hard and assumed the captaincy on occasion as he moved between the Nos 10 and 12 jerseys. Riley Hohepa ran the cutter manfully in the first half of the season, and goalkicked accurately, but did not appeal as the long-term answer in that position.

Jonathan Taumateine played well at times in the No 9 jersey, and Liam Daniela added value as his sub.

Malgene Ilaua played strongly at No 8, but was less effective when he moved to openside flanker. Dan Hyatt was, as ever, a workhorse. Sam Henwood was again strong over the ball and able to win lineout ball at two, but he played just six games.

Daymon Leasuasu was the pick of the locks, proving one of the best ball-winners in the Mitre 10 Cup, while Viliame Rarasea passed 50 games and had several good moments.

The scrum was always a strong set-piece for the Steelers, and Metcher and O'Donnell both performed in this area, if susceptible to penalties.

Hooker Joe Royal was rugged around the park, vigorous on the drive, and accurate enough at the lineout, but his replacement Donald Maka, while bustling with the ball, struggled to hit his lineout targets.

Tai Lavea will be the 2020 Steelers head coach and will need to harness the union's young talent.

Higher honours went to:
New Zealand: N. Laulala, K. Read, S. Williams
New Zealand Under 20:   E. Nanai-Seturo

COUNTIES MANUKAU REPRESENTATIVES 2019

	Club	Games for Union	Points for Union		Club	Games for Union	Points for Union
Nathaniel Apa	Bombay	5	0	Orbyn Leger	Karaka	27	27
Sue Asomua	Waiuku	6	0	Donald Maka	Bombay	10	5
Sean Bagshaw	Onewhero	59	0	Tim Metcher	Patumahoe	9	0
Liam Daniela	Bombay	22	5	Sikeli Nabou	Ardmore-Marist	62	40
Liam Fitzsimons	Ardmore-Marist	3	5	Etene Nanai-Seturo	Karaka	7	5
Nikolai Foliaki	Marist [1]	9	5	Siaosi Nginingini	Ardmore-Marist	1	0
Sam Furniss	Patumahoe	10	0	Conan O'Donnell	Bombay	9	5
Josh Gray	Ardmore-Marist	2	0	Viliame Rarasea	Overseas	50	15
Kali Hala	Karaka	15	15	Savelio Ropati	Ardmore-Marist	12	0
Sam Henwood	Pukekohe	32	35	Joe Royal	Ponsonby [2]	30	35
Riley Hohepa	Patumahoe	7	34	Mark Royal	Patumahoe	9	0
Leigh Hughes	Pukekohe	1	0	Samuel Slade	Pukekohe	6	0
Dan Hyatt	Waiuku	31	30	Jonathan Taumateine	Ardmore-Marist	19	10
Malgene Ilaua	Papakura	9	10	Rodney Tongotea	Karaka	1	5
Johnny Kawau	Bombay	20	10	Cardiff Vaega	Karaka	39	25
Andrew Kellaway	Overseas	10	2	Sonny Bill Williams	Puni	3	0
Kris Kuridrani	Waiuku	10	20	Mickey Woolliams	University [3]	6	0
Daymon Leasuasu	Ardmore-Marist	14	5				

1 Loaned from Auckland   2 Loaned from Auckland   3 Loaned from Manawatu

INDIVIDUAL SCORING

	Tries	Con	PG	DG	Points		Tries	Con	PG	DG	Points
Hohepa	1	10	3	–	34	Kawau	1	–	–	–	5
Kuridrani	4	–	–	–	20	Leasuasu	1	–	–	–	5
Leger	1	3	2	–	17	Maka	1	–	–	–	5
Hala	3	–	–	–	15	Nanai-Seturo	1	–	–	–	5
Ilaua	2	–	–	–	10	J. Royal	1	–	–	–	5
Nabou	2	–	–	–	10	Tongotea	1	–	–	–	5
O'Donnell	2	–	–	–	10	Kellaway	–	1	–	–	2
Penalty try	1	–	–	–	7						
Fitzsimons	1	–	–	–	5	**Totals**	**26**	**14**	**5**	**0**	**175**
Foliaki	1	–	–	–	5						
Henwood	1	–	–	–	5	Opposition scored	45*	32	9	0	318
Hyatt	1	–	–	–	5						

*Includes penalty try (worth 7 points)

COUNTIES MANUKAU 2019

	Taranaki	North Harbour	Waikato	Wellington	Tasman	Auckland	Southland	Canterbury	Hawke's Bay	Manawatu	Totals
A.J.H. Kellaway	15	15	15	15	15	15	15	15	15	15	10
K.C.J. Kuridrani	14	14	14	14	14	14	14	14	14	14	10
E. Nanai-Seturo	11	–	–	–	–	–	–	–	–	–	1
L.P. Fitzsimons	–	–	s	–	–	–	–	–	11	11	3
N.N. Apa	s	13	13	–	–	–	–	s	s	–	5
K.H.K. Hala	s	11	11	11	11	11	11	11	–	s	9
C.K. Vaega	13	12	12	s	s	12	s	12	12	12	10
R.F. Tongotea	–	–	–	–	–	–	–	–	–	s	1
N.K. Foliaki	–	s	s	13	13	13	13	13	13	13	9
J. Gray	–	–	–	–	–	s	–	–	s	–	2
S. Williams	12	–	–	–	–	–	–	–	–	–	1
O.N.T. Leger (capt)	–	–	–	12	12	10	12	10	10	10	7
R. H.T.M. Hohepa	10	10	10	10	10	–	10	s	–	–	7
L.T. Daniela	s	s	s	s	s	9	s	s	s	s	10
S.T.K.H. Nginingini	–	–	–	–	–	s	–	–	–	–	1
J.A. Taumateine	9	9	9	9	9	–	9	9	9	9	9
M.O. Ilaua	8	8	8	8	s	7	7	7	s	–	9
D.T. Hyatt	s	s	s	s	8	8	–	8	8	8	9
S. Ropati	–	–	–	–	–	s	8	–	–	s	3
S.T. Henwood (capt)	7	7	–	7	7	–	–	–	7	7	6
S.C. Furniss	–	–	7	–	–	–	–	–	–	–	1
S.V. Slade	6	6	–	–	6	6	s	6	–	–	6
J.D. Kawau	s	s	–	s	–	–	s	s	6	6	7
D.A. Leasuasu	5	5	5	5	5	5	5	5	–	5	9
M.R. Woolliams	–	4	4	–	4	s	–	–	4	4	6
V.L. Rarasea	–	–	s	4	s	4	4	4	5	–	7
S. Nabou	4	–	6	6	s	s	6	s	s	s	9
S. Asomua	s	–	–	–	–	s	–	s	s	s	5
T.P. Metcher	3	3	3	3	3	3	3	–	3	3	9
L.A. Hughes	–	–	–	s	–	–	–	–	–	–	1
S. Bagshaw	–	s	s	1	1	s	1	s	s	s	9
M.J.T.K.T.R. Royal	s	–	s	s	s	–	s	1	–	–	6
C.F. O'Donnell	1	1	1	–	s	1	s	3	1	1	9
J.W. Royal	2	2	2	2	2	2	s	2	s	2	10
D.S.K.M. Maka	s	s	s	s	s	s	2	s	2	s	10

COUNTIES MANUKAU TEAM RECORD, 2019

Played 10   Won 1   Lost 9   Points for 175   Points against 318

Date	Opponent	Location	Score	Tries	Con	PG	DG	Referee
August 10	Taranaki (cr)	Pukekohe	29–34	Kuridrani, Nanai-Seturo, O'Donnell, Hyatt	Hohepa (2), Kellaway	Hohepa		A.W.B. Mabey
August 16	North Harbour (P)	Albany	39–25	Kuridrani (2), Hala, O'Donnell, penalty try	Hohepa (3)	Hohepa (2)		B.D. O'Keeffe
August 24	Waikato (P)	Pukekohe	26–31	Hala, Henwood, Hohepa, Maka	Hohepa (3)			N.P. Briant
August 29	Wellington (P)	Wellington	22–29	Nabou, Hala, Leger, Ilaua	Hohepa			N.J. Webster
September 6	Tasman (P)	Pukekohe	0–36					M.C.J. Winter
September 14	Auckland (P)	Pukekohe	13–28	J. Royal, Nabou		Leger		T.N. Griffiths
September 21	Southland (cr)	Invercargill	14–42	Foliaki, Ilaua	Hohepa, Leger			N.J. Webster
September 28	Canterbury (P)	Christchurch	5–38	Kuridrani				N.E.R. Hogan
October 3	Hawke's Bay (cr)	Pukekohe	10–22	Kawau	Leger	Leger		M.C.J. Winter
October 12	Manawatu (cr)	Palmerston North	17–33	Fitzsimons, Leasuasu, Tongotea	Leger			D.J. Waenga

NGATI POROU EAST COAST

2019 Status: Heartland Championship
Founded 1921 as East Coast. Affiliated 1922.
  Name changed to Ngati Porou East Coast 2017
President: B.N. (Bailey) Mackey
Chairman: C.W. (Campbell) Dewes
Chief executive officer: Cushla Tangaere-Manuel
Coach: W.L. (Wayne) Ensor
Assistant coach: T.D. (Troy) Para
Main ground: Whakarua Park, Ruatoria
Capacity: 3000
Colours: Sky blue

RECORDS

Highest attendance	4000	*v Poverty Bay (Div 3 final), 1999*
Most appearances	113	*E.M. Waitoa, 1979–2006*
	113	*C.F. Harrison, 2003-2017*
Most points	406	*E.J. Manuel, 1985–98*
Most tries	24	*J.R. Kururangi, 1979–96*
Most points in a season	145	*M.R. Flutey, 2000*
Most tries in a season	9	*S. Vorenasu, 2011*
Most conversions in a season	20	*M.R. Flutey, 2001*
		J.R. Semple, 2012
Most penalty goals in a season	30	*M.R. Flutey, 2000*
Most dropped goals in a season	3	*M.R. Flutey, 2000*
Most points in a match	22	*V.P. Taingahue v Buller, 1999*
Most tries in a match	3	*W. Peachy v Bush, 1954*
		T.M. Reedy v Horowhenua, 1958
		J.R. Kururangi v West Coast, 1992
		J. Higgins v Poverty Bay, 1993
		M. Vere v Buller, 1999
		T.W. Delamere v Horowhenua Kapiti, 2000
		H.F.Haerewa v Poverty Bay, 2012
		S.P. Destounis, v Poverty Bay, 2016
Most conversions in a match	8	*V.P. Taingahue v Buller, 1999*
Most penalty goals in a match	7	*M.R. Flutey v Nelson Bays, 2001*
Highest team score	74	*v Buller, 1999*
Record victory (points ahead)	69	*72–3 v West Coast, 1992*
Highest score conceded	116	*v North Otago, 2010*
Record defeat (points behind)	113	*3–116 v North Otago, 2010*

Once again it was another winless season for Ngati Porou East Coast in the Heartland Championship. However, there was a definite sign of rejuvenation as the team was certainly a stronger one in both personnel and performance for a number of years, and the fittest for a number of years as well. The supporters also sensed something as Whakarua Park twice had crowds of over 1500 for home games and must be looking forward to the 2020 season.

Only against the two eventual Meads Cup finalists Wanganui and North Otago did the scores blow out and the side held second half leads against West Coast and Poverty Bay. And the scoreline against King Country did not reflect Ngati Porou East Coast's dominance of possession and territory.

The side secured plenty of possession due to the fine lineout work from Adaam Ross, and his locking partner Scott Lasenby had an excellent all-round game against West Coast. The scrum was comparable to most packs, with prop Laman Davies having his best season, being a strong scrummager. Fellow prop Hakarangi Tichborne missed half the season by being with the NZ Defence Force team in Japan, but still scored four tries in his four games, while Perrin Manuel started at prop and finished at hooker.

Former Chiefs and Maori All Black loose forward Mitchell Crosswell arrived from Taranaki and set a high standard for the others to follow. Hoani Te Moana started the season on the bench but such was his form he was a first choice loose forward in the second half of the season. Captain Hone Haerewa was again the team's outstanding player, his selection for the NZ Heartland team's tour was well merited. This loose forward trio was a real strength of the side.

Experienced players Sam Parkes and Verdon Bartlett was not quite as influential as previous seasons but were steady. Debutant Chris Richardson, at first five-eighth, made an encouraging start to his first-class career and second five-eighth Tawhao Stewart (ex Poverty Bay) had an impressive game against Thames Valley.

Not wanted by Waikato, Zac Guildford was a valuable acquisition at centre, as you would expect from the former All Black. He organised the backline and against King Country he played his 200th first-class match, missing the final game through injury. Epeli Lotawa always looked dangerous on the wing and was top tryscorer with six.

Higher honours went to:
New Zealand Heartland: H. Haerewa

NGATI POROU EAST COAST REPRESENTATIVES 2019

	Club	Games for Union	Points for Union		Club	Games for Union	Points for Union
Hamuera Baker	Hikurangi	6	0	David Manuel	Hikurangi	16	0
Verdon Bartlett	TVC	77	41	Perrin Manuel [1]	Tech OB [4]	33	21
Pera Bishop	Ruatoria City	48	5	William Martin	Tokararangi	5	0
Manahi Brooking	Tokararangi	1	0	Moana Mato	TVC	9	0
John Brown	Ruatoria City	3	0	Buchanan Maxwell	Ruatoria City	8	5
Zane Crooks	Tokomaru Bay United	2	9	Tipene Meihana	Uawa	2	5
Mitchell Crosswell	Tukapa [2]	8	10	Sam Parkes	Uawa	43	78
Laman Davies	Uawa	19	5	Trent Proffit	Hikurangi	10	5
Lorne Goldsmith	Ruatoria City	7	0	Chris Richardson	Uawa	8	0
Zac Guildford	Fraser Tech [3]	7	10	Jack Richardson	Uawa	10	5
Benny Haerewa	Hicks Bay	14	0	Wyntah Riki	Uawa	11	0
Hone Haerewa	Tokararangi	39	34	Adaam Ross	Uawa	17	0
Rikki Kernohan	Uawa	12	0	BJ Sidney	Uawa	10	12
Anton King	Hicks Bay	7	0	Tawhao Stewart	TVC	7	10
Daniel Knubley	Uawa	15	0	Hoani Te Moana	TVC	18	0
Scott Lasenby	Uawa	18	0	Hakarangi Tichborne	Tokomaru Bay United	8	30
Epeli Lotawa	United Matamata Sports [3]	16	50	Sailosi Vatubua	Ardmore Marist [5]	9	20

1 Player of Origin   2 Taranaki RU   3 Waikato RU   4 Hawke's Bay RU   5 Counties Manukau RU

INDIVIDUAL SCORING

	Tries	Con	PG	DG	Points		Tries	Con	PG	DG	Points
Lotawa	6	–	–	–	30	P. Manuel	1	–	–	–	5
Parkes	1	7	2	–	25	Davies	1	–	–	–	5
Tichborne	4	–	–	–	20	Bartlett	1	–	–	–	5
H. Haerewa	2	1	–	–	12	Meihana	1	–	–	–	5
Crosswell	2	–	–	–	10						
Guildford	2	–	–	–	10	**Totals**	**24**	**11**	**3**	**0**	**153**
Stewart	2	–	–	–	10						
Crooks	–	3	1	–	9	Opposition scored	48*	34	3	0	319
Penalty Try	1	–	–	–	7						

* Includes one penalty try (7 points)

NGATI POROU EAST COAST 2019

	Buller	Mid Canterbury	Thames Valley	King Country	Wanganui	West Coast	Poverty Bay	North Otago	Totals
Z.P. Crooks	15	15	–	–	–	–	–	–	2
V.R.M. Bartlett	s	14	15	15	15	15	15	15	8
W. Martin	14	–	s	–	s	14	–	s	5
S. Vatuba	11	–	–	–	–	–	–	13	2
D.I. Manuel	s	–	14	s	s	s	s	s	7
E. Lotawa	–	11	11	11	11	12	11	11	7
R.B. Haerewa	–	s	s	14	14	–	s	14	6
T. Meihana	–	–	–	–	–	11	–	s	2
BJ Sidney	–	–	–	–	–	s	14	–	2
Z.R. Guildford	13	13	13	13	13	13	13	–	7
M.H. Mato	–	–	–	–	s	–	–	–	1
T.M.T.I.W. Stewart	12	12	12	12	12	–	12	12	7
C. Richardson	s	10	10	10	10	10	10	10	8
S.P. Parkes	10	–	s	9	9	9	9	9	7
H. Baker	9	9	9	s	–	s	s	–	6
M.C. Crosswell	8	8	8	7	6	6	8	6	8
T.C. Proffit	7	7	7	–	–	–	7	–	4
H. Haerewa (capt)	6	6	6	8	8	8	4	8	8
J. Richardson	s	–	–	–	–	–	6	–	2
H.J. Te Moana	–	s	s	6	7	7	–	7	6
R.M. Kernohan	–	–	–	s	–	–	s	–	2
M. Brooking	–	–	–	–	s	–	–	–	1
B.T.T. Maxwell	–	–	–	–	–	–	–	s	1
A.T. Ross	5	5	5	5	5	5	5	5	8
S.T. Lasenby	4	4	4	4	4	4	–	4	7
A.J. King	–	s	s	s	s	s	s	s	7
H.T.K. Tichborne	1	1	–	–	–	–	3	3	4
P.P. Bishop	s	s	3	s	3	3	s	s	8
L.L.A. Davies	s	–	1	1	1	1	1	1	7
D.W. Knubley	–	–	s	–	–	s	–	–	2
P.J. Manuel	3	3	2	3	2	2	2	2	8
W.W. Riki	2	2	–	2	–	–	–	–	3
J. Brown	–	–	s	s	s	–	–	–	3
L. Goldsmith	–	–	–	–	–	s	–	s	2

NGATI POROU EAST COAST TEAM RECORD, 2019

Played 8 · Lost 8 · Points for 153 · Points against 319

Date	Opponent	Location	Score	Tries	Con	PG	DG	Referee
August 24	Buller (H)	Westport	19–54	Tichborne (2), Crosswell	Crooks (2)			T. Griffiths
August 31	Mid Canterbury (H)	Ruatoria	15–22	Guildford, Lotawa	Crooks	Crooks		T. Griffiths
September 7	Thames Valley (H)	Paeroa	15–43	Stewart, H. Haerewa, Lotawa				A. Mabey
September 14	King Country (H)	Tokomaru Bay	12–27	Guildford, Penalty Try				M. Winter
September 21	Wanganui (H)	Wanganui	24–67	Lotawa, Parkes, P. Manuel	Parkes (3)	Parkes		S. Curran
September 28	West Coast (H)	Ruatoria	19–21	Lotawa, Crosswell, Davies	Parkes (2)			R. Gordon
October 5	Poverty Bay (H)	Gisborne	20–24	H. Haerewa, Bartlett, Lotawa	H. Haerewa	Parkes		A. Mabey
October 12	North Otago (H)	Ruatoria	29–61	Tichborne (2), Stewart, Lotawa, Meihana	Parkes (2)			T. Cottrell

HAWKE'S BAY

2019 Status: Mitre 10 Cup Championship
Founded 1884. Original member 1892
President: P.G. (Paul) Daniel
Chairman: B.J. (Brendon) Mahony
Chief executive officer: J.L. (Jay) Campbell
Coach: M.D. (Mark) Ozich
Assistant coach: J.D. (Josh) Syms
Main ground: McLean Park, Napier
Capacity: 16,500
Colours: Black and white

RECORDS

Most appearances	158	*N.W. Thimbleby, 1959–71*
Most points	998	*J.B. Cunningham, 1990–98*
Most tries	73	*B.A. Grenside, 1919–31*
Most points in a season	237	*J.B. Cunningham, 1994*
Most tries in a season	18	*B.A. Grenside, 1926*
		P.J. Cooke, 1986
Most conversions in a season	47	*J.B. Cunningham, 1995*
Most penalty goals in a season	37	*M.W. Berquist, 2009*
Most dropped goals in a season	7	*B.D.M. Furlong, 1968*
		M.K. Sisam, 1979
Most points in a match	36	*M.K. Sisam v East Coast, 1979*
Most tries in a match	6	*R.P. Hunter v East Coast, 1979*
Most conversions in a match	13	*J.B. Cunningham v Cook Islands, 1995*
Most penalty goals in a match	7	*J.B. Cunningham v Manawatu, 1993*
		J.B. Cunningham v King Country, 1994
		R.G.E. Lewis v North Harbour, 2001
Highest team score	99	*v Cook Islands, 1995*
		v Mid Canterbury, 2003
Record victory (points ahead)	99	*99–0 v Cook Islands, 1995*
Highest score conceded	86	*v Waikato, 1999*
Record defeat (points behind)	86	*0–86 v Waikato, 1999*

Despite narrowly falling to Bay of Plenty at the final hurdle in the Championship final, to just miss promotion to the Premiership, Hawke's Bay continued its upward swing in the Mitre 10 Cup. For the second year in a row the Magpies set a new try-scoring tally for the Union in first division/Mitre 10 Cup rugby by scoring 53 in 2019. But deficiencies in defence persisted with 41 tries conceded — by comparison Bay of Plenty conceded just 23.

Included in the eight wins were victories over Premiership teams Waikato and Counties Manukau, as well as a draw with another Premiership team, Wellington, in which the Magpies did well to come back from 12–24 down. The only losses were to eventual national champions Tasman and twice to Bay of Plenty. The effort against Bay of Plenty in the final was a big improvement on the loss to Bay of Plenty in the round robin.

The player of the season was undoubtedly hooker, and captain, Ash Dixon. His seven tries were not only the most by a Magpie this year, they were most tries scored by any forward in the Mitre 10 Cup competition. His captaincy was inspiring and calm, and it was not just a coincidence that the only game he missed was the big defeat to Bay of Plenty in the Magpies' worst performance of the season.

Pouri Rakete-Stones continues to get better and better at loosehead prop, gaining selection to the NZ Maori team and earning a Super Rugby contract with the Hurricanes. The seasoned Ben May was a powerful scrummager at tighthead, ably demonstrated against Tasman where the Hawke's Bay scrum struggled until he came on as a sub before halftime. The arriving Isaia Walker-Leawere was a welcome asset at lock, a position in which Hawke's Bay was well served with Michael Allardice, who missed the start through injury, and the underrated Tom Parsons who was again a workhorse. Parsons was first equal in most lineouts won by all individuals in the Mitre 10 Cup. The mobile Geoff Cridge spent more time at blindside flanker than at lock.

Gareth Evans, the returning Brendon O'Connor, and Devan Flanders were a well performed loose forward trio. Evans, the third most successful lineout winner in the Mitre 10 Cup, produced the form expected of him and O'Connor was always on the spot at the breakdown. Devan Flanders built nicely on last year's debut on both attack and defence, while Marino Mikaele-Tu'u made a late start to the season because of injury and Josh Kaifa was a lively openside, usually off the bench.

With Brad Weber only appearing once due to All Blacks commitments, there was much to enthuse about in the play of halfback Folau Fakatava. He has the speed around the field, good variety with a break and a kick, and the accuracy of pass required. Lincoln McClutchie grew more comfortably into the first five-eighth role as the season went along, although his goalkicking was not always reliable. Outside him at second five-eighth Danny Toala is another young player with potential, being a strong runner who gained six tries and kicked some valuable goals. This inside back trio are just 19, 20 and 20 years old respectively.

Stacey Ili was a steady centre. At wing Neria Fomai finished well for three tries against Northland but his try against Otago in the semi-final was his best effort while Mason Emerson scored a brace against Taranaki utilising his speed. Sam McNicol and Jonah Lowe both missed almost the entire season to injury while Caleb Makene was a safe fullback under the high ball and quick to counter-attack, scoring four tries. Tiaan Falcon made a welcome return from injury for the final four games, kicking 15 goals from 15 attempts, including a penalty goal against Counties Manukau from inside his own half.

The Magpies used 32 players, of whom seven were new, although six of the newcomers had previous provincial experience — Caleb Makene (Tasman and Canterbury), Ollie Sapsford (Mid Canterbury), Isaia Walker-Leawere (Poverty Bay and Wellington), Joel Hintz (Canterbury and Wellington), Namatahi Waa (Northland) and Neria Fomai (Southland). For Makene, Waa and Fomai it was a return to the province of their schooling, having represented Hawke's Bay in age-grade rugby. In addition, Brendon O'Connor had returned from overseas, having last appeared in 2015.

Regulars from last year who had departed were Joe Apikotoa (Wellington), Pasqualle Dunn (Japan), Ben Power (Wellington), JJ Taulagi (France), Sasa Tofilau (Auckland), and Sam Ulufonua (Auckland).

Higher honours went to:

New Zealand:	B. Retallick, B. Weber
New Zealand Under 20:	D. Flanders, K. Kereru-Symes, D. Toala
New Zealand Maori:	A. Dixon, P. Rakete-Stones, I. Walker-Leawere

HAWKE'S BAY REPRESENTATIVES 2019

	Club	Games for Union	Points for Union		Club	Games for Union	Points for Union
Michael Allardice	Pirates	57	20	Jason Long	Hastings RS	45	30
Geoff Cridge	Central HB	38	15	Jonah Lowe	Clive	38	82
Jacob Devery	Hastings RS	8	0	Caleb Makene	Taradale	11	20
Ash Dixon	Tech OB	96	80	Ben May	Central HB	27	5
Zac Donaldson	Napier OB Marist	7	0	Lincoln McClutchie	Tamatea	18	49
Mason Emerson	Hastings RS	45	60	Sam McNicol	Napier OB Marist	6	5
Gareth Evans	Havelock North	28	20	Marino Mikaele-Tu'u	Hastings RS	27	35
Folau Fakatava	Hastings RS	19	30	Brendon O'Connor	¹	45	95
Tiaan Falcon	Clive	28	82	Tom Parsons	Central HB	37	25
Tim Farrell	Tech OB	6	0	Pouri Rakete-Stones	Pirates	30	15
Devan Flanders	Havelock North	21	10	Ollie Sapsford	Taradale	10	5
Neria Fomai	Hastings RS	12	20	Danny Toala	Hastings RS	15	53
Joel Hintz	Central HB	10	0	Timo Vaiusu	Hastings RS	1	0
Stacey Ili	Napier OB Marist	22	10	Namatahi Waa	Taradale	7	0
Siosiua "Josh" Kaifa	Clive	23	15	Isaia Walker-Leawere	Clive	10	0
Kianu Kereru-Symes	MAC	18	10	Brad Weber	Napier OB Marist	28	54

1 Arrived from overseas

INDIVIDUAL SCORING

	Tries	Con	PG	DG	Points		Tries	Con	PG	DG	Points
Toala	6	10	1	–	53	Mikaele-Tu'u	2	–	–	–	10
McClutchie	3	14	2	–	49	Flanders	2	–	–	–	10
Dixon	7	–	–	–	35	Penalty Try	1	–	–	–	7
Falcon	–	11	4	–	34	Weber	1	–	–	–	5
Fakatava	4	–	–	–	20	Evans	1	–	–	–	5
Makene	4	–	–	–	20	Cridge	1	–	–	–	5
Fomai	4	–	–	–	20	Sapsford	1	–	–	–	5
Emerson	4	–	–	–	20	Lowe	1	–	–	–	5
O'Connor	3	–	–	–	15						
Rakete-Stones	3	–	–	–	15	**Totals**	**53**	**35**	**7**	**0**	**358**
Parsons	3	–	–	–	15						
Long	2	–	–	–	10	*Opposition scored*	*41*	*28*	*17*	*0*	*312*

HAWKE'S BAY 2019

	Manawatu	Wellington	Otago	Northland	Southland	Waikato	Taranaki	Bay of Plenty	Counties Manukau	Tasman	Otago (sf)	Bay of Plenty (f)	Totals
C.L. Makene	15	15	15	15	15	15	15	15	15	14	14	–	11
T.J. Falcon	–	–	–	–	–	–	–	–	s	15	15	15	4
O.R. Sapsford	14	14	s	s	s	–	s	s	s	s	s	–	10
M.R. Emerson	11	11	11	11	11	11	11	11	11	11	11	11	12
N. Fomai	s	s	s	14	14	14	14	14	14	13	13	13	12
J.H. Lowe	–	–	14	–	–	–	–	–	–	–	s	14	3
S.J. McNicol	13	–	–	–	–	–	–	–	–	–	–	–	1
S.I.A. Ili	s	13	13	13	13	13	13	13	13	s	12	12	12
D.S. Toala	12	12	12	12	12	12	12	12	12	12	–	s	11
T. Vaiusu	–	–	–	–	–	–	s	–	–	–	–	–	1
L.F. McClutchie	10	10	10	10	10	10	10	10	10	10	10	10	12
F.M.N. Fakatava	9	9	–	9	9	9	9	9	9	9	9	9	11
Z.G.C. Donaldson	s	–	–	s	s	–	s	s	–	s	–	–	6
B.M. Weber	–	–	9	–	–	–	–	–	–	–	–	–	1
G.O. Evans	8	8	–	8	8	8	–	8	8	–	8	8	9
B.R. O'Connor	7	7	7	7	s	7	7	7	–	7	7	7	11
D.J. Flanders	6	6	8	s	6	s	8	s	s	8	s	s	12
S.A. Kaifa	s	s	s	s	7	s	s	s	7	s	s	s	12
M.E.R. Mikaele-Tu'u	–	–	–	–	–	–	s	s	6	6	6	6	6
T.I. Parsons	5	5	5	5	s	–	5	5	5	5	5	5	11
G.O. Cridge	4	4	6	6	s	6	6	6	s	4	–	s	11
I.E.T. Walker-Leawere	s	s	4	4	4	4	4	–	–	s	s	4	10
M.G. Allardice	–	–	–	s	5	5	–	4	4	–	4	–	6
J.N. Hintz	3	3	3	–	s	s	s	s	3	–	s	s	10
P.G. Rakete-Stones	1	1	1	1	1	1	1	1	s	1	1	1	12
T.J. Farrell	s	–	–	–	–	–	–	–	–	–	–	–	1
N.T.A. Waa	s	s	s	s	3	–	–	–	s	3	–	–	7
B. May	–	s	s	3	–	3	3	3	–	s	3	3	9
J.B. Long	–	–	–	s	s	s	s	s	1	s	s	s	9
A.L. Dixon (capt.)	2	2	2	2	2	2	2	–	2	2	2	2	11
K.R. Kereru-Symes	s	s	s	s	s	–	s	2	s	s	–	s	10
J.D. Devery	–	–	–	–	–	–	s	–	–	–	–	–	1

G.O. Evans and B.R. O'Connor co-captained the match A.L. Dixon did not appear in.

HAWKE'S BAY TEAM RECORD, 2019

Played 12   Won 8   Drew 1   Lost 3   Points for 358   Points against 312

Date	Opponent	Location	Score	Tries	Con	PG	DG	Referee
August 11	Manawatu (C)	Palmerston North	31–13	Dixon (2), O'Connor, Rakete-Stones, Fakatava	Toala (3)			C. Stone
August 16	Wellington (cr)	Napier	27–27	O'Connor, Parsons, Toala, Makene	McClutchie (2)	McClutchie		F. Murphy (Ireland)
August 22	Otago (C)	Napier	29–21	Dixon, Parsons, Toala, Weber	McClutchie (2), Toala			M. Fraser
August 31	Northland (C)	Whangarei	43–28	Fomai (3), Makene (2), Dixon, Fakatava	Toala (4)			M. Winter
September 6	Southland (C)	Napier	41–23	Dixon (2), Evans, Toala, O'Connor, McClutchie, Long	Toala (2), McClutchie			R. Mahoney
September 12	Waikato (cr)	Hamilton	27–24	McClutchie, Fakatava, Rakete-Stones, Emerson	McClutchie (2)	McClutchie		N. Briant
September 20	Taranaki (C)	Napier	35–17	Emerson (2), Toala (2), Penalty Try	McClutchie (4)			N. Hogan
September 28	Bay of Plenty (C)	Tauranga	24–51	Toala, Cridge, Sapsford, Mikaele-Tu'u	McClutchie (2)			J. Doleman
October 3	Counties Manukau (cr)	Pukekohe	22–10	Parsons, Dixon, Fakatava	McClutchie, Falcon	Falcon		M. Winter
October 12	Tasman (cr)	Napier	28–47	Mikaele-Tu'u, Flanders, Makene, Long	Falcon (4)			R. Kelly
October 19	Otago (C sf)	Napier	44–39 a.e.t.	Fomai, Rakete-Stones, McClutchie, Flanders, Emerson	Falcon (5)	Falcon (3)		A. Mabey
October 25	Bay of Plenty (C f)	Rotorua	7–12	Lowe	Falcon			R. Kelly

HOROWHENUA KAPITI

2019 Status: Heartland Championship
Founded 1893: as Horowhenua. Affiliated 1893.
Name changed to Horowhenua Kapiti 1997.
President: G.B. (Gerald) De Castro
Chairman: J.R. (John) Mowbray
Chief executive officer: C.J. (Corey) Kennett
Coach: C.R.K. (Chris) Wilton
Assistant coach: M.P. (Mark) Rutene
Main ground: Levin Park Domain
Capacity: 12,000
Colours: Red, white and blue

RECORDS

Highest attendance	6500	*Hurricanes v Crusaders pre-season, 2014*
Most appearances	153	*P.M. Hirini, 1986–2000*
Most points	440	*C.W. Laursen, 1984–89*
Most tries	69	*D.C. Laursen, 1980–92*
		P.M. Hirini, 1986–2000
Most points in a season	136	*C.J. Spencer, 1993*
Most tries in a season	13	*D.C. Laursen, 1987*
		C.J. Kennett, 1993
Most conversions in a season	26	*C.J. Spencer, 1993*
		R.F. Aloe, 2008
Most penalty goals in a season	29	*C.W. Laursen, 1987*
Most dropped goals in a season	5	*M. Liddicoat, 1979*
Most points in a match	29	*J.P.M. Hamilton v West Coast, 2010*
		B.C. Laursen v Poverty Bay, 2015
Most tries in a match	5	*D.C. Laursen v West Coast, 1991*
Most conversions in a match	9	*D.P. Nepia v Buller, 1999*
	9	*R.F. Aloe v East Coast, 2008*
Most penalty goals in a match	6	*J. Proctor v Wanganui, 2009*
		J.S. So'oialo v Buller 2017
Highest team score	73	*v Buller, 1999*
		v East Coast, 2008
Record victory (points ahead)	73	*73–0 v Buller, 1999*
Highest score conceded	108	*v Counties, 1994*
Record defeat (points behind)	96	*12–108 v Counties, 1994*

The 2019 season was a frustrating one for Horowhenua Kapiti with just three wins, half the number of last year. There was a very good performance in defeating King Country at Te Kuiti and there were chances to win in the narrow losses to both West Coast and Wairarapa Bush.

The assembled team looked capable of challenging for the Meads Cup, but injury and unavailability to many first-choice players severely disrupted the campaign. Timoci Seruwalu, Cody Hemi, "Nardus" Erasmus and Scott Cameron missed half the season through injury, Jaxon Tagavaitau, Tainui Woodmass and Logan Broughton missed half the season due to being with the NZ Defence Force team, player of origin Atutahi Henare was recalled by Manawatu after the opening match, and Junior Laloifi left mid-season to take up a contract in Italy. This meant 38 players appeared with 20 of them being debutants. Only three players appeared in all eight games.

Both wings Himiona Henare and Willie Paia'aua had to be watched carefully by the opposition but had contrasting results. Henare built on last year's promising debut season with six tries while Paia'aua's solitary try did not reflect his contribution. Kameli Kuruyabaki was a strong defender and difficult to contain at centre.

The best of the forwards were lively flanker Nathan Kendrick and prop David McErlean. The latter spent the first half of the season coming off the subs bench at hooker and, contributing well, was then switched to starting prop for the second half of the season. Two promising discoveries were 2m lock Tuitonga Katoa and prop Jordan Tupai-Ui.

Not appearing in 2019 from last year's team were Leon Ellison in Japan, and Tyson Maki not playing. The absence due to injury of Ryan Shelford was a big blow. Star loan player of the previous two years James So'oialo was playing in Australia.

Of the newcomers, Junior Laloifi, on loan from Manawatu, had previously played Super Rugby for Queensland, "Nardus" Erasmus, also on loan from Manawatu, had played Currie Cup for the Free State Cheetahs, Cody Hemi had represented Wanganui, and Kameli Kuruyabaki, another on loan from Manawatu, had also played for Wanganui.

Andrew Knewstubb made the NZ Sevens team during the year but made no appearances for Horowhenua Kapiti.

Higher honours went to:

New Zealand Heartland: S. Cameron, H. Henare, N. Kendrick, A. Lahmert, W. Paia'aua,
T. Seruwalu, J. Tagavaitau

New Zealand Sevens: A. Knewstubb

HOROWHENUA KAPITI REPRESENTATIVES 2019

	Club	Games for Union	Points for Union		Club	Games for Union	Points for Union
Sedale Arthur	Toa	1	0	Sean Pape	Shannon	1	0
Logan Broughton	Shannon	5	0	Tiwana Paringatai [3]		18	0
Scott Cameron	Waikanae	51	53	Robin Praat	Foxton	44	0
Albertus Erasmus	Feilding OB Oroua [2]	3	5	Ethan Reti	Waikanae	16	39
Shae Gray	Foxton	3	0	Trent Reti	Waikanae	16	5
Cody Hemi	Foxton	5	11	Dean Ropata	Toa	16	0
Atutahi Henare [1]	Kia Toa [2]	1	0	Timoci Seruwalu	Ngamatapouri [4]	13	35
Himione Henare	Levin COB	17	68	Jaxon Tagavaitau	Shannon	4	0
Jono Ihaka	Kia Toa [2]	5	20	Christian Tahiwi-MacMillan	Shannon	2	0
Tuitonga Katoa	Foxton	6	0	Kane Tamou	Foxton	21	10
Nathan Kendrick	[3]	25	37	Dylan Taylor	Paraparaumu	15	10
Kameli Kuruyabaki	Palm Nth OB Marist [2]	4	0	Hamiora Thomas	Shannon	1	0
Aaron Lahmert	Waikanae	51	37	Jordan Tupai-Ui	Levin COB	7	10
Junior Laloifi	Feilding OB Oroua [2]	4	5	Pakaitore Turia	Poneke [5]	3	7
Michael Laursen	Foxton	1	0	Isaako Ulutoa	Levin COB	4	0
Pita Marshall	Foxton	5	5	Joel Winterburn	Rahui	20	10
David McErlean	Foxton	46	35	Sonny Woodmass	Shannon	6	0
Willie Paia'aua	Levin COB	31	72	Tainui Woodmass	Shannon	24	0
Ropati Paleaae	Foxton	1	0	Tom Zimmerman	Foxton	17	0

1 *Player of Origin*   2 *Manawatu RU*   3 *Returned from Overseas*   4 *Wanganui RU*   5 *Wellington RU*

INDIVIDUAL SCORING

	Tries	Con	PG	DG	Points
H. Henare	6	8	4	–	58
E. Reti	–	7	3	–	23
Ihaka	4	–	–	–	20
Hemi	1	3	–	–	11
Kendrick	2	–	–	–	10
Tupai-Ui	2	–	–	–	10
Turia	1	1	–	–	7
Cameron	1	–	–	–	5
Erasmus	1	–	–	–	5
Tamou	1	–	–	–	5

* Includes two penalty tries (14 points)

	Tries	Con	PG	DG	Points
Laloifi	1	–	–	–	5
McErlean	1	–	–	–	5
Seruwalu	1	–	–	–	5
Marshall	1	–	–	–	5
Taylor	1	–	–	–	5
Paia'aua	1	–	–	–	5
Totals	**25**	**19**	**7**	**0**	**184**
Opposition scored	37*	23	4	1	250

HOROWHENUA KAPITI 2019

	Mid Canterbury	West Coast	South Canterbury	Buller	King Country	Poverty Bay	Wairarapa Bush	Wanganui	Totals
J.D. Ihaka	–	–	13	15	15	15	15	–	5
H.T.W.K. Henare	15	15	14	11	11	11	11	11	8
J. Laloifi	14	11	13	15	–	–	–	–	4
W.E. Paia'aua	11	–	11	14	14	14	–	14	6
H.T. Thomas	–	14	–	–	–	–	–	–	1
S.V.C. Arthur	–	s	–	–	–	–	–	–	1
M. Laursen	–	–	s	–	–	–	–	–	1
D.C. Taylor	–	–	–	–	–	s	14	s	3
J.F. Tagavaitau	13	13	–	–	–	12	–	12	4
C. Tahiwi-MacMillan	–	–	s	–	s	–	–	–	2
K.N. Kuruyabaki	–	–	–	–	13	13	13	13	4
T.S. Seruwalu	12	–	12	12	–	–	–	–	3
S.G.R. Gray	s	12	–	–	12	–	–	–	3
C.T.A.M. Hemi	10	10	15	–	–	–	–	–	5
E.T. Reti	s	s	10	10	s	–	10	s	7
P. Turia	–	–	–	–	10	10	–	10	3
S.J. Pape	–	–	–	–	–	–	–	s	1
A.K.K. Henare	9	–	–	–	–	–	–	–	1
K.E.M. Tamou	s	9	9	9	9	9	9	9	8
T.C. Reti	–	–	s	s	s	–	–	–	3
A.B. Erasmus	8	8	8	–	–	–	–	–	3
T.L. Zimmerman	–	–	6	8	8	8	8	8	6
N.J. Kendrick	7	7	–	7	7	2	7	7	7
A.D. Lahmert (capt)	6	–	7	6	6	7	6	–	6
L.P.T. Broughton	s	6	–	–	–	6	12	6	5
P.W. Marshall	–	s	–	s	s	–	s	s	5
R.F. Paleaae	–	–	s	–	–	–	–	–	1
T.H.F.M. Katoa	5	–	–	4	4	4	s	4	6
F.T. Woodmass	4	4	–	–	–	–	5	–	3
S.R. Woodmass	–	5	5	5	5	–	–	5	5
I. Ulutoa	–	–	4	s	–	s	–	s	4
J.K.M. Winterburn	–	–	–	–	–	5	4	–	2
S.A. Cameron	3	–	–	3	–	s	–	3	4
R.A. Praat	1	3	1	1	1	–	1	–	6
D.J. McErlean	s	1	s	s	3	3	3	1	8
J.L. Tupai-Ui	–	s	3	s	s	1	s	s	7
D. Ropata	2	2	2	2	2	–	2	2	7
T.S. Paringatai	–	–	–	–	s	s	s	–	3

J.F. Tagavaitau captained v West Coast; W.E. Paia'aua captained v Wanganui

HOROWHENUA KAPITI TEAM RECORD, 2019

Played 8   **Won 3**   **Lost 5**   **Points for 184**   **Points against 250**

Date	Opponent	Location	Score	Tries	Con	PG	DG	Referee
August 24	Mid Canterbury (H)	Ashburton	17–10	Cameron, Erasmus	H. Henare (2)	H. Henare		S. Curran
August 31	West Coast (H)	Levin	21–27	Tamou, Kendrick, H. Henare	Hemi (3)			J.Bredin
September 7	South Canterbury (H)	Timaru	7–57	H. Henare	E. Reti			J. Bredin
September 14	Buller (H)	Levin	31–46	Laloifi, McErlean, Seruwalu, Tupai-Ui	E. Reti (4)	E. Reti		N. Morgan
September 21	King Country (H)	Te Kuiti	35–19	Ihaka (2), H. Henare (2), Marshall	Turia, H. Henare	H. Henare (2)		V. Ringrose
September 28	Poverty Bay (H)	Waikanae	38–28	Ihaka (2), Turia, Tupai-Ui, H. Henare, Taylor	H. Henare (4)			C. Stone
October 5	Wairarapa Bush (H) (BS)	Masterton	20–25	H. Henare, Kendrick	E. Reti (2)	E. Reti (2)		R. Gordon
October 12	Wanganui (H)	Levin	15–38	Paia'aua, Hemi	H. Henare	H. Henare		N. Hogan

BS Bruce Steel Cup

KING COUNTRY

2019 Status: Heartland Championship
Founded 1922. Affiliated 1922
President: L.M. (Max) Lamb
Chairman: I.C. (Ivan) Haines
General Manager: S.M. (Susan) Youngman
Coach: C.W. (Craig) Jeffries
Assistant coach: C.J. (Charles) Hubbard
Main grounds: Owen Delany Park, Taupo; Rugby Park, Te Kuiti
Capacity: 15,000; 5000
Colours: Gold and maroon

RECORDS

Highest attendance	12,000	*King Country v South Africa, 1994 (Taupo)*
Most appearances	147	*P.L. Mitchell, 1988–2001*
Most points	917	*H.C. Coffin, 1984–95*
Most tries	46	*M.R. Kidd, 1974–84*
Most points in a season	230	*H.C. Coffin, 1992*
Most tries in a season	11	*D.M. Flavell, 1981*
		S.J. Bradley, 1992
Most conversions in a season	40	*H.C. Coffin, 1992*
Most penalty goals in a season	45	*H.C. Coffin, 1992*
Most dropped goals in a season	8	*I.N. Ingham, 1966*
Most points in a match	33	*H.C. Coffin v Poverty Bay, 1992*
Most tries in a match	4	*C.A. Crossman v Auckland XV, 1936*
		J. Haitana & H. Dixon v Thames Valley, 1938
		T. Katene v Golden Bay-Motueka, 1955
		J.A.W. McIlroy v Horowhenua, 1965
		D.W. Koni v Taranaki, 1969
		D.M. Flavell v East Coast, 1979
		N.A. Harrison v East Coast, 1981
		N.A. Harrison v Horowhenua, 1984
		J.W. Wells v East Coast, 1992
Most conversions in a match	10	*H.C. Coffin v Poverty Bay, 1992*
Most penalty goals in a match	7	*L.W.T. Peina v Wanganui, 2000*
Highest team score	99	*v East Coast, 1992*
Record victory (points ahead)	99	*99–0 v East Coast, 1992*
Highest score conceded	97	*v Auckland, 1993*
Record defeat (points behind)	94	*3–97 v Auckland, 1993*

2019 was a big disappointment for King Country after last year's best ever season in the Heartland Championship. A promising start was made with two wins in the first four matches, but the remaining four matches were all lost to finish tenth and out of the playoffs.

There were 11 debutants in the season opening loss to West Coast, and the 19–21 loss to South Canterbury was a frustrating one where a last-minute penalty awarded to King Country in kickable range was reversed by the referee. The win over Ngati Porou East Coast was the best performance, being achieved with minority possession.

The team was weakened by the unavailability of five of last year's first choice players who missed the entire rep season due to injury — Dean Church, Joe Perawiti, Rob Sherson, Sean Wanden and Mike Horrocks – which left big gaps. In addition Oliver Kay was not playing, Baven Brown had retired and Manawa Veitayaki was at Waikato, which meant there were 16 newcomers in the 33 players used. Of the loan players Alefosio Tapili was a Samoa A and sevens rep, John Ika had represented Wairarapa Bush and Llisoni "Richie" Tuivanuavou had played for NZ Marist.

Alex Thrupp was again the standout in the backline, his power and pace making him a hard man to stop on the wing. Loan player Alefosio Tapili was a determined runner at centre, while the inside back combination of Zayn Tipping, Evaan Reihana and Brad Armstrong played every game together.

The best forward was undoubtedly number eight Chulainn Mabbett-Sowerby who built on the experience gained in last season's debut. Liam Rowlands, who played at both flanker and hooker, also improved on his debut last year. The experienced Carl Carmichael was again good value at loosehead prop, and the new lock pairing of Josh Balme and Brad Jeffries looked very promising.

Higher honours went to:
New Zealand Heartland: C. Carmichael, C. Mabbett-Sowerby, A. Thrupp

KING COUNTRY REPRESENTATIVES 2019

	Club	Games for Union	Points for Union		Club	Games for Union	Points for Union
Brad Armstrong	Te Puke [2]	8	5	Manawa Owens	Tongariro United	6	0
Josh Balme [1]	Hamilton Marist [3]	7	15	Jamin Pinkerton	Tongariro United	6	5
Nick Barnes	Taupo Sports	9	5	Jonty Powers [1]	Fraser Tech [3]	1	0
Daniel Baxter	Taupo Sports	15	0	Evaan Reihana	Waitete	17	144
Carl Carmichael	Taumarunui RS	35	10	Cameron Robinson	Taupo Sports	7	0
Doug Clapcott	Piopio	15	5	Dan Ross	Taumarunui RS	6	5
Brad Coulson	Taupo Sports	2	0	Liam Rowlands	Taupo Sports	17	20
Shilo Cullen	Taupo Sports	11	5	Alefosio Tapili	Mt Wellington [5]	7	20
Whakataki Cunningham	Tongariro United	29	124	Alex Thrupp	Waitete	30	87
Cruise Dunster	Tongariro United	2	0	Zayn Tipping	Taupo Sports	54	208
Karney Dunster	Kio Kio United	8	0	Tana Tuhakaraina	Te Puna [2]	8	15
Lachlan Foote	Piopio	2	0	Llisoni "Richie" Tuivanuavou	Marist St Michaels [2]	3	5
James Hemara	Waitete	53	98	Tayne Tupaea	Piopio	6	5
Charlie Henare	Taupo Sports	18	0	Stephan Turner	Piopio	23	27
John Ika	MAC [4]	2	0	Ratu Vosaki	Taupo Sports	18	15
Brad Jeffries	Piopio	8	5	Sisa Vosaki	Taupo Sports	13	10
Chulainn Mabbett-Sowerby	Piopio	16	30				

1 Player of Origin   2 Bay of Plenty RU   3 Waikato RU   Hawke's Bay RU   5 Auckland RU

INDIVIDUAL SCORING

	Tries	Con	PG	DG	Points
Reihana	–	15	5	–	45
Tapili	4	–	–	–	20
Thrupp	3	–	–	–	15
Balme	3	–	–	–	15
Tipping	2	2	–	–	14
Mabbett-Sowerby	2	–	–	–	10
S. Vosaki	2	–	–	–	10
Penalty Try	1	–	–	–	7
Turner	1	–	–	–	5
Jeffries	1	–	–	–	5
Armstrong	1	–	–	–	5
Tupaea	1	–	–	–	5

	Tries	Con	PG	DG	Points
Tuhakaraina	1	–	–	–	5
Barnes	1	–	–	–	5
Tuivanuavou	1	–	–	–	5
R. Vosaki	1	–	–	–	5
Ross	1	–	–	–	5
Pinkerton	1	–	–	–	5
Rowlands	1	–	–	–	5
Totals	**28**	**17**	**5**	**0**	**191**
Opposition scored	39 *	23	8	0	267

* Includes one penalty try (7 points)

KING COUNTRY 2019

	West Coast	Buller	Wairarapa Bush	Ngati Porou East Coast	Horowhenua Kapiti	South Canterbury	Wanganui	Thames Valley	Totals
S.K. Turner	15	s	–	–	s	s	s	14	6
J.T. Ika	–	15	15	–	–	–	–	–	2
J.T.T.R. Hemara	–	–	s	–	–	–	–	–	1
C.J. Robinson	–	–	–	–	–	15	15	s	3
R.S. Vosaki	14	s	s	s	11	11	11	11	8
S.A. Cullen	11	–	–	–	–	–	–	s	2
T.L.T.R. Tupaea	s	14	14	14	14	–	–	s	6
S. Vosaki	–	11	11	–	–	–	–	–	2
A.M. Thrupp	–	–	s	11	13	14	14	13	6
A. Tapili	13	13	13	15	–	13	13	15	7
T. Tuhakaraina	–	–	–	13	15	–	–	–	2
B. Armstrong	12	12	12	12	12	12	12	12	8
E.H. Reihana	10	10	10	10	10	s	10	10	8
B.A. Coulson	s	s	–	–	–	–	–	–	2
D.W. Cunningham	–	–	–	s	s	10	s	s	5
Z.J. Tipping	9	9	9	9	9	9	9	9	8
C. Mabbett-Sowerby	8	8	8	8	s	8	8	–	7
L.T. Foote	7	s	–	–	–	–	–	–	2
J.L. Powers	6	–	–	–	–	–	–	–	1
K.K.A.M. Dunster	s	6	6	6	6	s	s	6	8
M.K. Owens	–	s	s	s	s	–	s	7	6
D.W. Baxter	–	–	–	7	7	7	7	8	5
L.R. Tuivanuavou	–	–	–	–	8	6	6	–	3
J.H. Balme	5	5	5	5	5	5	–	5	7
C.K.T. Dunster	4	–	–	–	–	–	–	s	2
B.J. Jeffries	s	4	4	4	s	4	4	4	8
D.J. Clapcott	–	s	s	s	4	s	5	5	6
J.L. Pinkerton	3	3	–	3	–	s	s	s	6
C.W. Carmichael (capt)	1	–	1	1	1	1	1	1	7
C.K. Henare	s	s	s	s	s	s	3	–	7
D.S. Ross	–	1	3	–	3	3	s	3	6
L.A. Rowlands	2	7	7	2	2	2	2	2	8
N.G. Barnes	s	2	2	s	s	s	s	s	8

L. Rowlands captained v Buller.

KING COUNTRY TEAM RECORD, 2019

Played 8   Won 2   Lost 6   Points for 191   Points against 267

Date	Opponent	Location	Score	Tries	Con	PG	DG	Referee
August 24	West Coast (H)	Greymouth	27–56	Tapili, Turner, Mabbett-Sowerby, Jeffries	Reihana (2)	Reihana		N. Webster
August 31	Buller (H)	Taupo	34–12	Tapili (2), S. Vosaki (2), Tipping	Reihana (3)	Reihana		H. Reed
September 7	Wairarapa Bush (H)	Masterton	31–37	Armstrong, Mabbett-Sowerby, Thrupp, Balme, Tupaea	Reihana (3)			T. Cottrell
September 14	Ngati Porou East Coast (H)	Tokomaru Bay	27–12	Tuhakaraina, Tapili, Barnes	Reihana (2), Tipping	Reihana (2)		M. Winter
September 21	Horowhenua Kapiti (H)	Te Kuiti	19–35	Tuivanuavou, R. Vosaki, Penalty Try	Reihana			V. Ringrose
September 28	South Canterbury (H)	Taupo	19–21	Balme (2), Tipping	Reihana (2)			D. MacPherson
October 5	Wanganui (H)	Wanganui	19–57	Ross, Thrupp, Pinkerton	Reihana (2)			V. Ringrose
October 12	Thames Valley (H)	Te Kuiti	15–37	Thrupp, Rowlands	Tipping	Reihana		M. Playle

MANAWATU

2019 Status: Mitre 10 Cup Championship
Founded 1886. Original member 1892
President: B.S. (Bruce) Hemara
Chairman: T.J. (Tim) Myers
Chief executive officer: S.M. (Shannon) Paku
Coach: P.C. (Peter) Russell
Assistant coach: A.J. (Aaron) Good, Greg Fleming
Main ground: Central Energy Trust Arena, Palmerston North
Capacity: 17,000
Colours: Green and white

MANAWATU RUGBY

RECORDS

Highest attendance	17,100	Manawatu v British & Irish Lions, 2005
Most appearances	145	*G.A. Knight, 1975–86*
Most points	641	*J.J. Holland, 1991–96*
Most tries	66	*K.W. Granger, 1971–84*
Most points in a season	182	*J.M. Smith, 1991*
Most tries in a season	14	*P.L. Alston, 1991*
Most conversions in a season	38	*D.L. Rollerson, 1981*
		J.M. Smith, 1991
Most penalty goals in a season	27	*M.C. Finlay, 1984*
		A. McMaster, 1987
Most dropped goals in a season	9	*J.P.J. Carroll, 1978*
Most points in a match	35	*J.M. Smith v Horowhenua, 1992*
Most tries in a match	5	*J.P. Butt v Wanganui, 1944*
		N.J. Mears v Horowhenua, 1958
		G.P.D. Henare v Horowhenua, 1987
Most conversions in a match	11	*J.M. Smith v Poverty Bay, 1991*
Most penalty goals in a match	6	*M.R. Love v Waikato, 1983*
		M.C. Finlay v Wanganui, 1984
		A. McMaster v Waikato, 1987
		J.J. Holland v Counties, 1994
		I. Thompson v Northland, 2009
Highest team score	94	*v Poverty Bay, 1991*
Record victory (points ahead)	87	*94–7 v Poverty Bay, 1991*
Highest score conceded	109	*v British & Irish Lions, 2005*
Record defeat (points behind)	103	*6–109 v British & Irish Lions, 2005*

The omission of Ngani Laumape from the All Blacks squad for the Rugby World Cup was a surprise for many fans, but that disappointment was turned when he became the saviour of the Turbos. Seldom does one player have so much influence on a team's performance and match outcome. It seemed Manawatu had two teams, one without Laumape and one with him. He was available for only five games and was instrumental in the four wins Manawatu registered including the shock win over Canterbury. Thanks to Laumape, Manawatu reached the semifinals and such was his impact that it is accepted that had he been in Japan the Turbos would have lost every game.

The scrums were the major problem, the forwards being shunted often and conceding the inevitable penalty as a result. The front row simply battled to hold their ground. Sam Stewart and Nick Grogan shared the hooking duties and were, generally, accurate lineout throwers. Sam Tawake, Fa'aleilei Sione, Sione Asi and Paulo Leleisiuao (from Brisbane) tried their best at prop but rarely dominated. We would have liked to have seen Fraser Armstrong bring more of his Hurricanes form into the Turbos. Liam Mitchell was the best forward, outstanding in the lineout and busy in general play. He was partnered at lock by Fraser Stone who last appeared in 2015. The work rate of evergreen Nick Crosswell was an inspiration, a grand stalwart of local rugby who joins the few who have made 100 appearances for the union. Johnny Galloway had his moments and Brayden Iose, free from injury, improved with each game and should become more prominent in coming years. Sione Tu'ipulotu was an able substitute in the loose. Injury prevented former PNBHS player Tyler Laubscher, aged 18, from appearing in club rugby in 2019, but this promising loose forward made a brief appearance late in the season and more should be seen of him in the future.

Jamie Booth, after a season of Super Rugby with the Sunwolves, was perhaps the outstanding halfback in the competition, an inspiring captain, sharp on attack and a courageous tackler. Life was so often difficult for him behind a scrum in reverse. Otere Black was tidy in his work and an accurate goalkicker; like Booth, he had difficulties with a forward pack battling for dominance. In midfield James Tofa showed improvement alongside the experienced Hamish Northcott. It was unfortunate for Rob Thompson to see his season limited through injury and concussion issues. The wings seldom received opportunities. Adam Boult has good speed but there were too few chances to exhibit his pace. Back from Japan, Andre Taylor's season is best remembered for his two long-range penalty goals. Sam Malcolm returned from Canada to again be a reliable fullback. We hope to see more of young backs Stewart Cruden, Ben Werthmuller, Josiah Maraku and Drew Wild in coming years.

Injury ended the season early for Tom Hughes, Sam Wasley and Ben Wyness. The season's results could have improved if the forwards had been supported with the grunt of All Black Jackson Hemopo (injured) and an injury-free Rob Thompson. The Turbos' 2019 season will best be remembered for the remarkable contribution of Ngani Laumape in his few appearances, when his tackle-busting runs and tactical kicking so often resulted in tries.

Higher honours went to:

New Zealand:	J. Hemopo, N. Laumape, A.L. Smith
Maori All Blacks:	O. Black, R. Thompson
New Zealand Sevens:	K.T. Baker

MANAWATU REPRESENTATIVES 2019

	Club	Games for Union	Points for Union		Club	Games for Union	Points for Union
Fraser Armstrong	OB Marist	44	5	Josiah Maraku	Feilding	7	0
Sione Asi	Kia Toa	16	0	Liam Mitchell	Te Kawau	25	5
Otere Black	College OB	56	444	Hamish Northcott	University	63	30
Jamie Booth	University	53	55	Rhys Pedersen	OB Marist	7	5
Adam Boult	Te Kawau	8	10	Fa'alelei Sione	Freyberg OB	20	10
Nick Crosswell	Feilding	104	20	Sam Stewart	Te Kawau	21	0
Stewart Cruden	College OB	3	0	Fraser Stone	Kia Toa	75	30
Griffin Culver	Feilding	4	0	Samuela Tawake	Sumner[1]	10	5
Johnny Galloway	Feilding	9	10	Andre Taylor	College OB	40	100
Nick Grogan	University	35	0	Rob Thompson	University	12	15
Jackson Hemopo	Kia Toa	24	20	James Tofa	College OB	17	5
Atutahi Henare	Kia Toa	4	0	Sione Tu'ipulotu	Ardmore Marist[2]	11	0
Tom Hughes	University	11	0	Te Rangatira Waitokia	University	17	0
Brayden Iose	Kia Toa	12	10	Sam Wasley	Feilding	3	0
Tyler Laubscher	Manawatu RU	1	0	Ben Werthmuller	OB Marist	5	10
Ngani Laumape	Kia Toa	19	70	Drew Wild	Feilding	3	0
Paulo Leleisiuao	Souths (Brisbane)	8	0	Ben Wyness	Feilding	1	0
Sam Malcolm	Toronto Arrows (Canada)	27	53				

[1] *Canterbury RU*   [2] *Counties Manukau RU*

INDIVIDUAL SCORING

	Tries	Con	PG	DG	Points		Tries	Con	PG	DG	Points
Black	2	19	9	–	75	Malcolm	–	–	2	–	6
Taylor	3	–	2	–	21	Northcott	1	–	–	–	5
Booth	4	–	–	–	20	Pedersen	1	–	–	–	5
Laumape	4	–	–	–	20	Tawake	1	–	–	–	5
Galloway	3	–	–	–	15						
Boult	2	–	–	–	10	**Totals**	**25**	**19**	**13**	**0**	**202**
Iose	2	–	–	–	10						
Werthmuller	2	–	–	–	10	Opposition scored	58*	34	7	0	381

* Includes one penalty try (7 points)

MANAWATU 2019

	Hawke's Bay	Taranaki	Tasman	Otago	Northland	Southland	Canterbury	North Harbour	Bay of Plenty	Counties Manukau	Bay of Plenty	TOTALS
S.B. Malcolm	15	–	–	15	15	15	–	–	s	15	15	7
B. Wyness	–	15	–	–	–	–	–	–	–	–	–	1
D. Wild	–	s	15	14	–	–	–	–	–	–	–	3
A.S. Taylor	–	–	–	s	14	14	15	15	15	14	–	7
Te R.W. Waitokia	14	–	–	–	s	s	14	14	14	–	14	7
B.B. Werthmuller	s	14	–	–	–	–	–	–	–	s	11	4
J.M. Maraku	–	s	14	–	–	–	s	s	11	11	13	7
S.R. Cruden	–	–	s	s	–	–	–	–	–	–	s	3
A.C. Boult	11	11	11	11	11	11	11	11	–	–	–	8
R. Thompson	13	–	–	–	s	–	–	13	–	–	–	3
H.C. Northcott	12	13	13	13	13	13	13	12	13	–	s	10
J. Tofa	s	12	12	12	–	s	s	s	s	13	12	10
K.H. Laumape	–	–	–	–	12	12	12	–	12	12	–	5
O.W. Black	10	10	10	10	10	10	10	10	10	10	10	11
J.P. Booth (Capt)	9	9	9	9	9	9	9	9	9	9	9	11
G.J. Culver	s	–	s	s	s	–	–	–	–	–	–	4
A.K.K. Henare	–	–	–	–	–	–	–	s	s	s	s	4
B.D. Iose	8	8	–	s	8	8	8	8	8	8	8	10
S. Tu'ipulotu	s	s	8	8	s	s	s	s	s	s	s	11
T. Laubscher	–	–	–	–	–	–	–	–	–	s	–	1
J.B. Galloway	7	7	–	–	7	7	7	7	7	7	7	9
S.D. Wasley	s	–	s	–	–	–	–	–	–	–	–	2
R.C. Pedersen	–	–	7	–	–	s	s	s	s	s	s	7
N.J. Crosswell	6	6	6	7	6	6	6	6	6	6	6	11
L.F. Mitchell	5	4	4	6	5	5	5	5	5	5	5	11
F.P. Stone	4	5	s	s	4	4	4	4	4	4	4	11
T.W. Hughes	–	s	–	4	s	–	–	–	–	–	–	3
J.N. Hemopo	–	–	5	5	–	–	–	–	–	–	–	2
P. Leleisiuao	3	s	–	s	s	–	–	s	s	s	s	8
S.O.F. Tawake	s	3	3	3	3	3	3	3	3	3	–	10
S.F. Asi	–	–	s	s	s	s	s	–	–	–	3	6
F.P. Armstrong	1	1	–	–	–	s	1	1	1	1	1	8
F. Sione	s	s	1	1	1	1	s	s	s	s	s	11
S.W. Stewart	2	s	s	s	2	2	s	s	s	2	2	11
N.A.J. Grogan	s	2	2	2	s	s	2	2	2	s	s	11

MANAWATU TEAM RECORD, 2019

Played 11 Won 4 Lost 7 Points for 202 Points against 381

Date	Opponent	Location	Score	Tries	Con	PG	DG	Referee
August 11	Hawke's Bay (C)	Palmerston North	13–31	Northcott	Black			C.J. Stone
August 17	Taranaki (C)	Palmerston North	10–13	Werthmuller, Booth				Dan Jones (Wales)
August 24	Tasman (cr)	Blenheim	3–64			Black		N.E.R. Hogan
August 30	Otago (C, RS)	Dunedin	20–37	Booth, Boult	Black (2)	Black (2)		G.W. Jackson
September 5	Northland (C)	Palmerston North	31–25	Taylor (2), Galloway, Booth	Black (4)	Black		G.W. Jackson
September 14	Southland (C)	Invercargill	31–26	Laumape (2), Iose, Pedersen	Black (4)	Black		A.W.B. Mabey
September 19	Canterbury (cr)	Christchurch	32–29	Galloway, Taylor, Laumape, Iose	Black (3)	Black, Taylor		R.P. Kelly
September 29	North Harbour (cr)	Palmerston North	16–29	Boult, Black		Black (2)		H.G. Reed
October 5	Bay of Plenty (C)	Tauranga	10–46	Booth	Black	Taylor		D.J. Waenga
October 12	Counties Manukau (cr)	Palmerston North	33–17	Black, Laumape, Galloway, Tawake, Werthmuller	Black (4)	Malcolm		D.J. Waenga
October 18	Bay of Plenty (s-f)	Rotorua	3–64			Malcolm		R.P. Kelly

MID CANTERBURY

2019 Status: Heartland Championship
Founded 1904 as Ashburton sub-union affiliated
to South Canterbury RU. Name changed
to Ashburton County 1905 and affilated
to Canterbury RU 1905. Became a full union
with affiliation to NZRU 1927.
Name changed to Mid Canterbury 1952.
President: J.C. (Jock) Ross
Chairman: G.P. (Gerard) Rushton
Chief executive officer: I.J. (Ian) Patterson
Coach: D.D. (Dale) Palmer
Assistant coach: J.J. (Jason) Rickard
Main ground: Ashburton Showgrounds
Capacity: 10,000
Colours: Forest green and gold

RECORDS

Highest attendance	8656	*Mid Canterbury v British Isles, 1983*
Most appearances	158	*J.C. Ross, 1970–87*
Most points	598	*A.H.A. Smith, 1955–68*
Most tries	47	*G.R. Bryant, 1968–77*
Most points in a season	200	*S.R. Middleton, 1994*
Most tries in a season	13	*M.L. Sau, 2017*
Most conversions in a season	34	*S.R. Middleton, 1994*
		J.R. Percival, 2017
Most penalty goals in a season	44	*S.R. Middleton, 1994*
Most dropped goals in a season	12	*M.B. Roulston, 1982*
Most points in a match	22	*M.C. Williams v East Coast, 2014*
Most tries in a match	5	*G.R. Bryant v Nelson Bays, 1977*
Most conversions in a match	8	*S.R. Middleton v West Coast, 1998*
Most penalty goals in a match	6	*S.R. Middleton v Horowhenua Kapiti, 1998*
		D.J. Maw v West Coast, 2007
		M.C. Williams v Wanganui, 2014
Highest team score	90	*v West Coast, 1998*
Record victory (points ahead)	77	*90–13 v West Coast, 1998*
Highest score conceded	99	*v Hawke's Bay, 2003*
Record defeat (points behind)	91	*8–99 v Hawke's Bay, 2003*

Mid Canterbury suffered its worst ever season in the Heartland Championship. The one win recorded was the fewest ever achieved, and in finishing 11th missed both sets of playoffs for the very first time.

The forwards encountered a number of bigger opposition packs, and the team usually started strong in most games before a tendency to fall off the pace later on. Halftime leads were held against West Coast and Poverty Bay but poor second halves resulted in defeat. Against South Canterbury a last minute penalty kick was missed and the match ended drawn in what was probably the best performance of the season.

Jackson Donlan was the team's best performer. An excellent hooker, he was also effective around the field and as captain was an inspiring leader. Props Tom Heywood and Sorby Sovea scrummaged well and with their high workrate in general play formed a very good front row with their captain. Reserve prop Adam Williamson invariably made a good impact when coming off the bench. Eric Duff and Matt Bentley produced a good supply of ball from the lineouts, and flanker Seta Koroitamana maintained his usual high standard as the best of the loose forwards, and even made one appearance at centre. He topped the try scoring with four.

Loan player Corey McKay looked a good find at first five-eighth. Tyler Blackburn started the season at halfback but then an unexpected shift to second five-eighth, due to injuries, brought out some impressive defensive performances. Young wing Tololima Savaiinea looked a good find, and halfback Will Mackenzie's experience was an asset to the side.

Locals of last year's squad who were elsewhere in 2019 were Tom Hanham-Carter, Aron Einarrson and Brian Matoramusha, all in Canterbury, although the latter did return as a loan player for half the matches. In addition, Andrew Letham was out injured.

To help add experience and depth in the squad, a number of players agreed to make themselves available again for the Heartland Championship — Richard Catherwood, Jon Dampney, Tevita Ula, and Kody Nordqvist all had last represented Mid Canterbury in 2016. Newcomer Ata Ata Langilangi had previously represented South Canterbury and Josh McAtamney had played for both Poverty Bay and South Canterbury.

Higher honours went to:
New Zealand Heartland: S. Koroitamana

MID CANTERBURY REPRESENTATIVES 2019

	Club	Games for Union	Points for Union		Club	Games for Union	Points for Union
Manasi Bari	Methven	7	15	Hamish Mackenzie	Southern	5	0
Matt Bentley	Rakaia	17	0	Will Mackenzie	Southern	72	5
Tyler Blackburn	Methven	33	12	Sam Madden	Southern	4	0
Tom Blyth	Rakaia	13	0	Brian Matoramusha	Lincoln University [2]	12	47
Richard Catherwood	Darfield [2]	57	72	Josh McAtamney	Southern	5	10
Nete Caucau	Methven	41	35	Matt McAtamney	Southern	8	10
Jon Dampney	Southern	120	157	Corey McKay	Taieri [3]	7	47
Jackson Donlan	Rakaia	55	21	Timoci Nabakeke	Rakaia	27	33
Eric Duff	Southern	57	31	Kody Nordqvist	Rakaia	33	16
Matt Groom	Methven	28	15	Tololima "Lima" Savaiinaea	Celtic	8	0
Tom Heywood	Rakaia	23	5	Cory Sinclair	Rakaia	8	0
Seta Koroitamana	Rakaia	55	153	Sorby Sovea	Belfast [2]	6	0
Ata Ata Langilangi	Rakaia	3	0	Jacob Sutton	Celtic	3	0
Tim Lawn	Methven	1	0	Inoke Tonga	Rakaia	3	0
Ioelu "Joel" Leo [1]	Chch HSOB [2]	4	0	Tevita Ula	Hampstead	39	15
Angus Lindsay	Celtic	25	30	Adam Williamson	Southern	24	0

1 Player of Origin   2 Canterbury RU   3 Otago RU

INDIVIDUAL SCORING

	Tries	Con	PG	DG	Points
McKay	–	13	7	–	47
Koroitamana	4	–	–	–	20
Dampney	3	–	–	–	15
Bari	3	–	–	–	15
J. McAtamney	2	–	–	–	10
M. McAtamney	2	–	–	–	10
Groom	2	–	–	–	10
Penalty Try	1	–	–	–	7
Blackburn	–	2	1	–	7

	Tries	Con	PG	DG	Points
Donlan	1	–	–	–	5
W. Mackenzie	1	–	–	–	5
Nabakeke	1	–	–	–	5
Nordqvist	1	–	–	–	5
Totals	**21**	**15**	**8**	**0**	**161**
Opposition scored	*35*	*23*	*5*	*0*	*236*

MID CANTERBURY 2019

	Horowhenua Kapiti	Ngati Porou East Coast	West Coast	South Canterbury	Poverty Bay	Thames Valley	North Otago	Wairarapa Bush	Totals
R.L. Catherwood	15	–	–	s	–	10	s	13	5
M.S. McAtamney	s	15	15	15	15	15	15	s	8
T.N. Nabakeke	14	14	–	s	11	s	13	–	6
T.S. Savaiinaea	11	11	11	11	s	14	14	15	8
M. Bari	–	s	14	14	14	s	s	14	7
T.B. Matoramusha	–	–	s	–	–	11	11	11	4
T.J. Lawn	–	–	–	–	–	–	–	s	1
A.J. McAtamney	13	13	13	13	13	–	–	–	5
R.N. Caucau	12	12	12	–	12	–	–	–	4
T.A.C. Blackburn	s	9	9	12	s	12	12	12	8
C.M. McKay	10	10	10	10	10	–	10	10	7
I.F. Tonga	s	s	s	–	–	–	–	–	3
A.W. Mackenzie	9	–	–	9	9	9	9	9	6
C.W. Sinclair	–	s	s	s	s	s	s	s	7
J.R. Dampney (capt)	8	8	8	8	8	8	8	8	8
S.S. Koroitamana	7	–	7	7	7	13	7	–	6
T.H. Ula	6	–	6	6	6	s	–	s	6
K.J. Nordqvist	s	s	–	–	–	s	6	6	5
T.E.L. Blyth	s	6	s	s	–	6	–	–	5
A.J. Lindsay	–	7	s	–	–	–	–	–	2
J.R. Sutton	–	s	–	–	–	–	s	s	3
F.S. Madden	–	s	–	–	s	–	s	7	4
H.I. Mackenzie	–	–	–	–	–	7	–	–	1
A.A.M.H. Langilangi	5	–	–	s	s	–	–	–	3
E.J. Duff	4	4	4	4	4	4	4	4	8
M.J. Bentley	–	5	5	5	5	5	5	5	7
S.T. Sovea	3	3	3	3	3	3	–	–	6
T.J. Heywood	1	1	1	1	1	1	1	1	8
A.C.J. Williamson	s	s	s	s	–	s	3	3	7
M.R. Groom	–	–	–	–	s	s	s	s	4
J.L. Donlan	2	2	2	2	2	2	2	2	8
I. Leo	–	–	s	–	s	–	s	s	4

MID CANTERBURY TEAM RECORD, 2019

Played 8   Won 1   Drew 1   Lost 6   Points for 161   Points against 236

Date	Opponent	Location	Score	Tries	Con	PG	DG	Referee
August 24	Horowhenua Kapiti (H)	Ashburton	10–17	Koroitamana, J. McAtamney				S. Curran
August 31	Ngati Porou East Coast (H)	Ruatoria	22–15	Dampney, M. McAtamney, Bari	McKay (2)	McKay		T. Griffiths
September 7	West Coast (H)	Greymouth	41–43	Bari (2), Koroitamana (2). M. McAtamney, Donlan	McKay (4)	McKay		J. Munro
September 14	South Canterbury (H)	Ashburton	13–13	Dampney	McKay	McKay (2)		J. Munro
September 21	Poverty Bay (H)	Gisborne	38–52	J. McAtamney, Dampney, Penalty Try, W. Mackenzie, Groom	McKay (4)	McKay		A. Mabey
September 28	Thames Valley (H)	Ashburton	17–31	Koroitamana, Nabakeke	Blackburn (2)	Blackburn		N. Webster
October 5	North Otago (H) (HS)	Oamaru	10–34	Nordqvist	McKay	McKay		C. Paul
October 12	Wairarapa Bush (H)	Ashburton	10–31	Groom	McKay	McKay		D. Moore

HS Hanan Shield

NORTH HARBOUR

2019 Status: Mitre 10 Cup Premiership
Founded 1985. Affiliated 1985
President: J. (John) McKittrick
Chairman: G.R. (Gary) Howarth
General Manager: D.B. (David) Gibson
Coach: K.J. (Kieran) Keane
Assistant coaches: S.R.B (Sam) Ward, B.M. (Brett) Craies
Main ground: North Harbour Stadium, Albany
Capacity: 25,000
Colours: White, black and cardinal

RECORDS

Most appearances	145	*Ron Williams, 1985–94*
		Walter Little, 1987–2000
Most points	1052	*Warren Burton, 1990–96*
Most tries	63	*Richard Kapa, 1985–93*
Most points in a season	258	*Warren Burton, 1995*
Most tries in a season	16	*Glenn Davis, 1999*
Most conversions in a season	53	*Warren Burton, 1991*
Most penalty goals in a season	47	*Warren Burton, 1995*
Most dropped goals in a season	3	*Jamie Cameron, 1991*
Most points in a match	34	*Frano Botica v Queensland Country, 1985*
Most tries in a match	5	*Glenn Davis v Poverty Bay-East Coast, 1999*
		Tevita Li v Taranaki, 2017
Most conversions in a match	10	*Frano Botica v Taranaki, 1989*
		Jamie Cameron v Marlborough, 1990
		Warren Burton v Wanganui, 1991
Most penalty goals in a match	6	*Warren Burton v Counties, 1990*
		Warren Burton v Wellington, 1990
		Warren Burton v Otago, 1994
		Warren Burton v Hawke's Bay, 1996
Highest team score	99	*v Horowhenua Kapiti, 2008*
Record victory (points ahead)	93	*99–6 v Horowhenua Kapiti, 2008*
Highest score conceded	71	*v Auckland, 1995*
Record defeat (points behind)	55	*10–65 v Canterbury 2002*

North Harbour will be kicking itself for dropping two home crossover games — against Bay of Plenty and Otago — which ultimately cost the union a Premership semi-final berth.

A new coaching group of former All Black Kieran Keane, assisted by Sam Ward and Brett Craies, had the unenviable task of bringing a young squad swiftly up to task after several pre-season injuries decimated the numbers.

In the end, it was a fair effort to use just 32 players and, if goalkicks had been made in the final match against Canterbury, North Harbour may have won both the Ranfurly Shield and a top four berth.

Rugby people in the region will, however, look with envy upon Tasman, the country's newest provincial union, hoisting the Rugby Cup after just 14 seasons, while North Harbour's search for glory remains unrequited.

And yet, North Harbour reeled off several halves of top quality rugby. The struggle was to put it all together, which is why Keane's men won just four games, two less than in 2018, when they missed the playoffs by four points.

Down 28–0 to Auckland in the season opener, Harbour staged a rousing comeback to draw the clash, though the Battle of the Bridge trophy remained with its Blues brothers.

There was great disappointment that the Lion Red Challenge Cup was surrendered in a home defeat to Counties Manukau, while Bay of Plenty also toppled Harbour in Albany.

The season appeared to be turning for the better after a stirring second stanza comeback to edge Waikato in Albany. The next two games were lost, but Harbour acquitted itself admirably to push the Mako hard in Nelson. The loss to Otago, despite falling off just 12 tackles, in Albany, was inexplicable.

The win over Wellington was based on the best 40 minutes of the season in the first spell, when Harbour's set-piece dominance paved the way for some well-constructed team tries.

Things threatened to turn pear-shaped in Christchurch when Shaun Stevenson was switched to No 10 and the radar off the tee was astray, but the victory might still have been won. In the final analysis, just two more points were needed to sneak into the semi-finals.

Stevenson was again mightily effective at fullback, often hitting the blind incisively and combining well with his fellow backs. Matt Duffie shouldered most of the captaincy duties in the absence of the injured James Parsons and his general play, including seven tries, was superior to his 2018 output. Mark Telea had always been a fringe player, but his six tries showed a growing awareness of his game allied with his usual raw pace. He offset the loss of Tevita Li to Japan.

Veteran centre Asaeli Tikoirotuma showed his nous and strength over the ball and on the tackle, and proved an astute signing from London Irish. James Little often added impact as a replacement, while Harrison Groundwater made few mistakes and showed us more on attack.

Jared Page, who had previously played fullback for Counties Manukau, made three appearances before injury, but won a Blues contract. Matt McGahan stepped in, returning home from the Queensland Reds, and looked good in place of the injured Bryn Gatland.

Bryn Hall was the player of the season, his heads-up footy setting up several tries and staving off the challenge of Lewis Gjaltema.

The Inisi brothers, Fine in the backs and Lotu in the pack, both showed their talents, mostly as subs.

Such was Murphy Taramai's convincing form at No 8 that he was signed by the Hurricanes. Dillon Hunt may have slipped in the national No 7 pecking order, but he was always valuable for his province. The rookie No 6 Ethan Roots impressed in every outing, strong over the ball and making his tackles after a compelling club season.

North Harbour possessed three quality locks in Ben Nee-Nee, Jacob Pierce and Gerard Cowley-Tuioti, who passed 50 games. All three were prime lineout targets.

The scrum was never dominated, thanks in part to Sione Mafileo at tighthead and All Blacks reject Karl Tu'inukuafe, who impressed around the track as much as in the tight.

Parsons' back troubles allowed Luteru Tolai to shine at rake, aided by David Meki.

Higher honours went to:
New Zealand Maori: B. Hall, S. Stevenson
New Zealand Universities: K. Felise, H. McGahan

NORTH HARBOUR REPRESENTATIVES 2019

	Club	Games for Union	Points for Union		Club	Games for Union	Points for Union
Tomas Aoake	East Coast Bays	5	0	Brad McNaughton	North Shore	1	0
Gerard Cowley-Tuioti	Massey	56	20	David Meki	East Coast Bays	6	0
Xavier Cowley-Tuioti	Massey	1	0	Ben Nee-Nee	Northcote	19	0
Matt Duffie	Takapuna	39	110	Jared Page	Silverdale	3	13
Tate Evans	East Coast Bays	2	0	James Parsons	Takapuna	106	102
Lewis Gjaltema	East Coast Bays	21	5	Jacob Pierce	North Shore	17	0
Harrison Groundwater	East Coast Bays	27	30	Osea Qamasea	Mahurangi	1	5
Bryn Hall	Northcote	78	89	Ropate Rinakama	Silverdale	2	0
Dillon Hunt	Marist	16	20	Ethan Roots	East Coast Bays	10	0
Fine Inisi	Takapuna	5	5	Jimmy Roots	East Coast Bays	2	0
Lotu Inisi	Takapuna	9	10	Shaun Stevenson	Marist	30	68
Luatangi Li	East Coast Bays	17	10	Murphy Taramai	Northcote	41	15
James Little	North Shore	8	15	Mark Telea	Massey	25	35
Sione Mafileo	North Shore	53	15	Asaeli Tikoirotuma	Northcote	9	15
Nic Mayhew	Northcote	33	10	Luteru Tolai	Northcote	16	5
Matt McGahan	Kumeu	40	162	Karl Tu'inukuafe	Takapuna	27	15

INDIVIDUAL SCORING

	Tries	Con	PG	DG	Points		Tries	Con	PG	DG	Points
McGahan	1	17	3	–	48	Gjaltema	1	–	–	–	5
Duffie	7	–	–	–	35	F. Inisi	1	–	–	–	5
Telea	6	–	–	–	30	Li	1	–	–	–	5
Hall	3	1	1	–	20	Mafileo	1	–	–	–	5
Little	3	–	–	–	15	Parsons	1	–	–	–	5
Tikoirotuma	3	–	–	–	15	Qamasea	1	–	–	–	5
Stevenson	2	–	1	–	13	Taramai	1	–	–	–	5
Page	–	5	1	–	13	Tolai	1	–	–	–	5
Groundwater	2	–	–	–	10						
L. Inisi	2	–	–	–	10	**Totals**	**41**	**23**	**6**	**0**	**271**
Tu'inukuafe	2	–	–	–	10						
Penalty try	1	–	–	–	7	Opposition scored	36*	26	9	0	265
G. Cowley-Tuioti	1	–	–	–	5						

* Includes three penalty tries (21 points)

NORTH HARBOUR 2019

	Auckland	Counties Manukau	Southland	Bay of Plenty	Waikato	Tasman	Otago	Manawatu	Wellington	Canterbury	Totals
S.T. Stevenson	15	15	15	15	15	15	15	–	15	10	9
M.D. Duffie (capt)	14	14	14	14	14	s	14	15	14	15	10
O. Qamasea	–	–	–	–	–	–	–	–	–	14	1
M.E. Telea	11	11	–	11	11	11	11	11	11	11	9
T.J. Aoake	–	–	11	–	s	14	s	14	–	–	5
A.T. Tikoirotuma	13	13	13	13	13	13	–	13	13	13	9
J.O. Little	–	s	12	s	s	s	s	s	–	s	8
F. Inisi	–	–	s	–	–	–	13	s	s	–	5
H.H. Groundwater	12	12	s	12	12	12	12	12	12	12	10
M.T. McGahan	–	s	10	10	10	10	10	10	10	–	8
J.R. Page	10	10	–	s	–	–	–	–	–	–	3
B.D. Hall	9	9	9	9	9	9	9	9	9	9	10
L.M. Gjaltema	s	–	s	s	s	s	s	s	s	s	9
B.J. McNaughton	–	s	–	–	–	–	–	–	–	–	1
L. Inisi	s	s	8	8	s	s	s	–	s	s	9
M.V.U. Taramai	8	8	s	s	8	8	8	8	8	8	10
T.A. Evans	–	–	–	–	–	–	–	–	7	7	2
D. Hunt (capt)	7	7	7	7	7	7	7	7	–	–	8
E.J. Roots	6	6	6	6	6	6	6	6	6	6	10
J.W.L. Pierce	5	s	4	5	5	5	s	4	5	–	9
G.E. Cowley-Tuioti	4	4	s	4	4	4	4	s	4	4	10
X. Cowley-Tuioti	–	–	–	–	–	–	–	–	–	s	1
B.P. Nee-Nee	s	5	5	s	s	s	5	5	s	5	10
S.T. Mafileo	3	3	3	3	3	3	3	3	3	3	10
R.R. Rinakama	–	–	s	–	–	s	–	–	–	–	2
J.D. Roots	–	–	–	–	–	–	–	–	s	s	2
L. Li	s	s	s	s	s	s	s	s	s	–	9
G.Z.K. Tu'inukuafe	1	1	1	1	1	1	1	1	1	1	10
N.J. Mayhew	s	s	–	–	–	–	–	–	–	–	2
L.H.V. Tolai	2	2	s	2	s	s	2	2	2	2	10
J.W. Parsons (capt)	–	–	–	s	2	2	–	–	–	–	3
D.T. Meki	s	s	2	–	–	–	–	s	s	s	6

NORTH HARBOUR TEAM RECORD, 2019

Played 10 Won 4 Drew 1 Lost 5 Points for 271 Points against 265

Date	Opponent	Location	Score	Tries	Con	PG	DG	Referee
August 9	Auckland (P)	Auckland	28–28	G. Cowley-Tuioti, Tikoirotuma, Tu'inukuafe, Li	Page (4)			P.M. Williams
August 16	Counties Manukau (P)	Albany	25–39	Duffie (2), Telea, L. Inisi	Page	Page		B.D. O'Keeffe
August 25	Southland (cr)	Invercargill	33–12	Little, Tikoirotuma, Hall, Groundwater, Duffie	McGahan (4)			J.D. Munro
September 1	Bay of Plenty (cr)	Albany	19–27	L. Inisi, Little, Stevenson	McGahan (2)			N.E.R. Hogan
September 7	Waikato (P)	Albany	38–36	Telea (2), Taramai, Tolai, Little, McGahan	McGahan (4)			J.J. Doleman
September 15	Tasman (P)	Nelson	17–21	Parsons, penalty try	McGahan	McGahan		R.P. Kelly
September 21	Otago (cr)	Albany	15–21	Duffie, Hall	McGahan	McGahan		J.D. Munro
September 29	Manawatu (cr)	Palmerston North	29–16	Tikoirotuma, Mafileo, Duffie, Telea, F. Inisi	McGahan (2)			H.G. Reed
October 4	Wellington (P)	Albany	42–34	Duffie (2), Tu'inukuafe, Stevenson, Hall, Groundwater	McGahan (3)	McGahan, Stevenson		T.M.T. Cottrell
October 13	Canterbury (RS, P)	Christchurch	25–31	Telea (2), Qamasea, Gjaltema	Hall	Hall		J.J. Doleman

NORTH OTAGO

2019 Status: Heartland Championship
Founded 1904 as sub union affilated to Otago RU.
Became a full union in 1927 with affiliation to NZRU.
President: D.J.L. (David) Douglas
Chairman: W.L. (Warren) Prescott
Chief executive officer: C.S. (Colin) Jackson
Coach: J.A. (Jason) Forrest
Assistant coach: Nick Anderson
Main ground: Whitestone Contracting Stadium (since 2007)
Capacity: 7000
Colours: Gold

RECORDS

Highest attendance	6500	*North Otago v Marlborough (Div 3 final), 1997*
Most appearances	123	*M.J. Mavor, 1995–2009*
Most points	429	*P.M. Ford, 1964–74*
Most tries	39	*V.T. Fifita, 2000–04*
Most points in a season	159	*S.M. Porter, 2002*
Most tries in a season	15	*V.T. Fifita, 2002*
Most conversions in a season	42	*M. Adair, 2005*
Most penalty goals in a season	30	*C.J.W. Finch, 1997*
		S.M. Porter, 2000
Most dropped goals in a season	4	*M.E. Kenworthy, 1986*
Most points in a match	28	*C.J.W. Finch v Poverty Bay, 1998*
		S.M. Porter v Poverty Bay, 2000
Most tries in a match	5	*L.M. Herden v East Coast, 2010*
Most conversions in a match	9	*B. Patston v East Coast, 2010*
Most penalty goals in a match	7	*C.J.W. Finch v South Canterbury, 1998*
Highest team score	116	*v East Coast, 2010*
Record victory (points ahead)	113	*116–3 v East Coast, 2010*
Highest score conceded	139	*v Auckland, 1993*
Record defeat (points behind)	134	*5–139 v Auckland, 1993*

North Otago had a triumphant season in 2019, winning the Heartland Championship for the third time by defeating Wanganui 33–19 in the Meads Cup final, and also winning the prized Hanan Shield off South Canterbury in the opening match and successfully defending it against Mid Canterbury.

After four matches North Otago was top of the Heartland table as the only team with four wins. These were followed by two bonus-point defeats to West Coast and Wanganui which dropped them to fourth, but two more wins saw the side qualify second for the playoffs. In the semi-final North Otago held a 27–13 lead over Wairarapa Bush with 10 minutes left, and withstood a comeback to hold on 27–25. In the final against Wanganui North Otago led 25–7 at halftime and prevented any possibility of a comeback with a dominant display on the day.

The foundation of North Otago's success was laid by a superb set of forwards. The front row of Ralph Darling, captain Sam Sturgess, and Meli Kolinisau was too good for most opponents in the set scrums and also excelled around the field with carries and defensive work. The same could be said for the lock pairing of loan players Charles Elton and William Kirkwood with their lineout skills and mobility in the open. Kelepi Funaki was a more than useful reserve prop. It was a shame Sturgess missed the playoffs because of injury but Hayden Tisdall stepped up well in his absence. Darling's six tries made him equal top try scorer and he surprised everyone with a well taken drop goal in the final. In the Ranfurly Shield challenge he played his 100th match for the union.*

Player of origin Jacob Coghlan, who had last appeared in 2016, was the standout loose forward who always gave of his best in every game. The versatile flanker could play on both the openside and blindside. The only real change the coach had to make in the forward pack during the season was the introduction of Marcus Balchin at flanker to utilise his speed and mobility. Experienced number eight Josh Clark gave fine service to complete a good loose forward trio.

Robbie Smith was a very much in-form halfback throughout the campaign, and with his excellent goalkicking he scored 109 points which made him the top points scorer in the Heartland Championship. At first five-eighth Mike Williams usually took the right option and had a keen eye for the gap. He missed games in mid-season while with the NZ Universities Under 23 team.

Taina Tamou started the season on the wing but coach Jason Forrest returned him to second five-eighth after the Wanganui defeat, where the aggressive runner looked dangerous every time he received the ball. Centre Lemi Masoe returned from South Canterbury and at 38 he was naturally slower than he used to be, but showed enough dash when required as he showed when setting up Adam Johnson's try in the final. During the season he passed his century of games for the union. Having debuted in 2007, Masoe has played in all three of North Otago's winning Meads Cup finals.

Englishman Howard Packman was a fast wing and very good finisher, scoring six tries. Twenty-year-old fullback Patrick Pati made a huge impression in his debut season at first-class level. With his speed and swerve the livewire runner arrived in the province during the club season and was duly selected in the NZ Heartland team for the end of year tour.

From last year's team Anthony Amato was at South Canterbury, Frank Kelly had returned to England, Mikaele Mafi had gone to Otago and Filipo Veamatahau was in Canterbury. Of the newcomers Howard Packman had played for the England Under 20 and Sevens teams and Patrick Pati had played for the Samoa A and Sevens teams.

North Otago's home match versus Wairarapa Bush on August 30 was played at Forsyth Barr Stadium in Dunedin, as the curtain-raiser to the Otago v Manawatu Mitre 10 Cup match.

*The 2019 Almanack incorrectly reported Darling had played his 100th match in the final match of 2018 — when it was actually his 99th.

Higher honours went to:
New Zealand Heartland: J. Clark, R. Darling, M. Kolinisau, P. Pati, R. Smith

NORTH OTAGO REPRESENTATIVES 2019

	Club	Games for Union	Points for Union
Anthony Arty	Athletic Marist	6	7
Marcus Balchin	Maheno	10	5
Josh Clark	Maheno	40	5
Jacob Coghlan [1]	Alhambra Union [2]	14	10
Ralph Darling	Old Boys	109	101
Mathew Duff	Excelsior	56	11
Charles Elton	Harbour [2]	10	10
Andrew Fauoo	Athletic Marist	1	0
Kelepi Funaki	Old Boys	18	0
Clement Gasca	Maheno	5	5
Jake Greenslade	Valley	22	15
Joshua Hayward	Maheno	7	0
Adam Johnson	Maheno	10	5
Lachlan Kingan	Maheno	10	5
William Kirkwood	Green Island [2]	11	0
Melikisua Kolinisau	Valley	43	15

	Club	Games for Union	Points for Union
Lemi Masoe	Old Boys	104	136
Michael Mata'afa	Maheno	5	0
Howard Packman	Valley	10	30
Patrick Pati	Athletic Marist	10	5
Robbie Smith	Maheno	50	155
Sam Sturgess	Valley	32	35
Manulua Taiti	Old Boys	39	5
Taina Tamou	Excelsior	18	15
Samuel Tatupu	Maheno	9	5
Toni Taufa	Old Boys	1	0
Bailey Templeton	Kurow	1	0
Hayden Tisdall	Maheno	14	10
Matthew Vocea	Valley	33	71
Michael Williams	Otago University [2]	7	5
George Witana	Dunedin [2]	2	0

1 Player of Origin   2 Otago RU

INDIVIDUAL SCORING

	Tries	Con	PG	DG	Points
Smith	3	26	17	–	118
Darling	6	–	–	1	33
Packman	6	–	–	–	30
Kolinisau	3	–	–	–	15
Sturgess	3	–	–	–	15
Masoe	2	1	–	–	12
Elton	2	–	–	–	10
Tamou	2	–	–	–	10
Greenslade	2	–	–	–	10
Coghlan	2	–	–	–	10
Tisdall	2	–	–	–	10
Arty	1	1	–	–	7

	Tries	Con	PG	DG	Points
Tatupu	1	–	–	–	5
Williams	1	–	–	–	5
Gasca	1	–	–	–	5
Kingan	1	–	–	–	5
Pati	1	–	–	–	5
Balchin	1	–	–	–	5
Johnson	1	–	–	–	5
Totals	**41**	**28**	**17**	**1**	**315**
Opposition scored	35*	23	12	0	259

* Includes one penalty try (7 points)

NORTH OTAGO 2019	Otago	South Canterbury	Wairarapa Bush	Poverty Bay	Thames Valley	West Coast	Wanganui	Mid Canterbury	Ngati Porou East Coast	Wairarapa Bush (sf)	Wanganui (f)	Totals
P. Pati	15	–	15	15	15	15	15	15	15	15	15	10
H.F. Packman	14	14	14	14	–	14	14	11	11	11	11	10
A. Fauoo	11	–	–	–	–	–	–	–	–	–	–	1
T. Tamou	–	11	–	s	14	11	11	12	12	12	12	9
A.G. Johnson	–	s	11	11	11	–	–	14	14	14	14	8
M. Vocea	–	–	–	–	–	–	s	–	–	–	s	2
C. Gasca	13	15	s	13	s	–	–	–	–	–	–	5
L. Masoe	12	13	13	–	13	13	13	13	13	13	13	10
S.T. Tatupu	s	12	12	12	12	12	12	s	s	–	–	9
L.T. Kingan	10	10	s	s	10	10	s	s	s	–	s	10
M.D. Williams	–	s	10	10	–	–	–	10	10	10	10	7
G.F.T.R. Witana	–	–	–	–	–	s	10	–	–	–	–	2
R.L. Smith	9	9	9	9	9	9	9	9	9	9	9	11
A.P.A. Arty	s	–	s	–	s	–	s	s	s	–	–	6
J.A. Clark	8	8	–	s	8	8	6	8	–	8	8	9
M.S. Balchin	7	–	–	–	7	7	s	7	7	7	7	8
J.S. Greenslade	6	6	8	6	–	–	s	s	8	s	–	8
M.R.V. Duff	s	–	6	–	–	s	s	–	–	s	s	6
J.H. Coghlan	s	7	7	7	6	6	7	6	6	6	6	11
T. Taufa	s	–	–	–	–	–	–	–	–	–	–	1
W.O. Kirkwood	5	5	5	5	5	5	5	5	5	5	5	11
J.L.R. Hayward	4	s	s	4	s	–	4	–	s	–	–	7
C.H. Elton	–	4	4	8	4	4	8	4	4	4	4	10
M.M. Taiti	–	–	s	s	s	s	–	s	s	s	s	8
M. Kolinisau	3	3	–	3	–	3	s	3	3	3	3	9
R.K. Darling	1	1	–	s	1	1	1	1	1	1	1	10
M.A.I. Mata'afa	s	–	1	–	s	–	–	s	–	–	s	5
K.K. Funaki	s	s	3	1	3	s	3	s	s	s	s	11
B.C. Templeton	–	–	s	–	–	–	–	–	–	–	–	1
S.W. Sturgess (capt)	2	2	2	2	2	2	2	2	2	–	–	9
H.M. Tisdall	s	–	s	s	s	s	–	–	s	2	2	8

R.K. Darling captained the final two matches.

NORTH OTAGO TEAM RECORD, 2019

Date	Opponent	Location	Played 11 Score	Won 8 Tries	Drew 0	Lost 3 Con	Points for 315 PG	DG	Points against 259 Referee
July 26	Otago (RS)	Oamaru	14–49	Packman, Smith		Smith (2)			R. Mahoney
August 24	South Canterbury (H) (HS)	Timaru	26–20	Kolinisau, Packman		Smith (2)	Smith (4)		J. Bredin
August 30	Wairarapa Bush (H)	Dunedin	25–11	Packman, Tatupu, Masoe		Smith (2)	Smith (2)		S. Curran
September 7	Poverty Bay (H)	Gisborne	34–30	Williams, Elton, Gasca, Darling		Smith (4)	Smith (2)		H. Reed
September 14	Thames Valley (H)	Oamaru	22–21	Sturgess		Smith	Smith (5)		S. Curran
September 21	West Coast (H)	Greymouth	17–18	Kingan, Pati, Tamou		Smith			J. Bredin
September 28	Wanganui (H)	Oamaru	22–27	Tamou, Darling, Arty		Smith, Masoe	Smith		T. Cottrell
October 5	Mid Canterbury (H) (HS)	Oamaru	34–10	Darling (2), Masoe, Balchin, Greenslade, Kolinisau		Smith (2)			C. Paul
October 12	Ngati Porou East Coast (H)	Ruatoria	61–29	Sturgess (2), Darling (2), Coghlan (2), Greenslade, Smith, Tisdall		Smith (7), Arty			T. Cottrell
October 19	Wairarapa Bush (MC sf)	Oamaru	27–25	Packman (2), Tisdall, Kolinisau		Smith (2)	Smith		T. Cottrell
October 26	Wanganui (MC f)	Oamaru	33–19	Elton, Johnson, Packman, Smith		Smith (2)	Smith (2)	Darling	A. Mabey

HS Hanan Shield

NORTHLAND

2019 Status: Mitre 10 Cup Championship
Founded 1920 as North Auckland. Affiliated 1920.
Name changed to Northland 1994
President: S.L. (Sharon) Morgan
Chairman: A.C. (Ajit) Balasingham
Chief executive officer: A.K. (Alister) McGinn
Coach: D.J.C. (Derren) Witcombe
Assistant coaches: G.N. (George) Konia,
C.D. (Cam) Goodhue,
B.R. (Brad) Te Haara
Main ground: Semenoff Stadium, Whangarei
Capacity: 24,000
Colours: Cambridge blue

RECORDS

Most appearances	165	*Joe Morgan, 1967–81*
Most points	1656	*Warren Johnston, 1986–97*
Most tries	71	*Norman Berryman, 1991–2003*
Most points in a season	283	*David Holwell, 1997*
Most tries in a season	21	*Norman Berryman, 1994*
Most conversions in a season	85	*David Holwell, 1997*
Most penalty goals in a season	34	*Warren Johnston, 1989*
Most dropped goals in a season	10	*Eddie Dunn, 1979*
Most points in a match	38	*David Holwell v Thames Valley, 1997*
Most tries in a match	7	*Norman Berryman v Wairarapa Bush, 1994*
Most conversions in a match	14	*David Holwell v Thames Valley, 1997*
Most penalty goals in a match	6	*Chippie Semenoff v Thames Valley, 1978*
		Warren Johnston v Wairarapa Bush, 1993
		Warren Johnston v France, 1994
		Warren Johnston v Wairarapa Bush, 1995
		Ash Moeke v North Harbour, 2012
		Dan Hawkins v North Harbour, 2014
		Peter Breen v Otago, 2017
Highest team score	113	*v Thames Valley, 1997*
Record victory (points ahead)	99	*113–14 v Thames Valley, 1997*
Highest score conceded	84	*v Otago, 1998*
Record defeat (points behind)	74	*10–84 v Otago, 1998*

Northland lacked several key things that stymied their 2019 campaign — X-factor, depth and consistency — but there were glimpses of Taniwha magic even with a depleted squad.

The 2–8 record does not compare well to 2018, when they reached the Championship semi-final, and they only ensured sixth position, and thus avoiding the wooden spoon, with a sparkling 40–10 demolition of Otago on the final day of the regular season.

Some pundits predicted Northland would take the Championship crown but that was always going to be a pipe dream when injuries ruled out the likes of Tom Robinson and Rene Ranger, among others. It meant coach Derren Witcombe had to delve deep into the ranks of Northland club rugby. While this was the right thing to do, a lack of experience showed at crucial moments throughout the season.

Yet it all started so promisingly, grinding out a creditable 27–17 win in Invercargill on opening night. We saw outside backs Jordan Hyland and Scott Gregory used in a lineout drive which yielded a try. Alas, we saw little more of this innovation.

Northland struggled in its four crossover games, falling heavily to Auckland, Canterbury, Wellington and Tasman, but was competitive in patches in all those reverses.

At times the side would play with commitment, vigour and flair, but then a loose pass, a dropped ball or a turnover would hinder their progress. The Taniwha, in general, fell off too many tackles and scored just two tryscoring bonus points.

But it all came together under an October spring sun in Whangarei when they played like it was the unshackled 1970s under Ted Griffin and the Okara Park bank was packed. It was a hearty note for Witcombe to depart after his second stint as head coach, but with lingering questions of 'What if?'

Notable losses from 2018 included halfback Jono Kitto and captain/hooker Matt Moulds, both to Japan. A growing injury toll did not help matters. Incoming were Counties Manukau prop Coree Te Whata-Colley, who played in every game, Waikato lock Sam Caird, Southland second five Matt Johnson, and nomadic halfback Harrison Levien. All played well enough to varying degrees.

Scott Gregory was used at fullback and centre. He was prone to mistakes at times, but brought some much-needed X-factor on attack and was strong as an ox in and on the tackle. He scored three tries, as did Jordan Hyland, who played his way into a fulltime Super Rugby deal with the Blues. The Taniwha missed him in the four games in which he was not available.

Renata Roberts-Tenana, especially in the Otago match, and Pisi Leilua, both enjoyed good moments without being able to consistently crack the starting XV. Tamati Tua was injured for all but three games. Matt Johnson and Blake Hohaia were a useful midfield duo, but opponents were able to make headway through their channels.

No 10 Jack Debreczeni had another influential season, this time without posting 100 points. Sam Nock wore the captain's armband several times and tried hard. He is slowly making the sort of impact we know he can at this level.

Loose forward Aorangi Stokes offered real power off the bench or at the boot of the scrum, scoring three tries, and was always a handful with the ball. No one can ever question Matt Matich's commitment to the cause. Injury again hit Kane Jacobson, while Josh Goodhue also fell to the curse. Temo Mayanavanua stepped up when he had to, winning ball and driving with vigour.

Isis Tuungafasi and Ross Wright, who now has 97 caps, were the main looseheads, while hooker and original captain Jordan Olsen played his heart out, despite missing half the games.

That said, the Northland set-piece was not always reliable, and this proved costly.

Higher honours went to:

New Zealand:	Jack Goodhue
New Zealand Maori:	J. Hyland, R. Wright
New Zealand Under 20:	S. Gregory
New Zealand Sevens:	S. Gregory

NORTHLAND REPRESENTATIVES 2019

	Club	Games for Union	Points for Union
Paddy-Jo Atkins	Wellsford	16	5
Jarod Byrnes	Old Boys-Marist	6	0
Sam Caird	Old Boys-Marist	9	0
James Cherrington	Mid Northern	3	0
Jack Debreczeni	Eastern	21	186
Setefano Funaki	Waipu	6	0
Josh Goodhue	United Kawakawa	35	20
Will Grant	Hora Hora	3	0
Scott Gregory	Hikurangi	20	25
Dan Hawkins	Old Boys-Marist	49	329
Blake Hohaia	Kamo	25	15
Nick Hyde	Western Sharks	5	0
Jordan Hyland	Wellsford	46	65
Kane Jacobson	Kamo	6	0
Matt Johnson	Old Boys-Marist	7	0
Pisi Leilua	Waipu	9	5
Harrison Levien	Old Boys-Marist	6	5
Matt Matich	Western Sharks	35	35

	Club	Games for Union	Points for Union
Jaycob Matiu	Hora Hora	33	10
Temo Mayanavanua	Waipu	13	10
Sam McNamara	Waipu	16	0
Sam Nock	Kerikeri	46	42
Jordan Olsen	Mid Northern	43	10
Jonty Rae	Old Boys-Marist	4	5
Renata Roberts-Tenana	Old Boys-Marist	11	15
Tommy Smith	Kerikeri	6	2
Aorangi Stokes	Old Boys-Marist	17	30
Jack Straker	Kamo	19	5
Sean Sweetman	Wellsford	11	5
Corey Taylor	Kerikeri	1	0
Coree Te Whata-Colley	Western Sharks	10	10
Tamati Tua	Hikurangi	26	15
Isi Tuungafasi	Mid Northern	21	0
Simoni Uluinakauvadra	Waipu	1	0
Boyd Wiggins	Old Boys-Marist	2	0
Ross Wright	Wellsford	97	35

INDIVIDUAL SCORING

	Tries	Con	PG	DG	Points
Debreczeni	2	23	10	–	86
Hyland	3	–	–	–	15
Gregory	3	–	–	–	15
Stokes	3	–	–	–	15
Mayanavanua	2	–	–	–	10
Nock	2	–	–	–	10
Roberts-Tenana	2	–	–	–	10
Te Whata-Colley	2	–	–	–	10
Wright	2	–	–	–	10
Atkins	1	–	–	–	5
Leilua	1	–	–	–	5

	Tries	Con	PG	DG	Points
Levien	1	–	–	–	5
Matich	1	–	–	–	5
Matiu	1	–	–	–	5
Rae	1	–	–	–	5
Straker	1	–	–	–	5
Sweetman	1	–	–	–	5
Smith	–	1	–	–	2
Totals	**29**	**24**	**10**	**0**	**223**
Opposition scored	59	40	6	0	393

NORTHLAND 2019

	Southland	Auckland	Taranaki	Hawke's Bay	Manawatu	Canterbury	Bay of Plenty	Wellington	Tasman	Otago	Totals
S.J. Gregory	15	13	15	15	15	15	15	15	15	13	10
J.S.C. Hyland	14	14	14	–	14	–	–	–	14	14	6
R.C. Roberts-Tenana	–	s	s	14	–	14	14	–	s	11	7
P. Leilua	11	11	11	11	11	s	s	11	–	15	9
J.C. Rae	–	–	–	–	–	11	11	14	11	–	4
J.N. Cherrington	–	–	–	–	–	–	–	s	13	s	3
T.R. Tua	–	–	–	s	12	13	–	–	–	–	3
M.J. Johnson	13	12	13	13	13	–	13	13	–	–	7
B.M. Hohaia	12	s	12	12	s	12	12	12	12	12	10
T.E. Smith	–	–	–	s	–	s	s	s	s	s	6
J.M. Debreczeni	10	15	10	10	10	10	10	10	10	10	10
D.C. Hawkins	–	10	s	–	–	–	–	–	–	–	2
S.J. Nock (capt)	9	9	9	9	9	9	9	9	–	9	9
W.A. Grant	–	s	–	–	–	–	–	–	9	s	3
C.L. Taylor	–	–	–	–	–	–	–	–	s	–	1
H.C. Levien	–	–	s	s	s	s	s	s	–	–	6
J.T. Matiu	–	8	8	8	8	8	8	8	–	–	7
A.T.H. Stokes	8	–	s	7	7	s	s	s	8	8	9
M.E.S. Matich	7	7	7	–	–	7	7	–	s	s	7
K.P. Jacobson	s	–	–	–	–	–	–	–	–	–	1
S.J. McNamara	6	6	6	6	6	6	6	6	6	6	10
J.J. Byrnes	–	s	–	s	s	–	–	7	7	7	6
S. Funaki	–	–	–	s	–	s	s	s	s	4	6
S. Uluinakauvadra	–	–	–	–	–	–	–	–	–	s	1
S.W. Caird	s	s	4	5	4	5	5	5	5	–	9
T.S. Mayanavanua	4	4	–	4	s	–	–	4	4	5	7
S.M.Y. Sweetman	–	–	s	–	–	4	4	–	–	–	3
J.K. Goodhue	5	5	5	s	5	–	–	–	–	–	4
J.J. Straker	s	s	3	3	s	–	3	3	3	3	9
C.J.W. Te Whata-Colley	3	3	s	s	3	3	s	s	s	s	10
B.L. Wiggins	–	–	–	–	–	s	–	–	–	–	1
I.J. Tuungafasi	1	1	s	s	s	1	1	s	s	1	10
R.G. Wright	s	s	1	1	1	s	s	1	1	s	10
P-J. Atkins	s	s	s	2	2	2	2	2	2	s	10
J.D. Olsen (capt)	2	2	2	–	–	–	–	–	s	2	5
N.M.W. Hyde	–	–	–	s	s	s	s	s	–	–	5

NORTHLAND TEAM RECORD, 2019

Played 10   Won 2   Lost 8   Points for 225   Points against 393

Date	Opponent	Location	Score	Tries	Con	PG	DG	Referee
August 8	Southland (C)	Invercargill	27-17	Te Whata-Colley, Hyland, Mayanavanua	Debreczeni (3)	Debreczeni (2)		N.J. Webster
August 15	Auckland (cr)	Whangarei	10-43	Leilua	Debreczeni	Debreczeni		M.I. Fraser
August 25	Taranaki (C)	New Plymouth	19-52	Wright, Roberts-Tenana, Te Whata-Colley	Debreczeni (2)	Debreczeni (2)		P.M. Williams
August 31	Hawke's Bay (C)	Whangarei	28-43	Mayanavanua, Straker, Matiu	Debreczeni (2)	Debreczeni (3)		M.C.J. Winter
September 5	Manawatu (C)	Palmerston North	25-31	Nock, Wright, Gregory	Debreczeni (2)	Debreczeni (2)		G.W. Jackson
September 13	Canterbury (cr)	Whangarei	12-42	Sweetman, Debreczeni	Debreczeni			T.M.T. Cottrell
September 22	Bay of Plenty (C)	Whangarei	22-46	Roberts-Tenana, Nock, Levien	Debreczeni, Smith	Debreczeni		C.J. Stone
September 28	Wellington (cr)	Wellington	36-57	Stokes (2), Atkins, Rae, Debreczeni	Debreczeni (4)	Debreczeni		G.W. Jackson
October 6	Tasman (cr)	Nelson	6-52		Debreczeni (2)			H.G. Reed
October 13	Otago (C)	Whangarei	40-10	Hyland (2), Gregory (2), Stokes, Matich	Debreczeni (5)			J.D. Munro

OTAGO

2019 Status: Mitre 10 Cup Championship
Founded 1881. Affiliated 1895
President: D.G. (Des) Smith
Chairman: R.K. (Rowena) Davenport
General manager: R.P. (Richard) Kinley
Coach: B. (Ben) Herring
Assistant coaches: T.J.S. (Tom) Donnelly,
    R.H. (Ryan) Martin
Main ground: Forsyth Barr Stadium, Dunedin
Capacity: 28,000
Colours: Dark blue

RECORDS

Most appearances	170	*Richard Knight, 1981–92*
Most points	1520	*Greg Cooper, 1984–96*
Most tries	73	*Paul Cooke, 1990–96*
Most points in a season	279	*Greg Cooper, 1991*
Most tries in a season	16	*John Timu, 1988*
		John Timu, 1990
		Paul Cooke, 1995
		Brendan Laney, 1998
Most conversions in a season	50	*Greg Cooper, 1989*
Most penalty goals in a season	54	*Greg Cooper, 1989*
Most dropped goals in a season	9	*Lee Smith, 1986*
Most points in a match	39	*Paul Turner v East Coast, 1986*
Most tries in a match	5	*George Owles v South Canterbury, 1920*
		Bill Meates v South Canterbury, 1948
		Bruce Hunter v Marlborough, 1969
		Graham Sims v West Coast, 1972
Most conversions in a match	14	*Paul Turner v East Coast, 1986*
Most penalty goals in a match	7	*Greg Cooper v NZ Combined Services, 1989*
		Greg Cooper v Canterbury, 1991
		Blair Feeney v Wellington, 2002
Highest team score	91	*v East Coast, 1986*
Record victory (points ahead)	85	*88–3 v North Otago, 1983*
Highest score conceded	68	*v Wellington, 2007*
Record defeat (points behind)	61	*7–68 v Wellington, 2007*

It was fun while it lasted.

Otago's rousing Ranfurly Shield run and drive for the Championship made for compelling viewing. Making it even more creditable was the fact that Otago used no less than 51 players, 17 of whom appeared in just one match, and battled a crippling injury toll which decimated its meagre resources even before the first kickoff. So to hold the Log o' Wood until the final defence of the season — the seventh of the tenure — and to push Hawke's Bay in a Championship semi-final thriller in Napier was a tremendous effort under the circumstances.

In all, there were seven props and six hookers used by head coach Ben Herring, who was into the second year of his deal before a family sabbatical in America.

The season kicked off with two comfortable, if scratchy, Shield defences in Wanaka and

Oamaru, which exposed several promising club players to the jersey, as well as former Auckland pivot Ash Moeke, who slotted seven goals against North Otago. Centre Matt Faddes raised his 50 games against Thames Valley before departing for Ireland.

There were concerning early signs in the Championship, when Bay of Plenty put 50 on the Razorbacks and exposed scrummaging issues. Swapping sides for props Hisa Sasagi and Aki Seiuli seemed to work for the rest of the season.

Otago looked a different side at home, galvanised by the Shield. The notable exception was a 21–15 win at North Harbour, despite missing 36 tackles.

Southland, Manawatu, Taranaki and Waikato were all repulsed with gritty and, at times, opportunistic rugby. But the Razorbacks were exposed in Wellington and against Northland. Canterbury stole the Shield in the final defence of 2019, but Otago did not give it up without a fight.

Pre-season losses far outweighed the gains. Sam Anderson-Heather (hiatus), Donald Brighouse (Taranaki), Naulia Dawai (USA), Josh Larsen (USA Rugby World Cup), Melani Matavao (Samoa, RWC), Josh Renton (Italy) and Tom Rowe (Japan) were among the defections.

New signings were few, just halfback Kayne Hammington (Manawatu) and young prop Saula Ma'u (Auckland).

A groin injury saw captain Michael Collins make a slow start to the season, but he thereafter recaptured most of his best form from fullback. The star turns in the backline, however, were wing Jona Nareki, who scored nine tries and provided much-needed X-factor, and the versatile Vilimoni Koroi, who appeared in four positions, kicked goals when required, and was always dangerous on attack. His hat-trick against Manawatu and his virtuoso 20-point haul against Taranaki were among the season's highlights. English import Henry Purdy showed his speed and finishing ability.

Centre Aleki Morris-Lome enjoyed a fine rookie season, scoring seven tries, and was the sole Razorback to play in all 13 games. Inside one position, Sio Tomkinson continued his solid Highlanders form.

Josh Ioane's season was slightly disrupted by his All Blacks' call-ups, but he showed his maturity, sharpshooting and versatility, moving out to second five for the Northland clash.

Hammington offered good value until injured, Rowan Gouws was sparky off the bench, and NZ Universities halfback Connor McLeod looked promising later in the season.

As he did in 2018, No 8 Dylan Nel carried strongly in every outing. So well did Slade McDowall perform in the No 7 jersey, especially over the ball, that he often pushed captain designate James Lentjes to the blindside.

Adam Thomson, technically loaned from North Harbour, wound back the clock at 37 with some classy displays and must have gone close to winning a full Super Rugby contract.

Joe Latta, who played his blazer game, and Josh Dickson, who raised the half century and again pulled down more lineout ball than anyone in the Mitre 10 Cup, were industrious locks.

Ma'u made a promising introduction to first-class rugby behind the likes of George Bower, Sasagi and Seiuli.

Liam Coltman played just once at hooker, allowing Seko Pole to make 12 outings and push on to 49 games for the province.

Higher honours went to:

New Zealand:	L. Coltman, J. Ioane, B. Smith
New Zealand Sevens:	V. Koroi, J. Nareki
New Zealand Universities:	T. Haugh, J. Hill, K. Lea, C. McLeod, M. Taimalie

OTAGO REPRESENTATIVES 2019

	Club	Games for Union	Points for Union
Jonah Aoina	Kaikorai	21	15
James Arscott	Green Island	1	0
George Bower	Harbour	20	0
Harrison Boyle	Dunedin	1	0
Michael Collins	Wakatipu	60	80
Liam Coltman	Alhambra-Union	68	15
Louis Conradie	Taieri	9	0
Josh Dickson	University	53	25
Matt Faddes	University	50	90
Alex Frood	Alhambra-Union	1	0
Rowan Gouws	Kaikorai	10	10
Lisala Halaleva	Harbour	2	0
Kurt Hammer	Taieri	13	5
Kayne Hammington	Zingari-Richmond	8	0
Taylor Haugh	University	12	0
Josh Hill	University	7	0
Jeff Ikani	Harbour	1	0
Josh Ioane	Southern	29	230
Ricky Jackson	University	5	0
Joketani Koroi	Harbour	15	10
Vilimoni Koroi	Alhambra-Union	33	98
Joe Latta	Owaka	16	5
Kilipati Lea	University	1	0
James Lentjes	Taieri	45	55
Mika Mafi	Southern	15	15
Saula Ma'u	Harbour	4	5

	Club	Games for Union	Points for Union
Slade McDowall	Kaikorai	27	25
Connor McLeod	University	6	0
Ben Millar	Roxburgh	1	0
Ben Miller	Kaikorai	1	16
Steven Misa	Takapuna [1]	4	0
Sione Misiloi	Harbour	23	0
Ash Moeke	–	1	14
Ben Morris	Taieri	1	0
Aleki Morris-Lome	Harbour	13	35
Jona Nareki	Alhambra-Union	30	120
Dylan Nel	Green Island	21	20
Will Ngatai	Te Puna [2]	1	0
Sekonaia Pole	Harbour	49	10
Henry Purdy	–	10	15
Hisa Sasagi	Southern	56	0
Mitchell Scott	Taieri	28	50
Aki Seiuli	Taieri	73	25
Nic Souchon	Lincoln University [3]	6	0
Haru Tatekawa	–	4	0
Josh Timu	University	8	5
Hayden Todd	Cromwell	1	0
Sio Tomkinson	Harbour	47	69
Adam Thomson	Takapuna [4]	62	80
Matt Whaanga	Taieri	14	5
Angus Williams	University	2	0

1. Loaned from North Harbour
2. Loaned from Bay of Plenty
3. Loaned from Canterbury
4. Loaned from North Harbour

INDIVIDUAL SCORING

	Tries	Con	PG	DG	Points
Ioane	1	20	9	–	72
V. Koroi	7	8	4	–	63
Nareki	9	–	–	–	45
Morris-Lome	7	–	–	–	35
Collins	4	–	–	–	20
McDowall	4	–	–	–	20
Tomkinson	4	–	–	–	20
Miller	1	4	1	–	16
Lentjes	3	–	–	–	15
Purdy	3	–	–	–	15
Moeke	–	7	–	–	14
Dickson	2	–	–	–	10

	Tries	Con	PG	DG	Points
Gouws	2	–	–	–	10
Mafi	2	–	–	–	10
Nel	2	–	–	–	10
Ma'u	1	–	–	–	5
Pole	1	–	–	–	5
Thomson	1	–	–	–	5
Timu	1	–	–	–	5
Totals	**55**	**39**	**14**	**0**	**395**
Opposition scored	55*	45	13	0	406

* includes one penalty try (7 points)

OTAGO 2019

	Thames Valley	North Otago	Bay of Plenty	Southland	Hawke's Bay	Manawatu	Taranaki	Wellington	North Harbour	Waikato	Canterbury	Northland	Hawke's Bay (C, SF)	Totals
T.C. Haugh	15	–	15	15	–	s	–	–	–	s	s	15	s	8
M.W.V. Collins (capt)	–	–	–	s	s	15	15	s	15	15	15	–	15	9
V.T. Koroi	–	11	10	10	15	14	10	15	14	14	14	10	10	12
J.M. Nareki	s	15	–	11	11	11	11	s	–	11	11	s	11	11
H.J. Boyle	–	s	–	–	–	–	–	–	–	–	–	–	–	1
M.J. Scott	14	–	–	–	–	–	–	–	–	–	–	–	–	1
W.M. Ngatai	–	–	s	–	–	–	–	–	–	–	–	–	–	1
L. O. Halaleva	–	14	14	–	–	–	–	–	–	–	–	–	–	2
H.A. Purdy	–	–	11	14	14	–	14	11	11	s	s	11	14	10
J.C. Timu	11	–	–	–	–	–	–	14	s	–	–	14	–	4
M.A. Faddes	13	–	–	–	–	–	–	–	–	–	–	–	–	1
H. Tatekawa	–	–	–	–	s	s	s	12	–	–	–	–	–	4
A. Morris-Lome	s	13	13	13	13	13	12	13	13	13	13	13	13	13
H. Todd	–	s	–	–	–	–	–	–	–	–	–	–	–	1
M.A. Whaanga	12	–	–	s	–	–	–	–	–	–	–	s	s	4
P.F. Tomkinson	–	12	12	12	12	12	13	–	12	12	12	–	–	9
B. Miller	10	–	–	–	–	–	–	–	–	–	–	–	–	1
J.R. Ioane	–	–	–	–	10	10	–	10	10	10	10	12	12	8
A.K. Moeke	–	10	–	–	–	–	–	–	–	–	–	–	–	1
K.M. Hammer	9	–	–	–	–	–	–	–	–	–	–	–	–	1
K.W. Hammington	s	9	9	9	9	9	9	9	–	–	–	–	–	8
J.M. Arscott	–	–	–	–	–	–	–	–	–	–	–	s	–	1
R.P.C. Gouws	–	s	s	s	s	s	s	–	9	9	–	9	9	10
C.P.A. McLeod	–	–	–	–	–	–	s	s	s	9	s	s	–	6
D.M. Nel	8	8	8	8	s	8	–	8	8	8	7	8	–	11
M.T.T. Mafi	–	–	–	–	–	–	s	s	s	–	s	s	–	5
S.R. McDowall	7	7	7	7	–	7	7	–	7	7	7	–	7	10
J.A.R. Lentjes (capt)	s	s	6	6	7	s	s	7	6	–	–	–	–	9
A.J. Thomson	–	–	–	s	6	6	6	–	6	6	6	6	–	8
S.F. Misiloi	6	6	s	s	8	5	8	8	–	–	s	8	4	11
J. Ikani	–	–	–	–	–	–	–	–	–	–	–	s	–	1
J.R. Koroi	–	s	s	–	–	–	–	–	–	–	–	–	–	2
B.J. Morris	5	–	–	–	–	–	–	–	–	–	–	–	–	1
L.J. Conradie	–	–	s	–	s	4	4	4	s	s	4	4	–	9
J.J. Latta	4	4	4	4	4	–	–	s	4	4	–	–	–	8
J.M. Dickson	–	5	5	5	5	–	5	6	5	5	5	–	5	10
J. Hill	s	–	–	–	s	s	5	–	–	s	5	s	–	7
A.L. Williams	3	–	–	–	–	–	–	–	–	–	–	–	–	1
S. Ma'u	s	s	–	–	–	–	–	–	–	–	–	s	s	4
Y. Sasagi	–	3	1	3	s	3	3	s	3	3	3	–	3	11
B.J. Millar	s	–	–	–	–	–	–	–	–	–	–	–	–	1
J.T. Aoina	–	–	s	s	s	1	1	1	s	s	s	1	–	10
A. Seiuli	–	s	3	1	1	s	s	s	1	1	1	s	1	12
K.S.K. Lea	1	–	–	–	–	–	–	–	–	–	–	–	–	1
G.G. Bower	–	1	s	s	3	s	s	3	s	s	s	3	s	12
N.P. Souchon	–	–	2	s	–	s	–	s	2	2	–	–	–	6
S.J. Pole	2	2	s	2	s	2	2	2	–	s	s	s	s	12
R.D. Jackson	s	–	–	–	–	–	–	–	–	–	–	–	–	1
A.H. Frood	–	s	–	–	–	–	–	–	–	–	–	–	–	1
L.J. Coltman	–	–	–	–	2	–	–	–	–	–	–	–	–	1
S.J. Misa	–	–	–	–	–	–	–	–	s	–	2	2	2	4

OTAGO TEAM RECORD, 2019

Date	Opponent	Location	Score	Tries (Played 13 / Won 7)	Con (Lost 6)	PG (Points for 395)	DG	Referee (Points against 406)
July 13	Thames Valley (RS)	Wanaka	41–21	Pole, Lentjes, Miller, Morris-Lome, Nel, McDowall	Miller (4)	Miller		N. Watson
July 26	North Otago (RS)	Oamaru	49–14	V. Koroi, Dickson, Morris-Lome, Nareki, Gouws, Ma'u, Lentjes	Moeke (7)			R.M. Mahoney
August 11	Bay of Plenty (C)	Tauranga	7–50	Tomkinson	V. Koroi	V. Koroi		F. Murphy (Ireland)
August 17	Southland (RS, C)	Dunedin	41–22	Nareki (2), McDowall, Nel, Dickson, Gouws	V. Koroi (4)	V. Koroi		P.M. Williams
August 22	Hawke's Bay (C)	Napier	21–29	Nareki, Ioane, Collins	Ioane (3)			M.I. Fraser
August 30	Manawatu (RS,C)	Dunedin	37–20	V.Koroi (3), Nareki, Tomkinson	Ioane (3)	Ioane (2)		G.W. Jackson
September 8	Taranaki (RS, C)	Dunedin	35–27	Nareki (2), Morris-Lome, V. Koroi	V. Koroi (3)	V. Koroi (3)		N.P. Briant
September 15	Wellington (cr)	Wellington	24–54	Purdy, Collins, Morris-Lome, Mafi	Ioane (2)			D.J. Waenga
September 21	North Harbour (cr)	Albany	21–15	Lentjes, Tomkinson, Morris-Lome	Ioane (3)			J.D. Munro
September 29	Waikato (RS, cr)	Dunedin	45–35	V. Koroi (2), McDowall, Morris-Lome, Purdy, Nareki	Ioane (3)	Ioane (3)		R.P. Kelly
October 5	Canterbury (RS, cr)	Dunedin	25–35	Tomkinson, Thomson, Nareki	Ioane (2)	Ioane (2)		G.W. Jackson
October 13	Northland (C)	Whangarei	10–40	Purdy, Timu				J.D. Munro
October 19	Hawke's Bay (C, sf)	Napier	39–44	Collins (2), McDowall, Morris-Lome, Mafi	Ioane (4)	Ioane (2)		A.W.B. Mabey

POVERTY BAY

2019 Status: Heartland Championship
Founded 1890. Affiliated 1893
President: R.W. (Richard) Glover
Chairman: H.M. (Hayden) Swann
Chief executive officer: J.I. (Josh) Willoughby
Coach: T.J. (Tom) Cairns
Assistant coach: M.N. (Miah) Nikora
Main ground: Rugby Park, Gisborne
Capacity: 18,000
Colour: Scarlet

RECORDS

Highest attendance	15,000	*Poverty Bay-East Coast v British Isles, 1971*
Most appearances	150	*S.T. Ngatu, 2003–2018*
Most points	791	*S.C. Leighton, 2004–12*
Most tries	35	*P.S.R. Ransley, 1961–74*
Most points in a season	144	*S.C. Leighton, 2007*
Most tries in a season	11	*J. Moeke, 1997;*
		J. Stewart, 2010
		J. Stewart, 2011
Most conversions in a season	30	*S.C. Leighton, 2007*
Most penalty goals in a season	27	*D.M. Boyle, 1999*
Most dropped goals in a season	3	*G.B. Ross, 1976; J. Whittle, 1979*
Most points in a match	35	*S.C. Leighton v Thames Valley, 2007*
Most tries in a match	4	*J.L. Penny v Olympians Club, 1953*
		K.A. Twigley v East Coast, 1966
		I.A. Kirkpatrick v East Coast, 1971
		K.D. Ferris v East Coast, 1983
		A.B. Hansen v North Otago, 1987
Most conversions in a match	9	*R.P. Owen v East Coast, 1983*
Most penalty goals in a match	7	*S.P. Parkes v Buller, 2013*
Highest team score	75	*v East Coast, 1980*
Record victory (points ahead)	75	*75–0 v East Coast, 1980*
Highest score conceded	121	*v Waikato, 1998*
Record defeat (points behind)	121	*0–121 v Waikato, 1998*

Poverty Bay sneaked into the Lochore Cup semi-finals with an eighth place finish despite losing their final round robin match to Buller. Poverty Bay always looked to play an expansive game and, from broken play in particular, were dangerous. They, and Wanganui, scored the most four-try bonus points in the round robin with six each. However, in their nine games they conceded 34 points or more in seven of them.

The season started off strongly with a win over defending champions Thames Valley. The match with eventual Heartland Champions North Otago was lost by conceding a try with four minutes left, and there were stirring fightbacks against Wairarapa Bush and Horowhenua Kapiti which both just fell short, coming back from 0–26 and 0–33 deficits respectively. In the semi-final Poverty Bay were down 14–41 before scoring three tries in the final five minutes to finish at 35–41, all examples of the side's inconsistency within games.

Andrew Tauatevalu was always a threat with his pace and counter-attack, scoring six tries and kicking valuable goals, but his general play was inconsistent at times. Matt Raleigh on the wing had a good second season and was a strong defender. Tane McGuire was a useful utility back and Ethine Reeves was an elusive centre who distributed well to players in support. Poverty Bay are fortunate to have two well performing halfbacks in Willie Grogan and Mario Counsell.

Beaudein Waaka was an unexpected arrival from Sydney having played for Manly in the Shute Shield competition. The former Taranaki and NZ Sevens rep produced a classy performance in each of the four matches he played, scoring six tries. He had debuted for the province in 2012 while still at school.

Poverty Bay fielded a couple of outstanding flankers in Adrian Wyrill and Quade Tapsell. Wyrill was a strong carrier of the ball and quick to the breakdown. Tapsell, not picked by Waikato due to missing much of the club season, obtained a lot of possession at the back of the lineout, and showed pace around the field. Their work rate around the field was immense. Having appeared in the front row in the last couple of seasons, Tamanui Hill returned to number eight. Although not tall, he added to the loose forward effort with determined ball carrying.

A most promising player emerged in 21-year-old Gabe Te Kani who looked an athletic and strong lock. Captain Ken Houkamau was a solid grafter and retired after the last match. Hooker Rikki Terekia did his core jobs competently and got around the field well to score five tries. Prop Semisi Akana had his best season in the scarlet jersey.

Former Hawke's Bay and Manawatu loose forward Mark Atkins suffered concussion in the final pre-season match. He had already been named in the NZ Heartland team to play Samoa at Eden Park but was forced to subsequently withdraw from the fixture and did not appear in a Championship match.

Last year's standout flanker Callum McDonald was in Taranaki, last year's top try-scorer Te Peehi Fairlie was unavailable, and Anthony Karauria was not playing. Jody Allen, twin brother of lock Juston, returned to the province for the first time since 2016. He missed the middle part of the season being away with the NZ Defence Force team. Adrian Wyrill had previously represented Taranaki and Manawatu.

POVERTY BAY REPRESENTATIVES 2019

	Club	Games for Union	Points for Union		Club	Games for Union	Points for Union
Semisi Akana	Ngatapa	26	15	Tane McGuire [1]	Tech OB [2]	15	5
Jody Allen	Taradale [2]	9	30	Scott McKinley	OB Marist	20	5
Juston Allen	OB Marist	24	15	Hunter Mokomoko	Te Puna [3]	8	5
William Bollingford	Pirates GMC	8	0	Toru Noanoa	Waikohu	23	15
Nicholas Carrizo	OB Marist	2	0	Matthew Raleigh	Ngatapa	12	15
Campbell Chrisp	Ngatapa	50	5	Nathan Rangihuna	YMP	2	0
Jacob Cook	OB Marist	29	6	Morgan Reedy	OB Marist	2	0
Mario Counsell	Waikohu	56	15	Ethine Reeves	Waikohu	52	134
Lance Dickson	OB Marist	7	0	Kelvin Smith	Waikohu	46	83
William Grogan	OB Marist	35	5	Quade Tapsell	Hamilton Marist [4]	8	10
Tamanui Hill	HSOB	38	40	Andrew Tauatevalu	HSOB	25	184
Jake Holmes	OB Marist	20	25	Myles Tawa	HSOB	2	0
Ken Houkamau	Pirates GMC	39	16	Gabriel Te Kani	OB Marist	8	0
Jacob Leaf	Pirates GMC	9	0	Rikki Terekia	OB Marist	10	25
Korey Love	HSOB	10	5	Beaudein Waaka [5]		5	61
Jordan McFarlane	Gisborne BHS	1	0	Fawn White	YMP	16	0
Matekaeroa McGuire	HSOB	14	5	Adrian Wyrill	OB Marist	7	10

1 Player of Origin   2 Hawke's Bay RU   3 Bay of Plenty RU   4 Waikato RU   5 Arrived from overseas

INDIVIDUAL SCORING

	Tries	Con	PG	DG	Points
Tauatevalu	6	12	4	–	66
Waaka	6	11	–	–	52
Terekia	5	–	–	–	25
Penalty Try	3	–	–	–	21
Reeves	4	–	–	–	20
Smith	–	5	1	–	13
Wyrill	2	–	–	–	10
Raleigh	2	–	–	–	10
Noanoa	2	–	–	–	10
Tapsell	2	–	–	–	10
McKinley	1	–	–	–	5

	Tries	Con	PG	DG	Points
Houkamau	1	–	–	–	5
M. McGuire	1	–	–	–	5
Akana	1	–	–	–	5
T. McGuire	1	–	–	–	5
Hill	1	–	–	–	5
Holmes	1	–	–	–	5
Totals	**39**	**28**	**5**	**0**	**272**
Opposition scored	44 *	26	8	0	298

* Includes one penalty try (7 points)

POVERTY BAY 2019

	Thames Valley	South Canterbury	North Otago	Wairarapa Bush	Mid Canterbury	Horowhenua Kapiti	Ngati Porou East Coast	Buller	West Coast (sf)	Totals
S. McKinley	15	s	14	14	14	11	14	14	s	9
H.L. Mokomoko	14	14	–	–	11	–	–	–	–	3
A.H. Tauatevalu	13	15	15	11	15	14	–	13	11	8
K.D. Love	11	–	–	–	–	s	–	s	–	3
N.T. Rangihuna	s	11	–	–	–	–	–	–	–	2
M.W. Raleigh	–	–	11	s	s	–	11	11	14	6
J.G. Holmes	–	–	–	–	–	s	s	s	s	4
E.S. Reeves	–	13	13	13	s	15	–	–	13	6
T.R. McGuire	12	10	10	10	13	13	13	12	12	9
J.P. Leaf	s	12	12	12	12	12	12	s	s	9
K.M. Smith	10	–	–	s	10	10	15	15	15	7
B.R.T. Waaka	–	–	–	15	–	–	10	10	10	4
M.B. Counsell	9	9	s	s	s	s	s	9	9	9
W.D. Grogan	s	s	9	9	9	9	9	–	–	7
T.G. Hill	8	–	8	8	8	8	8	8	8	8
A.E. Wyrill	7	7	7	–	7	7	7	7	–	7
Q. Tapsell	6	8	6	–	6	6	6	6	7	8
W.C. Bolingford	s	s	–	s	s	s	s	s	6	8
F.D. White	–	6	–	–	–	–	–	–	–	1
N. Carrizo	–	–	–	7	–	–	–	–	s	2
M.J. Reedy	–	–	–	6	–	–	–	–	s	2
J.E. Cook	5	–	s	–	–	–	–	–	–	2
K.R. Houkamau (capt)	4	4	4	4	4	4	4	4	4	9
Juston N. Allen	s	s	–	s	s	s	s	s	–	7
G.C. Te Kani	–	5	5	5	5	5	5	5	5	8
Jody M. Allen	3	3	–	–	–	–	3	3	–	4
T.M. Noanoa	1	s	1	1	1	1	1	1	1	9
M.C.L.M. Tawa	s	–	–	–	–	3	–	–	–	2
L.A. Dickson	–	1	s	–	s	–	–	–	–	3
S.M. Akana	–	s	3	3	3	s	s	–	s	7
C.P.L. Chrisp	–	–	–	–	–	–	–	s	3	2
R.T. Terekia	2	2	2	2	2	2	2	2	2	9
M.W.E. McGuire	s	s	–	s	s	s	s	s	–	7
J. McFarlane	–	–	–	–	–	–	–	–	s	1

POVERTY BAY TEAM RECORD, 2019

Played 9 Won 3 Lost 6 Points for 272 Points against 298

Date	Opponent	Location	Score	Tries	Con	PG	DG	Referee
August 24	Thames Valley (H)	Paeroa	17–15	Tauatevalu (2), Terekia	Tauatevalu			D. Waenga
August 31	South Canterbury (H)	Gisborne	29–40	Wyrill (2), Reeves, Penalty Try	Tauatevalu (2)	Tauatevalu		T. Cottrell
September 7	North Otago (H)	Gisborne	30–34	Tauatevalu, McKinley, Penalty Try	Tauatevalu (2)	Tauatevalu (3)		H. Reed
September 14	Wairarapa Bush (H)	Masterton	31–36	Reeves, Terekia, Waaka, Raleigh	Tauatevalu (2), Waaka, Smith	Smith		N. Webster
September 21	Mid Canterbury (H)	Gisborne	52–38	Tauatevalu (3), Noanoa (2), Houkamau, Terekia, Tapsell	Tauatevalu (5), Smith			A. Mabey
September 28	Horowhenua Kapiti (H)	Waikanae	28–38	Penalty Try, Tapsell, M. McGuire, Reeves	Smith (3)			C. Stone
October 5	Ngati Porou East Coast (H)	Gisborne	24–20	Raleigh, Terekia, Waaka, Akana	Waaka (2)			A. Mabey
October 12	Buller (H)	Westport	26–36	Waaka (2), T. McGuire, Hill	Waaka (3)			J. Bredin
October 19	West Coast (LC sf)	Greymouth	35–41	Waaka (2), Terekia, Holmes, Reeves	Waaka (5)			H. Reed

SOUTH CANTERBURY

2019 Status: Heartland Championship
Founded 1888. Original member 1892
President: N.F. (Neville) Twaddell
Chairman: G.E. (Grant) Norton
Chief Executive Officer: C.W. (Craig) Calder
Coach: N.G. (Nigel) Walsh
Assistant coaches: S.P. (Shaun) Breen, C.S. (Chris) Gard
Main ground: Alpine Energy Stadium, Timaru
Capacity: 17,000
Colours: Emerald green and black

RECORDS

Highest attendance	17,000	*South Canterbury v France, 1961*
Most appearances	152	*S.J. Todd, 1986–2001*
Most points	1048	*B.J. Fairbrother, 1981–92*
Most tries	60	*S.J. Todd 1986–2001*
Most points in a season	175	*B.J. Fairbrother, 1991*
Most tries in a season	13	*J.S. Ellery, 1960*
		C.J. Dorgan, 1992
		B.J. Laney, 1992
Most conversions in a season	31	*B.J. Fairbrother, 1989*
Most penalty goals in a season	31	*B.J. Fairbrother, 1990*
Most dropped goals in a season	8	*B.J. Fairbrother, 1987*
		B.J. Fairbrother, 1991
Most points in a match	32	*G.I. Dempster v Wairarapa Bush, 1996*
Most tries in a match	4	*G.V. Gerard v Southland, 1926*
		E.W. Ryan v Ashburton County, 1935
		E.W. Ryan v Wellington XV, 1937
		J.M. Cole v North Otago, 1958
		E.C. Smith v Nelson, 1961
		B.J. Matthews v North Otago, 1992
		D.J. Hunter v Poverty Bay, 1993
		I.G. Howden v Marlborough, 1996
		S. Kiole v West Coast, 2002
		E. Tau v Poverty Bay, 2015
Most conversions in a match	8	*B.J. Fairbrother v West Coast, 1989*
		B.J. Fairbrother v North Otago, 1991
		B.J. Fairbrother v North Otago, 1992
		C.S. Gard v North Otago, 1993
		B.J. Laney v North Otago, 1994
		G.I. Dempster v Wairarapa Bush, 1996
Most penalty goals in a match	7	*B.J. Fairbrother v East Coast, 1990*
Highest team score	100	*v Ngati Porou East Coast, 2018*
Record victory (points ahead)	93	*100–7 v Ngati Porou East Coast, 2018*
Highest score conceded	103	*v Canterbury, 2001*
Record defeat (points behind)	103	*0–103 v Canterbury, 2001*

For the first time since 2014 South Canterbury missed out on a top four finish and a shot at the Meads Cup. After the sixth-round win over King Country, South Canterbury was tied for first place, but the final two round robin matches were lost to Thames Valley and West Coast after holding respective 21–7 and 17–0 leads in those two matches. This tumbled the team down to seventh place, three points outside the top four, and into the Lochore Cup.

After that disappointment South Canterbury achieved their biggest win of the season over Buller in the semi-final and set themselves another encounter with West Coast. In trying conditions South Canterbury led 17–5 at halftime, having had use of the strong wind. Within ten minutes of the second half, South Canterbury were down 17–19 and a repeat of the round robin match seemed to be unfolding. This time the forward pack responded and grew dominant, and Willie Wright kicked two superb pressure penalty goals into the wind for the 23–19 victory to win the Lochore Cup for the second time.

The first choice back three of fullback Zac Saunders and wings Clarence Moli and Kalavini Leatigaga showed a lot of speed and attacking running to score 13 tries between them. Saunders and Moli both missed the playoffs, and Leatigaga half the season, all due to injury. Brad Tunnicliffe showed himself to be a very determined backup wing, scoring five tries in his four appearances when Leatigaga was out. It is not often a player scores three tries in one game, as Tunnicliffe did against Poverty Bay, and can't find a place in the team for the next two matches.

Again on loan, Shayne Anderson played some very good rugby at centre on both attack and defence, being particularly effective in the second half of the campaign, and his midfield partner Joel Smith was steady in his debut season. Miles Medlicott directed play well at first five-eighth with his distribution and tactical kicking. Halfback Willie Wright was in superb form all season, his goalkicking again being excellent, which he underlined in the Lochore Cup final. Medlicott and Wright both moved out one position for the playoffs as Smith was ruled out due to concussion.

In a big forward pack, South Canterbury had a dynamic set of loose forwards. Siu Kakala, Cameron Russell and Anthony Amato were all in their debut season for the union and interacted superbly with strong ball carrying, speed to the breakdown and defensive work. Nick Strachan was not seen at his best, being bothered by a knee injury which caused him to miss three of the final four games. His captaincy was undoubtedly missed in the last two round robin matches.

Solomone Lavaka, Kieran Coll and 1.98m Reegan O'Gorman were all hard-working locks, with O'Gorman in particular earning plenty of lineout possession. The front row of Tokomata Fakatava, Ben Hewitson and Dan Suter was a good one, appearing together in every game. An arm injury to centurion Matt Fetu in the second match ended his season prematurely.

Newcomer Reegan O'Gorman has played for Canada, his father Pat being a Canterbury rep 1984–86 before emigrating. Dan Suter had represented Wales Under 20 and professional Welsh clubs Ospreys and Dragons. Anthony Amato had been a North Otago rep last year and Faalele Iosua was ex Wanganui. A number of last year's regulars were absent injured — Loni Toumohuni, Dominic Visesio, Garrett Casey — while elsewhere were Setefano Sauqaqa (retired), Timote Tuipulotu (Tonga), Veikoso "James" Poloniati (Wellington) and Pita Anae Ah Sue (Spain).

Higher honours went to:
New Zealand Heartland: K. Leatigaga, M. Medlicott, N. Strachan, W. Wright

SOUTH CANTERBURY REPRESENTATIVES 2019

	Club	Games for Union	Points for Union
Anthony Amato	Waimate	10	20
Shayne Anderson	Marist Albion [2]	24	25
Garrett Casey	Celtic	15	20
Kieran Coll	Christchurch [2]	41	58
Reilly Cormack [1]	Marist Albion [2]	6	3
Theo Davidson	Waimate	41	44
Tokomata Fakatava	Waimate	19	5
Matt Fetu	Celtic	105	35
Philip Fuls	Temuka	2	0
Pita Halaifonua	Harlequins	1	0
Ben Hewitson	Pleasant Point	66	5
Cameron Hucker	Pleasant Point	6	0
Faalele Iosua	Temuka	1	5
Siu Kakala	Harlequins	9	30
Molitoni Latu	Harlequins	3	0
Solomone Lavaka	Temuka	14	15
Kalavini Leatigaga	Temuka	30	131

	Club	Games for Union	Points for Union
Viliame Logovatu	Celtic	10	23
George Lott	Mackenzie	2	0
Ryan McNab	Mackenzie	2	5
Miles Medlicott	Waimate	61	38
Clarence Moli	Waimate	8	25
Reegan O'Gorman [3]		10	5
Cameron Russell	Mackenzie	10	15
Zac Saunders	Celtic	16	45
Joel Smith	Geraldine	8	10
Matthew Stewart	Celtic	5	0
Nick Strachan	Celtic	87	82
Dan Suter	Otorohanga [4]	10	0
Aifala Taelaga	Temuka	3	0
Jared Trevathan	Mackenzie	57	148
Brad Tunnicliffe	Old Boys	8	40
James Wilson-Bishop	Pleasant Point	10	0
Willie Wright	Celtic	46	316

1 Player of Origin   2 Canterbury RU   3 Arrived from Overseas   4 Waikato RU

INDIVIDUAL SCORING

	Tries	Con	PG	DG	Points
Wright	1	25	9	–	82
Kakala	6	–	–	–	30
Tunnicliffe	5	–	–	–	25
Moli	5	–	–	–	25
Saunders	5	–	–	–	25
Amato	4	–	–	–	20
Russell	3	–	–	–	15
Leatigaga	3	–	–	–	15
Strachan	2	–	–	–	10
Smith	2	–	–	–	10
Anderson	2	–	–	–	10
Davidson	–	3	1	–	9

	Tries	Con	PG	DG	Points
Penalty Try	1	–	–	–	7
Iosua	–	1	1	–	5
Lavaka	1	–	–	–	5
Fakatava	1	–	–	–	5
Medlicott	1	–	–	–	5
McNab	1	–	–	–	5
O'Gorman	1	–	–	–	5
Cormack	–	–	1	–	3
Totals	**44**	**29**	**12**	**0**	**316**
Opposition scored	30 *	17	11	0	219

* Includes one penalty try (7 points)

SOUTH CANTERBURY 2019

	North Otago	Poverty Bay	Horowhenua Kapiti	Mid Canterbury	Buller	King Country	Thames Valley	West Coast	Buller (sf)	West Coast (f)	Totals
J.L. Wilson-Bishop	15	s	s	s	s	s	15	s	15	15	10
Z.C.C. Saunders	s	15	15	15	15	15	–	15	–	–	7
C.M. Moli	14	14	14	14	14	14	14	14	–	–	8
K.V. Leatigaga	11	–	11	11	–	–	–	11	11	11	6
B.D. Tunnicliffe	–	11	–	–	11	11	11	–	–	–	4
M. Latu	–	–	–	–	–	–	s	–	14	14	3
S.W. Anderson	13	13	13	13	13	13	13	13	13	13	10
J.C. Smith	s	12	12	12	12	12	12	s	–	–	8
R.W. Cormack	–	s	s	–	s	s	s	–	s	–	6
M.W. Medlicott	12	10	10	10	10	10	10	10	12	12	10
F.A. Iosua	10	–	–	–	–	–	–	–	–	–	1
J.D. Trevathan	–	–	–	–	–	–	–	s	s	s	3
W.A. Wright	9	–	s	9	9	9	9	9	10	10	9
T.R. Davidson	s	9	9	–	s	s	s	s	9	9	9
G.M. Lott	–	s	–	–	–	–	–	–	–	–	1
S.I.F. Kakala	8	8	8	–	6	6	8	8	s	s	9
P. Fuls	s	s	–	–	–	–	–	–	–	–	2
K.P. Coll	–	–	s	8	8	8	5	5	5	5	8
R. McNab	–	–	–	–	–	–	–	–	8	8	2
N.J.C. Strachan (capt)	7	7	7	7	7	7	–	–	–	s	7
A. Amato	6	6	5	4	s	s	s	s	6	6	10
C.D.R. Russell	s	s	6	6	s	s	7	7	7	7	10
P.O. Halaifonua	–	–	–	s	–	–	–	–	–	–	1
M.J. Stewart	–	–	–	–	–	–	–	–	s	–	1
S.P. Lavaka	5	5	s	s	5	5	6	6	–	–	8
R.P. O'Gorman	4	4	4	5	4	4	4	4	4	4	10
D.J. Suter	3	3	3	3	3	3	3	3	3	3	10
M. Fetu	1	s	–	–	–	–	–	–	–	–	2
T.M.H.K. Fakatava	s	1	1	1	1	1	1	1	1	1	10
V.N. Logavatu	–	–	s	–	–	–	–	–	–	–	1
A. Taelaga	–	–	–	s	–	s	–	–	s	–	3
G.J. Casey	–	–	–	–	–	–	–	–	s	s	2
B.C. Hewitson	2	2	2	2	2	2	2	2	2	2	10
C.A. Hucker	–	s	s	–	s	s	–	s	s	–	6

M.W. Medlicott captained the final four games.

SOUTH CANTERBURY TEAM RECORD, 2019

Played 10   Won 6   Drew 1   Lost 3   Points for 316   Points against 219

Date	Opponent	Location	Score	Tries	Con	PG	DG	Referee
August 24	North Otago (H) (HS)	Timaru	20–26	Kakala (2), Strachan	Iosua	Iosua		J. Bredin
August 31	Poverty Bay (H)	Gisborne	40–29	Tunnicliffe (3), Moli (2), Saunders	Davidson (2)	Davidson, Cormack		T. Cottrell
September 7	Horowhenua Kapiti (H)	Timaru	57–7	Saunders, Russell, Moli, Kakala, Smith, Leatigaga, Lavaka, Fakatava	Wright (6), Davidson	Wright		J. Bredin
September 14	Mid Canterbury (H)	Ashburton	13–13	Strachan	Wright	Wright (2)		J. Munro
September 21	Buller (H)	Timaru	38–27	Tunnicliffe (2), Saunders (2), Anderson, Wright	Wright (4)			R. Mahoney
September 28	King Country (H)	Taupo	21–19	Kakala, Anderson, Smith	Wright (3)			D. MacPherson
October 5	Thames Valley (H)	Paeroa	24–28	Penalty Try, Russell, Moli	Wright (2)	Wright		D. MacPherson
October 12	West Coast (H)	Timaru	24–27	Kakala, Medlicott, Saunders, Moli	Wright (2)			T. Griffiths
October 19	Buller (LC sf)	Westport	56–24	Amato (3), McNab, O'Gorman, Leatigaga, Kakala, Russell	Wright (5)	Wright (2)		N. Webster
October 26	West Coast (LC f)	Greymouth	23–19	Amato, Leatigaga	Wright (2)	Wright (3)		T. Cottrell

HS Hanan Shield

SOUTHLAND

2019 Status: Mitre 10 Cup Championship
Founded 1887. Affiliated 1894
President: K.I. (Kim) McDowall
Chairman: B.J. (Bernie) McKone
General Manager: B. (Brian) Hopley
Coach: D.N. (Dave) Hewett
Assistant coaches: J.M. (Jason) Kawau, D.J. (Dale) McLeod
Main ground: Rugby Park Stadium, Invercargill
Capacity: 20,200
Colours: Maroon

**RUGBY
SOUTHLAND**

RECORDS

Most appearances	139	*Jason Rutledge, 2000–2016*
Most points	976	*Simon Culhane, 1988–98*
Most tries	46	*Bruce Pascoe, 1983–89*
Most points in a season	194	*Simon Culhane, 1994*
Most tries in a season	13	*Simon Forrest, 1992*
Most conversions in a season	38	*Simon Culhane, 1997*
Most penalty goals in a season	41	*Eion Crossan, 1989*
Most dropped goals in a season	10	*Brian McKechnie, 1977*
Most points in a match	37	*Simon Culhane v Manawatu, 1994*
Most tries in a match	5	*Simon Forrest v Poverty Bay, 1992*
Most conversions in a match	11	*Simon Culhane v Malborough, 1997*
Most penalty goals in a match	8	*Simon Culhane v Manawatu, 1994*
Highest team score	92	*v Marlborough, 1997*
Record victory (points ahead)	74	*79–5 v Poverty Bay, 1992*
Highest score conceded	95	*v Waikato, 1998*
Record defeat (points behind)	88	*7–95 v Waikato, 1998*

Southland will be heartened by the fact that it finally snapped a 27-match losing streak in the Mitre 10 Cup, but the Stags were again the cellar-dwellers of the Championship section.

The stats were very similar to the 2018 season, with two heavy defeats, competitive in several fixtures, but with an overall average losing score of 37–16. Second year coach Dave Hewett had roughly the same quality of personnel as in 2018, so it was no real surprise at the same placing. For all that, if Northland had not won its final game in style, then the Stags would have placed sixth in the Championship.

The Taniwha edged the Stags on opening night, before two losses to Otago in the Ranfurly Shield challenge and North Harbour in which the Stags were not far off the pace.

Southland will feel like the Manawatu game was there for the taking, and then it all clicked in the September 21 crossover clash against Counties Manukau in a thumping 42–14 victory to break a three-year drought. That was one of just two games in which the Stags recorded a try-scoring bonus point.

The 64–7 defeat to Auckland was not much better than the 80–0 blanking by Canterbury but seemed inconsistent with the efforts during the rest of the season. The manner in which the Stags held eventual Championship winner Bay of Plenty to 22–12 in Invercargill suggests there is some starch to this team.

Back surgery ruled out promising lock Manaaki Selby-Rickit before the season kicked off, while former All Blacks loose forward Elliot Dixon was keen to return for the Stags but insurance issues around his Japanese contract prevented him from playing. James Wilson had already taken the yen, while Matt Johnson signed with Northland. Aleki Morris-Lome was making a name for himself in Otago, while Tony Lamborn was involved with the USA's Rugby World Cup squad. Jackson Ormond returned to Taranaki, but marked his brother Lewis in round eight.

Incoming were some useful signings, specifically Marty McKenzie, who last played for the union in 2013 before heading north to Taranaki, loaned halfback Logan Crowley from the same union, Charles Alaimalo and Josh Moorby from Waikato and Greg Pleasants-Tate from Canterbury.

Moorby started every game, one of just two players to do so, and impressed with his willingness to counter-attack. He scored three tries. The most penetrative outside back was, however, Isaac Te Tamaki, who scored four tries and was dangerous at either wing or centre. Ray Nu'u impressed at second five in his second season.

Scott Eade returned from injury but then was hurt again halfway through the campaign. McKenzie had moments of brilliance but was not able to bring the same authority with which he had played for the Chiefs. He did combine well with Crowley, who was MVP in the victory over the Steelers. Nico Costa was injured early, allowing Jay Renton to show his wares off the bench.

No 8 Bill Fukofuka hoisted the 50-game milestone and again gave yeoman service. Matty James and Alaimalo acted as useful foils in the loose. Locks Mike McKee and Craig Smith won good lineout ball at times.

Morgan Mitchell was the rock of the pack. The tighthead prop started every match, raised the half century and kept his side of the scrum up. Joe Walsh was the main man on the other side of that set-piece. Captain Brayden Mitchell had early injury issues and was then forced onto the side of the scrum by the solid form of Pleasants-Tate, who was playing for his fifth province, but scored four tries and scrummaged well. Flynn Thomas' injury allowed Pleasants-Tate further opportunities.

SOUTHLAND REPRESENTATIVES 2019

	Club	Games for Union	Points for Union		Club	Games for Union	Points for Union
Charles Alaimalo	Woodlands	10	5	Ray Nu'u	Wyndham	16	5
Chris Apoua	Midlands	14	0	Lewis Ormond	Woodlands	27	40
Ryan Carter	Mossburn	2	0	Ben Paulin	Blues	3	0
Nico Costa	Woodlands	12	5	Greg Pleasants-Tate	Star	9	20
Logan Crowley	Coastal [1]	10	10	Jay Renton	Blues	25	0
Ethan de Groot	Blues	8	0	Howard Sililoto	Papakura [2]	7	0
Scott Eade	Marist	62	254	Craig Smith	Pirates-Old Boys	7	0
Javaan Fa'amoe-loane	Marist	2	0	Shaun Stodart	Marist	25	0
Moses Faletolu	Woodlands	7	0	Lausii Taliauli	–	5	0
Ben Fotheringham	Marist	14	0	Raymond Tatafu	Blues	20	0
Bill Fukofuka	Blues	57	35	Mitch Taylor	Blues	6	0
Phil Halder	Marist	29	5	Isaac Te Tamaki	EN Barbarians	18	35
Matthew James	Woodlands	10	5	Flynn Thomas	Marist	22	5
Mike McKee	EN Barbarians	29	5	Viliami Tosi	Marist	5	0
Marty McKenzie	Woodlands	35	128	Tauasosi Tuimavave	Woodlands	21	22
Brayden Mitchell	Star	54	15	Rory van Vugt	EN Barbarians	9	10
Morgan Mitchell	Star	50	20	Joseph Walsh	Woodlands	34	5
Josh Moorby	Woodlands	10	15	Seb Wileman	Marist	2	0

1. *Loaned from Taranaki*   2. *Loaned from Counties Manukau*

INDIVIDUAL SCORING

	Tries	Con	PG	DG	Points
McKenzie	1	14	6	–	51
Pleasants-Tate	4	–	–	–	20
Te Tamaki	4	–	–	–	20
Moorby	3	–	–	–	15
Crowley	2	–	–	–	10
Ormond	2	–	–	–	10
Alaimalo	1	–	–	–	5
Eade	1	–	–	–	5
Fukofuka	1	–	–	–	5

	Tries	Con	PG	DG	Points
Halder	1	–	–	–	5
James	1	–	–	–	5
Nu'u	1	–	–	–	5
van Vugt	1	–	–	–	5
Totals	**23**	**14**	**6**	**0**	**161**
Opposition scored	56	40	4	0	372

SOUTHLAND 2019

	Northland	Otago	North Harbour	Canterbury	Hawke's Bay	Manawatu	Counties Manukau	Taranaki	Auckland	Bay of Plenty	Totals
J.M. Moorby	15	15	15	15	15	15	15	15	15	14	10
T. Tuimavave	–	–	–	–	–	–	s	–	14	–	2
I.R. Te Tamaki	14	14	14	–	13	13	13	13	13	13	9
L.H. Ormond	s	s	–	14	14	14	14	14	–	11	8
S.W. Wileman	11	–	–	–	–	–	–	–	s	–	2
R.F. van Vugt	–	–	–	–	–	–	11	11	11	s	4
L. Taliauli	–	11	11	11	11	11	–	–	–	–	5
M. Faletolu	13	13	s	s	s	s	–	–	12	–	7
J.M.K. Fa'amoe-Ioane	–	–	13	13	–	–	–	–	–	–	2
R.I. Nu'u	12	12	12	12	12	12	12	12	–	12	9
S.R. Eade	s	s	s	10	–	–	–	–	–	–	4
M.R. McKenzie	10	10	10	–	10	10	10	10	10	15	9
M. Taylor	–	–	–	s	s	–	s	s	s	10	6
L.E. Crowley	9	9	9	s	9	9	9	9	9	9	10
N. Costa	s	s	–	–	–	–	–	–	–	–	2
J.L. Renton	–	–	s	9	s	s	s	s	s	s	8
B.S. Fukofuka	8	8	8	8	8	s	s	s	s	s	10
P.V. Tosi	–	–	s	s	s	–	–	–	–	–	3
P.W. Halder	7	7	–	–	–	–	–	–	–	–	2
M.D. James	s	s	7	7	7	7	7	7	7	7	10
C. Alaimalo	6	6	6	6	s	8	8	8	8	8	10
B.T. Mitchell (capt)	s	–	–	–	6	6	6	6	6	6	7
M.J.F. McKee	5	5	5	4	5	5	–	5	5	5	9
C.W. Smith	–	–	–	–	–	–	5	4	4	4	4
B. Paulin	–	–	–	s	–	s	s	–	–	–	3
R.K. Tatafu	4	4	s	5	4	4	4	s	s	s	10
B.J. Fotheringham	s	s	4	–	–	–	–	–	–	–	3
M.D. Mitchell	3	3	3	3	3	3	3	3	3	3	10
S.D.G. Stodart	–	–	s	s	s	s	s	–	–	–	5
C. Apoua	s	s	s	–	–	–	–	s	s	s	6
H.J.F. Sililoto	–	–	s	s	s	–	s	s	s	s	7
J.S. Walsh	s	s	1	1	1	1	1	1	1	1	10
E.L. de Groot	1	1	–	–	–	–	–	–	–	–	2
F.C. Thomas (capt)	2	2	2	2	s	s	–	–	–	–	6
G.W. Pleasants-Tate	–	s	s	s	2	2	2	2	2	2	9
R.J. Carter	–	–	–	–	–	–	s	s	–	–	2

SOUTHLAND TEAM RECORD, 2019

Played 10   Won 1   Lost 9

Date	Opponent	Location	Score	Tries	Con	PG	DG	Points for 161	Points against 372	Referee
August 8	Northland (C)	Invercargill	17–27	Te Tamaki, Halder, Moorby	McKenzie					N.J. Webster
August 17	Otago (RS, C)	Dunedin	22–41	Moorby, Alaimalo, Fukofuka	McKenzie (2)	McKenzie				P.M. Williams
August 25	North Harbour (cr)	Invercargill	12–33	McKenzie, Eade	McKenzie					J.D. Munro
August 31	Canterbury (cr)	Christchurch	0–80							D.J. Waenga
September 6	Hawke's Bay (C)	Napier	23–41	Te Tamaki (2), Moorby	McKenzie	McKenzie (2)				R.M. Mahoney
September 14	Manawatu (C)	Invercargill	26–31	Pleasants-Tate, Ormond, Crowley, Nu'u	McKenzie (3)					A.W.B. Mabey
September 21	Counties Manukau (cr)	Invercargill	42–14	Crowley, van Vugt, Te Tamaki, Pleasants-Tate, Ormond	McKenzie (4)	McKenzie (3)				N.J. Webster
September 26	Taranaki (C)	New Plymouth	0–19							D.J. Waenga
October 5	Auckland (cr)	Auckland	7–64	Pleasants-Tate	McKenzie					T.N. Griffiths
October 10	Bay of Plenty (C)	Invercargill	12–22	James, Pleasants-Tate	McKenzie					M.C.J. Winter

TARANAKI

2019 Status: Mitre 10 Cup Championship
Founded 1889. Original member 1892
President: R.J. (Robin) Houghton
Chairman: L.J. (Lindsay) Thomson
Chief executive officer: J.R. (Jeremy) Parkinson (to Sept)
P.J. (Paul) Veric (interim, from Sept)
Coach: W.T.C. (Willie) Rickards
Assistant coaches: C.B.J. (Craig) Clarke), T.M. (Tim) Stuck
Main ground: Yarrow Stadium, New Plymouth
Capacity: 12,000
Colours: Amber and black

RECORDS

Most appearances	222	*Ian Eliason, 1964–81*
Most points	1723	*Kieran Crowley, 1980–94*
Most tries	64	*Kieran Crowley, 1980–94*
Most points in a season	233	*Jamie Cameron, 1995*
Most tries in a season	13	*Charlie McAlister, 1985*
Most conversions in a season	49	*Kieran Crowley, 1983*
Most penalty goals in a season	39	*Jamie Cameron, 1995*
Most dropped goals in a season	11	*Ross Brown, 1964*
Most points in a match	34	*Jamie Cameron v Nelson Bays, 1995*
Most tries in a match	5	*George Loveridge v Wanganui, 1913*
		Dave Vesty v Thames Valley, 1971
		Mark Robinson v Southland, 1997
Most conversions in a match	13	*Kieran Crowley v East Coast, 1983*
Most penalty goals in a match	9	*Beauden Barrett v Bay of Plenty, 2011*
Highest team score	104	*v Nelson Bays, 1995*
Record victory (points ahead)	97	*97–0 v East Coast, 1983*
Highest score conceded	80	*v Otago, 1996*
Record defeat (points behind)	60	*16–76 v North Harbour, 1989*

The 2019 Mitre 10 Cup season was ultimately a disappointing one for this proud rugby province who failed to return to Premiership status since losing it in 2018. Three wins from the first three games gave fans and supporters some cause for optimism. However, this proved to be short lived, as only one further game was won.

Taranaki looked the better team for large parts of the unsuccessful Ranfurly Shield challenge, playing some beautiful attacking rugby. However, a series of handling errors at crucial times saw four very real try-scoring opportunities blown in what was a classic Shield encounter. A poor effort against Hawkes Bay in Napier followed, in what was certainly the team's worst performance of the year.

By this stage of the competition, injuries were starting to take their toll on many of the marquee players in the squad. Whilst an ugly win over a spirited Southland team in squally, wintry evening conditions at Yarrows Stadium did manage to break a four-game losing streak, the manner in which it was achieved only reinforced the team's inability at times to impose their style of game on opposition teams.

Despite the results, the team was superbly led by captain Mitch Brown who gave nothing less than 100 per cent in every single match he played. He was deservedly Taranaki's forward, player and players' player of the year.

Elsewhere in the forwards, Taranaki were well served in the front row stocks by former Otago rep Donald Brighouse, and fellow props Reuben O'Neill, Jared Proffit, Chris Gawler and Kyle Stewart who were all used at different times throughout the season in what was a solid scrum. Ricky Riccitelli was consistent and reliable at hooker and was well supported by Bradley Slater and Scott Mellow who both gave a good account of themselves in their limited number of appearances.

New Zealand Under 20 representative Tupou Vaa'i had an impressive season at lock, showing great aggression and ball skills and, together with new cap Joshua Lord, offered a glimpse of what the Taranaki locking combination of the future might look like. Vaa'i won the Union's most promising player award. Jesse Parete was an industrious, physical lock who was ably supported by the veteran Leighton Price who always answered the call when required.

Lachlan Boshier consistently showed his class at openside flanker with some standout performances until a shoulder injury in the shield match cruelly interrupted his season. His absence was certainly felt. Heiden Bedwell-Curtis was a bruising, rugged loose forward who always looked for work. Kaylum Boshier is another New Zealand Under 20s rep who showed his versatility in playing admirably in all three loose forward positions throughout the season. He has a bright future. Tom Florence continues to impress every time he pulls on a Bulls jersey.

Pita Gus Sowakula was a dominant force at No 8. His big, strong ball carrying runs and direct abrasive style were a constant feature of his play and a pleasure to watch.

In the backs, Jayson Potroz was a reliable and dependable fullback who showed some nice touches. He was the team's back of the year. Jackson Ormond showed yet again he has lost none of his finishing skills on the outside, and in conjunction with Waisake Naholo, scored some great tries on the wing. Naholo left for English club London Irish at season's end.

Newcomers Matt McKenzie and Lukas Halls and the returning Liam Blyde and Kini Naholo are all exciting young prospects, which suggests there is no shortage of speed and talent in the back division to look forward to in the coming years.

In the midfield, Tei Walden was consistently the glue in the Taranaki backline, starting in every match. His experience and leadership skills proved invaluable. He was the perfect foil for the dangerous Sean Wainui at centre, who breached the defensive line nearly every time he touched the ball. Both these players ended the season as the team's equal top tryscorers. Former Wellington representative Regan Verney looked handy in his few appearances.

Daniel Waite started at first five-eighth and his versatility was called upon once Stephen Perofeta returned to the ten jersey mid-season. Waite was Taranaki's top points scorer.

Te Toiroa Tahuriorangi provided stability and experience at halfback. He was well aided by former Auckland representative Lisati Milo-Harris, who looked sharp and busy, making the most of his chances. He was rewarded with a Super Rugby contract. Xavier Roe will continue to mature and develop as a halfback given more game time.

A total of 38 players were used throughout the season. For the first time since 1995, two sets of brothers — Lachlan and Kaylum Boshier and Waisake and Kini Naholo — appeared in the same team for Taranaki in the season opener against Counties Manukau.

Higher honours went to:

New Zealand:	B. Barrett, J. Barrett, S. Barrett, A. Ta'avao
New Zealand Under 20:	K. Boshier, T. Vaa'i
Maori All Blacks:	T. Tahuriorangi, S. Wainui, T. Walden

TARANAKI REPRESENTATIVES 2019

	Club	Games for Union	Points for Union
Heiden Bedwell-Curtis	Inglewood	9	5
Liam Blyde	Clifton	4	0
Kaylum Boshier	New Plymouth OB	10	5
Lachlan Boshier	New Plymouth OB	38	45
Donald Brighouse	Southern	9	0
Mitchell Brown	Inglewood	36	5
Johnny Faletagoa'i-Malase	Spotswood United	2	0
Tom Florence	New Plymouth OB	18	5
Chris Gawler	Coastal	21	0
Lukas Halls	Tukapa	1	0
Josh Lord	Coastal	4	0
Matthew McKenzie	Clifton	6	0
Scott Mellow	Tukapa	10	0
Lisati Milo-Harris	Inglewood	8	0
Kini Naholo	Clifton	5	15
Waisake Naholo	Spotswood United	44	110
Brayton Northcott-Hill	New Plymouth OB	12	17
Reuben O'Neill	New Plymouth OB	34	5
Jackson Ormond	Southern	65	80
Jesse Parete	Southern	13	5
Stephen Perofeta	Clifton	32	78
Jayson Potroz	Tukapa	13	32
Leighton Price	Tukapa	31	5
Jared Proffit	Spotswood United	32	5
Ricky Riccitelli	Tukapa	26	20
Xavier Roe	Tukapa	6	0
Brad Slater	Hautapu [1]	8	0
Asaeli Sorovaki	Spotswood United	8	0
Pita-Gus Sowakula	Spotswood United	24	20
Kyle Stewart	Stratford Eltham	15	0
Te Toiroa Tahuriorangi	New Plymouth OB	41	25
Tupou Vaa'i	New Plymouth OB	9	5
Regan Verney	New Plymouth OB	4	0
Sean Wainui	New Plymouth OB	43	70
Daniel Waite	New Plymouth OB	16	81
Tei Walden	Spotswood United	20	25

[1] Waikato RU

INDIVIDUAL SCORING

	Tries	Con	PG	DG	Points
Waite	1	14	8	–	57
Perofeta	1	5	3	–	24
Wainui	4	–	–	–	20
Ormond	4	–	–	–	20
Walden	4	–	–	–	20
Potroz	3	1	–	–	17
W. Naholo	3	–	–	–	15
Penalty Try	2	–	–	–	14
L. Boshier	2	–	–	–	10
Tahuriorangi	1	–	–	–	5
Vaa'i	1	–	–	–	5
Brown	1	–	–	–	5
Bedwell-Curtis	1	–	–	–	5
Sowakula	1	–	–	–	5
Riccitelli	1	–	–	–	5
Totals	**30**	**20**	**11**	**0**	**227**
Opposition scored	37*	23	9	0	260

* includes one penalty try (7 points)

TARANAKI 2019	Counties Manukau	Manawatu	Northland	Tasman	Otago	Bay of Plenty	Hawke's Bay	Southland	Waikato	Auckland	Totals
J.P. Potroz	15	15	15	15	15	15	15	15	15	11	10
L.G. Blyde	–	–	–	–	–	–	s	s	–	s	3
W.R. Naholo	14	–	14	14	14	14	14	14	14	14	9
J.T. Ormond	11	14	s	–	s	11	11	11	11	–	8
K.V. Naholo	s	11	11	–	–	–	–	–	–	–	3
L.J.M. Halls	–	–	–	11	–	–	–	–	–	–	1
S.T. Wainui	13	13	13	13	11	–	–	13	13	13	8
T.T. Walden	12	12	12	12	13	13	12	12	12	12	10
R.D. Verney	s	s	–	–	–	s	13	–	–	–	4
B.K. Northcott-Hill	–	s	s	–	–	–	–	–	–	–	2
D.S. Waite	10	10	10	10	12	12	s	–	s	15	9
S. Perofeta	–	–	–	s	10	10	10	10	10	10	7
M.R. McKenzie	–	–	–	s	s	s	–	s	s	s	6
H.J.T.T. Tahuriorangi	9	9	9	–	9	9	–	s	9	9	8
L.M. Milo-Harris	–	–	s	9	s	s	9	9	s	s	8
X.O. Roe	–	–	–	s	–	–	s	–	–	–	2
P.G.N. Sowakula	8	8	8	–	8	8	8	8	8	8	9
L.S. Boshier	7	7	7	7	7	–	–	–	s	s	7
K.L. Boshier	6	s	6	8	s	s	–	s	s	7	9
H.K. Bedwell-Curtis	–	6	–	–	6	6	6	6	6	6	7
T.H.T. Florence	–	–	s	6	s	7	7	7	7	s	8
J.M. Faletagoa'i–Malase	–	–	–	s	–	–	s	–	–	–	2
M.M. Brown (capt)	5	5	5	5	5	5	5	5	5	–	9
T.P.O. Vaa'i	4	s	4	4	–	–	–	–	4	4	6
J.W.Z. Parete	s	4	–	–	4	4	–	–	–	–	4
J.M.J. Lord	–	–	s	–	–	–	s	s	–	5	4
L.T. Price	–	–	–	s	–	s	4	4	–	–	4
D.I.M. Brighouse	3	3	3	–	3	3	3	3	3	3	9
R.G. O'Neill	1	1	1	1	–	–	–	–	–	–	4
C.M. Gawler	s	s	s	s	1	1	1	1	1	1	10
K.L. Stewart	s	s	s	3	s	s	s	s	s	s	10
A.S. Sorovaki	–	–	–	s	–	–	–	–	–	–	1
J.P. Proffit	–	–	–	–	s	s	s	s	s	s	6
S.B. Mellow	2	–	s	–	–	–	–	–	–	–	3
J.R. Riccitelli	–	2	2	2	2	2	2	–	2	2	8
B.A. Slater	–	–	–	s	s	s	s	2	s	s	7

TARANAKI TEAM RECORD, 2019

Played 10 Won 4 Lost 6 Points for 227 Points against 260

Date	Opponent	Location	Score	Tries	Con	PG	DG	Referee
August 10	Counties Manukau (cr)	Pukekohe	34–29	Wainui, W. Naholo, Penalty Try, L. Boshier, Ormond	Waite (2)	Waite		A. Mabey
August 17	Manawatu (C)	Palmerston North	13–10	Penalty Try		Waite (2)		D. Jones
August 25	Northland (C)	New Plymouth	52–19	Wainui (2), Ormond (2), Tahuriorangi, Vaa'i, Waite, Potroz	Waite (6)			P. Williams
September 1	Tasman (cr)	New Plymouth	18–28	L. Boshier, W. Naholo	Waite	Waite (2)		A. Mabey
September 8	Otago (C) (RS)	Dunedin	27–35	Brown, Perofeta, Walden	Waite (3)	Waite (2)		N. Briant
September 14	Bay of Plenty (C)	New Plymouth	17–31	Potroz, Walden	Waite (2)	Waite		J. Doleman
September 20	Hawke's Bay (C)	Napier	17–35	Potroz, Bedwell-Curtis	Potroz, Perofeta	Perofeta		N. Hogan
September 26	Southland (C)	New Plymouth	19–0	Walden, Ormond, W. Naholo	Perofeta (2)			D. Waenga
October 6	Waikato (cr)	Hamilton	19–38	Walden, Wainui, Sowakula	Perofeta (2)			J. Munro
October 11	Auckland (cr)	New Plymouth	11–35	Riccitelli		Perofeta (2)		G. Jackson

TASMAN

2019 Status: Mitre 10 Cup Premiership
Founded and **affiliated 2005** (December)
President: R.S. (Ramon) Sutherland
Chairman: W.A. (Wayne) Young
Chief executive officer: A.J.F. (Tony) Lewis
Co-coaches: A.D. (Andrew) Goodman, C. (Clarke) Dermody
Assistant coaches: S.A. (Shane) Christie, G.N. (Gray) Cornelius
Main ground: Trafalgar Park, Nelson; Lansdowne Park, Blenheim
Capacity: 18,000
Colours: Navy blue and red

RECORDS

Most appearances	104	*Robbie Malneek, 2006–2017*
Most points	628	*Marty Banks, 2013–2016*
Most tries	25	*Robbie Malneek*
Most points in a season	173	*Marty Banks, 2014*
Most tries in a season	10	*Peter Playford, 2006*
Most conversions in a season	37	*Marty Banks, 2014*
Most penalty goals in a season	33	*Marty Banks, 2016*
Most dropped goals in a season	1	*by five players*
Most points in a match	28	*Marty Banks v Northland, 2013*
Most tries in a match	4	*Peter Playford v Canada A, 2006*
		Peter Playford v Northland, 2006
Most conversions in a match	7	*Aaron Kimura v Northland, 2006*
		Marty Banks v Manawatu, 2013
Most penalty goals in a match	8	*Tom Marshall v Bay of Plenty, 2010*
Most dropped goals in a match	1	*by five players*
Highest team score	64	*v Waikato, 2013*
		v Manawatu, 2019
Record victory (points ahead)	61	*64-3 v Manawatu, 2019*
Highest score conceded	52	*v Counties Manukau, 2017*
Record defeat (points behind)	42	*7–49 v Auckland, 2007*

After just 14 seasons, the Tasman Mako have reached the pinnacle of New Zealand provincial rugby.

The Premiership final victory must rank as the finest day for rugby at the top of the South Island since Marlborough stunned the nation with the 1973 Ranfurly Shield upset of Canterbury.

The Mako had been knocking at the door since their 2013 Championship victory, and had contested three Premiership finals before 2019. In 2011 they were last in the Championship, and thus ranked 14th of the top tier unions.

The manner in which they went 10–0 through the regular season and then ground out their playoffs victories showed a team that was adaptable to all conditions and opponents to produce the first unbeaten season since Auckland in 2007.

In scoring 62 tries, 17 more than in 2018, the Mako could hurt you in several ways, be it a kick-pass from Mitch Hunt, a lineout drive or a slick backline move. But it was the parsimonious defence, organised by assistant coach Shane Christie, that was most telling. Conceding just 14 tries in 12 games, with an average winning score of 37–11, told of a tight group that played for each other and trusted the systems.

Tasman sounded an early warning to the competition with a 45–8 demolition of Wellington, and thereafter, barring the tight wins over North Harbour and Waikato, was untroubled, scoring try-scoring bonus points in all bar two games. Especially impressive was the 23–8 defeat to Canterbury in Christchurch, and the shutouts of Counties Manukau and Auckland.

The latter bounced back with a committed display in the semi-final, but the Mako, superbly led by David Havili, scored the points when they mattered.

In the final, they were always one step ahead of a competitive Wellington, but relied on a Will Jordan double and Mitch Hunt's accuracy off the tee to seal the triumph.

Pre-season gains included Atu Moli coming home from Waikato, though his All Blacks duties meant he appeared just once, and Australian hooker Hugh Roach, who offered immense value off the bench, and four times. Joe Wheeler was back from Japan, but was injured, as was Kane Hames, who found a home in the TV commentary box.

Losses included Alex Ainley (Bay of Plenty), Solomon Alaimalo (Waikato), Jed Brown (Japan) and Ray Niuia (Samoa RWC).

Havili was used almost exclusively at fullback, shifting back from the midfield, and continued his Crusaders' form with dangerous counter-attacking and astute decision-making.

Will Jordan was pushed to the right wing and scored seven tries, while Leicester Faingaanuku equalled that on the other wing. A player of the ilk of Jamie Spowart, who scored four tries, hardly got a look in.

Centre Fetuli Paea was promoted after being the Tasman club player of the year with Waitohi. His impact off the bench was telling, especially in the playoffs, and he won a Super Rugby contract. Alex Nankivell was an underrated second five, always straightening the attack and breaking the line in time of need.

Hunt played consistently well in the No 10 jersey and scored 102 points, while his halfback Finlay Christie gave him slick service and ran incisively.

The Mako enjoyed enviable depth in the loose trio. Liam Squire was at his bruising best in either the No 8 or No 6 jersey, while Jordan Taufua, who opted not to play for Manu Samoa at Rugby World Cup, signed off his Tasman days with a typically all-action campaign.

Sione Havili offered a good foil on the openside flank, as did indefatigable Ethan Blackadder on the blind. It was noticeable that, after he left injured during the semi-final, the pack was not as dominant.

Shannon Frizell was used mostly at lock before his RWC call-up. The Quinten Strange-Pari Pari Parkinson combination continues to grow.

The Mako used seven props, all of whom added to the solid scrum. Tyrel Lomax was again to the fore on the tighthead side. Wyatt Crockett's long career ended in glory.

Andrew Makalio again played a prominent role, and was one of the best hookers in the Mitre 10 Cup.

Higher honours went to:
New Zealand:	S. Frizell, A. Moli
New Zealand Maori:	T. Lomax, A. Nankivell, P. Parkinson
New Zealand Under 20:	L. Faingaanuku
New Zealand Sevens:	T. Joass, T. Ng Shiu

TASMAN REPRESENTATIVES 2019

	Club	Games for Union	Points for Union		Club	Games for Union	Points for Union
Levi Aumua	Riwaka	29	35	Atu Moli	Harlequins	1	0
Ethan Blackadder	Nelson	44	40	Sam Moli	Marist	5	5
Finlay Christie	Stoke	43	35	Alex Nankivell	Stoke	45	40
Te Ahiwaru Cirikidaveta	Stoke	10	15	Jacob Norris	Marist	7	10
Ryan Coxon	Wanderers	14	0	Tim O'Malley	Waitohi	28	72
Wyatt Crockett	Nelson	20	15	Fetuli Paea	Waitohi	9	0
Leicester Faingaanuku	Nelson	13	35	Paripari Parkinson	Stoke	32	5
Tima Faingaanuku	Nelson	35	50	Tim Perry	Nelson	70	25
Taina Fox-Matamua	Marist	6	0	Sam Prattley	Pakuranga [3]	30	0
Shannon Frizell	Marist	29	35	Hugh Roach	Nelson	10	20
David Havili	Nelson	53	116	Isaac Salmon	Nelson	21	0
Sione Havili-Talitui	College Rifles [1]	16	25	Declan Smith	Stoke	2	0
Mitch Hunt	Stoke	44	342	Jamie Spowart	Marist	6	25
Will Jordan	Nelson	32	105	Liam Squire	Nelson	47	60
Uchida Keisuke	Overseas	9	0	Braden Stewart	Central	8	0
Tyrel Lomax	Stoke	29	10	Quinten Strange	Nelson	38	25
Andrew Makalio	Marist	41	50	Jordan Taufua	Wanderers	30	20
Samuel Matenga	Sydenham [2]	3	0				

1. Loaned from Auckland   2. Loaned from Canterbury   3. Loaned from Auckland

INDIVIDUAL SCORING

	Tries	Con	PG	DG	Points		Tries	Con	PG	DG	Points
Hunt	1	32	11	–	102	Nankivell	2	–	–	–	10
L. Faingaanuku	7	–	–	–	35	Squire	2	–	–	–	10
Jordan	7	–	–	–	35	Fox-Matamua	1	–	–	–	5
D. Havili	3	4	2	–	29	Penalty try	1	–	–	–	7
O'Malley	1	7	1	–	22	Frizell	1	–	–	–	5
Christie	4	–	–	–	20	Lomax	1	–	–	–	5
S. Havili	4	–	–	–	20	S. Moli	1	–	–	–	5
Roach	4	–	–	–	20	Norris	1	–	–	–	5
Spowart	4	–	–	–	20	Strange	1	–	–	–	5
Blackadder	3	–	–	–	15	Taufua	1	–	–	–	5
T. Faingaanuku	3	–	–	–	15	Penalty try	1	–	–	–	5
Makalio	3	–	–	–	15						
Aumua	2	–	–	–	10	**Totals**	**62**	**43**	**14**	**0**	**440**
Cirikidaveta	2	–	–	–	10						
Crockett	2	–	–	–	10	Opposition scored	14*	7	17	0	137

* includes one penalty try (7 points)

TASMAN 2019

	Wellington	Canterbury	Manawatu	Taranaki	Counties Manukau	North Harbour	Waikato	Auckland	Northland	Hawke's Bay	Auckland	Wellington	Totals
D. K. Havili (capt)	15	15	s	12	15	15	15	15	–	15	15	15	11
W.T. Jordan	14	14	15	15	14	14	14	14	15	–	14	14	11
J.W. Spowart	–	–	14	–	–	–	–	–	14	s	–	–	3
L.T. Faingaanuku	s	s	11	14	s	s	11	s	–	14	–	–	9
L.O.K.W.T. Faingaanuku	11	11	–	11	11	11	s	11	11	11	11	11	11
L.J.T. Aumua	13	13	–	13	13	13	13	13	s	13	13	13	11
F.M.A. Paea	–	–	s	s	–	s	s	s	13	s	s	s	9
T.P. O'Malley	s	–	12	s	s	10	10	–	s	–	s	s	9
A.P. Nankivell	12	12	13	–	12	12	12	12	12	12	12	12	11
M.J. Hunt (capt)	10	10	10	10	10	–	–	10	10	10	10	10	10
F.T. Christie	9	9	9	9	9	9	s	9	9	9	9	9	12
D. Smith	s	–	–	–	–	–	–	–	s	–	–	–	2
U. Keisuke	–	–	s	s	s	s	9	s	–	s	s	s	9
L.I.J. Squire	8	s	6	8	–	6	–	8	6	–	8	6	9
T.J. Fox-Matamua	–	–	–	–	–	–	–	–	8	–	–	–	1
J. Taufua	s	8	8	s	8	8	8	s	–	–	s	8	10
S.T. Havili-Talitui	7	7	–	7	7	7	s	7	7	8	7	7	11
B.J. Stewart	–	–	–	–	–	–	–	–	–	s	–	–	1
J.K. Norris	–	–	7	–	s	–	7	–	–	7	–	s	5
T.A. Cirikidaveta	s	–	–	–	–	s	s	s	5	–	s	s	7
E.J. Blackadder	6	6	s	6	6	s	6	6	s	6	6	–	11
S.M. Frizell	5	5	5	s	s	–	–	–	–	–	–	–	5
P.M. Parkinson	–	s	s	5	5	5	5	5	s	5	5	5	11
Q.J. Strange (capt)	4	4	4	4	4	4	4	4	4	4	4	4	12
S.I. Matenga	–	–	–	–	s	s	–	–	s	–	–	–	3
T.S. Lomax	3	3	3	3	–	–	3	3	3	3	3	3	10
I.A. Salmon	s	s	s	s	3	3	s	s	–	s	s	s	11
A. Moli	–	s	s	–	–	–	–	–	–	–	–	–	1
S. M.J. Prattley	s	s	–	–	–	–	–	–	–	–	–	–	2
R.C. Coxon	1	1	–	–	–	–	–	–	1	s	–	–	4
W.W.V. Crockett	–	–	–	1	s	s	s	1	s	1	s	s	9
T.G. Perry	–	–	1	s	1	1	1	s	–	–	1	1	8
A. Makalio	2	2	–	2	2	–	–	2	2	2	2	2	9
H.E. Roach	s	s	2	s	–	–	2	s	s	s	s	s	10
S. Moli	–	–	s	–	s	2	s	–	–	–	–	–	4

TASMAN TEAM RECORD, 2019

Played 12 Won 12 Lost 0 Points for 440 Points against 137

Date	Opponent	Location	Score	Tries	Con	PG	DG	Referee
August 10	Wellington (P)	Blenheim	45–8	L. Faingaanuku (2), Squire, Makalio, Lomax, D. Havili, Cirikidaveta	Hunt (5)			J.J. Doleman
August 18	Canterbury (P)	Christchurch	23–8	Aumua, L. Faingaanuku, Frizell	Hunt	Hunt (2)		N.P. Briant
August 24	Manawatu (cr)	Blenheim	64–3	Spowart (3), Squire, Roach, Taufua, Christie, Jordan, Blackadder, Norris	Hunt (4), O'Malley (3)			N.E.R. Hogan
September 1	Taranaki (cr)	New Plymouth	28–18	T. Faingaanuku (2), Makalio, Christie	Hunt	Hunt (2)		A.W.B. Mabey
September 6	Counties Manukau (P)	Pukekohe	36–0	Jordan (2), Aumua, S. Moli, L. Faingaanuku, Hunt (3), O'Malley	Hunt (3), O'Malley	Hunt		M.C.J. Winter
September 15	North Harbour (P)	Nelson	21–17	Christie, S. Havili, penalty try	O'Malley (2)			R.P. Kelly
September 21	Waikato (P)	Hamilton	35–26	Roach, D. Havili, Blackadder, Crockett	D. Havili (2), O'Malley	D. Havili (2), O'Malley		T.M.T. Cottrell
September 27	Auckland (P)	Nelson	40–0	Blackadder, Makalio, L. Faingaanuku, Christie, Roach, S. Havili	Hunt (5)			J.D. Munro
October 6	Northland (cr)	Nelson	52–6	Jordan (2), Cirikidaveta, S. Havili, Spowart, Crockett, O'Malley, Fox-Matamua	Hunt (6)			H.G. Reed
October 12	Hawke's Bay (cr)	Napier	47–28	L. Faingaanuku (2), S. Havili, T. Faingaanuku, Hunt, Nankivell, Roach	Hunt (4), D. Havili (2)			R.P. Kelly
October 19	Auckland (P, sf)	Blenheim	18–9	Strange, Nankivell	Hunt	Hunt (2)		J.J. Doleman
October 26	Wellington (P, f)	Nelson	31–14	Jordan (2), D. Havili	Hunt (2)	Hunt (4)		G.W. Jackson

THAMES VALLEY

2019 Status: Heartland Championship
Founded and affiliated 1922
President: K.J. (Kelly) Plummer
Chairman: G.S. (Grant) Dickey
Chief executive officer: Edmond Leahy (to July)
General Manager: Brett Barnham (from September)
Coach: M.W. (Matthew) Bartleet
Assistant coaches: D.P. (David) Harrison,
J.R. (Joe) Murray
Main ground: Paeroa Domain
Capacity: 3000
Colours: Gold and red

RECORDS

Highest attendance	7000	*Thames Valley v Auckland (Ranfurly Shield), 1989*
Most appearances	144	*B.C. Duggan, 1970–84*
Most points	665	*D.P. Harrison, 2004–15*
Most tries	42	*I.F. Campbell, 1981–94*
Most points in a season	127	*J.R. Reynolds, 2011*
Most tries in a season	14	*I.F. Campbell, 1988*
Most conversions in a season	30	*D.B. McCallum, 1995*
Most penalty goals in a season	25	*J.R. Reynolds, 2011*
Most dropped goals in a season	4	*T.E. Shaw, 1962*
		R.W. Kemp, 1968
Most points in a match	27	*D.B. McCallum v East Coast, 1995*
		M. Griffin v King Country, 2003
Most tries in a match	4	*I.F. Campbell v North Otago, 1990*
		G.A. Ellis v North Otago, 1994
		G.W. McLiver v Marlborough, 1995
Most conversions in a match	8	*G.A. Ellis v West Coast, 1994*
		M.A. Handley v North Otago, 1994
Most penalty goals in a match	7	*D.P. Harrison v Mid Canterbury, 2009*
	7	*J.R. Reynolds v East Coast, 2011*
	7	*R.D. Crosland v Wanganui, 2019*
Highest team score	86	*v North Otago, 1994*
Record victory (points ahead)	79	*86–7 v North Otago, 1994*
Highest score conceded	113	*v Northland, 1997*
Record defeat (points behind)	99	*14–113 v Northland, 1997*

Although not reaching the heights of 2018, it was still a very good season for Thames Valley. Following a very creditable performance in their Ranfurly Shield challenge against Otago, the Swamp Foxes went on to top the points table in the round robin of the Heartland Championship. In their first ever home semi-final for the Meads Cup Thames Valley narrowly lost to Wanganui in a tense match which was an excellent example of hard-fought finals' rugby.

In all of their matches Thames Valley provided stern opposition for their opponents. At Wanaka the Swamp Foxes led Otago 13–7 at halftime in their Ranfurly Shield challenge and did not lose their lead until the 52nd minute. With eight minutes to go they were still in touch at 16–26, and in their three Heartland losses the margins were only two, three and five points.

Fifteen members of the 2018 team were again selected and they were joined by two former Thames Valley representatives — Jason Laurich who had last appeared in 2014 and Kieran Ramage in 2015. The side was further strengthened by the addition of former Bay of Plenty representative, Matty Axtens as a loan player, and Fred Kei Fotofili, an Auckland B representative. A further 15 players made their first-class debut.

In an interesting move the Union gained the services of former French international Rafael Ibanez as a Resource coach. He proved to be popular and informative, and left New Zealand at the end of the season to take up the position of French national team manager. The team's coaches Matt Bartleet, David Harrison and Joe Murray produced effective game plans which were well executed by the team. There was an emphasis on running rugby and 27 of the team's 33 tries were scored by the backs with Harry Lafituanai scoring nine times in his eight games. The next highest try scorer was the flanker, Lalea Mau, with five.

Regan Crosland started the season covering the first five-eighth position but then moved to fullback for the final six games where he proved to be a very able custodian. He equalled the Heartland record for the most penalty goals in a match with the seven he kicked against Wanganui. Harry Lafituanai, Kieran Lee and Jason Laurich formed a fine trio of outside backs. Lafituanai used his speed to great effect and fully deserved his selection in the New Zealand Heartland XV against Samoa.

Sam McCahon started the season at centre but moved in one place when loan player Danny Kayes was injured, producing some outstanding rugby both on attack and defence. Reece Boughton again proved his worth to the team as a points' scorer by kicking 33 goals in eight games as well as scoring three tries. Ben Bonnar is now a very experienced player and contributed a great deal to the team on and off the field.

A change in occupation limited Brett Ranga's availability in 2019 but Matty Axtens, Fred Kei Fotofili and Lalea Mau developed into a very effective loose forward combination. A head injury in the club final resulted in Cameron Dromgool, the promising lock from 2018, not being available for any Heartland games. Sione To'a adapted very well to the lock position and proved to be a good partner for Connor McVerry who was named as Thames Valley's Player of the Year.

Mainly as a result of injuries, nine different players were used in the front row. Kieran Ramage showed his versatility by playing both as a hooker and prop. Glen McIntyre did not have the impact that he displayed in the previous year but his brother, Lance, proved to be a strong scrummager and Nico Aandeweil, on loan from Waikato, also showed much promise.

Brett Ranga (Captain), Harry Lafituanai and Glen McIntyre represented the New Zealand Heartland XV in the early season match against Samoa but only Ranga was chosen for the end of season matches and he again led the team against New Zealand Marist and the Vanua XV in Fiji.

Higher honours went to:
New Zealand Heartland: H.Lafituanai, G.McIntyre, B. Ranga

THAMES VALLEY REPRESENTATIVES 2019

Club	Games for Union	Points for Union		Club	Games for Union	Points for Union
Nico Aandewiel	Hautapu [2]	5	0	Kieran Lee	Melville [2]	18	45
Matiu Abraham	Thames	10	20	Ryan Leopold	Thames	5	0
Matthew Axtens	Mt Maunganui [3]	10	5	Keegan Lewis	Waihou	12	0
Cole Berridge	Thames	7	2	Laulea Mau	Thames	9	25
Ben Bonnar	Waihou	36	28	Sam McCahon	Waihou	28	30
Reece Boughton	Thames	18	188	Lance McIntyre	Waihou	8	0
Regan Crosland	Mercury Bay	10	37	Glen McIntyre	Waihou	25	10
Sergio De La Fuente	Thames	11	5	Connor McVerry	Mercury Bay	37	0
Cameron Dromgool	Te Aroha COB	11	5	Logan Mitchell	Hauraki North	5	0
Brandon Dromgool	Te Aroha COB	1	0	Bobby Motuliki	Thames	5	5
Lance Easton	Tairua	79	97	William Newbold	Hauraki North	1	0
Mathew Fisher	Hauraki North	21	0	Dan Peace	Waihou	2	0
Manawa Hill	Waihi Athletic	1	0	Kieran Ramage	Mercury Bay	36	10
Danny Kayes	Mt Maunganui [3]	5	20	Brett Ranga	Waihi Athletic	47	40
Fred Kei Fotofili	Thames	10	0	Sione To'a	Thames	8	0
Harry Lafituanai	Waihou	26	80	Brooklyn Toia	Paeroa	3	0
Jason Laurich [1]	Auckland University [4]	30	40	Sitiveni Tupou	Thames	25	10

1 Player of Origin   2 Waikato RU   3 Bay of Plenty RU   4 Auckland RU

INDIVIDUAL SCORING

	Tries	Con	PG	DG	Points		Tries	Con	PG	DG	Points
Boughton	3	17	16	–	97	Bonnar	1	–	–	–	5
Lafituanai	9	–	–	–	45	Motuliki	1	–	–	–	5
Crosland	2	3	7	–	37	Axtens	1	–	–	–	5
Mau	5	–	–	–	25	Berridge	–	1	–	–	2
Kayes	4	–	–	–	20						
Lee	3	–	–	–	15	**Totals**	**33**	**21**	**23**	**0**	**276**
Laurich	3	–	–	–	15						
Abraham	1	–	–	–	5	Opposition scored	27 *	17	16	0	224

* Includes one penalty try (7 points)

THAMES VALLEY 2019	Otago	Poverty Bay	Wanganui	Ngati Porou East Coast	North Otago	Wairarapa Bush	Mid Canterbury	South Canterbury	King Country	Wanganui (sf)	Totals
J.K. Laurich	15	15	15	15	11	14	14	14	14	13	10
W.T.K. Newbold	–	–	–	–	–	–	–	–	s	–	1
H.K. Lafituanai	14	14	–	14	14	13	13	13	13	–	8
K.F. Lee	11	11	–	11	–	11	11	11	11	11	8
M.J.K. Abraham	s	s	14	–	–	–	–	–	–	–	3
L.M.N. Mitchell	–	–	11	s	–	–	s	–	s	14	5
B. Motuliki	–	–	s	s	s	s	s	–	–	–	5
S.M. McCahon	13	13	13	13	13	12	12	12	12	12	10
D.J. Kayes	12	12	12	12	12	–	–	–	–	–	5
R. Boughton	10	10	–	–	10	10	10	10	10	10	8
R.D. Crosland	s	s	10	10	15	15	15	15	15	15	10
B.T. Bonnar	9	–	s	9	9	9	9	9	9	9	9
C.M. Berridge	s	s	–	s	s	–	s	–	s	s	7
M.A. Fisher	–	9	9	–	–	–	–	–	–	s	3
M.S. Axtens	8	8	6	8	8	8	8	8	8	8	10
D.J. Peace	–	s	8	–	–	–	–	–	–	–	2
F.G.A. Kei Fotofili	7	7	7	7	7	7	7	7	7	7	10
B.D. Ranga (capt)	6	6	–	–	–	–	–	4	6	4	5
L.F. Mau	s	–	s	6	6	6	6	6	s	6	9
L.C. Easton	s	–	–	–	–	–	–	s	s	s	4
R.F. Leopold	–	–	–	s	s	–	s	s	–	s	5
C.E. McVerry	5	5	5	5	5	5	5	5	5	5	10
C.M. Dromgool	4	–	–	–	–	–	–	–	–	–	1
S.T. To'a	s	s	4	4	4	4	4	–	4	–	8
B. Dromgool	–	4	–	–	–	–	–	–	–	–	1
K.S. Lewis	–	–	s	s	s	s	s	–	–	s	6
S.V. Tupou	3	3	s	3	s	s	3	s	s	3	10
L.T. McIntyre	1	–	1	1	1	1	1	–	s	s	8
S. De La Fuente	s	s	–	s	–	–	s	–	–	s	5
K.J. Ramage	–	1	2	s	s	2	2	1	1	1	9
N.F.J. Aandewiel	–	–	3	–	3	3	–	3	3	–	5
G.F. McIntyre	2	–	–	2	2	–	s	2	2	2	7
B.D.K.W. Toia	s	2	–	–	–	s	–	–	–	–	3
M.R. Hill	–	s	–	–	–	–	–	–	–	–	1

B.D. Ranga captained the first two games; C.E. McVerry captained in the five matches Ranga did not play; Ranga and B.T. Bonnar co-captained the final three games.

THAMES VALLEY TEAM RECORD, 2019

Played 10   **Won 6**   **Lost 4**   **Points for 276**   **Points against 224**

Date	Opponent	Location	Score	Tries	Con	PG	DG	Referee
July 13	Otago (RS)	Wanaka	21–41	Lafituanai (2)	Boughton	Boughton (3)		N. Watson
August 24	Poverty Bay (H)	Paeroa	15–17	Lee (2), Kayes				D. Waenga
August 31	Wanganui (H)	Wanganui	36–30	Abraham, Laurich, Mau		Crosland (7)		R. Mahoney
September 7	Ngati Porou East Coast (H)	Paeroa	43–15	Lafituanai (2), Kayes (2), Bonnar, Mau, Motuliki	Crosland (3), Berridge			A. Mabey
September 14	North Otago (H)	Oamaru	21–22	Boughton (2), Kayes	Boughton (3)			S. Curran
September 21	Wairarapa Bush (H)	Paeroa	29–23	Mau, Laurich, Lee, Axtens	Boughton (3)	Boughton		H. Reed
September 28	Mid Canterbury (H)	Ashburton	31–17	Laurich, Lafituanai, Mau, Boughton	Boughton (4)	Boughton		N. Webster
October 5	South Canterbury (H)	Paeroa	28–24	Crosland, Mau, Lafituanai	Boughton (2)	Boughton (3)		D. MacPherson
October 12	King Country (H)	Te Kuiti	37–15	Lafituanai (3), Crosland	Boughton (4)	Boughton (3)		M. Playle
October 19	Wanganui (MC sf)	Paeroa	15–20			Boughton (5)		D. Waenga

WAIKATO

2019 Status: Mitre 10 Cup Premiership
Founded 1909 as South Auckland.
Affiliated 1909. Name changed to Waikato 1921
President: D.I. (Duane) Monkley
Chairman: C.J.R. (Colin) Groves
Chief executive officer: B.M. (Blair) Foote
Coach: A.H. (Andrew) Strawbridge
Assistant coaches: R.Q. (Roger) Randle, N.J. (Nathan) White
Main ground: FMG Stadium Waikato, Hamilton
Capacity: 27,000
Colours: Red, yellow and black

RECORDS

Most appearances	148	*Ian Foster, 1985–98*
Most points	1604	*Matthew Cooper, 1990–99*
Most tries	70	*Bruce Smith, 1979–84*
Most points in a season	269	*Brett Craies, 1989*
Most tries in a season	17	*Bruce Smith, 1981*
Most conversions in a season	69	*Brett Craies, 1989*
Most penalty goals in a season	57	*Matthew Cooper, 1993*
Most dropped goals in a season	10	*John Boe, 1981*
Most points in a match	35	*Bruce Reihana v North Otago, 2000*
Most tries in a match	5	*Gary Major v East Coast, 1981*
		Bruce Smith v Nadi, 1982
		Bruce Smith v South Australia, 1983
		Ian Wilson v South Canterbury, 1984
		Rob Gordon v Southland, 1990
		Roger Randle v Poverty Bay, 1998
		Sitiveni Sivivatu v Auckland, 2004
Most conversions in a match	12	*Matthew Cooper v Wairarapa Bush, 1990*
		Glen Jackson v West Coast, 2000
Most penalty goals in a match	7	*Andrew Strawbridge v Wellington, 1985*
		Trent Renata v Bay of Plenty, 2013
Highest team score	121	*v Poverty Bay, 1998*
Record victory (points ahead)	121	*121–0 v Poverty Bay, 1998*
Highest score conceded	96	*v Harlequins Invitation XV, 1995*
Record defeat (points behind)	71	*25–96 v Harlequins Invitation XV, 1995*

Waikato harboured high hopes of making the Premiership semi-finals after winning promotion from the Championship in 2018.

While the Mooloos played some sparkling rugby at times due to their sharp backline, they also dropped three tight mid-season games and three crossover games in all, which hurt them badly in the final analysis. Sixth place, though comfortably outside the relegation zone, would have been disappointing to new head coach Andrew Strawbridge and his assistants Roger Randle and Nathan White.

And yet it all started on a high note, defeating Canterbury 31–28 on opening weekend in

Hamilton. There followed just two more victories and a draw in the Stan Thomas Memorial Trophy clash with Auckland as Waikato showed some naivety and set-piece brittleness under pressure. But if they could bottle the first halves against Auckland, North Harbour and Hawke's Bay and turn those encounters into wins, it could all have been so different.

Pre-season departures included Atu Moli (Tasman), Adam Burn (retired), Sam Caird (Northland), Jordan Manihera (USA), among others. Former Wallabies prop Toby Smith never recovered from concussion symptoms and subsequently retired.

New signings included Solomon Alaimalo (Tasman), who did not turn out until halfway through the campaign, veteran Api Naikatini (USA), Carlos Price (Wellington), Taleni Seu (Auckland), who also never recovered enough to play, and Antonio Shalfoon (Canterbury).

Furthermore, Ayden Johnstone appeared in just the opening two games and Haereiti Hetet just thrice, causing something of a loosehead prop crisis, which was eventually solved with the loan of New Zealand Under 20s rep Rob Cobb from Auckland.

Lock Laghlan McWhannell only came right to play in the final two rounds, so Waikato probably did well to call on just 37 players.

Rivez Reihana, in just his first year out of First XV rugby, showed his attacking qualities in either the No 10, 15 or 22 jerseys. Matty Lansdown had an injury-plagued season.

Wing Declan O'Donnell scored four tries and had moments of brilliance, like Waikato in general. Bailyn Sullivan was a sound finisher but was exposed defensively on occasion. Sevu Reece was not there to provide 14 tries, as he did in 2018.

Quinn Tupaea did not suffer from second year syndrome, playing every game, scoring seven tries and providing attacking thrust in the Mooloos midfield, combining nicely with captain Dwayne Sweeney. The latter raised his ton in emotional fashion in the Tasman clash in Hamilton. Despite a light club season, Sweeney was full value for his province in 2019.

Fletcher Smith continued his 2018 form, goalkicking accurately and running the cutter with authority. His partnership with consistent halfback Jack Stratton was critical to setting the Waikato backline alight.

Murray Iti was industrious at No 8, but the best display of the season in that jersey came from new All Black Luke Jacobson against Counties Manukau, where he showed why he is one of the hardest tacklers in the land.

His older brother Mitch Jacobson further enhanced his growing reputation at openside flanker. Rookies Hamilton Burr and Samipeni Finau were both solid value on the blindside.

Lock James Tucker was arguably the pick of the Waikato forwards, strong on the carry and good in the air.

Josh Iosefa-Scott and Sefo Kautai both shared the tighthead prop duties to good effect, while NZ Under 20s loosehead Ollie Norris was one of the Mitre 10 Cup's rookies of the season and not just for his scrummaging prowess.

Samisoni Taukei'aho was omnipresent in the No 2 jersey and his prolific try scoring rate — of 18 five-pointers in 33 matches — continued unabated. He crossed for six in 2019 and was tough to stop on the lineout drive.

Higher honours went to:
New Zealand: L. Jacobson, A. Lienert-Brown, S. Reece
New Zealand Under 20: G. Dyer, S. Finau, O. Norris, S. Parker, R. Reihana, J. Thompson, Q. Tupaea
Maori All Blacks: H. Hetet, F. Smith
New Zealand Sevens: T. Mikkelson

WAIKATO REPRESENTATIVES 2019

	Club	Games for Union	Points for Union
Solomon Alaimalo	Hamilton Marist	5	15
Tim Bond	Morrinsville Sports	19	0
Hamilton Burr	Hautapu	7	10
Tyler Campbell	University	26	25
Rob Cobb	Ponsonby[1]	5	0
Sam Cooper	Hamilton Old Boys	3	0
Samipeni Finau	Hamilton Old Boys	5	0
Haereiti Hetet	Otorohanga	8	0
Josh Iosefa-Scott	Melville	30	10
Murray Iti	Otorohanga	33	20
Luke Jacobson	Hautapu	11	0
Mitch Jacobson	Hautapu	46	15
Ayden Johnstone	Hautapu	23	0
Sefo Kautai	Hamilton Marist	31	5
Matty Lansdown	Fraser Tech	27	47
Sekope Lopeti-Moli	Hautapu	13	10
Laghlan McWhannell	Hautapu	15	5
Api Naikatini	Taupiri	6	0
Hugo Nankivell	Fraser Tech	1	0

	Club	Games for Union	Points for Union
Ollie Norris	Hautapu	10	5
Declan O'Donnell	Melville	42	70
Simon Parker	Hautapu	6	10
Carlos Price	Hamilton Marist	6	0
Rivez Reihana	Melville	9	2
Louis Rogers	University	6	5
Antonio Shalfoon	Te Awamutu Sports	5	0
Fletcher Smith	University	22	213
Jack Stratton	Hautapu	21	5
Bailyn Sullivan	Hamilton Marist	26	50
Dwayne Sweeney	Morrinsville Sports	103	134
Raniera Takarangi	Hamilton Old Boys	12	15
Samisoni Taukei'aho	Fraser Tech	33	90
Valynce Te Whare	Fraser Tech	3	5
James Thompson	Hautapu	2	0
James Tucker	Hamilton Marist	42	30
Newton Tudreu	Hamilton Marist	2	5
Quinn Tupaea	Hamilton Old Boys	21	70

1. Loaned from Auckland

INDIVIDUAL SCORING

	Tries	Con	PG	DG	Points
Smith	1	27	8	–	83
Tupaea	7	–	–	–	35
Taukei'aho	6	–	–	–	30
Sullivan	5	–	–	–	25
O'Donnell	4	–	–	–	20
Alaimalo	3	–	–	–	15
Burr	2	–	–	–	10
Parker	2	–	–	–	10
Penalty try	1	–	–	–	7
Iosefa-Scott	1	–	–	–	5
M. Jacobson	1	–	–	–	5

	Tries	Con	PG	DG	Points
Norris	1	–	–	–	5
Rogers	1	–	–	–	5
Te Whare	1	–	–	–	5
Tucker	1	–	–	–	5
Tudreu	1	–	–	–	5
Reihana	–	2	–	–	4
Sweeney	–	1	–	–	2
Totals	**38**	**30**	**8**	**0**	**276**
Opposition scored	43	30	14	0	317

WAIKATO 2019

	Canterbury	Bay of Plenty	Counties Manukau	Auckland	North Harbour	Hawke's Bay	Tasman	Otago	Taranaki	Wellington	Totals
T.A.J. Campbell	15	–	–	–	–	–	–	–	–	–	1
R.W.M. Reihana	s	15	15	15	15	10	–	s	15	15	9
M.R.T. Lansdown	–	–	–	s	s	15	s	s	–	–	5
D.P.T.K. O'Donnell	–	–	14	14	14	s	14	14	14	14	8
S. Alaimalo	–	–	–	–	–	11	15	15	11	11	5
V.C. Te Whare	11	11	s	–	–	–	–	–	–	–	3
B.W.M. Sullivan	14	14	11	11	11	14	11	11	s	s	10
N.W.K. Tudreu	–	s	s	–	–	–	–	–	–	–	2
Q.P.C. Tupaea	13	13	–	13	13	13	13	13	13	13	9
L.S. Rogers	s	s	13	–	s	–	–	–	s	s	6
D.W.H. Sweeney (capt)	12	12	12	12	12	12	12	12	12	12	10
F.H. Smith	10	10	10	10	10	s	10	10	10	10	10
C.T. Price	–	–	–	s	s	–	s	s	s	s	6
J.B. Stratton	9	9	9	9	9	9	9	9	9	9	10
R. Takarangi	s	s	s	–	–	s	–	–	–	–	4
M.E. Iti	8	8	s	8	8	8	s	s	8	8	10
L.B. Jacobson	–	–	8	–	–	–	–	–	–	–	1
H.A. Nankivell	–	–	–	–	–	–	–	–	7	–	1
M.L. Jacobson	7	7	7	7	7	s	7	7	–	7	9
S.C. Parker	s	s	–	–	–	s	8	8	–	s	6
H.R. Burr	6	6	6	s	s	7	6	–	–	–	7
S.U. Finau	–	–	–	6	6	–	–	6	s	6	5
J.F. Tucker	–	–	5	5	5	6	5	5	6	5	8
A.N. Naikatini	–	–	–	4	4	–	4	4	4	4	6
J.M.P. Thompson	5	5	–	–	–	–	–	–	–	–	2
L.E. McWhannell	–	–	–	–	–	–	–	–	s	s	2
T.O. Bond	4	4	4	–	s	4	s	s	5	–	8
A.J. Shalfoon	s	s	s	s	–	5	–	–	–	–	5
J.Z.A. Iosefa-Scott	3	3	s	s	s	s	s	s	s	s	10
S.S.V. Kautai	s	s	3	3	3	3	3	3	3	3	10
R.L. Cobb	–	–	–	–	–	s	1	1	1	1	5
O.M. Norris	s	s	1	1	1	1	s	s	s	s	10
C.A. Johnstone	1	1	–	–	–	–	–	–	–	–	2
H.B.G. Hetet	–	–	s	s	s	–	–	–	–	–	3
S.F. Taukei'aho	2	2	2	2	2	2	2	2	2	2	10
S.D. Cooper	–	s	–	–	–	s	s	–	–	–	3
S. Lopeti-Moli	–	–	s	s	–	–	–	–	s	s	4

WAIKATO TEAM RECORD 2019

Played 10 · Won 3 · Drew 1 · Lost 6 · Points for 276 · Points against 317

Date	Opponent	Location	Score	Tries	Con	PG	DG	Referee
August 10	Canterbury (P)	Hamilton	31–28	Iosefa-Scott, Tupaea, Burr, Te Whare	Smith (4)	Smith		D. Jones (Wales)
August 18	Bay of Plenty (cr)	Rotorua	14–40	Tupaea (2)	Smith (2)			D.J. Waenga
August 24	Counties Manukau (P)	Pukekohe	31–26	O'Donnell, Sullivan, Tudreu, Burr	Smith (4)	Smith		N.P. Briant
August 31	Auckland (P)	Hamilton	20–20	Norris, O'Donnell	Smith (2)	Smith (2)		R.P. Kelly
September 7	North Harbour (P)	Albany	36–38	Taukei'aho (2), Sullivan, Tupaea, Smith	Smith (4)	Smith		J.J. Doleman
September 12	Hawke's Bay (cr)	Hamilton	24–27	Tupaea (2), Alaimalo, Parker	Reihana (2)			N.P. Briant
September 21	Tasman (P)	Hamilton	26–35	Sullivan (2), O'Donnell	Sweeney	Smith (3)		T.M.T. Cottrell
September 29	Otago (RS, cr)	Dunedin	35–45	Taukei'aho (2), Parker, M. Jacobson, penalty try	Smith (4)			R.P. Kelly
October 6	Taranaki (cr)	Hamilton	38–19	Alaimalo (2), O'Donnell, Taukei'aho, Tupaea, Tucker	Smith (4)			J.D. Munro
October 12	Wellington (P)	Wellington	21–39	Taukei'aho, Sullivan, Rogers	Smith (3)			A.W.B. Mabey

WAIRARAPA BUSH

2019 Status: Heartland Championship
Founded: Wairarapa 1886 and original member 1892.
Bush 1890 and affiliated 1893. Amalgamated 1971.
President: B.A. (Brian) Weatherstone
Chairman: T.H.G. (Tim) Nathan (to Feb)
J.N. (Jason) Carruthers (from March)
Chief executive officer: A.R. (Tony) Hargood
Coach: J.R. (Joe) Harwood
Assistant coach: Deon van Deventer
Main ground: Memorial Park, Masterton
Capacity: 10,000
Colours: Green

RECORDS

Highest attendance	12,000	*Wairarapa Bush v British Isles, 1971 and 1983*
Most appearances	132	*G.K. McGlashan, 1971–83*
Most points	561	*P. Harding-Rimene, 1999–2008*
Most tries	43	*M.T. Foster, 1984–92*
Most points in a season	166	*G.M. Walters, 2012*
Most tries in a season	14	*S.F. Simanu, 2005*
Most conversions in a season	28	*M.F.C. Benton, 1987*
Most penalty goals in a season	34	*G.M. Walters, 2012*
Most dropped goals in a season	7	*K.W. Carter, 1985*
Most points in a match	26	*M.J. Berry v South Canterbury, 1995*
Most tries in a match	5	*S. Malatai v Buller, 2018*
Most conversions in a match	11	*M.F.C. Benton v Horowhenua, 1987*
Most penalty goals in a match	6	*J.T. Te Huia v Buller, 2010*
		G.M. Walters v South Canterbury, 2012
Highest team score	82	*v Horowhenua, 1987*
Record victory (points ahead)	73	*82–9 v Horowhenua, 1987*
Highest score conceded	96	*v Canterbury, 2006*
Record defeat (points behind)	86	*10–96 v Canterbury, 2006*

Wairarapa Bush's upward trend continued in 2019, making the top four where they lost their Meads Cup semi-final by just two points to eventual Heartland champions North Otago. The opening round win over Wanganui would have given the team a lot of confidence, a match in which the valued Bruce Steel Cup was also attained. Although well beaten by North Otago in the following game, there was only one further loss in the remaining round robin matches. Wairarapa Bush's ability to grind out victories was a feature, with five of the six wins being by 10 points or less.

A spirited effort was made against North Otago in the semi-final, much superior to that displayed in the round robin defeat. In the final minute of play Wairarapa Bush attacked from their own 22 into the opposition 22 but a knock on at a ruck was called and the fulltime whistle sounded.

The side's fitness was very good and injuries were few, but the major reason for the side's fortunes was the performance of the forward pack. It was a bigger one than last year and the scrum bettered the majority of the teams it encountered.

Sam Gammie, Bruce Kauika-Petersen and Max Tufuga formed a powerful front row at scrum time, appearing in every game together, with Sam Tufuga a capable reserve. All were mobile around the field, particularly Kauika-Petersen who stood out in this regard. Lachie McFadzean consistently proved his worth in the lineouts as well as applying himself in the tight play, and was partnered for most matches by Andrew McLean who provided good go-forward. James Goodger was the designated captain for the season; however, he suffered a shoulder injury playing for the NZ Heartland team against Samoa, but recovered in time for the final three matches.

Number eight Kirk Tufuga took over the captaincy in Goodger's absence and retained it upon his return. Johan Van Vliet was an outstanding loose forward, be it tackling on defence, winning the ball at the breakdown or on attack. Brad Campbell showed up well in defence, and only lost his starting place due to the return of Goodger.

At halfback Daryl Pickering had his best season. Tipene Haira started the season in fine form at first five-eighth, but Tim Priest was moved there from fullback for the final few matches. His play throughout the season was of a uniformly high standard, launching counter-attacks and goalkicking superbly, twice landing valuable last-minute penalty goals — against Thames Valley for a vital bonus point and against Buller for the win.

When Robbie Anderson's season ended with injury, Ueta Tufuga moved out to centre where he scored a superb try against Poverty Bay. Brock Price was then brought into second five-eighth, proving solid on defence and a strong runner. The two wings, 21-year-old Logan Flutey and 18-year-old Logan Hebenton-Prendeville, created problems for opposition defences with their speed and evasive ability, scoring seven and three tries respectively. Hebenton-Prendeville scored a brilliant try on debut against Wanganui. Inia Katia was unpredictable on occasions at fullback, always willing to try things which sometimes worked and sometimes didn't.

Of last year's local regulars Soli Malatai was in Wellington, Tavita Isaac was unavailable and Matt Henderson was injured. Johan Van Vliet arrived back in the province having last played for Wairarapa Bush in 2013 after which he then went overseas to play for the Netherlands, while Brent Wilson had previously represented North Harbour and English clubs Northampton and Newcastle Falcons.

In the match against Poverty Bay the union fielded three sets of brothers — Flutey (2), Priest (2) and Tufuga (4). All four Tufuga brothers appeared together in eight of the nine matches.

Higher honours went to:
New Zealand Heartland: T. Flutey, J. Goodger, L. McFadzean, T. Priest

WAIRARAPA BUSH REPRESENTATIVES 2019

	Club	Games for Union	Points for Union
Robbie Anderson	Eketahuna	31	31
Bryan Arnold	East Coast	9	0
Lewis Bush	Greytown	1	0
Jock Cameron	Gladstone	1	0
Brendon Campbell	Eketahuna	36	15
Logan Flutey	Martinborough	4	5
Tristan Flutey	Martinborough	15	40
Sam Gammie	Eketahuna	32	42
James Goodger	Marist	54	59
Tipene Haira	Martinborough	39	66
Cameron Hayton	Gladstone	54	86
Logan Hebenton-Prendeville	Gladstone	7	15
Inia Katia	Gladstone	80	60
Bruce Kauika-Petersen	Northern United [2]	9	10
Lachlan McFadzean	Carterton	53	0
Andrew McLean	Gladstone	80	26

	Club	Games for Union	Points for Union
Elijah-James Pakoti	Martinborough	25	5
Raniera Petersen	Greytown	5	5
Daryl Pickering	Carterton	21	10
Brock Price	Carterton	10	25
Alex Priest	Martinborough	1	0
Tim Priest	Martinborough	38	276
Sam Shaw	Eketahuna	5	0
Andrew Smith	Gladstone	21	12
Joseva Tako	Gladstone	2	0
Terongo Tekii	Carterton	1	0
Kirk Tufuga [1]	Massey University [3]	19	5
Max Tufuga	Eketahuna	18	0
Sam Tufuga	Massey University [3]	8	10
Ueta Tufuga	Massey University [3]	9	15
Johan Van Vliet	Eketahuna	39	45
Brent Wilson	Carterton	2	0

1 Player of Origin   *2 Wellington RU*   *3 Manawatu RU*

INDIVIDUAL SCORING

	Tries	Con	PG	DG	Points
T. Priest	–	13	9	–	53
T. Flutey	7	–	–	–	35
Haira	1	5	6	–	33
Price	4	–	–	–	20
Hebenton-Prendeville	3	–	–	–	15
U. Tufuga	3	–	–	–	15
Campbell	3	–	–	–	15
S. Tufuga	2	–	–	–	10
Kauika-Petersen	2	–	–	–	10
Van Vliet	1	–	–	–	5

	Tries	Con	PG	DG	Points
K. Tufuga	1	–	–	–	5
L. Flutey	1	–	–	–	5
Hayton	1	–	–	–	5
Petersen	1	–	–	–	5
Pickering	1	–	–	–	5
Totals	**31**	**18**	**15**	**0**	**236**
Opposition scored	*28*	*19*	*9*	*1*	*208*

WAIRARAPA BUSH 2019	Wanganui	North Otago	King Country	Poverty Bay	Thames Valley	Buller	Horowhenua Kapiti	Mid Canterbury	North Otago (sf)	Totals
I.S.T. Katia	15	15	15	15	–	–	15	15	15	7
A.M.F. Priest	–	–	–	s	–	–	–	–	–	1
L.J. Hebenton-Prendeville	14	14	–	–	14	14	14	14	14	7
T.R. Flutey	11	11	11	11	11	11	11	11	11	9
J.W. Cameron	–	–	14	–	–	–	–	–	–	1
R.J. Anderson	13	13	–	–	–	–	–	–	–	2
U.F. Tufuga	12	12	13	13	13	13	13	13	13	9
C.M. Hayton	–	–	–	s	–	–	s	–	–	2
B.O.J. Price	–	s	12	12	12	s	–	s	s	7
R.W. Petersen	–	–	–	–	s	12	12	12	12	5
T.T. Haira	10	10	10	10	10	10	s	s	s	9
T.C. Priest	–	s	14	15	15	10	10	10	10	8
D.J. Pickering	9	9	9	9	9	9	s	s	9	9
B.M. Arnold	s	s	s	s	s	s	9	9	s	9
K.M.S. Tufuga	8	8	8	8	8	8	8	8	8	9
J.J.A. Van Vliet	7	7	7	7	7	7	7	7	7	9
J.V. Tako	6	6	–	–	–	–	–	–	–	2
B.J.W. Campbell	–	s	s	6	6	6	6	s	s	8
L.H.A. Flutey	–	–	–	s	s	s	–	s	–	4
L.J.M. McFadzean	5	4	4	4	4	4	4	4	4	9
J.W.P.R. Goodger (capt)	4	–	–	–	–	–	s	6	6	4
A.D. Smith	s	5	–	–	–	s	s	–	–	4
S.J. Shaw	–	s	6	–	5	–	–	–	–	3
B.A. Wilson	–	–	5	s	–	–	–	–	–	2
A.R. McLean	–	–	s	5	–	5	5	5	5	6
S.P.I. Tufuga	3	3	3	s	s	s	–	s	s	8
M.H.P.V. Tufuga	1	1	s	3	3	3	3	3	3	9
S.G. Gammie	s	s	1	1	1	1	1	1	1	9
L.P. Bush	–	–	–	–	–	–	s	–	–	1
B.K. Kauika-Petersen	2	2	2	2	2	s	2	2	2	9
E.J. Pakoti	–	s	–	s	s	2	s	s	s	7
T.T.A. Tekii	–	–	s	–	–	–	–	–	–	1

Goodger captained the opening match; Anderson captained the second match; K.M.S. Tufuga captained the last seven matches.

WAIRARAPA BUSH TEAM RECORD, 2019

			Played 9	Won 6	Lost 3	Points for 236		Points against 208
Date	Opponent	Location	Score	Tries	Con	PG	DG	Referee
August 24	Wanganui (H) (BS)	Masterton	28–18	T. Flutey, S. Tufuga, Hebenton-Prendeville	Haira (2)	Haira (3)		M. Winter
August 30	North Otago (H)	Dunedin	11–25	Price		Haira (2)		S. Curran
September 7	King Country (H)	Masterton	37–31	T. Flutey (2), Campbell (2), Van Vliet, U. Tufuga	Haira, T. Priest	Haira		T. Cottrell
September 14	Poverty Bay (H)	Masterton	36–31	U. Tufuga (2), Campbell, K. Tufuga, Haira	T. Priest (4)	T. Priest		N. Webster
September 21	Thames Valley (H)	Paeroa	23–29	T. Flutey, L. Flutey	Haira, T. Priest	T. Priest (3)		H. Reed
September 28	Buller (H)	Westport	20–17	T. Flutey, Price	T. Priest (2)	T. Priest (2)		S.Curran
October 5	Horowhenua Kapiti (H) (BS)	Masterton	25–20	T. Flutey (2), Hebenton-Prendeville, Hayton	T. Priest	T. Priest		R. Gordon
October 12	Mid Canterbury (H)	Ashburton	31–10	Kauika-Petersen (2), Petersen, Hebenton-Prendeville, Price	T. Priest (3)			D. Moore
October 19	North Otago (MC sf)	Oamaru	25–27	Pickering, S. Tufuga, Price	T. Priest, Haira	T. Priest (2)		T. Cottrell

BS Bruce Steel Cup

WANGANUI

2019 Status: Heartland Championship
Founded 1888. Original member 1892
President: T.C. (Tom) Kilgariff
Chairman: J.M. (Jeff) Phillips
Chief executive officer: B.S. (Bridget) Belsham
Coach: J.M. (Jason) Caskey
Assistant coach: J.P. (Jason) Hamlin
Main ground: Cooks Gardens
Capacity: 15,000
Colours: Royal blue, black and white

WANGANUI

RECORDS

Highest attendance	6500	*Wanganui v Scotland, 1996*
Most appearances	146	*T.T.T. Olney, 1973–90*
Most points	980	*R.B. Barrell, 1963–77*
Most tries	48	*J.D. Hainsworth, 1984–95*
Most points in a season	184	*G.R.J. Lennox, 1994*
Most tries in a season	14	*H.S. Gordon, 1988*
	14	*P. Fetuia, 2006*
Most conversions in a season	44	*M.K. Davis, 2008*
Most penalty goals in a season	39	*R.B. Barrell, 1975*
Most dropped goals in a season	6	*L.T. Head, 1952*
Most points in a match	32	*K.H. Chase v East Coast, 1989*
Most tries in a match	6	*D.F. Philipson v Taranaki, 1919*
Most conversions in a match	10	*L.K. Harding v West Coast, 1993*
		G.R.J. Lennox v Buller, 1994
Most penalty goals in a match	6	*R.B. Barrell v Manawatu, 1971*
		R.B. Barrell v Taranaki, 1975
		M.K. Davis v East Coast, 2011
Highest team score	81	*v West Coast, 1993*
		v Buller, 1994
Record victory (points ahead)	77	*80–3 v King Country, 2017*
Highest score conceded	88	*v Taranaki, 2000*
Record defeat (points behind)	84	*0–84 v Taranaki, 1995*

With the loss of their opening three matches it was a certainty that Wanganui would have to win all remaining five round robin matches to have any chance of making the top four playoffs for the Meads Cup. In a dramatic run, where every match was a virtual elimination match, not only were the last five matches won, they were all won with a bonus point for four tries to finish fourth.

The winning streak started with Wanganui's best performance of the season against unbeaten West Coast where Wanganui had to play with 14 men for the last 74 minutes, having had a player red carded. Victory over Thames Valley in the semi-final was achieved in a hard-fought encounter, but in the final Wanganui had to concede to a North Otago team that was better on the day.

Wanganui had a smaller forward pack than the majority of teams in the Heartland Championship but still functioned well. Angus Middleton, Jamie Hughes, and captain Campbell Hart were outstanding loose forwards, gaining turnovers and exhibiting strong defence. A change was made at number eight after the defeat to Buller with Ezra Meleisea brought in on loan and he fitted in well.

Locks Sam Madams and Josh Lane (along with Campbell Hart) frequently gave Wanganui an edge in the lineouts. Madams was strong in all departments of tight play and well supported in this regard by Lane who had made just two previous appearances in 2017. Wiremu Cottrell, Gabriel Hakaraia, Kamipeli Latu and newcomer Raymond Salu were all capable props in the scrums and around the field. Latu, in particular, was impressive, Hakaraia missed the final through injury, and Salu had very good pace for a front row forward, scoring five tries. Roman Tutauha was his usual consistent self at hooker.

Lindsay Horrocks was in top form throughout the season, comparing favourably with any other halfback in the Heartland Championship. Craig Clare's season ended prematurely with injury with Dane Whale taking over at first five-eighth. Whale's goalkicking unfortunately was erratic and Nick Harding was brought into fullback to assume the goalkicking duties. He proved to be most reliable, including one superb penalty goal from inside his own half in the semi-final.

Twenty-year-old wing Vereniki Tikoisolomone had a sensational debut season, scoring 13 tries to easily top the Heartland Championship try scoring and finish just one short of the Championship record. Tyler Rogers-Holden scored four tries against Ngati Porou East Coast, and unluckily lost his place when Harding was brought in. Loan player Shai Wiperi was a steady utility. The midfield combinations tried in the first half of the season seemed problematical, being resolved with the arrival of loan player Amos Pogia to strike an effective partnership with Penijamini Nabainivalu.

Locals missing from last year's line-up included Cameron Crowley (retired), Harry Symes (injured), Simon Dibben (semi-retired), Kaveni Dabenaise (Northland) and Kameli Kuruyabaki (Manawatu). Of the arrivals Shae Wiperi had previously played for Horowhenua Kapiti, Josaia Bogileka had represented NZ Marist and Ezra Meleisea had been a Samoa Under 20 rep.

Higher honours went to:
New Zealand Heartland: C. Clare, C. Hart, L. Horrocks, P. Nabainivalu

WANGANUI REPRESENTATIVES 2019

	Club	Games for Union	Points for Union		Club	Games for Union	Points for Union
Josaia Bogileka	Marist	2	0	Josh Lane	Kaierau	11	5
Chris Breuer	Border	3	0	Kamipeli Latu	Border	42	25
Troy Brown	Ruapehu	15	0	Sam Madams	Marist	60	15
Craig Clare	Border	28	267	Ezra Meleisea	Auckland University [1]	7	10
Wiremu Cottrell	Taihape	13	5	Angus Middleton	Border	26	30
Cameron Davies	Kaierau	2	0	Penijamini Nabainivalu	Marist	17	10
Joseph Edwards	Kaierau	3	0	Karl Pascoe	Kaierau	2	0
Dylan Gallien	Taihape	12	5	Amos Pogia	Auckland University [1]	6	10
Gabriel Hakaraia	Ruapehu	24	10	Ethan Robinson	Kaierau	17	10
Nick Harding	Border	22	136	Tyler Rogers-Holden	Taihape	17	50
Campbell Hart	Ruapehu	33	21	Raymond Salu	Kaierau	8	25
Peter-Travis Hay-Horton	Taihape	8	5	Tom Symes	Border	4	5
Jack Hodges	Border	2	5	Renato Tikoisolomone	Border	19	11
Lindsay Horrocks	Border	70	87	Vereniki Tikoisolomone	Border	10	65
Bryn Hudson	Ngamatapouri	40	46	Roman Tutauha	Ruapehu	72	36
Jamie Hughes	Ruapehu	38	38	Dane Whale	Taihape	45	114
Samu Kabunavanua	Ngamatapouri	38	81	Shai Wiperi	Feilding OB Oroua [2]	10	5

1 Auckland RU   2 Manawatu RU

INDIVIDUAL SCORING

	Tries	Con	PG	DG	Points
V. Tikoisolomone	13	–	–	–	65
Harding	1	18	4	–	53
Whale	1	12	3	–	38
Horrocks	5	–	–	–	25
Salu	5	–	–	–	25
Rogers-Holden	5	–	–	–	25
Tutauha	2	–	–	–	10
Latu	2	–	–	–	10
Meleisea	2	–	–	–	10
Hughes	2	–	–	–	10
Pogia	2	–	–	–	10
Clare	–	2	–	1	7
Wiperi	1	–	–	–	5

	Tries	Con	PG	DG	Points
Nabainivalu	1	–	–	–	5
Kubunavanua	1	–	–	–	5
Hart	1	–	–	–	5
Cottrell	1	–	–	–	5
Hay-Horton	1	–	–	–	5
Robinson	1	–	–	–	5
Lane	1	–	–	–	5
Middleton	1	–	–	–	5
Totals	**49**	**32**	**7**	**1**	**333**
Opposition scored	26*	15	23	1	232

* includes two penalty tries (14 points)

WANGANUI 2019

	Wairarapa Bush	Thames Valley	Buller	West Coast	Ngati Porou East Coast	North Otago	King Country	Horowhenua Kapiti	Thames Valley (sf)	North Otago (f)	Totals
N.R. Harding	s	15	–	s	s	s	15	15	15	15	9
T.T.H. Rogers-Holden	15	9	11	11	11	11	–	s	s	s	9
V.W. Tikoisolomone	14	14	14	14	14	14	14	14	14	14	10
T.O.H. Symes	11	11	–	–	–	–	–	–	–	–	2
K.A. Pascoe	–	–	–	s	–	–	s	–	–	–	2
S.T. Wiperi	13	13	15	15	15	15	11	11	11	11	10
A.I. Pogia	–	–	–	s	13	13	13	13	13	13	6
P.B. Nabainivalu	12	–	13	13	–	12	12	12	12	12	8
T.J. Brown	s	–	12	12	12	s	s	s	s	s	9
E. Robinson	–	12	–	s	13	s	s	s	s	s	8
J. Bogileka	–	s	s	–	–	–	–	–	–	–	2
C.D. Clare	10	–	10	–	–	–	–	–	–	–	2
D.J. Whale	s	10	s	10	10	10	10	10	10	10	10
L.D. Horrocks	9	–	9	9	9	9	9	9	9	9	9
C.T. Davies	–	s	–	–	s	–	–	–	–	–	2
B.D. Hudson	8	8	8	–	–	–	–	–	–	–	3
R. Tikoisolomone	–	s	–	s	–	s	–	–	–	–	3
E.F. Meleisea	–	–	–	8	8	8	8	8	8	8	7
A.H. Middleton	7	–	–	–	–	s	s	7	7	7	6
C.J. Hart (capt)	6	–	6	6	6	6	6	6	6	6	9
S.M. Kubunavanua	s	6	–	–	s	–	–	s	s	s	6
C.E. Breuer	s	s	s	–	–	–	–	–	–	–	3
J.N. Hughes	–	7	7	7	7	7	7	s	s	s	9
P.T. Hay-Horton	5	–	5	5	5	–	s	–	–	–	5
S.A. Madams	4	4	4	4	s	4	4	4	4	4	10
J.R.C. Lane	–	5	s	s	4	5	5	5	5	5	9
J.I. Hodges	–	s	–	–	–	–	–	–	–	–	1
W.H. Cottrell	3	s	–	3	–	3	–	–	–	3	5
G.T.E. Hakaraia	1	1	3	–	3	1	3	3	3	3	8
R. Salu	s	–	1	1	s	–	s	s	s	s	8
K.T. Latu	–	3	s	s	1	s	1	1	1	1	9
R.B.K. Tutauha	2	2	2	2	2	2	2	2	2	2	10
J.T. Edwards	s	s	–	–	–	s	–	–	–	–	3
D.R. Gallien	–	–	s	s	2	s	–	s	s	s	7

R.B.K. Tutauha captained the match Hart did not appear in.

WANGANUI TEAM RECORD, 2019

Played 10 Won 6 Lost 4 Points for 333 Points against 232

Date	Opponent	Location	Score	Tries	Con	PG	DG	Referee
August 24	Wairarapa Bush (H) (BS)	Masterton	18–28	Tutauha, Horrocks	Whale	Whale	Clare	M. Winter
August 31	Thames Valley (H)	Wanganui	30–36	Harding, Tutauha, Whale, Wiperi	Harding (2)	Harding (2)		R. Mahoney
September 7	Buller (H)	Westport	21–22	V. Tikoisolomone (2), Salu	Clare (2), Whale			N. Webster
September 14	West Coast (H)	Wanganui	36–18	Rogers-Holden, Salu, Nabainivalu, Horrocks, Latu	Whale (4)	Whale		C. Stone
September 21	Ngati Porou East Coast (H)	Wanganui	67–24	Rogers-Holden (4), V. Tikoisolomone (2), Salu (2), Meleisea, Hughes, Kubunavanua	Whale (3), Harding (3)			S. Curran
September 28	North Otago (H)	Oamaru	27–22	Horrocks, Hart, Cottrell, V. Tikoisolomone	Whale (2)	Whale		T. Cottrell
October 5	King Country (H)	Wanganui	57–19	V. Tikoisolomone (2), Hughes, Meleisea, Pogia, Horrocks, Hay-Horton, Robinson, Lane	Harding (6)			V. Ringrose
October 12	Horowhenua Kapiti (H)	Levin	38–15	V. Tikoisolomone (3), Latu, Pogia, Salu	Harding (3), Whale			N. Hogan
October 19	Thames Valley (MC sf)	Paeroa	20–15	V. Tikoisolomone (2)	Harding (2)	Harding (2)		D. Waenga
October 26	North Otago (MC f)	Oamaru	19–33	Horrocks, Middleton, V. Tikoisolomone	Harding (2)			A. Mabey

BS Bruce Steel Cup

WELLINGTON

2019 Status: Mitre 10 Cup Premiership
Founded 1879. Original member 1892
President: M.P. (Murray) Blandford
Chairman: I.G. (Iain) Potter
Chief Executive Officer: M.G. (Matt) Evans
Coach: C.J. (Chris) Gibbes
Assistant coaches: C.S. (Cory) Jane, L. (Leo) Crowley
Main ground: Westpac Stadium, Wellington
Capacity: 34,500
Colours: Black

RECORDS

Most appearances	173	*Graham Williams, 1964–76*
Most points	909	*Allan Hewson, 1977–86*
Most tries	105	*Bernie Fraser, 1975–86*
Most points in a season	199	*John Gallagher, 1987*
Most tries in a season	24	*Bernie Fraser, 1981*
Most conversions in a season	47	*Jackson Garden-Bachop, 2017*
Most penalty goals in a season	38	*Jon Preston, 1994*
Most dropped goals in a season	7	*John Dougan, 1971*
Most points in a match	34	*David Holwell v Bay of Plenty, 2002*
Most tries in a match	7	*Nigel Geany v Wanganui, 1991*
Most conversions in a match	14	*Peter O'Shaughnessy v Horowhenua, 1988*
		Simon Mannix v Rosario, 1995
Most penalty goals in a match	7	*Jackson Garden-Bachop v North Harbour, 2016*
Highest team score	118	*v Rosario, 1995*
Record victory (points ahead)	101	*118–17 v Rosario, 1995*
Highest score conceded	82	*v Otago, 1998*
Record defeat (points behind)	72	*10–82 v Otago, 1998*

It was a funny old season for the Wellington Lions — scratchy at the start, often brilliant in the second half and again, for the seventh time, suffering the heartache of finishing runners-up in the Premiership decider.

There was a six-game winning streak to savour and only three defeats, but the Lions scored fewer tries and conceded more than in 2018, when they only reached the semi-finals.

It looked like being a long campaign when Tasman put them to the sword to the tune of 45–8 on opening weekend. But slowly, inexorably, they righted the ship, having the better of a draw in Napier, and winning grinds against Canterbury, Counties Manukau (for the Jonah Lomu Memorial Trophy) and Bay of Plenty.

Then the Lions moved up several cogs, smashing Otago and Northland to bookend an impressive 34–15 victory at Eden Park for the Fred Lucas Memorial Trophy.

The loss to North Harbour seemed like an aberration, though they were exposed at the scrum and made too many unforced handling errors. It mattered not, as Wellington reeled off two impressive wins in the capital, against Waikato to close the regular season, and Canterbury in the semi-final.

Even in the final, while the 31–14 margin seems clearcut to Tasman, Wellington was very competitive, and was possibly unlucky to have a Pepesana Patafilo try ruled out by the TMO.

Personnel losses from 2018 included Sam Lousi (UK), Jeffery Toomaga-Allen (UK), Isaia Walker-Leawere (Hawke's Bay) and Thomas Waldrom (retired).

Gains were Auckland midfielder/wing Vince Aso, who has played several seasons for the Hurricanes, outside back Connor Garden-Bachop coming home from Canterbury, and prop Sef Fa'agase from Canterbury, though he was technically a loan player out of Otago.

There was a consistency about Wellington's selection, nine players appearing in every game, while Billy Proctor (one of four Wellington NZ Under 20 reps), James Blackwell and Xavier Numia started all 12 matches.

Trent Renata again proved his utility value, often off the bench. Wes Goosen, after starring at fullback in 2018, was most effective on the right wing, scoring a team-high six tries, and the Lions missed him when out with a hamstring in the playoffs. He would have brought up his 50 games milestone, but will now have to wait until 2020. Ben Lam had some injuries which prevented his full output, but Patafilo was effective as a backup.

At either centre or wing, Vince Aso produced the goods and five tries. Peter Umaga-Jensen tied up the No 12 jersey with his power and solid defence, keeping his twin brother Thomas on the pine.

Jackson Garden-Bachop is very much at home at this level, scoring a Mitre 10 Cup high 116 points and running the cutter with authority. He struck up a cohesive partnership with halfback Kemara Hauiti-Parapara.

Teariki Ben-Nicholas came of age at No 8, carrying with venom and lifting his work rate. Captain Du'Plessis Kirifi proved himself the best No 7 in the competition, with his all-action rugby, an effective fetcher and a menace both with and without the ball. Mateaki Kafatolu commanded the No 6 jersey with a consistent season.

Vaea Fifita played six games in three positions but has yet to show he is consistently All Blacks class. Josh Furno was an accurate lineout forward, while Blackwell drove standards in the pack with his work rate.

Alex Fidow's season bore the fruits of one who thrived when shaking off injury, and he continued his high try-scoring rate, with five. Xavier Numia was an admirable foil on the other side of the scrum, playing well all season and scoring a fine solo try against Hawke's Bay.

In Dane Coles' absence, Asafo Aumua cemented his spot, tightening his game. His hit in the final on Leicester Faingaanuku was thunderous. James O'Reilly was a reliable replacement, bringing up 50 games (in all) at this level.

Higher honours went to:

New Zealand:	D. Coles, V. Fifita, T. Perenara, A. Savea
New Zealand Maori:	J. Garden-Bachop
New Zealand Under 20:	N. Ah Kuoi, T. Plumtree, B. Proctor, K. Uluilakepa

WELLINGTON REPRESENTATIVES 2019

	Club	Games for Union	Points for Union
Naitoa Ah Kuoi	Marist-St Pat's	11	0
Vince Aso	Paremata-Plimmerton	11	25
Asafo Aumua	Avalon	42	95
Teariki Ben-Nicholas	Old Boys-University	28	15
James Blackwell	Petone	42	35
Connor Collins	Hutt Old Boys-Marist	9	0
Sef Fa'agase	N/A[1]	7	0
Alex Fidow	Oriental-Rongotai	30	75
Vaea Fifita	Wellington	42	65
Losi Filipo	Northern United	9	10
Josh Furno	Western Suburbs	11	5
Connor Garden-Bachop	Northern United	4	0
Jackson Garden-Bachop	Northern United	64	516
Wes Goosen	Old Boys-University	49	120
Kemara Hauiti-Parapara	Tawa	34	30
Mateaki Kafatolu	Petone	28	15

	Club	Games for Union	Points for Union
Du'Plessis Kirifi	Northern United	27	30
Ben Lam	Tawa	28	70
Xavier Numia	Oriental-Rongotai	19	10
James O'Reilly	Hutt Old Boys-Marist	38	15
Sitiveni Paongo	Tawa	21	25
Piri Paraone	Petone	1	0
Pepesana Patafilo	Tawa	10	10
Morgan Poi	Old Boys-University	4	0
Billy Proctor	Marist-St Pat's	25	25
Trent Renata	Oriental-Rongotai	26	51
Luke Tau'alupe	Oriental-Rongotai	2	0
Galu Taufale	Poneke	31	25
Kaliopasi Uluilakepa	Petone	10	5
Peter Umaga-Jensen	Wainuiomata	22	25
Thomas Umaga-Jensen	Wainuiomata	23	55
Campbell Woodmass	Northern United	3	0

1. *Loaned from Otago*

INDIVIDUAL SCORING

	Tries	Con	PG	DG	Points
J. Garden-Bachop	–	28	19	1	116
Goosen	6	–	–	–	30
Aso	5	–	–	–	25
Fidow	5	–	–	–	25
Kirifi	4	–	–	–	20
Hauiti-Parapara	4	–	–	–	20
Proctor	4	–	–	–	20
Renata	1	7	–	–	19
Blackwell	3	–	–	–	15
P. Umaga-Jensen	3	–	–	–	15
Aumua	2	–	–	–	10
Lam	2	–	–	–	10

	Tries	Con	PG	DG	Points
Patafilo	2	–	–	–	10
Ben-Nicholas	1	–	–	–	5
Furno	1	–	–	–	5
Kafatolu	1	–	–	–	5
Numia	1	–	–	–	5
Paongo	1	–	–	–	5
T. Umaga-Jensen	1	–	–	–	5
Totals	**47**	**35**	**19**	**1**	**365**
Opposition scored	*46*	*28*	*11*	*–*	*319*

WELLINGTON 2019	Tasman	Hawke's Bay	Canterbury	Counties Manukau	Bay of Plenty	Otago	Auckland	Northland	North Harbour	Waikato	Canterbury	Tasman	Totals
C.C. Garden-Bachop	15	–	–	–	–	–	–	–	–	s	s	s	4
T.W.K. Renata	–	s	15	s	15	10	s	s	s	15	15	15	11
L.F. Filipo	–	–	s	–	–	–	–	–	–	–	–	–	1
W.S. Goosen	14	14	–	14	14	14	14	14	14	14	–	–	9
M.B. Lam	11	–	–	s	11	11	11	11	–	–	14	14	8
B.D. Proctor	13	15	13	15	13	15	15	15	15	13	13	13	12
V.T. Aso	s	13	14	13	–	13	13	13	13	11	11	11	11
P. Patafilo	–	11	11	11	s	–	s	s	11	s	s	s	10
P.I.J. Umaga-Jensen	12	12	12	12	12	12	12	–	12	12	12	12	11
T.N.M. Umaga-Jensen	–	s	s	–	s	s	–	12	s	–	–	–	6
J.K. Garden-Bachop	10	10	10	10	10	s	10	10	10	10	10	10	12
P.P.K. Paraone	s	–	–	–	–	–	–	–	–	–	–	–	1
K.H. Hauiti-Parapara	9	9	9	9	s	9	9	9	9	9	9	9	12
C.D. Collins	s	s	s	s	9	s	–	–	–	s	s	s	9
C.T.J. Woodmass	–	–	–	–	–	–	s	s	s	–	–	–	3
T.G. Ben-Nicholas	8	8	8	8	8	8	s	8	s	8	8	8	12
V.T.L. Fifita	–	–	–	–	–	–	8	6	8	4	4	4	6
D.P.A. Kirifi (capt)	7	7	7	7	7	7	7	7	7	7	7	7	12
G.F. Taufale	s	s	s	–	s	s	–	–	–	s	–	–	6
M. Kafatolu	6	6	6	6	6	6	6	s	6	6	6	6	12
L.K. Tau'alupe	–	s	–	s	–	–	–	–	–	–	–	–	2
J. Blackwell	5	5	5	5	5	5	5	5	5	5	5	5	12
N.S. Ah Kuoi	4	–	s	s	s	s	s	4	s	s	s	s	11
R.J. Furno	s	4	4	4	4	4	4	s	4	–	s	s	11
A.F. Fidow	3	3	3	3	3	3	3	–	3	3	3	3	11
S.F. Fa'agase	s	s	s	–	s	–	–	3	–	–	s	s	7
S.F. Paongo	–	–	–	–	–	s	s	s	s	s	s	s	7
M.P. Poi	s	s	s	s	–	–	–	–	–	–	–	–	4
X.S. Numia	1	1	1	1	1	1	1	1	1	1	1	1	12
K. Uluilakepa	s	–	–	s	s	s	s	s	s	s	–	–	8
J.P. O'Reilly	2	s	s	s	s	s	s	s	s	s	s	s	12
A.J. Aumua	–	2	2	2	2	2	2	2	2	2	2	2	11

WELLINGTON TEAM RECORD, 2019

			Played 12	Won 8	Drew 1	Lost 3	Points for 365		Points against 319
Date	Opponent	Location	Score	Tries		Con	PG	DG	Referee
August 10	Tasman (P)	Blenheim	8–45	Fidow			J. Garden-Bachop		J.J. Doleman
August 16	Hawke's Bay (cr)	Napier	27–27	Ben-Nicholas, Aso, Hauiti-Parapara, Numia		J. Garden-Bachop (2)	J. Garden-Bachop		Frank Murphy (Ireland)
August 23	Canterbury (P)	Wellington	23–22	Aso, Kirifi, Fidow		J. Garden-Bachop	J. Garden-Bachop (2)		B.D. O'Keeffe
August 29	Counties Manukau (P)	Wellington	29–22	Goosen, Blackwell, B. Proctor, Kirifi		J. Garden-Bachop (3)	J. Garden-Bachop		N.J. Webster
September 7	Bay of Plenty (cr)	Rotorua	16–15	P. Umaga-Jensen		J. Garden-Bachop	J. Garden-Bachop (3)		T.N. Griffiths
September 15	Otago (cr)	Wellington	54–24	Goosen (3), Fidow (2), P. Umaga-Jensen, Hauiti-Parapara, Lam		Renata (7)			D.J. Waenga
September 22	Auckland (P)	Auckland	34–15	B. Proctor (2), P. Umaga-Jensen, Kafatolu		J. Garden-Bachop (4)	J. Garden-Bachop (2)		J.J. Doleman
September 28	Northland (cr)	Wellington	57–36	Kirifi (2), Patafilo (2), Aso, T. Umaga-Jensen, Furno, Goosen		J. Garden-Bachop (7)	J. Garden-Bachop		G.W. Jackson
October 4	North Harbour (P)	Albany	34–42	Blackwell, Aso, Hauiti-Parapara, Paongo, Goosen		J. Garden-Bachop (3)	J. Garden-Bachop		T.M.T. Cottrell
October 12	Waikato (P)	Wellington	39–21	Aumua (2), Aso, Proctor, Hauiti-Parapara		J. Garden-Bachop (4)	J. Garden-Bachop (2)		A.W.B. Mabey
October 19	Canterbury (P, sf)	Wellington	30–19	Renata, Blackwell, Lam		J. Garden-Bachop (3)	J. Garden-Bachop (2)	J. Garden-Bachop	G.W. Jackson
October 26	Tasman (P, f)	Nelson	14–31	Fidow			J. Garden-Bachop (3)		G.W. Jackson

WEST COAST

2019 **Status:** Heartland Championship
Founded 1890. Affiliated 1893
President: D.P. (David) Walklin
Chairman: M.J. (Mike) Meehan
Chief executive officer: Mike Connors
Coach: S.J. (Sean) Cuttance
Assistant coach: K.G. (Kyle) Parker
Main ground: John Sturgeon Park, Greymouth
Capacity: 8000
Colours: Red and white

RECORDS

Highest attendance	10,000	*West Coast–Buller v British Isles, 1959*
Most appearances	101	*M.T. Mudu, 2004–2019*
Most points	712	*M.A. Foster, 1992–2000*
Most tries	27	*K.J.J. Beams, 1965–78*
Most points in a season	176	*M.A. Foster, 1999*
Most tries in a season	9	*P.A. Teen, 1975*
Most conversions in a season	20	*M.A. Foster, 1999*
Most penalty goals in a season	38	*M.A. Foster, 1999*
Most dropped goals in a season	9	*A.P. O'Regan, 1987*
Most points in a match	24	*M.A. Foster v Horowhenua Kapiti, 1999*
Most tries in a match	4	*K. McNee v Buller, 1964*
		F.P. O'Donnell v Buller, 1970
		P.A. Teen v Nelson Bays, 1975
		R.J. Stanton v Ngati Porou East Coast, 2018
Most conversions in a match	6	*L.T. Martyn v Golden Bay-Motueka, 1933*
Most penalty goals in a match	6	*P.W. Hutchison v East Coast, 1991*
		C.N. Simpson v South Canterbury, 2007
Highest team score	62	*v Ngati Porou East Coast, 2018*
Record victory (points ahead)	42	*45–3 v Golden Bay-Motueka, 1933*
Highest score conceded	128	*v Canterbury, 1992*
Record defeat (points behind)	128	*0–128 v Canterbury, 1992*

West Coast came agonisingly close to winning a national trophy for the first time in 2019. Hosting South Canterbury in the final of the Lochore Cup, in difficult conditions, the side was behind 5–17 at halftime. Turning with the strong wind now behind them, West Coast gained the lead at 19–17 but ultimately went down 19–23, with a definite try-scoring chance missed with a couple of minutes left.

Six wins were achieved in the round robin but a top four place for the Meads Cup eluded the team, finishing fifth to contest the Lochore Cup. These six round robin wins are the most by a team in the history of the Heartland Championship not making the top four. The lack of bonus points cost West Coast in this regard, as a bonus point for scoring four tries was only achieved in three of the eight round robin matches. Too often promising attacking phases were not turned into tries. An unexpected poor performance against Buller was also costly. However, a win was achieved against eventual champions North Otago.

The strength of the team lay in its very efficient forward pack which was probably the biggest in the Heartland Championship and seldom bettered. Numerous scrum penalties were gained and lineout drives were a feature of their play. Daniel Davis, captain Troy Tauwhare and Tyler Kearns formed a powerful front row at scrum time and all were mobile around the field, with Dan Foord a very able backup. Sam Liebezeit and his locking partner Tumama Tu'ulua excelled in the lineouts and were always involved in the tight play.

Amenatave Tukana, Josh Tomlinson, Steve Soper and Brad Tauwhare were an outstanding set of loose forwards who exhibited a high work rate contesting the breakdown, using their size and speed to good advantage there and around the field with carries and defensive work.

The backline contributed just 12 of the 41 tries scored. Throughout the season Jesse Pitman-Joass and Kahu Tamatea both showed a good tactical appreciation in directing the team forward, and halfback Jarrod Ferguson served them both very well. The loss of fullback Todd Struthers to injury in the third match was keenly felt as he was in very good form and his attacking flair was missed. The dependable Sione Holani provided his usual hard running and strong defending at second five-eighth. Peter Te Rakau had some useful games and Jade Coleman looked a promising wing in his three appearances.

Regulars missing from last year's team included Duncan Wood, Tom Reekie, Oliver Dimmick, Kevin Curtis (all in Canterbury) and Regan Stanton (playing rugby league in Canterbury). Of the newcomers Nick Thomson had played for Canterbury and Hawke's Bay, Kahu Tamatea had represented Poverty Bay, East Coast and the NZ Heartland team, and Trent Lawn is a NZ Universities rep.

A Seddon Shield challenge to Marlborough sub-union was lost 17–20 on 3 August.

Higher honours went to:
New Zealand Heartland: S. Holani, T. Kearns, S. Liebezeit, T. Tauwhare

WEST COAST REPRESENTATIVES 2019

	Club	Games for Union	Points for Union		Club	Games for Union	Points for Union
Jade Coleman	Blaketown	3	15	Jesse Pitman-Joass [2]		17	26
Daniel Davis	South Westland	27	10	Steven Soper	Grey Valley	26	50
Ben Eder	Waimea OB [2]	1	0	Todd Struthers	Kiwi	6	39
Jarrod Ferguson	Kiwi	31	20	Kahu Tamatea	Grey Valley	9	0
Dan Foord	Kiwi	25	10	Brad Tauwhare	Kiwi	48	60
Sione Holani	Grey Valley	12	10	Troy Tauwhare	Kiwi	73	64
Tyler Kearns	Grey Valley	14	0	Peter Te Rakau	Kiwi	27	25
Trent Lawn [1]	Canterbury University [3]	5	0	Nick Thomson [4]		8	5
Alex Lean	Grey Valley	9	0	Josh Tomlinson	Wests	19	20
Sam Liebezeit	Grey Valley	10	25	Tumama Tu'ulua	Auckland University [5]	15	10
Sean McClure	Kiwi	60	114	Amenatave Tukana	Belfast [3]	34	51
Jared Mitchell	Wests	10	10	Boris Van Bruchem	New Brighton [3]	1	5
Maleli Mudu	Marist	101	146	Jasyn Van Vliet	Kiwi	11	0
Nick Muir	Kiwi	5	0	Logan Winter	Kiwi	23	16
Eric Munro	Blaketown	7	0				

1 Player of Origin   2 Tasman RU   3 Canterbury RU   4 Arrived from Overseas   5 Auckland RU

INDIVIDUAL SCORING

	Tries	Con	PG	DG	Points
McClure	1	9	4	–	35
Struthers	–	10	3	–	29
Pitman-Joass	3	4	–	1	26
Liebezeit	5	–	–	–	25
Tomlinson	4	–	–	–	20
Soper	4	–	–	–	20
B. Tauwhare	3	–	–	–	15
T. Tauwhare	3	–	–	–	15
Tukana	3	–	–	–	15
Coleman	3	–	–	–	15
Mitchell	2	–	–	–	10
Winter	2	–	–	–	10

	Tries	Con	PG	DG	Points
Penalty Try	1	–	–	–	7
Bruchem	1	–	–	–	5
Davis	1	–	–	–	5
Thomson	1	–	–	–	5
Holani	1	–	–	–	5
Tu'ulua	1	–	–	–	5
Ferguson	1	–	–	–	5
Foord	1	–	–	–	5
Totals	**41**	**23**	**7**	**1**	**277**
Opposition scored	41	29	9	0	290

WEST COAST 2019

	King Country	Horowhenua Kapiti	Mid Canterbury	Wanganui	North Otago	Ngati Porou East Coast	Buller	South Canterbury	Poverty Bay (sf)	South Canterbury (f)	Totals
T.R. Struthers	15	15	15	–	–	–	–	–	–	–	3
A.J. Lean	14	12	14	14	14	13	13	–	12	13	9
N.J. Muir	11	11	11	–	–	11	11	–	–	–	5
N.J. Thomson	s	14	s	11	11	–	s	–	s	s	8
P.E. Te Rakau	–	–	–	–	15	14	14	14	14	14	6
J.D. Coleman	–	–	–	–	–	–	–	11	11	11	3
M.T. Mudu	–	–	–	–	–	–	–	s	–	–	1
S.R. McClure	13	13	13	13	12	15	15	13	13	s	10
S.F. Holani	12	–	12	12	13	12	12	–	–	12	7
E.M. Munro	s	s	–	s	s	–	s	12	s	–	7
J. Pitman-Joass	10	10	10	15	10	10	10	15	15	15	10
K.D. Tamatea	–	s	s	10	s	s	s	10	10	10	9
J.C. Ferguson	9	9	9	s	s	9	9	9	9	9	10
J.V. Mitchell	s	s	s	9	9	s	s	s	s	s	10
A.V. Tukana	8	8	8	8	8	8	8	8	8	8	10
J.P. Tomlinson	7	7	7	s	6	s	s	6	6	6	10
B.G. Tauwhare	6	6	6	6	–	6	6	–	s	s	8
S.G. Soper	s	s	s	7	7	7	7	7	7	7	10
L.H.F. Winter	s	s	s	s	s	s	–	s	s	–	8
S.P. Liebezeit	5	5	5	5	5	5	5	5	5	5	10
B.P. Van Bruchem	4	–	–	–	–	–	–	–	–	–	1
J.P. Van Vliet	s	s	–	4	s	s	–	–	–	–	5
T.N.L. Tu'ulua	–	4	4	–	4	4	4	4	4	4	8
B.J. Eder	–	–	–	s	–	–	–	–	–	–	1
D.J. Davis	3	3	s	s	3	3	3	3	3	3	10
T.J. Kearns	1	1	1	1	1	1	1	1	1	1	10
D.M. Foord	s	s	3	3	s	s	s	s	s	s	10
T.K. Tauwhare (capt)	2	–	2	2	2	2	2	2	2	2	9
T.B.F. Lawn	–	2	–	s	–	s	s	–	s	–	5

T.J. Kearns captained the match T.K. Tauwhare did not appear in.

WEST COAST TEAM RECORD, 2019

Played 10   **Won 7**   **Drew 0**   **Lost 3**   **Points for 277**   **Points against 290**

Date	Opponent	Location	Score	Tries	Con	PG	DG	Referee
August 24	King Country (H)	Greymouth	56–27	Tomlinson (2), Van Bruchem, Davis, B. Tauwhare, Pitman-Joass, Thomson, Mitchell	Struthers (5)	Struthers (2)		N. Webster
August 31	Horowhenua Kapiti (H)	Levin	27–21	Tomlinson, Liebezeit, Pitman-Joass	Struthers (3)	Struthers	Pitman-Joass	J. Bredin
September 7	Mid Canterbury (H)	Greymouth	43–41	Liebezeit (2), T. Tauwhare, Holani, Mitchell, Winter, Tukana	Struthers (2), McClure, Pitman-Joass			J. Munro
September 14	Wanganui (H)	Wanganui	18–36	B. Tauwhare, Liebezeit	McClure	McClure (2)		C. Stone
September 21	North Otago (H)	Greymouth	18–17	T. Tauwhare, Tu'ulua	McClure	McClure (2)		J. Bredin
September 28	Ngati Porou East Coast (H)	Ruatoria	21–19	Tukana, Penalty Try, Soper	McClure (2)			R. Gordon
October 5	Buller (H)	Greymouth	7–47	Soper	McClure			M. Playle
October 12	South Canterbury (H)	Timaru	27–24	Ferguson, McClure, Soper, Coleman, Winter	McClure			T. Griffiths
October 19	Poverty Bay (LC sf)	Greymouth	41–35	Coleman (2), Liebezeit, Pitman-Joass, Tomlinson, B. Tauwhare, Soper	McClure (2), Pitman-Joass			H. Reed
October 27	South Canterbury (LC f)	Greymouth	19–23	Tukana, T. Tauwhare, Foord	Pitman-Joass (2)			T. Cottrell

RANFURLY SHIELD 2019

In the opening defence Heartland side Thames Valley led 13-0 after 30 minutes, and Otago did not get in front until Ben Miller's try in the 52nd minute.

Rebecca Mahoney became the first woman to referee a Ranfurly Shield match when she controlled the North Otago challenge.

The Shield changed hands in Otago's final defence of the season. Canterbury opened the scoring with an 11th minute Brett Cameron penalty goal and led all the way, although it was an 80th minute Cameron penalty goal that made the game safe at 35-25 for the challengers. Three tries resulted from intercepts in the match - two to Canterbury and one to Otago. It was Canterbury's 14th consecutive win over Otago, stretching back to 2006.

Canterbury's sole defence, against North Harbour, was the 700th match for the Ranfurly Shield.

Results

Otago

693	July 13	v Thames Valley	Wanaka	won	41-21
694	July 26	v North Otago	Oamaru	won	49-14
695	August 17	v Southland	Dunedin	won	41-22
696	August 30	v Manawatu	Dunedin	won	37-20
697	September 8	v Taranaki	Dunedin	won	35-27
698	September 29	v Waikato	Dunedin	won	45-35
699	October 5	v Canterbury	Dunedin	lost	25-35

Canterbury

700	October 13	v North Harbour	Christchurch	won	31-25

First and most recent Ranfurly Shield match	Played	Won	Lost	Drawn as		Points	
				holder	challenger	for	against
Auckland (1904–2015)	203	158	39	5	1	5849	2220
Bay of Plenty (1920–2015)	24	2	22	–	–	328	655
Buller (1907–2001)	12	–	11	–	1	36	328
Bush (1927–1968)	7	–	7	–	–	41	285
Canterbury (1904–2019)	197	150	40	6	1	5742	2561
Counties Manukau (1958–2017)	33	7	24	–	2	566	872
East Coast (1953–2013)	7	–	7	–	–	22	430
Golden Bay-Motueka (1958)	1	–	1	–	–	8	56
Hawke's Bay (1905–2018)	96	61[1]	31	3	1	2038	1474
Horowhenua Kapiti (1914–2015)	10	–	10	–	–	92	563
King Country (1922–2016)	20	–	20	–	–	120	664
Manawatu (1914–2019)	39	14	24	–	1	531	765
Manawhenua (1927–1929)	6	3	3	–	–	84	110
Marlborough (1908–2005)	20	7	13	–	–	245	539
Mid Canterbury (1933–2017)	15	–	15	–	–	111	620
Nelson (1924–1959)	2	–	2	–	–	17	66
Nelson Bays (1973–2005)	6	–	6	–	–	46	334
North Harbour (1986–2019)	21	4	17	–	–	487	639
North Otago (1938–2019)	14	–	14	–	–	92	787
Northland (1935–2015)	48	17	30	1	–	715	1053
Otago (1904–2019)	90	43	44	1	2	1466	1321
Poverty Bay (1911–2018)	17	–	17	–	–	78	790
South Auckland (1911)	1	–	1	–	–	5	21
South Canterbury (1920–2006)	26	3	23	–	–	273	821
Southland (1906-2019)	74	30	41	–	3	1099	1439
Taranaki (1906-2019)	101	49	46	3	3	1661	1653
Tasman (2008-2012)	2	–	2	–	–	60	75
Thames Valley (1951-2019)	16	–	16	–	–	97	706
Waikato (1932-2019)	109	67	38	3	1	3173	1713
Wairarapa (1905–1969)	30	12	17	–	1	431	504
Wairarapa Bush (1973–2015)	9	–	9	–	–	67	491
Wanganui (1907–2018)	31	–	30	–	1	239	985
Wellington (1904–2014)	98	50	42	1	5	1545	1343
West Coast (1932–2000)	15	–	15	–	–	107	588

[1] *Includes Hawke's Bay's 1927 winning challenge against Wairarapa that was subsequently overturned on protest.*

HIGHEST WINNING MARGIN BY A SHIELD HOLDER
134 points   Auckland 139   North Otago 5 at Oamaru 1993

HIGHEST WINNING MARGIN BY A CHALLENGER
45 points   Waikato 52   North Harbour 7 at Albany 2007

INDIVIDUAL PERFORMANCES

Most matches	57	*G.J. Fox, Auckland*
Most points	932	*G.J. Fox, Auckland*
Most tries	53	*T.J. Wright, Auckland*
Most conversions	233	*G.J. Fox, Auckland*
Most penalty goals	142	*G.J. Fox, Auckland*
Most dropped goals	14	*R.H. Brown, Taranaki;*
		D. Trevathan, Otago
Most goals from a mark	3	*J.H. Dufty, Auckland*
Most points in a match	40	*J.J. Kirwan, Auckland v North Otago, 1993*
Most tries in a match	8	*J.J. Kirwan, Auckland v North Otago, 1993*
Most conversions in a match	12	*B.M. Craies, Auckland v Horowhenua,1986;*
		G.J. Fox, Auckland v Nelson Bays, 1991;
		G.W. Jackson, Waikato v West Coast, 2000;
		L.H. Munro, Auckland v North Otago, 2008
Most penalty goals in a match	7	*R.M. Deans, Canterbury v Counties, 1984*
		C.J. McIntyre, Canterbury v Wellington, 2003
Most dropped goals in a match	3	*R.H. Brown, Taranaki v Wanganui, 1964;*
		R.H. Brown, Taranaki v North Auckland, 1964;
		G.P. Coffey, Canterbury v Auckland, 1990;
		A.P. Mehrtens, Canterbury v Southland, 1995

WINNING CHALLENGES

Canterbury	16	Taranaki	6	Marlborough	1
Auckland	15[1]	Otago	6	Manawatu	1
Waikato	11	Northland	4	Bay of Plenty	1
Wellington	10	Wairarapa	3	North Harbour	1
Southland	7	South Canterbury	2	Counties Manukau	1
Hawke's Bay	6[2]	Manawhenua	1		

[1] *Auckland were also the first holders, presented the Shield in 1902 by the NZRFU for having the best record that year.*
[2] *Includes Hawke's Bay's 1927 winning challenge against Wairarapa that was subsequently overturned on protest.*

TENURES

Longest tenure	Challenges resisted		Shortest tenure		Days
Auckland	1985–93	61	Hawke's Bay	2013	6
Auckland	1960–63	25	Wellington	1963	7
Canterbury	1982–85	25	Waikato	2007	7
Hawke's Bay	1922–27	24	Otago	2013	9
Auckland	1905–13	23	Auckland	1972	10
Canterbury	1953–56	23	North Auckland	1960	11
Canterbury	2000–03	23	Wairarapa	1950	14
Hawke's Bay	1966–69	21	South Canterbury	1950	14
Waikato	1997–00	21	Auckland	1952	14

North Auckland resisted one challenge;
the other unions were defeated by the first challenger.

HAPPENINGS

Yvette Corlett, who died in Auckland on April 13, 2019, aged 89, was one of New Zealand's greatest Olympians and in the judgement of most sports historians, the female equivalent of the triple Olympic gold medallist, Peter Snell. As Yvette Williams, she was the first New Zealand woman to win an Olympic gold medal, the long jump at Helsinki in 1952. She remained the country's only woman to win Olympic gold for another 40 years. She also won a gold medal at the 1950 Empire Games in Auckland and a further three at the 1954 Empire Games in Vancouver. Though her fame came from her track and field prowess, she also was a top basketballer and netballer. She also had a love of rugby and a considerable family connection with the game. One of her sons, Peter, played many Auckland premier club seasons with Pakuranga and as a midfield back represented Auckland in 22 games in 1980–82 and made two appearances for Auckland B. Her brother, Roy Williams, also a gold medallist in the decathlon at the 1966 Commonwealth Games in Jamaica, was a leading sports journalist and for many years was a rugby reporter for the *Auckland Star*, covering many All Blacks and international tours. Remarkably, despite her illustrious sporting career and involvement with the community, she was never made a Dame, which for many was an inexplicable oversight. *(Contributed by Lindsay Knight)*

•   •   •

There was a first in October's trans-Tasman schools international in Hamilton. For the first time since NZ Schools and their Australian counterparts started playing in 1978, two siblings were in opposing sides. NZ Schools fielded tighthead prop Tiaan Tauakipulu (St Kentigern College), who performed strongly, while off the bench for Australian Schools/Under 18s came loose forward Keynan Tauakipulu, who attends St Peter's Lutheran College in Brisbane. Keynan, who was previously at St Kentigern, won the family bragging rights as Australia edged the home side 18–14 to take the Trans-Tasman Shield for the first time since 2012. The boys' father Fraser, who played club rugby for Tamaki and Manukau in Auckland, and Dijon in France, was sideline cheering his boys on and said it was an emotional occasion. An older brother, front-rower Bronson Fotuali'i-Tauakipulu, has already played one test for Manu Samoa, against Wales in 2017. The younger Tauakipulus have open eligibility for New Zealand, Australia, Tonga and Samoa, the latter their mother's heritage.

•   •   •

When it was announced that the All Blacks game against Italy at RWC had been cancelled and would be treated as a 0–0 draw, Geoff Miller, former co-editor of the *Almanack*, was thrown into a panic. Match "abandoned" okay, match "not played" would do. "No result" would be satisfactory but the humiliation associated with a 0–0 draw would mean:
- That the All Blacks had been kept to nil in a test match for the first time since 1964, and by Italy.
- That Italy had halted the All Blacks' winning run at Rugby World Cup.
- It would lower the All Blacks' average winning score and average tries per match.
- Personal records such as winning sequences would all have to start at zero again.
- And more . . .

Some hurried correspondence to Japan saw a favourable response from World Rugby of "no result" arrive on a New Zealand desk that evening which meant an unblemished record and no change to New Zealand's world ranking.

•   •   •

TRY SCORING ANALYSIS

TOTAL TRIES BY WORLD CUP CYCLE	New Zealand	Australia	England	France	Ireland	South Africa	Wales
2000–03	226	147	199	143	173	127	135
2004–07	219	184	115	152	123	194	166
2008–11	200	155	92	94	99	126	112
2012–15	209	132	115	81	109	143	92
2016–19	287	164	176	99	171	148	120

AVERAGE TRIES PER TEST BY WORLD CUP CYCLE	New Zealand	Australia	England	France	Ireland	South Africa	Wales
2000–03	5.0	3.3	4.2	2.9	3.7	2.8	2.9
2004–07	4.6	3.7	2.8	3.1	2.8	3.6	3.4
2008–11	3.6	2.8	2.0	2.1	2.2	2.6	2.2
2012–15	3.9	2.4	2.5	1.8	2.5	3.0	1.9
2016–19	5.4	3.2	3.5	2.2	3.5	2.9	2.3

- In the current RWC cycle 2016–19 the All Blacks scored 287 tries. They are the only team in history to have scored more than 200 tries in a four-year period.
- The All Blacks have averaged 5.4 tries per game over the last four years. England, with 4.2 nearly 20 years ago, is the only non-New Zealand team to have averaged better than four tries per test.
- Note that the All Blacks' 5.4 tries average is better than 50 per cent superior to second-placed England.
- Not included in the tables but still relevant is that the All Blacks have been top try-scorers in the world for each of the last ten years.
- Last year it was noted that Beauden Barrett was the only goal-kicker in history to averaged better than three conversions per test — it helps if you score more than five tries per match.
- Surprising how modest are the French and Wales figures over this 20-year period.
- The four-year bracket coincides with some recycling of coaches worldwide.

• • •

When Brad Slater played for the Chiefs against the Sunwolves on March 2 at Hamilton, it was only his second first-class match. His sole previous first-class appearance had been for Taranaki in 2017. A total of 19 players★ have made their first-class debut in New Zealand rugby when playing for a Super Rugby team:

- Brad Fleming, Crusaders v Chiefs, 1996
- Xavier Rush, Blues v Northern Transvaal, 1997
- Finau Maka, Hurricanes v Northern Transvaal, 1997
- Sam Johnstone, Crusaders v Chiefs, 1998
- Tanner Vili, Hurricanes v Reds, 2000
- Nick Collins, Chiefs v Crusaders, 2001
- James Arlidge, Blues v Cats, 2001
- Paul Williams, Highlanders v Chiefs, 2003
- Mose Tuiali'i, Blues v Bulls, 2003
- Onosa'i Tololima-Auva'a, Blues v Bulls, 2006

- Steve Alfeld, Crusaders v Lions, 2008
- Ben Lam, Blues v Stormers, 2012
- Albert Nikoro, Blues v Brumbies, 2012
- Anton Lienert-Brown, Chiefs v Bulls, 2014
- Jordan Payne, Chiefs v Rebels, 2014
- Akira Ioane, Blues v Chiefs, 2015
- Airi Hunt, Blues v Crusaders, 2015
- Sam McNicol, Hurricanes v Chiefs, 2015
- Rameka Poihipi, Crusaders v French Barbarians, 2018

*New Zealand-based players only. It does not include players the Super Rugby clubs have signed from overseas or from rugby league to play for them.

Tanner Vili is on the list even though he played for Samoa during 1999, including at the World Cup that year. He was a New Zealand-based player who played for Auckland club Teachers-Eastern that won the Gallaher Shield in both 1998 and 1999.

•   •   •

Southland's 42–14 victory over Counties Manukau on September 21 ended a run of 27 consecutive Mitre 10 Cup defeats dating back to 2016.
 In first division/Mitre 10 Cup rugby, the biggest runs of consecutive losses are:

30	Northland	2003–04–05–06
27	Southland	2016–17–18–19
19	Southland	1990–95–97
19	Northland	2014–15–16
18	Northland	1992–98–99
15	Hawke's Bay	1992–93–2006

Promotion-relegation matches are excluded from the above table as they were not first division fixtures. One of the teams involved in those matches would always be a second division team.

•   •   •

The most consecutive losses each of the 14 Mitre 10 Cup unions have suffered in first division/Mitre 10 Cup rugby are:

Auckland	4	2013–14
Bay of Plenty	12	2013–14
Canterbury	5	1991–92
Counties Manukau	9	2001, 06
Hawke's Bay	15	1992–93, 2006
Manawatu	11	1988, 2006
North Harbour	10	2011–12
Northland	30	2003–04–05–06
Otago	8	1979–80
Southland	27	2016–17–18–19
Taranaki	13	1994–95–96
Tasman	8	2007–08
Waikato	10	2017–18
Wellington	10	2013–14

● ● ●

Hawke's Bay Tui's fullback Cortez Te Pou made her first-class debut against Northland on September 7. The 18-year-old Karamu High School student scored four tries for Hawke's Bay in their 64–31 win. Her four tries equalled the women's record of most tries on first-class debut, joining some illustrious names:

Louisa Wall, New Zealand v Australia Capital Territory, 1994
Vanessa Cootes, New Zealand v Australia, 1995
Dianne Kahura, New Zealand v Germany, 1998
Tammi Wilson, New Zealand v Germany, 1998
Kylie Shankland, Canterbury B v Nelson Bays, 2001
Cortez Te Pou, Hawke's Bay v Northland, 2019

Prior to 1999 when the national championship was introduced only Black Ferns fixtures held first-class status.

● ● ●

The New Zealand Defence Force team — the Defence Blacks — participated in the third International Defence Rugby Competition, the military equivalent of the World Cup. This tournament is always held just prior to the Rugby World Cup, and the 2019 event was held in Japan during September 11–23. Nations participating were: Australia, Fiji, France, Georgia, Korea, Japan, Papua New Guinea, New Zealand, Tonga and United Kingdom.

The Defence Blacks results were:
1st Round: Bye
Quarter-final: v Australia Defence Force, won 47–35
Semi-final: v Royal Fijian Military Forces, lost 7–50
3rd/4th playoff: v French Military Forces, lost 5–10

The team's matches at the 2011 and 2015 competitions carried first-class status, but their matches at the 2019 tournament do not as no match reports were supplied to NZ Rugby by team management for consideration. The squad was:

Jaxon Tagavaitau (captain — Army), Jody Allen (civilian — Hawke's Bay), Taine Aupori (Army), Ethan Bartle (Air Force), Jimmy Berghan (Army), Robert Brocklehurst (Army), Logan Broughton (Army), Sam Cadman (Air Force), James Coburn (Army), Jared Deal (Army), Zane Douglas (Navy), Vesi Luatua (Army), Trent Luka (Navy), Tejay Oliver (Army), Brent Pope (Army), Hamish Pyne (Navy), Tama Ropati (Army), Devon Scott (Air Force), Troy Sherriff (Army), Tiatoa Teariki (Navy), Hakarangi Tichborne (Army), Opeti Tuipulotu (Navy), Cole Waaka (Air Force), Reece White (Army), Tainui Woodmass (Army), Aidan Woodward (Army).
Manager: Simon Vissers (Navy). *Head Coach:* Tim Kareko (Army).

● ● ●

Four players were invited to play for the London-based Barbarians club's women's team against a Wales XV at Cardiff on November 30. The Barbarians won 29–15. The four were: Stephanie Te Ohaere-Fox (captain, hooker), Eloise Blackwell (lock), Charmaine McMenamin (No 8, 1 try) and Ruahei Demant (first five-eighth). This was the first women's team to be fielded by the club.

• • •

Sarah Hirini, captain of the successful Black Ferns Sevens team, became the first female recipient of the Tom French Cup which since 1949 has been awarded annually to the Maori player of the year.

• • •

Emily Hsieh joined NZ Rugby as Women's Referee Development Manager in September 2019. It is not often an experienced referee from overseas joins the national panel. Emily was born in Massachusetts, USA, in 1990, her parents having immigrated from Taiwan. She played rugby for Brown University 2008–12 and then, briefly, for Boston club Beantown Rugby until taking up the whistle in 2013. In 2014 she attended the South Africa Referee Academy. In 2018 she was appointed to the World Series referee panel and officiated at the USA, Dubai, Canada and France rounds of the 2018/19 series. For the 2019/20 series Emily was a referee at the USA round in October and is scheduled to do three rounds in 2020.

• • •

Sir Peter Snell, triple Olympic champion, who died during the year, played rugby at Mt Albert Grammar School, being in the first XV for three years. He was halfback in 1955, second five-eighth 1956 and first five-eighth and wing in 1957. His father George represented Bush against Nelson in 1924. George played on the wing and was from Eketahuna club.

• • •

The loss in December of Jazz Muller and Sam Strahan (see Obituaries) leaves Ian Kirkpatrick the sole survivor of the 11 forwards who played in the four tests during the 1967 tour of Britain and France. Kirkpatrick played in the test against France, his test debut. Strahan died suddenly just four days after delivering the eulogy at Muller's funeral. Kirkpatrick attended Strahan's funeral which was held in front of the grandstand at the Kimbolton ground. The ranks of surviving All Blacks who played during coach Fred Allen's unbeaten era 1966–68 are thinning.

• • •

The 2019 ASB Rugby Awards were held at Sky City Convention Centre, Auckland, on December 12. The winners are recorded elsewhere in this publication, but we note here the finalists for some of the awards (winner in bold).

- Sky Television Fans Try of the Year — Sheree Hume (Otago Spirit), Stuart Leach (Rotorua BHS), **TJ Perenara** (All Blacks).
- Charles Monro Rugby Volunteer of the Year — Sue Mitchell (Taranaki), Kevin Pulley (Wellington), **Ian Spraggon** (Bay of Plenty).
- New Zealand Rugby Referee of the Year — Rebecca Mahoney, Ben O'Keeffe, **Paul Williams**.
- New Zealand Rugby Age Grade Player of the Year — Zach Gallagher (Canterbury), **Fletcher Newell** (Canterbury), Tupou Vaa'i (Taranaki).
- Mitre 10 Heartland Championship Player of the Year — **Josh Clark** (North Otago), Campbell Hart (Wanganui), Robbie Smith (North Otago).
- Richard Crawshaw Memorial All Blacks Sevens Player of the Year — Dylan Collier, Andrew Knewstubb, **Tone Ng Shiu**.
- Black Ferns Sevens Player of the Year — Kelly Brazier, Sarah Hirini, **Tyla Nathan-Wong**.
- Duane Monkley Medal — Gareth Evans (Hawke's Bay), Salesi Rayasi (Auckland), Fletcher Smith (Waikato), **Chase Tiatia** (Bay of Plenty).
- Fiao'o Faamausili Medal — **Chelsea Bremner** (Canterbury), Ayesha Leti-I'iga (Wellington), Patricia Maliepo (Auckland).

- Investec Super Rugby Player of the Year — Scott Barrett (Crusaders), **Ardie Savea** (Hurricanes), Brad Weber (Chiefs).
- Tom French Memorial Māori Player of the Year — Ash Dixon, **Sarah Hirini**, TJ Perenara.
- ASB National Coach of the Year — Andrew Goodman (Tasman, Crusaders) and Clarke Dermody (Tasman), Kieran Kite (Canterbury Women), **Scott Robertson** (Crusaders).
- ASB New Zealand Coach of the Year — Steve Hansen (All Blacks), Glenn Moore (Black Ferns), **Allan Bunting and Cory Sweeney** (Black Ferns Sevens).
- Black Ferns Player of the Year — Kendra Cocksedge, Ayesha Leti-I'iga, **Charmaine McMenamin**.
- All Blacks Player of the Year — Beauden Barrett, Anton Lienert-Brown, **Ardie Savea**.
- adidas National Team of the Year — Canterbury Women, **Crusaders**, Tasman.
- adidas New Zealand Team of the Year — All Blacks, Black Ferns, **Black Ferns Sevens**.

2019 SEASON'S STATISTICS

LEADING SCORERS IN ALL FIRST-CLASS MATCHES IN NEW ZEALAND AND FOR NEW ZEALAND TEAMS OVERSEAS

(Record: 519, G.J. Fox, 1989 in 32 games, 2 Tries, 122 Con, 88 PG, 1 DG)

	Teams	M	Tries	Con	PG	DG	Total
R. Mo'unga	Crusaders/New Zealand	24	9	74	23	–	262
J.R. Ioane	Highlanders/Otago/New Zealand	23	5	56	19	–	194
B.J. Barrett	Hurricanes/New Zealand	22	7	46	15	–	172
O.W. Black	Blues/NZ Maori/Manawatu	28	3	42	22	–	165
J.M. Debreczeni	Chiefs/Northland	17	4	36	12	–	128
J.K. Garden-Bachop	Hurricanes/Wellington	15	–	32	20	1	127
R.L. Smith	North Otago/NZ Heartland	14	3	27	17	–	120
M.J. Hunt	Crusaders/Tasman	20	2	37	11	–	117
H.R.J. Plummer	Blues/Auckland	24	2	25	17	–	111
B.D. Cameron	Crusaders/Canterbury	16	1	35	11	–	108
J.M. Barrett	Hurricanes/New Zealand	23	8	15	11	–	103

LEADING TRY-SCORERS

(Record: 36, J.J. Kirwan, 1987 in 32 games)

Tries	Games		Teams
19	21	S.L. Reece	Crusaders/New Zealand
19	24	K.H. Laumape	Hurricanes/New Zealand/Manawatu
15	20	W.T. Jordan	Crusaders/Tasman
14	23	W.T. Goosen	Hurricanes/Wellington
14	15	J.A. McKay	Highlanders/Canterbury
13	10	V.W. Tikoisolomone	Wanganui
12	20	R.E. Ioane	Blues/New Zealand/Auckland
12	30	D.K. Havili	Crusaders/Tasman/UK Barbarians
11	16	Q.P.C. Tupaea	NZ Under 20/Waikato
11	23	B.M. Ennor	Crusaders/New Zealand/Canterbury
11	23	M.B. Lam	Hurricanes/Wellington
11	21	G.C. Bridge	Crusaders/New Zealand
10	22	P.F. Tomkinson	Highlanders/Otago

THREE (or more) TRIES IN A MATCH

(Record: 8, T.R. Heeps, New Zealand v Northern NSW, 1962;
J.J. Kirwan, Auckland v North Otago, 1993)

4	R.E. Ioane	Blues v Sunwolves
4	G.C. Bridge	New Zealand v Tonga
4	T.T.H. Rogers-Holden	Wanganui v Ngati Porou East Coast
3	K.H. Laumape	Hurricanes v Brumbies
3	K.J. Herbert	New Zealand Under 20 v Japan Under 20
3	S.L. Reece	Crusaders v Bulls
3	B.M. Ennor	Crusaders v Rebels
3	S.L. Reece	Crusaders v Rebels
3	S.T. Stevenson	Chiefs v Rebels
3	J.W. Spowart	Tasman v Manawatu
3	V.T. Koroi	Otago v Manawatu
3	B.D. Tunnicliffe	South Canterbury v Poverty Bay
3	N. Fomai	Hawke's Bay v Northland
3	W.T. Goosen	Wellington v Otago
3	A.H. Tauatevalu	Poverty Bay v Mid Canterbury
3	C.J. Tiatia	Bay of Plenty v Hawke's Bay, 28 September
3	J. Ravouvou	Bay of Plenty v Manawatu, 5 October
3	V.W. Tikoisolomone	Wanganui v Horowhenua Kapiti
3	H.K. Lafituanai	Thames Valley v King Country
3	E.R. Narawa	Bay of Plenty v Manawatu, 18 October
3	A. Amato	South Canterbury v Buller, 19 October

21 (or more) POINTS IN A MATCH

(Record: 45, S.D. Culhane, New Zealand v Japan, 1995, 1 try, 20 conversions)

27	R.W.M. Reihana	New Zealand Under 20 v Japan Under 20, 1t, 11c
27	J.J. Lash	Buller v West Coast, 2t, 4c, 3pg
25	A.H. Tauatevalu	Poverty Bay v Mid Canterbury, 3t, 5c
24	J.J. Lash	Buller v Ngati Porou East Coast, 2t, 7c
23	R. Mo'unga	Crusaders v Highlanders, June 21, 2t, 5c, 1pg
21	D.S. McKenzie	Chiefs v Bulls, 6c, 3pg
21	C.D. Bosch	Sharks v Crusaders, 7pg
21	R.D. Crosland	Thames Valley v Wanganui, 7pg
21	J.M. Barrett	New Zealand v Namibia, 1t, 8c

SIX (or more) CONVERSIONS IN A MATCH
(Record: 20, J.P. Preston, Canterbury v West Coast, 1992;
S.D. Culhane, New Zealand v Japan, 1995)

11	R.W.M. Reihana	New Zealand Under 20 v Japan Under 20
8	R. Mo'unga	New Zealand v Canada
8	J.M. Barrett	New Zealand v Namibia
7	R. Mo'unga	Crusaders v Rebels
7	A.K. Moeke	Otago v North Otago
7	J.J. Lash	Buller v Ngati Porou East Coast
7	B.J. Barrett	New Zealand v Tonga
7	T.W.K. Renata	Wellington v Otago
7	J.K. Garden-Bachop	Wellington v Northland
7	H.R.J. Plummer	Auckland v Southland
7	R.L. Smith	North Otago v Ngati Porou East Coast
6	D.S. McKenzie	Chiefs v Bulls
6	B.J. Barrett	Hurricanes v Chiefs
6	F.W. Burke	New Zealand Under 20 v Scotland Under 20
6	J.M. Debreczeni	Chiefs v Rebels
6	D.S. Waite	Taranaki v Northland
6	B.D. Cameron	Canterbury v Southland
6	W.A. Wright	South Canterbury v Horowhenua Kapiti
6	N.R. Harding	Wanganui v King Country
6	M.J. Hunt	Tasman v Northland

SIX (or more) PENALTY GOALS IN A MATCH
(Record: 9, A.P. Mehrtens, New Zealand v Australia, at Auckland, 1999;
A.P. Mehrtens, New Zealand v France, at Paris, 2000;
B.J. Barrett, Taranaki v Bay of Plenty, 2011)

7	C.D. Bosch	Sharks v Crusaders
7	R.D. Crosland	Thames Valley v Wanganui

TWO (or more) DROPPED GOALS IN A MATCH
(Record: 5, M.K. Sisam, Hawke's Bay v East Coast, 1979)

No player drop kicked more than one goal in a match in 2019

SCORED IN ALL FOUR WAYS
No player scored all four ways in a match in 2019

CURRENT PLAYER STATISTICS
by Geoff Miller

CAREER RECORDS OF PLAYERS APPEARING IN FIRST-CLASS RUGBY IN NEW ZEALAND, 2019

100 GAMES OF FIRST-CLASS RUGBY

W.W.V. Crockett	375	J.L. To'omaga-Allen	168	A.P. Stephens	122
M.A. Nonu	344	A.W. Pulu	164	R. Thompson	121
K.J. Read	333	J.P.T. Moody	164	T.J. Smith	119
O.T. Franks	286	D.W.H. Sweeney	163	L.I.J. Squire	119
S.L. Whitelock	285	C.J.D. Taylor	158	J.R. Marshall	118
B.R. Smith	283	C.I. Eves	156	N.P. Harris	117
A.L. Smith	280	B.M. Weber	155	M. Fetu	116
R.S. Crotty	279	W.R. Naholo	154	D.P. Lienert-Brown	116
D.S. Coles	263	R.T. Malneek	152	L. Masoe	114
S.R. Donald	243	N.C. Crosswell	151	A. Seiuli	111
B. May	243	A.N. Ainley	148	T.T. Walden	111
B.J. Barrett	242	M.D. Drummond	147	V.T.L. Fifita	110
M.B. Todd	241	S.M.J. Prattley	144	R.J. Prinsep	110
A.L. Dixon	227	A.R. Lienert-Brown	140	M.S. Ala'alatoa	108
J.W. Parsons	218	D.K. Havili	137	M.J. Hunt	108
T.T.R. Perenara	218	N.E. Laulala	137	C.D. Clare	107
L. Romano	210	R.J. Buckman	136	O.W. Black	106
S.J. Cane	205	T. Li	136	M.G. Allardice	104
B.A. Retallick	204	M.P. Proctor	134	K.D. Tamatea	104
Z.R. Guildford	203	R. Mo'unga	133	J.R. Riccitelli	104
L.C. Whitelock	202	S.K. Barrett	132	M.T. Mudu	103
E.C. Dixon	188	A.L. Ioane	131	M.B. Lam	102
L.J. Coltman	184	G.O. Evans	130	P.B. Nabainivalu	102
T.E.S. Bateman	183	S.B. Williams	129	G. Cowley-Tuioti	101
S.J. Taufua	177	J.R. Dampney	128	M.A. Faddes	101
B.C.F. Funnell	175	D.S. McKenzie	128	A.T.O.A. Hodgman	101
A.S. Savea	175	R.K. Darling	127	S.T. Mafileo	101
T.S.G. Franklin	171	M.R. McKenzie	126	M. Nanai	101
A.W.F. Ta'avao-Matau	171	P.T. Tuipulotu	126	V.T. Aso	100
A.O.H.M. Tu'ungafasi	169	T.G. Perry	124	K.W. Hammington	100
B.D. Hall	168	S.T. Tokolahi	124		

500 POINTS IN FIRST-CLASS RUGBY

B.J. Barrett	2106	O.W. Black	673	M.J. Hunt	552
S.R. Donald	1842	M.R. McKenzie	663	T.J. Manawatu	545
R. Mo'unga	1177	J.J. Lash	659	J.M. Barrett	544
D.S. McKenzie	991	M.A. Nonu	600	J.K. Garden-Bachop	542
M. Banks	967	F.H. Smith	557	C.D. Clare	505

50 TRIES IN FIRST-CLASS RUGBY

M.A. Nonu	120	T.T.R. Perenara	73	G.C. Bridge	56
Z.R. Guildford	99	T. Li	69	R.S. Crotty	56
W.R. Naholo	93	R.E. Ioane	70	A.L. Smith	54
B.R. Smith	91	K.H. Laumape	66	R.T. Malneek	53
B.J. Barrett	79	K.J. Read	63	M.B. Lam	51

FIRST-CLASS STATISTICS

to January 1, 2020

by Geoff Miller

250 GAMES OF FIRST-CLASS RUGBY

K.F. Mealamu	2000-15	384	A.P. Mehrtens	1993-2005	282
W.W.V. Crockett	2005-19	375	A.L. Smith	2008-19	280
C.E. Meads	1955-74	361	R.S. Crotty	2008-19	279
S.B.T. Fitzpatrick	1983-97	346	A.J. Wyllie	1964-80	279
M.A. Nonu	2002-19	344	A.M. Stone	1980-94	275
R.H. McCaw	2000-15	334	C.J. Spencer	1992-2005	273
K.J. Read	2005-19	333	J.A. Collins	1994-2010	273
T.D. Woodcock	2000-15	331	M.J.A. Cooper	1985-99	270
J.F. Umaga	1994-2011	329	D.E. Holwell	1995–2010	270
A.M. Haden	1971-86	327	J.M. Muliaina	1999-2014	270
L.J. Messam	2003-18	327	B.G. Williams	1968-84	269
Q.J. Cowan	2000-16	326	K.R. Tremain	1957-72	268
R.W. Loe	1980-97	321	J.J. Kirwan	1983-94	267
G.W. Whetton	1979-95	313	A.M. Ellis	2004-16	266
Z.V. Brooke	1985-97	311	L.R. MacDonald	1994-2009	266
A.K. Hore	1999-2016	311	C.G. Smith	2003-15	265
W.F. McCormick	1958-78	310	C.C. King	2002-18	265
C.S. Ralph	1996-2008	306	D.S. Coles	2007-19	263
G.J. Fox	1982-95	303	G.L. Slater	1991-2005	262
A.D. Oliver	1993-2007	298	R.D. Thorne	1996-2	262
N.J. Hewitt	1988-2001	296	H.T.P. Elliot	2005-17	261
J. Kaino	2003-18	295	K.J. Crowley	1980-94	260
S.C. McDowell	1982-98	294	T.J. Blackadder	1990-2001	260
R.M. Brooke	1987-2001	289	C.H. Hoeft	1993-2005	260
C.R. Flynn	2001-17	289	I.A. Eliason	1964-82	259
D.W. Carter	2002-15	287	E. Clarke	1990-2005	259
I.D. Jones	1988-2000	287	S.J. Bachop	1986-99	257
O.T. Franks	2007-19	286	C.S. Jane	2003-17	257
I.A. Kirkpatrick	1966-79	285	G.A. Knight	1972-86	254
S.L. Whitelock	2008-19	285	G.M. Somerville	1997-2008	254
J.W. Marshall	1992-2005	284	I.J. Clarke	1951-63	253
P.A.T. Weepu	2003-17	284	S.M. Going	1962-78	251
W.K. Little	1988-2000	283	C.R. Jack	1998-11	250
B.R. Smith	2007-19	283	B.J. Robertson	1971-84	250

1000 POINTS IN FIRST-CLASS RUGBY

	Career	Games	Tries	Con	PG	DG/Mark	Points
G.J. Fox	1982–95	303	29	901	683	47	4112
D.W. Carter	2002–2015	287	78	649	646	19	3683
A.P. Mehrtens	1993–2005	282	40	556	572	54	3190
M.J.A. Cooper	1985–99	270	79	475	420	2	2577
K.J. Crowley	1980–94	260	86	375	376	9	2261
G.J.L Cooper	1984–96	188	60	385	388	14	2221
D.E. Holwell	1995–2010	270	39	451	366	2	2201
W.B. Johnston	1986–2001	220	29	421	396	5	2179
B.J. Barrett	2010-19	242	79	428	282	3	2106
R.M. Deans	1979–90	187	45	390	370	1	2073
W.F. McCormick	1958–78	310	57	457	314	9	2065
T.E. Brown	1995–2011	211	29	345	373	14	1996
A.R. Cashmore	1992–2005	185	64	351	290	2	1898
C.J. Spencer	1992–2005	273	101	329	222	11	1860
D.B. Clarke	1951–64	226	22	365	318	28/3	1851
S.R. Donald	2001-19	243	68	337	274	2	1842
S.D. Culhane	1988–99	155	20	292	312	19	1671
J.B. Cunningham	1990–98	136	52	316	226	1	1569
B.A. Blair	1999–2006	148	59	302	221	–	1562
L.Z. Sopoaga	2010-18	171	26	299	267	5	1544
A.W. Cruden	2008–17	201	33	245	267	2	1462
G.W. Jackson	1996–2004	175	41	267	215	8	1408
D.W. Hill	1997–2006	177	30	279	230	1	1401
A.R. Hewson	1973–88	154	19	247	229	17	1308
J.P. Preston	1987–98	171	21	242	231	–	1281
M. Williment	1958–68	121	17	296	188	16	1255
F.M. Botica	1985–2001	149	37	262	171	7	1213
L.W. Mains	1967–76	142	13	213	227	13	1193
R. Mo'unga	2013–2019	133	39	306	123	–	1177
E.J. Crossan	1987–96	91	29	189	220	–	1157
G.D. Rowlands	1969–82	179	41	198	186	15	1151
C.L. McAlister	2002–11	151	19	205	207	1	1129
I.T. West	2012–18	139	26	224	179	2	1121
J.W. Wilson	1992–2002	233	151	76	68	4	1123
W.J. Burton	1990–96	93	10	215	204	5	1099
J.A. Gallagher	1984–90	139	67	196	144	1	1095
J.A. Gopperth	2002–09	125	27	228	167	2	1094
B.J.W. Fairbrother	1981–92	118	20	132	183	61	1076
R.B. Barrell	1963–79	147	20	125	225	10	1030
D.P. Lilley	1993–2003	162	41	139	176	6	1029
G.W. Anscombe	2010–14	83	27	163	182	1	1010

100 TRIES IN FIRST-CLASS RUGBY

	Games	Tries		Games	Tries
J.J. Kirwan	267	199	I.A. Kirkpatrick	285	114
T.J. Wright	217	177	N.R. Berryman	188	114
D.C. Howlett	240	173	J. Vidiri	154	112
B.G. Fraser	201	171	E. Clarke	259	111
C.M. Cullen	233	164	C.I. Green	159	111
Z.V. Brooke	311	161	J.T. Rokocoko	214	111
J.F. Umaga	329	156	H.E. Gear	228	111
J.W. Wilson	233	151	G.B. Batty	142	109
R.A. Jarden	134	145	B.R. Ford	196	109
R.Q. Randle	188	141	J.K.R. Timu	182	108
B.G. Williams	269	137	R.L. Gear	197	108
K.R. Tremain	268	136	T.W. Mitchell	155	106
P.J. Cooke	192	134	S.S. Wilson	202	106
C.S. Ralph	306	133	E.J. Rush	196	104
J.T. Lomu	203	126	B.W. Smith	146	102
S.W. Sivivatu	191	125	R.M. Smith	152	102
M. Clamp	141	123	A.R. Sutherland	208	102
S.J. Savea	212	121	P. Bale	129	101
M.A. Nonu	344	120	C.J. Spencer	273	101
A.E. Cooke	131	119			

MOST DROPPED GOALS IN FIRST-CLASS RUGBY

B.J.W. Fairbrother	61	M.A. Herewini	47	P. Martin	34
A.P. Mehrtens	54	R.J. Preston	39	B.J. McKechnie	33
M.B. Roulston	49	J.W. Boe	37	E.J. Dunn	32
G.J. Fox	47	R.H. Brown	35	D. Trevathan	31

MOST POINTS IN A FIRST-CLASS MATCH

	Match	Tries	Con	PG	DG	Total
S.D. Culhane	New Zealand v Japan, 1995	1	20	–	–	45
J.P. Preston	Canterbury v West Coast, 1992	1	20	–	–	44
R.M. Deans	New Zealand v South Australia, 1984	3	14	1	–	43
A.R. Cashmore	Auckland v Mid Canterbury, 1995	5	9	–	–	43
J.F. Karam	New Zealand v South Australia, 1974	2	15	1	–	41
J.J. Kirwan	Auckland v North Otago, 1993	8	–	–	–	40
P.W. Turner	Otago v East Coast, 1986	2	14	1	–	39
J.W. Wilson	New Zealand Colts v Thames Valley, 1993	4	5	3	–	39
D.J. Kellett	Western Samoa v Marlborough, 1993	3	12	–	–	39
R.A. Jarden	New Zealand v Central West (Aust), 1951	6	10	–	–	38
D.E. Holwell	Northland v Thames Valley, 1997	2	14	–	–	38
B.A. Blair	New Zealand v Ireland A, 2001	3	4	5	–	38
R.J. du Preez	Sharks v Blues 2018	1	6	7	–	38
J.L. Graham	Counties v East Coast, 1972	–	14	3	–	37
S.D. Culhane	Southland v Manawatu, 1994	1	1	8	2	37
J.B. Cunningham	Central Vikings v South Canterbury, 1997	3	11	–	–	37
B.A. Blair	Canterbury v Counties Manukau, 1999	3	11	–	–	37

REFEREES

by Chris Jansen

2019 NEW ZEALAND RUGBY NATIONAL REFEREES SQUAD

	Union	Squad Debut	Tests	SR	P	HC	FPC	Sevens	Nat[1]	Prov[2]	RS[3]	Total
N.P. Briant	Bay of Plenty	2009	8	58	59	11	2	29	15	–	11	182
J.R. Bredin	Otago	2019	–	–	–	5	1	–	–	–	–	6
T.M.T. Cottrell	Hawke's Bay	2017	–	–	5	14	2	1	–	1	–	23
S.T.W. Curran	Otago	2019	–	–	–	5	1	–	–	–	–	6
J.J. Doleman	Auckland	2014	–	–	20	18	2	26	8	–	2	75
M.I. Fraser	Wellington	2007	8	60	60	17	2	5	17	1	8	170
R.J.M. Gordon	Wellington	2015	–	–	–	20	–	–	1	–	–	21
T.N. Griffiths	Manawatu	2016	–	–	5	17	1	–	–	–	–	23
G. Haswell	Canterbury	2019	–	–	–	–	2	1	–	–	–	3
N.E.R. Hogan	Wellington	2017	–	–	7	10	4	3	–	–	–	24
G.W. Jackson	Bay of Plenty	2010	32	88	60	8	–	–	7	1	8	196
R.P. Kelly	Taranaki	2009	–	–	50	15	1	63	4	3	3	136
A.W.B. Mabey	Auckland	2014	–	–	24	20	1	–	2	–	1	47
D.J. Macpherson	Poverty Bay	2018	–	–	–	2	1	1	–	1	–	5
J.D. Munro	Canterbury	2011	–	–	10	14	3	3	1	–	1	31
Dr. B.D. O'Keeffe	Wellington	2012	20	45	43	6	1	1	1	7	6	124
C.D. Paul	S. Canterbury	2018	–	–	–	1	1	1	–	–	–	3
B.E. Pickerill	North Harbour	2012	5	25	38	8	1	3	10	–	3	90
M.E. Playle	Auckland	2016	–	–	–	2	2	–	–	–	–	4
H.G. Reed	Hawke's Bay	2016	–	–	2	19	1	–	1	–	–	23
V.F. Ringrose	Wellington	2014	–	–	–	23	1	2	2	–	–	28
C.J. Stone	Taranaki	2012	–	–	17	22	2	2	–	1	–	44
D.J. Waenga	Hawke's Bay	2018	–	–	6	2	2	1	–	–	–	11
N.J. Webster	North Otago	2016	–	–	5	21	–	–	1	–	1	27
M.C.J. Winter	Waikato	2015	–	–	9	21	2	6	1	–	–	39
P.M. Williams	Taranaki	2014	14	29	29	7	–	3	6	2	4	89

SR   Super Rugby
P   Mitre 10 Cup (total includes former ITM Cup fixtures)
HC   Heartland Championship
FPC   Farah Palmer Cup
[1]NZR appointment — international tour, Ranfurly Shield (non-Mitre 10 Cup), national trial, and women's international.
[2]interprovincial (non-Mitre 10 Cup, non-Heartland Championship, non-Ranfurly Shield)
[3]Ranfurly Shield — also included within N1 or Nat (if a non-Mitre 10 Cup match)
[4]Men refereeing FPC fixtures are credited with a first-class appointment.

REFEREE APPOINTMENTS 2019

Jono Bredin

August	24	HC	Buller v East Coast	Westport
	31	HC	Horowhenua Kapiti v West Coast	Levin
September	7	HC	South Canterbury v Horowhenua Kapiti	Timaru
	15	FPC	Wellington v Counties Manukau	Wellington
	21	HC	West Coast v North Otago	Greymouth
October	12	HC	Buller v Poverty Bay	Westport

Nick Briant

February	16	SR	Blues vs Crusaders	Auckland
March	1	SR	Hurricanes v Brumbies	Palmerston North
	30	SR	Blues v Stormers	Auckland
April	13	SR	Sharks v Jaguares	Durban
	20	SR	Stormers v Brumbies	Cape Town

May	10	SR	Blues v Hurricanes	Auckland
	25	SR	Sunwolves v Rebels	Tokyo
June	8	SR	Jaguares v Sharks	Buenos Aires
August	18	P	Canterbury v Tasman	Christchurch
	24	P	Counties Manukau v Waikato	Pukekohe
September	8	P/RS	Otago v Taranaki	Dunedin
	12	P	Waikato v Hawke's Bay	Hamilton

Tipene Cottrell

August	31	HC	Poverty Bay v South Canterbury	Gisborne
September	7	HC	Wairarapa Bush v King Country	Masterton
	13	P	Northland v Canterbury	Whangarei
	21	P	Waikato v Tasman	Hamilton
	28	HC	North Otago v Wanganui	Oamaru
October	4	P	North Harbour v Wellington	Albany
	12	HC	East Coast v North Otago	Ruatoria
	19	HC s-f	North Otago v Wairarapa Bush	Oamaru
	27	LC f	West Coast v South Canterbury	Greymouth
December	14/15		National Sevens	Tauranga

Stu Curran

August	24	HC	Mid Canterbury v Horowhenua Kapiti	Ashburton
	30	HC	North Otago v Wairarapa Bush	Dunedin
September	8	FPC	Otago v Taranaki	Dunedin
	14	HC	North Otago v Thames Valley	Oamaru
	21	HC	Wanganui v East Coast	Wanganui
	28	HC	Buller v Wairarapa Bush	Westport

James Doleman

January	26/27		New Zealand World Rugby Sevens	Hamilton
February	2/3		Australia World Rugby Sevens	Sydney
March	1-3		USA World Rugby Sevens	Las Vegas
	8	PCC	Fiji Warriors v Tonga A	Suva
	12	PCC	Fiji Warriors v Junior Japan	Suva
April	5-7		Hong Kong World Rugby Sevens	Hong Kong
	13/14		Singapore World Rugby Sevens	Singapore
June	8	JWC	England U20 v Italy U20	Sante Fe
	12	JWC	Georgia U20 v Scotland U20	Rosario
	17	JWC s-f	Argentina U20 v Australia U20	Rosario
	22	JWC f	France U20 v Australia U20	Rosario
August	10	P	Tasman v Wellington	Blenheim
September	7	P	North Harbour v Waikato	Albany
	14	P	Taranaki v Bay of Plenty	New Plymouth
	22	P	Auckland v Wellington	Auckland
	28	P	Bay of Plenty v Hawke's Bay	Tauranga
October	13	P	Canterbury v North Harbour	Christchurch
	19	P s-f	Tasman v Auckland	Blenheim
December	5-7		Dubai World Rugby Sevens	Dubai
	13-15		South Africa World Rugby Sevens	Cape Town

Mike Fraser

February	16	SR	Jaguares v Lions	Buenos Aires
March	9	SR	Blues v Sunwolves	Albany
	15	SR	Chiefs v Hurricanes	Hamilton

	30	SR	Sharks v Bulls	Durban
April	5	SR	Lions v Sharks	Johannesburg
	12	SR	Rebels v Stormers	Melbourne
May	4	SR	Highlanders v Chiefs	Dunedin
	18	SR	Rebels v Bulls	Melbourne
	25	SR	Crusaders v Blues	Christchurch
	31	SR	Blues v Bulls	Auckland
June	14	SR	Highlanders v Waratahs	Invercargill
	22	SR q-f	Brumbies v Sharks	Canberra
	28	SR s-f	Jaguares v Brumbies	Buenos Aires
July	27	PNC	Samoa v Tonga	Apia
August	3	PNC	Fiji v Canada	Suva
	15	P	Northland v Auckland	Whangarei
	22	P	Hawke's Bay v Otago	Napier

Richard Gordon

| September | 28 | HC | East Coast v West Coast | Ruatoria |
| October | 5 | HC | Wairarapa Bush v Horowhenua Kapiti | Masterton |

Tim Griffiths

August	24	HC	South Canterbury v North Otago	Timaru
	31	HC	East Coast v Mid Canterbury	Ruatoria
September	7	P	Bay of Plenty v Wellington	Rotorua
	14	P	Counties Manukau v Auckland	Pukekohe
October	5	P	Auckland v Southland	Auckland
	12	HC	South Canterbury v West Coast	Timaru

George Haswell (Canterbury)

September	28	FPC	Wellington v Waikato	Wellington
October	5	FPC	Hawke's Bay v Otago	Napier
December	14/15		National Sevens	Tauranga

Nick Hogan

August	24	P	Tasman v Manawatu	Blenheim
September	1	P	North Harbour v Bay of Plenty	Albany
	8	P	Auckland v Canterbury	Auckland
	14	HC	Horowhenua Kapiti v Buller	Levin
	20	P	Hawke's Bay v Taranaki	Napier
	28	P	Canterbury v Counties-Manukau	Christchurch
October	12	HC	Horowhenua Kapit v Wanganui	Levin
December	14/15		National Sevens	Tauranga

Glen Jackson

February	15	SR	Chiefs vs Highlanders	Hamilton
	24	6N	Italy v Ireland	Rome
March	9	SR	Waratahs v Reds	Sydney
	16	SR	Brumbies v Waratahs	Canberra
	23	SR	Hurricanes v Stormers	Wellington
April	5	SR	Highlanders v Hurricanes	Dunedin
	13	SR	Bulls v Reds	Pretoria
	27	SR	Stormers v Bulls	Cape Town
May	18	SR	Blues v Chiefs	Auckland
June	7	SR	Crusaders v Rebels	Christchurch
	15	SR	Hurricanes v Blues	Wellington

	21	SR q-f	Jaguares v Chiefs	Buenos Aires
August	30	P/RS	Otago v Manawatu	Dunedin
September	5	P	Manawatu v Northland	Palmerston North
	28	P	Wellington v Northland	Wellington
October	5	P/RS	Otago v Canterbury	Dunedin
	11	P	Taranaki v Auckland	New Plymouth
	19	P s-f	Wellington v Canterbury	Wellington
	26	P f	Tasman v Wellington	Nelson

Richard Kelly

January	26/27		New Zealand World Rugby Sevens	Hamilton
February	2/3		Australia World Rugby Sevens	Sydney
March	1-3		USA World Rugby Sevens	Las Vegas
	9/10		Canada World Rugby Sevens	Vancouver
April	5-7		Hong Kong World Rugby Sevens	Hong Kong
	13/14		Singapore World Rugby Sevens	Singapore
May	25/26		England World Rugby Sevens	London
June	1-2		France World Rugby Sevens	Paris
August	31	P	Waikato v Auckland	Hamilton
September	15	P	Tasman v North Harbour	Nelson
	19	P	Canterbury v Manawatu	Christchurch
	29	P/RS	Otago v Waikato	Dunedin
October	12	P	Hawke's Bay v Tasman	Napier
	18	P s-f	Bay of Plenty v Manawatu	Rotorua
	25	P c f	Bay of Plenty v Hawke's Bay	Rotorua
December	5-7		Dubai World Rugby Sevens	Dubai
	13/15		South Africa World Rugby Sevens	Cape Town

Angus Mabey

August	10	P	Counties Manukau v Canterbury	Pukekohe
September	1	P	Taranaki v Tasman	New Plymouth
	7	HC	Thames Valley v East Coast	Paeroa
	14	P	Southland v Manawatu	Invercargill
	21	HC	Poverty Bay v Mid Canterbury	Gisborne
October	5	HC	Poverty Bay v East Coast	Gisborne
	13	P	Northland v Otago	Whangarei
	19	P s-f	Hawke's Bay v Otago	Napier
	26	MC f	North Otago v Wanganui	Oamaru

Damian Macpherson

September	28	HC	King Country v South Canterbury	Taupo
October	5	HC	Thames Valley v South Canterbury	Paeroa

Daniel Moore (Canterbury)

September	21	FPC	Canterbury v Manawatu	Christchurch
October	12	HC	Mid Canterbury v Wairarapa Bush	Ashburton

James Munro

August	25	P	Southland v North Harbour	Invercargill
	31	FPC	Bay of Plenty v Counties Manukau	Tauranga
September	7	HC	West Coast v Mid Canterbury	Greymouth
	14	HC	Mid Canterbury v South Canterbury	Ashburton
	21	P	North Harbour v Otago	Albany
	27	P	Tasman v Auckland	Nelson

October	6	P	Waikato v Taranaki	Hamilton
	12	P	Wellington v Waikato	Wellington
December	14/15		National Sevens	Tauranga

Ben O'Keeffe

February	15	SR	Brumbies v Rebels	Canberra
	23	SR	Crusaders v Hurricanes	Christchurch
March	10	6N	Ireland v France	Dublin
	29	SR	Hurricanes v Crusaders	Wellington
April	12	SR	Crusaders v Highlanders	Christchurch
	26	SR	Sunwolves v Highlanders	Tokyo
May	11	SR	Highlanders v Jaguares	Dunedin
	18	SR	Reds v Waratahs	Brisbane
June	1	SR	Chiefs v Crusaders	Suva
	8	SR	Waratahs v Brumbies	Sydney
July	27	RC	Australia v Argentina	Brisbane
August	16	P	North Harbour v Counties Manukau	Albany
	23	P	Wellington v Canterbury	Wellington
	31		Fiji v Tonga	Auckland
September	6		England v Italy	London
	21	RWC	Australia v Fiji	Sapporo
October	2	RWC	France v USA	Fukuoka
	13	RWC	Japan v Scotland	Yokohama

Chris Paul

| October | 5 | HC | North Otago v Mid Canterbury | Oamaru |
| December | 14/15 | | National Sevens | Tauranga |

Brendon Pickerill

February	23	SR	Jaguares v Bulls	Buenos Aires
March	9	SR	Crusaders v Chiefs	Christchurch
April	6	SR	Bulls v Jaguares	Pretoria
	19	SR	Chiefs v Lions	Hamilton
May	3	SR	Crusaders v Sharks	Christchurch
	17	SR	Hurricanes v Jaguares	Wellington
June	7	SR	Reds v Blues	Brisbane
August	10	PNC	Fiji v Samoa	Suva
	24	P	Auckland v Bay of Plenty	Auckland

Marcus Playle

September	20	FPC	Hawke's Bay v Taranaki	Napier
October	5	HC	West Coast v Buller	Greymouth
	12	HC	King Country v Thames Valley	Te Kuiti

Hugh Reed

August	30	HC	King Country v Buller	Taupo
September	7	HC	Poverty Bay v North Otago	Gisborne
	21	HC	Thames Valley v Wairarapa Bush	Paeroa
	29	P	Manawatu v North Harbour	Palmerston North
October	6	P	Tasman v Northland	Nelson
	19	HC s-f	West Coast v Poverty Bay	Greymouth

Vincent Ringrose

September	21	HC	King Country v Horowhenua Kapiti	Te Kuiti
October	5	HC	Wanganui v King Country	Wanganui

Cameron Stone

August	11	P	Manawatu v Hawke's Bay	Palmerston North
September	14	HC	Wanganui v West Coast	Wanganui
	22	P	Northland v Bay of Plenty	Whangarei
	28	HC	Horowhenua Kapiti v Poverty Bay	Waikanae

Daniel Waenga

August	18	P	Bay of Plenty v Waikato	Rotorua
	24	HC	Thames Valley v Poverty Bay	Paeroa
	31	P	Canterbury v Southland	Christchurch
September	7	FPC	Hawke's Bay v Northland	Napier
	15	P	Wellington v Otago	Wellington
	26	P	Taranaki v Southland	New Plymouth
October	5	P	Bay of Plenty v Manawatu	Tauranga
	12	P	Manawatu v Counties Manukau	Palmerston North
	19	HC s-f	Thames Valley v Wanganui	Paeroa

Nick Webster

July	13	RS	Otago v Thames Valley	Wanaka
August	8	P	Southland v Northland	Invercargill
	24	HC	West Coast v King Country	Greymouth
	29	P	Wellington v Counties Manukau	Wellington
September	9	HC	Buller v Wanganui	Westport
	14	HC	Wairarapa Bush v Poverty Bay	Masterton
	21	P	Southland v Counties Manukau	Invercargill
	28	HC	Mid Canterbury v Thames Valley	Ashburton
October	19	HC s-f	Buller v South Canterbury	Westport

Michael Winter

August	24	HC	Wairarapa Bush v Wanganui	Masterton
	31	P	Northland v Hawke's Bay	Whangarei
September	6	P	Counties Manukau v Hawke's Bay	Pukekohe
	14	HC	East Coast v King Country	Ruatoria
	22	FPC	Auckland v Wellington	Auckland
October	3	P	Counties Manukau v Hawke's Bay	Pukekohe
	10	P	Southland v Bay of Plenty	Invercargill
December	14/15		National Sevens	Tauranga

Paul Williams

February	23	SR	Sharks v Blues	Durban
March	2	SR	Lions v Bulls	Johannesburg
	16	6N	England v Scotland	London
	24	SR	Reds v Brumbies	Brisbane
	29	SR	Waratahs v Sunwolves	Newcastle
April	20	SR	Highlanders v Blues	Dunedin
	26	SR	Crusaders v Lions	Christchurch
May	25	SR	Waratahs v Jaguares	Sydney

	31	SR	Rebels v Waratahs		Melbourne
June	15	SR	Brumbies v Reds		Canberra
August	8	P	Auckland v North Harbour		Auckland
	17	P/RS	Otago v Southland		Dunedin
	25	P	Taranaki v Northland		New Plymouth
September	22	RWC	England v Tonga		Sapporo
October	3	RWC	Georgia v Fiji		Hanazono
	9	RWC	Argentina v USA		Kumagaya

PCC   *Pacific Champions Cup*
RWC   *Rugby World Cup*
RWCQ *Rugby World Cup Qualifier*
JWC   *Junior World Championship*
RC   *Rugby Championship*
SR   *Super Rugby*
6N   *Six Nations*

Two overseas referees controlled four Mitre 10 Cup fixtures:
Frank Murphy (*Ireland*) Aug 11 Bay of Plenty v Otago, Aug 16 Hawke's Bay v Wellington,
Dan Jones (*Wales*) Aug 10 Waikato v Canterbury, Aug 17 Manawatu v Taranaki,
Federico Anselmi (*Argentina*) replaced Nick Briant (injury) in the Super 15 fixture Hurricanes
v Brumbies in Palmerston North March 1st.

INTERNATIONAL ASSISTANT REFEREES AND TELEVISION MATCH OFFICIALS

Nick Briant

August	3		Fiji v Canada		Suva

Mike Fraser

September	6		Japan v South Africa		Kumagaya

Shane McDermott

September	6		Japan v South Africa	(TMO)	Kumagaya

Glenn Newman

February	2	6N	Ireland v England	(TMO)	Dublin
	10	6N	England v France	(TMO)	London
July	27	PNC	Japan v Fiji (TMO)		Kamaishi
August	3	PNC	Japan v Tonga	(TMO)	Hanazono

Ben O'Keeffe

March	16	6N	Wales v Ireland		Cardiff
August	9	PNC	Tonga v Canada		Lautoka
September	23	RWC	Wales v Georgia		Aichi
	28	RWC	Argentina v Tonga		Hanazono
October	5	RWC	England v Argentina		Tokyo
	20	RWC q-f	Japan v South Africa		Tokyo
	27	RWC s-f	Wales v South Africa		Yokohama
November	2	RWC f	England v South Africa		Yokohama

Aaron Paterson

August	31		Fiji v Tonga		Auckland

Brendon Pickerill

February	1	6N	France v Wales	Paris
	10	6N	England v France	London
July	27	RC	Australia v Argentina	Brisbane
August	3	PNC	Japan v Tonga	Hanazono
September	7		Australia v Samoa	Sydney
	21	RWC	France v Argentina	Tokyo
	24	RWC	Russia v Samoa	Kumagaya
	28	RWC	Argentina v Tonga	Hanazono
October	3	RWC	Ireland v Russia	Kobe
	9	RWC	Argentina v USA	Kumagaya
	12	RWC	Ireland v Samoa	Fukuoka

Ben Skeen

March	10	6N	Ireland v France	(TMO)	Paris
	16	6N	England v Scotland	(TMO)	London
July	27	RC	Australia v Argentina	(TMO)	Brisbane
September	7		Australia v Samoa	(TMO)	Sydney
	20	RWC	Japan v Russia	(TMO)	Tokyo
	22	RWC	England v Tonga	(TMO)	Sapporo
	26	RWC	England v USA	(TMO)	Kobe
	28	RWC	Japan v Ireland	(TMO)	Shizuoka
	29	RWC	Australia v Wales	(TMO)	Tokyo
October	3	RWC	Ireland v Russia	(TMO)	Kobe
	5	RWC	Australia v Uruguay	(TMO)	Otia
	6	RWC	France v Tonga	(TMO)	Kumamoto
	9	RWC	Wales v Fiji (TMO)		Otia
	13	RWC	Japan v Scotland	(TMO)	Yokohama
	19	RWC q-f	Australia v England	(TMO)	Oita
	27	RWC s-f	Wales v South Africa	(TMO)	Yokohama
November	2	RWC f	England v South Africa	(TMO)	Yokohama

Cameron Stone

July	27	PNC	Japan v Fiji	Kamaishi
August	31		Fiji v Tonga	Auckland
September	7		Australia v Samoa	Sydney

Paul Williams

March	9	6N	England v Italy	London
July	27	RC	Australia v Argentina	Brisbane
September	26	RWC	England v USA	Kobe
	29	RWC	Georgia v Uruguay	Kumagaya
October	6	RWC	France v Tonga	Kumamoto
	20	RWC q-f	Wales v France	Oita

(TMO)	Television Match Official
JWC	Junior World Championship
PNC	Pacific Nations Cup
RC	Rugby Championship
6N	Six Nations

2019 INTERNATIONAL REFEREES

M.I. Fraser	2013 Georgia v USA, Wales v Tonga; 2014 Canada v Scotland, Tonga v USA; 2018 Fiji v Samoa, Samoa v Germany (RWCQ), 2019 Samoa v Tonga, Fiji v Canada.
G.W. Jackson	2012 England v Fiji, Georgia v Japan; 2013 Italy v Australia, France v Tonga; 2014 Argentina v Ireland, South Africa v Scotland, Australia v Argentina, France v Fiji, Ireland v Australia; 2015 France v Scotland, Wales v Ireland, Argentina v South Africa, Ireland v Canada (RWC), Australia v Fiji (RWC), Tonga v Namibia (RWC), USA v Japan (RWC); 2016 Italy v England, Scotland v France, South Africa v Ireland, South Africa v Argentina, France v Australia; 2017 Italy v Ireland, South Africa v France, Australia v South Africa, Wales v Australia; 2018 Ireland v Wales, South Africa v England, Australia v South Africa, Italy v Georgia, France v Argentina; 2019 Italy vs Ireland, USA v Japan.
Dr B.D. O'Keeffe	2016 Samoa v Georgia, Japan v Scotland, Scotland v Argentina; 2017 Italy v France, South Africa v France, South Africa v Australia, Ireland v South Africa, England v Australia; 2018 Wales v France, South Africa v England, South Africa v Argentina, Wales v Australia, Ireland v USA; 2019 Ireland v France, Australia v Argentina, Fiji v Tonga, England vs Italy, Australia v Fiji (RWC), France v USA (RWC), Japan v Scotland (RWC).
B.E. Pickerill	2017 Germany v USA; 2018 Tonga v Georgia, Tonga v Samoa, Cook Islands v Hong Kong (RWCQ), 2019 Fiji v Samoa.
P.M. Williams	2016 Romania v USA; 2017 Italy v Scotland, Fiji v Italy, Samoa vs Fiji (RWCQ), Ireland v Fiji; 2018 Australia v Ireland, England v Japan, Scotland v Argentina; 2019 England v Scotland, South Africa v Australia, Australia v Samoa, England v Tonga (RWC), Georgia v Fiji (RWC), Argentina v USA (RWC).

INTERNATIONAL REFEREES
to 1 January, 2020

Bishop, D.J. (Southland) 1986–95	26	McKenzie, E. (Wairarapa) 1921	1
Bray, L.E. (Wellington) 2001–08	9	McKenzie, H.J. (Wairarapa) 1936	1
Briant, N.P. (Bay of Plenty) 2014–18	8	McLachlan, L.L. (Otago) 1989–94	7
Brown, K.W. (Southland) 2008–11	8	McMullen, R.F. (Auckland) 1973	1
Campbell, A. (Auckland) 1908	2	Matheson, A.M. (Taranaki) 1946	1
Dainty, C.J. (Wellington) 1982–86	2	Millar, D.H. (Otago) 1965–78	8
Deaker, K.M. (Hawke's Bay) 2001–08	23	Moffit, J. (Wellington) 1936	1
Doocey, T.F. (Canterbury) 1976–83	3	Munro, V.G. (Canterbury) 2009–10	2
Downes, A.D. (Otago) 1913	1	Murphy, J.P. (North Auckland) 1959–69	13
Duffy, B.W. (Taranaki) 1977	1	Neilson, A.E. (Wellington) 1921	2
Duncan, J. (Otago) 1908	1	Nicholson, G.W. (Auckland) 1913	1
Evans, F.T. (Canterbury) 1904	1	O'Brien, P.D. (Southland) 1994–2005	37
Farquahar, A.B. (Auckland) 1961–64	6	O'Keeffe, Dr B.D. (Wellington) 2016–19	20
Fleury, A.L. (Otago) 1959	1	Parkinson, F.G.M. (Manawatu) 1955–56	3
Fong, A.S. (West Coast) 1946–50	2	Pickerill, B.E. (North Harbour) 2017–19	5
Forsyth, R.A. (Taranaki) 1958	1	Pollock, C.J. (Hawke's Bay) 2005–15	22
Francis, R.C. (Wairarapa Bush) 1984–86	10	Pring, J.P.G. (Auckland) 1966–72	8
Fraser, M.I. (Wellington) 2013–19	8	Robson, C.F. (Waikato) 1963	1
Fright, W.A. (Canterbury) 1956	2	Simpson, J.L. (Wellington) 1913	1
Frood, J. (Otago) 1952	1	Skeen, B.D. (Auckland) 2008–09	2
Garrard, W.G. (Canterbury) 1899	1	Sullivan, G. (Taranaki) 1950	1
Gillies, C.R. (Waikato) 1958–59	4	Sutherland, F.E. (Auckland) 1930	1
Griffiths, A.A. (Waikato) 1952	1	Taylor, A.R. (Canterbury) 1965–72	3
Harrison, G.L. (Wellington) 1979–83	4	Thompson, M.W. (Auckland) 1983	2
Hawke, C.J. (South Canterbury) 1990–2001	24	Tindill, E.W.T. (Wellington) 1950–55	3
Hill, E.D. (Auckland) 1949	1	Wahlstrom, G.K. (Auckland) 1994–97	6
Hollander, S. (Canterbury) 1930–31	4	Walsh, L. (Canterbury) 1949	1
Honiss, P.G. (Canterbury & Waikato) 1997–2008	46	Walsh, S. (Wellington) 1994–97	5
Jackson, G.W. (Bay of Plenty) 2012–19	32	Walsh, S.R. (North Harbour) 1998–2008	33
King, J.S. (Wellington) 1937	2	White, J.M (Auckland) 2013	2
Lawrence, B.J. (Bay of Plenty) 2005–11	25	Williams, J. (Otago) 1905	1
Lawrence, K.H. (Bay of Plenty) 1985–91	13	Williams, P.M. (Taranaki) 2016–19	14
Macassey, L.E. (Otago) 1937	1	Williamson G.L. (Wellington) 2010–13	2
McAuley, C.J. (Otago) 1962	1	Wise, G.J. (Hawke's Bay) 2004	1
McDavitt, P.A. (Wellington) 1972–77	5	Wolstenholme, B. (Poverty Bay) 1955	1

100 AND MORE FIRST-CLASS MATCHES
to 1 January, 2020

PP.D. O'Brien	1988-2005	230	R.P. Kelly	2009-2019	136
P.G. Honiss	1992-2008	227	G.K. Wahlstrom	1985-2002	132
S.R. Walsh	1994-2008	214	Dr. B.D. O'Keeffe	2012-2019	124
B.J. Lawrence	1997-2012	205	G.L. Williamson	2003-2014	117
C.J. Pollock	2000-2016	204	Dr. J.M. White	2000-2013	116
G.W. Jackson	2010-2019	196	D.J. Bishop	1976-1995	114
C.J. Hawke	1983-2001	183	G.J. Wise	1996-2007	114
N.P. Briant	2009-2019	182	K.W. Brown	1999-2012	112
K.M. Deaker	1996-2008	181	S. Walsh	1980-2000	103
M.I. Fraser	2007-2019	170	K.H. Lawrence	1971-1992	100
L.E. Bray	1991-2008	144			

SEVENS RUGBY
NEW ZEALAND SEVENS SQUADS 2019

The All Blacks Sevens finished the 2018/19 HSBC Sevens Series in third place behind Fiji (winners) and USA. New Zealand won two of the tournaments, at Dubai (December 2018) and at Sydney and was second at Paris and third at Hamilton and Las Vegas. The 2019/20 series commenced strongly with second place at Dubai and first place at Cape Town.

		New Zealand	Australia	USA	Canada	Hong Kong	Singapore	England	France	Dubai	South Africa	TOTALS
Kurt Baker	Manawatu	*	*	*	–	*	*	*	–	*	*	8
Dylan Collier	Waikato	*	–	–	–	*	*	*	*	*	*	7
Scott Curry	Bay of Plenty	*	–	–	–	*	*	*	*	*	*	7
Sam Dickson	Canterbury	*	*	*	*	*	*	–	–	*	*	8
Scott Gregory	Northland	s	*	*	*	–	–	*	–	–	–	5
Trael Joass	Tasman/BOP	–	s	*	*	–	–	–	–	–	–	3
Andrew Knewstubb	Horowhenua Kapiti	*	*	–	*	*	*	*	*	*	*	9
Vilimoni Koroi	Otago	*	*	*	*	–	–	*	s	–	–	6
Ngarohi McGarvey-Black	Bay of Plenty	–	–	–	*	–	–	–	*	*	*	4
Tim Mikkelson	Waikato	*	*	*	*	*	*	*	*	*	*	10
Sione Molia	Counties Manukau	*	*	*	*	*	–	*	*	*	–	8
Jona Nareki	Otago	*	*	*	*	*	*	*	*	–	–	8
Tone Ng Shiu	Tasman	*	*	*	*	*	*	*	*	*	*	10
Amanaki Nicole	Canterbury	–	*	–	–	–	s	–	*	–	–	3
Joe Ravouvou	Auckland	*	*	*	*	*	*	s	*	–	–	8
Salesi Rayasi	Auckland	–	–	–	–	–	–	–	–	*	*	2
Akuila Rokolisoa	Counties Manukau	–	–	*	–	s	*	–	–	s	*	5
Te Puoho Stephens	Tasman	–	–	–	s	–	–	–	–	–	–	1
William Warbrick	Bay of Plenty	–	–	–	–	–	–	–	–	–	s	1
Regan Ware	Bay of Plenty	*	*	*	*	*	*	*	*	*	*	10
Joe Webber	Bay of Plenty	–	–	–	–	*	*	*	*	*	*	6

Captaincy was shared during the year: Curry and Mikkelson (New Zealand, Hong Kong, Singapore, England, France, Dubai, South Africa); Mikkelson and Molia (Australia, USA, Canada).

Coach: Clark Laidlaw (*Taranaki*)
Manager: Ross Everiss (*Bay of Plenty*)
Assistant coach: Tomasi Cama (*Manawatu*)
Physiotherapist: Damian Banks (*Bay of Plenty*)

INDIVIDUAL SCORING

	Tries	Con	Points		Tries	Con	Points
Knewstubb	23	87	289	Webber	10	–	50
Ware	37	–	185	Collier	8	–	40
Ravouvou	27	–	135	Curry	7	1	37
Baker	17	23	131	Bregory	6	–	30
Koroi	9	32	109	Rayasi	5	–	25
Nareki	19	–	95	Nicole	2	–	10
Molia	18	–	90	Penalty try	1	–	7
Ng Shiu	18	–	90	Stephens	1	–	5
Mikkelson	17	2	89				
Dickson	14	1	72	**TOTALS**	**252***	**166**	**1594**
McGarvey-Black	7	10	55				
Rokolisoa	6	10	50	Opposition scored 730 points			

* includes one penalty try (7 points)

Final points for 2018/19 World Rugby Sevens Series: Fiji 186, USA 177, New Zealand 162, South Africa 148, England 114, Samoa 107, Australia 104, France 99, Argentina 94, Scotland 72, Canada 59, Spain 49, Kenya 37, Wales 31, Japan 27, Ireland 19, Chile 6, Tonga 5, Zimbabwe 2, Portugal 1, Hong Kong 1. The series was held over ten tournaments between November 2018 and June 2019.

Previous winners: New Zealand 2000, 2001, 2002, 2003, 2004, 2005, 2007, 2008, 2011, 2012, 2013, 2014; Fiji 2006, 2015, 2016; South Africa 2009, 2017, 2018; Samoa 2010.

World Rugby Sevens Series Cup championship titles (1999 to 1 January 2020): New Zealand 54, Fiji 41, South Africa 29, England 19, Samoa 10, Australia 7, United States 3, Argentina 2, Scotland 2, France 1, Kenya 1, Canada 1.

NEW ZEALAND AT HSBC NEW ZEALAND SEVENS
Waikato Stadium, Hamilton   January 26/27, 2019

Date	Opponent	Result	Tries	Conversions
Jan 26	Japan	won 52–0	Nareki (2), Molia, Knewstubb, Collier, Ware, Koroi, Ravouvou	Knewstubb (5), Koroi
Jan 26	Canada	won 49–10	Ware (2), Koroi, Curry, Ravouvou, Molia, Knewstubb	Koroi (4), Knewstubb (3)
Jan 26	Spain	won 24–0	Collier, Mikkelson, Molia, Baker	Knewstubb, Baker
Jan 27	Australia (Cup q-f)	won 24–17	Collier, Nareki, Ware, Mikkelson	Knewstubb, Koroi
Jan 27	USA (Cup s-f)	lost 7–17	Ware	Koroi
Jan 27	South Africa (for 3rd)	won 29–7	Ng Shiu (2), Mikkelson, Ravouvou, Dickson	Knewstubb (2)

Fiji defeated USA 38–0 in the Cup final

NEW ZEALAND AT HSBC AUSTRALIA SEVENS
Spotless Stadium, Sydney   February 2/3, 2019

Date	Opponent	Result	Tries	Conversions
Feb 2	Wales	won 27–14	Ravouvou, Ng Shiu, Baker, Ware, Molia	Knewstubb
Feb 2	Spain	won 41–0	Dickson (2), Ravouvou (2), Ware, Nareki, Baker	Knewstubb (2), Koroi
Feb 2	Scotland	won 42–0	Knewstubb (2), Gregory (2), Ware, Nareki	Knewstubb (3), Koroi (3)
Feb 3	France (Cup q-f)	won 28–5	Nareki, Ware, Dickson, Ng Shiu	Knewstubb (2), Koroi (2)
Feb 3	Fiji (Cup s-f)	won 36–14	Baker (2), Koroi (2), Ng Shiu, Gregory	Koroi (2), Baker
Feb 3	USA (Cup final)	won 21–5	Ware, Dickson, Ng Shiu	Koroi (3)

NEW ZEALAND AT HSBC USA SEVENS
Sam Boyd Stadium, Las Vegas   March 1–3, 2019

Date	Opponent	Result	Tries	Conversions
Mar 1	Samoa	won 33–0	Ware (2), Molia (2), Baker	Koroi (3), Rokolisoa
Mar 1	Canada	won 33–19	Mikkelson (2), Ravouvou, Rokolisoa, Nareki	Rokolisoa (4)
Mar 2	Spain	won 19–7	Ravouvou, Koroi, Dickson	Koroi (2)
Mar 2	Fiji (Cup q-f)	won 19–14	Molia (2), Baker	Baker (2)
Mar 3	USA (Cup s-f)	lost 19–24	Molia, Baker, Mikkelson	Baker (2)
Mar 3	Argentina (for 3rd)	won 26–19	Molia (2), Ravouvou, Ng Shiu	Koroi (2), Baker

USA defeated Samoa 27–0 in the Cup final

NEW ZEALAND AT HSBC CANADA SEVENS
BC Place Stadium, Vancouver   March 9/10, 2019

Date	Opponent	Result	Tries	Conversions
Mar 9	France	won 45–7	Molia, Koroi, Ravouvou, Mikkelson, Dickson, Knewstubb, Ng Shiu	Koroi (4), Knewstubb
Mar 9	Spain	lost 24–26	Ravouvou (2), Knewstubb, Dickson	Knewstubb (2)
Mar 9	Australia	won 36–12	Ravouvou (2), Dickson, Mikkelson, McGarvey-Black, Koroi	Knewstubb (2), McGarvey-Black
Mar 10	Fiji (Cup q-f)	lost 21–22	Dickson, Mikkelson, Koroi	Knewstubb (3)
Mar 10	Argentina (s-f for 5th)	won 26–21	Molia, Gregory, Nareki, Stephens	Knewstubb (2), Koroi
Mar 10	England (for 5th)	won 26–19	Nareki (2), Koroi, McGarvey-Black	Knewstubb, Koroi, McGarvey-Black

South Africa defeated France 21–12 in the Cup final

NEW ZEALAND AT HSBC HONG KONG SEVENS
Hong Kong Stadium, Hong Kong
April 5–7, 2019

Date	Opponent	Result	Tries	Conversions
Apr 5	Australia	won 40–19	Ravouvou (2), Ware, Dickson, Nareki, Webber	Knewstubb (5)
Apr 6	Kenya	won 36–0	Ravouvou (2), Ware (2), Webber, Curry	Knewstubb (3)
Apr 6	Fiji	lost 5–24	Ravouvou	
Apr 7	France (Cup q-f)	lost 12–14	Baker, Knewstubb	Knewstubb
Apr 7	England (s-f for 5th)	won 17–10	Webber, Collier, Ng Shiu	Rokolisoa
Apr 7	Argentina (for 5th)	lost 14–21	Baker, Ng Shiu	Rokolisoa (2)

Fiji defeated France 21–7 in the Cup final

NEW ZEALAND AT HSBC SINGAPORE SEVENS
National Stadium, Singapore
April 13/14, 2019

Date	Opponent	Result	Tries	Conversions
Apr 13	Japan	won 43–0	Ware (2), Knewstubb (2), Nareki, Baker, Ravouvou	Knewstubb (3), Baker
Apr 13	Spain	won 53–0	Rokolisoa (2), Dickson, Curry, Nareki, Baker, Ware, Webber, Ravouvou	Baker (2), Mikkelson, Knewstubb
Apr 13	Samoa	won 26–22	Ware (2), Mikkelson, Rokolisoa	Baker (2), Knewstubb
Apr 14	Fiji (Cup q-f)	lost 5–19	Mikkelson	
Apr 14	Australia (s-f for 5th)	won 27–22	Ravouvou (2), Webber, Nareki, Mikkelson	Rokolisoa
Apr 14	Samoa (for 5th)	lost 17–19	Ravouvou (2), Dickson	Knewstubb

South Africa defeated Fiji 20–19 in the Cup final

NEW ZEALAND AT HSBC ENGLAND SEVENS
Twickenham, London
May 25/26, 2019

Date	Opponent	Result	Tries	Conversions
May 25	Scotland	won 21–7	Mikkelson, Curry, Gregory	Knewstubb (3)
May 25	Ireland	won 34–7	Knewstubb (2), Ware (2), Ng Shiu, Collier	Knewstubb (2)
May 25	England	lost 12–17	Gregory, Ng Shiu	Knewstubb
May 26	France (Cup q-f)	lost 14–19	Knewstubb, Mikkelson	Knewstubb (2)
May 26	South Africa (s-f for 5th)	won 21–17	Molia, Knewstubb, Mikkelson	Koroi, Knewstubb, Mikkelson
May 26	Ireland (for 5th)	won 35–14	Ravouvou (2), Ng Shiu (2), Ware	Knewstubb (4), Curry

Fiji defeated Australia 43–7 in the Cup final

NEW ZEALAND AT HSBC FRANCE SEVENS
Stade Jean Bouin, Paris   June 1/2, 2019

Date	Opponent	Result	Tries	Conversions
June 1	Scotland	won 14–12	Ware, Nareki	Knewstubb (2)
June 1	Japan	won 31–14	Nareki (2), Ware, Nicole, Knewstubb	Knewstubb (2), McGarvey-Black
June 1	France	won 17–10	Curry, Molia, Ware	Knewstubb
June 2	Argentina (Cup q-f)	won 21–12	Molia (2), Knewstubb	Knewstubb (3)
June 2	South Africa (Cup s-f)	won 33–7	Ware (2), Nareki, Knewstubb, Nicole	Knewstubb (4)
June 2	Fiji (Cup final)	lost 24–35	Ware (2), Nareki, Collier	Knewstubb, McGarvey-Black

NEW ZEALAND AT HSBC DUBAI SEVENS
The Sevens, Dubai   December 5–7, 2019

Date	Opponent	Result	Tries	Conversions
Dec 5	Wales	won 36–7	Baker (2), Ng Shiu (2), McGarvey-Black (2)	Baker (3)
Dec 6	Canada	won 33–7	Rayasi (3), Webber, Ware	Knewstubb (3), Baker
Dec 6	Samoa	won 40–7	Knewstubb (2), McGarvey-Black, Curry, Molia, Rayasi	Knewstubb (3), McGarvey-Black (2)
Dec 7	USA (Cup q-f)	won 26–5	Ware (2), Webber, Collier	Baker (3)
Dec 7	England (Cup s-f)	won 19–12	Knewstubb, Ware, Rayasi	McGarvey-Black (2)
Dec 7	South Africa (Cup final)	lost 0–15		

NEW ZEALAND AT HSBC SOUTH AFRICA SEVENS
Cape Town Stadium, Cape Town   December 13–15, 2019

Date	Opponent	Result	Tries	Conversions
Dec 13	Wales	won 43–7	Rokolisoa (2), Knewstubb, Ware, Webber, Mikkelson, McGarvey-Black	Knewstubb (3), Dickson
Dec 14	Canada	won 33–5	Collier, Curry, Mikkelson, Ware, Dickson	Baker (2), McGarvey-Black (2)
Dec 14	Argentina	won 19–14	Webber (2), Knewstubb	Knewstubb (2)
Dec 15	Scotland (Cup q-f)	won 35–19	Ng Shiu (2), Baker (2), Knewstubb	Knewstubb (4), Baker
Dec 15	Fiji (Cup s-f)	won 24–7	Penalty try, Baker, Ware, Knewstubb	Baker
Dec 15	South Africa (Cup final)	won 7–5	McGarvey-Black	Rokolisoa

PLAYING RECORD OF NEW ZEALAND SEVENS TEAMS

	Tournaments			Games				Points	
	Attended	Won	Runner-up	Played	Won	Draw	Lost	For	Against
1973	1	–	–	3	2	–	1	58	50
1983	1	–	–	5	4	–	1	114	4
1984	1	–	1	5	4	–	1	74	40
1985	1	–	–	4	3	–	1	88	18
1986	3	3	–	16	15	–	1	414	72
1987	2	1	1	11	10	–	1	284	66
1988	2	1	1	11	10	–	1	274	37
1989	2	2	–	11	11	–	–	316	71
1990	1	–	1	5	4	–	1	134	44
1991	1	–	1	5	4	–	1	150	18
1992	1	–	1	5	4	–	1	130	34
1993	3	–	–	17	12	–	5	420	175
1994	2	1	–	10	9	–	1	361	89
1995	5	2	1	22	19	–	3	681	182
1996	5	3	2	29	27	–	2	1263	236
1997	4	1	1	21	18	–	3	670	287
1998	11	6	2	59	54	–	5	2134	473
1999	10	7	2	54	49	1	4	1574	426
2000	10	6	3	59	55	–	4	2048	354
2001	10	7	1	60	56	–	4	2042	330
2002	13	8	2	75	68	1	6	2377	565
2003	7	1	3	40	34	–	6	1285	411
2004	8	3	2	46	39	–	7	1396	395
2005	8	3	1	48	41	–	7	1509	441
2006	9	2	1	48	36	2	10	1380	551
2007	8	4	–	44	40	–	4	1391	355
2008	8	4	2	47	43	–	4	1350	367
2009	9	2	2	49	37	–	12	1262	514
2010	9	2	2	51	43	1	7	1531	541
2011	9	4	1	50	43	–	7	1479	519
2012	9	3	4	54	46	–	8	1375	556
2013	10	3	4	60	52	–	8	1651	584
2014	10	4	3	60	50	–	10	1645	511
2015	8	1	3	47	33	1	13	1039	692
2016	11	3	1	64	45	3	16	1357	860
2017	11	1	2	64	48	–	16	1396	802
2018	13	3	1	73	52	–	21	1746	887
2019	10	2	2	60	47	-	13	1594	730
TOTALS	**246**	**93**	**54**	**1392**	**1167**	**9**	**216**	**39992**	**13287**

SEVENS RECORDS

to January 1, 2020

BY NEW ZEALAND TEAMS

Most successive wins	47	2007–08
Most successive tournament wins	7	2007–08
Most successive appearances in finals	12	1986–92

Tournament records

Most points	463	Portugal, 1996
Most tries	69	Portugal, 1996
Most conversions	59	Portugal, 1996

Match records

Highest team score	94	v Moldova, Portugal, 1996
Record victory (*points ahead*)	94	94–0, v Moldova, 1996
Highest score conceded	61	v Fiji, Japan, 1996
Record defeat (*points behind*)	56	5–61, v Fiji, Japan, 1996
Most tries	14	v Moldova, Portugal, 1996
Most conversions	12	v Moldova, Portugal, 1996
		v Hungary, Portugal, 1996

BY THE PLAYERS

Career records

Attended most tournaments	94	DJ Forbes; T.J. Mikkelson
Most points	2122	T. Cama
Most tries	233	T.J. Mikkelson

Tournament records

Most points	136	C.M. Cullen, Hong Kong, 1996
Most tries	20	B.R.M. Fleming, Portugal, 1996
Most conversions	28	D.A. Smith, Portugal, 1996

Match records

Most points	37	C.M. Cullen, v Sri Lanka, Hong Kong, 1996
Most tries	7	C.M. Cullen, v Sri Lanka, Hong Kong, 1996
Most conversions	9	T.J. Wright, v Korea, Sydney, 1989
		M. Ashford, v Sri Lanka, Dubai, 2001

NEW ZEALAND SEVENS REPRESENTATIVES, 1973–2019

	Tournaments
Ahki, P.J. (*North Harbour*) 2013–14–16	7
Ai'i, O. (*Auckland*) 1999–00–01–02–04–05	25
Alley, G. (*North Harbour*) 1992–93	2
Andrews, L.S. (*Otago*) 1999	2
Anesi, S.R. (*Waikato*) 2004–06	7
Arnold, T.C. (*Bay of Plenty*) 2009–10–11–12	19
Ashford, M.R. (*Auckland*) 2001–05	10
Atiga, B.A.C. (*Auckland*) 2007	1
Austin, H.S.E. (*Taranaki*) 1999	1
Auva'a, O.J. (*Auckland*) 2006–09	5
Bachop, G.T.M. (*Canterbury*) 1990–91–92–94	5
Baker, K.T. (*Manawatu*) 2008–09–17–18–19 (*Taranaki*) 2010–12–13–14–16	45
Bale, P. (*Canterbury*) 1990–92–93	3
Barrett, B.J. (*Taranaki*) 2010	2
Batty, G.B. (*Wellington*) 1973	1
Baxter, C.N.O. (*Bay of Plenty*) 2003–06–07	9
Berryman, N.R. (*Northland*) 1997	1
Blackadder, T.J. (*Canterbury*) 1993	2
Blackie, J.M. (*Otago*) 2002–03–04–05–06	12
Blowers, A.F. (*Auckland*) 1995	3
Blythe, T.G. (*Waikato*) 1999 (*Bay of Plenty*) 2001	3
Booth, J.P. (*Manawatu*) 2017	2
Botica, F.M. (*North Harbour*) 1985–86–87–88	8
Bourke, C.R. (*Hawke's Bay*) 2004	3
Brooke, Z.V. (*Auckland*) 1986–87–88–89–90	10
Brooke-Cowden, M. (*Auckland*) 1986–87	5
Bruning, K.T. (*Waikato*) 1994 (*Nelson Bays*) 1995	3
Bryant, R.J. (*Taranaki*) 1997	1
Bunce, F.E. (*North Harbour*) 1993	2
Bunce; J.F. (*Manawatu*) 2015 (*Waikato*) 2018	4
Bunting, A.M. (*Bay of Plenty*) 2002–03	6
Cama, T. (*Manawatu*) 2005–07–08–	

	Tournaments
09–10–11–12–13–14	63
Camburn, M. (*North Harbour*) 2005	3
Cashmore, A.R. (*Auckland*) 1995	4
Christie, S.A. (*Tasman*) 2011	2
Clamp, M. (*Wellington*) 1984–85–86	4
Clarke, C.D. (*Auckland*) 2018	2
Clarke, E. (*Auckland*) 1993	1
Clutterbuck, M.J. (*Bay of Plenty*) 2014	1
Cocker, E. (*Otago*) 2005–06–07 (*Auckland*) 2008–09	28
Collier, D.J. (*Waikato*) 2015–16–17–18–19	40
Colling, G.L. (*Otago*) 1973	1
Collins, N.I. (*Bay of Plenty*) 2001–02	6
Crowley, A.E. (*Taranaki*) 1987–88–89–91	6
Cullen, C.M. (*Manawatu*) 1995–96 (*Wellington*) 1998–00	7
Curry, S.B. (*Manawatu*) 2010–12–13 (*Bay of Plenty*) 2011–14–15–16–17–18–19	57
Curtis, A.A.D. (*Wellington*) 2013–14–15 (*Manawatu*) 2017	19
Dagg, I.J.A. (*Hawke's Bay*) 2007–08	6
Daniel, B.W. (*Bay of Plenty*) 1997	2
Dauwai, A. (*Thames Valley*) 2006	2
Dawson, A.J. (*Counties*) 1983–85	2
De Goldi, C.D. (*Bay of Plenty*) 1998–99–00 (*Auckland*) 2001–02–03–04	41
Dickson, S.N. (*Canterbury*) 2012–13–14–15–16–17–18–19	55
Donald, A.J. (*Wanganui*) 1983	1
Duggan, R.J.L. (*Waikato*) 1997	1
Ellis, M.C.G. (*Otago*) 1993	1
Ellison, T.E. (*Wellington*) 2005–06	5
Ensor A.C. (*Otago*) 2014	1
Erenavula, L. (*Counties*) 1994	2
Evans, N.J. (*North Harbour*) 2002	8
Faddes, M.A. (*Otago*) 2013	3
Fainga'anuku, L.T. (*Tasman*) 2018	1
Farani, D. (*Wellington*) 1997	1
Flavell, T.V. (*North Harbour*) 1998	2

Tournaments

Fleming, B.R.M.
  (Bay of Plenty) 1995
  (Canterbury) 1996–97–98
  (Wellington) 1998–99–00–01–02
  (Otago) 2003–04 — 35
Foote, B.M. *(Waikato)* 1997
  (North Harbour) 1998 — 3
Forbes, D.J. *(Auckland)* 2006–07
  (Counties Manukau) 2008–09–10–
  11–12–13–14–15–16–17 — 94
Forster, S.T. *(Otago)* 1993 — 2
Fry, R.J. *(Auckland)* 1983–84 — 2
Fuatai, F. *(Otago)* 2017 — 2

Gallagher, J.A. *(Wellington)* 1989–90 — 3
Gear, R.L. *(Auckland)* 1998–99–01 — 9
Gear, H.E. *(North Harbour)* 2003
  (Wellington) 2010–12 — 4
Going, S.J.
  (Northland) 1999–00–01–02–03 — 29
Goodhue, E.J. *(Northland)* 2015 — 2
Granger, K.W. *(Manawatu)* 1983 — 1
Grant, P.W. *(Otago)* 2008–09–10 — 15
Green, C.I. *(Canterbury)* 1986 — 2
Gregory, S.J. *(Northland)* 2018–19 — 8
Grice, R.J.L. *(Waikato)* 2011 — 3
Guildford, Z.R. *(Hawke's Bay)* 2010 — 1

Haami, B.D. *(Taranaki)* 2000 — 2
Halai, F. *(Waikato)* 2010–11–12 — 15
Hales, D.A. *(Canterbury)* 1973 — 1
Hamilton, L.G. *(North Harbour)* 2009 — 1
Hamilton, A.R.
  (Hawke's Bay) 1994–95–96 — 5
Haugh, T.C. *(Otago)* 2018 — 2
Heem, B.I. *(Auckland)* 2010–11–12
  (Tasman) 2013–14 — 22
Hoeata, J.M.R.A. *(Taranaki)* 2006 — 2
Holmes, B. *(North Auckland)* 1973 — 1
Hona, J. *(Bay of Plenty)* 2005 — 4
Houston, J.D.W. *(Canterbury)* 2017 — 1
Howarth, S.P. *(Auckland)* 1991 — 1
Hudson, C. *(Canterbury)* 1999–00 — 6
Hunt, N. *(Wellington)* 2005–06–07–08
  (Bay of Plenty) 2009 — 28

Ieremia, A. *(Wellington)* 1997 — 1
Ioane, A. *(Counties Manukau)* 1997 — 2
Ioane, A.L. *(Auckland)* 2014–16 — 11

Tournaments

Ioane, R.E. *(Auckland)* 2015–16 — 11
Ioasa, T.S.J.
  (Hawke's Bay) 2001–04–05–06–07–08
  (Wellington) 2002–03 — 48
Iopu, I.P. *(Auckland)* 2012
  (Taranaki) 2016–17 — 9
Izatt, C.S. *(Manawatu)* 1999 — 2

Jackman, M.B. *(HB/Cant)* 2012–13
  –14 — 10
Jane, C.S. *(Wellington)* 2006 — 5
Joass, T.J. *(Tasman)* 2017
  (Tas/BOP) 2018–19 — 17
John, O.W. *(Counties Manukau)* 1996 — 2
Jones, M.T.
  (Bay of Plenty) 1993–94–95–96–97 — 11

Kaino, J. *(Auckland)* 2005 — 2
Kaka, G.G. *(Hawke's Bay)*
  2013–14–15–16 — 33
Kamana, T.J.K.J. *(Waikato)* 2007 — 2
Karauna, D.T. *(Waikato)* 1996–97–
  98–00–01–02–03 — 35
Kepu, S.K.M. *(Auckland)* 2001 — 1
Keresoma, M.M. *(Auckland)* 2012–13 — 3
Khan, R.N. *(Auckland)* 2013–16–17–18 — 12
King, P.S.V.
  (Bay of Plenty) 2006–07–08–09–10
  (North Harbour) 2011–12 — 33
Kinikinilau, R.U.
  (Wellington) 2002–03–04–05–06
  (Waikato) 2007 — 13
Kiri Kiri, A.I. *(Manawatu)* 2015–16 — 4
Kirk, D.E. *(Otago)* 1984
  (Auckland) 1985–86 — 5
Kirwan, J.J. *(Auckland)*
  1984–85–86–88 — 5
Knewstubb, A.S. *(Tasman)* 2017
  (Tas/Horo Kap) 2018
  (Horowhenua Kapiti) 2019 — 27
Koloto, E.T. *(Manawatu)* 1987 — 2
Konia, G.N. *(Hawke's Bay)* 1997 — 1
Koonwaiyou, A. *(Auckland)* 2002 — 1
Koroi, V.T. *(Otago)* 2017–18–19 — 20

Lahmert, W.H. *(Taranaki)* 2012–13 — 5
Lam, M.B. *(Auckland)* 2012–13–
  14–16 — 15
Lam, P.R.
  (Auckland) 1989–90–91–92–93 — 7

Latimer, T.D.
(*Bay of Plenty*) 2004–05–06   15
Lawrence, Z.W.
(*North Harbour*) 2005–06–07
(*Bay of Plenty*) 2008–09–10   35
Lee, F.A. (*Counties Manukau*) 2010   4
Leo'o, J.J. (*Canterbury*) 2000–01   8
Lewis, A.J. (*Otago*) 1984   1
Lindsay, A.C. (*Canterbury*) 1983–84   2
Llewellyn, R.A.M. (*Canterbury*) 2012   1
Lomu, J.T. (*Counties Manukau*)
1994–95–96–98–99
(*Wellington*) 2000–01   13
Lynn, K.G. (*Southland*) 2008   2

McMaster, A. (*Manawatu*) 1987   2
McPhee, J.B. (*North Harbour*) 2010   2
McQuoid, G.A. (*Bay of Plenty*) 2004   3
MacDonald, L.T.J.
(*Bay of Plenty*) 2005–09   3
McGarvey-Black, N.M.
(*Bay of Plenty*) 2018–19   10
McKenzie, M.R. (*Southland*) 2014   2
Mafi, L.O. (*Manawatu*) 2003
(*Taranaki*) 2004–05   8
Maher, J.T. (*Counties Manukau*) 2006   2
Maidens, T.K. (*Hawke's Bay*) 1995   1
Malo, J.R. (*Waikato*) 2012   1
Marshall, J.R. (*Tasman*) 2011   2
Martin, E.M. (*Waikato*) 1996   1
Martin, R.E. (*Bay of Plenty*) 2001–02   11
Martine, H.R.I.
(*King Country*) 2000   1
Masirewa, L.R. (*Waikato*) 2012–13
(*Bay of Plenty*) 2018   12
Masirewa, W.
(*Counties Manukau*) 1996–97–98   10
Masoe, M.C. (*Taranaki*) 2001–02–04   22
Messam, L.J. (*Bay of Plenty*) 2002
(*Waikato*) 2003–04–05–06–10–16   26
Mikkelson, T.J. (*Waikato*) 2007–08–09
–10–11–12–13–14–15–16–17–18–19   94
Miller, A.J. (*Bay of Plenty*) 1997   1
Mills, J.G. (*Auckland*) 1984   1
Milne, B.W.T. (*Southland*) 2002   2
Molia, S.L.J.
(*Counties Manukau*) 2016–17–18–19   37
Monaghan, A.C.
(*Northland*) 1998–00   18

Muliaina, J.M.
(*Auckland*) 1999–00–01–02   11
Munro, L.H. (*Auckland*) 2006   4
Murray, C.D. (*Counties*) 1994   1

Naholo, W.R. (*Taranaki*) 2012–13–14   8
Nanai-Seturo, E.W.P.S.
(*Counties Manukau*) 2018   8
Nanai-Williams, T.T.
(*Counties Manukau*) 2008–09   7
Naoupu, G.E. (*Canterbury*) 2005   3
Nareki, J.M. (*Otago*) 2018–19   14
Nepia, D.S.M.
(*Bay of Plenty*) 2000–01   5
Newby, C.A. (*Bay of Plenty*) 1999
(*North Harbour*) 1999–00–01–02   13
Ng Shiu, I.J.S. (*Tasman*) 2017–18–19   25
Ngaluafe, N.S.J. (*Southland*) 2016   1
Nicole, A.P. (*Canterbury*) 2018–19   7
Nonoa, S.I. (*Waikato*) 1998   1
Nonu, M.A. (*Wellington*) 2004   2
Nowell, B.C. (*Canterbury*) 2008   2

O'Donnell, D.P.T. (*Waikato*)
2010–11–14–15   12
O'Donnell, K.F.T. (*Taranaki*) 2011–12   5
Ormsby, K.M.T.
(*Counties Manukau*) 2000   1
Ormond, J.T. (*Taranaki*) 2010–11   3
Ormond, L.H. (*Taranaki*) 2015–16–17   12
Osborne, G.M.
(*Nth Harbour*) 1992–93–94–96–97   6

Paramore, J. (*Counties*) 1993   2
Parkinson, D.T. (*Auckland*) 1998–99
(*Otago*) 2001
(*North Harbour*) 2003   15
Parkinson, M.T.
(*North Harbour*) 1999–2003–04
(*Bay of Plenty*) 2005   14
Peacocke, G.M.
(*North Harbour*) 1996–97   3
Pearson, M.B. (*Wellington*) 2015   1
Pedersen, H.L. (*Otago*) 2005   2
Pelenise, A.
(*Canterbury*) 2005–06–07   13
Phillips, C.M.
(*North Auckland*) 1986   3
Philpott, S. (*Canterbury*) 1988   2

Tournaments

Pierce, M.S.L.
(*North Harbour*) 1989–91–92–93–95 6
Piutau, S.T. (*Auckland*) 2011–12 8
Popoali'i, B. (*Wellington*) 2009
(*Otago*) 2011 8
Puletua, J.R. (*Auckland*) 2009 1
Pulu, A.W.
(*Counties Manukau*) 2015–16 7
Putt, K.B. (*Waikato*) 1987–89 2

Qio, J. (*NZ Fijians*)[1] 1999 1

Raikabula, L.
(*Wellington*) 2006–11–12–13–14–15
(*Hawke's Bay*) 2007
(*Manawatu*) 2008–09–10 70
Raikuna, D.A. (*Counties Manukau*) 2011
(*North Harbour*) 2013–14 12
Raki, L.E. (*Counties Manukau*) 1985–87 3
Ralph, C.S.
(*Bay of Plenty*) 1996–97–98
(*Canterbury*) 2000 7
Ranby, R.M. (*Waikato*) 2005 2
Randle, R.Q.
(*Hawke's Bay*) 1995–96–97–98
(*Waikato*) 2000–01–02 10
Ranger, R.M.N.
(*Northland*) 2006–07–08 8
Ravouvou, J. (*Auckland*) 2017–18–19 22
Rayasi, P. (*Wellington*) 1993 1
Rayasi, S.T.M. (*Auckland*) 2018–19 6
Reid, H.B. (*Otago*) 2001
(*North Harbour*) 2002–03–04
(*Bay of Plenty*) 2005–06 28
Reid, H.R. (*Bay of Plenty*) 1983 1
Reihana, B.T. (*Waikato*) 1998–02 2
Rich, G.J.W. (*Auckland*) 1983–84–85 3
Rickards, W.T.C.
(*Southland*) 2006–07–08–09 8
Robertson, G.A. (*Waikato*) 2011 3
Rokocoko, J.T. (*Auckland*) 2002–05 8
Rokolisoa, A.T.
(*Counties Manukau*) 2018–19 12
Ropiha, B.J. (*Hawke's Bay*) 2016 1
Ruddell, N.K. (*North Auckland*) 1986 1
Ruru, J.L. (*Otago*) 2016 2
Rush, E.J. (*Auckland*) 1988–89–90–91
(*North Harbour*) 1992–93–94–95–
96–97–98–99–00–01–02–03–04 62

Samuels, T.D.G. (*Hawke's Bay*) 2017 1
Savea, A.S. (*Wellington*) 2012–16 8
Savea, S.J. (*Wellington*) 2008–09 7
Savou, T.H. (*Manawatu*) 1998 1
Schmidt-Uili, P.T. (*Manawatu*) 1998 2
Schrijvers, D.J. (*Wellington*) 2018 1
Schuster, N.J.
(*Wellington*) 1986–88–89–90 6
Scown, A.I. (*Taranaki*) 1973 1
Scrimgeour, O.J.
(*Bay of Plenty*) 1995–96
(*Waikato*) 1995–96–97–98–99 22
Senio, K. (*Auckland*) 2001 2
Seymour, D.J.
(*Canterbury*) 1988–89–90–91–
92–93–99–00–02
(*Hawke's Bay*) 1994–95–96
(*Wellington*) 1997–98–99 35
Shelford, W.T.
(*North Harbour*) 1985–86–87 5
Simonsson, B.G. (*Bay of Plenty*) 2017–18 3
Skudder, G.R. (*Waikato*) 1973 1
Smith, B.R. (*Otago*) 2010 1
Smith, B.W. (*Waikato*) 1983 1
Smith, David (*Auckland*) 2008 1
Smith, D.A. (*Canterbury*) 1996 3
Smith, W.R. (*Canterbury*)
1984–85–86 4
Smylie, C.B. (*North Harbour*) 2002 2
Soakai, A. (*Otago*) 2006–07 9
So'oialo, R. (*Wellington*) 2000–01–02 6
Souness, B.J. (*Taranaki*) 2009–10–11 17
Spooner-Neera, T.A. (*Hawke's Bay*)
2013 4
Stanaway, T.Z.B.P. (*Bay of Plenty*)
2015–16–17–18 9
Stanley, J.T. (*Auckland*) 1983 1
Steinmetz, P.C. (*Wellington*) 1999 3
Stephens, T.P.O.T.R. (*Tasman*) 2019 1
Stevens, I.N. (*Wellington*) 1973 1
Stowers, S.L. (*Auckland*) 2004
(*Counties Manukau*) 2009–10–12–
13–14–15–16–17 42
Sutherland, A.R.
(*Marlborough*) 1973 1
Sweeney, D.W.H. (*Waikato*) 2006 6

Tagaloa, T.D.L. (*Wellington*) 1991 1
Tairea, F.T. (*Auckland*) 2009 1

[1]Tournament reserve players called upon when injuries prevented New Zealand from having fit reserves for the final.

NEW ZEALAND INTERNATIONAL SEVENS

FMG Waikato Stadium, Hamilton

January 26/27, 2019

POOL PLAY

A   Australia 17 Argentina 12; Fiji 54 Wales 7; Australia 26 Wales 5;
Fiji 33 Argentina 24; Argentina 36 Wales 7; Fiji 26 Australia 19.

B   Samoa 12 England 10; USA 29 Tonga 7; England 36 Tonga 7;
USA 34 Samoa 14; Samoa 28 Tonga 12; USA 19 England 7.

C   Scotland 26 France 21; South Africa 29 Kenya 10; Scotland 19 Kenya 10;
South Africa 17 France 5; Kenya 19 France 15; South Africa 26 Scotland 7.

D   Spain 12 Canada 12; New Zealand 52 Japan 0; Spain 22 Japan 19;
New Zealand 49 Canada 10; Canada 26 Japan 0; New Zealand 24 Spain 0.

CUP CHAMPIONSHIP

Quarter-finals	Fiji 33, Canada 7; South Africa 28, Samoa 19; New Zealand 24, Australia 17; USA 19, Scotland 14.
Semi-finals	Fiji 29, South Africa 7; USA 17, New Zealand 7.
Final	Fiji 38, USA 0.
Play off for 3rd	New Zealand 29, South Africa 7.
5th place semi-final	Samoa 28, Canada 19; Scotland 24, Australia 14.
5th place play-off	Scotland 24, Samoa 19.

CHALLENGE TROPHY

Quarter-finals	Argentina 35, Japan 0; Kenya 19, Tonga 12; Spain 19, Wales 10; England 21, France 5.
Semi-finals	Kenya 24, Argentina 7; England 38, Spain 7.
Final	England 36, Kenya 7.

13th place semi-final Tonga 31, Japan 7; France 35, Wales 19.
13th place play-off   Tonga 33, France 10.

Tournament referees: James Doleman (*New Zealand*), Craig Evans (*Wales*), Sam Grove-White (*Scotland*), Richard Kelly (*New Zealand*), Damon Murphy (*Australia*), Rasta Rasivhenge (*South Africa*), Matt Rodden (*Hong Kong*), Tevita Rokovereni (*Fiji*), Jordan Way (*Australia*).

New Zealand International Sevens Tournaments

	Cup final	Plate winner	Bowl winner	Shield winner
2000	Fiji 24, New Zealand 14	Canada	France	
2001	Australia19, Fiji 17	Samoa	South Africa	Japan
2002	South Africa 17, Samoa 14	Argentina	France	Cook Is
2003	New Zealand 38, England 26	Samoa	Canada	Tonga
2004	New Zealand 33, Fiji 15	Tonga	Argentina	USA
2005	New Zealand 31, Argentina 7	Australia	Kenya	Niue
2006	Fiji 27, South Africa 22	England	Scotland	Tonga
2007	Samoa 17, Fiji 14	England	Argentina	Portugal
2008	New Zealand 22, Samoa 7	South Africa	England	USA
2009	England 19, New Zealand 17	South Africa	Cook Is	Scotland
2010	Fiji 19, Samoa 14	Australia	Wales	USA
2011	New Zealand 29, England 14	Fiji	Kenya	USA
2012	New Zealand 24, Fiji 7	South Africa	Kenya	Scotland
2013	England 24, Kenya 19	Australia	Canada	Wales
2014	New Zealand 21, South Africa 0	Australia	Kenya	USA
2015	New Zealand 27, England 21	Fiji	France	Canada
2016	New Zealand 24, South Africa 21	Australia	Samoa	France

	Cup final	Challenge Trophy winner
2017	South Africa 26, Fiji 5	Kenya
2018	Fiji 24, South Africa 17	USA
2019	Fiji 38, USA 0	England

NEW ZEALAND SEVENS SELECTION

Squads, minus several regular sevens players involved in Mitre 10 Cup campaigns, attended tournaments in Germany (September) and Fiji (November).

		Germany	Fiji	TOTALS
Kurt Baker	Manawatu	–	*	1
Rewita Biddle	Bay of Plenty	*	–	1
Dylan Collier	Waikato	–	*	1
Scott Curry (co-capt)	Bay of Plenty	–	s	1
Sam Dickson	Canterbury	*	–	1
Dan Fransen	Canterbury	*	–	1
Taylor Haugh	Otago	–	*	1
Trael Joass	Tasman	*	*	2
Niko Jones	Auckland	–	*	1
Andrew Knewstubb	Horowhenua Kapiti	*	–	1
Ngarohi McGarvey-Black	Bay of Plenty	*	*	2
Luke Masirewa	Bay of Plenty	*	–	1
Tim Mikkelson (capt)	Waikato	*	*	2
Sione Molia	Counties Manukau	*	–	1
Tone Ng Shiu	Tasman	*	–	1
Amanaki Nicole	Canterbury	*	*	2
Akuila Rokolisoa	Counties Manukau	–	*	1
Jamie Spowart	Tasman	–	*	1
Te Rangatira Waitokia	Manawatu	–	*	1
William Warbrick	Bay of Plenty	–	*	1
Regan Ware	Bay of Plenty	*	–	1

Coach: Tomasi Cama (in Germany), Clark Laidlaw (Fiji)
Manager: Ross Everiss
Physiotherapist: Damian Banks (Germany), Kate Niederer (Fiji)

NEW ZEALAND SELECTION AT OKTOBERFEST SEVENS
Olympic Stadium, Munich, Germany · September 21/22, 2019

Date	Opponent	Result	Tries	Conversions
Sept 21	South Africa	lost 12–19	Ware, Molia	Knewstubb
Sept 21	Australia	won 17–14	McGarvey-Black (2), Joass	Knewstubb
Sept 21	England	won 38–7	Ware (2), Masirewa, Fransen, Joass, McGarvey-Black	Fransen (3), Biddle
Sept 22	Fiji (Cup semi-final)	lost 12–14	Knewstubb, McGarvey-Black	Knewstubb
Sept 22	Germany (for 3rd)	won 22–12	Biddle (2), Fransen, McGarvey-Black	Biddle
South Africa defeated Fiji 12–10 in the Cup final				

NEW ZEALAND SELECTION AT OCEANIA SEVENS
ANZ Stadium, Suva, Fiji · November 7–9, 2019

Date	Opponent	Result	Tries	Conversions
Nov 7	New Caledonia	won 57–0	Rokolisoa (3), Baker (3), Spowart, Collier, Waitokia	Baker (3), Rokolisoa, McGarvey-Black, Haugh
Nov 7	Niue	won 38–0	Collier (2), Warbrick, Joass, Spowart, Waitokia	McGarvey-Black (2), Mikkelson, Baker
Nov 8	Japan	lost 14–17	Rokolisoa, McGarvey-Black	Rokolisoa, McGarvey-Black
Nov 8	Fiji	lost 15–21	Collier (2), Jones	
Nov 9	Cook Islands (s-f for 7th – 10th place)	won 64–0	Warbrick (2), Curry (2), Rokolisoa (2), Haugh (2), Baker, McGarvey-Black	Haugh (3), McGarvey-Black (2), Rokolisoa, Curry
Nov 9	Solomon Islands (final for 7th place)	won 39–7	McGarvey-Black (3), Warbrick (2), Baker, Mikkelson	Baker, Haugh
Australia defeated Fiji 22–7 in the Cup final.				

NATIONAL SEVENS

Tauranga Domain   December 14/15, 2019

POOL PLAY

A   Canterbury 38, Wairarapa Bush 7; Auckland 14, Counties Manukau 5;
        Canterbury 21, Counties Manukau 14; Auckland 45, Wairarapa Bush 10;
        Auckland 26, Canterbury 12; Counties Manukau 28, Wairarapa Bush 12.

B   Waikato 38, South Canterbury 0; Tasman 24, Otago 12;
        Waikato 7, Otago 5; Tasman 41, South Canterbury 12;
        Waikato 19, Tasman 7; Otago 31, South Canterbury 12.

C   Wellington 40, Thames Valley 0; Hawke's Bay 22, Southland 19;
        Southland 7, Wellington 5; Hawke's Bay 31, Thames Valley 5;
        Hawke's Bay 24, Wellington 17; Southland 40, Thames Valley 7.

D   Bay of Plenty 35, Manawatu 12; North Harbour 17, Taranaki 12;
        Taranaki 40, Manawatu 14; Bay of Plenty 22, North Harbour 14;
        North Harbour 19, Manawatu 17; Taranaki 22, Bay of Plenty 12.

CUP CHAMPIONSHIP

Quarter-finals   Auckland 22, Tasman 19; Taranaki 17, Southland 7;
                   Bay of Plenty 12, Hawke's Bay 10; Waikato 17, Canterbury 12.
Semi-finals   Auckland 12, Taranaki 5; Waikato 19, Bay of Plenty 10.
Final   Waikato 31, Auckland 5.

PLATE CHAMPIONSHIP

Semi-finals   Tasman 19, Southland 17; Hawke's Bay 28, Canterbury 26.
Final   Tasman 33, Hawke's Bay 19.

BOWL CHAMPIONSHIP

Quarter-finals   Counties Manukau 46, South Canterbury 7;
                   North Harbour 41, Thames Valley 7;
                   Wellington 17, Manawatu 14; Otago 24, Wairarapa Bush 7.
Semi-finals   Counties Manukau 24, North Harbour 0; Otago 35, Wellington 12
Final   Counties Manukau 24, Otago 19.

SHIELD CHAMPIONSHIP

Semi-finals   South Canterbury 24, Thames Valley 19; Manawatu 14, Wairarapa Bush 10.
Final   Manawatu 26, South Canterbury 14.

Tournament referees: Tipene Cottrell, George Haswell, Nick Hogan, James Munro, Chris Paul,
        Michael Winter.

Joe Tauiwi Memorial Trophy *(Player of the Tournament)*
2001 Rua Tipoki (*North Harbour*), 2002 Tafai Ioasa (*Wellington*), 2004 Rudi Wulf (*North Harbour*), 2005 Amasio Valence (*Auckland*), 2006 Gary Saifoloi (*Auckland*), 2007 Tomasi Cama (*Manawatu*), 2008 David Raikuna (*Counties Manukau*), 2009 Luke Hamilton (*North Harbour*), 2010 Ben Souness (*Taranaki*), 2011 Malakai Fekitoa (*Auckland , 2012 Buxton Popoaili'i (*Otago*), 2013 David Raikuna (*North Harbour*), 2014 George Tilsley (*Manawatu*), 2015 Luke Masirewa (*Waikato*), 2016 Augustine Pulu (*Counties Manukau*) , 2017 Andrew Knewstubb (*Tasman*), 2018 (*January*) Jordan Bunce (*Waikato*); (*December*) James Lash (*Tasman*), 2019 Liam Coombes-Fabling (*Waikato*).

NATIONAL SEVENS

TOURNAMENT TROPHY WINNERS

	Venue	Cup	Plate	Bowl	Shield
1975	Auckland	Marlborough			
1976	Christchurch	Marlborough			
1977	Blenheim	Manawatu			
1978	Hamilton	Manawatu			
1979	Palmerston Nth	Manawatu			
1980	Palmerston Nth	Auckland			
1981	Palmerston Nth	Taranaki			
1982	Feilding	Taranaki			
1983	Feilding	Auckland			
1984	Feilding	Auckland			
1985	Feilding	Counties			
1986	Feilding	Nth Harbour			
1987	Christchurch	Nth Harbour	Canterbury	Horowhenua	
1988	Pukekohe	Auckland	Manawatu	Wai Bush	
1989	Palmerston Nth	Auckland	Taranaki	Wanganui	Hawke's Bay
1990	Palmerston Nth	Canterbury	Bay of Plenty	Wanganui	Manawatu B
1991	Palmerston Nth	Auckland	Counties	Canterbury	East Coast
1992	Palmerston Nth	Nth Harbour	Counties	Auckland	Manawatu B
1993	Palmerston Nth	Canterbury	Nth Harbour	Taranaki	King Country
1994	Palmerston Nth	Counties	Nth Harbour	Canterbury	Manawatu B
1995	Palmerston Nth	Counties	Wellington	King Country	Manawatu B
1996	(*Mar*) Palm Nth	Waikato	C'nties M'kau	Wai Bush	Poverty Bay
1996	(*Nov*) Palm Nth	Waikato	Wellington	Wai Bush	Wanganui
1997	Rotorua	Waikato	Auckland	Otago	Wai Bush
1998	Rotorua	Waikato	Canterbury	Wai Bush	Otago
1999	Palmerston Nth	Nth Harbour	Canterbury	King Country	Nelson Bays
2000	Palmerston Nth	Nth Harbour	Wanganui	Nelson Bays	Southland
2001	Palmerston Nth	Nth Harbour	C'nties M'kau	Manawatu	West Coast
2002	Palmerston Nth	Wellington	Waikato	Marlborough	West Coast
2004	Queenstown	Nth Harbour	Auckland	Canterbury	Manawatu
2005	Queenstown	Auckland	Wellington	Otago	Manawatu
2006	Queenstown	Auckland	Bay of Plenty	Southland	Cantabrians
2007	Queenstown	Auckland	C'nties M'kau	Wellington	Northland

	Venue	*Cup*	*Plate*	*Bowl*	*Shield*
2008	Queenstown	Auckland	Manawatu	Wellington	Tasman
2009	Queenstown	Nth Harbour	Wellington	Otago	Southland
2010	Queenstown	Waikato	Nth Harbour	Horo' Kapiti	Tasman
2011	Queenstown	Auckland	Nth Harbour	Manawatu	Canterbury
2012	Queenstown	Auckland	Taranaki	Tasman	Bay of Plenty
2013	Queenstown	Taranaki	Auckland	Hawke's Bay	C'nties M'kau
2014	Rotorua	Wellington	Manawatu	Nth Harbour	Waikato
2015	Rotorua	Waikato	Taranaki	NthHarbour	Canterbury
2016	Rotorua	C'nties M'kau	Auckland	Northland	Wanganui
2017	Rotorua	C'nties M'kau	Auckland	Bay of Plenty	Otago
2018					
(Jan)	Rotorua	Waikato	Bay of Plenty	C'nties M'kau	Northland
(Dec)	Tauranga	Tasman	Taranaki	Auckland	Manawatu
2019	Tauranga	Waikato	Tasman	C'nties M'kau	Manawatu

NEW ZEALAND
RUGBY FOOTBALL UNION 2019

Founded 1991

Argentina Deaf visited for three tests against New Zealand Deaf. The fixtures do not have first-class status.

NEW ZEALAND DEAF 2020		Argentina	Argentina	Argentina	TOTALS
Matt Hollis	Central Zone	15*	–	15*	2
Kamau Wise	Central Zone	s	15*	s	3
Petaera Meihana	Paramatta-Plimmerton, Wellington	14*	14*	13	3
Henry Tangiwai-Scott	Southern Zone	11*	s	11*	3
Matthew Findsen	Southern Zone	s	11	14*	3
Joseph Konelio	Suburbs, Auckland	s	–	s	2
Henare Browne	Suburbs, Auckland	–	–	s	1
Mitchell MacPherson (vc)	Silverdale, North Harbour	13	13	8	3
Paul Walker	Southern Zone	12	s	12	3
Rhys Sticklings	Southern Zone	–	12	–	1
James Copeland	College Rifles, Auckland	10	10	10	3
Herbie Agnew	Linwood, Canterbury	9	9	9	3
Doug Brand	Valley, North Otago	8	8*	–	2
Daniel Eastwood	College Rifles, Auckland	–	s	–	1
Reuben Buzzard	Christchurch, Canterbury	7	7	7	3
Toby Agnew (capt)	Linwood, Canterbury	6*	–	–	1
Ashley Bensley	Linwood, Canterbury	s	6	2*	3
Kristofer Jonsson	Southern Zone	–	–	6	1
Wiremu Ellis	Saracens, Canterbury	5	–	s	2
Ryan Cassidy	Central Zone	s	5*	–	2
Samuel Lane	Kaierau, Wanganui	s	s	s	3
Phillip King	Ponsonby, Auckland	4*	4	4*	3
Maara Tuare	Southern Zone	3*	s	3*	3
David Dayberg	Northern Zone	s	3*	s	3
Kenneth Tafai	Belfast, Canterbury	1*	1	1*	3
Simona Fauena	Upper Hutt OB, Wellington	s	–	s	2
Ben Webb	Paramatta-Plimmerton, Wellington	2*	2	s	3

MacPherson was captain in second and third tests.

Manager: Riaan Van Vuuren (*Wellington*)
Assistant manager: Evelyn Pateman (*Christchurch*)
Coach: Clive Morgan (*Wellington*)
Assistant coach: Ben Robertson (*Christchurch*)
Physiotherapists: Dina Lewis (*Waikato*), Gareth O'Loughlin (*Auckland*), Kelly Powell (*Auckland*).

May 26 v **Argentina Deaf**, at Waitemata RFC, Henderson, Auckland. Won 24–8. Hollis, Walker, Ellis tries; H. Agnew 3 penalty goals.
Referee: Jeremy Kannemeyer (Auckland).

May 29 v **Argentina Deaf**, at Waitemata RFC, Henderson, Auckland. Won 20–3. Bensley 2, Buzzard tries; Copeland conversion; H. Agnew penalty goal.
Referee: Maggie Cogger-Orr (Auckland).

June 1 v **Argentina Deaf**, at Ponsonby RFC, Western Springs, Auckland. Won 29–0. Copeland 3, Hollis, Ellis tries; Copeland 2 conversions.
Referee: Charles Visser (Wellington).

INTERNATIONAL MATCH RECORD

1995	v South Africa	Christchurch	lost	15	22
	v South Africa	Palmerston North	won	17	8
	v South Africa	Takapuna	lost	0	46
1998	v Wales	Newport	won	35	10
	v Wales	Neath	won	55	3
	v Wales	Llanelli	won	57	5
2001	v Australia	Sydney	won	25	0
	v Australia	Sydney	lost	12	15
2002	v Australia	Sydney	won	19	17
	v Wales (WC)	Auckland	lost	5	11
	v Australia (WC)	Auckland	won	23	13
	v Wales (WC final)	Auckland	lost	14	28
2005	v Australia	Wanganui	lost	10	22
	v Australia	Christchurch	won	10	8
2012	v Australia	Auckland	lost	20	22
2013	v Australia	Canberra	won	30	13
2015	v Australia	Christchurch	lost	13	15
2016	v Argentina	Cordoba	won	19	15
	v Argentina	San Salvador de Jujuy	won	18	16
2019	v Argentina	Auckland	won	24	8
	v Argentina	Auckland	won	20	3
	v Argentina	Auckland	won	29	0

WC   World Cup

The 26th national Deaf tournament between the three zones was held at College Rifles RFC, Remuera, Auckland during April 19–21. The results were: Southern 49 Northern 7; Central 26 Northern 25; Southern 25 Central 14. Southern Zone was awarded the NZ Rugby Shield.

CLUB FINALS

Results of the 2019 senior club finals.

Auckland – Gallaher Shield:

20 July: Ponsonby 27 v Marist 24
Down 3-17 at halftime Ponsonby went ahead 27-17 and held on to win their 50th title.

Bay of Plenty – Baywide Premier Trophy:

20 July: Te Puna 23 v Tauranga Sports 10
Halftime 13-7. Celebrating their 100th anniversary Te Puna won their first ever title.

Buller – Senior Shield:

13 July: Ngakawau-Karamea 46 v Westport 31
Haftime 24-17.

Canterbury

Ellesmere-Mid Canterbury-North Canterbury combined – Luisetti Combined Country Cup:
3 June: Glenmark-Cheviot 34 a.e.t. v Southern 34 a.e.t.
Postponed from the Saturday (1st) due to bad weather. 26-26 after 80 minutes. Shared title

Metropolitan – Hawkins Trophy:
28 July: HSOB 34 v Lincoln University 29
Down 5-29 after 35 minutes HSOB came back to win 34-29.

Ellesmere sub union – Coleman Shield:
27 July: Southbridge 16 v Darfield 12
Halftime 5-5. Darfield were held up on the line with four minutes left but could not get the ball down for the winning try.

North Canterbury sub union – Hunnibel Memorial Trophy:
27 July: Glenmark-Cheviot 16 v Kaiapoi 10
Halftime 9-0, but down 9-10 Glenmark-Cheviot needed a late try to complete an unbeaten season with 17 wins and one draw.

Counties Manukau – McNamara Cup:

20 July: Bombay 33 v Ardmore Marist 18
Halftime 14-10. Bombay scored four tries to two.

Ngati Porou East Coast – Rangiora Keelan Memorial Shield:

27 July: Uawa 24 v Tihirau Victory Club 23
The lead changed hands five times. TVC missed a last minute penalty goal to win the game.

Hawke's Bay – Maddison Trophy Cup:

20 July: Napier OB Marist 43 a.e.t. v Hastings RS 24 a.e.t.
24-24 after 80 minutes. Down 10-24 after 64 minutes, Napier OB Marist scored a last minute converted try to force extra time, then scored three tries in the first half of extra time.

Wairoa sub union – Garry Allen Memorial Shield
10 August-28 September: 1st Tapuae 15 points, YMP 15 points
A shared title. Both teams won three out of three but the match between them set for 31 August was postponed, and subsequently not rescheduled.

Horowhenua Kapiti – Ramsbotham Cup:

20 July: Foxton 31 v Waikanae 25
Foxton led 24-0 after 20 minutes but Waikanae edged ahead 25-24. Foxton scored a converted try with four minutes left to regain the lead and the match ended with Waikanae turning over possession five metres from the Foxton posts. Foxton's first title since 1988.

King Country – Meads Shield:

27 July: Taupo Sports 38 v Waitete 6
Halftime 22-6, Taupo Sports defended their title.

Manawatu – Hankins Shield:

13 July: Feilding 16 v Massey University 14
Halftime 10-6. Massey University scored a try in the right corner in the final minute. The conversion from the sideline, to force extra time, missed. Feilding's first title since 1984.

Mid Canterbury – Watters Cup:

20 July: Rakaia 19 a.e.t. v Methven 12 a.e.t.
Played in the rain, it was 12-12 after 80 minutes. The match ended with a Methven player pushed into touch a metre from the Rakaia tryline.
For combined competition with Ellesmere and North Canterbury sub-unions see Canterbury.

Northland

Northland Premiership – Joe Morgan Memorial Trophy:
13 July: Waipu 31 v Old Boys Marist 20
Halftime 19-3. Waipu won their first title.

Bay of Islands sub union – Championship Shield:
13 July: Moerewa-United Kawakawa 40 v Kaikohe 31
Halftime 18-12. The match doubled as a Northland North Zone Championship final. Moerewa-United Kawakawa subsequently won a promotion-relegation match into the Northland Premiership for 2020 to complete a perfect 18 wins from 18 games.

Mangonui sub union – Bell Shield:
27 July: Awanui 36 a.e.t. v Eastern United 29 a.e.t.
29-29 after 80 minutes. Eastern United scored a try close to the posts in the 80th minute, but the conversion, to win, missed, forcing extra time. There was a Harvey brother on each side and a Ngaruhe brother on each side.

North Harbour – A.S.B. Cup:

20 July: East Coast Bays 21 v Northcote 17
East Coast Bays led all the way for their first title since 1991. Both teams scored two tries.

North Otago – Citizen's Shield:

20 July: Maheno 18 v Old Boys 7
Old Boys led 7-0 after 16 minutes, but did not score again.

Otago

Metropolitan – Speight's Championship Shield:
27 July: University 38 v Taieri 31
University led 31-3 at halftime but Taieri levelled at 31-31 with five minutes left. In the 80th minute Angus Williams scored a try for University to win the match.

Central Region – Super Liquor Trophy:
27 July: Arrowtown 24 v Cromwell 21.
Arrowtown led 21-7 during the second half but Cromwell levelled at 21-21. A 76th minute penalty goal was the difference for Arrowtown's first title since 2009. Cromwell had won both previous matches this year.

Southern Region – Speight's Cup:
27 July: Clutha 34 v Crescent 28.
Third year in a row these two teams have met in the final. A Crescent try in the final minute closed the gap but Clutha won their fifth title in a row.

Central Region-Southern Region: Countrywide Shield
3 August: Clutha 24 v Arrowtown 14
Clutha came from 3-14 down at halftime to win the Countrywide Shield for the fifth consecutive time.

Poverty Bay – Lee Brothers Shield:

20 July: Old Boys Marist 65 v YMP 5.
Old Boys Marist's first title since 2004.

Southland – Galbraith Shield:

13 July: Blues 16 v Star 9
In the rain, Blues scored the only try of the match with 15 minutes left, and with the conversion went ahead 16-9 for their first title since 2005.

South Canterbury – Hamersley Cup:

27 July: Temuka 41 v Celtic 10
Temuka scored three tries for a 27-0 halftime lead towards their first title since 2001, and deny Celtic an 11th successive title.

Taranaki – McMasters Shield:

13 July: Spotswood United 18 v Coastal 13
Halftime 8-8. Neither team had won the title. Coastal had won both previous matches this year and were beaten in the final for the third successive year.

Tasman – Tasman Trophy:

8 June: Nelson Marist 32 a.e.t. v Waimea Old Boys 29 a.e.t.
An 80th minute penalty goal by Waimea OB forced extra time at 29-29. James Hawkey scored the only points in extra time with a penalty goal for Marist two minutes from the end. The round robin match had been a 26-26 draw.

Marlborough sub union – Champion of Champions Trophy:
20 July: Waitohi 26 v Central 20
It was 20-20 midway through the second half. Remaining scoring was two Corey Bovey penalty goals.

Nelson Bays sub union – Strange Memorial Cup + Centennial Cup:
20 July: Waimea Old Boys 25 a.e.t. v Marist 23 a.e.t.
Having gone into extra time in the Tasman final, these two teams went into extra time again. Marist scored an 80th minute try to make it 20-20 but the conversion, to win, missed, forcing extra time.

Thames Valley – McClinchy Cup:

3 August: COBRAS 25 v Thames 23.
Having led twice, Thames missed a last minute 40 metre penalty goal to win.

Waikato – Breweries Shield:

20 July: Hautapu 22 v Fraser Tech 13
In the rain, with two minutes left, a penalty goal made the game safe for Hautapu who completed a perfect season 18 wins from 18 games. Each side scored one try.

Wanganui – President's Rosebowl:

27 July: Taihape 31 a.e.t. v Border 26 a.e.t.
Border led 20-6 during the first half, but a late penalty goal for Taihape levelled 26-26 for extra time. A Richard Irons try in the first period put Taihape in front for the first time. Border had won both previous matches in 2019.

Wairarapa Bush – Tui Cup:

27 July: Martinborough 36 v Gladstone 32
Down 12-20 after 22 minutes, Martinborough went out to a 36-20 lead. Gladstone scored a last minute try to close the gap to 36-32. Martinborough's first title since 1991.

Wellington – Jubilee Cup:

27 July: Northern United 25 v Wainuiomata 16
Halftime 19-13. Only scoring in the second half was through penalty goals.

West Coast – Taylorville Wallsend Trophy:

13 July: Kiwi 50 v Grey Valley 27
Halftime 26-15. Kiwi's 6th consecutive final and 4th consecutive title completed a perfect season of 12 wins from 12 games. They have now won their last 39 games.

Most consecutive championships:
14 Star (Southland) 1890-1903
10 Athletic (North Otago) 1906-1915; Celtic (South Canterbury) 2009-2018
8 Star (Southland) 1919-1926; Westport (Buller) 1963-1970; Invercargill (Southland) 1987-1994; Ponsonby (Auckland) 2004-2011

Most consecutive Sub Union championships:
13 Mahia (Wairoa) 1981-1993
11 Dannevirke O.B. (Dannevirke) 1946-1955, (Central HB-Dannevirke) 1956

JOCK HOBBS MEMORIAL NATIONAL UNDER 19 TOURNAMENT

The sixth edition was played from 8 – 14 September at Owen Delany Park, Taupo. On the final day four of the eight matches were shown live on Sky TV. The matches are not of first-class status.

The seedings for the National Tournament, based on placings in prior tournaments held within each Super Rugby franchise (Crusaders and Highlanders combined), were:

Premiership (top eight) – Graham Mourie Cup
Auckland *(Blues 1)*, Auckland Development *(Blues 2)*, Bay of Plenty *(Chiefs 1)*, Canterbury *(Southern 1)*, Manawatu *(Hurricanes 2)*, Otago *(Southern 2)*, Waikato *(Chiefs 2)*, Wellington *(Hurricanes 1)*.

Championship (bottom eight) – Michael Jones Trophy
Counties Manukau *(Chiefs 4)*, Hawke's Bay *(Hurricanes 3)*, Heartland, North Harbour *(Blues 3)*, Northland *(Blues 4)*, Southland *(Southern 4)*, Taranaki *(Chiefs 3)*, Tasman *(Southern 3)*.

2019 RESULTS

PREMIERSHIP (1ST - 8TH) – GRAHAM MOURIE CUP

Day One: September 8
Canterbury 27 – Manawatu 7; Wellington 22 – Otago 3; Auckland 30 – Waikato 25; Bay of Plenty 50 – Auckland Development 0
Day Two: September 11
Semi-finals: Auckland 21 a.e.t. – Wellington 18 a.e.t.; Canterbury 16 – Bay of Plenty 14
Ranking: Manawatu 36 – Auckland Development 24; Otago 21 – Waikato 10
Day Three: September 14
1st/2nd Final: Canterbury 26 – Auckland 17
3rd/4th Wellington 34 – Bay of Plenty 7   *5th/6th* Otago 17 – Manawatu 3   *7th/8th* Waikato 36 – Auckland Development 19

CHAMPIONSHIP (9TH – 16TH) – MICHAEL JONES TROPHY

Day One: September 8
Taranaki 58 – Northland 0; North Harbour 27 – Counties Manukau 26; Hawke's Bay 44 – Southland 0; Tasman 33 – Heartland 3
Day Two: September 11
Semi-finals: Hawke's Bay 10 – North Harbour 9; Taranaki 47 – Tasman 27
Ranking: Heartland 41 – Northland 26; Counties Manukau 81 – Southland 12
Day Three: September 14
9th/10th Final: Taranaki 52 – Hawke's Bay 25
11th/12th North Harbour 29 – Tasman 17   *13th/14th* Counties Manukau 52 – Heartland 20
15th/16th Northland 45 – Southland 18

D.J. Graham Award (player of the tournament)	Fletcher Newell	*(Canterbury)*
Top Try-scorers	(4)	Jamahl Hapi *(Taranaki)*, Josh Jacomb *(Taranaki)*, Saul Lewis *(Tasman)*, Ioane Moananu *(Counties Manukau)*, Millennium Sanerivi *(Taranaki)*, Bailey Tautau *(Tasman)*
Top Points-scorer	(52)	Josh Jacomb *(Taranaki)*

2019 SQUADS (APPEARANCES IN BRACKETS):

Auckland: *Co Captains* – Lemeki Namoa, Niko Jones   *Coach* – Greg Aldous
Sione Ahio (3); Patrick Elia (3); Joseph Fabish (3); Cameron Finefeuiaki (2); Taufa Funaki (3); Jack Gray (3); Niko Jones (3); John Latu (3); Junior Mafelo (0); Leweni Mocevakaca (3); Heremaia Murray (3); Lemeki Namoa (3); Damien Naufahu (3); Mase Neemia (2); Terrell Peita (3); Noah Perelini (0); Robert Rush (3); Danny Silivelio (2); Champagnat Solomon-Mua (3); Zarn Sullivan (3); Mateo Taiseni (1); Soane Vikena (3); Shalom Viliamu (3); Jerry Wilson (2); Samuel Wye (3).

Auckland Development: *Captain* – Thomas Strachan   *Coach* – Ramsey Tomokino
Valentino Adam (3); Likau Alatini (3); Thomas Drumm (2); Levi Filiga (0); Foliga Gabriel (3); Terepai King (2); Folau Latu (3); Tui Aso Lene (3); Sione Ma'asi (3); Va'a Maelega (3); Jermaine Malaga (3); Sosene Mataena (3); Jared Mataia (1); Eric McLoughlin (3); Cody Mitchell (3); Connor Moors (2); Benjamin Plummer (3); Louis Saena (3); Pio Sefo (3); Thomas Strachan (3); Reece Suesue (3); Sake Tafea (2); Sione Takai (3); Tualamiu Tauasosi (1); Dominic Tevao (2); Abraham Tongotongo (2).

Bay of Plenty: *Captain* – Benet Kumeroa   *Coach* – James Porter
Nikora Broughton (3); Louis Brunisma (3); Josh Calvert (3); Lockie Devereux (3); Bailey Gordon (3); Chris Hemi (3); Jackson Hollinshead (3); Tamarau Karepa (1); Benet Kumeroa (3); Peni Lasaqa (3); Izhan Le Compte (0); Malupo Ma'afu (3); Rory Marsh (3); Connor McEldowney (1); Cassius Misa (3); Simione Ofa (3); Connor Paki (2); Fritz Rayasi (3); Pena Taumata (2); Jamaine Tawa (3); Poukohe Tawhara-Sorenson (3); Tamaikoha Te Aute (3); Sam Tuibua (3); Hunter Wharerau (2); Taituha Woller (3).

Canterbury: *Captain* – Isaiah Punivai   *Coach* – Grant Keenan
Liam Allen (3); Finlay Brewis (3); Louie Chapman (3); Joshua Corrigan (1); Sam Darry (3); Luke Donaldson (3); Thomas Edwards (3); Chay Fihaki (3); Angus Fletcher (2); Daniel Johnson (1); Tahu Kaa (3); Oscar Koller (3); Harry McKay (1); Lachlan McNair (3); Cullen Moody (3); Fletcher Morgan (3); Michael Naitokani (3); Fletcher Newell (3); Mahonri Ngakuru (3); George Prain (3); Isaiah Punivai (3); Joshua Ree (0); Patrick Thacker (1); Tamaiti Williams (3); Hunter Wilson (3).

Counties Manukau: *Captain* – Ioane Moananu   *Coach* – Stephen Donald
Eric Ah Hing (2); Setaliki Baker (3); Atonio Efaraimo (3); Paul Faoagali (3); Tevita Hala (3); Michael Hoeft (2); Chey Jacobs (3); Ailepata Lemalu (3); Ioane Moananu (3); Leo Ngatai-Tafau (3); Aue Parima (3); Tuhikiterangi Pompey (3); Sione Pulu (3); Cameron Roigard (3); Toara Ruben (3); Mark Samuelu (2); Zachary Smith (3); Irirangi Taniere (3); Jonwa Taumateine (1); Ethan Taylor (2); Ethan Thomas (1); Shammah Tiumalu (2); Zion Tofilau (3); Larenz Tupaea-Thomsen (3); Malkome Vaka (3); Aporosa Vuniyayaawa (3).

Hawke's Bay: *Captain* – Patrick Teddy   *Coach* – Blair Cross
Sean Baker (3); Tama Dunn (3); Tiaki Fabish (3); Joshua Gimblett (3); Samuel Henderson (3); Damarus Hokianga (3); Gideon Kautai (3); Ben Kelt (3); Miracle Lolofie (3); Oskar Lynch (3); Troy McIvor (3); Lee Moleli (3); Arana Murphy (3); Vince Onesi (1); Blake Patterson (3); Luke Russell (3); Leighton Shaw (2); Zac Southwick (3); Kyaan Tawhai (2); Ethan Taylor (2); Patrick Teddy (3); Te Kahika Thompson (3); Joeli Tora (0); Liam Udy-Johns (3); Sam Walton-Sexton (3).

Heartland: *Captain* – Jason Myers   *Coach* – Aleni Feagaiga
Caleb Aldridge *Buller* (3); Jaide Barlow *King Country* (3); Harvey Blyth *Mid Canterbury* (2); Austin Brear *Thames Valley* (3); Kohlt Coveney *Wanganui* (3); Cruise Dunster *King Country* (2); James Gilland *Horowhenua Kapiti* (3); Aaron Gordon *Wairarapa Bush* (3); Shae Gray *Horowhenua Kapiti* (3); Paddy Henwood *North Otago* (3); Te Huia Kutia *Thames Valley* (3); Ben McCarthy *North Otago* (3); Tipene Meihana *Ngati Porou East Coast* (3); Sam Morrison *Wairarapa Bush* (2); Jason Myers *Wanganui* (3); Raniera Petersen *Wairarapa Bush* (1); Logan Prenderville *Wairarapa Bush* (2); Toroa Rapana *Horowhenua Kapiti* (3); Josh Rauhihi *Horowhenua Kapiti* (3); Reeve Satherley *King Country* (1); Chase Sheriden *Poverty Bay* (3); Oliver Toma *King Country* (2); Taniela Wacokecoke *South Canterbury* (3); Stanley Wright *Wairarapa Bush* (3); Lance Wylie *West Coast* (3).

Manawatu: *Captain* – Flyn Yates   *Coach* – Shane Ratima
Trevor-Shane Baker (3); Stewart Cruden (3); Thomas Finlay (2); Jack Fleury (3); Michael Halatuituia (3); Dylan Hall (3); Max Harris (3); Chase Jordan (3); Jekope Kitou (2); Darel Lander (3); Tyler Laubscher (3); Josh Maoate (3); Josiah Maraku (3); Harry Newman (3); Alec Odel (1); Gus Robertson (3); Potene Rolls-Paewai (3); Johnny Shannon (3); William Treder (3); Atonio Walker-Leawere (3); Drew Wild (3); Stefan Williams (1); Bryn Wilson (3); Korie Winters (3); Flyn Yates (3).

North Harbour: *Captain* – Jed Melvin   *Coach* – Bill Wigglesworth
Kade Banks (3); Braedyn Collins (3); Fraser Ditchfield (3); Nikau Drage (2); Maasi Fakahokotau (2); AJ Frost (2); Zack Godfrey (3); Maine Kitson (2); Dave Koelman (2); Tevita Langi (3); Caleb Leef (3); Josh Mackenzie (3); Jayden Marsters (2); Jed Melvin (3); Carlos Muru (2); Jimmy Roots (3); Ben Ruzich (3); Vili Sio (3); Lewis Swann (1); Sekuini Tanimo (3); Tupou Uhi (3); Sean Vete (3); Sam Waterworth (3); Timothy Webster (2); Daniel Windleburn (3).

Northland: *Co Captains* – Mason Hohaia, Sage Walters-Hansen   *Coach* – Mark Kapa
Maka Ahio (3); Davarn Amosa-Bodman (3); Tomislav Baker (3); Ratu-Kuli Baleisomosomo (2); Connor Bolton (3); Gill Cann-Vaana (3); Jack Doyle (3); Walton Edwards (2); Esile Fono (3); Tyler Foster (1); Te Are Haika (2); Kingi Herewini (3); Mason Hohaia (3); Jayden Kemp (2); Chase Killen (3); Cullen Lowe (2); Craven Martin (3); Jake McClure (2); Kory McShane (2); Memphis Ngaruhe (3); Javahn Repia (3); Ethan Sherwood (3); D'Angelo Tahitahi (2); Aisea Tuifeleaki (3); Sage Walters-Hansen (3).

Otago: *Captain* – Sean Withy   *Coach* – Seilala Mapusua
Cameron Allan-McNeill (1); Arthur Allen (2); James Arscott (3); Austin Atiga (3); Geordie Bean (3); James Bolton (3); Harrison Boyle (3); Keegan Christian-Goss (3); Shane Fikken (3); Riley Forbes (2); Nathan Giles (2); Michael Graham (3); Jakob Harrex (2); Jesse Hutton (1); Jeff Ikani (3); Siaki Kata (3); Brayden Laing (2); Simeon Latu (3); Bob Martin (2); Saula Ma'u (2); Corrigan Miller (3); Jake Russ (3); Oscar Schmidt-Uili (3); Jesse Va'afusuaga (3); Sean Withy (3).

Southland: *Captain* – Morgan Riordan   *Coach* – Chris McIlwrick
Callum Carter (3); Josh Cavanagh (3); Kane Collins (2); Allan Gillies (1); Sam Hogan (3); Motai Hogg-Kingi (3); Campbell Hosie (2); Osika Kaufononga (3); Hamish Kennelly (2); Elisara Kuresa (3); Junior Lafoga (3); Ezekiel Maheno (3); Jordan Maher (3); Josh Mason (3); Caleb McKenzie (3); Sam Mitchell (3); James Riordan (1); Morgan Riordan (3); Jacob Robertson (3); Kyle Sinclair (1); Keahn Tipu (3); Eliot Warrender (3); Adam Webster (3); Kuki Wickliffe (3); Leo Wiki (3).

Taranaki: *Captain* – Millennium Sanerivi   *Coach* – Rhys Connell
Jackson Clarke (3); Christian Fa'avae (3); Ricco Falaniko (3); Crusader Faletagoai (3); Harris Gemmell (2); Reece Gray (3); Daniel Guthrie (1); Jamahl Hapi (3); Josh Iwikau (3); Josh Jacomb (3); Lachlan Jones (3); Bailey Kingi-Hayward (3); Josh Lord (3); Nathaniel Peters (3); Daniel Rona (3); Deken Rooks (0); Jordan Roylance (3); Millennium Sanerivi (3); Benny Shelford-Katene (3); Jackson Sinclair (3); Adam Smith (3); Kristian Standen (3); Brent Tucker (3); Luka Walker (2); Joel Williamson (2).

Tasman: *Captain* – Taine Robinson   *Coach* – Dan Perrin
Mitchell Barry (3); Tom Bassett-Eason (0); Seth Brown (3); Levi Carew (3); Ryan Churchill (2); Poihipi Clayton (3); Cody Delleca (3); Max Fraine (3); Jake Goeddert (0); Mathew Graham-Williams (3); Christopher Hala'ufia (3); Jaydn Holdaway (2); Zyon Holo (3); Daniel Jones (3); Jan Lammers (3); Saul Lewis (3); Sione Lonitenisi (3); Campbell Morgan-Parata (3); Max Nalder (3); Tyler Palmer (2); Conor Rhind (3); Taine Robinson (3); Kershawl Sykes-Martin (3); Bailey Tautau (3); Apetone Vaka (3).

Waikato: *Captain* – Thomas Martin (2), Stanley Paese (1)   *Coach* – Mark McConnell
Brad Burkhart (1); Quinn Collard (2); Vainakola Halafihi (2); Nicolas Jeffcoat (3); Logan Karl (0); Dion Keogh (2); Paula Mahe (2); Dillon Martin (2); Thomas Martin (2); Jack McConnell (3); Albert Nadan (1); Quintony Ngatai (3); Simon Parker (1); Stanley Pease (3); Terry Pongi (3); Jared Ruwhiu-Bott (3); Brendan Sanders (3); Daniel Sinkinson (2); Lewis Taitoko (3); Junior Taumaoe (1); Valynce Tewhare (3); Lisiate To'ofohe (3); Aaron Vercoe (2); Andrew Viane (3); Joel Waru (2), Shi Jie Yong (3).

Wellington: *Captain* – Leo Thompson   *Coach* – Dion Waller
Iona Apineru (3); Isaac Bracewell (3); Luke Chisholm (3); Sanasco Crichton (3); Caleb Delany (2); Cameron Ferreira (1); Luke Gilbert (1); Kienan Higgins (3); Shamus Langton (3); Niko Manaena (3); Kayden Muller (1); Hugo Plummer (3); Taine Plumtree (3); PJ Sheck (0); Kaleb Sinclair (1); Angelo Smith (1); Sam Smith (3); Josh Southall (3); Malo Tevita-Manuao (3); Leo Thompson (3); Tyrone Thompson (3); Junior Time-Taotua (3); Jaylen Tuapola (3); Steven Va'a (3); Keelan Whitman (3).

SECONDARY SCHOOLS RUGBY

The New Zealand Schools fell to their first defeat in the trans-Tasman Shield since 2012.

They had kicked off their campaign with a Game of Three Halves in Palmerston North against the NZ Barbarians Schools and New Zealand Maori Under 18s. On the first official game day at Hamilton BHS, NZ Schools comfortably dispatched Fijian Schools but found Australia to be too aggressive at the breakdown and well-drilled on day two at St Paul's Collegiate.

Cameron Church continued a tradition of top-quality loose forwards by winning the coveted Rugby News/Jerry Collins Memorial Bronze Boot from the trans-Tasman international.

NEW ZEALAND SCHOOLS, 2019

	School	Date of birth	Height	Weight
Seb Calder	St Andrew's College	16/03/02	1.84	119
Cameron Church	St Kentigern College	03/11/01	1.85	85
Allan Craig	St Kentigern College	19/04/02	1.97	102
Matt Dobbyn	Hamilton BHS	09/07/01	1.83	94
Vaiolini Ekuasi	St Peter's School, Cambridge	11/10/01	1.86	107
Zach Gallagher (capt)	Christ's College	04/09/01	1.95	103
Dom Gardiner	St Bede's College	12/07/01	1.88	93
Meihana Grindlay	King's College	07/04/01	1.87	109
Wil Gualter	Lincoln High School	05/06/01	1.87	81
Max Hughes	Christchurch BHS	18/10/01	1.68	74
Corey Kellow	Sacred Heart College	25/05/01	1.87	102
Jacob Kneepkens	Francis Douglas Memorial College	03/08/01	1.86	85
Ollie Lewis	Christchurch BHS	24/07/01	1.83	79
Ben Lopas	Christchurch BHS	28/12/00	1.77	114
Ruben Love	Palmerston North BHS	28/04/01	1.82	87
Michael Manson	Otago BHS	05/07/01	1.76	79
Aidan Morgan	King's College	07/06/01	1.69	85
Blair Murray	New Plymouth BHS	09/10/01	1.73	71
Manu Paea	Rotorua BHS	17/09/01	1.74	85
Te Rama Reuben	St Kentigern College	26/02/02	1.88	106
Anton Segner	Nelson College	24/07/01	1.93	106
Jack Sexton	St Andrew's College	17/04/01	1.87	104
Roderick Solo	Scots College	07/07/01	1.75	79
Ben Strang	Whanganui Collegiate	23/12/01	1.79	95
Tiaan Tauakipulu	St Kentigern College	03/05/01	1.87	122
Gideon Wrampling	St Paul's Collegiate	26/07/01	1.85	102

NB. Original selections Finau Halafihi of Auckland Grammar School and Vincent Green of Hamilton BHS withdrew with injury.

Calder and Dobbyn were promoted from NZ Barbarians Schools before the first game due to injuries, while Manson joined after the first match day.

Manager: Nick Reid (*Awatapu College*)
Head coach: Mark Hammett (*Highlanders*)
Assistant coaches: Sam Rasch (*Scots College*), Kevin Harding (*Canterbury*)
Strength & conditioning coach: Stephen van Gruting (*Canterbury*)
Physiotherapist: Richie Marsden (*Tasman*)
Video analyst: Doug Neilson (*NZ Rugby*)
Campaign manager: Matt Sexton (*NZ Rugby*)
Campaign support: Ezra Iupeli (*NZ Rugby*)

INDIVIDUAL SCORING

	Tries	Con	PG	DG	Points
Wrampling	3	–	–	–	15
Church	3	–	–	–	15
Murray	2	–	–	–	10
Morgan	–	5	–	–	10
Gardiner	1	–	–	–	5
Lewis	–	1	–	–	2
Totals	**9**	**6**	**0**	**0**	**57**
Opposition scored	3	1	3	0	26

NEW ZEALAND SCHOOLS 2019

	Fiji	Australia	TOTALS
Murray	s	15	2
Solo	s	14	2
Love	15	11	2
Gualter	14	–	1
Manson	–	s	1
Grindlay	13	13	2
Wrampling	11	12	2
Kneepkens	12	–	1
Morgan	10	10	2
Lewis	s	s	2
Paea	s	9	2
Hughes	9	s	2
Ekuasi	8	8	2
Reuben	s	–	1
Church	7	7	2
Segner	6	6	2
Gardiner	s	s	2
Kellow	s	s	2
Gallagher	5	5	2
Craig	4	4	2
Calder	s	s	2
Tauakipulu	3	3	2
Sexton	s	s	2
Lopas	1	1	2
Strang	2	2	2
Dobbyn	s	s	2

NEW ZEALAND SCHOOLS, 2019

PLAYED 2 WON 1 LOST 1 POINTS FOR 57 POINTS AGAINST 26

Date	Opponent	Location	Score	Tries	Con	PG	DG	Referee
September 30	Fiji Schools	Hamilton	43–8	Wrampling (3), Church (2), Murray (2)	Morgan (4)			Chris Paul
October 4	Australian Schools	Hamilton	14–18	Church, Gardiner	Morgan, Lewis			Jono Bredin

NEW ZEALAND BARBARIANS SCHOOLS

Results:

September 30 v **Australian Schools** at Hamilton BHS, Hamilton. Lost 17–30
Tries: Manson (2), Cook-Savage; *Con:* Smiler-Ah Kiong

October 4 v **Fijian Schools** at St Paul's Collegiate, Hamilton. Won 52–22
Tries: Pepe, Bainivalu, Richards-Coxhead, Goerke, J. Brown, Iobu, Smiler-Ah Kiong, Mataiciwa; *Cons:* Cook-Savage (6)

Backs: Etonia Bainivalu (*St Bede's College*), Te Paea Cook-Savage (*St Paul's Collegiate*), Dayton Iobu (*King's College*), Carlos Karaitiana (*Rotorua BHS*), Treyah Kingi-Taukamo (*St Kentigern College*), Brian Leali'ifano (*Sacred Heart College*), Giovanni Leituala (*King's HS*), Michael Manson (*Otago BHS*), Jona Mataiciwa (*St Kentigern College*), Alfred Nonu (*Tangaroa College*), Jermaine Pepe (*Rangiora HS*), Latrell Smiler-Ah Kiong (*Hastings BHS*)

Forwards: George Bell (*John McGlashan College*), James Brown (*King's College*), Taya Brown (*Nelson College*), Leroy Ferguson (*John McGlashan College*), Joseph Gavigan (*Manukura*), Julian Goerke (*Hastings BHS*), Jamie Hannah (*Christchurch BHS*), TK Howden (*Feilding HS*), Sosaia Moala (*Auckland Grammar School*), Monu Moli (*Marlborough BC*), Harrison Press (*Hutt International BS*), Hakaraia Richards-Coxhead (*Hamilton BHS, captain*), Leandro Vakatini (*King's College*), Jayden Walker (*Napier BHS*)

Manager: Chris Back (*Wanganui*)
Head coach: Gus Leger (*Sacred Heart College*)
Assistant coach: Mark Hooper (*Kelston BHS*)
Strength & conditioning coach: Anthony Joseph (*Waikato*)
Physiotherapist: Miles Ganley (*Wellington*)
Video analyst: Ryan Runciman (*Wellington*)
Campaign manager: Ben Fisher (*NZ Rugby*)

NEW ZEALAND BARBARIANS AREA SCHOOLS 2019

Now into its seventh season under the sponsorship of the NZ Barbarians club, the Area Schools squad is chosen from the smaller rural high schools after an annual regional tournament and assembles for several days each September in Palmerston North.

September 11 v **Wanganui Under 18** in Palmerston North. Won 27–5
Tries: A. Farrant, Vea, Atutola, Hallam-Doole, Mataira; *Con:* Smith

September 14 v **Manawatu Under 16** in Palmerston North. Won 25–21
Tries: Beck, McQueen, Kitto, White, Hallam-Doole

Squad: Connor Guest (*captain*), Danny Henderson (*Tauraroa Area School, Northland*), Luke Stern, Jacob Paton, Caleb Beck (*Hurunui College, Canterbury*), Rui Farrant, Anam Farrant (*Waiheke home schooled, Auckland*), Brett McKay, Clay Morgan (*Collingwood AS, Tasman*), Te Ratu Makoare Mataira (*Raglan AS, Waikato*), William Haywood (*Lawrence AS, Otago*), Carter Hodge, Bradley Ray, Trinity McQueen (*Mercury Bay AS, Thames Valley*), Samson Vea (*Rangiora New Life, Canterbury*), Teihana Senior, Sheldyn Hemana-Paira (*Te Wharekura o Te Kaokaoroa o Paterere, Waikato*), Doug Smith (*Maniototo AS, Otago*), Ethan Kitto, Bradyn White (*Roxburgh AS, Otago*), Kayleb Te Whare (*Te Kura Kaupapa Maori o Haurouta Wananga, Poverty Bay*), Kaharau Atutola (*Broadwood AS, Northland*), Tyler Hallam-Doole (*Coromandel AS, Thames Valley*)

Guest, Henderson, Beck, Morgan, McQueen, Mataira, Smith and Senior were also members of the 2018 squad.

Manager: Mike Smith (*Mercury Bay AS*)
Head Coach: Justin Marsh (*Tongariro AS, King Country*)
Assistant coach: Hone Manuel (*Te Wharekura o Manaia, Thames Valley*)

SCHOOLS RUGBY REVIEW

Much of the commentary around the supposed problems inherent in First XV rugby emanated from those who have not even deigned to watch — live or on the box — this often exciting, and always passionate, level of the game.

That made for emotional, but not knowledgeable, engagement, especially on social media.

While New Zealand Rugby's independent review highlighted key areas of concern, much of the pre-season spotlight fell on the saga surrounding Auckland's St Kentigern College, which was prohibited from playing its scholarship players until round six of the 1A competition.

But once the season actually started, the rugby itself commanded the headlines, from St Peter's College's worthy run in the April Sanix tournament in Japan right up until the October trans-Tasman schools international, won by Australia for the first time since 2012.

The NZ Barbarians Schools again showed why this second-tier national schools team is still of vital importance, while the NZ Barbarians Area Schools won its annual fixture.

NATIONAL TOP FOUR

Hastings BHS repeated its 2017 success in the boys' competition, winning in some style in inclement conditions in Palmerston North.

St Kentigern, Auckland runner-up, won the co-ed title, as it did in 2011, capping a remarkable season for the Presbyterian private school.

Hamilton GHS went back to back in the girls' competition for the Hine Pounamu Trophy, overrunning Christchurch GHS.

Finals:
Boys: Hastings BHS 27 King's College 14
Co-ed: St Kentigern College 29 Feilding HS 22
Girls: Hamilton GHS 58 Christchurch GHS 7

MOASCAR CUP

As in 2018, there were four different holders of the coveted and iconic Moascar Cup, the Ranfurly Shield equivalent of First XV rugby.

The Moascar was in Auckland control right up until the September 8 boys' final of the Top 4 competition in Palmerston North.

St Peter's, which had won the trophy in such brilliant style in the 2018 Top 4 final, made one successful Moascar defence in May before relinquishing the silverware 15–13 to St Kentigern, which was still without its five scholarship players. A resilient St Kent's made four successful defences until the 1A final, falling 29–22 to fellow private school King's College.

King's, which had not held the Moascar since 1998, in turn defended the trophy in the Top 4 semi-final, 49–17 over Nelson College. But Hastings BHS was not to be denied in the final, taking King's 27–14 in the wet to clinch the cup for the first time since 2004 and just the second occasion in that school's history.

OTHER HIGHLIGHTS

- Auckland Grammar School topped its 150th celebrations with a 19–15 home win over old rival King's before more than 10,000, one of the largest crowds in the city below the All Blacks in 2019.
- Palmerston North BHS won the 115th Polson Banner clash, 27–15 over Napier BHS, its first victory in this traditional match since 2015.
- Hamilton BHS won its 12th Super 8 title, 13–5 over Hastings BHS in the wet at home in the decider.
- Westlake BHS won yet another North Harbour title, 31–12 over first-time finalist Whangarei BHS.
- Scots College beat St Patrick's Silverstream 20–15 in the Wellington final, its first crown since 2014, thus denying Stream a three-peat.
- Nelson College's 35–31 win over Christchurch BHS was its first UC Championship title since 2007.
- King's won its first Auckland 1A title since 2005, beating St Kentigern in the final.
- Hamilton BHS won an unprecedented fifth straight Condors Sevens crown (and record seventh in all), defeating King's 27–12 in the boys' Cup final in Auckland.
- Led by a virtuoso four-try effort from Jorja Miller in the final, Christchurch GHS won its first Condors title, beating Howick College 29–14 in the girls' Cup final.
- The World Schools Sevens saw Australia defeat Japan SDS 21–12 in the girls' Cup final, while NZ Condors were too slick, to the tune of 43–5, for NZ Fijians, in the boys' Cup final.

WOMEN'S RUGBY
THE ALMANACK NEW ZEALAND XV

Olivia McGoverne
Canterbury

Renee Wickliffe
Bay of Plenty

Grace Brooker
Canterbury

Ayesha Leti-I'iga
Wellington

Chelsea Alley
Waikato

Ruahei Demant
Auckland

Kendra Cocksedge
Canterbury

Charmaine McMenamin
Auckland

Lesley Elder (capt)
Bay of Plenty

Chelsea Bremner
Canterbury

Eloise Blackwell
Auckland

Pia Tapsell
North Harbour

Aleisha Nelson
Auckland

Te Kura Ngata-Aerengmate
Northland

Toka Natua
Waikato

Reserves –

Stephanie Te Ohaere-Fox (*Canterbury*), Phillipa Love (*Canterbury*), Leilani Perese (*Counties Manukau*), Charmaine Smith (*Auckland*), Leanne Thompson (*Auckland*), Rosie Kelly (*Otago*), Kilisitina Moata'ane (*Otago*), Carla Hohepa (*Waikato*).

COMMENTS

The Farah Palmer Cup contained many highly promising young players as well as experienced campaigners. We considered the season's performance by some players to be superior to those involved in the earlier Black Ferns fixtures. Injury prevented some Black Ferns to fully participate in the provincial competition.

Fullbacks: Olivia McGoverne (Canterbury) was in outstanding form and there were pleasing performances from Natahlia Moors (Auckland), Sapphire Tapsell (Bay of Plenty), Emily Kitson (Counties Manukau) and Krysten Cottrell (Hawke's Bay). Sheree Hume (Otago) and Selica Winiata (Manawatu) continue to serve their unions well although Winiata played at first five-eighth for Manawatu.

Wings: The Black Ferns pairing of Ayesha Leti-I'iga (Wellington) and Renee Wickliffe (Bay of Plenty) were the best performers and in the championship we saw fine efforts from Mayalin Lolohea (Canterbury), the Auckland pair Princess Elliot and Isla Norman-Bell, Lanulangi Veainu (Counties Manukau), Simone Small (North Harbour), Savannah Bodman (Northland) and Rebecca Kersten (Tasman).

Midfield: Canterbury had a formidable pair in Grace Brooker and Lucy Anderson, as did Otago with Kilisitina Moata'ane and Amy du Plessis and the Manawatu pair of Janna Vaughan and Lauren Balsillie. Chelsea Alley (Waikato) was the best seen at second five-eighth. Carla Hohepa gave strong performances for the Black Ferns but did not appear for Waikato. Amanda Rasch (Wellington) was effective in either five-eighths positions.

First five-eighths: Ruahei Demant (Auckland) directed play well with the Black Ferns before moving out one position to accommodate the 16-year-old talent Patricia Maliepo in the Auckland team. Rosie Kelly was outstanding for Otago and there were solid efforts from Hazel Tubic (Counties Manukau) and Cassie Siataga (Canterbury).

Halfbacks: Kendra Cocksedge (Canterbury) remains the best performer and has appeared in all 45 tests played by the Black Ferns since 2011. Arihiana Marino-Tauhinu (Counties Manukau), Kiritapu Demant (Auckland) and Emma Jensen (Hawke's Bay) were prominent and Melanie Puckett (Canterbury) could play equally well on the wing.

Loose forwards: The Black Ferns trio of Charmaine McMenamin (Auckland), Lesley Elder (Bay of Plenty) and Pia Tapsell (North Harbour) were very effective. Leanne Thompson (Auckland), Alana Bremner (Canterbury), Kendra Reynolds (Bay of Plenty), Kennedy Simon (Waikato), Larissa Lima (Counties Manukau) were very effective. Experienced performers Linda Itunu (Auckland), Justine Lavea (Counties Manukau), Jackie Patea-Fereti (Wellington), Greer Muir (Otago) and Jessica Foster-Lawrence (Tasman) served their unions well. Two promising players are Bree Thomas (Otago) and Liana Mikaele-Tu'u (Hawke's Bay).

Locks: Eloise Blackwell (Auckland) and Chelsea Bremner (Canterbury) are our choices with Charmaine Smith (Auckland), Joanah Ngan-Woo (Wellington), Hanna Brough (Hawke's Bay), Lisa Molia (Counties Manukau), and beach volley baller Kelsie Wills (Bay of Plenty) also standing out.

Props: There was little between Aleisha Nelson (Auckland), Toka Natua (Waikato), Phillipa Love (Canterbury) and Leilani Perese (Counties Manukau) with Eilis Doyle (Otago) and Olivia Ward-Duin (North Harbour) also showing out. Amy Rule (Canterbury) and Angel Mulu (Bay of Plenty) show promise.

Hookers: Te Kura Ngata-Aerengamate (Northland), Stephanie Te Ohaere-Fox (Canterbury), Luka Connor (Bay of Plenty) and Forne Burkin (Hawke's Bay) were the leading players. Sapphire Abraham (Auckland) shows promise.

PLAYER OF THE YEAR

Charmaine Jacqueline McMenamin (*Auckland*) played a full part in all six tests, the No 8 scoring two tries against Australia at Perth and a further try in the return match at Eden Park. For Auckland she was consistently in outstanding form in a team making a remarkable recovery from its form slump of 2018. She possesses a wide range of skills, is a strong ball carrier, solid defender, leads by example and works hard at her game both on and off the field. In November she was honoured with selection in the London-based Barbarians club for a fixture against Wales at Cardiff.

Born in Lower Hutt on 13 May 1990 Charmaine McMenamin attended Waterloo School before the family moved to Gisborne where she attended Te Hapara School and Ilminster Intermediate prior to Gisborne Girls' High School 2003–07. She started playing rugby in 2005 but league became an attraction and during her last year of school her father made many road trips to Lower Hutt for Charmaine to play for the Te Aroha Eels team in the Wellington competition. After two years with the club she made the move to Auckland in 2009, playing for Richmond Roses and Te Atatu Roosters. She appeared for the Auckland representative team Akarana and in 2012 played for the Kiwi Ferns. McMenamin played both league and union until focusing on union from 2016.

From an early age McMenamin had an ambition to become a Black Fern. Her first-class debut was at Petone in 2009 when she was on the bench for Hawke's Bay's game against Wellington, a friend having asked her to join the Tuis for the game. She joined Takapuna club in 2010, a year in which no provincial competition was held, and was chosen for an Auckland team for a competition held in Taupo. The next year she made her Auckland debut in the championship and has been a regular member since and has now played 53 games for the Storm. She moved from Takapuna to Ponsonby club in 2012. In 2013 McMenamin joined the Black Ferns and is now one of the senior members with 25 tests

PROMISING PLAYER OF THE YEAR

Patricia Maliepo (*Auckland*) played a prominent role in her Marist team's winning of the Auckland senior club championship and this was followed by inclusion in the Storm squad for the Farah Palmer Cup campaign. She played at first five-eighth in the opening game and scored a try within 20 minutes. In the second game she went on at halftime with Ruahei Demant moving out to second five-eighth.

The combination worked and Maliepo retained the first-five spot for the rest of the season, she being on the field for all but six minutes of the remaining six games. The Storm marched to the final where it was beaten by Canterbury. Maliepo was the team's goalkicker, contributing 78 points, but it was her general play that impressed most, as she possesses a fine ability to read a game, a calm attitude, can kick, pass, tackle and dart though a gap on attack. These are qualities expected from an experienced campaigner not from a 16-year-old schoolgirl. The youngster played with a maturity far beyond her years and promises to rise to higher honours in a very short time. Over the years there have been many boys of Maliepo's age appear in first-class rugby but, surely, no one as young as Maliepo (aged 16 years five months) has made such an impact in their first season at first-class level.

Born in Auckland on 13 March 2003 Patricia Maliepo received her primary education at Ellerslie School followed by two years at Edgewater College 2016–17 and is currently at Southern Cross Campus. Her rugby commenced in 2012, joining Marist club when aged nine. Maliepo's talent was recognised early, and she was in both Auckland Under 15 and Under 18 representative teams 2016 and 2017 and captained both teams in 2018.

SEASON IN REVIEW
By Rikki Swannell

After two years of unprecedented commitment to the women's game, 2019 was another season of significant growth led by the two flagship teams, the Black Ferns and Black Ferns Sevens, who again set high standards during their international campaigns.

Continuing where they left off in 2018, the Black Ferns Sevens dominated the World Series, while also playing on home soil for the first time. A Fast Four competition against England, France and China was held as part of the men's round in Hamilton, giving fans a taste of what they'll see in 2020 when a full round of the women's series will be played in New Zealand for the first time.

Having won the first two tournaments in Glendale and Dubai, Sarah Hirini's team took the same form into 2019 with victory in Sydney. However, their remarkable run of 37 wins in a row came to an abrupt end in Kitakyushu, drawing with Russia and beaten by France in pool play before eventually finishing fifth. They bounced back strongly to win the title in Langford, Canada and secured qualification for the Tokyo 2020 Olympics at the same time. While they couldn't finish the season off with victory in the final tournament in Biarritz, beaten by a very strong USA side in the final, New Zealand won the overall World Series title and lost just three games all season in doing so.

Such was New Zealand's dominance, Hirini, Ruby Tui and Tyla Nathan-Wong were not only named in the overall season Dream Team but were also nominated for World Rugby's women's sevens player of the year, with Tui winning that award. However, as a sign of just how competitive the series has become, USA won the opening event of the 2020 campaign on home soil in Colorado and will be a huge threat to New Zealand's Olympic hopes. Australia is also returning to form, finishing runners-up in Glendale, with New Zealand third.

As the sevens season wrapped up, the XVs campaign for the Black Ferns was getting underway. With six test matches on the schedule, 2019 was the biggest for New Zealand in a non-World Cup year and also marked something of a changing of the guard. With the retirement, this time for good, of the legendary Fiao'o Fa'amausili, Bay of Plenty's Les Elder was appointed as the new Black Ferns captain, while four players, Luka Connor, Karli Faneva, Arihiana Marino-Tauhinu and Nathalia Moors, were given national contracts for the first time to take the number of semi-professional XVs players to 29.

The Super Series in San Diego pitted the Black Ferns against England, France, USA and Canada. After fairly routine wins over Canada and the United States to start the tournament, New Zealand stumbled badly against France who have rapidly become the Black Ferns biggest rival after winning their last two meetings. It also perhaps highlighted the challenge women's teams still face with that match the Black Ferns' third in nine days. However, they bounced back strongly a week later with an impressive win over England which also saw them hold on to the number one world ranking, having provisionally lost it to England after that defeat by France. While the return of the Super Series was a real positive, the disappointment at seeing substandard facilities and a poor-quality pitch used for the majority of games must be noted.

Six weeks later the Black Ferns were back in action with a two-test series against Australia, where both matches were played as double-headers alongside the Bledisloe Cup. In front of large crowds at Perth's new Optus Stadium and Eden Park, the Black Ferns dominated both matches to comfortably retain the Laurie O'Reilly Memorial trophy. While Australia showed signs of improvement, the Black Ferns record now stands at 19 wins, no losses against the Wallaroos.

The rapid improvement and growing depth at the top level was highlighted by the number of players who made their international debuts in 2019. When Grace Brooker took the field in the second test against Australia, she became the 10th debutant of the season and 19th since winning the World Cup in 2017. That match at Eden Park was notably the 99th NZ Rugby sanctioned test for the Black Ferns and also saw Kendra Cocksedge receive her official cap from Prime Minister Jacinda Ardern, having played her 50th match in the Super Series loss to France.

The momentum continued into the Farah Palmer Cup season. The arrival of Northland expanded the competition to 13 teams with all the Mitre 10 Cup provincial unions, bar Southland, now included. It was a massive achievement for a small union like Northland to make such a big statement of commitment and a fourth new team in the space of three seasons is something very few sports leagues globally could lay claim to. Auckland was most grateful for Northland's arrival, as it earned them a reprieve from relegation and a place in the top tier Premiership. Keeping two divisions in the competition remains important as there is still a big discrepancy between the quality of the teams and the pool of talent unions have to call on.

Despite some of those divides, the quality of rugby went to a new level and some exciting young talent stamped their marks on the competition. Auckland 16-year-old Patricia Maliepo stunned with her composure, game-management and ball-playing skills while Canterbury's Chelsea Bremner took her game to a new level. Cemented on the left wing for the Black Ferns, Ayesha Leti-I'iga continued her form for Wellington with a season high 12 tries, and Rosie Kelly had a breakout season for Otago, finishing as the competition's top points scorer with 107.

Canterbury continued its dominance in the Premiership, completing an unbeaten season en route to a third straight title. However, they were pushed all the way by both Counties and Auckland during the playoffs and with Wellington and Bay of Plenty continuing to develop, strong rivalries are starting to show. At the other end of the premiership, Manawatu had a season to forget and were relegated to the Championship.

They'll be replaced in the top tier by Otago, who went through the Championship season unbeaten and have benefited from having a major university in the city in assembling a hugely talented squad of players to help complement their home-grown players. Beaten finalists Hawke's Bay showed significant growth to reach the final and go close to victory in just their third year since returning to the competition, while Northland thrilled by making the semi-finals in their first year,

A record 27 games were broadcast live on Sky Sport as either stand-alone fixtures or double-headers, but although the final two games at Rugby Park in Christchurch were played in front of strong, vocal home supporters, the small crowd numbers overall remain a problem to be solved.

Following the Farah Palmer Cup, a New Zealand women's development team was named for the first time and competed at the Oceania Championships in November. Featuring a mixture of recently capped internationals and standouts from the FPC, New Zealand dominated the tournament in Lautoka, beating Fiji 53-nil, Australia A 50-nil and PNG 131-nil. While it shows the continued strength and depth of the game in New Zealand, there is much work to be done to develop women's rugby throughout the region.

Great strides were made on other fronts in 2019. Rebecca Mahoney continued to set the standard for aspiring referees, becoming the first woman to control a Ranfurly Shield challenge and then a men's provincial Mitre 10 cup match when she took charge of the game between Hawke's Bay and Southland. Black Ferns star Selica Winiata also carved a new path, officiating at the Oceania Sevens and then at the Dubai World Series event, while New Zealand Rugby appointed a women's referee development manager for the first time, American Emily Hsieh. Cheryl Smith became the first female head coach in the FPC, teaming up with Sue Dawson to guide Northland in its first season, while fellow former Black Ferns Anna Richards (Auckland) and Aimee Sutorius (Otago) were new assistant coaches this year.

With playing numbers among women and girls continuing to move north year on year, the Black Ferns Sevens heading into Olympic year and the World Cup to be hosted here in 2021, now is the time to be bold and innovative for everyone involved in the women's game.

NEW ZEALAND BLACK FERNS

The Women's Rugby Super Series was held in San Diego, California during June-July. Five nations took part in the round-robin tournament with New Zealand winning with 14 competition points followed by England 13, France 10, Canada 7, USA 4.

Results: England 38, USA 5; New Zealand 35, Canada 20; Canada 36, France 19; New Zealand 33, USA 0; France 25, New Zealand 16; England 19, Canada 17; England 20, France 18; USA 20, Canada 18; France 53, USA 14; New Zealand 28, England 13.

In August two tests were played with Australia for the Laurie O'Reilly trophy.

NEW ZEALAND, 2019

	Union	Date of Birth	Height	Weight	Tests at 1/1/19
C.H. (Chelsea) Alley	Waikato	7/11/92	1.78	81	18
E.S. (Eloise) Blackwell	Auckland	28/12/90	1.82	89	37
K.A. (Kelly) Brazier	Bay of Plenty	28/10/89	1.73	68	37
G.E. (Grace) Brooker	Canterbury	20/6/99	1.73	75	0
F.K. (Forne) Burkin	Canterbury	28/10/98	1.66	76	0
K.M. (Kendra) Cocksedge	Canterbury	1/7/88	1.57	61	47
L.H.J. (Luka) Connor	Bay of Plenty	24/9/96	1.71	95	0
K.J. (Krysten) Cottrell	Hawke's Bay	17/2/92	1.62	65	5
D.R. (Ruahei) Demant	Auckland	21/4/95	1.69	81	5
L.T. (Lesley) Elder (capt)	Bay of Plenty	10/1/87	1.66	62	13
K.J.K. (Karli) Faneva	Bay of Plenty	20/5/98	1.76	92	0
T.M. (Theresa) Fitzpatrick	Auckland	25/2/95	1.68	75	9
C.G.T.O. (Carla) Hohepa	Waikato	27/7/85	1.75	71	19
A.A. (Ayesha) Leti-I'iga	Wellington	3/1/99	1.66	79	3
P.E.A. (Phillipa) Love	Canterbury	8/4/90	1.73	90	7
C.J. (Charmaine) McMenamin	Auckland	13/5/90	1.73	84	19
A.A.H. (Arihiana) Marino-Tauhinu	Counties Manukau	29/3/92	1.61	74	0
Kilisitina Moata'ane	Otago	23/11/97	1.67	79	0
D.B. (Natahlia) Moors	Auckland	7/12/95	1.63	71	1
T.I.Te O. (Toka) Natua	Waikato	22/11/91	1.70	101	16
A.P. (Aleisha) Nelson	Auckland	2/3/90	1.82	104	29
J.M.F. (Joanah) Ngan-Woo	Wellington	15/12/95	1.82	88	0
T.R. (Te Kura) Ngata-Aerengamate	Counties Manukau	21/10/91	1.64	96	23
M.J. (Marcelle) Parkes	Wellington	9/9/97	1.77	78	2
J.S. (Jackie) Patea-Fereti	Wellington	30/9/86	1.78	83	17
L.L.R. (Leilani) Perese	Counties Manukau	1/1/93	1.79	125	5
A.F. (Alena) Saili	Southland	13/12/98	1.73	79	2
K.W. (Kennedy) Simon	Waikato	1/10/96	1.72	80	0
C.B. (Charmaine) Smith	Auckland	15/11/90	1.83	77	21
P.H. (Pia) Tapsell	North Harbour	2/8/98	1.78	86	0
O.Y. (Olivia) Ward-Duin	North Harbour	23/12/93	1.83	105	0
R.W.M. (Renee) Wickliffe	Bay of Plenty	30/5/87	1.64	63	35
S.C. (Selica) Winiata	Manawatu	14/11/86	1.55	58	36

Coach: Glenn Moore
Manager: Lauren Cournane
Physiotherapist: Georgia Milne
Strength & conditioning coach: Jamie Tout

Assistant coach: Wesley Clarke, John Haggart
Campaign manager: Cate Sexton
Doctor: Dr Steve Smith
Analyst: Arran Hodge

INDIVIDUAL SCORING

	Tries	Con	PG	DG	Points
Cocksedge	–	12	12	–	60
Wickliffe	4	–	–	–	20
Blackwell	3	–	–	–	15
Hohepa	3	–	–	–	15
McMenamin	3	–	–	–	15
Demant	2	1	–	–	12
Leti-I'iga	2	–	–	–	10
Alley	1	1	–	–	7
penalty try	1	–	–	–	7
Elder	1	–	–	–	5

	Tries	Con	PG	DG	Points
Moors	1	–	–	–	5
Ngan-Woo	1	–	–	–	5
Ngata-Aerengamate	1	–	–	–	5
Smith	1	–	–	–	5
Tapsell	1	–	–	–	5
Winiata	1	–	–	–	5
Totals	**26**	**14**	**12**	**–**	**196**
Opposition scored	9	5	7	–	76

NEW ZEALAND IN 2019

	Canada	USA	France	England	Australia	Australia	TOTALS
Winiata	15*	–	15*	–	15	15*	4
Saili	S	–	S	S	–	–	3
Brooker	–	–	–	–	–	S	1
Wickliffe	14	15	14	14*	14*	14	6
Moors	–	14*	–	–	–	–	1
Leti-I'iga	11	11	11	11	11	11	6
Moata'ane	–	–	–	–	S	–	1
Hohepa	13	13	13	13	13	13	6
Fitzpatrick	–	S	–	S	–	–	2
Alley	12	12*	S	12*	12*	12*	6
Brazier	–	S	12	15	–	–	3
Demant	10*	10	10*	10	10	10	6
Cottrell	S	–	–	–	S	S	3
Cocksedge	9*	9*	9*	9*	9*	9*	6
Marino-Tauhinu	S	S	S	S	S	S	6
Tapsell	8	8	6*	6	6	6*	6
Patea-Fereti	–	–	–	–	–	S	1
Elder	7*	7*	–	7*	7*	7*	5
Parkes	S	–	7*	S	–	–	3
Simon	–	S	S	–	S	S	4
McMenamin	6	6	8	8	8	8	6
Smith	5	5*	5	5	5*	5	6
Blackwell	4*	4	4	4*	4	4	6
Faneva	S	–	S	–	–	–	2
Ngan-Woo	–	S	–	S	S	–	3
Nelson	3*	3*	3*	3*	3*	3*	6
Perese	S	S	S	S	S	S	6
Natua	1*	S	1*	1*	1*	1*	6
Love	S	1*	S	S	–	–	4
Ward-Duin	–	–	–	–	S	S	2
Ngata-Aerengamate	2*	2*	2*	2*	2*	2*	6
Connor	S	–	S	S	–	S	4
Burkin	–	S	–	–	S	–	2

Cocksedge was captain against France

NEW ZEALAND IN 2019

				Played 6	Won 5	Lost 1	Points for 196		Points against 76
Date	Opponent	Location	Score	Tries		Con	PG	DG	Referee
June 28	Canada	San Diego	35–20	Blackwell, Hohepa, Alley, Leti-I'iga		Cocksedge (3)	Cocksedge (3)		Sara Cox *(England)*
July 2	USA	San Diego	33–0	Hohepa, Ngata-Aerengamate, Moors, Tapsell, Blackwell		Cocksedge (4)			Hollie Davidson *(Scotland)*
July 6	France	San Diego	16–25	penalty try			Cocksedge (3)		Joy Neville *(Ireland)*
July 14	England	San Diego	28–13	Wickliffe (3)		Cocksedge (2)	Cocksedge (3)		Amy Perrett *(Australia)*
August 10	Australia	Perth	47–10	McMenamin (2), Wickliffe, Demant, Winiata, Elder, Leti-I'iga, Ngan-Woo		Cocksedge, Demant	Cocksedge		Hollie Davidson *(Scotland)*
August17	Australia	Auckland	37–8	Demant, Blackwell, Hohepa, McMenamin, Smith		Cocksedge (2), Alley	Cocksedge (2)		Aimee Barrett-Theron *(South Africa)*

Test venues: Chula Vista Elite Athlete Training Centre, San Diego; San Diego State University's Torero Stadium (v England); Optus Stadium,

Perth; Eden Park, Auckland.

NEW ZEALAND WOMEN'S REPRESENTATIVES, 1989–2019

	Internationals Games	Points
Aiatu, Muteremoana S. 1981– (Wellington) 2011	1	–
Alley, Chelsea H. 1992– (Waikato) 2013–14–17–18–19 (North Harbour) 2015–16	24	27
Andrew, Shannon R. 1972– (Auckland) 1996	2	–
Aniseko, Fa'anati 1989– (Auckland) 2007	2	5
Apiata, Jacquileen W. 1966– (Canterbury) 1989–90–91–92–93–94–95	5	–
Atkins, Leanne T. 1976– (Northland) 1994	–	–
Baker, Lise (Wellington) 1990	–	–
Baker, Miriama 1962– (Auckland) 1989–91	–	–
Baker, Shakira J. 1992– (Wellington) 2011 (Manawatu) 2012–14	13	40
Ballinger, Shona 1970– (Wellington) 1990–91	–	–
Barclay, F.J. see King, F.J.		
Berry, Zoey P. 1987– (Canterbury) 2012	1	–
Blackledge, V.E. see Grant, V.E.		
Blackwell, Eloise S. 1990– (Auckland) 2011–12–13–14–15–16–17–18–19	43	50
Blyde, Cherrie (Taranaki) 1992	–	–
Borthwick, Nicole M. 1980– (Auckland) 2005	2	7
Bosman (nee Ngatai), Melodie, 2010. see Ngatai, M.M.		
Brazier, Kelly A. 1989– (Otago) 2009–10–12–13–14–16 (Canterbury) 2011 (Bay of Plenty) 2017–19	40	190
Brett, Lesley 1968– (Canterbury) 1990–91	3	12
Brooker, Grace E. 1999– (Canterbury) 2019	1	0
Broughton, Florence (Wellington) 1990	–	–
Burkin, Forne K. 1998– (Canterbury) 2019	2	0
Canterbury, Marina R. 1984– (Hawke's Bay) 2005	5	10
Chase, Debbie P.M. 1966– (Canterbury) 1990–91–93	3	12
Chittock, Barbara J. 1985– (Canterbury) 2009	–	–
Coady, Olivia R. 1990– (Canterbury) 2008–09	4	5
Cobley, Rhonda J. 1971– (Canterbury) 1992–94	–	–
Cocksedge, Kendra M. 1988– (Canterbury) 2007–08–09–10–11–12–13–14–15–16–17–18–19	53	342
Codling, Monalisa M. 1977– (Otago) 1998 (Auckland) 1999–02–03–04–05–06–07–08–10	30	25
Connor, Luka H.J. 1996– (Bay of Plenty) 2019	4	0
Cootes, Vanessa 1969– (Waikato) 1995–96–97–98–00–01–02	16	215
Cottrell, Krysten J. 1992– (Hawke's Bay) 2018–19	8	–
Crossman, Lydia J. 1986– (Hawke's Bay) 2011 (Auckland) 2012	5	–
Cunningham, Vicky (Auckland) 1997	1	–
Davie, Mary (Canterbury) 1992–93	–	–
Dawson, Susan 1971– (Northland) 1999–00–02	4	5
de Jong, Catherine L. 1984– (Otago) 2005	1	–
Demant, D. Ruahei 1995– (Auckland) 2018–19	11	14
Demant, Kiritapu W. 1996– (Auckland) 2015	2	–
Edwards (nee Shelford), Exia T. 1975– (Bay of Plenty) 1998–99–00–01–02–03–04–05–06	27	90
Edwards, Maree 1975– (Otago) 1998–00 (Canterbury) 2003	4	5
Edwards, Tangaloa (Auckland) 1989	–	–
Elder (nee Ketu), Lesley T. 1987– (Waikato) 2015–17 (Bay of Plenty) 2018–19	18	10
Ellis, Judith M. 1966– (Canterbury) 1993–94–95	1	–
Engebretsen, Lauren J. 1983– (Waikato) 2004	3	–

	Internationals	
	Games	Points
Epiha, Eva A. 1974– (Auckland) 1994	–	–
Everitt, Rawinia P. 1986–	21	25
(Auckland) 2011–12		
(Counties Manukau) 2013–14–16–17		
Ewe, Donna 1964– (Auckland) 1990–	3	–
91		
Fa'amausili, Fiao'o 1980–	57	85
(Auckland) 2002–03–05–06–07–08–		
09–10–11–12–13–14–15–16–17–18		
Fa'aope, Lili (Canterbury) 1989–90	–	–
Faneva, Karli J.K. 1998– (Bay of	2	0
Plenty) 2019		
Farr, Amy M. 1982– (Wellington) 2007	1	0
Fereti (nee Patea), Jackie S. see		
Patea, J.S.		
1966– (Canterbury) 1989–90–91	3	–
Fitzpatrick, Theresa M. 1995–	11	15
(Auckland) 2017–18–19		
Ford, Amanda 1970–	1	4
(Canterbury) 1989–90–91		
Ford, Deborah 1965–	–	–
(Canterbury) 1989–90–91		
Frost, Seuga 1966–	–	–
(Canterbury) 1990–91		
Garden, Susan 1961–2008	–	–
(Canterbury) 1989–90–91		
(Otago) 1992		
Gavet, Sandra 1961–	–	–
(Auckland) 1990–92		
Goss, Sarah L. 1992–	10	5
(Manawatu) 2016 –17		
Grant (nee Blackledge),Victoria E.	17	35
1982– (Auckland) 2006–07–08–09–		
10–11		
(Waikato) 2013		
Gray, Isabel 1974– (Wellington) 1999–	5	5
02–05		
Gubb (nee Halapua), Charlene P.T. see		
Halapua, C.P.T.		
Halapua, Charlene P.T. 1988–	9	5
(Auckland) 2015–16–17		
Harrison, Sarah (Wellington) 1999	2	–
Hayes, Carol 1970– (Southland) 1989–	–	–
91–92–93		
Heenan, Janet M. 1969–	5	–
(Northland) 1996–98		
Heighway, Victoria L 1980–	32	10
(Auckland) 2000–01–02–03–04–05–		
06–07–08–09–10		
Hiemer, Riki (Wellington) 1997	2	–
Hina, Trisha R. 1977– (Auckland) 2010	4	–

	Internationals	
	Games	Points
Hireme, A. Honey 1981–	18	75
(Waikato) 2014–15–16–17		
Hirovanaa, Monique J. 1966–	24	65
(Auckland) 1994–95–96–97–98–99–		
00–01–02		
Hohepa, Carla G. 1985–	25	95
(Otago) 2007–08–09–10		
(Waikato) 2016–17–19		
Hull, R.M. see Mahoney, R.M.		
Hopkins, Anna 1970–	–	–
(Wellington) 1991		
Huxford, Sarah (Wellington) 1993	–	–
Inwood, Nicola A. 1970–	3	–
(Canterbury) 1989–90–91		
Itunu, Aldora T. 1991–	20	30
(Auckland) 2015–16–17–18		
Itunu, Linda F. 1984–	39	10
(Auckland) 2003–04–06–07–08–09–		
10–14–15–17–18		
Jensen, Emma M. 1977–	49	53
(Waikato) 2002–03–04		
(Auckland) 2005–06–07–08–09–10–		
11–12–13–14–15		
John, Chris (Canterbury) 1990	–	–
Johnson, Fiona C. 1970–	–	–
(Wellington) 1990		
Kahura, Dianne M.T. 1969–	12	95
(Auckland) 1998–99–00–02		
Kay, Rhonda 1976– (Waikato) 2000	1	–
Ketu, Lesley T. see Elder, L.T.		
King (nee Barclay), Fiona J. 1972–	18	5
(Otago) 1996–97–98–99–00–01–02		
Kingi, Mere A. 1974–	5	10
(Auckland) 2003–04		
Kiwi, Kellie H. 1972– (Bay of	8	15
Plenty) 1996–97–98		
Knight, Neroli 1974–	4	–
(Wellington) 1990–91–99–00–01		
Konui, Toni R.H. 1966–	3	–
(Auckland) 1998		
Kupa, Mel (Hawke's Bay) 1997	2	–
Lavea, Justine 1984–	34	30
(Auckland) 2004–05–07–09–10–11–		
12–13–14		
(Counties Manukau) 2015		
Lavea, Vaniya N.H. 1981–	5	–
(Auckland) 2003–04–07		
Leiataua, Onjeurlina F. 1995–	1	–
(Auckland) 2013		
Lemon, Tracey M. 1970–2012	2	–
(Auckland) 1991–94–95		

	Internationals	
	Games	Points
Lene, Stacey O. 1980– (Canterbury) 2003–04–05	7	35
Leti-I'iga, Ayesha A. 1999– (Wellington) 2018–19	9	15
Levave, Sanita D. 1988– (Wellington) 2014	5	–
Lili'i, Adrienne P. 1970– (Auckland) 1999–02–03–04 (Waikato) 2000	12	5
Littleworth, Helen M. 1966– (Canterbury) 1989–90–91–92–93–94 (Otago) 1995–96	8	20
Liua'ana, Rebecca 1970– (Wellington) 1999–00–01–02	10	10
Lotui'iga, L. Brigitta 1968– (Auckland) 1998	5	–
Love, Phillipa E.A. 1990– (Otago) 2014 (Canterbury) 2017–18–19	11	5
McKay, K. Ruth 1986– (Manawatu) 2007–08–09–10–12–13–14	25	–
McKenzie, Margaret J. 1970– (Otago) 2000–05	5	5
McMenamin, Charmaine J. 1990– (Auckland) 2013–16–17–18–19	25	20
Mahon, Helen L. 1968– (Canterbury) 1989 (Wellington) 1991 (Waikato) 1992	3	12
Mahoney (nee Hull), Rebecca M. 1983– (Manawatu) 2004–08 (Hawke's Bay) 2006 (Wellington) 2009–10–11	16	25
Makata, Rachel J. 1974– (Auckland) 2006	2	5
Maliukaetau, F. Diane L. 1986– (Auckland) 2005–06	6	5
Mallard, Beth L. 1981– (Otago) 2006–07–08–09	8	–
Manuel, Huriana R. 1986– (Auckland) 2005–06–07–08–09–10–14	25	70
Marino-Tauhinu, Arihiana A.H. 1992– (Counties Manukau) 2019	6	–
Marsh, A. see Rule, A.		
Martin, Rochelle L. 1973– (Wellington) 1994–95 (Auckland) 1996–97–98–99–00–02–04–05–06	32	70
Matapo, P.E.A. 'Kelani' 1983– (Auckland) 2011	1	–
Mata'u, Aotearoa K. 1997– (Counties Manukau) 2016–17	8	5

	Internationals	
	Games	Points
Mihinui, M.T. Eliza 1960– (Auckland) 1994	–	–
Moata'ane, Kilisitina 1997– (Otago) 2019	1	–
Moore, Aroha 1978– (Auckland) 2004	3	–
Moors, D.B. 'Natahlia' 1995– (Auckland) 2018–19	2	5
Mortimer, Stephanie A. 1981– (Canterbury) 2003–04–05–06	11	50
Mulipola, Tala 1981– (Auckland) 2000–01–03	7	5
Murphy, Amanda J. 1985– (Canterbury) 2009–11	2	–
Myers, H.J. see Porter, H.J.		
Natua Toka I. 1991– (Waikato) 2015–16–17–19	22	25
Nelson, Aleisha P. 1990– (Auckland) 2012–14–15–16–17–18–19	35	10
Nemaia, Ana (Auckland) 1989	–	–
Nesbit, Joanne (Canterbury) 1989	–	–
Ngan-Woo, Joanah M.F. 1995– (Wellington) 2019	3	5
Ngata-Aerengamate, Te Kura R. 1991– (Counties Manukau) 2014–15–16–17–18–19	29	10
Ngatai, Melodie M. 1976– (Auckland) 2004 (Waikato) 2005 (Hawke's Bay) 2006–11 (Canterbury) 2010–13	17	–
Nielsen, Jacinta 1972– (Otago) 1997–98–00	7	–
O'Leary, Pauline (Wanganui) 1993	–	–
O'Reilly, Lauren M. 1967– (Canterbury) 1992–93–94	1	–
Paasi, Poinisitia 1970–2018 (Wellington) 2001–07	4	–
Paitai, Elsie 1963– (Auckland) 1990–91	–	–
Palmer, Farah R. 1972– (Otago) 1996–98–99–00 (Waikato) 1997 (Manawatu) 2001–02–03–04–05–06	35	25
Papalii, Christine 1962– (Auckland) 1989–90–92	–	–
Parkes, Marcelle J. 1997– (Wellington) 2018–19	5	–
Patea-Fereti, Jackie S. 1986– (Wellington) 2012–13–14–16–18–19	18	–

	Internationals Games	Points		Internationals Games	Points

Paul, Geraldine 1965– (Bay of 4   10
Plenty) 1989–91–97
(Taranaki) 1994
Paul, Tamaku 1979– (Bay of 1   –
Plenty) 2001
Penetito, Karina E. see Stowers, K.E.
Perese, Leilani L.R. 1993– 11   –
(Counties Manukau) 2018–19
Piho, Mata 1972– (Otago) 1998–00 3   –
Porter (nee Myers), Hannah J. 1979– 22   169
(Otago) 2000–02
(Auckland) 2003–04–05–06–08

Reader, Heidi C. 1971– (Otago) 1993 3   38
(Waikato) 1994–96
(Bay of Plenty) 1995
Rees, Vivian L. 1971– 2   2
(Wellington) 1993–94–95
Rere (Ratu), Ericka 1963– 3   –
(Wellington) 1990–91–92
(Bay of Plenty) 1993
Reynolds, Julie 1966– –   –
(Canterbury) 1993–94
Richards, Anna M. 1964– 49   89
(Auckland) 1990–91–92–93–94–96–
97–98–99–00–01–02–03–04–05–
06–07–08–10
Richards, Fiona C. 1970– 14   –
(Canterbury) 1993–94–95–96
(Auckland) 1997–98–99
Richardson, Claire 1984– 23   54
(Otago) 2003–04–05–06–07–12
(Auckland) 2013–14
Rikihana-Broughton, Julie –   –
(Wellington) 1990
Robertson, Casey J. 1981– 38   10
(Canterbury) 2002–03–04–05–06–09–
10–11–12–13–14
Robinson, Melodie C. 1973– 18   20
(Wellington) 1996–97–98–99
(Auckland) 2001–02
Robinson, Vita J. 1982– 14   –
(Auckland) 2007–09–10–11–13
Rodd, Christine A. 1959– 2   –
(Canterbury) 1990–91
Ross, L. Christine 1964– (Mid 5   52
C'bury) 1989–92–96
(Canterbury) 1990–91
Rowat, Claire L. 1983– –   –
(Wellington) 2009
Rule (nee Marsh), Amiria 1983– 34   75
(Canterbury) 2000–01–02–03–5–06–
09–11–13–14
Ruscoe, Melissa J. 1976– 22   32
(Canterbury) 2004–05–06–07–08–10

Rush, Annaleah M. 1976– 20   156
(Otago) 1996–97–98–99
(Auckland) 2000–01–02
Rush, Erin 1970– (Wellington) 2003 2   –
Saili, Alena F. 1998– 5   –
(Southland) 2018–19
Savage, Aroha 1990– 33   20
(Auckland) 2010–11–12
(Counties Manukau) 2013–14–16–
17–18
Sheck, Regina 1969– 25   25
(Auckland) 1994–96–97–98
(Waikato) 1999–00–01–02–03–04
Shelford, Exia T. see Edwards, E.T.
Shortland, Suzanne 1974– 18   20
(Auckland) 1997–98–99–00–01–02
Simon, Kennedy W. 1996– 4   –
(Waikato) 2019
Simpson-Brown, Lenadeen H. 1964– 8   15
(Canterbury) 1994
(Waikato) 1995–96–97
Sio, Nina 1963– (Auckland) 1989– 4   –
91–92
(Waikato) 1994
Sione, Joan L. 1986– (Auckland) 2005– 6   5
10
Sisifa, Angelene A.F. 1989– 7   –
(Otago) 2015–16
Smith, Charmaine B. 1990– (North 27   20
Harbour) 2015–16–17
(Auckland) 2018–19
Smith, Kimberly M. 1985– 11   –
(Canterbury) 2005–06–07–08–09
Solomon, Pikihuia P. 1983– 2   10
(Otago) 2005
Stowers, Karina E. (nee 18   –
Penetito) 1986– (Auckland) 2005–
09–10–11–12–13
Su'a, S.M.A. 'Nara' 1969– 2   5
(Auckland) 1996
Suasua-White, D. see White, D.M.
Subritzky-Nafatali, Victoria S. 1991– 19   34
(Otago) 2012–14
(Counties Manukau) 2015–16–17
Sue, Kristina J. 1987– 15   –
(Manawatu) 2016–17–18
Sutorius, Aimee E. 1979– 3   –
Wellington) 2007–08–09

Tagoai, Monica F. 1998– 3   –
(Wellington) 2018
Tahu, Bella M. 1970– (Auckland) 1996 3   –
Talawadua, Sosoli J. 1989– 8   5
(Waikato) 2016–17

	Internationals	
	Games	Points
Tamihana, Florence (Wellington) 1995	1	–
Tapsell, Pia H. 1998– (North Harbour) 2019	6	5
Taufateau, Doris J.T. 1987– (Auckland) 2008–10–11	5	–
Taylor, Karen 1968– (Bay of Plenty) 1996	2	5
Teddy, Waimania L. 1979– (Auckland) 2005–06–07	6	–
Te Tamaki, Teresa K. 1981– (Auckland) 2007–08–11 (Waikato) 2012–15	10	–
Tekeu, No'o (–) 1990	–	–
Te Ohaere-Fox,Stephanie A. 1985– (Canterbury) 2008–09–10–12–13–14 (Wasps) 2011	24	–
Thomas, Emma H. 1958– (Bay of Plenty) 1996–97–98	9	–
Tiplady, Anika M. 1980– (Manawatu) 2007 (Canterbury) 2009	2	–
Tiplady-Hurring, Halie A. 1986– (Canterbury) 2008–10–14 (Otago) 2012	13	15
Tiriamai, Kimi 1964– (Auckland) 1990–91	2	–
Tofa, L. Cristo. S. 1987– (North Harbour) 2018	2	–
Tubic, Hazel S. 1990– (Auckland) 2011–12 (Counties Manukau) 2016–17	11	12
Va'aga, Helen 1977– (Auckland) 2002–03–05–06	10	10
Vaeteru, Teina (–) 1990	–	–
Vaughan, Janna M. 1988– (Manawatu) 2015–16	6	10
Waaka, Cheryl M. 1970– (Auckland) 1997–98–00–01–02–03–04 (Northland) 1999	20	35
Waaka, Stacey J.A.K. 1995– (Waikato) 2015–17–18	16	30

	Internationals	
	Games	Points
Wall, Louisa H. 1972– (Waikato) 1994 (Auckland) 1995–96–97–98–99	15	95
Ward-Duin, Olivia Y. 1993– (North Harbour) 2019	2	–
Waters, Tracey J.R. 1973– (Canterbury) 1995–96–98	10	5
Wharton, Julie (Auckland) 1990	–	–
Whata-Simpkins, Katarina R. 1990– (Wellington) 2011	1	0
White, Davida M. 1967– (Auckland) 1993–94–95–96–98–00	13	0
Wickliffe, Renee W.M. 1987– (Auckland) 2009–10–11 (Counties Manukau) 2013–14–15–16–17 (Bay of Plenty) 2018–19	41	105
Wihongi, Kamila T. 1982– (Otago) 2005	1	–
Williams, Amy L. 1986– (Hawke's Bay) 2005–06	6	–
Williams, Tasha H. 1973– (Manawatu) 1994	1	10
Willoughby, Shannon M. 1982– (Otago) 2005–06	8	–
Wilson, Tammi 1973– (Auckland) 1998–99–00–01–02	16	196
Wilton, Kathleen A. 1984– (Otago) 2007–11–12–13–14	18	–
Winiata, Selica C. 1986– (Manawatu) 2008–12–13–14–15–16–17–18–19	40	195
Wong, Natasha A. 1967– (Canterbury) 1990–91–92–93–94	3	–
Wood, Rebecca J. 1987– (North Harbour) 2017	7	–
Woodman, Portia L. 1991– (Auckland) 2013 (Counties Manukau) 2016–17	16	110
Woodman, Sharnita K. 1986– (Counties Manukau) 2016	2	–
Yates, Sandy 1979– (Counties Manukau) 2001	1	–

BLACK FERNS RECORDS

NEW ZEALAND INTERNATIONAL CAPTAINS

Fiao'o Faamausili	2012–18	35
Farah Palmer	1997–2006	30
Melissa Ruscoe	2007–10	8
Lenadeen Simpson-Brown	1994–96	6
Leslie Elder	2019	5
Helen Littleworth	1991	3
Victoria Grant	2010–11	3
Rochelle Martin	2005–06	2
Victoria Heighway	2009	2
Davida White	1998	1
Anna Richards	2005	1
Casey Robertson	2011	1
Amiria Rule	2014	1
Kendra Cocksedge	2019	1

MOST APPEARANCES IN INTERNATIONALS

F.M. Faamausili	2002–18	57	K.A. Brazier	2009–19	40
K.M. Cocksedge	2007–19	53	S.C. Winiata	2008–19	40
A.M. Richards	1991–10	49	C.J. Robertson	2002–14	38
E.M. Jensen	2002–15	49	L.F. Itunu	2003–18	38
E.S. Blackwell	2011–19	43	F.R. Palmer	1996–06	35
R.W.M. Wickliffe	2009–19	41	A.P. Nelson	2012–19	35

MOST SUCCESSIVE INTERNATIONALS

K.M. Cocksedge	2011–19	45

MOST POINTS IN INTERNATIONALS

	Tries	Con	PG	DG	Total		Tries	Con	PG	DG	Total
K.M. Cocksedge	16	86	30	–	342	K.A. Brazier	11	45	15	–	190
V. Cootes	43	–	–	–	215	H.J. Porter	5	42	20	–	169
T. Wilson	21	29	11	–	196	A.M. Rush	14	34	6	–	156
S.C. Winiata	39	–	–	–	195						

MOST POINTS IN AN INTERNATIONAL

V. Cootes	v France, 1996	45	(9 tries)
P.L. Woodman	v Hong Kong, 2017	40	(8 tries)
T. Wilson	v USA, 1999	36	(6 tries, 3 conversions)
L.C. Ross	v France, 1996	34	(2 tries, 12 conversions)
K.M. Cocksedge	v Hong Kong, 2017	31	(1 try, 13 conversions)
T. Wilson	v Germany, 1998	30	(4 tries, 5 conversions)

MOST TRIES IN AN INTERNATIONAL

V. Cootes	v France, 1996	9	V. Cootes	v USA, 1998	5
P.L. Woodman	v Hong Kong, 2017	8	V. Cootes	v Germany, 2002	5
T. Wilson	v USA, 1999	6	S.C. Winiata	v Samoa, 2014	5
V. Cootes	v USA, 1996	5			

MOST PENALTY GOALS IN AN INTERNATIONAL

K.A. Brazier	v England, 2013	4	K.M. Cocksedge	v England, 2015	4

MOST CONVERSIONS IN AN INTERNATIONAL

K.M. Cocksedge	v Hong Kong, 2017	13	L.C. Ross	v Canada, 1996	9
L.C. Ross	v France, 1996	12	H.C. Reader	v USA, 1996	8

INTERNATIONAL MATCH RECORD

Year		Opponent	Venue	Result		
1991	v	Canada[1]	Glamorgan	won	24	8
	v	Wales[1]	Llanharen	won	24	6
	v	USA[1] (semi-final)	Cardiff	lost	0	7
1994	v	Australia	Sydney	won	37	0
1995	v	Australia	Auckland	won	64	0
1996	v	Australia	Sydney	won	28	5
	v	Canada	St Albert	won	88	3
	v	USA	Edmonton	won	86	8
	v	France	Edmonton	won	109	0
1997	v	England	Burnham	won	67	0
	v	Australia	Dunedin	won	40	0
1998	v	Germany[1]	Amsterdam	won	134	6
	v	Scotland[1]	Amsterdam	won	76	0
	v	Spain[1] (quarter-final)	Amsterdam	won	46	3
	v	England[1] (semi-final)	Amsterdam	won	44	11
	v	USA[1] (final)	Amsterdam	won	44	12
	v	Australia	Sydney	won	27	3
1999	v	Canada	Palmerston North	won	73	0
	v	USA	Palmerston North	won	65	5
2000	v	Canada	Winnipeg	won	41	0
	v	USA	Winnipeg	won	45	0
	v	England	Winnipeg	won	32	13
2001	v	England	Rotorua	won	15	10
	v	England	Albany	lost	17	22
2002	v	Germany[1]	Barcelona	won	117	0
	v	Australia[1]	Barcelona	won	36	3
	v	France[1] (semi-final)	Barcelona	won	30	0

	v	England[1] (final)	Barcelona	won	19	9
2003	v	World XV	Auckland	won	37	0
	v	World XV	Whangarei	won	38	19
2004	v	Canada	Vancouver	won	32	5
	v	USA	Calgary	won	35	0
	v	England	Edmonton	won	38	0
2005	v	Scotland	Ottawa	won	30	9
	v	Canada	Ottawa	won	43	3
	v	Canada	Ottawa	won	32	5
	v	England	Auckland	won	33	8
	v	England	Hamilton	won	24	15
2006	v	Canada[1]	Edmonton	won	66	7
	v	Samoa[1]	Edmonton	won	50	0
	v	Scotland[1]	Edmonton	won	21	0
	v	France[1] (semi-final)	Edmonton	won	40	10
	v	England[1] (final)	Edmonton	won	25	17
2007	v	Australia	Wanganui	won	21	11
	v	Australia	Wellington	won	29	12
2008	v	Australia	Canberra	won	37	3
	v	Australia	Canberra	won	22	16
2009	v	England	London	won	16	3
	v	England	London	lost	3	10
2010	v	South Africa[1]	London	won	55	3
	v	Australia[1]	London	won	32	5
	v	Wales[1]	London	won	41	8
	v	France[1] (semi-final)	London	won	45	7
	v	England[1] (final)	London	won	13	10
2011	v	England	London	lost	0	10
	v	England	London	lost	7	21
	v	England	London	draw	8	8
2012	v	England	Esher	lost	13	16
	v	England	Aldershot	lost	8	17
	v	England	London	lost	23	32
2013	v	England	Auckland	won	29	10
	v	England	Hamilton	won	14	9
	v	England	Pukekohe	won	29	8
2014	v	Australia	Rotorua	won	38	3
	v	Samoa	Auckland	won	90	12
	v	Canada	Tauranga	won	16	8
	v	Canada	Whakatane	won	33	21
	v	Kazakhstan[1]	Marcoussis	won	79	5
	v	Ireland[1]	Marcoussis	lost	14	17
	v	USA[1]	Marcoussis	won	34	3
	v	Wales[1]	Paris	won	63	7
	v	USA[1]	Paris	won	55	5
2015	v	Canada	Calgary	won	40	22
	v	England	Red Deer	won	26	7
	v	USA	Edmonton	won	49	14

2016	v	Australia	Auckland	won	67	3
	v	Australia	Albany	won	29	3
	v	England	London	won	25	20
	v	Canada	Dublin	won	20	10
	v	Ireland	Dublin	won	38	8
2017	v	Canada	Wellington	won	28	16
	v	Australia	Christchurch	won	44	17
	v	England	Rotorua	lost	21	29
	v	Wales[1]	Dublin	won	44	12
	v	Hong Kong[1]	Dublin	won	121	0
	v	Canada[1]	Dublin	won	48	5
	v	USA[1] (semi-final)	Belfast	won	45	12
	v	England[1] (final)	Belfast	won	41	32
2018	v	Australia	Sydney	won	31	11
	v	Australia	Auckland	won	45	17
	v	USA	Chicago	won	67	6
	v	France	Toulon	won	14	0
	v	France	Grenoble	lost	27	30
2019	v	Canada	San Diego	won	35	20
	v	USA	San Diego	won	33	0
	v	France	San Diego	lost	16	25
	v	England	San Diego	won	28	13
	v	Australia	Perth	won	47	10
	v	Australia	Auckland	won	37	8

[1]World Cup

SUMMARY OF INTERNATIONALS

Played:	99	Points for:	3905
Won:	86	Points against:	888
Lost:	12		
Drawn:	1		

NEW ZEALAND DEVELOPMENT XV

For the first time, a Black Ferns Development team was assembled and participated in the Oceania championship in Fiji. In its three games the team amassed 234 points while conceding none.

NEW ZEALAND DEVELOPMENT XV AT
OCEANIA RUGBY WOMEN'S CHAMPIONSHIP

	Union	Date of Birth	Height	Weight
S.C.R. (Saphire) Abraham	Auckland	3/7/01	1.69	88
L.N.Y. (Lauren) Balsillie	Manawatu	13/6/98	1.69	70
A.J. (Alana) Bremner	Canterbury	10/2/97	1.78	80
C.J. (Chelsea) Bremner	Canterbury	11/4/95	1.81	88
G.E. (Grace) Brooker*	Canterbury	20/6/99	1.73	75
F.K. (Forne) Burkin*	Hawke's Bay	28/10/98	1.66	76
L.H.J. (Luka) Connor*	Bay of Plenty	24/9/96	1.71	95
E.O. (Eilis) Doyle	Otago	21/3/97	1.76	96
Joanna Fanene	Auckland	11/11/98	1.78	105
R.C. (Rosie) Kelly	Otago	16/1/00	1.59	62
M.M. (Mayalin) Lolohea	Canterbury	19/7/99	1.68	79
O.B. (Olivia) McGoverne	Canterbury	2/6/97	1.75	79
A.A.H. (Arihiana) Marino-Tauhinu* (capt)	Counties Manukau	29/3/92	1.61	74
Kilisitina Moata'ane*	Otago	23/11/97	1.67	80
I.M.P. (Ilisapeta) Molia	Counties Manukau	16/8/01	1.80	96
D.B. (Natahlia) Moors*	Auckland	7/12/95	1.63	71
A.J. (Angel) Mulu	Bay of Plenty	21/11/99	1.64	98
J.M.F. (Joanah) Ngan-Woo*	Wellington	15/12/95	1.82	88
L.L.R. (Leilani) Perese*	Counties Manukau	1/1/93	1.76	125
M.C. (Melanie) Puckett	Canterbury	6/7/99	1.60	67
A.A. (Amanda) Rasch	Wellington	9/8/93	1.74	87
K.L. (Kendra) Reynolds	Bay of Plenty	25/1/93	1.63	73
A.M. (Amy) Rule	Canterbury	15/7/00	1.70	95
K.W. (Kennedy) Simon*	Waikato	1/10/96	1.73	80
P.H. (Pia) Tapsell*	North Harbour	2/8/98	1.78	85
H.S. (Hazel) Tubic*	Counties Manukau	31/12/90	1.66	70
L.L. (Langi) Veainu	Counties Manukau	3/11/93	1.65	71
K.P. (Kelsie) Wills	Bay of Plenty	8/1/93	1.84	81

*Black Fern

Original selection Krysten Cottrell* (Hawke's Bay) was injured and replaced by Rosie Kelly. Brooker captained the team v Papua New Guinea.

Coach: Wayne Maxwell (*Waikato*)
Assistant coaches: Kieran Kite (*Canterbury*), Whitney Hansen (*Canterbury*)
Strength & conditioning: Amanda Murphy (*Canterbury*)
Manager: Faamoana Leilua (*Counties Manukau*)
Physiotherapist: Gabrielle McCullough

Teams: Australia A, Fiji, NZ Development, Papua New Guinea, Samoa, Tonga.

Results

November 18	Samoa 65 Papua New Guinea 12; NZ Development 53 Fiji 0.
November 22	NZ Development 50 Australia A 0; Fiji 26 Samoa 7.
November 26	NZ Development 131 Papua New Guinea 0; Australia 27 Samoa 5.
November 30	Fijiana B v Papua New Guinea; Fiji v Samoa.

All games were played at Churchill Park, Lautoka.

A Tongan team member, on arrival in Fiji, was suspected of having measles and after tests were made Fiji health authorities placed the Tongan team in quarantine for 18 days forcing Tonga to withdraw from the tournament.

NEW ZEALAND DEVELOPMENT XV	Fiji	Australia A	Papua New Guinea	TOTALS
McGoverne	15*	15*	–	2
Moors	14	14	11*	3
Lolohea	11	s	12	3
Veainu	–	11*	14	2
Brooker	13	13	15*	3
Kelly	s	–	s	2
Balsillie	12	–	s	2
Moata'ane	–	12	13*	2
Tubic	10	10	s	3
Rasch	s	s	10	3
Marino-Tauhinu	9*	9*	–	2
Puckett	s	s	9	3
Fanene	8*	s	–	2
Tapsell	s	8*	8*	3
Reynolds	7	–	s	2
Simon	–	7	7	2
A. Bremner	6	s	6	3
Molia	–	6*	s	2
Ngan-Woo	5	–	5	2
Wills	4*	5	–	2
C. Bremner	s	4	4*	3
Rule	3*	s	s	3
Perese	1*	3*	3	3
Mulu	s	1*	s	3
Doyle	s	s	1*	3
Connor	2*	2*	s	3
Abraham	s	–	2*	2
Burkin	–	s	–	1

INDIVIDUAL SCORING

	Tries	Con	PG	DG	Points
Moors	6	–	–	–	30
Tubic	2	6	–	–	22
Rasch	–	11	–	–	22
Abraham	3	–	–	–	15
Balsillie	3	–	–	–	15
Brooker	3	–	–	–	15
Lolohea	3	–	–	–	15
Perese	3	–	–	–	15
Veainu	3	–	–	–	15
Kelly	1	5	–	–	15
Connor	2	–	–	–	10
Moata'ane	2	–	–	–	10
Molia	2	–	–	–	10
Tapsell	2	–	–	–	10
McGoverne	1	–	–	–	5
Ngan-Woo	1	–	–	–	5
Rule	1	–	–	–	5
Totals	**38**	**22**	**0**	**0**	**234**
Opposition scored	0	0	0	0	0

NEW ZEALAND DEVELOPMENT XV IN FIJI

Played 3 · Won 3 · Points for 234 · Points against 0

Date	Opponent	Location	Score	Tries	Con	PG	Referee
Nov 18	Fiji	Lautoka	53–0	Moors (2), Perese (2), Ngan-Woo, Brooker, Lolohea, Balsillie, Tubic	Tubic (3), Rasch		Brittany Andrews *(New Zealand)*
Nov 22	Australia A	Lautoka	50–0	Connor (2), McGoverne, Molia, Veainu, Perese, Lolohea, Moata'ane	Tubic (3), Rasch (2)		Avii Fa'alpega *(Samoa)*
Nov 26	Papua New Guinea	Lautoka	131–0	Moors (4), Abraham (3), Tapsell (2), Veainu (2), Brooker (2), Balsillie (2), Lolohea, Moata'ane, Rule, Molia, Kelly, Tubic	Rasch (8), Kelly (5)		Tyler Miller *(Australia)*

RESULTS FROM 2019 FIRST-CLASS SEASON IN NEW ZEALAND

AND TEAMS OF NEW ZEALANDERS OVERSEAS

Key:

P	Farah Palmer Cup Premiership
C	Farah Palmer Cup Championship
sf	semi-final
f	final
ST	J.J. Stewart Trophy
*	not first-class

January

Sat/Sun 26/27	*	Fast Four Sevens				Hamilton

February

Fri-Sun 1-3	*	Australia WR Sevens				Sydney

April

Sat/Sun 20/21	*	Japan WR Sevens				Kitakyushu

May

Sat/Sun 11/12	*.	Canada WR Sevens				Victoria

June

Sat/Sun	15/16	*	France WR Sevens				Biarritz
Fri	28		New Zealand	35	Canada	20	San Diego

July

Tue	2		New Zealand	33	USA	0	San Diego
Sat	6		France	25	New Zealand	16	San Diego
Sun	14		New Zealand	28	England	13	San Diego

August

Sat	10		New Zealand	47	Australia	10	Perth
Sat	17		New Zealand	37	Australia	8	Auckland
Sat	31	P,ST	Canterbury	57	Wellington	19	Christchurch
		P	Counties Manukau	34	Bay of Plenty	24	Tauranga
		P	Auckland	41	Waikato	23	Hamilton

September

Fri	6	P	Counties Manukau	43	Manawatu	14	Pukekohe
Sat	7	P	Wellington	32	Bay of Plenty	29	Porirua
		C	Hawke's Bay	64	Northland	31	Napier
		C	North Harbour	22	Tasman	10	Blenheim
Sun	8	P	Canterbury	45	Auckland	12	Auckland
		C	Otago	57	Taranaki	5	Dunedin
Sat	14	P	Waikato	15	Manawatu	12	Palmerston North
		P	Auckland	28	Bay of Plenty	19	Whakatane
		C	Hawke's Bay	39	North Harbour	10	North Shore
		C	Otago	40	Northland	7	Whangarei
		C	Tasman	36	Taranaki	22	New Plymouth
Sun	15	P	Wellington	38	Counties Manukau	36	Wellington
Fri	20	C	Hawke's Bay	74	Taranaki	0	Napier
Sat	21	P	Bay of Plenty	26	Waikato	21	Hamilton
		P,ST	Canterbury	54	Manawatu	7	Christchurch

Day	Date		Team				Venue
		C	Otago	58	Tasman	15	Oamaru
Sun	22	P	Auckland	38	Wellington	10	Auckland
		C	Northland	27	North Harbour	21	Whangarei
Fri	27	C	Hawke's Bay	55	Tasman	5	Nelson
Sat	28	P	Canterbury	32	Counties Manukau	12	Pukekohe
		P	Wellington	59	Waikato	31	Wellington
		C	Northland	22	Taranaki	12	Inglewood
Sun	29	P	Auckland	50	Manawatu	26	Palmerston North
		C	Otago	90	North Harbour	0	Dunedin

October

Day	Date		Team				Venue
Fri	4	C	North Harbour	33	Taranaki	21	Albany
Sat	5	P	Bay of Plenty	30	Manawatu	17	Tauranga
		P	Auckland	38	Counties Manukau	31	Auckland
		C	Otago	34	Hawke's Bay	26	Napier
		C	Northland	35	Tasman	27	Whangarei
Sat/Sun	5/6	*	USA WR Sevens				Glendale
Sun	6	P	Canterbury	45	Waikato	5	Hamilton
Sat	12	P	Counties Manukau	28	Waikato	19	Pukekohe
		P	Wellington	42	Manawatu	26	Palmerston North
		C qf	Tasman	25	North Harbour	19	Albany
Sun	13	P, ST	Canterbury	40	Bay of Plenty	7	Christchurch
		C qf	Northland	32	Taranaki	14	Whangarei
Sat	19	P sf	Auckland	43	Wellington	24	Auckland
		C sf	Otago	64	Tasman	10	Dunedin
		C sf	Hawke's Bay	46	Northland	31	Napier
Sun	20	P sf	Canterbury	31	Counties Manukau	22	Christchurch
Sat	26	P f	Canterbury	30	Auckland	20	Christchurch
Sun	27	C f	Otago	24	Hawke's Bay	20	Dunedin

November

Day	Date		Team				Venue
Thu-Sat	7-9	*	Oceania Sevens				Suva
Mon	18		New Zealand Development	53	Fiji	0	Lautoka
Thu	22		New Zealand Development	50	Australia A	0	Lautoka
Tue	26		New Zealand Development	131	Papua New Guinea	0	Lautoka

December

Day	Date		Event				Venue
Thu-Sat	5-7	*	Dubai WR Sevens				Dubai
Fri-Sun	13-15	*	South Africa WR Sevens				Cape Town
Sat/Sun	14/15	*	National Sevens				Tauranga

WOMEN'S CLUB FINALS

Results of the 2019 senior club finals. Counties Manukau and North Harbour clubs participated in the Auckland competition.

Union	Winner		Runner-up	
Auckland	Marist	32	College Rifles	22
Bay of Plenty	Rangiuru	29	Whakarewarewa	0
Canterbury	Christchurch[2]	55	Canterbury University	14
Hawke's Bay	Napier Tech	27	Hastings RS	24
Manawatu	Kia Toa	17	Feilding OB Oroua	12
Northland	Kaikohe	17	Te Rarawa	12
Otago	University[1]	32	Pirates	19
Taranaki	Coastal[1]	25	Clifton	10
Tasman	Waimea OB	27	Moutere	17
Waikato	Melville[1]	34	Hamilton OB	19
Wellington	Oriental Rongotai	43	Northern United	10

[1] also won in 2018   [2] also won in 2017 and 2018

FARAH PALMER CUP

The number of teams increased to thirteen with the return of Northland. Teams were ranked based on the 2018 results with the top seven teams playing in the premiership division and the remaining six in the championship division. Wellington was promoted after winning the 2018 Championship. The addition of Northland to the Championship enabled Auckland, bottom-placed in the 2018 Premiership, to retain its place in the higher division.

Final standings after round robin:

	P	W	D	L	B⁴	B⁷	Pts	T	C	PG	DG	Total	T	C	PG	DG	Total
										FOR					AGAINST		
PREMIERSHIP DIVISION																	
Canterbury	6	6	–	–	6	–	**30**	43	29	–	–	273	11	6	–	–	67
Auckland	6	5	–	1	5	–	**25**	32	22	1	–	207	23	15	3	–	154
Wellington	6	4	–	2	4	–	**20**	30	22	2	–	200	35	21	–	–	217
Counties Manukau	6	3	–	3	5	2	**19**	31	14	2	–	189	26	16	1	–	165
Bay of Plenty	6	2	–	4	4	1	**13**	23	10	–	–	135	26	15	4	–	172
Waikato	6	1	–	5	1	1	**6**	16	8	5	1	114	33	20	2	–	211
Manawatu	6	–	–	6	2	1	**3**	16	11	–	–	102	37	23	–	1	234
TOTALS								**191**	**116**	**10**	**1**	**1220**	**191**	**116**	**10**	**1**	**1220**
CHAMPIONSHIP DIVISION																	
Otago	5	5	–	–	5	–	**25**	45	27	–	–	279	8	5	1	–	53
Hawke's Bay	5	4	–	1	5	–	**21**	41	25	1	–	258	13	6	1	–	80
Northland	5	3	–	2	3	–	**15**	19	9	3	–	122	26	18	–	–	166
North Harbour	5	2	–	3	1	1	**10**	12	10	2	–	86	28	19	3	–	187
Tasman	5	1	–	4	2	–	**6**	15	7	2	–	95	32	13	2	–	192
Taranaki	5	–	–	5	1	–	**1**	10	5	–	–	60	35	22	1	–	222
TOTALS								**142**	**83**	**8**	**0**	**900**	**142**	**83**	**8**	**0**	**900**

B⁴ bonus points for four or more tries in a match.   *B⁷ bonus points for loss by seven or fewer points.*

PREMIERSHIP

Semi-finals: Auckland 43 Wellington 24, at Auckland;
Canterbury 31 Counties Manukau 22, at Christchurch

Final: Canterbury 30 Auckland 20, at Christchurch

CHAMPIONSHIP

Quarter-finals: Tasman 25 North Harbour 19, at Albany;
Northland 32 Taranaki 14, at Whangarei

Semi-finals: Otago 64 Tasman 10, at Dunedin;
Hawke's Bay 46 Northland 31, at Napier

Final: Otago 24 Hawke's Bay 20, at Dunedin

LEADING POINTS-SCORERS

Rosie Kelly	Otago	107
Kendra Cocksedge	Canterbury	92

LEADING TRY-SCORERS

Ayesha Leti-I'iga	Wellington	12
Kilisitina Moata'ane	Otago	9

CAREER CHAMPIONSHIP RECORDS

Points

892	Kendra Cocksedge (Canterbury)
545	Emma Jensen (Waik/Auck/HB)
463	Selica Winiata (Manawatu)

Tries

68	Selica Winiata (Manawatu)
57	Kendra Cocksedge (Canterbury)
46	Fiao'o Faamausili (Auckland)

Games

120	Emma Jensen (Waik/Auck/HB)
113	Justine Lavea (Auckland/Counties Manukau)
106	Fiao'o Faamausili (Auckland)
102	Stephanie Te Ohaere-Fox (Canterbury)

GRAND FINAL RESULTS

	Winner		Runner-up		Venue
1999	Auckland	22	Wellington	0	Wellington
2000	Auckland	22	Otago	12	Auckland
2001	Auckland	28	Wellington	3	Auckland
2002	Auckland	53	Wellington	3	Auckland
2003	Auckland	35	Wellington	0	Auckland
2004	Auckland	29	Canterbury	10	Auckland
2005	Auckland	36	Canterbury	3	Auckland
2006	Wellington	11	Auckland	10	Auckland
2007	Auckland	32	Otago	27	Auckland
2008	Auckland	13	Canterbury	12	Auckland
2009	Auckland	24	Canterbury	20	Christchurch
2011	Auckland	34	Wellington	8	Hamilton
2012	Auckland	38	Canterbury	12	Christchurch
2013	Auckland	20	Canterbury	10	Wellington
2014	Auckland	28	Waikato	14	New Plymouth
2015	Auckland	39	Wellington	9	Napier
2016	Counties Manukau	41	Auckland	22	Pukekohe

	Premiership	Championship
2017	Canterbury	Bay of Plenty
2018	Canterbury	Wellington
2019	Canterbury	Otago

CHAMPIONSHIP RECORDS

BY THE TEAMS

	BEST PERFORMANCE 2019	RECORD
Season Totals		
Most points	367 by Otago	449 by Wellington, 2018
Most tries	58 by Otago	69 by Wellington, 2018
Most conversions	37 by Otago	49 by Wellington, 2018
Most penalty goals	5 by Northland and Waikato	14 by Otago, 2013
Most dropped goals	1 by Canterbury and Waikato	2 by Manawatu, 2002; Auckland, 2012
Match Records		
Most points	90 by Otago v North Harbour	118 by Wellington v Taranaki, 2018
Most tries	14 by Otago v North Harbour	18 by Auckland v North Harbour, 1999; by Wellington v Taranaki, 2018
Most conversions	10 by Otago v North Harbour	14 by Wellington v Taranaki, 2018
Most penalty goals	3 by (i) Waikato v Bay of Plenty; (ii) Canterbury v Counties M'kau (s-f)	6 by Auckland v Wellington, 2001
Most dropped goals	1 by (i) Waikato v Manawatu; (ii) Canterbury v Auckland (final)	1 on 10 occasions
Biggest winning margin	90 by Otago v North Harbour (90–0)	118 by Wellington v Taranaki (118–0), 2018

BY THE PLAYERS

	BEST PERFORMANCE 2019		RECORD	
Season Totals				
Most points	107	Rosie Kelly (Otago)	118	Amanda Rasch (Wellington), 2018
Most tries	12	Ayesha Leti-I'iga (Wellington)	16	Mele Hufanga (Auckland), 2015
Most conversions	32	Rosie Kelly (Otago)	46	Amanda Rasch (Wellington), 2018
Most penalty goals	5	Chelsea Alley (Waikato); Krystal Murray (Northland)	12	Chelsea Alley (Waikato), 2013
Most dropped goals	1	Chelsea Alley (Waikato); Kendra Cocksedge (Canterbury)	2	Rebecca Hull (Manawatu), 2002; Bella Milo (Auckland), 2012
Match Totals				
Most points	30	Rosie Kelly (Otago) v North Harbour	45	Kelly Brazier (Otago) v Hawke's Bay, 2012
Most tries	5	Ayesha Leti-I'iga (Wellington) v Manawatu	8	Annaleah Rush (Otago) v Hanan Shield Dist), 1999
Most conversions	10	Rosie Kelly (Otago) v North Harbour	14	Amanda Rasch (Wellington) v Taranaki, 2018
Most penalty goals	2	(i) Chelsea Alley (Waikato) v Bay of Plenty; (ii) Kendra Cocksedge (Canterbury) v Counties M'kau (s-f); (iii) Hayley Hutana (Tasman) v North Harbour	6	Annaleah Rush (Auckland) v Wellington, 2001
Most dropped goals	1	(i) Chelsea Alley (Waikato) v Manawatu; (ii) Kendra Cocksedge (Canterbury) v Auckland (final)	1	by 8 players on 10 occasions

AUCKLAND STORM

2019 Status: Premiership
NPC participation: 1999–
Coach: Richie Walker
Assistant coaches: Anna Richards, Craig Hall
Home grounds: Eden Park

RECORDS

Most appearances	106	*Fiao'o Fa'amausili, 1999–2018*
Most points	452	*Emma Jensen, 2004–17*
Most tries	46	*Fiao'o Fa'amausili, 1999–2017*
Most points in a season	101	*Tammi Wilson, 1999;*
Most tries in a season	16	*Mele Hufanga, 2015*
Most conversions in a season	27	*Bella Milo, 2012*
		Patricia Maliepo, 2019
Most penalty goals in a season	9	*Emma Jensen, 2014*
Most dropped goals in a season	2	*Bella Milo, 2012*
Most points in a match	31	*Tammi Wilson v North Harbour, 1999*
Most tries in a match	4	*Louisa Wall v North Harbour, 1999;*
		v Northland, 1999;
		Victoria Grant v Otago, 2008;
		Jade Le Pesq v Manawatu, 2012
		Mele Hufanga v Wellington, 2014;
		v Hawke's Bay, 2014;
		v Canterbury 2015;
		Natahlia Moors v Bay of Plenty, 2015
Most conversions in a match	13	*Tammi Wilson v North Harbour, 1999*
Most penalty goals in a match	6	*Annaleah Rush v Wellington, 2001*
Highest team score	116	*v North Harbour, 1999*
Record victory (points ahead)	116	*116–0 v North Harbour, 1999*
Highest score conceded	45	*14–45 v Waikato, 2018;*
		12–45 v Canterbury, 2019
Record defeat (points behind)	33	*12–45 v Canterbury, 2019*

The entry of Northland into the Championship division enabled Auckland, bottom placed in 2018, to avoid relegation and remain in the Premiership division. The Storm's reputation was restored with the forwards, mostly Black Ferns, providing a sound platform for a young backline to take advantage. Canterbury was the only team to upset the much improved Storm.

A dozen of the newcomers were teenagers with many establishing permanent places in the team. These include the wings Princess Elliot and Isla Norman-Bell and prop Chryss Viliko. First five-eighth Patricia Maliepo, aged 16, was a star performer who played with a maturity beyond her years. The form of this highly promising youngster enabled Ruahei Demant to move to midfield where she benefitted from more attacking possibilities.

Linda Itunu was a fine captain and was accompanied in the forwards by Black Ferns Charmaine McMenamin, Eloise Blackwell, Charmaine Smith, Aleisha Nelson and Cristo Tofa who had returned after two years with North Harbour. McMenamin enjoyed an outstanding year, so did Leanne Thompson who last appeared in 2017 and must be close to higher honours. Aimee Lenssen last appeared in 2016.

Higher honours went to:

New Zealand: E. Blackwell, R. Demant, T.M. Fitzpatrick, C. McMenamin, N. Moors, A. Nelson, C. Smith.

New Zealand Development: S. Abraham, J. Fanene, N. Moors

New Zealand Sevens: T.M. Fitzpatrick, T.B. Nathan-Wong, N.L.V. Williams

AUCKLAND REPRESENTATIVES 2019

	Club	Games for Union	Points for Union		Club	Games for Union	Points for Union
Saphire Abraham	College Rifles	8	10	Vainga Moimoi	College Rifles	5	0
Eloise Blackwell	Eden	57	60	Natahlia Moors	Ponsonby	20	75
Moana Cook	Ponsonby	7	0	Joeannah Naime-Purcell	Ponsonby	7	10
Rosie Cox	College Rifles	9	12	Daynah Nankivell	Ponsonby	4	10
Kiritapu Demant	College Rifles	36	101	Aleisha Nelson	College Rifles	68	60
Ruahei Demant	College Rifles	36	159	Isla Norman-Bell	Ponsonby	8	25
Princess Elliot	Ponsonby	8	30	Abigail Roache	Ponsonby	5	0
Joanna Fanene	Marist	17	30	Maiakawana-kaulani Roos	College Rifles	8	0
Grace Freeman	College Rifles	3	0	Jennifer-Rose Reu	Marist	8	0
Meriana Hokianga	Ponsonby	3	0	Lauren Sa'u	Marist	6	5
Aldora Itunu	Ponsonby	40	70	Charmaine Smith	College Rifles	12	10
Linda Itunu	Ponsonby	60	45	Leanne Thompson	College Rifles	24	15
Tafito Lafaele	Papatoetoe	1	0	Cristo Tofa	Ponsonby	9	5
Aimee Lenssen	College Rifles	22	10	Alanis Toia	Ponsonby	2	0
Charmaine McMenamin	Ponsonby	53	70	Leianne Tufuga	Marist	1	0
Lose Mafi	Marist	20	15	Mele Tui'nukuafe	Ponsonby	1	0
Patricia Maliepo	Marist	8	78	Chryss Viliko	Marist	8	0

INDIVIDUAL SCORING

	Tries	Con	PG	DG	Points		Tries	Con	PG	DG	Points
Maliepo	3	27	3	–	78	Naime-Purcell	2	–	–	–	10
R. Demant	7	1	–	–	37	Nankivell	2	–	–	–	10
Elliot	6	–	–	–	30	Mafi	1	–	–	–	5
Norman-Bell	5	–	–	–	25	Tofa	1	–	–	–	5
McMenamin	4	–	–	–	20						
K. Demant	3	–	–	–	15	**Totals**	**41**	**28**	**3**	**0**	**270**
Moors	3	–	–	–	15						
Abraham	2	–	–	–	10	Opposition scored	29	21	6	1	208
Blackwell	2	–	–	–	10						

AUCKLAND 2019

	Waikato	Canterbury	Bay of Plenty	Wellington	Manawatu	Counties Manukau	Wellington	Canterbury	TOTALS
D.B. Moors	15	15	15	15	15	15	15	15	8
L.E.F. Tufuga	–	–	–	–	s	–	–	–	1
A-P.P. Elliot	14	14	14	14	14	14	14	14	8
I.G.M. Norman-Bell	11	11	11	s	11	11	11	11	8
L. Mafi	s	s	s	11	–	s	–	–	5
A.S. Roache	13	–	13	–	–	s	s	s	5
L.T. Sa'u	12	13	–	–	–	–	–	–	2
J. Naime-Purcell	s	6	–	12	13	13	12	12	7
D.L. Nankivell	–	12	s	s	s	–	–	–	4
D.R. Demant	–	10	12	13	12	12	13	13	7
P. Maliepo	10	s	10	10	10	10	10	10	8
G.A. Freeman	s	–	–	–	–	–	s	s	3
M.E. Cook	9	s	s	s	s	s	–	s	7
J. Rose-Reu	s	–	–	–	–	–	–	–	1
K.W. Demant	–	9	9	9	9	9	9	9	7
J. Fanene	8	–	–	s	–	s	s	s	5
C.J. McMenamin	s	–	8	8	8	8	8	8	7
L.P. Thompson	7	7	7	7	7	7	7	7	8
L.F. Itunu (capt)	6	8	6	6	6	6	6	6	8
T. Lafaele	–	s	–	–	–	–	–	–	1
R.E. Cox	–	–	–	–	s	–	–	–	1
M.C.T. Roos	5	4	s	s	s	s	s	s	8
A.J. Lenssen	s	–	–	–	–	–	–	–	1
C.B. Smith	–	5	5	5	5	5	5	5	7
E.S. Blackwell	4	–	4	4	4	4	4	4	7
A.C.J. Toia	–	s	s	–	–	–	–	–	2
A.P. Nelson	3	–	3	3	3	3	3	3	7
M.L.T. Tui'nukuafe	–	–	–	–	s	–	–	–	1
A.T. Itunu	–	–	–	–	–	s	s	s	3
L.C.S. Tofa	1	3	1	1	2	2	2	2	8
M. Hokianga	–	s	s	s	–	–	–	–	3
C.Z.F. Viliko	2	1	2	2	1	1	1	1	8
S.C.R. Abraham	s	s	s	s	s	s	s	s	8
V.L. Moimoi	–	2	–	–	–	–	–	–	1

AUCKLAND TEAM RECORD, 2019

Played 8   Won 6   Lost 2   Points for 270   Points against 208

Date	Opponent	Location	Score	Tries	Con	PG	DG	Referee
August 31	Waikato (P)	Hamilton	41–23	Elliot (2), Maliepo, Norman-Bell, McMenamin, Moors, Blackwell	Maliepo (3)			Lauren Jenner
September 8	Canterbury (P)	Auckland	12–45	Nankivell, Elliott	R. Demant			Lauren Jenner
September 14	Bay of Plenty (P)	Whakatane	28–19	Norman-Bell, K. Demant, Maliepo, Moors	Maliepo (4)			Monique Dalley
September 22	Wellington (P)	Auckland	38–10	K. Demant, Mafi, Blackwell, R. Demant, Norman-Bell, Abraham	Maliepo (4)			Michael Winter
September 29	Manawatu (P)	Palmerston North	50–26	R. Demant (2), McMenamin, Tofa, Norman-Bell, Elliot, Moors, Nankivell	Maliepo (5)			Larissa Collingwood
October 5	Counties Manukau (P)	Auckland	38–31	McMenamin (2), R. Demant, Naime-Purcell, Maliepo	Maliepo (5)	Maliepo		Tyler Miller
October 19	Wellington (semi-final)	Auckland	43–24	Elliot (2), R. Demant, Naime-Purcell, Abraham, K. Demant	Maliepo (5)	Maliepo		Rebecca Mahoney
October 26	Canterbury (final)	Christchurch	20–30	R. Demant (2), Norman-Bell	Maliepo	Maliepo		Rebecca Mahoney

BAY OF PLENTY VOLCANIX

2019 Status: Premiership
NPC participation: 1999–2005, 2014–
Coach: Rodney Gibbs
Assistant coaches: Tanerau Latimer, Matt Wallis
Home Grounds: Tauranga Domain; Rugby Park, Whakatane.

RECORDS

Most appearances	38	*Janina Khan, 2001–19*
Most points	96	*Sapphire Tapsell, 2016–19*
Most tries	18	*Tamaku Paul, 1999–2002*
Most points in a season	55	*Tamaku Paul, 1999*
Most tries in a season	11	*Tamaku Paul, 1999*
Most conversions in a season	12	*Puawai Hohepa, 2004*
Most penalty goals in a season	4	*Renee Wickliffe, 2018*
Most dropped goals in a season	1	*Puawai Hohepa, 2000*
Most points in a match	20	*Tamaku Paul v Counties Manukau, 1999*
Most tries in a match	4	*Tamaku Paul v Counties Manukau, 1999*
Most conversions in a match	5	*Exia Shelford v Counties Manukau, 2003*
Most penalty goals in a match	2	*Heidi Reader v Northland, 1999;*
		Puawai Hohepa v Waikato, 2000
		Kymbillie Raynes v North Harbour, 2016
		Renee Wickliffe v Auckland 2018
Highest team score	73	*v Taranaki, 2018*
Record victory (points ahead)	73	*73–0 v Taranaki, 2018*
Highest score conceded	101	*v Auckland, 2015*
Record defeat (points behind)	101	*0–101 v Auckland, 2015*

The Volcanix won only two games but Canterbury was the only team to comfortably defeat the Bay side. The team continues to improve and possesses a competitive forward pack and speed out wide. Christie Yule again captained the team and had good support in the loose from Kendra Reynolds and Natalie Delamere who had returned home after several years with Waikato. Black Fern Karli Faneva was partnered at lock by the tall Kelsie Wills who was in her first year of rugby. A talented sportswoman, Wills represented New Zealand at beach volleyball at the 2018 Commonwealth Games. Wills quickly adjusted to rugby and her potential was recognised late in the year with selection in the Black Ferns Development team for the Oceania Championship. Hooker Luka Connor was a powerful runner and well supported by props Janina Khan and 19-year-old Angel Mulu whose promising season was rewarded with selection in the Black Ferns Development team.

The outside backs showed speed with Waikato loan player Danielle Paenga at centre and Natalie Walford and Autumn-Rain Stephens-Daly on the wings. Fullback Sapphire Tapsell was the leading try-scorer and the best back. Two 19-year-olds impressed in their first season. Nadia Flavell showed speed and a good fend and scored two tries during her three appearances off the bench. Arorangi Tauranga became the first choice first five-eighth, a good reader of play, an eye for a gap and a sound defender. Goalkicking was the Volcanix weakness and no penalties were converted into points.

Injury prevented Black Ferns captain Lesley Elder from appearing for the team. The best is yet to be seen from the rapidly improving Volcanix.

Higher honours went to:

New Zealand:	K.A. Brazier, L. Connor, L-A.Te A. Elder, K. Faneva, R. Wickliffe
New Zealand Development:	L. Connor, A. Mulu, K. Reynolds, K. Wills
New Zealand Sevens:	M.G. Blyde, K.A. Brazier, R.M. Tui

BAY OF PLENTY REPRESENTATIVES 2019

	Club	Games for Union	Points for Union		Club	Games for Union	Points for Union
Amanda Aldridge	Rangiuru	15	0	Danielle Paenga	Melville[1]	6	0
Tahlia Brody	Mt Maunganui	1	0	Tania-Rose Raharuhi	Whakarewarewa	20	0
Luka Connor	Rangataua	31	65	Kendra Reynolds	Rangiuru	32	20
Natalie Delamere	Rangiuru	13	5	Olivia Richardson	Rangataua	6	0
Karli Faneva	Mt Maunganui	6	0	Autumn-Rain Stephens-Daly	Whakarewarewa	22	30
Tynealle Fitzgerald	Rangiuru	11	5	Sapphire Tapsell	Rangiuru	26	96
Nadia Flavell	Whakarewarewa	3	10	Arorangi Tauranga	Mt Maunganui	5	0
Lily Florence	Whakarewarewa	26	0	Layla Te Riini	Rangiuru	2	0
Baye Jacob	Rangiuru	24	10	Jade Tuilaepa	Rangataua	16	15
Janina Khan	Whakarewarewa	38	5	Natalie Walford	Whakarewarewa	6	10
Tracey Lemon	Rangataua	3	0	Braxton Walker	Rangiuru	10	0
Azalleyah Maaka	Rangataua	3	0	Renee Wickliffe	Rangataua	8	51
Mystery McLean Kora	Rangiuru	16	25	Kelsie Wills	Mt Maunganui	6	0
Anahera Mohi	Rangiuru	8	0	Christie Yule	Rangiuru	25	15
Angel Mulu	Rangiuru	11	10				

1 Waikato RU

INDIVIDUAL SCORING

	Tries	Con	PG	DG	Points		Tries	Con	PG	DG	Points
Tapsell	5	10	–	–	45	Jacob	1	–	–	–	5
Connor	3	–	–	–	15	Mulu	1	–	–	–	5
Reynolds	3	–	–	–	15	Wickliffe	1	–	–	–	5
Flavell	2	–	–	–	10	Yule	1	–	–	–	5
Stephens-Daly	2	–	–	–	10						
Walford	2	–	–	–	10	**Totals**	**23**	**10**	**0**	**0**	**135**
Delamere	1	–	–	–	5						
Fitzgerald	1	–	–	–	5	Opposition scored	26	15	4	0	172

BAY OF PLENTY 2019

	Counties Manukau	Wellington	Auckland	Waikato	Manawatu	Canterbury	TOTALS
S.N.K. Tapsell	15	15	15	15	15	15	6
N.J. Walford	14	14	14	14	14	14	6
O.D. Richardson	11	–	–	–	–	s	2
A.C. Mohi	s	–	–	–	–	s	2
A-R. Stephens-Daly	–	11	11	11	11	11	5
D.R. Paenga	13	13	13	13	13	13	6
T-R.N. Raharuhi	s	s	s	s	s	s	6
A.A.M. Maaka	12	s	–	12	–	–	3
R.W.M. Wickliffe	–	12	12	–	–	–	2
T.D. Brody	–	–	s	–	–	–	1
N.A.A. Flavell	–	–	s	s	s	–	3
L.M. Te Riini	–	–	–	–	12	12	2
M.A. McLean Kora	10	10	10	–	–	–	3
A.S.W.T. Tauranga	s	s	–	10	10	10	5
J.U. Tuilaepa	9	9	9	9	9	9	6
N. Delamere	8	s	8	8	8	8	6
K.L. Reynolds	7	6	7	7	6	7	6
T.A. Fitzgerald	s	7	s	s	7	s	6
C.E. Yule (capt)	6	8	6	6	s	6	6
K.P. Wills	5	5	5	5	5	5	6
K.J.K. Faneva	4	4	4	4	4	4	6
A.V.H. Aldridge	s	s	s	–	–	–	3
T.M. Lemon	–	–	–	s	s	–	2
B.L. Jacob	3	3	s	s	s	s	6
J.L. Khan	s	s	3	3	3	3	6
A.J. Mulu	1	1	1	1	1	1	6
B.M.M. Walker	–	–	–	s	s	s	3
L.H.J. Connor	2	2	2	2	2	2	6
L.J. Florence	s	s	s	s	s	s	6

BAY OF PLENTY TEAM RECORD, 2019

Played 6   Won 2   Lost 4   Points for 135   Points against 172

Date	Opponent	Location	Score	Tries	Con	PG	DG	Referee
August 31	Counties Manukau (P)	Tauranga	24–34	Tapsell (2), Reynolds, Walford	Tapsell (2)			James Munro
September 7	Wellington (P)	Porirua	29–32	Wickliffe, Jacob, Connor, Reynolds, Stephens-Daly	Tapsell (2)			Larissa Collingwood
September 14	Auckland (P)	Whakatane	19–28	Yule, Tapsell, Flavell	Tapsell (2)			Monique Dalley
September 21	Waikato (P)	Hamilton	26–21	Tapsell, Mulu, Walford, Stephens-Daly	Tapsell (3)			Brittany Andrew
October 5	Manawatu (P)	Tauranga	30–17	Connor (2), Delamere, Reynolds, Tapsell, Flavell				Lara West *Australia*
October 13	Canterbury (P, ST)	Christchurch	7–40	Fitzgerald	Tapsell			Lauren Jenner

CANTERBURY

2019 Status: Premiership
NPC participation: 1999–
Coach: Kieran Kite
Assistant coaches: James Jowsey, Melissa Ruscoe
Home Ground: Christchurch Stadium;
　　　　　　　Rugby Park (v Manawatu, and final)

RECORDS

Most appearances	97	*Stephanie Te Ohaere-Fox, 2004–19*
Most points	892	*Kendra Cocksedge, 2007–19*
Most tries	57	*Kendra Cocksedge, 2007–19*
Most points in a season	116	*Kendra Cocksedge, 2018*
Most tries in a season	10	*Kendra Cocksedge, 2018*
Most conversions in a season	27	*Kendra Cocksedge, 2018*
		Kendra Cocksedge, 2019
Most penalty goals in a season	11	*Kendra Cocksedge, 2014*
Most dropped goals in a season	1	*Charntay Poko, 2017;*
		Kendra Cocksedge, 2019
Most points in a match	30	*Kendra Cocksedge, v Taranaki, 2013*
		v North Harbour, 2016
Most tries in a match	4	*Stephanie Mortimer v Waikato, 2004;*
		Kendra Cocksedge, v Taranaki, 2013
		v Auckland, 2018
Most conversions in a match	8	*Kendra Cocksedge v Hawke's Bay, 2012*
Most penalty goals in a match	5	*Kendra Cocksedge v Auckland, 2009*
		v Waikato, 2016
Highest team score	92	*v Taranaki, 2013*
Record victory (points ahead)	80	*92–12 v Taranaki, 2013*
Highest score conceded	70	*v Auckland, 2015*
Record defeat (points behind)	62	*8–70 v Auckland, 2015*

Canterbury were undefeated during their march towards retaining the Premiership title and the Stewart Trophy, scoring 50 tries while conceding only 17. The experienced captain Stephanie Te Ohaere-Fox ended the season three short of one hundred appearances for the union. Chelsea Bremner had an outstanding year, being partnered at lock by Canadian international Cindy Nelles. In the loose Alana Bremner and 18-year-old Lucy Jenkins were joined by former Otago Black Fern Angie Sisifa who missed the 2018 season because of injury. Phillipa Love's partner at prop was the highly promising teenager Amy Rule who had represented Otago the previous season. Forne Burkin returned to Hawke's Bay. Rebecca Todd returned to Canterbury after a season with Otago.

　　Kendra Cocksedge was again a very busy halfback and added the drop kick to her many skills. Outside her the trio of Cassie Siataga, Lucy Anderson and Grace Brooker played every game, the two midfielders being strong runners in outstanding form. Fullback Olivia McGoverne continues to impress. Sam Curtis was on the left wing with Te Rauoriwa Gapper and promising Mayalin Lolohea appearing on the other flank. American Olivia Bernadel-Huey made appearances off the bench. Melanie Puckett shows promise whether at halfback or on the wing.

Higher honours went to:

New Zealand: G. Brooker, F.K. Burkin, K. Cocksedge, P. Love

New Zealand Development: A. Bremner, C. Bremner, G. Brooker, M. Lolohea, O. McGoverne, M. Puckett, A. Rule.

CANTERBURY REPRESENTATIVES 2019

	Club	Games for Union	Points for Union
Taylor Aldridge	Canterbury Univ	2	0
Lucy Anderson	Christchurch	45	100
Olivia Bernadel-Huey	Canterbury Univ	3	0
Alana Bremner	Lincoln Univ	40	35
Chelsea Bremner	Lincoln Univ	24	5
Grace Brooker	HSOB	23	70
Kendra Cocksedge	Canterbury Univ	82	892
Sam Curtis	Christchurch	26	90
Taylor Curtis	Christchurch	14	0
Becky Davidson	Lincoln Univ	18	70
Te Rauoriwa Gapper	Canterbury Univ	18	30
Catriona Greenslade	Lincoln Univ	17	5
Lucy Jenkins	Christchurch	24	10
Bunty Kuruwaka-Crowe	Christchurch	1	0
Mayalin Lolohea	Christchurch	4	15
Phillipa Love	Christchurch	35	50
Irene MacArthur	Suburbs	6	0
Olivia McGoverne	Canterbury Univ	35	94
Cindy Nelles	Canterbury Univ	8	10
Greer O'Rourke	Canterbury Univ	14	5
Nina Poletti	Christchurch	19	15
Georgia Ponsonby	Lincoln Univ	16	5
Melanie Puckett	Lincoln Univ	16	25
Amy Rule	Lincoln Univ	8	0
Cassie Siataga	Linwood	24	29
Angie Sisifa	Christchurch	7	5
Kalesi Taga	Suburbs	1	0
Stephanie Te Ohaere-Fox	Christchurch	97	100
Rebecca Todd	Christchurch	18	20
Estelle Uren	Christchurch	42	60

INDIVIDUAL SCORING

	Tries	Con	PG	DG	Points
Cocksedge	4	27	5	1	92
Anderson	8	–	–	–	40
A. Bremner	5	–	–	–	25
McGoverne	4	1	–	–	22
Brooker	4	–	–	–	20
S. Curtis	4	–	–	–	20
Siataga	1	5	–	–	15
Gapper	3	–	–	–	15
Lolohea	3	–	–	–	15
Te Ohaere-Fox	3	–	–	–	15
Davidson	2	–	–	–	10
Nelles	2	–	–	–	10
Greenslade	1	–	–	–	5
Love	1	–	–	–	5
Poletti	1	–	–	–	5
Ponsonby	1	–	–	–	5
Puckett	1	–	–	–	5
Sisifa	1	–	–	–	5
Uren	1	–	–	–	5
Totals	**50**	**33**	**5**	**1**	**334**
Opposition scored	17	9	2	0	109

CANTERBURY 2019

	Wellington	Auckland	Manawatu	Counties Manukau	Waikato	Bay of Plenty	Counties Manukau	Auckland	TOTALS
O.B. McGoverne	15	15	15	15	15	15	15	15	8
T.R.B. Curtis	14	–	–	s	s	–	–	–	3
B.L. Davidson	–	14	14	–	–	–	–	–	2
M.M. Lolohea	–	–	s	14	14	–	14	–	4
Te R. Gapper	11	11	–	–	–	–	s	11	4
O.N. Bernadel-Huey	s	s	–	–	–	s	–	–	3
S.G.B. Curtis	–	–	11	11	11	11	11	11	6
G.E. Brooker	13	13	13	13	13	13	13	13	8
L.E. Anderson	12	12	12	12	12	12	12	12	8
T.R. Aldridge	–	s	–	–	–	s	–	–	2
C.M.T. Siataga	10	10	10	10	10	10	10	10	8
K.M. Cocksedge	9	–	9	9	9	9	9	9	7
M.C. Puckett	s	9	s	s	s	14	–	–	6
A.A.F. Sisifa	8	8	s	8	8	–	s	8	7
G.R.A. Ponsonby	s	s	8	s	s	8	8	s	8
I.A.S. MacArthur	–	–	–	–	–	s	–	–	1
L.V.M. Jenkins	7	s	7	7	s	7	7	7	8
G.R. O'Rourke	s	7	s	s	7	s	s	–	7
A.J. Bremner	6	6	6	6	6	6	6	6	8
C.L. Nelles	5	5	s	5	5	5	5	5	8
E.D. Uren	s	s	5	s	s	–	–	–	5
C.J. Bremner	4	4	4	4	4	4	4	4	8
K.L.S. Taga	–	–	–	–	–	s	–	–	1
A.M. Rule	s	3	3	3	3	3	3	3	8
P.E.A. Love	1	1	1	1	1	–	1	1	7
C.J. Greenslade	s	s	s	–	s	1	–	–	5
N.J.N. Poletti	–	s	s	s	–	s	–	–	4
B.A. Kuruwaka-Crowe	–	–	–	–	s	–	–	–	1
R.A. Todd	2	–	–	–	–	s	–	–	2
S.A. Te Ohaere-Fox (capt)	3	2	2	2	2	2	2	2	8

CANTERBURY TEAM RECORD, 2019

Played 8   Won 8   Lost 0   Points for 334   Points against 109

Date	Opponent	Location	Score	Tries	Con	PG	DG	Referee
August 31	Wellington (P, ST)	Christchurch	57–19	Nelles, Cocksedge, Sisifa, Anderson, McGoverne, Gapper, Greenslade, Ponsonby	Cocksedge (6)			Maggie Cogger-Orr
September 8	Auckland (P)	Auckland	45–12	Gapper (2), Love, McGoverne, Davidson, Anderson, Poletti	Siataga (4), McGoverne			Lauren Jenner
September 21	Manawatu (P, ST)	Christchurch	54–7	Anderson (2), Davidson, Te Ohaere-Fox, Cocksedge, Brooker, Lolohea, Uren	Cocksedge (7)			Dan Moore
September 28	Counties Manukau (P)	Pukekohe	32–17	Anderson (2), Lolohea, S. Curtis, A. Bremner, Brooker	Cocksedge			Rebecca Mahoney
October 6	Waikato (P)	Hamilton	45–5	S. Curtis, Lolohea, Cocksedge, Siataga, A. Bremner, Puckett	Cocksedge (4), Siataga			Rebecca Mahoney
October 13	Bay of Plenty (P, ST)	Christchurch	40–7	Te Ohaere-Fox (2), Cocksedge, A. Bremner, Anderson, S. Curtis	Cocksedge (5)			Lauren Jenner
October 20	Counties Manukau (semi-final)	Christchurch	31–22	A. Bremner (2), Brooker, McGoverne	Cocksedge	Cocksedge (3)		Brittany Andrew
October 26	Auckland (final)	Christchurch	30–20	McGoverne, Brooker, Anderson	Cocksedge (3)	Cocksedge (2)	Cocksedge	Rebecca Mahoney

COUNTIES MANUKAU HEAT

2019 Status: Premiership
NPC participation: 1999–2005, 2013–
Coach: Chad Shepherd
Assistant coach: Davida Suasua
Home grounds: Navigation Homes Stadium

RECORDS

Most appearances	51	*Arihiana Marino-Tauhinu, 2013–19*
Most points	250	*Hazel Tubic, 2005–19*
Most tries	26	*Te Kura Ngata-Aerengamate, 2013–18*
Most points in a season	78	*Hazel Tubic, 2017*
Most tries in a season	10	*Renee Wickliffe, 2015*
Most conversions in a season	28	*Hazel Tubic 2017*
Most penalty goals in a season	8	*Hazel Tubic, 2013*
Most dropped goals in a season	0	
Most points in a match	27	*Hazel Tubic v Taranaki, 2013*
Most tries in a match	4	*Renee Wickliffe v Otago, 2015*
		Portia Woodman v Wellington 2016
Most conversions in a match	7	*Hazel Tubic v Taranaki, 2013*
Most penalty goals in a match	4	*Hazel Tubic v Auckland, 2013*
Highest team score	84	*v North Harbour, 2017*
Record victory (points ahead)	77	*84–7 v North Harbour, 2017*
Highest score conceded	65	*v Auckland B, 2005*
Record defeat (points behind)	65	*0–65 v Auckland B, 2005*

With wins over Bay of Plenty, Manawatu and Waikato, the Heat secured a semi-final spot but was beaten by Canterbury. Long-serving hooker Te Kura Ngata-Aerengamate had moved to Northland but there were gains with the return of Hazel Tubic, Badinlee Munro-Smith and Shontelle Woodman. Munro-Smith represented Taranaki in 2018. Another arrival was former Auckland lock Rebecca Burch.

Halfback Arihiana Marino-Tauhinu captained the team for the sixth year and combined well with first five-eighth Hazel Tubic who set a new points record for the team. Woodman and Shyanne Thompson were the midfield pairing, Lanulangi Veainu and Waikohika Flesher on the wings and 19-year-old Emily Kitson at fullback.

Justine Lavea led the forwards with support from fellow Black Ferns props Leilani Perese and Aotearoa Matau. Hooker Grace Gago and Lavea were the only forwards to start every game. The large forward pack was again troublesome for most opponents.

Higher honours went to:
New Zealand: A. Marino-Tauhinu, T.R. Ngata-Aerengamate, L. Perese
New Zealand Development: A. Marino-Tauhinu, L. Molia, L. Perese, H. Tubic, L. Veainu

COUNTIES MANUKAU REPRESENTATIVES 2019

	Club	Games for Union	Points for Union
Glory Aiono	Manurewa	12	5
Jacqui Aiono	Manurewa	6	0
Juvina Auva'a	Ardmore Marist	2	0
Rebecca Burch	Ardmore Marist	4	0
Makayla Eli	Manurewa	3	0
Waikohika Flesher	Manurewa	14	30
Grace Gago	Manurewa	19	15
Emily Kitson	Ardmore Marist	18	27
Justine Lavea	Ardmore Marist	32	35
Larissa Lima E Silva	Ardmore Marist	19	0
Anastasia Mamea	Manurewa	12	20
Arihiana Marino-Tauhinu	Manurewa	51	225
Temira Mataroa	Manurewa	6	5
Aotearoa Matau	Ardmore Marist	42	105

	Club	Games for Union	Points for Union
Victoria Meki	Ardmore Marist	29	15
Ilisapeta 'Lisa' Molia	Ardmore Marist	7	5
Badinlee Munro-Smith	Manurewa	18	5
Yuki Ono	Ardmore Marist	13	15
Leilani Perese	Manurewa	27	35
Lauryn Steed	Ardmore Marist	18	15
Lavinia Tauhalaliku	Manurewa	7	15
Harono Te Iringa	Manurewa	18	10
Shyanne Thompson	Ardmore Marist	10	5
Ocean Tierney	Drury	3	0
Hazel Tubic	Manurewa	34	250
Leititia Vaka	Wesley College	5	5
Lanulangi Veainu	Ardmore Marist	21	70
Shontelle Woodman	Manurewa	31	20

INDIVIDUAL SCORING

	Tries	Con	PG	DG	Points
Tubic	2	12	2	–	40
Kitson	4	1	–	–	22
Flesher	4	–	–	–	20
Veainu	4	–	–	–	20
Gago	3	–	–	–	15
Matau	3	–	–	–	15
Perese	3	–	–	–	15
Marino-Tauhinu	1	3	1	–	14
Lavea	2	–	–	–	10
Tauhalaliku	2	–	–	–	10

	Tries	Con	PG	DG	Points
G. Aiono	1	–	–	–	5
Mataroa	1	–	–	–	5
Molia	1	–	–	–	5
Steed	1	–	–	–	5
Thompson	1	–	–	–	5
Vaka	1	–	–	–	5
Totals	**34**	**16**	**3**	**0**	**211**
Opposition scored	30	17	4	0	196

COUNTIES MANUKAU 2019	Bay of Plenty	Manawatu	Wellington	Canterbury	Auckland	Waikato	Canterbury	TOTALS
E.F. Kitson	15	15	15	15	15	15	15	7
L.L. Veainu	14	14	–	14	14	14	14	6
L. Tauhalaliku	–	s	14	–	–	–	–	2
W. Flesher	11	11	11	11	11	11	11	7
O. Tierney	–	–	s	s	–	s	–	3
S. Thompson	13	13	13	13	13	13	13	7
S.E. Woodman	12	12	12	12	–	s	12	6
H.S. Tubic	10	10	10	–	10	12	10	6
B.C.R. Munro-Smith	–	s	–	10	12	–	–	3
M. Eli	–	–	–	s	s	s	–	3
A.A.H. Marino-Tauhinu (capt)	9	9	9	–	9	10	9	6
L. Vaka	s	s	s	9	–	s	–	5
Y. Ono	–	–	–	s	–	9	s	3
J. Lavea	8	8	8	8	8	7	7	7
A. Mamea	s	s	s	–	s	8	–	5
L. Lima	7	7	7	7	7	–	–	5
G. Aiono	6	s	s	6	6	6	–	6
I.M.P. Molia	s	6	6	5	5	4	6	7
R.M. Burch	5	5	5	–	–	–	5	4
H. Te Irirangi	–	–	–	–	–	5	8	2
T. Mataroa	4	4	4	4	4	–	4	6
A.K. Matau	3	–	3	s	3	s	3	6
L. Steed	s	s	–	–	–	3	–	3
L.R.R. Perese	–	3	1	3	1	1	1	6
J.F. Aiono	1	1	s	1	s	–	s	6
G.L.F. Gago	2	2	2	2	2	2	2	7
V. Meki	s	–	s	–	–	–	–	2
J. Auva'a	–	s	–	–	–	s	–	2

Lavea was captain in Marino-Tauhina's absence

COUNTIES MANUKAU TEAM RECORD, 2019

Played 7 **Won 3** **Lost 4** **Points for 211** **Points against 196**

Date	Opponent	Location	Score	Tries	Con	PG	DG	Referee
August 31	Bay of Plenty (P)	Tauranga	34–24	Veainu (2), Matau, Gago, Flesher	Marino-Tauhinu (3)	Marino-Tauhinu		James Munro
September 6	Manawatu (P)	Pukekohe	43–14	Kitson, Marino-Tauhinu, Perese, Flesher, Lavea, Steed, Tubic	Tubic (4)			Maggie Cogger-Orr
September 15	Wellington (P)	Wellington	36–38	Tauhalaliku (2), Kitson, Flesher, Matau, Vaka	Tubic (3)			Jono Bredin
September 28	Canterbury (P)	Pukekohe	17–32	Perese, Gago, Kitson	Kitson			Rebecca Mahoney
October 5	Auckland (P)	Auckland	31–38	Lavea, Mataroa, Kitson, Molia, G. Aiono	Tubic (3)			Tyler Miller
October 12	Waikato (P)	Pukekohe	28–19	Flesher, Perese, Thompson, Tubic, Veainu		Tubic		Brittany Andrew
October 20	Canterbury (semi-final)	Christchurch	22–31	Veainu, Gago, Matau	Tubic (2)	Tubic		Brittany Andrew

HAWKE'S BAY TUI

2019 Status: Championship
NPC participation: 1999–2012, 2014–2015, 2017–
Coach: Stephen Woods
Assistant coach: Shaun Bell
Home grounds: Tremain Field, Park Island, Napier;
McLean Park (v Taranaki, Northland sf)

RECORDS

Most appearances	75	*Chanel Atkin 2001–19*
Most points	192	*Nerina Hawkins, 1999–2004*
Most tries	21	*Deidre Hakopa, 1999–2009*
Most points in a season	61	*Nerina Hawkins, 2003*
Most tries in a season	9	*Deidre Hakopa, 2003*
Most conversions in a season	16	*Nerina Hawkins, 2003;*
		Sylvia Bockman, 2019
Most penalty goals in a season	8	*Nerina Hawkins, 2003*
Most dropped goals in a season	0	
Most points in a match	25	*Deidre Hakopa v Southland, 2003*
Most tries in a match	5	*Deidre Hakopa v Southland, 2003*
Most conversions in a match	7	*Nerina Hawkins v Poverty Bay, 2000*
Most penalty goals in a match	4	*Nerina Hawkins v Auckland, 2003*
Highest team score	100	*v Southland, 2003*
Record victory (points ahead)	95	*100–5 v Southland, 2003*
Highest score conceded	93	*v Auckland, 2014*
Record defeat (points behind)	93	*0–93 v Auckland, 2014*

There was very little between the two leading Championship division teams, Otago having the better defensive record and twice defeated the Tuis to gain promotion for 2020. The Tuis were decisively stronger than the other four teams in the division and look to be the front-runners in the 2020 competition. It was a balanced squad of youth and experience, from eight Under 18 players to three players receiving their Hawke's Bay blazers — Chanel Atkin (nee Huddleston) 70 games, with both Gemma Woods and Te Maari MacGregor reaching their 50-game milestone. Hooker Forne Burkin returned to the Bay from Canterbury, this giving Tuis a second current Black Fern alongside Krysten Cottrell who was selected for the Development team to Fiji but forced to withdraw through injury.

The Tuis went from strength to strength over the 2019 season with the forwards dominating in most games. In midfield Chanel Atkin led by example, playing alongside a very experienced backline. Once again Emma Jensen controlled play from halfback. Holly MacDonald had represented Wellington in 2017 and former Otago player Michaela Baker returned after a stint playing in Spain. Cortez Te Pou, aged 18, made her debut at fullback against Northland and scored four tries, she has potential at both fullback and wing. Nicolette Adamson is new to the game this year and has speed to burn.

Hanna Brough (co-captain) was a consistent performer and the only player to play every minute of every game for Tui this season. She was named as best forward. Flanker Niamh Jefferson is a young talent with lots of experience and game knowledge. Kathleen Brown was another top performer in what was a very strong and dynamic forward pack. Liana Mikaele-Tu'u, aged 17, is a name to look out for in the future. Moomooga Palu is a crowd pleaser and for good reason: she has power, strength and size.

Higher honours went to:

New Zealand: K. Cottrell
New Zealand Development: F. Burkin

HAWKE'S BAY REPRESENTATIVES 2019

	Club	Games for Union	Points for Union
Nicolette Adamson	Taradale	2	5
Chanel Atkin (nee Huddleston)	Napier Technical	75	60
Davina Atkin	Taradale	13	0
Michaela Baker	Taradale	13	20
Sylvia Bockman	Taradale	25	86
Hanna Brough	Hastings R&S	12	25
Kathleen Brown	Napier Technical	14	35
Forne Burkin	Taradale	19	20
Krysten Cottrell	Taradale	30	96
Iukika Faavae	Hastings R&S	4	5
Teani Feleu	Clive	1	0
Kara Huata	Clive	7	0
Te Aroha Hunt	Napier Technical	21	5
Rebekah Hurae	Clive	20	0
Tori Iosefo	Napier Technical	11	60
Niamh Jefferson	Clive	19	25

	Club	Games for Union	Points for Union
Emma Jensen	Hastings R&S	14	21
Holly MacDonald	Clive	4	5
Te Maari MacGregor	Clive	51	94
Amber-Jane McKenzie	Taradale	3	0
Whitley Mareikura	Taradale	23	15
Teagan Meyer	Taradale	6	0
Līana Mikaele-Tu'u	Hastings R&S	6	10
Whitney Olsen	Napier Technical	5	0
Moomooga Palu	Hastings R&S	7	20
Felicity Powdrell	Taradale	24	20
Jennifer Simati	Napier Technical	11	0
Jessie Taueki	Clive	26	0
Shaylee Tipiwai	Clive	39	60
Cortez Te Pou	Clive	7	35
Gemma Woods	Taradale	54	55

INDIVIDUAL SCORING

	Tries	Con	PG	DG	Points
Bockman	–	16	1	–	35
Te Pou	7	–	–	–	35
Cottrell	1	12	1	–	32
Brown	6	–	–	–	30
Iosefo	6	–	–	–	30
Baker	4	–	–	–	20
Palu	4	–	–	–	20
Brough	3	–	–	–	15
Burkin	3	–	–	–	15
Jefferson	3	–	–	–	15
Tipiwai	3	–	–	–	15

	Tries	Con	PG	DG	Points
Woods	3	–	–	–	15
Adamson	2	–	–	–	10
C. Atkin	2	–	–	–	10
Mikaele-Tu'u	2	–	–	–	10
Jensen	1	1	–	–	7
Faavae	1	–	–	–	5
MacDonald	1	–	–	–	5
Totals	**52**	**29**	**2**	**0**	**324**
Opposition scored	20	13	3	0	135

HAWKE'S BAY 2019

	Northland	North Harbour	Taranaki	Tasman	Otago	Northland	Otago	TOTALS
K.J. Cottrell	–	15	10	15	15	15	10	6
C.P. Te Pou	15	14	s	s	s	14	14	7
F.R. Powdrell	14	s	–	11	s	s	s	6
S.T. Tipiwai	s	–	15	14	14	s	15	6
T.P.L.A. Iosefo	11	s	11	–	11	11	11	6
T.I. Feleu	–	11	–	–	–	–	–	1
N.A. Adamson	–	–	s	s	–	–	–	2
M.S.D. Baker	13	13	14	–	–	13	13	5
Te M.T. MacGregor	s	–	13	13	s	s	12	6
H.B.A. MacDonald	–	s	–	s	13	–	s	4
C.A. Atkin	12	12	12	12	12	12	–	6
S.C. Bockman	10	10	s	10	10	10	s	7
E.M. Jensen	9	9	9	9	9	9	9	7
G.L. Woods (co-capt)	8	8	8	–	–	8	8	5
N.W. Jefferson	7	7	7	7	7	7	7	7
K.M.T. Brown	6	6	–	8	–	3	6	5
T.J. Meyer	s	–	s	s	6	s	s	6
D.S. Atkin	–	s	–	–	–	–	–	1
A-J. McKenzie	–	–	–	s	s	–	s	3
R.K. Hurae	5	s	–	–	–	–	–	2
Te A. Hunt	s	5	4	4	5	4	–	6
L.E.T. Mikaele-Tu'u	–	s	5	5	8	5	5	6
H.L. Brough (co-capt)	4	4	6	6	4	6	4	7
W.A.M. Olsen	s	–	s	–	s	–	–	3
K.T.I. Huata	3	–	s	–	–	–	–	2
J.L. Simati	–	3	3	3	3	s	3	6
W.E.D.A. Mareikura	1	1	1	1	1	1	1	7
M.A. Palu	s	s	s	s	s	s	s	7
I. Faavae	–	–	–	s	s	s	s	4
F.K. Burkin	2	2	2	2	2	2	2	7
J.M. Taueki	s	–	–	–	–	–	–	1

HAWKE'S BAY TEAM RECORD, 2019

Played 7   Won 5   Lost 2   Points for 324   Points against 135

Date	Opponent	Location	Score	Tries	Con	PG	DG	Referee
September 7	Northland (C)	Napier	64–31	Te Pou (4), Brown (2), Baker (2), Iosefo, Brough	Bockman (6), Jensen			Dan Waenga
September 14	North Harbour (C)	North Shore	39–10	Palu (2), Baker, Brown, C. Atkin, Iosefo	Cottrell (2), Bockman	Bockman		Larissa Collingwood
September 20	Taranaki (C)	Napier	74–0	Woods (2), Brough (2), Palu (2), Jefferson, Tipiwai, Iosefo, C. Atkin, Te Pou, Adamson	Bockman (4), Cottrell (3)			Marcus Playle
September 27	Tasman (C)	Nelson	55–5	Brown (2), Tipiwai (2), Mikaele-Tu'u, Faavae, Macdonald, Adamson, Te Pou	Cottrell (3), Bockman (2)	Cottrell (2)		Maggie Cogger-Orr
October 5	Otago (C)	Napier	26–34	Burkin (2), Iosefo, Jefferson	Bockman (3)			George Haswell
October 19	Northland (semi-final)	Napier	46–31	Jensen, Iosefo, Baker, Cottrell, Burkin, Te Pou, Brown, Mikaele-Tu'u	Cottrell (3)			Lauren Jenner
October 27	Otago (final)	Dunedin	20–24	Jefferson, Woods, Iosefo	Cottrell	Cottrell		Brittany Andrew

MANAWATU CYCLONES

2019 Status: Premiership
NPC participation: 1999–
Coach: Fusi Feaunati
Assistant coach: Caleb Agnew-Jones
Home ground: Central Energy Trust Arena

MANAWATU RUGBY

RECORDS

Most appearances	81	*Selica Winiata, 2002–19*
Most points	463	*Selica Winiata, 2002–19*
Most tries	68	*Selica Winiata, 2002–19*
Most points in a season	110	*Selica Winiata, 2012*
Most tries in a season	14	*Selica Winiata, 2012*
Most conversions in a season	17	*Selica Winiata, 2012*
Most penalty goals in a season	8	*Anika Tiplady, 2004*
Most dropped goals in a season	2	*Rebecca Hull, 2002*
Most points in a match	38	*Selica Winiata v Waikato, 2012*
Most tries in a match	4	*Catherine Doyle v Poverty Bay-East Coast, 2002;*
		Selica Winiata v Waikato, 2012;
		Selica Winiata v Wellington, 2012
Most conversions in a match	9	*Elizabeth Goulden v Hawke's Bay, 2017*
Most penalty goals in a match	4	*Anika Tiplady v Bay of Plenty, 2004*
Highest team score	86	*v Hawke's Bay, 2017*
Record victory (points ahead)	78	*86–8 v Hawke's Bay, 2017*
Highest score conceded	70	*v Auckland, 2011*
Record defeat (points behind)	65	*5–70 v Auckland, 2011*

The Cyclones were competitive in most games, often holding a halftime lead, before being worn down by bigger forward packs during the second halves. Against Wellington the team had a healthy 26–7 halftime lead only to fall away during the last 35 minutes to lose 42–26. The Cyclones finished the season winless and drop to the Championship grade in 2020. Former Black Fern Sosoli Talawadua, from Wanganui, added experience at hooker and there were good efforts from Kahli Tipene and Samantha Tipene but, generally, the forward pack struggled against larger opposition and this hindered a talented backline.

Midfielder Janna Vaughan returned wearing a face mask to protect a broken cheekbone suffered while playing in Japan. Her experience and that of Crystal Mayes and Selica Winiata provided valuable guidance in a youthful set of backs. Winiata remains an exceptional attacking player but her opportunities were limited at first five-eighth compared with the freedom at fullback she had been accustomed to. Late in the year Winiata became a referee at sevens tournaments. Lauren Balsillie continues to develop as a strong attacker. Injuries and commitments to college teams disrupted the season for several players. A major loss was halfback Kristina Sue who left to join Spark and TVNZ as a panellist covering the Rugby World Cup. Japan international Yuki Sue came into the squad for the later games. Teenagers Rangimarie Sturmey (wing) and Kaipo Olsen-Baker (No 8) are the most promising of the younger brigade.

Manawatu has only two clubs of strength which is insufficient for a competitive Premier team and needs to attract teams from Levin, Wanganui and Wairarapa to create a more meaningful club competition. However, the Cyclones, providing they don't again suffer injuries, should regain confidence in 2020 where Hawke's Bay could be the major opponent.

Higher honours went to:

New Zealand: S. Winiata
New Zealand Development: L. Balsillie
New Zealand Sevens: R.R. Ferris, S.L. Hirini

MANAWATU REPRESENTATIVES 2019

	Club	Games for Union	Points for Union		Club	Games for Union	Points for Union
Lauren Balsillie	Feilding OB Oroua	28	72	Mahalia Polson	Kia Toa	23	0
Lucy Brown	Feilding OB Oroua	12	5	Layla Sae	University	4	0
Nicola Chase	Kia Toa	5	5	Shanna Solomon (nee Porima)	Kia Toa	24	20
Laura Claridge	Feilding OB Oroua	4	0	Kahurangi Sturmey	University	5	5
Carys Dallinger	Kia Toa	9	5	Rangimarie Sturmey	University	6	10
Tiana Davison	Kia Toa	1	0	Kristina Sue	Feilding OB Oroua	58	35
Jessica Fagan-Pease	Kia Toa	15	5	Yuki Sue	Mie Pearls (Japan)	2	0
Sequita Hemmingway	Kia Toa	16	0	Kalyn Takitimu-Cook	Feilding OB Oroua	5	24
Ashleigh Knight	Feilding OB Oroua	11	0	Sosoli Talawadua	University	6	0
Nicola Kuiti	Kia Toa	44	10	Ngano Tavake	University	1	0
Maggie Leota	Kia Toa	9	0	Kahli Tipene	Kia Toa	38	0
Marilyn Live	Kia Toa	20	5	Samantha Tipene	Kia Toa	34	25
Crystal Mayes	Kia Toa	26	55	Janna Vaughan	Kia Toa	39	95
Jayme Nuku	Kia Toa	29	0	Corrineke Windle	Feilding OB Oroua	17	8
Samantha Olsen	Feilding OB Oroua	9	0	Selica Winiata	Kia Toa	81	463
Kaipo Olsen-Baker	Feilding OB Oroua	4	0				

INDIVIDUAL SCORING

	Tries	Con	PG	DG	Points
Winiata	3	11	–	–	37
Balsillie	3	–	–	–	15
Mayes	3	–	–	–	15
Vaughan	3	–	–	–	15
R. Sturmey	2	–	–	–	10
Dallinger	1	–	–	–	5
K. Sturmey	1	–	–	–	5
Totals	**16**	**11**	**0**	**0**	**102**
Opposition scored	37	23	0	1	234

MANAWATU 2019

	Counties Manukau	Waikato	Canterbury	Auckland	Bay of Plenty	Wellington	TOTALS
C.A.M. Mayes	15	15	–	15	13	13	5
C.N. Dallinger	13	13	15	11	15	15	6
K. Takitimu-Cook	14	11	–	–	–	–	2
R.T. Sturmey	s	14	14	14	14	14	6
M.N. Leota	s	s	11	s	–	–	4
L.I. Claridge	–	–	s	s	s	s	4
J.M. Vaughan	12	12	13	13	–	11	5
S.J.T. Solomon	s	–	–	–	–	s	2
L.N.Y. Balsillie	11	s	12	12	12	12	6
S.C. Winiata (capt)	10	10	10	10	10	10	6
L. Brown	9	s	9	9	9	9	6
K.J. Sue	–	9	–	–	–	–	1
C.M. Windle	–	–	s	s	–	–	2
Y. Sue	–	–	–	–	s	s	2
T.L. Davison	8	–	–	–	–	–	1
K.T. Olsen-Baker	–	–	s	8	8	8	4
N. Chase	–	–	–	–	–	s	1
S.J. Tipene	7	7	7	7	7	7	6
J.R.Te O. Nuku	6	8	8	2	6	6	6
S. Olsen	s	s	s	6	–	–	4
L. Sae	–	6	6	s	–	s	4
N. Tavake	–	–	–	–	–	s	1
A.J. Knight	5	5	s	s	4	4	6
M.R. Polson	4	s	s	5	5	–	5
K.J. Sturmey	s	–	4	s	11	5	5
J.K. Fagan-Pease	–	4	5	4	–	–	3
S.M. Hemingway	3	3	s	s	1	s	6
K.M. Tipene	s	s	3	3	3	3	6
N.B. Kuiti	1	s	–	–	–	–	2
M. Live	s	1	1	–	s	1	5
S.J. Talawadua	2	2	2	1	2	2	6

MANAWATU TEAM RECORD, 2019

Played 6 Won 0 Lost 6 Points for 102 Points against 234

Date	Opponent	Location	Score	Tries	Con	PG	DG	Referee
September 6	Counties Manukau (P)	Pukekohe	14–43	Balsillie, Mayes	Winiata (2)			Maggie Cogger-Orr
September 14	Waikato (P)	Palmerston North	12–15	Dallinger, R. Sturmey	Winiata			Rebecca Mahoney
September 21	Canterbury (P, ST)	Christchurch	7–54	Balsillie	Winiata			Dan Moore
September 29	Auckland (P)	Palmerston North	26–50	Winiata (2), Vaughan (2)	Winiata (3)			Larissa Collingwood
October 5	Bay of Plenty (P)	Tauranga	17–30	Mayes, Balsillie, K. Sturmey	Winiata			Lara West *Australia*
October 12	Wellington (P)	Palmerston North	26–42	Vaughan, R. Sturmey, Mayes, Winiata	Winiata (3)			Maggie Cogger-Orr

NORTH HARBOUR HIBISCUS

2019 Status: Championship
NPC participation: 1999–2005, 2016–
Coach: Duncan McGrory
Assistant coach: Willie Walker
Home grounds: QBE Stadium, Albany;
  East Coast Bays RFC, North Shore

RECORDS

Most appearances	23	*Joanne Cherrington, 1999–2004*
		Nicole Brown, 2000–19;
		Olivia Ward-Duin, 2016–19
Most points	94	*Sophie Fisher, 2017–19*
Most tries	9	*Pia Tapsell, 2016–19*
Most points in a season	52	*Sophie Fisher, 2018*
Most tries in a season	5	*Caitlyn Cox, 2017*
		Simone Small, 2019
Most conversions in a season	14	*Sophie Fisher, 2018*
Most penalty goals in a season	7	*Rachel Howard, 2003*
Most dropped goals in a season	0	
Most points in a match	24	*Sophie Fisher v Taranaki, 2018*
Most tries in a match	3	*Simone Small v Taranaki, 2019*
Most conversions in a match	7	*Sophie Fisher v Taranaki, 2018*
Most penalty goals in a match	3	*Rachel Howard v Auckland B, 2003*
Highest team score	59	*v Taranaki, 2018*
Record victory (points ahead)	59	*59–0 v Taranaki, 2018*
Highest score conceded	116	*v Auckland, 1999*
Record defeat (points behind)	116	*0–116 v Auckland, 1999*

North Harbour Hibiscus enjoyed wins over Tasman and Taranaki but suffered a heavy 90-point loss to Otago. The team's outstanding player was midfielder Caroline Sio who had played 26 games as a loose forward for Wellington 2013–16. Fijian-born Tearren Nanjan, aged 18, appeared in four games in 2018 and became the regular No 8 in 2019. She is a highly promising player. Simone Small (wing) came off the bench in three games before gaining her first start against Taranaki, celebrating with three tries followed by a further two against Tasman. Small also successfully took over the goalkicking duties in Sophie Fisher's absence.

Prop Olivia Ward-Duin gained Black Ferns honours and returned to captain Hibiscus. The team's other Black Fern, Pia Tapsell, was in grand form for her country but, unfortunately, could make only two appearances for Hibiscus. Ashleigh Nathan had previously represented Bay of Plenty and Tasman. Nicole Brown, aged 40, was a regular reserve prop who had last represented 16 years earlier in 2003.

Neither East Coast Bays nor Glenfield clubs had the numbers to field senior teams in the Auckland competition and chose to combine to enter a team and became commonly known as Bayfield.

Higher honours went to:

New Zealand: P. Tapsell, O. Ward-Duin
New Zealand Development: P. Tapsell

NORTH HARBOUR REPRESENTATIVES 2019

	Club	Games for Union	Points for Union
Natasha Abel	ECB-Glenfield	5	0
Renee Adams	ECB-Glenfield	5	5
Hailey Beale	ECB-Glenfield	6	0
Anita Berry	ECB-Glenfield	6	0
Madison Brooke	ECB-Glenfield	1	0
Nicole Brown	Kumeu	23	5
Caitlyn Cox	ECB-Glenfield	17	35
Natasha Dallow	ECB-Glenfield	11	0
Raquel Garcia Godin	ECB-Glenfield	4	0
Sophie Fisher	ECB-Glenfield	18	94
Tenaija Fletcher	Mahurangi	6	0
Danjela Haigh	ECB-Glenfield	5	0
Katelyn Hilton	ECB-Glenfield	12	5
Tearren Nanjan	ECB-Glenfield	10	0

	Club	Games for Union	Points for Union
Ashleigh Nathan	ECB-Glenfield	4	0
Christine Quedley	Kumeu	12	0
Amy Robertshaw	ECB-Glenfield	16	15
Mikayla Robinson	ECB-Glenfield	4	5
Caroline Sio	ECB-Glenfield	6	0
Simone Small	ECB-Glenfield	5	37
Pia Tapsell	ECB-Glenfield	22	45
Jayjay Taylor	ECB-Glenfield	7	5
Inga Timani	ECB-Glenfield	15	5
Justine Vizirgianakis	ECB-Glenfield	21	5
Olivia Ward-Duin	ECB-Glenfield	23	15
Rona-Latisha Wharawhara	ECB-Glenfield	11	10
Kate Williams	ECB-Glenfield	14	5

INDIVIDUAL SCORING

	Tries	Con	PG	DG	Points
Small	5	6	–	–	37
Fisher	–	6	2	–	18
Tapsell	2	–	–	–	10
Ward-Duin	2	–	–	–	10
Adams	1	–	–	–	5
Brown	1	–	–	–	5
Cox	1	–	–	–	5

	Tries	Con	PG	DG	Points
Robertshaw	1	–	–	–	5
Robinson	1	–	–	–	5
Timani	1	–	–	–	5
Totals	**15**	**12**	**2**	**0**	**105**
Opposition scored	31	21	5	0	212

NORTH HARBOUR 2019

	Tasman	Hawke's Bay	Northland	Otago	Taranaki	Tasman	TOTALS
J. Vizirgianakis	15	11	–	s	s	s	5
R. Garcia Godin	10	15	15	15	–	–	4
C.R. Cox	14	14	14	14	14	14	6
R.A. Adams	11	–	11	11	15	15	5
S.L. Small	s	–	s	s	11	11	5
M.M.A. Robinson	13	13	13	13	–	–	4
R.C. Sio	12	12	12	12	13	12	6
C.M. Quedley	–	s	–	–	12	13	3
R–L.H. Wharawhara	–	10	10	10	10	10	5
N.P. Dallow	s	s	–	–	s	s	4
H.D. Beale	9	9	9	9	9	9	6
K.A. Hilton	s	s	s	s	s	–	5
T.A. Nanjan	8	8	8	8	8	6	6
P.H. Tapsell	–	–	–	–	s	8	2
K.R. Williams	7	7	–	7	–	–	3
T.V. Fletcher	6	6	7	s	7	7	6
N.L. Abel	s	s	s	–	s	s	5
A.R. Berry	5	4	6	6	6	4	6
S.R. Fisher	4	5	5	5	–	–	4
A.R. Nathan	s	–	–	s	4	s	4
M.F.A. Brooke	–	s	–	–	–	–	1
J. Taylor	–	–	4	4	5	5	4
A.S. Timani	3	1	1	1	1	1	6
N. Brown	s	s	s	s	s	s	6
O.Y. Ward-Duin (capt)	1	3	3	3	3	3	6
A.G. Robertshaw	2	2	2	2	2	2	6
D. Haigh	s	s	s	s	s	–	5

NORTH HARBOUR TEAM RECORD, 2019

				Played 6	Won 2	Lost 4	Points for 105		Points against 212
Date	Opponent	Location	Score	Tries		Con	PG	DG	Referee
September 7	Tasman (C)	Blenheim	22–10	Robertshaw, Adams, Brown		Fisher (2)	Fisher		Monique Dalley
September 14	Hawke's Bay (C)	North Shore	10–39	Ward-Duin		Fisher	Fisher		Larissa Collingwood
September 22	Northland (C)	Whangarei	21–27	Timani, Robinson, Cox		Fisher (3)			Lauren Jenner
September 29	Otago (C)	Dunedin	0–90						Brittany Andrew
October 4	Taranaki (C)	Albany	33–21	Small (3), Tapsell (2)		Small (4)			Maggie Cogger-Orr
October 12	Tasman (quarter-final)	Albany	19–25	Small (2), Ward-Duin		Small (2)			Monique Dalley

NORTHLAND KAURI

2019 Status: Championship
NPC participation: 1999–2005, 2019–
Coach: Cheryl Smith
Assistant coaches: Susan Dawson, Scott Collins
Home grounds: Semenoff Stadium (v North Harbour, Tasman);
         Trigg Sports Arena.

RECORDS

Most appearances	26	*Paula Yates, 1999–2005*
Most points	58	*Krystal Murray, 2019*
Most tries	9	*Stacey Neho, 2004–05*
Most points in a season	58	*Krystal Murray, 2019*
Most tries in a season	8	*Savannah Bodman, 2019;*
		Te Kura Ngata-Aerengamate, 2019
Most conversions in a season	14	*Krystal Murray, 2019*
Most penalty goals in a season	5	*Krystal Murray, 2019*
Most dropped goals in a season	0	
Most points in a match	17	*Krystal Murray v North Harbour, 2019*
Most tries in a match	3	*Savannah Bodman v Hawke's Bay, 2019;*
		Te Kura Ngata-Aerengamate v Taranaki, 2019
Most conversions in a match	4	*Krystal Murray v Hawke's Bay, 2019*
Most penalty goals in a match	2	*by four players*
Highest team score	49	*v North Harbour, 2004*
Record victory (points ahead)	31	*36–5 v North Harbour, 1999*
Highest score conceded	65	*v Auckland, 2000*
Record defeat (points behind)	58	*7–65 v Auckland, 2000*

After an absence of 13 years Northland returned to the national championship, the new team attracting players who had appeared for other provinces, some returning to their home region. The most valuable addition was Black Ferns hooker Te Kura Ngata-Aerengamate who captained the Kauri. The services of Black Fern Victoria Subritzky-Nafatali were also obtained. Another former Black Fern was Kamila Wihongi whose last appearance in first-class rugby was in 2008 when with Otago. Amanda Nepia had played for Northland during 2000–04. Other players with previous first-class experience include Stacey Tupe (ex-North Harbour), Timara Leaf, Kararaina Wira-Kohu, Krystal Murray and Harono Te Iringa (all from Counties Manukau).

The Farah Palmer Cup campaign commenced with losses to the two teams later to meet in the final, Hawke's Bay and Otago. Kauri improved with each game, winning the next four games before meeting Hawke's Bay again in the semi-final. Again, Kauri scored 31 points but this time reduced the Bay's tally from 64 to 46 points, a clear indication of the progress made during the season. Ngata-Aerengamate scored eight tries, the number being matched by a 17-year-old on the wing, Savannah Bodman.

Northland Kauri should meet with more success during 2020.

NORTHLAND REPRESENTATIVES 2019

	Club	Games for Union	Points for Union
Mia Anderson	Kaikohe	7	5
Jurney Blair	Te Rarawa	5	0
Savannah Bodman	Kamo Hawks	7	40
Jaimee Brown	Kamo Hawks	5	0
Leilani Erwin	Kaikohe	4	0
Eva-Star Fulton	Kaikohe	7	0
Bronwyn Hames	Kamo Hawks	5	0
Taylah Hodson-Tomokino	Horahora	1	0
Jherhi-kah Hoet	Papatoetoe[1]	1	0
Naomi Judd	City	3	0
Helen Kapa	Kaikohe	7	0
Justice Karena	Te Rarawa	6	0
Timara Leaf	Manurewa[2]	1	0
Tui McGeorge	Horahora	6	0

	Club	Games for Union	Points for Union
Cheryl Murray	Te Rarawa	7	0
Krystal Murray	Te Rarawa	7	58
Tyler Nankivell	Kaikohe	7	5
Amanda Nepia	City	12	5
Te Kura Ngata-Aerengamate	Te Rarawa	7	40
Alisha Proctor	Kaikohe	4	0
Kahurangi Shelford	Kaikohe	7	0
Victoria Subritzky-Nafatali	Ardmore Marist[2]	5	20
Harono Te Iringa	Manurewa[2]	1	5
Stacey Tupe	Kamo Hawks	7	5
Patricia Vaka	Kaikohe	5	0
Manaia Webb	Kaikohe	7	0
Kamila Wihongi	Kaikohe	7	0
Kararaina Wira-Kohu	Manurewa[2]	6	7

1 Auckland RU   2 Counties Manukau RU

INDIVIDUAL SCORING

	Tries	Con	PG	DG	Points
K. Murray	3	14	5	–	58
Bodman	8	–	–	–	40
Ngata-Aerengamate	8	–	–	–	40
Subritzky-Nafatali	4	–	–	–	20
Wira-Kohu	1	1	–	–	7
Anderson	1	–	–	–	5
Nankivell	1	–	–	–	5
Te Iringa	1	–	–	–	5
Tupe	1	–	–	–	5
Totals	**28**	**15**	**5**	**0**	**185**
Opposition scored	36	23	0	0	226

NORTHLAND 2019	Hawke's Bay	Otago	North Harbour	Taranaki	Tasman	Taranaki	Hawke's Bay	TOTALS
A.M. Nepia	15	15	13	s	s	–	s	6
C.M. Murray	14	s	14	13	13	13	13	7
S.J. Bodman	11	11	11	15	14	14	14	7
T.R. Leaf	s	–	–	–	–	–	–	1
J.L.W. Brown	–	s	s	11	s	s	–	5
L.C. Erwin	–	–	s	–	11	11	11	4
A.A.H. Proctor	13	s	15	14	–	–	–	4
S.A. Tupe	12	13	12	12	15	15	15	7
K.I.T. Wira-Kohu	s	12	–	s	12	12	12	6
V.S. Subritzky-Nafatali	10	10	–	–	10	10	10	5
T.B. Nankivell	s	s	10	10	s	s	s	7
M.H. Webb	9	14	9	9	9	9	9	6
J. Karena	–	9	s	4	s	s	s	6
J-K.H. Hoet	–	–	–	s	–	–	–	1
K.R. Murray	8	8	8	8	8	8	8	7
J.M. Blair	7	7	7	7	7	–	–	5
T.M. McGeorge	–	4	s	s	s	7	7	6
M.T. Anderson	6	s	6	6	6	6	6	7
H. Te Iringa	5	–	–	–	–	–	–	1
E-F. Fulton	s	5	5	5	5	5	5	7
T.C. Hodson-Tomokino	4	–	–	–	–	–	–	1
P.A. Vaka	–	6	4	–	4	4	4	5
K.T. Wihongi	3	1	3	3	3	1	1	7
K.W. Shelford	s	3	s	s	s	s	s	7
H.J. Kapa	1	s	1	s	1	3	3	7
B.M. Hames	s	s	s	1	s	–	–	5
N. Judd	–	–	–	s	–	s	s	3
Te K.R. Ngata-Aerengamate (capt)	2	2	2	2	2	2	2	7

NORTHLAND TEAM RECORD, 2019

Played 7 Won 4 Lost 3 Points for 185 Points against 226

Date	Opponent	Location	Score	Tries	Con	PG	DG	Referee
September 7	Hawke's Bay (C)	Napier	31–64	Bodman (3), Te Iringa, K. Murray	K. Murray (3)			Dan Waenga
September 14	Otago (C)	Whangarei	7–40	Bodman	Wira-Kohu			Maggie Cogger-Orr
September 22	North Harbour (C)	Whangarei	27–21	Nankivell, Ngata-Aerengamate, K. Murray	K. Murray (3)	K. Murray (2)		Lauren Jenner
September 29	Taranaki (C)	Inglewood	22–12	Ngata-Aerengamate, Tupe, Wira-Kohu, Anderson	K. Murray			Monique Dalley
October 5	Tasman (C)	Whangarei	35–29	Bodman (2), Ngata-Aerengamate (2), K. Murray, Subritzky-Nafatali	K. Murray	K. Murray		Lauren Jenner
October 13	Taranaki (quarter-final)	Whangarei	32–14	Ngata-Aerengamate (3), Subritzky-Nafatali (2)	K. Murray (2)	K. Murray		Larissa Collingwood
October 19	Hawke's Bay (semi-final)	Napier	31–46	Bodman (2), Subritzky-Nafatali, Ngata-Aerengamate	K. Murray (4)	K. Murray		Monique Dalley

OTAGO SPIRIT

2019 Status: Championship
NPC participation: 1999–
Coach: Scott Manson
Assistant coaches: Aimee Sutorius, Jamie Angus
Home grounds: Forsyth Barr Stadium;
        Whitestone Contracting Stadium, Oamaru

RECORDS

Most appearances	60	*Greer Muir, 2011–19*
Most points	221	*Claire Richardson, 2002–12*
Most tries	27	*Greer Muir, 2011–19*
Most points in a season	107	*Rosie Kelly, 2019*
Most tries in a season	11	*Annaleah Rush, 1999*
Most conversions in a season	32	*Rosie Kelly, 2019*
Most penalty goals in a season	12	*Hannah Myers, 2000*
Most dropped goals in a season	0	
Most points in a match	45	*Kelly Brazier v Hawke's Bay, 2012*
Most tries in a match	8	*Annaleah Rush v Mid/South Canterbury, 1999*
Most conversions in a match	10	*Kelly Brazier v Hawke's Bay, 2012*
		Rosie Kelly v North Harbour, 2019
Most penalty goals in a match	5	*Anika Tiplady v Auckland, 2013*
Highest team score	90	*v North Harbour, 2019*
Record victory (points ahead)	90	*90–0 v North Harbour, 2019*
Highest score conceded	86	*v Auckland, 2011*
Record defeat (points behind)	81	*5–86 v Auckland, 2011*

Otago Spirit had no difficulty during the march through the round-robin and posted five large scores including a record 90 points against North Harbour. Only Hawke's Bay threatened and the Spirit had to dig deep to overcome the Bay's strong challenge in the final. Otago were deserving winners, scoring 58 tries while conceding only 13, the defence was outstanding and promotion to the Premiership division was just reward for the hard work this province has done to raise the standard of rugby. One home game was taken to Oamaru, the town having contributed players to the Spirit squad in recent years.

Outstanding performances were produced by first five-eighth Rosie Kelly, aged 19, who was the only points centurion in the Farah Palmer Cup. She scored eight tries, is a reliable goal-kicker and has the versatility to also play at halfback. The teenager was in her third first-class season. It was a youthful backline with Rosie Buchanan-Brown at halfback and Amy du Plessis, a highly promising centre, pairing very well with new Black Fern Kilisitina Moata'ane who was the team's top try-scorer. The experienced Sheree Hume was again at fullback. Trisha Hopcroft and Kiana Wereta were on the wings. Others to appear in the backline include Hinemoa Watene (ex-Auckland), Teilah Ferguson (ex-Hawke's Bay) and the experienced USA Eagles international Hannah Stolba.

Eilis Doyle was the standout forward, a hard-working prop supporting regular frontrowers Isla Pringle and captain Tegan Hollows. Jess Kendall, Kate Smith and Julia Gorinski were experienced locks. The loose trio was unchanged through the campaign. Greer Muir, aged 26, made the successful transition from midfield to No 8 and extended her record of appearances for the Spirit to 60 games. Her sister Larissa, father Neville and grandfather Ernie have also represented Otago. Morgan Henderson, from the North Otago club Waitaki, continues to improve. A highly promising newcomer is 18-year-old flanker Bree Thomas, fresh out of Southland Girls' High School. She played every minute of every game and is a sister of Southland Stags player Flynn Thomas.

Higher honours went to:

New Zealand: K. Moata'ane

New Zealand Development: E. Doyle, R. Kelly, K. Moata'ane

OTAGO REPRESENTATIVES 2019

	Club	Games for Union	Points for Union
Meg Breen	University	3	10
Rosie Buchanan-Brown	Alhambra Union	12	15
Paige Church	Alhambra Union	13	0
Cheyenne Cunningham	Waitaki	22	50
Eilis Doyle	Alhambra Union	32	5
Amy du Plessis	Alhambra Union	10	35
Teilah Ferguson	Alhambra Union	7	20
Julia Gorinski	University	36	15
Morgan Henderson	Waitaki	23	20
Claudia Hobbs	University	6	0
Tegan Hollows	University	34	30
Patricia Hopcroft	University	13	15
Sheree Hume	Pirates	46	96
Rosie Kelly	University	15	150

	Club	Games for Union	Points for Union
Jessica Kendall	University	28	5
Gemma Millar	Pirates	10	0
Kilisitina Moata'ane	Pirates	36	110
Greer Muir	Pirates	60	135
Isla Pringle	University	20	10
Kate Smith	University	28	5
Hannah Stolba	Waitaki	10	5
Jordyn Tereu	Taieri	1	0
Bree Thomas	University	7	10
Rebecca Wairau	University	1	0
Morgan Walker	Pirates	13	0
Hinemoa Watene	University	6	10
Kiana Wereta	Alhambra Union	22	45

INDIVIDUAL SCORING

	Tries	Con	PG	DG	Points
Kelly	8	32	1	–	107
Moata'ane	9	–	–	–	45
Hume	5	5	–	–	35
du Plessis	5	–	–	–	25
Wereta	5	–	–	–	25
Ferguson	4	–	–	–	20
Hollows	3	–	–	–	15
Hopcroft	3	–	–	–	15
Breen	2	–	–	–	10
Buchanan-Brown	2	–	–	–	10
Cunningham	2	–	–	–	10

	Tries	Con	PG	DG	Points
Muir	2	–	–	–	10
Thomas	2	–	–	–	10
Watene	2	–	–	–	10
Doyle	1	–	–	–	5
Gorinski	1	–	–	–	5
Henderson	1	–	–	–	5
Stolba	1	–	–	–	5
Totals	**58**	**37**	**1**	**0**	**367**
Opposition scored	13	6	2	0	83

OTAGO 2019

	Taranaki	Northland	Tasman	North Harbour	Hawke's Bay	Tasman	Hawke's Bay	TOTALS
S.J. Hume	15	15	–	15	–	15	15	5
H.H. Watene	s	s	–	s	15	s	s	6
C.B. Cunningham	14	14	15	s	s	s	s	7
P.A. Hopcroft	–	s	14	14	14	14	14	6
K.M.P.Y. Wereta	11	11	11	–	11	11	11	6
M.E. Breen	s	–	s	s	–	–	–	3
A. du Plessis	13	13	13	13	13	13	–	6
K. Moata'ane	12	12	12	12	12	–	12	6
T.N.W. Ferguson	s	s	s	11	s	12	13	7
H.L. Stolba	10	10	s	s	–	s	–	5
R.C. Kelly	9	s	10	10	10	10	10	7
R.M. Buchanan-Brown	–	9	9	9	9	9	9	6
J.T.G. Tereu	–	–	s	–	–	–	–	1
G.A. Muir	8	8	8	8	8	8	8	7
M.A. Henderson	7	7	7	7	7	7	7	7
M.J. Walker	s	–	–	–	–	–	–	1
B-A.J. Thomas	6	6	6	6	6	6	6	7
J.B. Kendall	5	s	s	s	4	s	s	7
R.L. Wairau	s	–	–	–	–	–	–	1
J.F. Gorinski	–	5	5	5	5	5	5	6
K.E. Smith	4	4	4	4	s	4	4	7
E.O. Doyle	3	3	3	3	3	3	3	7
P.L.L. Church	–	–	–	–	s	s	–	2
I.R. Pringle	1	1	1	1	1	1	1	7
C.M. Hobbs	s	s	s	s	s	s	–	6
T.J. Hollows (capt)	2	2	2	2	2	2	2	7
G.A. Millar	s	s	s	s	–	s	–	5

OTAGO TEAM RECORD, 2019

Played 7 Won 7 Lost 0 Points for 367 Points against 83

Date	Opponent	Location	Score	Tries	Con	PG	DG	Referee
September 8	Taranaki (C)	Dunedin	57–5	Moata'ane (2), Wereta (2), Cunningham, Hume, Hollows, Muir, du Plessis	Kelly (6)			Stuart Curran
September 14	Northland (C)	Whangarei	40–7	du Plessis (2), Gorinski, Moata'ane, Hume, Stolba	Hume (5)			Maggie Cogger-Orr
September 21	Tasman (C)	Oamaru	58–15	Hopcroft (2), Wereta (2), Thomas, Buchanan-Brown, Doyle, Kelly, Breen, Moata'ane	Kelly (4)			Larissa Collingwood
September 29	North Harbour (C)	Dunedin	90–0	Moata'ane (4), Hollows (2), Kelly (2), Hume, Hopcroft, du Plessis, Ferguson, Breen, Thomas	Kelly (10)			Brittany Andrew
October 5	Hawke's Bay (C)	Napier	34–26	Kelly (2), Ferguson (2), Watene, du Plessis	Kelly (2)			George Haswell
October 19	Tasman (semi-final)	Dunedin	64–10	Kelly (2), Buchanan-Brown, Muir, Wereta, Henderson, Hume, Cunningham, Ferguson, Watene	Kelly (7)			Maggie Cogger-Orr
October 27	Hawke's Bay (final)	Dunedin	24–20	Kelly, Moata'ane, Hume	Kelly (3)	Kelly		Rebecca Mahoney

TARANAKI WHIO

2019 Status: Championship
NPC participation: 2000–01, 2013, 2018–
Coach: Matt Stone
Assistant coaches: Braydon Peterson, Daniel Brooks
Home grounds: Yarrow Stadium, New Plymouth;
　　　　　　TET Stadium, Inglewood

RECORDS

Most appearances	17	*Leah Barnard, 2013–19;*
		Victoria McCullough, 2013–19
Most points	29	*Chelsea Fowler, 2019*
Most tries	4	*Michaela Blyde, 2013*
Most points in a season	29	*Chelsea Fowler, 2019*
Most tries in a season	4	*Michaela Blyde, 2013*
Most conversions in a season	7	*Chelsea Fowler, 2019*
Most penalty goals in a season	2	*Kate Broadmore, 2013*
Most dropped goals in a season	0	
Most points in a match	11	*Chelsea Fowler v North Harbour, 2019*
Most tries in a match	2	*Michaela Blyde v Manawatu, 2013*
		Iritana Hohaia v Tasman, 2019
Most conversions in a match	3	*Chelsea Fowler v North Harbour, 2019*
Most penalty goals in a match	1	*Kate Broadmore v Otago, 2013;*
		v Wellington, 2013
Highest team score	22	*v Tasman, 2019*
Record victory (points ahead)	–	
Highest score conceded	118	*v Wellington, 2018*
Record defeat (points behind)	118	*0–118 v Wellington, 2018*

After a run of 25 games Taranaki Whio have yet to register a win in the national championship but the 2019 results reflect a big improvement in performance on the hammerings suffered the previous year. Twelve tries were scored and 40 conceded compared with only four tries in 2018 and 71 conceded. In 2018 the lowest points differential was 45 when losing to Hawke's Bay 55–10. On three occasions in 2019 the points differential was 14 or less, the closest game being the 22–12 loss to Northland. Clearly, the team is making progress and it is just a matter of time before an opponent is upset and celebrations commence.

Of the 2018 squad only nine returned for the 2019 campaign. Flanker Jalana Smith and first five-eighth Brooke Sim were the co-captains. The locks Victoria McCullough and Sharee Brown were prominent in the forwards. Halfback Iritana Hohaia, aged 19, was the team's outstanding player and Elle Johns the best of the outside backs. On the wing Kaya-Rose Kaui, aged 18, shows promise.

Higher honours went to:
New Zealand Sevens:　　　　Gayle Broughton

TARANAKI REPRESENTATIVES 2019

	Club	Games for Union	Points for Union		Club	Games for Union	Points for Union
Lisa Appert	Coastal	11	0	Donia King	Southern	6	0
Leah Barnard	Coastal	17	0	Jessica Lampe	Coastal	13	0
Sharee Brown	Southern	11	0	Victoria McCullough	Coastal	17	0
Mikaylah Callaghan	Clifton	6	0	Lavenia Nauga-Grey	Clifton	3	5
Anna Cole	Southern	4	0	Brooke Neilson	Inglewood United	6	0
Chelsea Fowler	Clifton	6	29	Catherine Parkinson	Stratford-Eltham	10	0
Bethany Gibbs	Coastal	7	0	Brooke Sim	Coastal	14	5
Natale-Ann Haupapa	Clifton	12	0	Jalana Smith	Coastal	12	15
Natasha Hintz	Coastal	10	0	Tiaan Taylor	Clifton	2	0
Iritana Hohaia	Coastal	6	15	Catriona Tulloch	Southern	5	0
Elle Johns	Waikato Univ[1]	12	0	Alesha Williams	Coastal	6	5
Kaya-Rose Kahui	Southern	5	5	Sarah Winter	Southern	3	0
Miriam Karalus	Coastal	6	0	Petra Zwart	Okaiawa	4	0

1 Waikato RU

INDIVIDUAL SCORING

	Tries	Con	PG	DG	Points
Fowler	3	7	–	–	29
Hohaia	3	–	–	–	15
Smith	2	–	–	–	10
Kahui	1	–	–	–	5
Nauga-Grey	1	–	–	–	5
Sim	1	–	–	–	5
Williams	1	–	–	–	5
Totals	**12**	**7**	**0**	**0**	**74**
Opposition scored	40	24	2	0	254

TARANAKI 2019

	Otago	Tasman	Hawke's Bay	Northland	North Harbour	Northland	TOTALS
A.M. Williams	15	15	s	s	11	s	**6**
C. Parkinson	–	–	s	15	15	15	**4**
B. Neilson	14	14	15	11	s	s	**6**
C.A. Tulloch	–	s	14	14	14	14	**5**
K-R. Kahui	11	11	11	–	s	11	**5**
A.M. Cole	s	–	s	s	s	–	**4**
S.J. Winter	–	s	–	s	–	s	**3**
E. Johns	13	13	13	13	13	13	**6**
C.M. Fowler	12	12	12	12	12	12	**6**
T.K. Taylor	s	–	–	–	s	–	**2**
B.A. Sim (co-capt)	10	10	10	10	10	10	**6**
I. Hohaia	9	9	9	9	9	9	**6**
N-A. Haupapa	8	8	s	8	8	8	**6**
M.A. Karalus	7	7	7	7	7	7	**6**
J.R. Smith (co-capt)	6	6	8	6	6	6	**6**
V.L. McCullough	5	5	6	5	s	5	**6**
J.A. Lampe	s	s	5	s	5	4	**6**
S.E. Brown	4	4	4	4	4	–	**5**
L. Barnard	3	3	3	3	3	–	**5**
M.T. Callaghan	s	s	s	s	s	3	**6**
B.C. Gibbs	1	1	s	1	–	s	**5**
L. Nauga-Grey	s	s	1	–	–	–	**3**
D. King	s	s	s	s	1	1	**6**
N.A. Hintz	2	2	–	–	–	s	**3**
L.C. Appert	s	s	–	s	s	s	**5**
P.D. Zwart	–	–	2	2	2	2	**4**

TARANAKI TEAM RECORD, 2019

					Played 6	Won 0	Lost 6	Points for 74			Points against 254
Date	Opponent	Location	Score	Tries			Con	PG	DG		Referee
September 8	Otago (C)	Dunedin	5–57	Smith							Stuart Curran
September 14	Tasman (C)	New Plymouth	22–36	Hohaia (2), Nauga-Grey			Fowler				Lauren Jenner
September 20	Hawke's Bay (C)	Napier	0–74								Marcus Playle
September 28	Northland (C)	Inglewood	12–22	Fowler, Smith			Fowler				Monique Dalley
October 4	North Harbour (C)	Albany	21–33	Sim, Kahui, Fowler			Fowler (3)				Maggie Cogger-Orr
October 13	Northland (quarter-final)	Whangarei	14–32	Hohaia, Fowler			Fowler (2)				Larissa Collingwood

TASMAN MAKO

2019 Status: Championship
NPC participation: 2017–
Coach: Chris Binns
Assistant coach: Bevan Thompson
Home Grounds: Trafalgar Park, Nelson; Lansdowne Park, Blenheim

RECORDS

Most appearances	19	*Jessica Foster-Lawrence, 2017–19;*
		Stephanie Mitchell, 2017–19;
		Tamara Silcock, 2017–19
Most points	71	*Hayley Hutana, 2018–19*
Most tries	7	*Wairakau Greig, 2017–19*
Most points in a season	45	*Hayley Hutana, 2019*
Most tries in a season	6	*Rebecca Kersten, 2019*
Most conversions in a season	9	*Hayley Hutana, 2018*
		Hayley Hutana, 2019
Most penalty goals in a season	4	*Hayley Hutana, 2019*
Most dropped goals in a season	0	
Most points in a match	15	*Amelia Hammett v Taranaki, 2018*
Most tries in a match	3	*Amelia Hammett v Taranaki, 2018*
Most conversions in a match	5	*Hayley Hutana v Taranaki, 2018*
Most penalty goals in a match	2	*Hayley Hutana v North Harbour, 2019*
Highest team score	65	*v Taranaki, 2018*
Record victory (points ahead)	53	*65–12 v Taranaki, 2018*
Highest score conceded	88	*v Wellington, 2018*
Record defeat (points behind)	85	*3–88 v Wellington, 2018*

Tasman won two games and are gradually gaining experience in the Farah Palmer Cup competition. Again the team was led by Jessica Foster-Lawrence and again she was the outstanding forward. Leah Miles, aged 17, is a highly promising flanker. Wing Rebecca Kersten top-scored with six tries and was the best of the backs. The experienced Wairakau Greig and Jessica Drummond were a very sound midfield pairing.

Higher honours went to:
New Zealand Sevens: R.I.R. Pouri-Lane

TASMAN REPRESENTATIVES 2019

	Club	Games for Union	Points for Union
Pippa Andrews	Moutere	11	0
Hannah Beech	Motueka HS	9	10
Anna Bradley	Waimea OB	13	5
Courtney Clarke	Motueka HS	13	0
Alesha Dempster	Waimea OB	3	0
Gabi Dixson	Rangataua[1]	7	0
Jessica Drummond	Motueka HS	10	20
Jordan Foster	Moutere	5	0
Jessica Foster-Lawrence	Waimea OB	19	7
Hannah Gillespie	Moutere	12	0
Wairakau Greig	Moutere	10	35
Amelia Hammett	Wanderers	6	15
Paris Hart	Rangataua[1]	7	0
Jess Harvie	Waimea College	1	0

	Club	Games for Union	Points for Union
Hayley Hutana	Moutere	12	71
Rebecca Kersten	Rangataua[1]	7	30
Bethan Manners	Waimea OB	6	5
Leah Miles	Waimea OB	10	0
Stephani Mitchell	Waimea OB	19	15
Louise Nalder	Waimea OB	11	0
Meika Newman	Waimea OB	1	0
Jamie Paenga	Waimea OB	11	0
Demi Salton	Waimea OB	12	5
Anya Schultz	Waimea OB	5	0
Tamara Silcock	Wanderers	19	10
Jaunita Thomson	Waimea OB	12	0
Sydnee Wilkins	Massey University[2]	10	15

1 Bay of Plenty RU   2 Manawatu RU

INDIVIDUAL SCORING

	Tries	Con	PG	DG	Points
Hutana	3	9	4	–	45
Kersten	6	–	–	–	30
Greig	3	–	–	–	15
Wilkins	3	–	–	–	15
Drummond	2	–	–	–	10
Manners	1	–	–	–	5
Mitchell	1	–	–	–	5
Silcock	1	–	–	–	5
Totals	**20**	**9**	**4**	**0**	**130**
Opposition scored	45	22	2	0	275

TASMAN 2019	North Harbour	Taranaki	Otago	Hawke's Bay	Northland	North Harbour	Otago	TOTALS
S.L. Wilkins	15	s	s	15	15	11	11	**7**
B. Manners	–	15	15	s	s	15	15	**6**
R. Kersten	14	14	14	s	14	14	14	**7**
A. Dempster	11	–	11	11	–	–	–	**3**
A. Schultz	s	–	–	14	11	s	s	**5**
A. Hammett	–	11	–	–	–	–	–	**1**
W. Greig	13	13	13	13	13	13	–	**6**
J.A. Drummond	12	12	12	–	12	12	12	**6**
D. Salton	s	s	s	12	s	s	13	**7**
H.S. Hutana	10	10	10	10	10	10	10	**7**
P.S. Andrews	9	s	9	9	9	9	–	**6**
J. Paenga	s	9	s	s	s	–	9	**6**
J. E-M. Foster-Lawrence (capt)	8	8	8	8	8	8	8	**7**
L. Miles	7	7	7	7	7	7	7	**7**
T. Silcock	6	6	6	6	6	6	6	**7**
H. Beech	s	–	–	s	–	s	s	**4**
C.E. Clarke	5	5	5	5	5	5	5	**7**
J. Thomson	4	4	4	s	s	s	s	**7**
J. Foster	s	s	s	–	s	–	s	**5**
H.E. Gillespie	–	s	s	4	4	4	4	**6**
J. Harvie	–	–	–	–	–	–	s	**1**
G. Dixson	3	s	s	s	s	3	3	**7**
A. Bradley	1	3	3	3	3	1	1	**7**
P. Hart	s	1	1	1	1	s	s	**7**
L. Nalder	–	s	s	s	s	s	s	**7**
S.L. Mitchell	2	2	2	2	2	2	2	**7**
M. Newman	s	–	–	–	–	–	–	**1**

TASMAN TEAM RECORD, 2019

					Played 7	Won 2	Lost 5	Points for 130		Points against 275
Date	Opponent	Location	Score	Tries		Con	PG	DG		Referee
September 7	North Harbour (C)	Blenheim	10–22	Greig, Drummond						Monique Dalley
September 14	Taranaki (C)	New Plymouth	36–22	Kersten (2), Mitchell, Silcock, Greig		Hutana (4)	Hutana			Lauren Jenner
September 21	Otago (C)	Oamaru	15–58	Drummond, Hutana		Hutana	Hutana			Larissa Collingwood
September 27	Hawke's Bay (C)	Nelson	5–55	Wilkins						Maggie Cogger-Orr
October 5	Northland (C)	Whangarei	29–35	Hutana (2), Kersten (2), Greig		Hutana (2)				Lauren Jenner
October 12	North Harbour (quarter-final)	Albany	25–19	Manners, Kersten, Wilkins		Hutana (2)	Hutana (2)			Monique Dalley
October 19	Otago (semi-final)	Dunedin	10–64	Wilkins, Kersten						Maggie Cogger-Orr

WAIKATO

W.R.U

2019 Status: Premiership
NPC participation: 1999–2005, 2012–
Coach: Wayne Maxwell
Assistant coaches: Warren Hodges, Joe Nayacakalou
Home Grounds: FMG Stadium Waikato

RECORDS

Most appearances	44	*Victoria Edmonds, 2012–18*
Most points	324	*Chelsea Alley, 2012–19*
Most tries	19	*Honey Hireme, 2001–16*
Most points in a season	81	*Chelsea Alley, 2014*
Most tries in a season	11	*Stacey Waaka, 2014*
Most conversions in a season	21	*Chelsea Alley, 2014, 2018*
Most penalty goals in a season	12	*Chelsea Alley, 2013*
Most dropped goals in a season	1	*Emma Jensen, 2000*
		Chelsea Alley, 2019
Most points in a match	18	*C. Alley v Bay of Plenty, 2014*
Most tries in a match	3	*Jordon Webber v Manawatu, 2012;*
		Honey Hireme v Manawatu, 2014;
		Stacey Waaka v Canterbury, 2014;
		v Bay of Plenty, 2015
Most conversions in a match	5	*C. Alley v Manawatu, 2014;*
		v Bay of Plenty, 2014
		v Auckland, 2018
Most penalty goals in a match	4	*Emma Jensen v Northland, 2000*
		Tenika Willison v North Harbour, 2016
Highest team score	48	*v Bay of Plenty, 2014*
Record victory (points ahead)	48	*48–0 v Bay of Plenty, 2014*
Highest score conceded	78	*v Auckland, 2002*
Record defeat (points behind)	78	*0–78 v Auckland, 2002*

It was a disappointing season for Waikato with only one win, against Manawatu, and that was achieved in the 75th minute when the scores were locked 12–12 and Chelsea Alley kicked a fine drop goal. Alley captained the team and was again the backline general and a talented footballer.

For various reasons only three players started in every game, Calista Ruruku (fullback), Rina Paraone (centre) and Renee Holmes (first five-eighth and halfback). Holmes previously represented Hawke's Bay and Bay of Plenty.

Higher honours went to:
New Zealand: C. Alley, Carla Hohepa, T. Natua, K. Simon
New Zealand Development: K. Simon
New Zealand Sevens: S.J. Baker, H.R. Harding, S.T. Kaka, C.R.A. Robins-Reti, M.G.T. Tairakena, T.L.R. Te Tamaki, S.J.A.K. Waaka, T.R. Willison

WAIKATO REPRESENTATIVES 2019

	Club	Games for Union	Points for Union
Chelsea Alley	University	36	324
Raquel Anderson-Pitman	University	26	14
Tyra Begbie	Putaruru	2	0
Jade Coates	Hamilton OB	3	0
Hope Fraser	Hamilton OB	1	0
Ashlee Gaby-Sutherland	Melville	20	15
Tazmin Gaby-Sutherland	Melville	4	0
Francea Hansen	University	17	10
Ryleigh Hayes	Melville	20	32
Emma-Lee Heta	Kihikihi	21	10
Renee Holmes	Hamilton OB	6	9
Chyna Hohepa	Kihikihi	23	15
Mereana Hyde	University	3	0
Tanya Kalounivale	Hamilton OB	15	5
Leomie Kloppers	Hamilton OB	11	0

	Club	Games for Union	Points for Union
Stephanie Lualua	Hamilton OB	2	0
Sophie Millar	University	4	0
Lena Mitchell	Hamilton OB	13	5
Toka Natua	University	28	15
Lonita Ngalu-Lavemei	Melville	10	35
Josina Ngare	University	4	0
Kiriana Nolan	Melville	2	5
Rina Paraone	Kihikihi	20	15
Donna Reynolds (nee Fermanis)	Hamilton OB	17	15
Calista Ruruku	University	19	42
Kennedy Simon	Hamilton OB	17	10
Kennedy Tahau	Hamilton OB	4	0
Awhina Tangen-Wainohu	Hamilton OB	10	10
Esther Tilo-Faiaoga	Melville	9	0
Azusa Yama	Hamilton OB	11	5

INDIVIDUAL SCORING

	Tries	Con	PG	DG	Points
Alley	1	5	5	1	33
Ngalu-Lavemei	4	–	–	–	20
Ruruku	2	1	–	–	12
Simon	2	–	–	–	10
Holmes	1	2	–	–	9
Mitchell	1	–	–	–	5
Natua	1	–	–	–	5
Nolan	1	–	–	–	5

	Tries	Con	PG	DG	Points
Reynolds	1	–	–	–	5
Tangen-Wainohu	1	–	–	–	5
Yama	1	–	–	–	5
Totals	**16**	**8**	**5**	**1**	**114**
Opposition scored	33	20	2	0	211

WAIKATO 2019

	Auckland	Manawatu	Bay of Plenty	Wellington	Canterbury	Counties Manukau	TOTALS
C.A. Ruruku	15	15	15	15	15	15	6
D.B. Reynolds	14	14	14	14	–	–	4
S. Millar	–	s	s	–	14	14	4
L. Ngalu-Lavemei	11	11	11	11	–	–	4
T.K. Begbie	–	–	–	–	11	11	2
R. Paraone	13	13	13	13	13	13	6
C.H. Alley (capt)	12	12	10	10	–	–	4
R. Hayes	–	s	12	12	12	s	5
M. Hyde	–	s	s	s	–	–	3
K.L.A. Nolan	–	–	–	–	s	12	2
R.M.M. Holmes	10	10	9	9	10	10	6
R. Anderson-Pitman	9	–	–	–	s	s	3
K.P.L. Tahau	–	9	–	s	9	9	4
L.J. Mitchell	8	s	s	8	8	8	6
F. Hansen	s	–	–	–	s	s	3
K.W. Simon	–	8	8	7	7	7	5
E-L. Heta	7	7	7	–	s	s	5
A.J. Gaby-Sutherland	6	6	–	6	6	6	5
E. Tilo-Faiaoga	5	–	–	s	5	5	4
T.J. Gaby-Sutherland	4	5	5	5	–	–	4
C. Hohepa	s	s	6	4	4	4	6
L. Kloppers	s	–	s	s	s	–	4
J. Coates	–	4	4	–	–	s	3
T.J.M. Kalounivale	3	3	–	3	–	–	3
A.K. Tangen-Wainohu	1	1	3	s	3	3	6
T.I. Natua	s	s	1	1	1	1	6
S.N. Lualua	–	–	–	–	s	s	2
A. Yama	2	2	s	2	2	2	6
J.T. Ngare	–	s	2	s	s	–	4
H.P. Fraser	–	–	–	–	–	s	1

Ashlee Gaby-Sutherland was captain in final two games.

WAIKATO TEAM RECORD, 2019

Played 6   Won 1   Lost 5   Points for 114   Points against 211

Date	Opponent	Location	Score	Tries	Con	PG	DG	Referee
August 31	Auckland (P)	Hamilton	23–41	Alley, Ngata-Lavemei, Natua	Alley	Alley (2)		Lauren Jenner
September 14	Manawatu (P)	Palmerston North	15–12	Ngalu-Lavemei, Reynolds	Alley		Alley	Rebecca Mahoney
September 21	Bay of Plenty (P)	Hamilton	21–26	Ngalu-Lavemei, Ruruku	Alley	Alley (3)		Brittany Andrew
September 28	Wellington (P)	Wellington	31–59	Mitchell, Holmes, Yama, Ngalu-Lavemei, Simon	Alley (2), Ruruku			George Haswell
October 6	Canterbury (P)	Hamilton	5–45	Nolan				Rebecca Mahoney
October 13	Counties Manukau (P)	Pukekohe	19–28	Tangen-Wainohu, Simon, Ruruku	Holmes (2)			Brittany Andrew

WELLINGTON PRIDE

2019 Status: Premiership
NPC participation: 1999–
Coach: Ross Bond
Assistant coach: Brendan Reidy
Home ground: Porirua Park; Westpac Stadium

RECORDS

Most appearances	61	*Jackie Patea-Fereti, 2006–19*
Most points	209	*Amanda Rasch, 2014–19*
Most tries	41	*Ayesha Leti-I'iga, 2015–19*
Most points in a season	118	*Amanda Rasch, 2014–18*
Most tries in a season	12	*Ayesha Leti-I'iga, 2019*
Most conversions in a season	21	*Elizabeth Goulden, 2015*
Most penalty goals in a season	46	*Amanda Rasch, 2018*
Most dropped goals in a season	0	
Most points in a match	43	*Amanda Rasch v Taranaki, 2018*
Most tries in a match	5	*Ayesha Leti-I'iga v Manawatu, 2019*
Most conversions in a match	14	*Amanda Rasch v Taranaki, 2018*
Most penalty goals in a match	5	*Elizabeth Goulden v Taranaki, 2013*
Highest team score	118	*v Taranaki, 2018*
Record victory (points ahead)	118	*118–0 v Taranaki, 2018*
Highest score conceded	65	*v Auckland, 2012*
Record defeat (points behind)	65	*0–65 v Auckland, 2012*

Wellington Pride returned to the Premiership division where they met stronger competition than the previous year, and were only beaten by Auckland and Canterbury. There were anxious moments at halftime against Manawatu when behind 26–7 but the big forwards soon wore down the home team and spun the ball wide where wing Ayesha Leti-I'iga scored four tries to add to the one she scored early in the game. The Black Fern ended the season scoring a third of the team's 33 tries (12), a record by a Pride player. It seemed simply a matter of getting the ball to the powerful runner and she would do the rest.

Some of the 2018 squad were unavailable but this was compensated by the return of several players from earlier years including Raylene Lolo, Moana Solia and Alice Soper. Loose forward Maki Takano had represented Japan. Thamsyn Newton had represented New Zealand in cricket. The only players to start in every game were Bernadette Robertson (midfield), Sinead Ryder-Toala (flanker) and Janet Taumoli (prop) who was regularly substituted by younger sister Barbra. Te Amohaere Ngata-Aerengamate is a sister of Black Fern Te Kura.

Amanda Rasch was again an accurate goalkicker and was successful with 20 conversions in succession during the last five games, an achievement rare in women's rugby.

Higher honours went to:
New Zealand:	A. Leti-I'iga, J. Ngan-Woo, M.J. Parkes, J. Patea-Fereti
New Zealand Development:	J. Ngan-Woo, A. Rasch
New Zealand Sevens:	D.S. Faleafaga, K.R. Whata-Simpkins

WELLINGTON REPRESENTATIVES 2019

	Club	Games for Union	Points for Union		Club	Games for Union	Points for Union
Ana-Maria Afuie	Marist St Pats	15	5	Te Amohaere Ngata-Aerengamate	Northern United	6	5
Precious Auimatangi	Petone	3	0	Jackie Patea-Fereti	Petone	61	80
Jane Bryce	Marist St Pats	8	11	Alicia Print	Oriental Rongotai	30	15
Emily Dalley	OB University	5	0	Amanda Rasch	Oriental Rongotai	25	209
Lyric Faleafaga	Northern United	2	0	Bernadette Robertson	Oriental Rongotai	21	30
Nina Foaese	Northern United	11	5	Sinead Ryder-Toala	Oriental Rongotai	17	20
Montana Heslop	OB University	8	5	Mary-Lee Sa'u	Petone	7	0
Emma Hopoi	OB University	2	0	Sauimoana 'Moana' Solia	OB University	16	5
Losaline Hopoi	OB University	1	0	Alice Soper	Wainuiomata	26	5
Ayesha Leti-I'iga	Oriental Rongotai	30	205	Rosie Stirling	Hutt OB Marist	20	5
Sanita Levave	Northern United	53	25	Elieta Taito	Petone	18	25
Raylene Lolo	Oriental Rongotai	21	20	Maki Takano	Marist St Pats	4	0
Kolora Lomani	Northern United	7	25	Barbra Taumoli	Oriental Rongotai	7	0
Fa'asua Makisi	Oriental Rongotai	40	15	Janet Taumoli	Oriental Rongotai	30	15
Sieni Mose-Samau	Petone	5	10	Angelica Uila	Petone	17	35
Thamsyn Newton	OB University	4	7	Rejieli Uluinayau	Oriental Rongotai	22	15
Joanah Ngan-Woo	Oriental Rongotai	48	60				

INDIVIDUAL SCORING

	Tries	Con	PG	DG	Points		Tries	Con	PG	DG	Points
Rasch	1	24	3	–	62	Ryder-Toala	1	–	–	–	5
Leti-I'iga	12	–	–	–	60	Soper	1	–	–	–	5
Lomani	5	–	–	–	25	Stirling	1	–	–	–	5
Ngan-Woo	3	–	–	–	15	J. Taumoli	1	–	–	–	5
Robertson	3	–	–	–	15						
Lolo	2	–	–	–	10	**Totals**	**33**	**25**	**3**	**0**	**224**
Newton	1	1	–	–	7						
Afuie	1	–	–	–	5	Opposition scored	41	26	1	0	260
Ngata-Aerengamate	1	–	–	–	5						

WELLINGTON 2019

	Canterbury	Bay of Plenty	Counties Manukau	Auckland	Waikato	Manawatu	Auckland	TOTALS
T.M.M. Newton	15	15	–	–	–	s	s	4
E.J. Dalley	–	–	15	15	15	15	15	5
K.R. Lomani	14	11	s	s	14	14	14	7
S. Mose-Samau	s	14	–	–	–	–	–	2
S.M. Solia	–	s	–	–	s	–	–	2
A.A. Leti-I'iga	11	–	11	–	11	11	11	5
L. Faleafaga	–	–	s	11	–	–	–	2
M.B.J. Robertson	13	13	14	14	13	12	12	7
F.A.R.M. Makisi	–	12	13	13	12	13	13	6
A.A. Rasch	12	–	12	12	10	10	10	6
M. Heslop	10	10	10	10	s	s	s	7
R. Uluinayau	9	s	s	s	s	s	s	7
A-M. Afuie	s	9	9	9	9	9	9	7
J.S. Patea-Fereti (capt)	8	8	8	–	–	8	8	5
S. Ryder-Toala	7	7	7	7	7	7	7	7
M-L. Sau	6	5	–	–	–	s	–	3
M. Takano	s	6	s	8	–	–	–	4
E. Hopoi	–	s	–	s	–	–	–	2
N. Foaese	–	–	6	6	6	6	–	4
P.S. Auimatagi	–	–	–	–	s	s	s	3
S.D. Levave	5	s	5	5	5	5	5	7
J.M.P. Ngan-Woo	4	4	4	4	8	–	6	6
Te A.E. Ngata-Aerengamate	s	–	s	s	4	4	4	6
J. Taumoli	3	3	3	3	3	3	3	7
B. Taumoli	s	s	s	s	s	s	s	7
A. Uila	1	1	–	–	s	–	–	3
R. Lolo	s	s	1	1	1	1	1	7
L.V. Hopoi	–	–	–	s	–	–	–	1
E. Taito	–	–	–	–	–	–	s	1
A. Print	2	2	–	–	–	–	–	2
J. Bryce	s	s	2	–	–	–	–	3
A. Soper	–	–	s	2	2	2	2	5
R. Stirling	–	–	–	s	s	s	s	4

Levave was captain in Patea-Fereti's absence.

WELLINGTON TEAM RECORD, 2019

Played 7   Won 4   Lost 3   Points for 224   Points against 260

Date	Opponent	Location	Score	Tries	Con	PG	DG	Referee
August 31	Canterbury (P, ST)	Christchurch	19–57	Ngan-Woo, J. Taumoli, Leti-I'iga	Rasch (2)			Maggie Cogger-Orr
September 7	Bay of Plenty (P)	Porirua	32–21	Lomani (2), Afuie, Lolo, Newton, Robertson	Newton			Larissa Collingwood
September 15	Counties Manukau (P)	Wellington	38–36	Leti-I'iga (3), Ryder-Toala, Soper, Ngan-Woo	Rasch (4)			Jono Bredin
September 22	Auckland (P)	Auckland	10–38	Robertson	Rasch	Rasch		Michael Winter
September 28	Waikato (P)	Wellington	59–31	Lomani (3), Ngan-Woo, Leti-I'iga, Lolo, Rasch, Stirling	Rasch (8)	Rasch		George Haswell
October 12	Manawatu (P)	Palmerston North	42–26	Leti-I'iga (5), Robertson	Rasch (6)			Maggie Cogger-Orr
October 19	Auckland (semi-final)	Auckland	24–43	Leti-I'iga (2), Ngata-Aerengamate	Rasch (3)	Rasch		Rebecca Mahoney

WOMEN'S FIRST-CLASS STATISTICS

to January 1, 2020

100 GAMES IN FIRST-CLASS RUGBY

	Career	Games		Career	Games
Emma Jensen	1999–2019	171	Selica Winiata	2001–19	121
Fiao'o Faamausili	1999–2018	164	Casey Robertson	1999–2014	118
Justine Lavea	2001–19	151	Aleisha Nelson	2008–19	103
Kendra Cocksedge	2007–19	136	Eloise Blackwell	2009–19	100
Stephanie Te Ohaere-Fox	2003–19	128	Linda Itunu	2003–19	100
Anna Richards	1990–2011	125			

300 POINTS IN FIRST-CLASS RUGBY

	Career	Games	Tries	Con	PG	DG	Points
Kendra Cocksedge	2007–19	136	74	289	96	1	1239
Selica Winiata	2001–19	121	107	45	11	–	658
Emma Jensen	1999–2019	171	12	148	81	1	602
Hannah Porter	1999–2008	59	20	115	61	–	513
Tammi Wilson	1998–2001	45	40	92	24	1	459
Kelly Brazier	2005–17	75	35	84	27	–	424
Chelsea Alley	2011–19	71	24	80	39	–	400
Hazel Tubic	2005–19	66	22	101	21	–	375
Claire Richardson	2001–14	79	36	33	25	–	321
Fiao'o Faamausili	1999–2018	164	63	–	–	–	315

45 TRIES IN FIRST-CLASS RUGBY

	Tries	Games		Tries	Games
Selica Winiata	107	121	Victoria Grant	51	69
Kendra Cocksedge	74	136	Renee Wickliffe	51	76
Fiao'o Faamausili	63	164	Louisa Wall	48	32
Vanessa Cootes	54	50	Carla Hohepa	48	50
Dianne Kahura	53	35	Ayesha Leti-I'iga	44	39

MOST DROPPED GOALS IN FIRST-CLASS RUGBY

	DG	Games
Rebecca Mahoney (*nee* Hull)	4	69

100 POINTS IN A SEASON

	Teams	M	Tries	Con	PG	DG	Total
Kendra Cocksedge	Canterbury/NZ, 2018	13	13	45	6	–	173
Kendra Cocksedge	Canterbury/NZ, 2017	14	11	52	4	–	171
Tammi Wilson	Auckland/NZ, 1999	10	15	34	4	–	155
Kendra Cocksedge	Canterbury/NZ, 2016	12	11	32	12	–	155
Kendra Cocksedge	Canterbury/NZ 2019	13	4	39	17	1	152
Kendra Cocksedge	Canterbury/NZ, 2014	17	5	32	16	–	137
Tammi Wilson	Auckland/NZ, 2002	11	8	20	14	1	125
Rosie Kelly	Otago/NZ Development 2019	9	9	37	1	–	122
Amanda Rasch	Wellington, 2018	8	4	46	2	–	118
Selica Winiata	Manawatu/NZ, 2012	9	15	17	2	–	115
Hannah Myers	Auckland/NZ, 2003	7	6	25	9	–	107
Hannah Myers	Auckland/NZ, 2005	12	4	27	11	–	107

MOST TRIES IN A SEASON

	Teams	Tries	Games
Dianne Kahura	Auckland/NZ, 2002	19	11
Vanessa Cootes	New Zealand, 1996	18	3
Selica Winiata	Manawatu/NZ, 2016	18	11
Mele Hufanga	Auckland 2015	16	7
Portia Woodman	New Zealand, 2017	16	8
Tammi Wilson	Auckland/NZ, 1999	15	10
Selica Winiata	Manawatu/NZ, 2012	15	9
Selica Winiata	Manawatu/NZ, 2014	15	13

MOST POINTS IN A GAME

	Match	Tries	Con	PG	DG	Points
Vanessa Cootes	New Zealand v France, 1996	9	–	–	–	45
Kelly Brazier	Otago v Hawke's Bay, 2012	5	10	–	–	45
Amanda Rasch	Wellington v Taranaki, 2018	3	14	–	–	43
Annaleah Rush	Otago v Hanan Shield Unions, 1999	8	1	–	–	42
Portia Woodman	New Zealand v Hong Kong, 2017	8	–	–	–	40
Selica Winiata	Manawatu v Waikato, 2012	4	6	2	–	38
Tammi Wilson	New Zealand v USA, 1999	6	3	–	–	36
Christine Ross	New Zealand v France, 1996	2	12	–	–	34
Kelly Brazier	Otago v Manawatu, 2009	4	7	–	–	34
Tammi Wilson	Auckland v North Harbour, 1999	1	13	–	–	31
Kendra Cocksedge	New Zealand v Hong Kong, 2017	1	13	–	–	31
Ruahei Demant	Auckland v Tasman, 2018	3	8	–	–	31
Tammi Wilson	New Zealand v Germany, 1998	4	5	–	–	30
Kendra Cocksedge	Canterbury v Taranaki, 2013	4	5	–	–	30
Kendra Cocksedge	Canterbury v North Harbour, 2016	4	5	–	–	30
Rosie Kelly	Otago v North Harbour 2019	2	10	–	–	30

MOST TRIES IN A GAME

	Match	Tries
Vanessa Cootes	New Zealand v France, 1996	9
Annaleah Rush	Otago v Hanan Shield Unions, 1999	8
Portia Woodman	New Zealand v Hong Kong, 2017	8
Tammi Wilson	New Zealand v USA, 1999	6
Helen Reader	New Zealand v New South Wales, 1994	5
Vanessa Cootes	New Zealand v USA, 1996	5
Vanessa Cootes	New Zealand v USA, 1998	5
Vanessa Cootes	New Zealand v Germany, 2002	5
Deidre Hakopa	Hawke's Bay v Southland, 2003	5
Kelly Brazier	Otago v Hawke's Bay, 2012	5
Selica Winiata	New Zealand v Samoa, 2014	5
Kilisitina Moata'ane	Otago v Tasman, 2017	5
Ayesha Leti-I'iga	Wellington v Manawatu 2019	5

MOST CONVERSIONS IN A GAME

	Match	Con
Amanda Rasch	Wellington v Taranaki, 2018	14
Tammi Wilson	Auckland v North Harbour, 1999	13
Kendra Cocksedge	New Zealand v Hong Kong, 2017	13
Christine Ross	New Zealand v France, 1996	12
Kelly Brazier	Otago v Hawke's Bay, 2012	10
Rosie Kelly	Otago v North Harbour 2019	10

MOST PENALTY GOALS IN A GAME

	Match	PG
Annaleah Rush	Auckland v Wellington, 2001	6
Kendra Cocksedge	Canterbury v Auckland, 2009	5
Elizabeth Goulden	Wellington v Taranaki, 2013	5
Kendra Cocksedge	Canterbury v Waikato, 2016	5

HIGHEST TEAM SCORES

Score	Match	Result
134	New Zealand v Germany, 1998	134-6
131	NZ Development v Papua New Guinea, 2019	131–0
121	New Zealand v Hong Kong, 2017	121-0
118	Wellington v Taranaki, 2018	118-0
117	New Zealand v Germany, 2002	117-0
116	Auckland v North Harbour, 1999	116-0
109	New Zealand v France, 1996	109-0
101	Auckland v Bay of Plenty 2015	101-0
100	Hawke's Bay v Southland, 2003	100-5

WOMEN'S RUGBY REFEREES 2019

by Chris Jansen

WOMEN'S RUGBY REFEREE SQUAD 2019

	Union	Squad Debut	Tests	SR	P	HC	FPC	Sevens	Nat[1]	Prov[2]	RS[3]	Total
B.J. Andrew	Manawatu	2015	–	–	–	–	19	2	1	–	–	22
M. Cogger-Orr	Auckland	2017	–	–	–	–	18	2	–	–	–	20
L.J. Collingwood	Waikato	2018	–	–	–	–	5	3	–	–	–	8
M.L. Dalley	Wellington	2018	–	–	–	–	5	2	–	–	–	7
E.K. Hsieh	Wellington	2019	–	–	–	–	–	2	–	–	–	2
L.M. Jenner	Counties Manukau	2017	–	–	–	–	16	11	–	–	–	27
R.M. Mahoney	Wairarapa Bush	2015	8	–	1	5	24	12	4	–	1	54
T.A. Ngawati	Bay of Plenty	2019	–	–	–	–	–	2	–	–	–	2
S.C. Winiata	Manawatu	2019	–	–	–	–	–	3	–	–	–	3

P   Mitre 10 Cup
HC   Heartland Championship
FPC   Farah Palmer Cup
Nat1   NZR appointment — international tour, Ranfurly Shield (non-Mitre 10 Cup), national trial, and women's international.

REFEREE APPOINTMENTS 2019

Brittany Andrew

September	21	FPC	Waikato v Bay of Plenty	Hamilton
	29	FPC	Otago v North Harbour	Dunedin
October	12	FPC	Counties Manukau v Waikato	Pukekohe
	20	FPC s-f	Canterbury v Counties Manukau	Christchurch
	27	FPC c f	Otago v Hawke's Bay	Dunedin
November	18	WRWCQ	New Zealand A v Fiji	Lautoka

Maggie Cogger-Orr

August	31	FPC	Canterbury v Wellington	Christchurch
September	6	FPC	Counties Manukau v Manawatu	Pukekohe
	14	FPC	Northland v Otago	Whangarei
	27	FPC	Tasman v Hawke's Bay	Nelson
October	4	FPC	North Harbour v Taranaki	Albany
	12	FPC	Manawatu v Wellington	Palmerston North
	19	FPC s-f	Otago v Tasman	Dunedin
December	14/15		National Sevens	Tauranga

Larissa Collingwood

September	7	FPC	Wellington v Bay of Plenty	Porirua
	14	FPC	North Harbour v Hawke's Bay	Albany
	21	FPC	Otago v Tasman	Oamaru
	29	FPC	Manawatu v Auckland	Palmerston North
October	13	FPC	Northland v Taranaki	Whangarei
December	14/15		National Sevens	Tauranga

Monique Dalley

September	7	FPC	Tasman v North Harbour	Blenheim
	14	FPC	Bay of Plenty v Auckland	Whakatane
	20	FPC	Hawke's Bay v Taranaki	Napier
	28	FPC	Taranaki v Northland	Inglewood
October	12	FPC	North Harbour v Tasman	Albany

Emily Hsieh

October	5/6		USA World Rugby Sevens	Glendale
December	14/15		National Sevens	Tauranga

Lauren Jenner

January	26/27		Fast Four Women's Sevens	Hamilton
February	1-3		Australia World Rugby Women's Sevens	Sydney
April	20/21		Japan World Rugby Women's Sevens	Kitakyushu
August	31	FPC	Waikato v Auckland	Hamilton
September	8	FPC	Auckland v Canterbury	Auckland
	14	FPC	Taranaki v Tasman	New Plymouth
	22	FPC	Northland v North Harbour	Whangarei
October	5	FPC	Northland v Tasman	Whangarei
	13	FPC	Canterbury v Bay of Plenty	Christchurch
	19	FPC s-f	Hawke's Bay v Northland	Napier
November	7/9		Oceania Women's Sevens	Suva
December	5-7		Dubai World Rugby Women's Sevens	Dubai
	13/15		South Africa World Rugby Women's Sevens	Cape Town

Rebecca Mahoney

May	24		Fijiana v Hong Kong	Nadi
July	10		USA v Canada	San Diego
	26	RS	Otago v North Otago	Oamaru
August	31	HC	Wanganui v Thames Valley	Wanganui
September	6	P	Hawke's Bay v Southland	Napier
	14	FPC	Manawatu v Waikato	Palmerston North
	21	HC	South Canterbury v Buller	Timaru
	28	FPC	Counties-Manukau v Canterbury	Pukekohe
October	6	FPC	Waikato v Canterbury	Hamilton
	19	FPC s-f	Auckland v Wellington	Auckland
	26	FPC p-f	Canterbury v Auckland	Christchurch
November	2		NZ Heartland XV v NZ Marist	Te Aroha
	10		Ireland v Wales	Dublin
	16		England v France	Exeter
	26	WRWCQ	Australia A v Samoa	Lautoka
	30	WRWCQ	Fijiana v Samoa	Lautoka

Tiana Ngawati

December	14/15		National Sevens	Tauranga

Selica Winiata

November	7-9		Oceania Women's Sevens	Suva
December	5-7		Dubai World Rugby Women's Sevens	Dubai
	13-15		South Africa World Rugby Women's Sevens	Cape Town

2019 INTERNATIONAL REFEREES

R.M. Mahoney   2016 Hong Kong v Japan (WRWCQ);2018 Ireland v USA,
                    Wales v Canada; 2019 Scotland v Wales, Fijiana v Hong Kong,
                    USA v Canada, England v France; Fijiana v Samoa (WRWCQ).

Two overseas referees controlled Farah Palmer Cup fixtures:
Lara West (*Australia*) Oct 5 Bay of Plenty v Manawatu.
Tyler Miller (*Australia*) Oct 5 Auckland v Counties-Manukau.

INTERNATIONAL ASSISTANT REFEREES

Brittany Andrew

August	17		New Zealand v Australia		Auckland
November	22	WRWCQ	Samoa v Fiji		Lautoka

Maggie Cogger-Orr

November	18	WRWCQ	Samoa v Papua New Guinea		Lautoka
	22	WRWCQ	Samoa v Fiji		Lautoka

Lee Jeffrey

August	17		New Zealand v Australia	(TMO)	Auckland

Rebecca Mahoney

July	14		France v USA	San Diego
August	17		New Zealand v Australia	Auckland

(TMO)   Television Match Official

INTERNATIONAL REFEREES
to 1 January, 2020

Beard, J.D.L. (Counties Manukau) 2014–16	10
Inwood, N.A. (Wanganui & Canterbury) 2002–14	32
Mahoney, R.M. (Wairarapa Bush) 2016–19	8
Mellor, K.E. (North Harbour) 2006	1

TWENTY-FIVE AND MORE FIRST-CLASS MATCHES
to 1 January, 2020

N.A. Inwood (Ewins)	2000-14	86	L. Jeffrey	2003-16	42
R.M. Mahoney	2015-19	54	C.F. Gurr	2011-16	37
J.D.L. Beard	2012-16	50	L.M. Jenner	2017-19	26

WOMEN'S SEVENS RUGBY

The Black Ferns continue to dominate international sevens winning five of their eight tournaments. The year commenced in January with four nations competing in a tournament in Hamilton run in conjunction with the men's HSBC series. The Black Ferns Sevens regained the HSBC title by winning four of the six rounds held between October 2018 and June 2019. From April 2018 to April 2019 the team won 50 games in succession during 10 tournaments, the record being halted by Russia in a drawn game at the Japan event. The 2019/20 HSBC series commenced in October at Glendale and the year ended with the winning of the Dubai and Cape Town rounds in December. These two wins were achieved without captain Sarah Hirini and speedster Michaela Blyde, both recovering from injuries. Portia Woodman missed the whole year while recovering from surgery.

A New Zealand Selection took part in the Oceania Sevens in Fiji but was twice defeated by a similar selection from Australia.

		Hamilton	Australia	Japan	Canada	France	USA	Dubai	South Africa	TOTALS
Shakira Baker	Waikato	*	*	*	*	*	*	*	–	7
Michaela Blyde	Bay of Plenty	*	*	–	*	*	*	–	–	5
Kelly Brazier	Bay of Plenty	–	–	–	*	*	*	*	*	5
Gayle Broughton	Taranaki	*	*	–	–	–	*	*	*	5
Dhys Faleafaga	Wellington	–	–	*	*	*	–	–	–	3
Rhiarna Ferris	Manawatu	s	–	*	–	–	–	–	–	2
Theresa Fitzpatrick	Auckland	*	*	–	–	*	*	*	*	6
Huia Harding	Waikato	–	–	–	–	–	–	*	*	2
Sarah Hirini (capt)	Manawatu	*	*	*	*	*	*	–	–	6
Shiray Kaka	Waikato	–	–	–	–	–	–	*	*	2
Tyla Nathan-Wong	Auckland	*	*	*	*	*	–	*	*	7
Mahina Paul	Bay of Plenty	–	–	–	–	–	–	–	*	1
Risi Pouri-Lane	Tasman	–	–	–	*	–	*	–	*	3
Cheyelle Robins-Reti	Waikato	–	–	*	*	*	–	–	–	3
Alena Saili	Southland	*	*	*	*	*	–	*	*	7
Montessa Tairakena	Waikato	–	–	–	–	–	*	–	–	1
Terina Te Tamaki	Waikato	*	*	*	*	*	*	–	–	6
Ruby Tui	Bay of Plenty	*	*	*	*	*	*	*	*	8
Stacey Waaka	Waikato	*	*	*	–	–	*	*	*	6
Katarina Whata-Simpkins	Wellington	*	*	–	–	–	–	–	–	2
Niall Williams	Auckland	*	*	*	*	*	*	*	*	8
Tenika Willison	Waikato	–	–	*	–	–	*	*	–	3

Nathan-Wong was captain for final two tournaments.

Coach: Allan Bunting (head coach at New Zealand and Australia), Cory Sweeney (head coach at Japan, Canada, France), co-coaches from USA.
Assistant coach: Stu Ross.
Manager: Toni Young.
Strength & conditioning trainer: Bradley Anderson.
Video analyst: Stu Ross.
Physiotherapist: Nicole Armstrong.

INDIVIDUAL SCORING

	Tries	Con	Points
Nathan-Wong	13	77	219
Blyde	27	–	135
Waaka	27	–	135
Brazier	21	4	113
Baker	21	–	105
Saili	19	–	95
Tui	16	–	80
Hirini	14	–	70
Broughton	12	–	60
Williams	11	–	55
Faleafaga	8	–	40
Pouri-Lane	–	19	38
Whata-Simpkins	1	8	21
Te Tamaki	3	–	15
Robins-Reti	2	1	12
Willison	1	3	11
Fitzpatrick	2	–	10
Harding	2	–	10
Kaka	2	–	10
Paul	2	–	10
Tairakena	2	–	10
TOTALS	**206**	**112**	**1254**
Opposition scored			430

Final points for 2018/19 World Rugby Sevens Series: New Zealand 110, USA 100, Canada 94, Australia 86, France 70, England 50, Russia 48, Ireland 41, Spain 36, Fiji 21, China 21, Scotland 2, Japan 1, Kenya 1, Brazil 1, Papua New Guinea 1, Mexico 1. The series was held over six tournaments from October 2018 to June 2019.

Previous winners: New Zealand 2013, 2014, 2015,2017; Australia 2016, 2018.
World Rugby Sevens Series Cup championship titles (2012 to 1 January 2020): New Zealand 24, Australia 8, Canada 4, England 2, USA 2.

NEW ZEALAND AT FAST FOUR TOURNAMENT
Waikato Stadium, Hamilton
January 26/27, 2019

Date	Opponent	Result	Tries	Conversions
Jan 26	England	won 19–14	Blyde, Hirini, Broughton	Nathan-Wong (2)
Jan 26	France	won 24–5	Waaka (3), Blyde	Nathan-Wong (2)
Jan 27	China	won 41–0	Saili (3), Baker (2), Broughton, Blyde	Whata-Simpkins (2), Nathan-Wong
Jan 27	France (final)	won 31–0	Waaka (3), Blyde, Baker	Nathan-Wong (3)

Round 1: France 33 China 7; New Zealand 19 England 14.
Round 2: England 33 China 14; New Zealand 24 France 5.
Round 3: New Zealand 41 China 0; France 24 England 12.
Playoff for third: England 26 China 7.

NEW ZEALAND AT HSBC AUSTRALIA SEVENS
Spotless Stadium, Sydney
February 1–3, 2019

Date	Opponent	Result	Tries	Conversions
Feb 1	Papua New Guinea	won 38–5	Hirini, Nathan-Wong, Williams, Broughton, Baker, Tui	Nathan-Wong (3), Whata-Simpkins
Feb 1	France	won 31–7	Blyde (2), Waaka, Broughton, Nathan-Wong	Nathan-Wong (3)
Feb 1	England	won 29–0	Williams, Broughton, Blyde, Baker, Saili	Nathan-Wong (2)
Feb 2	Canada (Cup q-f)	won 17–7	Tui, Hirini, Fitzpatrick	Whata-Simpkins
Feb 3	USA (Cup s-f)	won 29–5	Blyde, Tui, Broughton, Baker, Whata-Simpkins	Whata-Simpkins (2)
Feb 3	Australia (Cup final)	won 34–10	Blyde (3), Waaka (2), Baker	Whata-Simpkins (2)

NEW ZEALAND AT HSBC JAPAN SEVENS
Mikuni World Stadium, Kitakyushu
April 20/21, 2019

Date	Opponent	Result	Tries	Conversions
Apr 20	Japan	won 43–0	Waaka (2), Faleafaga (2), Willison, Williams, Baker	Nathan-Wong (3), Willison
Apr 20	Russia	draw 17–17	Baker, Nathan-Wong, Saili	Nathan-Wong
Apr 20	France	lost 7–29	Robins-Reti	Robins-Reti
Apr 21	USA (Cup q-f)	lost 19–26	Williams (2), Faleafaga	Nathan-Wong (2)
Apr 21	Russia (s-f for 5th)	won 36–0	Hirini (2), Tui, Nathan-Wong, Baker, Faleafaga	Nathan-Wong (3)
Apr 21	Australia (for 5th)	won 34–26	Hirini (2), Faleafaga, Saili, Tui, Nathan-Wong	Nathan-Wong (2)

Canada defeated England 7–5 in the Cup final

NEW ZEALAND AT HSBC CANADA SEVENS
Westhills Stadium, Langford, Victoria, British Columbia
May 11/12, 2019

Date	Opponent	Result	Tries	Conversions
May 11	Russia	won 26–7	Blyde (2), Brazier, Williams	Nathan-Wong (3)
May 11	China	won 45–0	Williams, Blyde, Tui, Faleafaga, Brazier, Robins-Reti, Te Tamaki	Nathan-Wong (4), Pouri-Lane
May 11	England	won 12–10	Saili, Hirini	Nathan-Wong
May 12	Spain (Cup q-f)	won 17–7	Tui, Nathan-Wong, Faleafaga	Nathan-Wong
May 12	USA (Cup s-f)	won 26–12	Brazier (3), Blyde	Nathan-Wong (3)
May 12	Australia (Cup final)	won 21–17	Hirini, Williams, Nathan-Wong	Nathan-Wong (3)

NEW ZEALAND AT HSBC FRANCE SEVENS
Parc des Sports Aguilera, Biarritz
June 15/16, 2019

Date	Opponent	Result	Tries	Conversions
June 15	Scotland	won 44–7	Blyde (2), Tui, Nathan-Wong, Hirini, Brazier, Saili, Baker	Nathan-Wong (2)
June 15	Russia	won 31–0	Baker (2), Faleafaga, Tui, Saili	Nathan-Wong (3)
June 15	England	won 27–14	Saili (2), Baker (2), Blyde	Nathan-Wong
June 16	China (Cup q-f)	won 36–0	Blyde (3), Saili, Te Tamaki, Tui	Nathan-Wong (3)
June 16	Canada (Cup s-f)	won 21–12	Saili, Nathan-Wong, Tui	Nathan-Wong (3)
June 16	USA (Cup final)	lost 10–26	Tui, Baker	

NEW ZEALAND AT HSBC USA SEVENS
Infinity Park, Glendale, Colorado
October 5/6, 2019

Date	Opponent	Result	Tries	Conversions
Oct 5	Japan	won 40–7	Baker (2), Hirini (2), Brazier, Blyde,	Pouri-Lane (4), Brazier
Oct 5	Russia	won 40–12	Brazier (3), Waaka, Te Tamaki, Tairakena	Pouri-Lane (5)
Oct 5	England	won 36–0	Hirini (2), Brazier, Williams, Waaka, Blyde	Pouri-Lane (2), Brazier
Oct 6	Ireland (Cup q-f)	won 36–10	Blyde (3), Waaka, Williams, Baker	Pouri-Lane (2), Brazier
Oct 6	USA (Cup s-f)	lost 17–19	Waaka (2), Baker	Brazier
Oct 6	France (for 3rd)	won 31–14	Tairakena, Brazier, Broughton, Blyde, Waaka	Pouri-Lane (3)

USA defeated Australia 26–7 in the Cup final.

NEW ZEALAND AT HSBC DUBAI SEVENS
The Sevens, Dubai
December 5–7, 2019

Date	Opponent	Result	Tries	Conversions
Dec 5	Japan	won 48–0	Waaka (2), Harding (2), Brazier, Fitzpatrick, Baker, Saili	Nathan-Wong (2), Willison (2)
Dec 6	England	won 40–12	Waaka (3), Brazier, Saili, Kaka	Nathan-Wong (5)
Dec 6	France	lost 14–19	Brazier (2)	Nathan-Wong (2)
Dec 7	Fiji (Cup q-f)	won 24–10	Tui, Waaka, Brazier, Broughton	Nathan-Wong (2)
Dec 7	USA (Cup s-f)	won 24–7	Nathan-Wong (2), Brazier, Waaka	Nathan-Wong (2)
Dec 7	Canada (Cup final)	won 17–14	Waaka (2), Broughton	Nathan-Wong

NEW ZEALAND AT HSBC SOUTH AFRICA SEVENS
Cape Town Stadium, Cape Town
December 13–15, 2019

Date	Opponent	Result	Tries	Conversions
Dec 13	South Africa	won 40–0	Saili (2), Nathan-Wong, Kaka, Broughton, Paul	Nathan-Wong (3), Pouri-Lane (2)
Dec 14	Fiji	won 12–10	Broughton, Waaka	Nathan-Wong
Dec 14	Russia	won 12–0	Saili, Broughton	Nathan-Wong
Dec 15	England (Cup q-f)	won 26–21 aet	Brazier, Nathan-Wong, Tui, Paul	Nathan-Wong (3)
Dec 15	Canada (Cup s-f)	won 15–5	Saili, Williams, Brazier	
Dec 15	Australia (Cup final)	won 17–7	Tui (2), Brazier	Nathan-Wong

SEVENS RECORDS

to January 1, 2020

BY NEW ZEALAND TEAMS

Most successive wins	50	2018-19
Most successive tournament wins	9	2018-19
Most successive appearances in finals	10	2013–15, 2018-19

Tournament records

Most points	293	Hong Kong, 2000
Most tries	47	Hong Kong, 2000
Most conversions	30	New Zealand 2001

Match records

Highest team score	83	v International Selection, Japan 2001
Record victory (points ahead)	83	83–0 v International Selection, Japan 2001
Highest score conceded	35	v Australia (final), Dubai 2013
Record defeat (points behind)	31	0–31 v Australia, Sydney 2018
Most tries	13	v International Selection, Japan 2001
Most conversions	10	v Tahiti, Fiji 2017

BY THE PLAYERS

Career records

Attended most tournaments	45	S.L. Hirini (nee Goss)
Most points	1200	P.L. Woodman
Most tries	240	P.L. Woodman
Most conversions	478	T.B. Nathan-Wong

Tournament records

Most points	70	P.L. Woodman, USA 2015
Most tries	14	P.L. Woodman, USA 2015
Most conversions	29	A.M. Richards, New Zealand 2001

Match records

Most points	25	M. Blyde, v Samoa, Noosa 2013
		P.L. Woodman v France, Brazil 2015;
		P.L. Woodman v USA, USA 2015
		M. Blyde v England, Canada 2017;
		T.R. Willison v Tahiti, Fiji 2017
Most tries	5	M. Blyde, v Samoa, Noosa 2013
		P.L. Woodman v France, Brazil 2015;
		P.L. Woodman v USA, USA 2015
		M. Blyde v England, Canada 2017
Most conversions	10	T.R. Willison v Tahiti, Fiji 2017

NEW ZEALAND SEVENS REPRESENTATIVES, 2000–19

	Tournaments
Alley, C.H. (*Waikato*) 2014	1
Aniseko, F. (*Auckland*) 2008	1
Baker, S.J. (*Wellington*) 2012 (*Manawatu*) 2013 (*Waikato*) 2016–17–18–19	21
Bird, O.M. (*Canterbury*) 2013	1
Blyde, M.G. (*Taranaki*) 2013–14–15–16 (*Bay of Plenty*) 2017–18–19	31
Brazier, K.A. (*Otago*) 2013–14 (*Bay of Plenty*) 2015–16–17–18–19	34
Broughton, G.P. (*Taranaki*) 2014–15–16–17–18–19	26
Burgess, L.A. (*Taranaki*) 2012–13	2
Cocksedge, K.M. (*Canterbury*) 2008–12–13	3
Cootes, V. (*Waikato*) 2001	3
Drummond, J.A. (*Tasman*) 2017	2
Davis, M.F. (*Counties Manukau*) 2012	1
Faleafaga, D.S. (*Wellington*) 2019	3
Ferguson, J. (*Hawke's Bay*) 2009	1
Ferris, R.R. (*Manawatu*) 2019	2
Fitzpatrick, T.M. (*Auckland*) 2016–17–18–19	23
Forbes, M.H. (*Tasman*) 2012	1
Gould, L. (*Canterbury*) 2000 (*Wellington*) 2001 (*Bay of Plenty*) 2012	4
Grant, K.M. (*Canterbury*) 2014	1
Grant, V.E. (*Auckland*) 2008–09	2
Greig, V.A.P. (*Manawatu*) 2013	2
Halapua, C. (*Auckland*) 2012	1
Hansen, S. (*Wanganui*) 2000	1
Harding, H.R. (*Waikato*) 2018–19	3
Hira-Herangi, A.P. (*Waikato*) 2014	1
Hireme, A.H. (*Waikato*) 2013–14–15	11
Hirini, S.L. (nee **Goss**) (*Manawatu*) 2012–13–14–15–16–17–18–19	45
Hohepa, C.G. (*Otago*) 2009 (*Waikato*) 2012–13–14–15	10
Hohepa, C.H. (*Waikato*) 2012	1
Holden, S.E. (*Manawatu*) 2000 (*Wellington*) 2001	2

	Tournaments
Hurring, H.A. (*Otago*) 2013	2
Hutana, H.S. (*Manawatu*) 2013	2
Itunu, L.F. (*Auckland*) 2009–12–13–14	11
Kahura, D.M.T. (*Auckland*) 2000–01	4
Kaka, S.T. (nee Tane) (*Waikato*) 2013–14–15–16–18–19	13
Karanga, P. (*Manawatu*) 2001	1
Kurei, N. (*Bay of Plenty*) 2000	1
Lavea, J. (*Auckland*) 2009	1
Lavea, V.N.H. (*Auckland*) 2008	1
McAlister, K.M. (*Auckland*) 2012–13–14–15–16–17	20
McGregor, A. (*Auckland*) 2008–09	2
Manuel, H.R. (*Auckland*) 2008–09–12–13–14–16	16
Mayes, C.A.M. (*Manawatu*) 2013–17	3
Morrow, M.L. (*Bay of Plenty*) 2014–15	3
Naoupo, T. (*Auckland*) 2001	3
Nathan-Wong, T.B. (*Auckland*) 2012–13–14–15–16–17–18–19	42
Ngawati, T.A. (*Auckland*) 2012	1
Paul, M.A. (*Bay of Plenty*) 2019	1
Paul, T. (*Bay of Plenty*) 2001	3
Porter, H.J. (nee Myers) (*Otago*) 2000–01 (*Auckland*) 2008–09	6
Pouri-Lane, R.I.R. (*Tasman*) 2018–19	4
Reti, T.C. (*Manawatu*) 2017	1
Richards, A.M. (*Auckland*) 2000–01	4
Robins-Reti, C.R.A. (*Waikato*) 2017–19	6
Ruscoe, M.J. (*Canterbury*) 2008	1
Rush, A.M. (*Auckland*) 2000–01	3
Saili, A.F. (*Southland*) 2017–18–19	18
Scanlan, C.R. (*Auckland*) 2014–15	3
Shelford, E.T. (*Bay of Plenty*) 2001	3
Shortland, S. (*Auckland*) 2000–01	4
Sue, K.J. (*Manawatu*) 2013	2
Sutorius, A.E. (*Wellington*) 2008	1
Tane, S.T. (*Waikato*) 2013–14–15–16	10
Tairakena, M.G.T. (*Waikato*) 2019	1
Tapsell, A.N.O. (*Canterbury*) 2013 (*Bay of Plenty*) 2015	5

Te Tamaki, T.K. (*Auckland*) 2008–09   2

Te Tamaki, T.L.R. (*Waikato*)
2016–17–18–19   17

Townsend, M.A. (*Manawatu*) 2008   1

Tubic, H.S. (*Counties Manukau*)
2012–13–14–15–16   15

Tufuga, R. (*Manawatu*) 2016–17   3

Tui, R.M. (*Canterbury*) 2012–13–14–
15–16–17–18–19   37

Vaughan, J.M. (*Manawatu*) 2016   1

Waaka, S.J.A.K. (*Waikato*)
2016–17–18–19   17

Webber, J.B.M. (*Waikato*) 2014–15–16   10

Whata-Simpkins, K.R. (*Wellington*)
2014–15–16–17–18–19   20

Wickliffe, R.W.M. (*Counties Manukau*)
2009–13–16–17   7

Wikeepa, R. (*Waikato*) 2009   1

Williams, N.L.V. (*Auckland*)
2015–16–17–18–19   28

Willison, T.R. (*Waikato*) 2016–17–18–19   12

Wilson, T. (*Auckland*) 2000   1

Winiata, S.C. (*Manawatu*)
2008–09–13–14–15–16   15

Woodman, P.L. (*Auckland*)
2012–13–14–15–
(*Counties Manukau*) 2016–17–18   35

PLAYING RECORD OF NEW ZEALAND SEVENS TEAMS

	Tournaments			Games				Points	
	Attended	Won	Runner-up	Played	Won	Draw	Lost	For	Against
2000	1	1	–	7	7	–	–	293	20
2001	3	3	–	15	15	–	–	661	17
2008	1	–	1	6	4	–	2	174	57
2009	1	–	1	6	5	–	1	177	37
2012	2	2	–	12	10	2	–	378	69
2013	6	3	1	36	30	–	6	958	279
2014	6	5	1	37	36	–	1	1102	262
2015	6	3	–	36	30	–	6	1011	402
2016	6	1	3	36	30	–	6	915	279
2017	7	5	–	41	39	–	2	1018	251
2018	8	7	1	45	44	–	1	1432	307
2019	8	5	1	46	40	1	5	1254	430
TOTALS	**55**	**35**	**9**	**323**	**290**	**3**	**30**	**8458**	**2410**

NEW ZEALAND SEVENS SELECTION

In November a squad attended the Oceania Sevens in Fiji. The squad was largely chosen from the wider training group and development players.

Squad: Shakira Baker (*Waikato*), Amy Du Plessis (*Otago*), Rhiarna Ferris (*Manawatu*), Theresa Fitzpatrick (*Auckland*), Jazmin Hotham (*Waikato*), Huia Harding (*Waikato*), Tysha Ikenasio (*Auckland*), Mahina Paul (*Bay of Plenty*), Cheyelle Robins-Reti (*Waikato*), Alena Saili (*Southland*), Montessa Tairakena (*Waikato*), Tenika Willison (*Waikato*), Portia Woodman (*Counties Manukau*).
Co-coaches: Allan Bunting and Cory Sweeney
Manager: Toni Young

NEW ZEALAND SELECTION AT OCEANIA SEVENS

ANZ Stadium, Suva, Fiji

November 7–9, 2019

Date	Opponent	Result	Tries	Conversions
Nov 7	Japan	won 26–5	Ferris, Tairakena, Woodman, Saili	Willison (3)
Nov 8	Australia	lost 5–17	Tairakena	
Nov 8	Canada	won 19–12	Ferris, Hotham, Willison	Willison (2)
Nov 9	Australia (s-f)	lost 0–12		
Nov 9	Papua New Guinea (for 3rd place)	won 29–0	Ikenasio (2), Fitzpatrick (2), Harding	Robins-Reti (2)

Australia defeated Fiji 24–12 in the Cup final.

NATIONAL SEVENS

Tauranga Domain   December 14/15, 2019

POOL

A   Manawatu 29 Taranaki 0; Counties Manukau 38 Hawke's Bay 5;
        Manawatu 29 Hawke's Bay 5; Counties Manukau 59 Taranaki 0;
        Counties Manukau 24 Manawatu 21; Hawke's Bay 28 Taranaki 19.

B   Waikato 35 Wellington 19; Canterbury 17 Tasman 7;
        Waikato 21 Tasman 14; Wellington 26 Canterbury 7;
        Waikato 24 Canterbury 5; Wellington 12 Tasman 10.

C   Auckland 26 North Harbour 12; Otago 17 Bay of Plenty 10;
        Auckland 26 Otago 0; Bay of Plenty 36 North Harbour 7;
        Bay of Plenty 17 Auckland 12; Otago 40 North Harbour 7.

CUP CHAMPIONSHIP

Quarter-finals   Counties Manukau 29 Canterbury 12; Bay of Plenty 17 Wellington 10;
                       Auckland 20 Manawatu 17; Waikato 19 Otago 10.
Semi-finals   Counties Manukau 24 Bay of Plenty 19; Waikato 14 Auckland 12.
Final   Counties Manukau 12 Waikato 5.
Play-off for 3rd/4th Auckland 33 Bay of Plenty 10.

PLATE CHAMPIONSHIP

Semi-finals   Canterbury 32 Wellington 0; Manawatu 22 Otago 0.
Final (5th/6th)   Manawatu 17 Canterbury 0.
Play-off for 7th/8th Otago 20 Wellington 5.

BOWL CHAMPIONSHIP

Semi-finals   Taranaki 26 Hawke's Bay 22; Tasman 34 North Harbour 0.
Final   Tasman 24 Taranaki 5
Play-off for 11th/12th North Harbour 19 Hawke's Bay 14.

Tournament referees: Maggie Cogger-Orr, Larissa Collingwood, Emily Hsieh, Tiana Ngawati

Anna Richards Trophy *(Player of the Tournament):*
2013   Selica Winiata (*Manawatu*)
2014   Hazel Tubic (*Counties Manukau*)
2015   Kayla McAlister (*Auckland*)
2016   Katarina Whata-Simpkins (*Wellington*)
2017   Kelly Brazier (*Bay of Plenty*)
2018   (January) Tenika Willison (*Waikato*);
           (December) Sarah Goss (*Manawatu*).
2019   Hazel Tubic (*Counties Manukau*).

TOURNAMENT TROPHY WINNERS

	Venue	*Cup*	*Plate*	*Bowl*
1998	Rotorua	Auckland		
1999	Palmerston North	Wellington		
2000	Palmerston North	Bay of Plenty		
2001	Palmerston North	Auckland		
2002	Palmerston North	Canterbury		
2013	Queenstown	Manawatu		
2014	Rotorua	Manawatu	Taranaki	Canterbury
2015	Rotorua	Auckland	Wellington	Otago
2016	Rotorua	Manawatu	Waikato	Tasman
2017	Rotorua	Counties Manukau	Bay of Plenty	Taranaki
2018	Rotorua (Jan)	Manawatu	Bay of Plenty	Southland
	Tauranga (Dec)	Manawatu	Canterbury	Tasman
2019	Tauranga	Counties Manukau	Manawatu	Tasman

CHRONICLE OF EVENTS

JANUARY 2019

5   Dave Rennie, currently coaching Scottish club Glasgow, re-signs for another season, taking him through to June 2020. The leading contenders for the All Blacks coaching job after the World Cup are considered to be Rennie, Warren Gatland (stepping down as Wales coach after the World Cup), Jamie Joseph (his contract as Japan coach expires after the World Cup), Ian Foster (current All Blacks assistant coach) and Crusaders coach Scott Robertson. Joe Schmidt is stepping down as Ireland coach after the World Cup but in November declared he will take a break from coaching.

7   Super Rugby teams resume training after the Christmas break.

10   The finalists for the Halberg Awards are announced. The All Black Sevens and Black Ferns Sevens are up for Team of the Year; Allan Bunting *(Black Ferns Sevens)*, Clark Laidlaw *(All Black Sevens)* and Joe Schmidt *(Ireland)* for Coach of the Year.

11   English club Northampton announce the signing of Matt Proctor.

12   World Rugby declares a change to Law 15.4 (Ruck). Each team has an offside line that runs parallel to the goal-line through *any hindmost point* of any ruck participant. Previously it was *the hindmost foot* of any participant. This change recognises that players involved in a ruck are likely to be on the ground and not necessarily on their feet.

17   English club Wasps announce the signing of Jeff To'omaga-Allen.

22   NZR release their commissioned review into secondary school rugby. The 31 recommendations include: 1) NZR being the governing body for secondary school rugby. 2) Establishing a NZ Secondary Schools Rugby Union as an advisory group. 3) NZR appointing a fulltime Manager for secondary school rugby. 4) Establishing a clear definition of performance grades with other grades existing primarily to maximise the appeal of the game. 5) The current Rugby Administrator in Schools (RAIS) funding to provincial unions be tagged to meaningful competition development/coaching with a focus on schools with low participation, rather than equal amounts to each school. 6) The establishment of a provincial under 18 tournament for girls. 7) NZR to investigate how the E Tu Rangatahi programme could be expanded in secondary schools to support Maori learners.

29   World Rugby's Executive Committee meets in Los Angeles where it gives further consideration for a Nations League held in years not containing the World Cup or a British and Irish Lions tour. According to *The Times* (London) newspaper it will feature 12 nations in a first division, containing the 10 countries participating in the Six Nations and Rugby Championship plus two others, who would play each other culminating in playoffs. It would start in 2022. A second division would also be played with promotion-relegation between the two divisions.

FEBRUARY

4   SANZAAR release their list of referees for Super Rugby matches in 2019. The 15-man list is down from the 17 last year. The six New Zealand referees are Nick Briant, Mike Fraser, Glen Jackson, Ben O'Keeffe, Brendon Pickerill and Paul Williams. Jamie Nutbrown, on last year's list, has retired. As much as possible, the 15 will work in the same five groups of three throughout the season to help teamwork, efficiency and support on and off the field.

7   NZ Secondary School Sports Council release their schools sports census for 2018, with rugby dropping from second to third place in participation. The top three sports are: first, Netball 27,139 (-1,306 from 2017); second, Basketball 26,481 (+832); third, Rugby 25,317 (-1634).

11   Liam Squire has signed for Japanese club NTT Docomo after the World Cup.

15   Owen Franks confirms signing for English club Northampton after the World Cup. . . .

As Super Rugby starts, a number of last year's All Blacks will only play 180 minutes in the first three matches, not play more than six consecutive weeks (a bye week resets the count at zero), and were excused the pre-season matches in an agreement made between NZR and the Super Rugby clubs in December. This is in addition to their usual two rest weeks during the competition. Kieran Read and Sam Whitelock are also excused the opening four matches and Beauden Barrett the opening two matches.

18 Crusader's coach Scott Robertson has re-signed for two more years to end of 2021.

20 SANZAAR Judicial Committee cancels the red card issued to Highlanders Petelisio Tomkinson against the Chiefs. The match officials ruled Tomkinson went shoulder first into Brodie Retallick's head when attempting a tackle when issuing the card. The Judicial Committee ruled Tomkinson's shoulder contacted Retallick's shoulder and no contact was made with the head.

21 Two club players — one in Hawke's Bay and one in Southland — receive two-year suspensions for the purchase of banned drug clenbuterol in the continuing 2017 investigation by Medsafe into now banned website NZ Clenbuterol . . . Halberg Awards: Black Fern Sevens win Team of the Year. NZR Board member Dr Farah Palmer is presented with a Sport NZ Leadership Award.

23 North Harbour have scrapped their representative Under 14 and Roller Mills (Under 13 and Under 55kg) teams and their end of season Junior Club Representative tournament, as a counter to falling schoolboy numbers with evidence that players who do not make high performance pathways at these early ages have a tendency to then just give up the game. (Most other provincial unions follow.)

25 The draws for the Mitre 10 Cup and Heartland Championship are released. The Mitre 10 Cup will start a week earlier due to the Wednesday night matches having been scrapped . . . Canterbury a loss of $128,541 for 2018.

26 The 29 players to receive Black Ferns contracts this year are named. There are four new players — Luka Connor, Karli Faneva, Arihiana Marino-Tauhinu and Natahlia Moors . . . Taranaki Regional Council vote to spend $55 million on repairing the East and West Stands at Yarrow Stadium. They considered eight options ranging from demolishing both stands and replacing with grassed banks ($6 million) to building a new stadium with roof ($271 million) . . . Hawke's Bay a profit of $109,934 — their 20th consecutive profit.

28 In an exclusive the *New Zealand Herald* "understands" the proposed World Rugby Nations League will now be restricted to just 12 teams — the Six Nations countries, the four Rugby Championship countries plus Japan and USA; the participants are locked in for 10 years; no promotion-relegation at all in those 10 years; start in 2020; the participating nations will earn NZ$10–14 million per year . . . Cue much criticism of World Rugby with the main theme being the exclusion of the Tier Two nations, particularly the Pacific Islands nations.

MARCH

1 NZR CEO Steve Tew counters with a release that the *New Zealand Herald*'s revelation was just one of a number of options presented for a proposed Nations League. Nothing has been agreed and the next opportunity for discussion is later this month at a World Rugby meeting . . . The jersey worn by All Black Hubert Turtill in the 1905 home test v Australia, plus his All Blacks and Canterbury caps, sells at a Cardiff auction house for £39,000 (NZ$74,500). The jersey was put up for sale by Turtill's great-great-grandson who lives in London and bought by a New Zealand consortium who intend to return it to New Zealand.

2 The Blues, Chiefs and Crusaders wear arm bands for their matches today in honour of Mike Tamoaieta who died suddenly yesterday aged 23. He had represented the Blues last year.

4   SANZAAR confirm match officials made a mistake in the Reds v Crusaders match on Brisbane on Saturday night (2 March). The Crusaders had used all eight subs when Mitchell Hunt left the field in the 72nd minute for an HIA assessment, with Richie Mo'unga returning to the field to replace him. The match officials ruled that Hunt had not left the field for an HIA, instead they believed he had suffered injury and was therefore not entitled to be replaced, so Mo'unga was asked to return to the sideline, leaving the Crusaders with 14 men. SANZAAR confirm that Hunt did leave the field for an HIA and was entitled to be replaced.

6   Kieran Read confirms he will exit NZ rugby after the World Cup and join Japanese club Toyota Verblitz . . . World Rugby issues a statement on the favoured plan under consideration since September 2018 for the proposed Nations League: to start in 2022; the Six Nations, Rugby Championship and British and Irish Lions completely retained; two divisions — merit based with promotion and relegation; two conferences in the top division comprising the Six Nations in one conference and the Rugby Championship plus two tier two nations in the other; each of the 12 teams will play the other 11 teams once, either home or away with points accumulated towards a league table; top two teams in each conference would play cross conference semi-finals, followed by a final; would run in two of the four years in the World Cup cycle — not in a World Cup year or British and Irish Lions tour year; broadcast rights to be aggregated and collectively sold; the competition would provide qualification and seeding for future World Cups; the World Cup could potentially move to 24 teams in 2027.

7   Manawatu announce a profit of $226,135.

9   Jackson Hemopo signs with Japanese club Mitsubishi for after the World Cup.

13   World Rugby announce the next four-year cycle of the HSBC World Rugby Sevens Series (2019/20–2022/23) will include at least six combined men's and women's events, with the women's series increased to eight events and men's series remaining at 10 events, with NZ confirmed as a host. The NZ leg at Hamilton will be a combined men's and women's event.

14   Spark's online service Sparksport starts streaming. . . . Three more club players have received bans for having purchased clenbuterol — one in Otago, one in Wairarapa Bush and one in North Harbour. Two receive two-year bans and one receives a four-year ban (two violations). . . . World Rugby meeting in Dublin: a final version of the proposed Nations League is settled on for further discussion. It is the same as outlined by World Rugby earlier this month but with the semi-final round now removed and a third division added. A commercial partnership with sports marketing company Infront Sports & Media could guarantee £6.1 billion (NZ $11.7 billion) for investment over the initial 12-year period.

15   Luke Whitelock signs for French club Pau for three years, effective after this year's World Cup. . . . Between 1.30pm and 2.00pm a lone gunman kills 50 Muslims in two Christchurch mosques and wounds 50 more. Some members of the Bangladesh cricket team arrived outside one of the mosques while the gunman was inside, and hurriedly left. . . . Before the start of the Chiefs–Hurricanes match, both teams mix and link arms in a circle in one-minute silence.

16   Tonight's Highlanders v Crusaders match at Dunedin is cancelled as a mark of respect to yesterday's killings. Both teams will receive two competition points.

17   Crusaders issue a statement that a name change will be considered by the club in the wake of Friday's killings. The name Crusaders has a usage with the Christian Crusaders who fought Muslims in the Middle East in the 11th-13th centuries. The club's use of the name Crusaders is meant to convey the crusading spirit of the community.

19   Wellington a $131,236 loss.

22   SANZAAR announces Super Rugby will reduce to 14 teams in 2021 and be a full round-robin competition (as it was from 2006 to 2010) with the top six entering the playoff phase. The Sunwolves will not be retained as the Japan RU would not agree to the financial terms imposed by SANZAAR for their continued participation after 2020. . . . Black Ferns will participate in a round robin Super Series tournament with Canada, England, France and USA in San Diego in July.

22–23   Before Super Rugby matches, a minute's silence is held with the teams mixing and linking arms in a circle as a mark of respect to those lost in the Christchurch mosque killings.

24   College Sport Auckland releases the review undertaken by an independent panel into last year's complaint against St Kentigern College by 10 of the other 11 Auckland 1A competition first XV schools. The review finds that St Kentigern broke no current CSA rules with their recruiting, in a sustained period of annual strengthening of its first XV, including the providing of scholarships. However, the review does criticise St Kentigern for not recognising/responding to a changed mood on this by their fellow competition schools, and relationships between them have suffered as a result. The review also noted: (1) That other schools in the competition were not immune from similar allegations, (2) The threatened boycott of matches against St Kentigern's by 10 of the other 11 schools, if St Kentigern's would not agree to a new policy of new to school players who have transferred from any first XV competition be excluded from the first six matches and the playoffs, would be a breach of current CSA rules. To resolve the impasse the review recommended that St Kentigern not play their new to school players in the opening six matches, which St Kentigern and also King's College agreed to. . . . Counties Manukau a profit of $84,340.

26   Bay of Plenty a profit of $901,576 . . . Northland a profit of $52,840.

27   Otago a profit of $131,589 . . . Taranaki a record loss of $818,445. Most of it is due to loss of revenue with the closure of the two earthquake-prone grandstands last year. . . . North Harbour a loss of $177,885 . . . Waikato a profit of $132,309.

28   A 1905 All Blacks jersey, one of the team swapped with Irish international Basil MacLear, sells at a Shropshire, England auction house for £30,000 (NZ$57,250).

31   Ryan Crotty announces he has signed for Japanese club Kubota Spears after the World Cup.

APRIL

3   NZR and Crusaders announce they have engaged independent research company Research First to seek feedback and provide recommendations on the Crusaders name and brand. Two possible options are: 1) Retaining Crusaders name but changing branding and imagery, 2) A complete rebranding including name and imagery. The name Crusaders will remain for, at least, the remainder of the 2019 season. The home pre-match ritual of riding horsemen in their medieval costume brandishing swords will not be seen again in 2019.

4   Another two club players receive bans for the purchase of clenbuterol — one in Waikato receives a four-year ban (two violations) and one in West Coast receives a two-year ban. This brings the number of players receiving bans to 26 since the investigation started in 2017.

5   Israel Dagg announces his injury-enforced retirement on medical advice. . . . NZ U20 team for the Oceania Championship is announced. At both the Oceania U20 Championship and World U20 Championship a World Rugby trial will operate where teams will announce a subs bench of 13 in each match, but will only be able to use eight of the 13 as subs during a match.

6   Christchurch Stadium will be renamed Orangetheory Stadium, after the global gym chain who have bought the naming rights, effective June 10.

8   Tasman a profit of $595,884.

9   41 players are named to attend an All Blacks foundation day in Wellington next Monday (15th). The players were selected before Super Rugby started and are drawn from last year's All Blacks, and are not necessarily the in-form 41 players from this year's Super Rugby. There will be no mini-camps as there was last year, but there will be further foundation days for North Island-based players in Auckland on May 20 and for South Island based players in Christchurch on June 3.

10   A Waihora club player receives a 20-week suspension for racial abuse in a pre-season match.

16   Spark announce that their service to watch all 48 World Cup matches live and on demand will cost $59.99 if subscribers sign up in May. It will increase to $79.99 in June and $89.99 nine days before the tournament starts. TVNZ will screen 12 matches free to air: seven will be live including both semi-finals and final. The All Blacks' four pool matches and (assumed) quarter-final will be delayed by one hour.

17   NZR AGM: An under budget loss of $1.863 million for 2018; Bill Osborne is the new President replacing Maurice Trapp who has completed his two-year term; Shaun Nixon (North Harbour) is elected to the Board in a ballot against Colin Groves (Waikato) to replace Steve Morris; Chairman Brent Impey and Mark Robinson were both reappointed to the Board by the Appointments Committee.

20   A One News/Colmar Brunton poll of 1009 New Zealanders: 76 per cent say the name Crusaders should be retained, 14 per cent say it should be changed, 10 per cent did not know/did not want to say.

26–27   Prior to the Crusaders–Lions and Hurricanes–Chief matches, homage is paid to the Anzacs and service men and women across the country with the traditional reading of "The Ode", playing of the "Last Post", a moment's silence, and "The Reveille".

29   Southland a profit of $45,648 and have completed repayment of a $500,000 loan from NZ Rugby taken out in 2011.

MAY

1   Sam Whitelock re-signs with NZR for another four years (2020–2023), but he does have exit clauses in his contract. With NZR Board approval, he will miss next year's Super Rugby competition to take up a short-term contract with Japanese club Panasonic and still be eligible for the All Blacks immediately upon return.

6   Mark Hammett is appointed NZ Schools coach for 2019.

7   World Rugby announce the squad of 23 match officials who will officiate at the World Cup. There are 12 referees (including Ben O'Keeffe and Paul Williams of NZ), seven assistant referees (including Brendon Pickerill) and four TMOs (including Ben Skeen). Glen Jackson, last year's NZ referee of the year, and who has refereed 30 tests, the most by a current NZ ref, misses selection.

8   Waisake Naholo confirms he has signed for England club London Irish after the World Cup.

9   The NZ Under 20 team is named for the World Championship in Argentina. The 28-man squad includes seven of last year's team. Eleven of the squad have played Mitre 10 Cup.

11   Second capping ceremony (first in 2019) for the Black Ferns, at Auckland, with 31 players officially capped.

12   The Black Ferns Sevens win the Canadian sevens event and qualify for the 2020 Tokyo Olympics. With one event to go on the 2018–19 circuit, they top the current series standings and cannot be caught by the current fifth-placed team, France, as the top four in the final standings will automatically qualify for Tokyo.

14   The Maori All Blacks will play two matches against Fiji in July — one in Suva and one in Rotorua. . . . The Black Ferns squad for 2019 is announced. Of the 35 players, 10 are uncapped and Lee Elder is the new captain.

18   Third Black Ferns capping ceremony, Christchurch: 17 players are officially capped.

20   All Blacks Foundation Day at Ardmore Marist rugby club for North Island All Blacks. . . . The Crusaders arrive home from South Africa and receive an apology from SANZAAR for a disallowed try in their 19–19 draw against the Stormers. A Sevu Reece try was ruled out by the TMO Marius Jonker for a forward pass, which SANZAAR says was not forward. The try would have put the Crusaders 24–16 ahead with five minutes left. Scheduled to be the TMO for this week's Sharks v Lions match, Jonker has been stood down from the game. . . . Reports emerge on social media of separate off-field incidents involving Crusaders' George Bridge and Richie Mo'unga in South Africa.

21   NZR and the Crusaders announce they are jointly reviewing the allegations into the two Crusaders players and will be investigated through NZR's Complaints Management Service which are handled by independent lawyer Steph Dyhrberg.

22   A Rolleston club player receives a four-year ban for strangling an opponent and punching him in the testicles during a recent second division club match against Prebbleton. The Rolleston player was red carded as a result of the incident. . . . World Rugby Council meets: Algeria is admitted as an Associate Member, taking the number of countries in World Rugby to 124. Samoa and Fiji (one seat each) participate in their first Council meeting. There is now 51 seats (17 countries, six regional associations and the Chairman) on the Council.

25   All Blacks Sevens team end day one of the London sevens top of their pool and into tomorrow's quarter-finals. The points gained qualify the team for next year's Olympic Games, and cannot be caught in the standings by the fifth-placed team as the top four in the final World Series points standings automatically qualify for the 2020 Olympics.

28   The Hawke's Bay club player who had a four-year doping ban imposed in November 2018 for the purchase of prohibited substances in 2014 and 2015 has his ban overturned. Submissions by the player satisfied the NZR Post-Hearing Review body that he was not playing or coaching at the time and was registered to his Hawke's Bay club without his knowledge or consent, so was not subject to NZR's anti-doping rules at the time.

JUNE

3   Queen's Birthday Honours List: Black Ferns Sevens captain Sarah Hirini becomes a Member of the NZ Order of Merit; Former Wairarapa Bush rep Bryan Styles receives the Queen's Service Medal. . . . All Blacks Foundation Day for the South Island All Blacks in Christchurch.

4   ACC release statistics that show an alarming spike in sports injuries in children aged 10–14. From 2008 to 2017 there has been a 60 per cent surge in the age bracket, double the increase of any other age range in that period. Attribution is partly due to the growing professionalism of junior sport with structured sports training and competition.

5   NZR CEO Steve Tew announces he will step down from the role at the end of the year.

8   NZR/Crusaders announce the name Crusaders will definitely stay for 2020 due to existing contracts in place, but the knight and sword image will be dropped from the club's apparel and marketing.

12   Brodie Retallick re-signs with NZR for 2021–2023. He will play in Japan in 2020 and 2021 and return to NZ in May 2021 and be immediately available for All Blacks selection (approved by NZR Board). . . . Eden Park will host the Pasifika Challenge on August 31. As preparation for the World Cup Fiji will play Tonga and Manu Samoa will play the NZ Heartland team in a double-header. . . . Taranaki issue a formal warning and up to eight weeks' suspensions for an after-fulltime brawl involving players, management, executive members and supporters of the Tukapa and Spotswood United premier teams on June 1. One official and four players were sanctioned, and both clubs were deducted five competition points. . . . Warren Gatland rules himself out of being the next All Black coach by agreeing to coach the 2021 British and Irish Lions team in South Africa. He hopes to return to New Zealand for a Super Rugby coaching position after it.

18   Black Ferns squad for the Super Series in San Diego is named. The 30-strong squad contains eight uncapped players.

19   World Rugby announce their proposed plans for a World Nations Championship have been discontinued. For the plan to continue further, unanimous approval from the 10 countries involved in the Rugby Championship and Six Nations championship was required, but unanimous approval from the Six Nations countries could not be obtained, with the promotion-relegation feature being the biggest hurdle.

20   Taranaki's home ground of Yarrow Stadium will have a $50 million upgrade after approval by both the Taranaki Regional Council (owner) and New Plymouth District Council (operator). As well as the repairing of the East and West stands (both closed last year), the field and lighting will be upgraded. Taranaki RU will bring in temporary seating for this year in front of the closed East Stand. (See Nov 15).

21   The All Blacks will host tests against Wales (two) and Scotland next year before the Rugby Championship. . . . For the Crusaders v Highlanders quarter-final, the Crusaders horsemen return for their pre-match ritual, but without the medieval costume and swords. Instead they parade with the colours of the six provincial unions that make up the Crusaders.

27   Chiefs coach Colin Cooper stands down from the role with one-year still to go on his contract.

28   Chiefs announce Warren Gatland has signed a four-year contract to coach the team through to 2023. He has been given NZR approval to take 2021 off to fulfil his commitment to coach the 2021 British and Irish Lions in South Africa.

JULY

1   The All Blacks World Cup jersey is unveiled. The design bears hand-drawn koru and fern motifs and the jersey is of seamless, woven technology and 25 per cent lighter than previous designs. . . . NZR/Crusaders announce the investigations into the conduct of George Bridge and Richie Mo'unga in South Africa in May by independent lawyer Steph Dyhrberg have concluded with the allegation against George Bridge being not upheld and the allegations against Richie Mo'unga being not substantiated. However, NZR have asked Crusaders to review their protocols for team post-match activity.

2   The All Blacks selectors name 39 players for the first two tests this year against Argentina and South Africa. Four newcomers are Braydon Ennor, Josh Ioane, Luke Jacobson and Sevu Reece, while Ryan Crotty, Scott Barrett and Liam Squire are currently unavailable and not included. A squad of 34 will then be named for the two Bledisloe Cup tests and a 31-man squad for the World Cup.

3   The Maori All Blacks squad is named. . . . A supporter of the Hampstead club receives a six-month ban from attending any rugby matches in Mid Canterbury for verbally abusing the referee as he walked back to the changing sheds after a recent match against Celtic.

5   Seven players — Karl Tu'inukuafe, Ofa Tu'ungafasi, Patrick Tuipulotu, Rieko Ioane, Dalton Papali'i, Brodie Retallick, Luke Jacobson — have been released by the All Blacks to play club rugby tomorrow.

9   This year's Farah Palmer Cup will feature 13 teams, with Northland being a new addition. Nineteen matches will be broadcast live as double headers alongside Mitre 10

Cup fixtures. The only Mitre 10 Cup union without a women's team in the Farah Palmer Cup is Southland.

12   Beauden Barrett re-signs with NZR for four years through to 2023 and will move to the Blues. He will take a break from the game after the World Cup and join the Blues midway through 2020. He also has an option to play one season in Japan (instead of Super Rugby) with the break to be negotiated with NZR and the Blues.

15   World Rugby announce a minor amendment to the scrum law, effective immediately. Pre-loading — where front rows place their heads on opponents' shoulders between the "bind" and "set" calls — is outlawed. The action causes axial or rotation loading on front rows' cervical spines during scrum engagement.

19   On the advice of official NZR ticket seller Ticketek, NZR have cancelled more than 700 tickets for the test against South Africa at Wellington. The cancelled tickets had been (re)sold on secondary market channels.

25   In the *New Zealand Herald* new Sky TV CEO Martin Stewart (since February), reflecting on Spark last year gaining the rights to this year's Rugby World Cup, and NZR's 2021–2025 broadcast rights coming up for negotiation this year, among others Sky TV holds, says "we dropped the ball", "we're not going to drop it again", and "if someone outbids us they are going to go broke".

30   Jordie Barrett re-signs with NZR. His three-year deal 2020–2022 is for the Hurricanes in 2020 but allows for a switch to another Super Rugby club for 2021–2022 if he chooses. . . . Otago re-sign former All Black Adam Thomson who has returned to New Zealand this year and been playing club rugby in North Harbour. He left New Zealand at end of 2012.

31   The 34-man squad for the two Bledisloe Cup matches is named. Of the 39 players named on July 2, the five to miss out are Asafo Aumua, Karl Tu'inukuafe, Shannon Frizell, Dalton Papali'i and Josh Ioane. Scott Barrett is now available and selected with Brodie Retallick now unavailable due to injury. Ryan Crotty and Liam Squire remain unavailable. . . . Japanese club Toshiba announce the signing of Matt Todd for their upcoming season which starts after the World Cup.

AUGUST

6   The Highlanders and Invercargill City Council reach agreement to terminate a contract a year early. In 2016 the Invercargill City Council agreed to underwrite the cost of staging Highlanders' matches at Rugby Park if the cost of staging the matches did not at least break even financially for the Highlanders. In return the Highlanders guaranteed a fixture at Invercargill for five years to 2020. The four matches staged so far have not required the City Council to write a cheque. A game at Invercargill in 2020 is not now guaranteed.

8–11   A one-minute silence in remembrance of Sir Brian Lochore is held before each Mitre 10 Cup match and the Black Ferns–Australia and All Blacks–Australia tests. The All Blacks wear Lochore's All Blacks number 637 on their sleeves.

8   The schedule for the 2019–2020 HSBC World Series Sevens is confirmed by World Rugby. The women's competition will increase to eight rounds (from six) and the men's will remain at 10 rounds. Six of the rounds will be combined men's and women's events. Los Angeles will host the USA men's round in place of Las Vegas. . . . World Rugby also announce six law trials to take place in various countries around the world. (1) 50:22 kick. A team who kicks the ball from their own half indirectly into touch in their opponent's 22, or from their own 22 into the opponent's half, will get the throw into the resultant lineout. (2) A high-tackle warning to be issued to a player post-match by a citing commissioner if a high tackle has not been picked up during the match by match officials. The issue of a second such warning to a player will result in a one-match suspension. (This has been trialled at the last two Under 20 World Championships). (3) Reducing the height of a tackle to the waist. (4) Ability to review a yellow card for dangerous foul play when a player is in the sin bin. (5) Introduction of a penalty/free-kick limit for teams. Once the limit has been reached a mandatory yellow card is given to the last offender. (6) A goal-line drop-out by the defending team when an attacking player is held up over the line.

15 Northland's home ground, the Northland Events Centre, has a new naming rights sponsor and will now be known as Semenoff Stadium.

18/25 Two-part drama *Jonah*, on the life of Jonah Lomu, screens on TV3.

18 The All Blacks release nine players to play Mitre 10 Cup this weekend.

19 Wales go to number one in the world rankings after defeating England 13–6 with the All Blacks dropping to number two despite defeating Australia 36–0 on the same weekend. The All Blacks record 509 weeks' reign at number one comes to an end, having reached the top spot on November 16, 2009.

20 World Rugby announce a law change effective immediately. If a player leaves the field for a blood injury or HIA, the match cannot restart until a replacement has come on.

21 World Rugby announce its World Cups in both 15s and 7s will no longer include gender in their titles. The Women's World Cup 2021 in New Zealand is now renamed Rugby World Cup 2021.

22 Four Super Rugby players have been released by their clubs to concentrate on the NZ Sevens team for next year's Tokyo Olympics: Caleb Clarke (Blues), Etene Nanai-Seturo (Chiefs), Salesi Rayasi (Hurricanes), Scott Gregory (Highlanders). . . . Sky Network Television secure the naming rights to Wellington's home ground, the Wellington Regional Stadium, for six years. Currently known as Westpac Stadium, the new deal begins on January 1, 2020.

28 The 31-man squad for the World Cup is named. Of the 34 players named on July 31 for the Bledisloe Cup matches, Owen Franks, Jackson Hemopo, Vaea Fifita, Ngani Laumape and Braydon Ennor miss out. Brodie Retallick and Ryan Crotty are now both available and selected. Liam Squire was still unavailable. . . . Government passes the Sale and Supply of Alcohol (Rugby World Cup 2019 Extended Trading Hours) Amendment Bill allowing licensed premises to open for live screening of matches during this year's World Cup that fall outside normal trading hours. Venues can open one hour before the match and must close 30 minutes after the match. Similar legislation had been passed for the last World Cup.

29 The All Blacks head out across the country on their ninth annual All Blacks to The Nation tour. The World Cup squad split into groups to travel to Whangarei, Matamata, Mount Maunganui, Gisborne, Rolleston, Christchurch and Wakatipu for the day. . . . Feature-length documentary film *Dan Carter: A Perfect 10* premieres in Auckland before going on nationwide release.

30 In Papakura District Court a 39-year-old man pleads guilty to an assault charge on a 15-year-old referee of a Counties Manukau Under 12s' match on July 27. The referee had sent the man's son off the field, whereupon after the final whistle the spectator assaulted the referee. The man will be sentenced in November (see Nov 21). . . . World Rugby announce a law change effective immediately. If the referee determines a high tackle warrants a red card, the referee must verify with the TMO whether a red card is the correct sanction.

SEPTEMBER

2 The All Blacks return to number one in the world rankings despite not playing. Wales's 17–22 loss to Ireland drops Wales down to number four.

3 NZ Rugby, along with NZ Cricket, NZ Football, Hockey NZ and Netball NZ, have signed a statement of intent with Sport NZ to improve the experience of youth sport with fun and player development under a six-point Statement of Intent.

5 World Rugby announce the three finalists for their Women's Sevens Player of the Year. They are all Black Ferns — Ruby Tui, Tyla Nathan-Wong and Sarah Hirini.

9 Former All Black, and current NZR Board member, Mark Robinson is confirmed as the replacement to succeed Steve Tew as NZR CEO. Robinson will start in January. . . . Ireland go to number one in the world rankings after their 19–10 win over Wales. The All Blacks defeat Tonga 92–7 on the same weekend but drop to number two as Ireland picked up more points for defeating a closer ranked team.

10 SANZAAR releases the draw for the 2020 Super Rugby competition. The opening round starts on Friday, January 31, its earliest ever start, to allow the competition to complete a clear one week before the national teams need to assemble for the home tests in the new July test window. Instead of evening matches starting at their traditional time of 7.35pm, they will now start at 7.05pm.

18 Highlanders announce a two-year strategic partnership with Japanese Top League club Mitsubishi Dynaboars. . . . Black Ferns coach Glen Moore is reappointed through to the 2021 World Cup. The role will now change to a fulltime one, and include talent identification with the provincial unions.

20 NZR open an Official All Blacks Store at Christchurch Airport.

21 For the All Blacks opening match at the World Cup (day two), streaming faults occur for many of Spark's customers, so that for the second half of the match Spark switch to simulcast coverage on to TVNZ's Duke free-to-air channel. This contingency had been signalled by Spark as a back-up before the tournament should a need arise. Spark also announce all three games tomorrow will also be simulcast on Duke.

23 The All Blacks return again to number one in the world rankings after defeating South Africa 23–13 in their World Cup opener, while Ireland drop to second despite defeating Scotland 27–3.

OCTOBER

5 Thames Valley wear special jerseys with coloured images of fox heads for their game against South Canterbury at Paeroa. The jerseys are sold at a charity auction after the match, raising $19,500 for Goldfields School.

10 World Rugby announce the All Blacks final pool match v Italy (at Toyota on the 12th) is one of two games that have been cancelled due to being in the forecast path of Typhoon Hagibis which is expected to arrive on the 12th. England v France at Yokohama is the other match cancelled. The four teams will receive two points each.

13 World Rugby cancels today's match between Namibia and Canada in Kamaishi due to Typhoon Hagibis.

14 NZR and Sky TV announce they have obtained the broadcast rights for New Zealand Rugby for 2021–2025. The current contract expires end of 2020. NZR have also purchased a 5 per cent stake in Sky TV of 21.8 million ordinary shares. The value of the new contract is not revealed. The deal was signed yesterday, on the last day Sky TV had in an exclusive negotiating period. The deal will require shareholder approval at Sky's annual meeting on the 17th because the value of the contract is worth more than half of Sky's current market value ($470 million) on the NZ Stock Exchange. . . . Sky's share price closes the day at $1.06 having started the day at 89 cents.

17 Sky TV's shareholders approve Sky TV's broadcast rights deal with NZR. The value of the contract is not disclosed but a reported figure of $400 million in the media "should be ignored" says the Sky TV CEO Martin Stewart.

21 Seventeen-year old Francis Douglas High School first XV co-captain Jacob Kneepkens has signed a two-year contract with the All Blacks Sevens.

22 Ninety-six athletes (48 male, 48 female) have been chosen from more than 500 applicants to compete at the 2019 Red Bull Ignite7 tournament at Waitakere, November 20–23. They will be competing for six places at the 2020 NZ Sevens Development Camps.

24 *Sydney Morning Herald* reports that Rugby Australia are in negotiations with Dave Rennie to be the next Australian coach. . . . South Canterbury have been censured and handed a suspended $500 fine for having unknowingly fielded a player classed as a local player when he had played one senior club match in another province this year. When realising this South Canterbury stood the player down and brought the issue to NZR's attention.

28 With their semi-final loss to England, the All Blacks have dropped to number three in the world rankings, their lowest ever position. England are now top, with South Africa second.

29 Spark announce the All Blacks v Wales third/fourth place playoff match will be screened on TVNZ on a one-hour delay. Originally the match was to be streamed on Spark only but Spark have relented with the All Blacks now involved in the match. . . . World Rugby Council interim meeting: 2022 World Cup Sevens is awarded to Cape Town, South Africa; Uruguay (one seat) is voted to membership on the Council.

31 Steve Hansen is one of five nominees for World Rugby's Coach of the Year, and the All Blacks are one of five nominees for Team of the Year.

NOVEMBER

1 Kendra Cocksedge is one of five nominees for World Rugby Women's 15s Player of the Year, and Ardie Savea is one of six nominees for Men's 15s Player of the Year.

3 At the World Rugby Awards Ruby Tui wins Women's Sevens Player of the Year.

4 Work has started on Waikato and Chief's home ground of FMG Stadium with the removal of the turf, drainage and irrigation. The new turf will be Desso hybrid turf — a product that includes 5 per cent artificial fibre. The project is funded through the Hamilton City Council. . . . The All Blacks rise to number two in the world rankings by virtue of their third/fourth playoff win against Wales. South Africa go to the top and England drop to three following South Africa's win in the World Cup final.

5 Spark Sport report they sold 192,000 tournament passes for the World Cup, with individual match passes taking the number of subscriptions to over 200,000. Some 212,000 streams were in use for the All Blacks v Ireland quarter-final, which was the most watched. One in five customers reported issues with two-thirds received in the first 10 days of the tournament, most relating to set-up issues.

6 NZR announce the make-up of a five-member panel to conduct the interviews for the next All Blacks coach and make a recommendation — NZR chairman Brent Impey, incoming CEO and current NZR board member Mark Robinson, NZR head of high performance Mike Anthony, former All Blacks coach Sir Graham Henry, former Silver Ferns netball coach Waimarama Taumaunu. NZR has written to 26 candidates to outline the process and invite them to apply. Candidates who apply must inform the panel who their assistants will be. The NZR Board will select the successful applicant.

7 The crossover matches for next year's Mitre 10 Cup are revealed.

8 Sonny Bill Williams announces he has signed for Canadian rugby league club Toronto Wolfpack who play in the UK Super League. According to one source he reputedly will receive $10 million for his two-year deal.

10 Chiefs announce the re-signing of Aaron Cruden for 2020 only. He has left his French

club Montpellier a season early, and will move on to Japanese club Kobelco Steelers after next year's Super Rugby season.

12   Our five Super Rugby squads are announced for 2020. A total of 46 newcomers are among the 195 contracted players.

15   Taranaki's home games next year will be staged at TET Stadium in Inglewood with Yarrow Stadium closed for repair and refurbishment (see June 20). . . . In Invercargill District Court Highlanders lock Manaaki Selby-Rickit is convicted of assault and ordered to pay $8000 reparations to the victim of an incident in the early hours of September 8 (see Dec 23). . . . Otago RU issues a life ban to a club player who received a red card then punched the referee in a club final on July 27. Police issued an assault charge but was subsequently withdrawn. The player will be able to return to the game as a coach, administrator or referee after 2020, but not as a player.

18   Japan RU announces Jamie Joseph has signed a new contract with them to the 2023 World Cup.

20   Rugby Australia announce Dave Rennie has been appointed their national coach through to the 2023 World Cup. . . . *SportBusiness Media* reports that Sky TV paid $500 million for the new five-year deal. For the current deal which expires end of 2020, the same outlet reports Sky TV paid US$160 million (NZ$250 million) for the five years.

21   In the Papakura District Court the spectator who assaulted a 15-year-old referee of an Under 12s match between two Ardmore Marist teams on July 27 is sentenced to 100 hours community work and ordered to pay $1000 to the victim (see Aug 30).

23   The Northern Roller Mills tournament (Under 13 and Under 55kg) played by the nine provinces in the Blues and Chiefs regions will now cease as an interprovincial tournament in a decision made by the Northern Region Rugby Council, in line with the current climate towards the restructuring of provincial age grade rugby. North Harbour and Taranaki did not send a team to this year's Roller Mills tournament. It was first played for in 1925. . . . NZR select six players (three men, three women) from the Red Bull Ignite 7s into the All Blacks Sevens and Black Ferns Sevens national development programme — Grace Kukutai, Renee Holmes, Isla Norman-Bell, Roderick Solo, Joel Cobb, Jona Mataiciwa.

26   Canterbury announce their two Ranfurly Shield defences against Heartland opposition next year will be against Buller at Westport and North Otago at Christchurch.

29   NZR announce changes to club and school rugby. (1) Game On will be used in all Club and Secondary School rugby — although provincial unions can select some school/club grades it will not be applied to if they wish. In Game On if one or both teams don't have 15 players, or enough front rowers, then instead of the game being defaulted or cancelled, the game will be played if: there is a minimum 10 players per side; scrums to be uncontested if not enough front rowers; rolling subs can be used; matches can be from 40 to 80 minutes in length; and be played for competition points. Game On can occur only if both teams and the referee agree before kickoff. (2) Under 11 rugby will change from 15-a-side on a full field to 10-a-side on a half field. This is the current model for Under 10 rugby. (3) Rip Rugby grades for children, teenagers and adults which are non-contact, based on the current Rippa Rugby played by Under 7s. . . .NZR and the Crusaders announce the outcome of the comprehensive review into the Crusaders brand. The name Crusaders will stay as no better name could be found. The new logo is a black (top) and red (bottom) tohu (symbol) in the form of the letter C.

DECEMBER

2   Steve Hansen announces his next job is as a coaching consultant to Japanese club Toyota. It is not a fulltime role. . . . NZR announce the venues for the six home tests next year — Auckland (2), Wellington (2), Hamilton, Dunedin. . . . Nominations for the ASB Rugby Awards are announced. In a new change, the All Blacks and Black Ferns will each have their own Player of the Year award, and the supreme award, the Kelvin R Tremain Memorial Player of the Year, will be chosen from the Player of the Year winners in all categories.

4 The Broadcasting Standards Authority describes a comment made by Bryn Hall — referring to Crusaders teammate Jack Goodhue as a Jew, on Sky Sport show *Kick Off* on June 13 — as "casual anti-Semitism". The BSA received a complaint and decided the slur was not serious enough to warrant a breach of broadcasting standards as it did not contain the level of malice or nastiness required. Sky TV have apologised and this has been addressed with Bryn Hall.

5 The 21 match officials for the 2020 Six Nations Championship are announced. New Zealanders involved are referees Ben O'Keefe and Paul Williams, assistant referees Mike Fraser and Brendon Pickerill, and TMO Glenn Newman. TMO Ben Skeen retired after the World Cup.

9 Ian Foster and Scott Robertson have their interviews for the All Blacks Head Coach role. . . . Auckland declare a loss of $262,000 for 2019.

10 Rebecca Mahoney will referee two of next year's Womens' Six Nations championship matches. She had been scheduled to referee two in the 2019 tournament but had been a late withdrawl due to a family bereavement.

11 NZR announce Ian Foster will be All Blacks coach for the next two years.

12 Christchurch City Council approve the plan for a new 25,000 seat covered multi-use arena eight years after the demise of AMI Stadium (Lancaster Park) caused by the 2011 earthquake. The arena will have a roof that is mostly clear and cost $473 million to build with $220 million coming from the Government's Christchurch Regeneration fund. Some 5000 temporary seats can be added. Construction to start in early 2022 and hopefully finished by spring 2024. It is at a different location to where AMI Stadium was. . . . ASB New Zealand Rugby Awards: Ardie Savea wins the supreme award, the Kelvin Tremain Memorial Trophy as NZ Player of the Year; outgoing NZR CEO Steve Tew is the recipient of the Steinlager Salver for outstanding service; Black Ferns Sevens captain Sarah Hirini becomes the first female winner of the Tom French Cup.

13 The 30-strong National Referee Squad for 2020 is announced. Of the 2019 squad, six have left and the two newcomers are Emily Hsieh and Tiana Ngawati. James Doleman is a new fulltime referee replacing Nick Briant who remains in the national squad.

18 High Performance Sport NZ announce their funding for 2020. The Black Ferns Sevens receive $1.2 million and the All Blacks Sevens receive $900,000.

19 Ian Foster reveals his coaching team. John Plumtree is assistant coach (and selector), Greg Feek is scrum coach and Scott McLeod stays on as defence coach. Grant Fox continues as third selector with no coaching role. There is one more coach to be added. . . . Hurricanes announce assistant coach Jason Holland will assume their head coach role now that Plumtree is in the All Blacks set-up.

23 Highlanders lock Manaaki Selby-Rickit is suspended from rugby for four weeks in a NZR misconduct hearing after being convicted for assault last month (see Nov 15). The four weeks covers the Highlanders two pre-season matches and opening two Super Rugby matches.

24 Former Crusaders assistant coach Brad Mooar, now head coach at Welsh club Scarlets, is confirmed as the final member of Ian Foster's coaching structure as backs coach. Mooar is in the first year of a two-year contract with Scarlets with NZR negotiating financial compensation for his early release.

31 New Year Honour's List: Steve Hansen receives a Knighthood; Steve Tew an Officer of the NZ Order of Merit; former Black Fern Honey Hireme a Member of the NZ Order of Merit; former NZ Maori rep Lehi Hohaia a Queen's Service Medal.

INTERNATIONAL ROUNDUP

There are now more than 600 professional rugby players playing outside New Zealand annually, who were either born in New Zealand, commenced their rugby careers here, or played Super Rugby or Mitre 10 Cup rugby here.

However, many of these players now travel abroad for short-term contracts, between New Zealand seasons, becoming 'whole of year' professional rugby players.

Several new professional leagues have increased these numbers, with 45 involved in Global Rapid Rugby in 2019, and 60 signed for North American Major League Rugby. Japan is the most preferred destination, attracting 163 players, with France close behind on 145 and England attracting 100.

The South American Superliga Americana and the European Continental Shield and Supercopa may attract more in coming years.

Numbers travelling to the Celtic Nations and Italy for the Guinness Pro14 have declined as these countries seek to broaden their own domestic base. In 2019, over 170 players with New Zealand links represented other countries, with a number qualifying residentially after travelling overseas to play rugby.

There are fewer numbers of offshore players involved in first-class rugby in New Zealand, although a number of Australian and Pacific Island age group internationals choose New Zealand for their rugby overseas experience. These factors all emphasise that rugby is a career choice for many young players and that New Zealand provides a great apprenticeship to build and maximise a player's commercial value.

INTERNATIONAL RESULTS 2019

Date	Home		Away		Location	Referee
AMERICAS RUGBY CHAMPIONSHIP						
Feb 02	Argentina XV	54	Brazil	3	Neuquen	J Montes (*Uruguay*)
Feb 02	United States	71	Chile	8	Santiago	D Schneider (*Argentina*)
Feb 02	Uruguay	20	Canada	17	Montevideo	F Anselmi (*Argentina*)
Feb 08	Uruguay	20	Chile	5	Montevideo	F Anselmi (*Argentina*)
Feb 09	Argentina XV	45	United States	14	Rio Negro	F Gonzalez (*Uruguay*)
Feb 09	Brazil	18	Canada	10	Sao Jose	F Mendez (*Chile*)
Feb 23	Argentina XV	35	Uruguay	10	Buenos Aires	D Summers (*USA*)
Feb 23	Canada	56	Chile	0	Langford	H Platais (*Brazil*)
Feb 24	United States	33	Brazil	28	Austin	D Schneider (*Argentina*)
Mar 02	Argentina XV	39	Canada	23	Langford	D Summers (*USA*)
Mar 02	Uruguay	32	United States	25	Seattle	P Deluca (*Argentina*)
Mar 03	Brazil	15	Chile	10	Sao Paulo	J Montes (*Uruguay*)
Mar 09	United States	30	Canada	25	Seattle	P Deluca (*Argentina*)
Mar 09	Uruguay	42	Brazil	20	Montevideo	T Chaudry (*Canada*)
Mar 09	Argentina XV	85	Chile	10	Santiago	H Platais (*Brazil*)

Date	Home		Away		Location	Referee

RUGBY EUROPE INTERNATIONAL CHAMPIONSHIP

Date	Home		Away		Location	Referee
Feb 09	Belgium	29	Germany	22	Brussels	S Tevzadze (*Georgia*)
Feb 09	Georgia	18	Romania	9	Cluj	S Gallagher (*Ireland*)
Feb 10	Spain	16	Russia	14	Madrid	J Neville (*Ireland*)
Feb 16	Romania	38	Germany	10	Botosani	N Amashukeli (*Georgia*)
Feb 16	Russia	64	Belgium	7	Sochi	C Serban (*Romania*)
Feb 17	Georgia	24	Spain	10	Tbilisi	C Ridley (*England*)
Mar 02	Russia	26	Germany	18	Heidelberg	L Cayre (*France*)
Mar 02	Georgia	46	Belgium	6	Brussels	B Blain (*England*)
Mar 03	Spain	21	Romania	18	Madrid	A Jones (*Wales*)
Mar 09	Romania	22	Russia	20	Botosani	P Brousset (*France*)
Mar 10	Georgia	52	Germany	3	Tbilisi	K Allen (*Scotland*)
Mar 10	Spain	47	Belgium	9	Madrid	M Mitrea (*Romania*)
Mar 17	Romania	43	Belgium	17	Brussels	C Evans (*Wales*)
Mar 17	Spain	33	Germany	10	Cologne	A Piardi (*Italy*)
Mar 17	Georgia	22	Russia	6	Sochi	T Foley (*England*)

RUGBY CHAMPIONSHIP

Date	Home		Away		Location	Referee
Jul 20	New Zealand	20	Argentina	16	Buenos Aires	A Gardner (*Australia*)
Jul 20	South Africa	35	Australia	17	Johannesburg	P Williams (*NZ*)
Jul 27	New Zealand	16	South Africa	16	Wellington	N Berry (*Australia*)
Jul 27	Australia	16	Argentina	10	Brisbane	B O'Keeffe (*NZ*)
Aug 10	Australia	47	New Zealand	26	Perth	J Garces (*France*)
Aug 10	South Africa	46	Argentina	13	Buenos Aires	R Poite (*France*)

PACIFIC NATIONS CUP

Date	Home		Away		Location	Referee
Jul 27	Japan	34	Fiji	21	Kamaishi	L Pearce (*England*)
Jul 27	United States	47	Canada	19	Glendale	A Brace (*Ireland*)
Jul 27	Samoa	25	Tonga	17	Apia	M Fraser (*NZ*)
Aug 03	Japan	41	Tonga	7	Hanozono	J Garces (*France*)
Aug 03	United States	13	Samoa	10	Suva	N Owens (*Wales*)
Aug 03	Fiji	38	Canada	13	Suva	M Fraser (*NZ*)
Aug 09	Tonga	33	Canada	23	Lautoka	N Owens (*Wales*)
Aug 10	Japan	34	United States	20	Suva	G Jackson (*NZ*)
Aug 10	Fiji	10	Samoa	3	Suva	B Pickerill (*NZ*)

Date	Home		Away		Location	Referee

OCEANIA RUGBY CUP

Date	Home		Away		Location	Referee
Aug 23	Papua New Guinea	89	Nauru	5	Port Moresby	P Isamaeli (*Samoa*)
Aug 23	Niue	19	Solomon Islands	17	Port Moresby	K Talemaivalagi (*Fiji*)
Aug 27	Papua New Guinea	29	Niue	10	Port Moresby	P Isamaeli (*Samoa*)
Aug 27	Solomon Islands	61	Nauru	7	Port Moresby	D Vosalevu (*Fiji*)
Aug 31	Papua New Guinea	15	Solomon Islands	13	Port Moresby	K Talemaivalagi (*Fiji*)
Aug 31	Niue	87	Nauru	0	Port Moresby	D Vosalevu (*Fiji*)

OTHER INTERNATIONALS

Date	Home		Away		Location	Referee
Jun 04	Uruguay	48	Russia	26	Montevideo	F Murphy (*Ireland*)
Jun 08	Namibia	30	Uruguay	28	Montevideo	B Whitehouse (*Wales*)
Jun 08	Russia	48	Argentina XV	40	Montevideo	F Gonzalez (*Uruguay*)
Jun 08	Romania	27	Chile	11	Valparaiso	C Antonio (*Argentina*)
Jun 08	Spain	22	Brazil	16	Sao Paulo	J Federico (*Argentina*)
Jun 15	Russia	20	Namibia	0	Montevideo	F Gonzalez (*Uruguay*)
Jun 15	Uruguay	28	Argentina XV	15	Montevideo	F Murphy (*Ireland*)
Jun 16	Spain	29	Chile	22	Curico	S Romero (*Uruguay*)
Jun 16	Romania	22	Brazil	21	Jundiai	D Schneider (*Argentina*)
Jun 22	Spain	41	Uruguay	21	Montevideo	F Anselmi (*Argentina*)
Jul 13	Fiji	27	NZ Maoris	10	Suva	D Murphy (*Australia*)
Jul 20	NZ Maoris	26	Fiji	17	Rotorua	N Berry (*Australia*)
Aug 10	Ireland	29	Italy	10	Dublin	L Pearce (*England*)
Aug 11	England	33	Wales	19	London	M Raynal (*France*)
Aug 17	Wales	13	England	6	Cardiff	P Gauzere (*France*)
Aug 17	France	32	Scotland	3	Paris	N Owens (*Wales*)
Aug 17	Italy	85	Russia	15	San Benedetto	K Dickson (*England*)
Aug 17	New Zealand	36	Australia	0	Auckland	J Peyper (*SA*)
Aug 17	South Africa	24	Argentina	18	Pretoria	L Pearce (*England*)
Aug 24	England	57	Ireland	15	London	N Owens (*Wales*)
Aug 24	Scotland	17	France	14	Edinburgh	W Barnes (*England*)
Aug 30	France	47	Italy	19	Paris	M Carley (*England*)
Aug 31	Fiji	29	Tonga	19	Auckland	B O'Keeffe (*NZ*)
Aug 31	Ireland	22	Wales	17	Cardiff	R Poite (*France*)
Aug 31	Scotland	44	Georgia	10	Tbilisi	M Raynal (*France*)

Date	Home		Away		Location	Referee
Aug 31	Samoa	36	NZ Heartland XV	19	Auckland	P Williams (*NZ*)
Sep 06	South Africa	41	Japan	7	Kumagaya	N Berry (*Australia*)
Sep 06	England	37	Italy	0	Newcastle	B O'Keeffe (*NZ*)
Sep 06	Scotland	36	Georgia	9	Edinburgh	R Poite (*France*)
Sep 07	New Zealand	92	Tonga	7	Hamilton	A Gardner (*Australia*)
Sep 07	Australia	34	Samoa	15	Sydney	P Williams (*NZ*)
Sep 07	Ireland	19	Wales	10	Dublin	A Ruiz (*France*)
Sep 07	United States	15	Canada	10	Vancouver	A Ruiz (*France*)
Nov 09	Brazil	26	Portugal	24	Sao Paulo	F Gonzalez (*Uruguay*)
Nov 16	Portugal	23	Chile	18	Santiago	D Schneider (*Argentina*)
Nov 16	Hong Kong	36	Belgium	17	Brussels	T Charabas (*France*)
Nov 23	Spain	29	Hong Kong	7	Madrid	I Tempest (*England*)

RUGBY WORLD CUP FINALS

Date	Home		Away		Location	Referee
Sep 20	Japan	30	Russia	10	Tokyo	N Owens (*Wales*)
Sep 21	Australia	39	Fiji	21	Sapporo	B O'Keeffe (*NZ*)
Sep 21	France	23	Argentina	21	Tokyo	A Gardner (*Australia*)
Sep 21	New Zealand	23	South Africa	13	Yokohama	J Garces (*France*)
Sep 22	England	35	Tonga	3	Sapporo	P Williams (*NZ*)
Sep 22	Ireland	27	Scotland	3	Yokohama	W Barnes (*England*)
Sep 22	Italy	47	Namibia	22	Osaka	N Berry (*Australia*)
Sep 23	Wales	43	Georgia	14	Aichi	L Pearce (*England*)
Sep 24	Samoa	34	Russia	9	Kumagaya	R Poite (*France*)
Sep 25	Uruguay	30	Fiji	27	Kamaishi	P Gauzere (*France*)
Sep 26	England	45	United States	7	Kobe	N Berry (*Australia*)
Sep 26	Italy	48	Canada	7	Fukuoka	N Owens (*Wales*)
Sep 28	Argentina	28	Tonga	12	Osaka	J Peyper (*SA*)
Sep 28	Japan	19	Ireland	12	Shizuoka	A Gardner (*Australia*)
Sep 28	South Africa	57	Namibia	3	Aichi	M Raynal (*France*)
Sep 29	Wales	29	Australia	25	Tokyo	R Poite (*France*)
Sep 29	Georgia	33	Uruguay	7	Kumagaya	W Barnes (*England*)
Sep 30	Scotland	34	Samoa	0	Kobe	P Gauzere (*France*)
Oct 02	France	33	United States	9	Fukuoka	B O'Keeffe (*NZ*)
Oct 02	New Zealand	63	Canada	0	Oita	R Poite (*France*)
Oct 03	Fiji	45	Georgia	10	Osaka	P Williams (*NZ*)
Oct 03	Ireland	35	Russia	0	Kobe	J Garces (*France*)

Date	Home		Away		Location	Referee
Oct 04	South Africa	49	Italy	3	Shizuoka	W Barnes (*England*)
Oct 05	Australia	45	Uruguay	10	Oita	M Raynal (*France*)
Oct 05	England	39	Argentina	10	Tokyo	N Owens (*Wales*)
Oct 05	Japan	38	Samoa	19	Aichi	J Peyper (*SA*)
Oct 06	France	23	Tonga	21	Kumamoto	N Berry (*Australia*)
Oct 06	New Zealand	71	Namibia	9	Tokyo	P Gauzere (*France*)
Oct 08	South Africa	66	Canada	7	Kobe	L Pearce (*England*)
Oct 09	Argentina	47	United States	17	Kumagaya	P Williams (*NZ*)
Oct 09	Scotland	61	Russia	0	Shizuoka	M Raynal (*France*)
Oct 09	Wales	29	Fiji	17	Oita	J Garces (*France*)
Oct 11	Australia	27	Georgia	8	Shizuoka	P Gauzere (*France*)
Oct 12	Ireland	47	Samoa	5	Fukuoka	N Berry (*Australia*)
Oct 13	Japan	28	Scotland	21	Yokohama	B O'Keeffe (*NZ*)
Oct 13	Tonga	31	United States	19	Osaka	N Owens (*Wales*)
Oct 13	Wales	35	Uruguay	13	Kumamoto	W Barnes (*England*)

Quarter-Finals

Date	Home		Away		Location	Referee
Oct 19	England	40	Australia	16	Tokyo	J Garces (*France*)
Oct 19	New Zealand	46	Ireland	14	Oita	N Owens (*Wales*)
Oct 20	Wales	20	France	19	Tokyo	J Peyper (*SA*)
Oct 20	South Africa	26	Japan	3	Tokyo	W Barnes (*England*)

Semi-Finals

Date	Home		Away		Location	Referee
Oct 26	England	19	New Zealand	7	Yokohama	N Owens (*Wales*)
Oct 27	South Africa	19	Wales	16	Yokohama	J Garces (*France*)

Bronze Match

Date	Home		Away		Location	Referee
Nov 01	New Zealand	40	Wales	17	Tokyo	W Barnes (*England*)

Final

Date	Home		Away		Location	Referee
Nov 02	South Africa	32	England	12	Yokohama	J Garces (*France*)

Date	Home		Away		Location	Referee

SIX-NATIONS CHAMPIONSHIP

Date	Home		Away		Location	Referee
Feb 01	Wales	24	France	19	Paris	W Barnes (*England*)
Feb 02	Scotland	33	Italy	20	Edinburgh	L Pearce (*England*)
Feb 02	England	32	Ireland	20	Dublin	J Garces (*France*)
Feb 09	Ireland	22	Scotland	13	Edinburgh	R Poite (*France*)
Feb 09	Wales	26	Italy	15	Rome	M Raynal (*France*)
Feb 10	England	44	France	8	London	N Owens (*Wales*)
Feb 23	Wales	21	England	13	Cardiff	J Peyper (*SA*)
Feb 23	France	27	Scotland	10	Paris	N Berry (*Australia*)
Feb 24	Ireland	26	Italy	16	Rome	G Jackson (*NZ*)
Mar 09	Wales	18	Scotland	11	Edinburgh	P Gauzere (*France*)
Mar 09	England	57	Italy	14	London	N Berry (*Australia*)
Mar 10	Ireland	26	France	14	Dublin	B O'Keeffe (*NZ*)
Mar 17	Wales	25	Ireland	7	Cardiff	A Gardner (*Australia*)
Mar 17	France	25	Italy	14	Rome	M Carley (*England*)
Mar 17	England	38	Scotland	38	London	P Williams (*NZ*)

FINAL TABLE

	P	W	D	L	For	Against	Pts
Wales	5	5	0	0	114	65	23
England	5	3	1	1	184	101	18
Ireland	5	3	0	2	101	100	14
France	5	2	0	3	93	118	10
Scotland	5	1	1	3	105	125	9
Italy	5	0	0	5	79	167	0

THE FOREIGN LEGION
by John Lea

These New Zealand origin players were either contracted with professional overseas clubs for play in 2019/20, or commenced and completed an overseas contract during 2019 (denoted by ★). Those no longer eligible for New Zealand have their country of allegiance shown in brackets.

AUSTRALIA

Super Rugby

ACT Brumbies:	Wharenui Hawera★, Christian Lealifano (Australia)★,Toni Pulu (Niue), Peter Samu (Australia), Irae Simone
Melbourne Rebels:	Robbie Abel★, Jermaine Ainsley (Australia), Solomone Kata, Anaru Rangi ★, Michael Ruru★, Jordan Uelese (Australia)
NSW Waratahs:	Tetera Faulkner (Australia), Lalakai Foketi, Karmichael Hunt (Australia), Sekope Kepu (Australia), Curtis Rona (Australia), JPSauni★
Queensland Reds:	Chris Feauai-Sautia (Australia), Adam Korczyk★, Brandon Paenga-Amosa (Australia), Lukhan Sakalaia-Lolo (Australia), Henry Speight (Australia), Caleb Timu (Australia)★, Taniela Tupou (Australia)

NRC

Brisbane City:	Adam Korczyk, Brandon Paenga-Amosa (Australia)
Canberra Vikings:	Toni Pulu (Niue), Peter Samu (Australia), Irae Simone
Melbourne Rising:	Jermaine Ainsley (Australia), Tetera Faulkner (Australia), Anaru Rangi, Michael Ruru, JP Sauni, James So'oialo (Samoa)
NSW Country Eagles:	Nigel Ah Wong★
Queensland Country:	Chris Feauai-Sautia (Australia), Jethro Felemi (Samoa), Dillon Wihongi
Sydney Rays:	Jake Abel, Lalakai Foketi, Charlie Gamble
Western Force:	Johan Bardoul, Leon Power, Henry Stowers (Samoa), Jeremy Thrush

Global Rapid Rugby

Asia Pacific Dragons:	Ha'amea Ahio, Naulia Dawai (Fiji), Irwin Finau, Rowan Gouws, Kurt Hammer, Zac Harrison-Jones, Stacey Ili (Samoa), Joketani Koroi, Junior Laloifi, Nili Latu (Tonga), Michael Lea, Meli Matavao (Samoa), Sekonaia Pole, Ropate Rinakama (Fiji), Michael Scott, Latu Talakai (Tonga), Asaeli Tikoirotuma (Fiji)
Fiji Warriors:	Johnny Dyer (Fiji), John Stewart (Fiji)
Kagifa Samoa:	Callum Adams, Sam Aiono, Latiume Fosita (Tonga), Zac Guildford, Leon Fukofuka (Tonga), Kali Hala (Tonga), Maui Hausia (Tonga), Taniela Koroi (Fiji), Dylan Lam, Fotu Lokotui (Tonga), Leon Makris, Matiaha Martin, Mike McKee, Otenili Moala, Siaosi Ngingini, Mark Royal, JP Sauni, Gafatasi Sua
South China Tigers:	Josh Dowsing (Hong Kong), Nathan de Thierry (Hong Kong), Ruan Du Plooy, Tau Koloamatangi (Hong Kong)

BRAZIL

Superliga Americana

Corinthians:	Josh Reeves (Brazil)

CANADA
Major League Rugby
Toronto Arrows   Tayler Adams, Richie Asiata, Sam Malcolm, Aaron McLelland*

ENGLAND
Aviva Premiership

Bath: Jackson Willison, Jack Wilson (England)*

Bristol Bears: John Afoa, Adrian Choat, Jake Heenan, Nathan Hughes
                        (England), James Lay (Samoa), Jordan Lay (Samoa), Alapati Leuia
                        (Samoa), Steven Luatua, Charles Piutau, Chris Vui (Samoa)

Exeter Chiefs: Tom Hendrickson

Gloucester: Willie Heinz (England), Josh Hohneck, Tom Marshall, Jason
                        Woodward (England)

Harlequins: Tevita Cavubati (Fiji), Elia Elia (Samoa),Paul Lasike (USA),
                        Francis Saili, Winston Stanley (Samoa)

Leicester Tigers: Brendon O'Connor*, Jordan Taufua, Joe Thomas, Telusa Veianu
                        (Tonga)

London Irish: Mike Coman*, Blair Cowan (Scotland), Terrence Hepetema, TJ
                        Ioane (Samoa), Sekope Kepu (Australia), William Lloyd, Motu
                        Matu'u (Samoa), Waisake Naholo, Curtis Rona (Australia)

London Wasps: Malakai Fekitoa, Jimmy Gopperth, Brad Shields (England), Lima
                        Sopoaga, Jeff To'omaga-Allen, Jacob Umaga

Northampton Saints: Piers Francis (England), Ben Franks, Owen Franks, Teimana
                        Harrison (England), Dylan Hartley (England), Ken Pisi (Samoa)*,
                        Matt Procter, Apisoloma Ratuniyarawa (Fiji), Ahsee Tuala
                        (Samoa), Nafi Tuitavake (Tonga)*

Sale Sharks: Bryn Evans, Johnny Leota (Samoa)*, Denny Solomona (England)

Saracens: Sean Maitland (Scotland), Hisa Sasagi (Samoa)*, Will Skelton
                        (Australia), Mako Vunipola (England)

Worcester Warriors: Michael Fatialofa, Ed Fidow (Samoa), Jono Kitto, Matt Moulds,
                        Melani Nanai

RFU Championship

Bedford Blues: Grayson Hart (Scotland), Daniel Temm

Cornish Pirates: Jake Ashby (Netherlands)*, Antonio Kirikiri, Fa'atiga Lemalu
                        (Samoa), Jordan Payne*, Shae Tucker, Marien Walker

Coventry: Jack Ram (Tonga)

Doncaster Knights: Mike Mayhew, Kurt Morath (Tonga), Dwayne Politaivao (Samoa),
                        Matt Talaese (Samoa)

Ealing Trailfinders: Paul Grant, Elijah Niko

Hartpury College: Jake Heenan, Don Koster

Jersey Reds: Adam Batt*, Samisoni Fisilau (Tonga), Liam Hall, Liam Howley,
                        Regan King, Uili Kolo'ofai (Tonga), Leroy Van Dam

London Scottish: Mark Bright (England), Chris Walker

Newcastle Falcons: Rodney Ah You (Ireland), John Hardie (Scotland), Sinoti Sinoti
                        (Samoa), Sonatane Takulua (Tonga), Cooper Vuna (Australia)

Nottingham: Tom Hill

Yorkshire Carnegie   Nick Mayhew, Richard Mayhew, Myles Thoroughgood, Jade Te Rure

FRANCE

Top 14

Agen:	Paul Ngauamo (Tonga), Jordan Puletua, Jamie-Jerry Taulagi (Samoa), Sam Vaka
Bayonne:	Alofa Alofa (Samoa), Matt Graham, Census Johnston (Samoa), Matt Luamanu (Samoa), Edwin Maka, Michael Ruru
Bordeaux Begles:	Ole Avei (Samoa), Ben Botica, Simon Hickey, Seta Tamanivalu
Brive:	So'otala Fa'aso'o, James Johnston (Samoa), Wesley Tapueluelu
Castres:	Paea Fa'anunu (Tonga), Filipo Nakosi (Fiji), Alex Tulou (Samoa), Ma'ama Vaipulu (Tonga), Karena Wihongi
Clermont:	Peter Betham, (Australia), Fritz Lee, Faifili Levave (Samoa), George Moala, Tim Nanai-Williams (Samoa), Isaia Toeava, Loni Uhila, John Ulugia
La Rochelle:	Uini Atonio (France), Tawera Kerr-Barlow, Teddy Stanaway, Victor Vito, Ihaia West
Lyon:	Toby Arnold, Cameron Mapusua, Charlie Ngatai, Rudi Wulf
Montpellier:	Aaron Cruden*, Kahn Fotuali'i (Samoa), Jarrad Hoeata, Nemani Nadolo (Fiji), Caleb Timu (Australia)
Pau:	Ziegfried Fisi'ihoi (Tonga), Jamie Mackintosh, Daniel Ramsey, Colin Slade, Ben Smith, Benson Stanley, Tom Taylor, Dominiko Waqaniburotu (Fiji), Luke Whitelock
Racing 92:	Dominic Bird, Ope Peleseuma (Samoa), Joe Rokocoko*, Ben Tameifuna (Tonga), Anthony Tuitavake, Virimi Vakatawa (France), Ben Volavola (Fiji)
Stade Francais:	Paul Alo-Emile (Samoa), Joketani Koroi
Toulon:	Brian Alainu'uese, Bryce Heem, Liam Messam, Nehe Milner-Skudder, Duncan Paia'aua (Australia), Julian Savea
Toulouse:	Pita Ahki, Carl Axtens, Charlie Faumuina, Jerome Kaino, Paul Perez (Samoa), Joe Tekori (Samoa)

Second Division

Aurillac:	Jack McPhee, Adrian Smith
Beziers Herault:	Nick Fitisemanu, Joe Tuineau (Tonga), Tyrone Viiga
Biarritz:	Sione Anga'aelangi (Tonga), Matt Clarkin, Tyrone Elkington-McDonald, Sefulu Gaugau, Leroy Houston (Australia), Adam Knight, Elvis Levi, Guy Millar, Sikeli Nabou (Fiji), Joseph Penetito, Jarred Poi
Colomiers:	Jonny Fa'amatuainu (Tonga), Daniel Faleafa (Tonga), Randall Kamea, Peni Rokodoguni, Chris Tuatara-Morrison
Grenoble:	Leva Fifita (Tonga), Hoani Matenga, Steven Setephano (Cook Islands), James So'oialo (Samoa), Albert Toetu, Taiasina Tu'ifua (Tonga), Edgar Tuinukuafe
Montauban:	Richard Haddon, Alex Luatua
Mont De Marsan:	Maselino Paulino (Samoa)
Oyonnax:	Tony Ensor, Rory Grice, Roimata Hansell-Pune, Quentin MacDonald, Tusi Pisi (Samoa), Nuku Swerling, Hoani Tui, Josh Tyrell (Samoa)

Perpignan:	Shahn Eru (Cook Islands), Piua Fa'aselele (Samoa), Lotima Fa'inganuku★, Michael Faleafa (Tonga), Manu Leiataua (Samoa), Genesis Mamea (Samoa), Tevita Mailau (Tonga), Eric Sione, George Tilsley
Provence:	Joe Edwards, Hikairo Forbes, Poutasi Luafutu (Australia), Lachie Munro, Sona Taumalolo (Tonga)
Rouen-Normandie:	Valentino Mapapalangi (Tonga), Anthony Perenise (Samoa)
Soyaux-Angouleme:	Tim Cowley (Samoa), Dylan Hayes, Kimami Sitauti (Australia), Pingi Tala'apitaga
USON Nevers:	Fa'atoina Autagavaia (Samoa), Auvasa Faleali'i (Samoa), Zac Guildford
Valence-Romans	Nigel Hunt, Matiaha Martin, Peter Saili
Vannes:	Hugh Chalmers, Ambrose Curtis, Ash Moeke, Albert Vulivuli (Fiji)

IRELAND

Guinness Pro 14

Connacht:	Bundee Aki (Ireland), Jarrad Butler, Tom McCartney, Dominic Robertson-McCoy
Leinster:	Michael Bent (Ireland), Jamison Gibson-Park, James Lowe, Joseph Tomane (Australia)
Munster:	Tyler Bleyendaal, Joey Carbery (Ireland), Rhys Marshall, Alby Matthewson
Ulster:	Matt Faddes, Sean Reidy (Ireland)

ITALY

Guinness Pro 14

Benetton Treviso:	Dean Budd (Italy), Hame Faiva, Monty Ioane, Jayden Hayward (Italy), Nasi Manu (Tonga), Iliesa Ratuva Tavuyara (Fiji)
Zebre:	Junior Laloifi, Josh Renton, Matu Tevi★, Jimmy Tuivaiti (Italy)

JAPAN

Super Rugby

Sunwolves	Mark Abbott★, Jarred Adams, Asaeli Ai Valu (Japan)★, Leni Apisai, Sione Asi, Jamie Booth★, Phil Burleigh (Scotland), Jason Emery★, Chris Eves, Jamie Henry (Japan)★, Mitchell Jacobson, Mateaki Kafatolu, Timothy Lafaele (Japan)★, Michael Little★, Pauliasi Manu★, Semisi Masirewa★, Craig Millar★, Brendan O'Connor, Hayden Parker ★, Sam Prattley★, Dan Pryor★, Kara Pryor★, Rene Ranger★, Tom Rowe, Ben Te'o (England), Luke Thompson (Japan)★, Josh Timu★, Hendrik Tui (Japan)★ (England), Nathan Vella★, Alex Woonton (Cook Islands)★

Top League

Canon Eagles:	Israel Dagg, Blair Tweed★
Coca Cola Red Sparks:	Solomon King, James Marshall★, Will Mangos, Joe Tupe, Will Tupou (Japan), Nathan Vella★

Hino Red Dolphins:	Hayden Cripps (Japan), Jack Debreczeni, Joel Everson, Gillies Kaka, Nili Latu (Tonga), Pauliasi Manu, Liaki Moli, Ash Parker (Japan), Chance Peni-Ataera, Augustine Pulu
Honda Heat:	Josh Bekhuis, Baden Kerr, Lomano Lemeki (Japan), Lelia Masaga, David Milo, Tetuhi Roberts, Tomasi Soqeta (Fiji), Shaun Treeby
Kobelco Steelers:	Nigel Ah Wong, Fraser Anderson (Tonga), Richard Buckman, Dan Carter, Nick Ealey, Andrew Ellis, Tom Franklin, Sefo Kautai, Tim Lafaele (Japan), Charlie Lawrence, Ata'ata Moeakiola (Japan), Hayden Parker, Brodie Retallick, Aidan Rodd, Jeff Thwaites★, Toni Vaihu, Matt Vant Leven
Kubota Spears	Ryan Crotty, Wharenui Hawera
Munakata Sanix Blues:	Mark Abbott, Siliva Ahio, Sam Chongkit, Jason Emery, Josh Gordon, Karne Hesketh (Japan), Jone Macilai★, Hare Makiri, Jake Paringatai, Dan Pryor, Bryce Robbins (Japan), Andre Taylor★
NEC Green Rockets:	Stephen Donald, Sam Henwood, Jack Lam (Samoa), Hapakuki Moala- Liavaa, Maritino Nemani, Tim O'Malley, George Risale, Amanaki Savieti, Lolagi Visinia, Sanaila Waqa
NTT Shining Arcs:	Brackin Karauria-Henry (Australia), Luteru Laulala, Christian Leali'ifano (Australia), Leilua Murphy, Sekonaia Pole, Isaac Ross, Jimmy Tupou
Ricoh Black Rams:	Colin Bourke, Mike Broadhurst (Japan), Elliot Dixon, Tamati Ellison, Ben Funnell, Damon Leasuasu, Josh Mau, Matt McGahan, Robbie Robinson (Japan), Jacob Skeen, Alex Woonton (Cook Islands)
Panasonic Wild Knights:	Asaeli Ai Valu (Japan), Harrison Brewer★, Wyatt Crockett, Ash Dixon★, Michael Hobbs, Justin Ives (Japana), Craig Millar, Emerson Tamura-Paki, Matt Todd, Tevita Tupou, George Whitelock
Suntory Sun-Goliath:	Richard Judd, Joe Latta, Kosei Ono (Japan), Jordan Smiler (Australia), Hendrik Tui (Japan), Joe Wheeler
Toshiba Brave Lupus:	Tim Bateman, Lyndon Dunshea, Johnny Fa'auli, Michael Harris (Australia), Richard Kahui, Michael Leitch (Japan), Tevita Li, Tom Parsons, Jack Stratton
Toyota Industries Shuttles:	Scott Fuglistaller, Jono Hickey, Taleni Seu, Tevita Taufu'i (Tonga)
Toyota Verblitz:	Jamie Henry (Japan), Male Sa'u (Japan), Shneil Singh, Stephen Yates
Yamaha Jubilo:	Mose Tuiali'I, Malo Tuitama

Top Challenge

Kamaishi Seawaves:	Mike Fitzgerald, Morgan Mitchell, Cody Rei, Dallas Tatana (Japan)
Kintetsu Liners:	Jed Brown, Quade Cooper (Australia), Pasqualle Dunn, Iopu Iopu-Aso, Semi Masirewa, Mike Stolberg, Luke Thompson (Japan), Solomon T-Pole
Kurita Water Gush:	Jacob Ellison (Japan), Ben Paltridge
Kyuden Voltex:	Phil Burleigh (Scotland), Tom Rowe
Mazda Blue Zoomers:	Joseph Kamana (Cook Islands)

Mitsubishi Dynaboars:	Albert Anae, Heiden Bedwell-Curtis, Dan Hawkins, Jackson Hemopo, Tevita Lepolo, Michael Little, Alaia'sa Roland, Matt Vaega, James Wilson
NTT Docomo:	Marty Banks, Jamason Fa'anana-Schultz (USA), Lincoln McClutchie, Keepa Mewett, Liam Squire
Shimizu Blue Sharks:	Pek Cowan (Australia)

PARAGUAY
Superliga Americana

Olimpia Lions: Matt Matich

ROMANIA
Continental Shield

Timisoara Saracens:	Viliami Moala, Michael Stewart, Stephen Shennan (Romania), Jack Umaga (Romania)
Bucharest Wolves:	Paula Kinikinilau (Romania), Luke Samoa (Romania), Mike Wiringi (Romania)

RUSSIA
Continental Shield:

Yenisei: Thomas Halse, Richard Kingi (Australia), Robbie Malneek

SCOTLAND
Guinness Pro 14

Edinburgh:	Simon Berghan (Scotland), Murray Douglas, Simon Hickey, Mungo Mason (Scotland)
Glasgow:	Corey Flynn, Callum Gibbins, Nick Grigg (Scotland), Siosiua Halanukonuka (Tonga), Aki Seuli, Samu Vunisa (Italy)

SPAIN
Supercopa

Alcobendas:	Brad Linkater (Spain), Manawanua Williams
Bathco:	Rex Pollock
Ciencias Cajasol:	Sione Fifita, Tomas Hanham, Grayson Knapp, Patrick Tulafasa
El Salvador:	James Faiva (Tonga), Liam Fitzsimons, Matthew Smith, Joshua Tafili, Sione Teu, Jacob Wainwright, Kade Whiting
Ordizia:	Jo Apikotoa, Pohutukawa Leauma, Siosiua Moala
Santboiana:	Pita Anae, Joseph Ikenasio, Faavae Sila, Afa Tauli (Spain)
VRAC Quesos:	Broc Hooper, Tuki Raimona

SOUTH AFRICA
Super Rugby

Bulls: Nafi Tu'itavake (Tonga)

UNITED STATES
Major League Rugby

Austin Herd:	Dan Faleafa (Tonga), Frank Halai, Potu Leavasa (Samoa)
Colorado Raptors:	Mickey Bateman, Michael Curry, Peter Dahl (USA)*, Mason Emerson, Marco Fepuleai, Digby Ioane (Australia), Rene Ranger, Samuel Slade, Michael Stewart, Murphy Taramai*, Zak Taulafo (Samoa)
Houston Sabercats:	Tim Cadwallader, Mathew Faoagali*, Taylor Howden, Siua Maile (Tonga), Baden Wardlaw*, Boyd Wiggins
New England Free Jacks:	Sam Beard, Donald Brighouse (Samoa), Naulia Dawai (Fiji), Tolu Fahamakioa (Samoa), Brad Hemopo, Josh Larsen (Canada), Liam Steel, Beaudein Waaka, Poasa Waqanibau (Fiji)
New Orleans Gold:	Tony Lamborn*, Kane Thompson (Samoa)
Old Glory DC:	Jamason Fa'anana-Schultz (USA), Gordon Fullerton, Apisai Naikatini (Fiji), Jason Robertson, Mike Sosene-Fegai (USA), Dylan Taikato-Simpson, Danny Tusitala (Samoa)
Rugby United New York:	Kara Pryor
San Diego Legion:	Chris Eves, Devereaux Ferris, Jordan Manihera*, Ma'a Nonu
Seattle Seawolves:	Brad Tucker
Utah Warriors:	Ara Elkington, Logan Daniels*, Jahmin Gernhoefer, Blake Hohaia, Johnny Ika (Tonga)*, Jackson Kaka, Dwayne Polataivao (Samoa), Hagen Schulte (Germany), James Semple*, Les Soloai*, Adam Thomson*, Kalolo Tuiloma, Fetu'u Vainikolo (Tonga)

URUGUAY
Superliga Americana

Penarol:	Afa Pakalani (Tonga)

WALES
Guinness Pro 14

Cardiff Blues:	Willis Halaholo, Rey Lee-Lo (Samoa), Filo Paulo (Samoa), Nick Williams
Dragons:	Jacob Botica, Brandon Nansen (Samoa)
Ospreys:	Gareth Anscombe (Wales), Ma'afu Fia (Tonga), Marty McKenzie
Llanelli Scarlets:	Danny Drake, Kieron Fonotia (Samoa), Sam Lousi (Tonga), Johnny McNicholl (Wales), Hadleigh Parkes (Wales), Blade Thomson (Scotland)

NEW ZEALAND ORIGIN AND FIRST-CLASS PLAYERS CAPPED OVERSEAS, 2019

Compiled by John Lea

Provincial Union and Year indicate most recent first-class play when applicable.

Player	Country	Provincial Union	Year
Sekope Kepu	Australia	Counties Manukau	2007
Christian Leali'ifano	Australia	Waikato	2010
Lukhan Sakalaia-Lolo	Australia	Auckland	-
Taniela Tupou	Australia	Auckland	-
Jordan Uelese	Australia	Wellington	-
Josh Reeves	Brazil	Canterbury	2018
Tyler Ardron	Canada	Chiefs	2019
Hubert Buydens	Canada	Manawatu	2014
Jake Ilnicki	Canada	Manawatu	2016
Josh Larsen	Canada	Otago	2018
Evan Olmstead	Canada	Auckland	2018
Jordan Olsen	Canada	Northland	2019
Djustice Sears-Duru	Canada	North Otago	2014
Othniel Joseph	Cook Islands Sevens	Auckland	-
Junior Kiria	Cook Islands Sevens	Auckland	-
Ben Marsters	Cook Islands Sevens	Auckland	-
Junior Napara	Cook Islands Sevens	Auckland	-
Stephen Willis	Cook Islands Sevens	Auckland	-
Joshua Brajkovic	Croatia	Auckland	-
Piers Francis	England	Blues	2017
Willie Heinz	England	Canterbury	2015
Nathan Hughes	England	Auckland	2013
Brad Shields	England	Hurricanes	2018
Ben Te'o	England	Auckland	-
Mako Vunipola	England	Auckland	-
Leroy Atalifo	Fiji	Canterbury	2017
Tevita Cavubati	Fiji	Tasman	2014
Johnny Dyer	Fiji	South Canterbury	2016
Temo Mayanavanua	Fiji XV	Northland	2019
Sikeli Nabou	Fiji	Counties Manukau	2018
Nemani Nagusa	Fiji	Tasman	2012
Filipo Nakosi	Fiji	Northland	2015

Player	Country	Provincial Union	Year
Patrick Osborne	Fiji	Highlanders	2017
Apisoloma Ratuniyarawa	Fiji	North Harbour	2012
John Stewart	Fiji Warriors	Poverty Bay	2010
Samuela Tawake	Fiji XV	Manawatu	2019
Asaeli Tikoirotuma	Fiji XV	Manawatu	2014
Ben Volavola	Fiji	North Harbour	2017
Dominiko Waqaniborotu	Fiji	Waikato	2010
Uini Atonio	France	Counties Manukau	2011
Virimi Vakatawa	France	Canterbury	-
Vito Lammers	Germany	Tasman	-
Hagen Schulte	Germany	Buller	2015
Nathan De Thierry	Hong Kong	Counties Manukau	2016
Josh Dowsing	Hong Kong	Counties Manukau	2016
Ruan Du Plooy	Hong Kong Dragons	Waikato	2016
Tau Koloamatangi	Hong Kong	Waikato	2016
Bundee Aki	Ireland	Counties Manukau	2014
Joey Carberry	Ireland	Auckland	-
Dean Budd	Italy	Northland	2011
Jayden Hayward	Italy	Taranaki	2012
Jimmy Tuivaiti	Italy	North Harbour	2014
Asaeli Ai Valu	Japan	Otago	-
Shota Horie	Japan	Otago	2012
Timothy Lafaele	Japan	Auckland	-
Michael Leitch	Japan	Chiefs	2017
Lomano Lemeki	Japan	Auckland	-
Ata'ata Moeakiola	Japan	Chiefs	2019
Kaito Shigeno	Japan	Auckland	2015
Fumiaki Tanaka	Japan	Highlanders	2016
Luke Thompson	Japan	Canterbury	-
Hendrik Tui	Japan	Auckland	-
Will Tupou	Japan	Auckland	-
Willie Ambaka	Kenya Sevens	Manawatu	2017
Josh Gascoigne	Netherlands	Waikato	2016
Liam McBride	Netherlands	Taranaki	2015
Shaun Atamu	Niue	Auckland	-
Lepau Feau	Niue Sevens	Auckland	-
Anthony Freddie	Niue	Wellington	-
Randy Freddie	Niue	Manawatu	-

Player	Country	Provincial Union	Year
Luka Gibb	Niue	Wellington	-
Khalum Halo	Niue	Wellington	-
Abraham Jackson	Niue	Horowhenua-Kapiti	-
Sebastian Jackson	Niue	Horowhenua-Kapiti	-
Jahsiah Keil	Niue Sevens	Auckland	-
Nicholas Laufoli	Niue	Auckland	-
Austin Masiutama	Niue Sevens	Auckland	-
Leslie McIlroy-Taleni	Niue Sevens	Auckland	-
Dawson Mele	Niue Sevens	Auckland	-
Bono Napota	Niue Sevens	Auckland	-
Logan Norman	Niue	Bay of Plenty	-
Cyruss Payne	Niue	Auckland	-
Keonte Tiauli	Niue Sevens	Auckland	-
Juston Vaimalu	Niue Sevens	Counties Manukau	-
Vaitagutu Williams	Niue Sevens	Auckland	-
Donald Coleman	Philippines Sevens	North Harbour	-
David Robinson-Polkey	Philippines	Auckland	-
Michael Ala'alatoa	Samoa	Canterbury	2019
Paul Alo-Emile	Samoa	Waikato	2013
Thomas Alosio	Samoa Sevens	Wellington	2015
Pele Cowley	Samoa	Waikato	2017
Elia Elia	Samoa	Canterbury	-
Piua Fa'asalele	Samoa	Wellington	-
Auvasa Faleali'i	Samoa	Auckland	2009
Ed Fidow	Samoa	Auckland	-
Losi Filipo	Samoa Sevens	Wellington	2019
Kieron Fonotia	Samoa	Tasman	2016
TJ Ioane	Samoa	Otago	2014
Jack Lam	Samoa	Waikato	2013
James Lay	Samoa	Bay of Plenty	2018
Jordan Lay	Samoa	Bay of Plenty	2017
Kane Leaupepe	Samoa	Hurricanes	2019
Rey Lee-Lo	Samoa	Hurricanes	2015
Alapati Leuia	Samoa	Wellington	2014
D'Angelo Leuila	Samoa A	Auckland	2019
Meli Matavao	Samoa	Otago	2018
Motu Matu'u	Samoa	Hurricanes	2015
Tim Nanai-Willliams	Samoa	Chiefs	2017

Player	Country	Provincial Union	Year
Ray Niuia	Samoa	Highlanders	2018
Filo Paulo	Samoa	North Harbour	2012
Tusi Pisi	Samoa	Hurricanes	2013
Dwayne Polataivao	Samoa	Auckland	2015
Paul Scanlan	Samoa Sevens	Auckland	-
Henry Stowers	Samoa	Bay of Plenty	2017
Sakaria Taulafo	Samoa A	Tasman	2009
Jamie-Jerry Taulagi	Samoa	Hawke's Bay	2018
Ahsee Tuala	Samoa	Counties Manukau	2014
Belgium Tuatagaloa	Samoa	Wellington	2014
Danny Tusitala	Samoa Sevens	Auckland	-
Josh Tyrell	Samoa	North Harbour	2017
Chris Vui	Samoa	North Harbour	2016
Simon Berghan	Scotland	Canterbury	-
Nick Grigg	Scotland	Wellington	-
Sean Maitland	Scotland	Canterbury	2012
Byron McGuigan	Scotland	Bay of Plenty	2014
Blade Thomson	Scotland	Hurricanes	2018
Brad Linklater	Spain	Auckland	-
Afa Tauli	Spain	Manawatu	-
Sione Anga'aelangi	Tonga	Counties Manukau	2016
Paea Fa'anunu	Tonga	Canterbury	2013
James Faiva	Tonga	Counties Manukau	-
Daniel Faleafa	Tonga	Northland	2012
Ma'afu Fia	Tonga	Manawatu	2015
Leva Fifita	Tonga	Waikato	2017
Ziegfried Fisi'ihoi	Tonga	Chiefs	2017
Samisoni Fisilau	Tonga	Bay of Plenty	2015
Latiume Fosita	Tonga	Auckland	2018
Leon Fukofuka	Tonga	Auckland	2018
Kali Hala	Tonga	Counties Manukau	2019
Siosiua Halanukonuka	Tonga	Tasman	2017
Sione Ika	Tonga Sevens	Hawke's Bay	2019
Fine Inisi	Tonga Sevens	North Harbour	2019
Lotu Inisi	Tonga Sevens	North Harbour	2019
Zane Kapeli	Tonga	Bay of Plenty	2018
Fotu Lokotui	Tonga	Counties Manukau	2018
Vili Lolohea	Tonga	Tasman	2017

Player	Country	Provincial Union	Year
Sam Lousi	Tonga	Wellington	2018
Siua Maile	Tonga	Canterbury	-
Nasi Manu	Tonga	Highlanders	2015
Otumaka Mausia	Tonga	Auckland	2017
Kurt Morath	Tonga	Taranaki	2008
Paul Ngauamo	Tonga	Canterbury	2011
Atieli Pakalani	Tonga	Auckland	2010
Fetuli Paea	Tonga	Tasman	2019
Siale Piutau	Tonga	Highlanders	2012
Sonatane Takulua	Tonga	Northland	2014
Latu Talakai	Tonga	Waikato	2017
Ben Tameifuna	Tonga	Waikato	2015
John Tapueluelu	Tonga	Otago	-
Nafi Tuitavake	Tonga	North Harbour	2015
Ma'ama Vaipulu	Tonga	Chiefs	2016
Telusa Veianu	Tonga	Crusaders	2013
Cooper Vuna	Tonga	Auckland	-
Jamason Fa'anana-Schultz	United States	Auckland	2017
Eric Fry	United States	Manawatu	2012
Tony Lamborn	United States	Southland	2018
Paul Lasike	United States	Auckland	-
Gannon Moore	United States	North Harbour	-
Mike Sosene-Feagai	United States	Auckland	2019
Gareth Anscombe	Wales	Auckland	2014
Johnny McNicholl	Wales XV	Canterbury	2016
Hadleigh Parkes	Wales	Auckland	2014

OVERSEAS PLAYERS IN NEW ZEALAND FIRST-CLASS RUGBY 2019

For previously capped players the most recent year and level of selection are shown. Some players have since, or soon will, also become eligible for New Zealand.

Player	Country	Year	NZ Team in 2019
Robbie Abel	Australia Schools	2007	Auckland
Tyler Campbell	Australia Schools	2015	Waikato
Jack Debreczeni	Australia Schools	2011	Northland
Sef Fa'agase	Australia XV	2016	Wellington
Matthew Garland	Australia Schools	2009	Bay of Plenty
Andrew Kellaway	Australia Under 20	2015	Counties Manukau
Chris Kuidrani	Australia Under 20	2011	Counties Manukau
Junior Laloifi	Australia Sevens	2013	Horowhenua-Kapiti
Tyrel Lomax	Australia Under 20	2016	Tasman
Tim Metcher	Australia Under 20	2011	Counties Manukau
Hugh Roach	Australia Under 20	2012	Tasman
Faalelei Sione	Australia Under 20	2016	Manawatu
Toby Smith	Australia	2017	Hurricanes
Reegan O'Gorman	Canada	2017	South Canterbury
Howard Packman	England Under 20	2015	North Otago
Henry Purdy	England Under 20	2014	Otago
Alex Hodgman	Fiji Under 20	2012	Auckland
Mitieli Kaloudigibeci	Fiji	Uncapped	Buller
Taniela Koroi	Fiji	2016	Auckland
Apisai Naikatini	Fiji	2014	Waikato
Viliame Rarasea	Fiji Under 20	2014	Counties Manukau
Ropate Rinakama	Fiji	2018	Northland
Asaeli Sorovaki	Fiji Under 20	2015	Taranaki
Pita-Gus Sowakula	Fiji	Uncapped	Taranaki
Oliver Jager	Ireland Under 18	2013	Canterbury
Conan O'Donnell	Ireland Under 20	2016	Counties Manukau
Josh Furno	Italy	2017	Wellington
Tim Bond	Japan A	2012	Waikato
Malgene Ilaua	Japan	2017	Counties Manukau
Harumichi Tatekawa	Japan	2018	Otago
Keisuke Uchida	Japan	2017	Tasman
Jared Adams	Samoa Under 20	2015	Auckland

Player	Country	Year	NZ Team in 2019
Michael Ala'alatoa	Samoa Under 20	2011	Canterbury
Nathaniel Apa	Samoa Under 20	2014	Counties Manukau
Donald Brighouse	Samoa	2018	Taranaki
Folau Fakatava	Samoa	Uncapped	Hawke's Bay
Moo Moo Falaniko	Samoa Under 20	2018	Wairarapa Bush
Marco Fepuleai	Samoa Under 20	2015	Auckland
Losi Filipo	Samoa Sevens	2017	Wellington
Neria Fomai	Samoa Sevens	2018	Hawke's Bay
Stacey Ili	Samoa	2018	Hawke's Bay
Josh Ioane	Samoa Under 20	2015	Otago
Fa'alele Iosua	Samoa A	2018	South Canterbury
Orbyn Leger	Samoa Under 20	2015	Counties Manukau
Pisi Leilua	Samoa Under 20	2015	Northland
Jeff Lepa	Samoa	2016	Buller
Melani Nanai	Samoa Under 20	2012	Blues
Ben Nee Nee	Samoa	2018	North Harbour
Pepesana Patafilo	Samoa Under 20	2015	Wellington
Savelio Ropati	Samoa Sevens	2017	Counties Manukau
Hisa Sasagi	Samoa	2018	Otago
Howard Sililoto	Samoa A	2018	Southland
Galu Taufale	Samoa	2017	Wellington
Jordan Taufua	Samoa Under 20	2011	Tasman
Jonathan Taumateine	Samoa Under 20	2015	Counties Manukau
Tanielu Tele'a	Samoa Under 20	2017	Auckland
Chase Tiatia	Samoa Under 20	2015	Bay of Plenty
Hugh Blake	Scotland Sevens	2018	Bay of Plenty
Hamilton Burr	Scotland Under 20	2016	Waikato
Ross Geldenhuys	South Africa	Uncapped	Bay of Plenty
Rowan Gouws	South Africa	Uncapped	Otago
Dylan Nel	South Africa	Uncapped	Otago
Vaea Fifita	Tonga Under 18	2010	Wellington
Shannon Frizzell	Tonga Under 20	2014	Tasman
Billy Fukofuka	Tonga Under 20	2015	Southland
Kali Hala	Tonga	2017	Counties Manukau
Samisoni Taukeiaho	Tonga Under 15	2013	Waikato
Mike Sosene-Feagai	United States	2016	Auckland
Declan Smith	Wales Under 20	2016	Tasman
Dan Suter	Wales	2013	South Canterbury

ALL BLACKS
TEST MATCH RECORD

to January 1, 2020

Opponents	Played	Won	Lost	Drawn	For	Against
Argentina	29	28	–	1	1150	422
Australia	166	115	44	7	3552	2365
British Isles	41	30	7	4	700	399
Canada	6	6	–	–	376	54
England	42	33	8	1	992	594
Fiji	5	5	–	–	364	50
France	61	48	12	1	1596	801
Georgia	1	1	–	–	43	10
Ireland	32	29	2	1	917	389
Italy	14	14	–	–	820	131
Japan	4	4	–	–	351	61
Namibia	2	2	–	–	129	23
Pacific Islands	1	1	–	–	41	26
Portugal	1	1	–	–	108	13
Romania	2	2	–	–	99	14
Samoa	7	7	–	–	411	72
Scotland	31	29	–	2	922	349
South Africa	99	59	36	4	2050	1577
Tonga	6	6	–	–	418	42
United States	3	3	–	–	171	15
Wales	35	32	3	–	1110	391
World XV	3	2	1	–	94	69
	602	**465**	**115**	**22**	**16,854**	**8,025**

The All Blacks have won 77.24 per cent of all test matches.

ALL BLACK STATISTICS

to January 1, 2020

LEADING ALL BLACK APPEARANCES IN ALL MATCHES

R.H. McCaw	149	S.S. Wilson	85	M.W. Shaw	69
C.E. Meads	133	B.R. Smith	85	D.S. Coles	69
K.F. Mealamu	133	B.J. Barrett	84	S.J. Cane	69
S.B.T. Fitzpatrick	128	I.J. Clarke	83	B.J. Lochore	68
K.J. Read	128	A.K. Hore	83	C.W. Dowd	67
T.D. Woodcock	118	J. Kaino	83	C.R. Jack	67
A.M. Haden	117	S.C. McDowall	81	A.D. Oliver	67
S.L. Whitelock	117	B.A. Retallick	81	G.M. Somerville	67
I.A. Kirkpatrick	113	J.F. Umaga	79	I.J.A. Dagg	66
B.G. Williams	113	G.J. Fox	78	G.A. Knight	66
D.W. Carter	112	R.W. Loe	78	A.J. Whetton	65
O.T. Franks	108	A.J. Williams	78	T.T.R. Perenara	65
I.D. Jones	105	W.J. Whineray	77	A.R. Sutherland	64
M.A. Nonu	104	W.K. Little	75	T.J. Wright	64
J.M. Muliaina	102	M.N. Jones	74	D.C. Howlett	63
B.J. Robertson	102	J.T. Lomu	73	K.L. Skinner	63
G.W. Whetton	101	P.A.T. Weepu	73	R. So'oialo	63
Z.V. Brooke	100	W.W.V. Crockett	72	M.R. Brewer	61
J.J. Kirwan	96	A.P. Mehrtens	72	M.J. Brownlie	61
C.G. Smith	94	M.G. Mexted	72	G.N.K. Mourie	61
A.L. Smith	92	J.W. Wilson	71	R.W. Norton	61
D.B. Clarke	89	R.M. Brooke	69	T.C. Randell	61
J.W. Marshall	88	O.M. Brown	69	D. Young	61
S.M. Going	86	F.E. Bunce	69	C.M. Cullen	60
K.R. Tremain	86	J.T. Rokocoko	69	B.C. Thorn	60

LEADING POINTS-SCORERS IN
ALL MATCHES FOR NEW ZEALAND

		Matches	Points
D.W. Carter	2003–15	112	1598
G.J. Fox	1985–93	78	1067
A.P. Mehrtens	1995–2004	72	994
D.B. Clarke	1956–64	89	781
B.J. Barrett	2012–19	84	655
W.F. McCormick	1965–71	44	453
B.G. Williams	1970–78	113	401t
C.J. Spencer	1995–2004	44	383
W.J. Wallace	1903–08	51	379
A.R. Hewson	1979–84	34	357
J.F. Karam	1972–75	42	345
A.W. Cruden	2010–17	50	322
K.J. Crowley	1983–91	35	316
J.W. Wilson	1993–2001	71	299
M.F. Nicholls	1921–30	51	284
J.J. Kirwan	1984–94	96	275
R.G. Wilson	1976–80	25	272
C.M. Cullen	1996–2002	60	266
R.M. Deans	1983–85	19	252
J.A. Gallagher	1986–89	41	251

includes a penalty try

LEADING TRY-SCORERS IN ALL MATCHES

		Matches	Tries
J.J. Kirwan	1984–94	96	67
B.G. Williams	1970–78	113	66t
C.M. Cullen	1996–2002	60	52
I.A. Kirkpatrick	1967–77	113	50
J.W. Wilson	1993–2001	71	50
S.S. Wilson	1976–83	85	50
D.C. Howlett	2000–07	63	49
T.J. Wright	1986–92	64	49t
J. Hunter	1905–08	36	48
J.T. Rokocoko	2003–10	69	47
B.G. Fraser	1979–84	55	46
S.J. Savea	2012–17	54	46
G.B. Batty	1972–77	56	45
J.T. Lomu	1994–2002	73	43
Z.V. Brooke	1987–97	100	42
M.J. Dick	1963–70	55	42

ᵗincludes a penalty try

MOST APPEARANCES IN INTERNATIONALS

R.H. McCaw	2001–15	148	G.M. Somerville	2000–08	66
K.F. Mealamu	2002–15	132	T.T.R. Perenara	2014–19	64
K.J. Read	2008–19	127	J.J. Kirwan	1984–94	63
T.D. Woodcock	2002–15	118	J.T. Lomu	1994–2002	63
S.L. Whitelock	2010–19	117	R.M. Brooke	1992–99	62
D.W. Carter	2003–15	112	D.C. Howlett	2000–07	62
O.T. Franks	2009–19	108	R. So'oialo	2002–09	62
M.A. Nonu	2003–15	103	C.W. Dowd	1993–2000	60
J.M. Muliaina	2003–11	100	J.W. Wilson	1993–2001	60
C.G. Smith	2004–15	94	A.D. Oliver	1997–2007	59
S.B.T. Fitzpatrick	1986–97	92	B.C. Thorn	2003–11	59
A.L. Smith	2012–19	92	Z.V. Brooke	1987–97	58
B.R. Smith	2009–19	84	G.W. Whetton	1981–91	58
A.K. Hore	2002–13	83	C.M. Cullen	1996–2002	58
B.J. Barrett	2012–19	83	S. Williams	2010–19	58
J. Kaino	2004–17	81	B.T. Kelleher	1999–2007	57
J.W. Marshall	1995–2005	81	O.M. Brown	1992–98	56
B.A. Retallick	2012–19	81	L.R. MacDonald	2000–08	56
I.D. Jones	1990–99	79	F.E. Bunce	1992–97	55
A.J. Williams	2002–12	77	M.N. Jones	1987–98	55
J.F. Umaga	1997–2005	74	C.E. Meads	1957–71	55
W.W.V. Crockett	2009–17	71	J.A. Kronfeld	1995–2000	54
P.A.T. Weepu	2004–13	71	S.J. Savea	2012–17	54
A.P. Mehrtens	1995–2004	70	C.S. Jane	2008–14	53
D.S. Coles	2012–19	69	Q.J. Cowan	2004–11	51
J.T. Rokocoko	2003–10	68	T.C. Randell	1997–2002	51
S.J. Cane	2012–19	68	W.K. Little	1990–98	50
C.R. Jack	2001–07	67	R.D. Thorne	1999–2007	50
I.J.A. Dagg	2010–17	66	C.J.Taylor	2015-19	50

MOST POINTS FOR NEW ZEALAND IN INTERNATIONALS

	Matches	Tries	Con	PG	DG	Mark	Points
D.W. Carter	112	29	293	281	8	–	1598
A.P. Mehrtens	70	7	169	188	10	–	967
B.J. Barrett	83	36	149	55	2	–	649
G.J. Fox	46	1	118	128	7	–	645
A.W. Cruden	50	5	63	56	1	–	322
C.J. Spencer	35	14	49	41	–	–	291
D.C. Howlett	62	49	–	–	–	–	245
C.M. Cullen	58	46	3	–	–	–	236
J.W. Wilson	60	44	1	3	1	–	234
J.T. Rokocoko	68	46	–	–	–	–	230
S.J. Savea	54	46	–	–	–	–	230
D.B. Clarke	31	2	33	38	5	2	207
A.R. Hewson	19	4	22	43	4	–	201
B.R. Smith	84	39	–	–	–	–	195
J.T. Lomu	63	37	–	–	–	–	185
J.F. Umaga	74	37ᵗ	–	–	–	–	185
T.E. Brown	18	5	43	20	–	–	171
J.M. Muliaina	100	34	–	–	–	–	170
M.A. Nonu	103	31	–	–	–	–	155
C.L. McAlister	30	7	26	22	–	–	153
L.R. MacDonald	56	15ᵗ	25	7	–	–	146
S.W. Sivivatu	45	29	–	–	–	–	145
J.J. Kirwan	63	35¹	–	–	–	–	143
R.H. McCaw	148	28ᵗ	–	–	–	–	140
I.J.A. Dagg	66	26	1	2	–	–	138
R. Mo'unga	17	3	45	9	·	·	132
C.G. Smith	94	26	–	–	–	–	130
K.J. Read	127	26	–	–	–	–	130
W.F. McCormick	16	–	23	24	1	–	121
J.W. Marshall	81	24	–	–	–	–	120
R.E. Ioane	29	24	–	–	–	–	120
S.D. Culhane	6	1	32	15	–	–	114
K.J. Crowley	19	5	5	23	2	–	105
N.J. Evans	16	5	30	6	–	–	103
P.A.T. Weepu	71	7	10	16	–	–	103

1 includes three tries at five points
t includes penalty try

MOST STARTS IN EACH POSITION
FOR NEW ZEALAND IN INTERNATIONALS

Fullback	J.M. Muliaina	2003–11	83	No 8	K.J. Read	2009–19	118
Wing	J.T. Rokocoko	2003–10	66	Flanker	R.H. McCaw	2001–15	139
Centre	C.G. Smith	2004–15	90	Lock	S.L. Whitelock	2010–19	97
2nd five-eighth	M.A. Nonu	2003–15	81	Prop	T.D. Woodcock	2002–15	105
1st five-eighth	D.W. Carter	2004–15	94	Hooker	S.B.T. Fitzpatrick	1986–97	91
Halfback	A.L. Smith	2012–19	84	Substitute	K.F. Mealamu	2002–15	55

The player must have started the match in that position. Appearances as replacements are not included except in this case Mealamu.

MOST TRIES FOR NEW ZEALAND IN INTERNATIONALS

	Matches	Tries		Matches	Tries
D.C. Howlett	62	49	M.A. Nonu	103	31
C.M. Cullen	58	46	D.W. Carter	112	29
J.T. Rokocoko	68	46	S.W. Sivivatu	45	29
S.J. Savea	54	46	R.H. McCaw	148	28t
J.W. Wilson	60	44	C.G. Smith	94	26
B.R. Smith	85	39	I.J.A. Dagg	66	26
J.T. Lomu	63	37	K.J. Read	127	26
J.F. Umaga	74	37t	J.W. Marshall	81	24
B.J. Barrett	83	36	R.E. Ioane	29	24
J.J. Kirwan	63	35	F.E. Bunce	55	20
J.M. Muliaina	100	34			

Includes one penalty try

MOST TRIES IN AN INTERNATIONAL

M.C.G. Ellis	v Japan, 1995	6	J.W. Wilson	v Samoa, 1999	4
J.W. Wilson	v Fiji, 1997	5	J.M. Muliaina	v Canada, 2003	4
D. McGregor	v England, 1905	4	S.W. Sivivatu	v Fiji, 2005	4
C.I. Green	v Fiji, 1987	4	Z.R. Guildford	v Canada, 2011	4
J.A. Gallagher	v Fiji, 1987	4	B.J. Barrett	v Australia, 2018	4
J.J. Kirwan	v Wales, 1988	4	J.M. Barrett	v Italy, 2018	4
J.T. Lomu	v England, 1995	4	G.C. Bridge	v Tonga, 2019	4
C.M. Cullen	v Scotland, 1996	4			

MOST PENALTY GOALS IN AN INTERNATIONAL

A.P. Mehrtens	v Australia, 1999	9	D.W. Carter	v Australia, 2007	7
A.P. Mehrtens	v France, 2000	9	P.A.T. Weepu	v Argentina, 2011	7
G.J. Fox	v W Samoa, 1993	7	B.J. Barrett	v BI Lions, 2017	7
A.P. Mehrtens	v South Africa, 1999	7			

MOST CONVERSIONS IN AN INTERNATIONAL

S.D. Culhane	v Japan, 1995	20	D.W. Carter	v Canada, 2003	9
N.J. Evans	v Portugal, 2007	14	C.R. Slade	v Japan, 2011	9
T.E. Brown	v Tonga, 2000	12	G.J. Fox	v Italy, 1987	8
L.R. MacDonald	v Tonga, 2003	12	G.J. Fox	v Wales, 1988	8
T.E. Brown	v Italy, 1999	11	A.P. Mehrtens	v Italy, 2002	8
G.J. Fox	v Fiji, 1987	10	R. Mo'unga	v Canada, 2019	8
C.J. Spencer	v Argentina, 1997	10	J.M. Barrett	v Namibia, 2019	8

HIGHEST POINTS-SCORERS IN AN INTERNATIONAL

	Opponent	Tries	Con	PG	DG	Points
S.D. Culhane	Japan, 1995[1]	1	20	–	–	45
T.E. Brown	Italy, 1999	1	11	3	–	36
D.W. Carter	Lions, 2005	2	4	5	–	33
C.J. Spencer	Argentina, 1997[1]	2	10	1	–	33
A.P. Mehrtens	Ireland, 1997	1	5	6	–	33
N.J. Evans	Portugal, 2007	1	14	–	–	33
T.E. Brown	Tonga, 2000	1	12	1	–	32
M.C.G. Ellis	Japan, 1995	6	–	–	–	30
B.J. Barrett	Australia, 2018	4	5	–	–	30
T.E. Brown	Samoa, 2001	3	3	3	–	30
A.P. Mehrtens	Australia, 1999	–	1	9	–	29
A.P. Mehrtens	France, 2000	–	1	9	–	29
L.R. MacDonald	Tonga, 2003	1	12	–	–	29
D.W. Carter	Canada, 2007	3	7	–	–	29
A.P. Mehrtens	Canada, 1995[1]	1	7	3	–	28
D.W. Carter	Wales, 2010	2	4	3	–	27
A.R. Hewson	Australia, 1982	1	2	5	1	26
G.J. Fox	Fiji, 1987	–	10	2	–	26
D.W. Carter	Wales, 2005	2	5	2	–	26
D.W. Carter	England, 2006	1	3	5	–	26
T.E. Brown	Samoa, 1999[1]	–	7	4	–	26
B.J. Barrett	Wales, 2016	2	5	2	–	26
D.W. Carter	South Africa, 2006	–	2	7	–	25
G.J. Fox	Western Samoa, 1993	–	2	7	–	25
J.W. Wilson	Fiji, 1997	5	–	–	–	25
C.J. Spencer	South Africa, 1997	1	4	4	–	25
D.W. Carter	France, 2004	1	4	4	–	25
W.F. McCormick	Wales, 1969	–	3	5	1	24
B.J. Barrett	Samoa, 2017	2	7	–	–	24
D.S. McKenzie	France, 2018	2	7	–	–	24

[1] *international debut*

NEW ZEALAND INTERNATIONAL CAPTAINS

R.H. McCaw	2004–15	110	J. Collins	2006–07	3
K.J. Read	2012–19	52	R.R. King	1937	3
S.B.T. Fitzpatrick	1992–97	51	D.J. Graham	1964	3
W.J. Whineray	1958–65	30	D.S. Loveridge	1980	3
R.D. Thorne	2002–07	23	K.F. Mealamu	2008–11	3
T.C. Randell	1998–2002	22	J.M. Muliaina	2009	3
J.F. Umaga	2004–05	21	F.J. Oliver	1978	3
G.N.K. Mourie	1977–82	19	J. Richardson	1924	3
B.J. Lochore	1966–70	18	F. Roberts	1910	3
A.G. Dalton	1981–85	17	R.W. Roberts	1914	3
G.W. Whetton	1990–91	15	S.J. Cane	2015–19	3
W.T. Shelford	1988–90	14	G.G. Aitken	1921	2
D.E. Kirk	1986–87	11	R.H. Duff	1956	2
T.J. Blackadder	2000	10	J.L. Griffiths	1936	2
A.R. Leslie	1974–76	10	A. McDonald	1913	2
A.D. Oliver	2001	10	N.A. Mitchell	1938	2
I.A. Kirkpatrick	1972–73	9	M.J. O'Leary	1913	2
C.G. Porter	1925–30	7	A.R. Reid	1957	2
F.R. Allen	1946–49	6	K.L. Skinner	1952	2
S.L. Whitelock	2017–19	6	J.B. Smith	1949	2
R.R. Elvidge	1949–50	5	P.B. Vincent	1956	2
R. So'oialo	2008–09	5	S.S. Wilson	1983	2
R.C. Stuart	1953–54	5	J. Duncan	1903	1
M.J. Brownlie	1928	4	P.W. Henderson	1995	1
D. Gallaher	1905–06	4	A.K. Hore	2011	1
M.J.B. Hobbs	1985–86	4	C.R. Laidlaw	1968	1
J. Hunter	1907–08	4	H.T. Lilburne	1929	1
P. Johnstone	1950–51	4	R.M. McKenzie	1938	1
F.D. Kilby	1932–34	4	J.R. Page	1934	1
J.E. Manchester	1935–36	4	E.J. Roberts	1921	1
J.W. Marshall	1997	4	B.R. Smith	2017	1
C.E. Meads	1971	4	J.C. Spencer	1905	1
R.W. Norton	1977	4	W.A. Strang	1931	1
J.W. Stead	1904–08	4	K.R. Tremain	1968	1
I.J. Clarke	1955	3	L.C. Whitelock	2018	1

HIGHEST SCORES IN TEST MATCHES

Opponent	Home		Away		Opponent	Home		Away	
Argentina	93–8	(1997)	54–18	(2012)	Namibia	–	–	58–14	(2015)
Australia	51–20	(2014)	54–34	(2017)	Pacific Islands	41–26	(2004)	–	
British Isles	48–18	(2005)	–		Portugal		–	108–13	(2007)
Canada	79–15	(2011)	68–8	(2003)	Romania		–	85–8	(2007)
England	64–22	(1998)	45–29	(1995)	Samoa	101–14	(2008)	25–16	(2015)
Fiji	91–0	(2005)	–		Scotland	69–20	(2000)	51–15	(1993)
								51–22	(2012)
France	61–10	(2007)	62–13	(2015)	South Africa	57–0	(2017)	57–15	(2016)
Georgia	–	–	43–10	(2015)	Tonga	102–0	(2000)	91–7	(2003)
Ireland	66–28	(2010)	63–15	(1997)	USA		–	74–6	(2014)
Italy	70–6	(1987)	101–3	(1999)	Wales	55–3	(2003)	53–37	(2003)
Japan	83–7	(2011)	145–17	(1995)					

MOST POINTS BY AN ALL BLACK AGAINST AN OPPONENT

Opponent	In an International			In a Career	
Argentina	33	C.J. Spencer	1997	103	G.J. Fox
Australia	30	B.J. Barrett	2018	366	D.W. Carter
British Isles	33	D.W. Carter	2005	46	A.R. Hewson
Canada	29	D.W. Carter	2007	47	D.W. Carter
England	26	D.W. Carter	2006	178	D.W. Carter
Fiji	26	G.J. Fox	1987	29	C.M. Cullen
France	29	A.P. Mehrtens	2000	146	D.W. Carter
Georgia	15	S.J. Savea	2015	15	S.J. Savea
Ireland	33	A.P. Mehrtens	1997	81	A.P. Mehrtens
Italy	36	T.E. Brown	1999	53	D.W. Carter
Japan	45	S.D. Culhane	1995	45	S.D. Culhane
Namibia	21	J.M. Barrett	2019	21	J.M. Barrett
Pacific Islands	11	D.W. Carter	2004	11	D.W. Carter
Portugal	33	N.J. Evans	2007	33	N.J. Evans
Romania	17	N.J. Evans	2007	17	N.J. Evans
Samoa	30	T.E. Brown	2001	56	T.E. Brown
Scotland	23	A.P. Mehrtens	1995	108	A.P. Mehrtens
South Africa	25	C.J. Spencer	1997	255	D.W. Carter
	25	D.W. Carter	2006		
Tonga	32	T.E. Brown	2000	32	T.E. Brown
USA	14	J.P. Preston	1991	14	J.P. Preston
Wales	27	D.W. Carter	2010	162	D.W. Carter

PLAYING RECORDS
OF NEW ZEALAND TEAMS
1884–2019

		Played	Won	Lost	Drawn	Points for	Points against
1884	in **New South Wales** and **New Zealand**	9	9	–	–	176	17
1893	in **New Zealand, New South Wales** and **Queensland**	11	10	1	–	175	48
1894	**New South Wales** in **New Zealand**	1	–	1	–	6	8
1896	**Queensland** in **New Zealand**	1	1	–	–	9	0
1897	in **New Zealand, New South Wales** and **Queensland**	11	9	2	–	238	83
1901	**New South Wales** in **New Zealand**	2	2	–	–	44	8
1903	in **Australia** and **New Zealand**	11	10	1	–	281	27
1904	**Great Britain** in **New Zealand**	1	1	–	–	9	3
1905	in **Australia** and **New Zealand**	7	4	1	2	89	30
	Australia in **New Zealand**	1	1	–	–	14	3
1905/06	in **the British Isles, France** and **North America**	35	34	1	–	976	59
1907	in **Australia**	8	6	1	1	115	53
1908	**Anglo-Welsh** in **New Zealand**	3	2	–	1	64	8
1910	in **Australia** and **New Zealand**	8	7	1	–	138	78
1913	**Australia** in **New Zealand**	4	3	1	–	79	52
	in **North America**	16	16	–	–	610	6
1914	in **Australia** and **New Zealand**	11	10	1	–	260	69
1920	in **Australia** and **New Zealand**	10	9	–	1	352	91
1921	**South Africa** and **New South Wales** in **New Zealand**	4	1	2	1	18	31
1922	in **Australia** and **New Zealand**	8	6	2	–	198	102
1923	**New South Wales** in **New Zealand**	3	3	–	–	91	26
1924/25	in **Australia, New Zealand, the British Isles, France** and **Canada**	38	36	2	–	981	180
1925	in **Australia** and **New Zealand**	8	6	2	–	132	67
	New South Wales in **New Zealand**	1	1	–	–	36	10
1926	in **Australia** and **New Zealand**	8	6	2	–	187	109
1928	in **South Africa** and **Australia**	23	17	5	1	397	153
	New South Wales in **New Zealand**	4	3	1	–	79	40
1929	in **Australia**	10	6	3	1	186	80
1930	**Great Britain** in **New Zealand**	5	4	1	–	87	40
1931	**Australia** in **New Zealand**	1	1	–	–	20	13
1932	in **Australia** and **New Zealand**	11	9	2	–	331	135
1934	in **Australia** and **New Zealand**	9	7	1	1	201	107
1935/36	in **the British Isles** and **Canada**	30	26	3	1	490	183
1936	**Australia** in **New Zealand**	3	3	–	–	65	32
1937	**South Africa** in **New Zealand**	3	1	2	–	25	37
1938	in **Australia**	9	9	–	–	279	73
1946	**Australia** in **New Zealand**	2	2	–	–	45	18
1947	in **Australia** and **New Zealand**	10	8	2	–	263	113
1949	in **South Africa**	25	14	7	4	241	157
	Australia in **New Zealand**	2	–	2	–	15	27

		Played	Won	Lost	Drawn	Points for	Points against
1950	**British Isles** in **New Zealand**	4	3	–	1	34	20
1951	in **Australia** and **New Zealand**	13	13	–	–	375	86
1952	**Australia** in **New Zealand**	2	1	1	–	24	22
1953/54	in the **British Isles, France** and **North America**	36	30	4	2	598	152
1955	**Australia** in **New Zealand**	3	2	1	–	27	16
1956	**South Africa** in **New Zealand**	4	3	1	–	41	29
1957	in **Australia** and **New Zealand**	14	13	1	–	472	94
1958	**Australia** in **New Zealand**	3	2	1	–	45	17
1959	**British Isles** in **New Zealand**	4	3	1	–	57	42
1960	in **Australia** and **South Africa**	32	26	4	2	645	187
1961	**France** in **New Zealand**	3	3	–	–	50	12
1962	in **Australia**	10	9	1	–	426	49
	Australia in **New Zealand**	3	2	–	1	28	17
1963	**England** in **New Zealand**	2	2	–	–	30	17
1963/64	in the **British Isles, France** and **Canada**	36	34	1	1	613	159
1964	**Australia** in **New Zealand**	3	2	1	–	37	32
1965	**South Africa** in **New Zealand**	4	3	1	–	55	25
1966	**British Isles** in **New Zealand**	4	4	–	–	79	32
1967	**Australia** in **New Zealand**	1	1	–	–	29	9
	in the **British Isles, France** and **Canada**	17	16	–	1	370	135
1968	in **Australia** and **Fiji**	12	12	–	–	460	66
	France in **New Zealand**	3	3	–	–	40	24
1969	**Wales** in **New Zealand**	2	2	–	–	52	12
1970	in **Australia** and **South Africa**	26	23	3	–	789	234
1971	**British Isles** in **New Zealand**	4	1	2	1	42	48
1972	**Internal Tour**	9	9	–	–	355	88
	Australia in **New Zealand**	3	3	–	–	97	26
1972/73	in the **British Isles, France** and **North America**	32	25	5	2	640	266
1973	**Internal Tour** and **England** in **New Zealand**	5	2	3	–	88	83
1974	in **Australia** and **Fiji**	13	12	–	1	446	73
	in **Ireland, Wales** and **England**	8	7	–	1	127	50
1975	**Scotland** in **New Zealand**	1	1	–	–	24	–
1976	**Ireland** in **New Zealand**	1	1	–	–	11	3
	in **South Africa**	24	18	6	–	610	291
	in **Argentina** and **Uruguay**	9	9	–	–	321	72
1977	**British Isles** in **New Zealand**	4	3	1	–	54	41
	in **France** and **Italy**	9	8	1	–	216	86
1978	**Australia** in **New Zealand**	3	2	1	–	51	48
	in the **British Isles**	18	17	1	–	364	147
1979	**France** in **New Zealand**	2	1	1	–	42	33
	in **Australia**	2	1	1	–	41	15
	Argentina in **New Zealand**	2	2	–	–	33	15
1979	in **England** and **Scotland**	11	10	1	–	192	95
1980	in **Australia** and **Fiji**	16	12	3	1	507	126

		Played	Won	Lost	Drawn	Points for	Points against
	Fiji in **New Zealand**	1	1	–	–	33	–
	in **North America** and **Wales**	7	7	–	–	197	41
1981	**Scotland** in **New Zealand**	2	2	–	–	51	19
	South Africa in **New Zealand**	3	2	1	–	51	55
	in **Romania** and **France**	10	8	1	1	170	108
1982	**Australia** in **New Zealand**	3	2	1	–	72	53
1983	**British Isles** in **New Zealand**	4	4	–	–	78	26
	in **Australia**	1	1	–	–	18	8
	in **Scotland** and **England**	8	5	2	1	162	116
1984	**France** in **New Zealand**	2	2	–	–	41	27
	in **Australia**	14	13	1	–	600	117
	in **Fiji**	4	4	–	–	174	10
1985	**England** in **New Zealand**	2	2	–	–	60	28
	Australia in **New Zealand**	1	1	–	–	10	9
	in **Argentina**	7	6	–	1	263	87
1986	**France** in **New Zealand**	1	1	–	–	18	9
	Australia in **New Zealand**	3	1	2	–	34	47
	in **France**	8	7	1	–	218	87
1987	**World Cup**	6	6	–	–	298	52
	in **Australia**	1	1	–	–	30	16
	in **Japan**	5	5	–	–	408	16
1988	**Wales** in **New Zealand**	2	2	–	–	106	12
	in **Australia**	13	12	–	1	476	96
1989	**France** in **New Zealand**	2	2	–	–	59	37
	Argentina in **New Zealand**	2	2	–	–	109	21
	Australia in **New Zealand**	1	1	–	–	24	12
	in **Canada, Wales** and **Ireland**	14	14	–	–	454	122
1990	**Scotland** in **New Zealand**	2	2	–	–	52	34
	Australia in **New Zealand**	3	2	1	–	57	44
	in **France**	8	6	2	–	175	110
1991	in **Argentina**	9	9	–	–	358	80
	in **Australia**	1	–	1	–	12	21
	Australia in **New Zealand**	1	1	–	–	6	3
	World Cup	6	5	1	–	143	74
1992	**Centenary matches** in **New Zealand**	3	2	1	–	94	69
	Ireland in **New Zealand**	2	2	–	–	83	27
	in **Australia** and **South Africa**	16	13	3	–	567	252
1993	**British Isles** in **New Zealand**	3	2	1	–	57	51
	Australia in **New Zealand**	1	1	–	–	25	10
	Western Samoa in **New Zealand**	1	1	–	–	35	13
	in **England** and **Scotland**	13	12	1	–	386	156
1994	**France** in **New Zealand**	2	–	2	–	28	45
	South Africa in **New Zealand**	3	2	–	1	53	41
	in **Australia**	1	–	1	–	16	20
1995	**Canada** in **New Zealand**	1	1	–	–	73	7
	World Cup	6	5	1	–	327	119
	Australia in **New Zealand**	1	1	–	–	28	16

		Played	Won	Lost	Drawn	Points for	Points against
	in **Australia**	1	1	–	–	34	23
	in **Italy** and **France**	8	7	1	–	339	126
1996	**Western Samoa, Scotland** in **NZ**	3	3	–	–	149	53
	Tri Nations	4	4	–	–	119	60
	in **South Africa1**	7	5	1	1	190	139
1997	**Fiji, Argentina, Australia1** in **NZ**	4	4	–	–	256	36
	Tri Nations	4	4	–	–	159	109
	in **British Isles**	9	8	–	1	395	119
1998	**England** in **New Zealand**	2	2	–	–	104	32
	Tri Nations	4	–	4	–	65	88
	in **Australia1**	1	–	1	–	14	19
1999	**Internal, Samoa, France** in **NZ**	3	3	–	–	147	31
	Tri Nations	4	3	1	–	103	61
	World Cup	6	4	2	–	255	111
2000	**Tonga, Scotland** in **New Zealand**	3	3	–	–	219	34
	Tri Nations	4	2	2	–	127	117
	in **France** and **Italy**	3	2	1	–	128	87
2001	**Samoa, Argentina, France** in **NZ**	3	3	–	–	154	37
	Tri Nations	4	2	2	–	79	70
	in **Ireland, Scotland** and **Argentina**	5	5	–	–	179	98
2002	**Italy, Ireland, Fiji** in **New Zealand**	4	4	–	–	187	42
	Tri Nations	4	3	1	–	97	65
	in **England, France** and **Wales**	3	1	1	1	91	68
2003	**England, Wales, France** in **New Zealand**	3	2	1	–	99	41
	Tri Nations	4	4	–	–	142	65
	World Cup	7	6	1	–	361	101
2004	**England, Argentina, Pacific Islands** in **New Zealand**	4	4	–	–	154	48
	Tri Nations	4	2	2	–	83	91
	in **Europe**	4	4	–	–	177	60
2005	**Fiji, Lions** in **New Zealand**	4	4	–	–	198	40
	Tri Nations	4	3	1	–	111	86
	in **Europe**	4	4	–	–	138	39
2006	**Ireland** in **New Zealand**						
	New Zealand in **Argentina**	3	3	–	–	86	59
	Tri Nations	6	5	1	–	179	112
	in **Europe**	4	4	–	–	156	44
2007	**France, Canada** in **New Zealand**	3	3	–	–	167	34
	Tri Nations	4	3	1	–	100	59
	World Cup	5	4	1	–	327	55
2008	**Ireland, England, Samoa** in **New Zealand**	4	4	–	–	203	57
	Tri Nations	6	4	2	–	152	106
	in **Hong Kong, United Kingdom** and **Ireland**	6	6	–	–	152	54
2009	**France, Italy** in **New Zealand**	3	2	1	–	63	43
	Tri Nations	6	3	3	–	141	131
	in **Japan** and **Europe**	6	5	1	–	147	80

		Played	Won	Lost	Drawn	Points for	Points against
2010	**Ireland, Wales** in **New Zealand**	3	3	–	–	137	47
	Tri Nations	6	6	–	–	184	111
	in **Hong Kong, United Kingdom** and **Ireland**	5	4	1	–	174	88
2011	**Fiji** in **New Zealand**	1	1	–	–	60	14
	Tri Nations	4	2	2	–	95	64
	World Cup	7	7	–	–	301	72
2012	**Ireland** in **New Zealand**	3	3	–	–	124	29
	Rugby Championship and **Bledisloe Cup**	7	6	–	1	195	84
	In **Europe**	4	3	1	–	147	80
2013	**France** in **New Zealand**	3	3	–	–	77	22
	Rugby Championship and **Bledisloe Cup**	7	7	–	–	243	148
	In **Japan** and **Europe**	4	4	–	–	134	69
2014	**England** in **New Zealand**	3	3	–	–	84	55
	Rugby Championship and **Bledisloe Cup**	7	5	1	1	193	119
	In **USA** and **United Kingdom**	4	4	–	–	156	59
2015	In **Samoa, Rugby Championship** and **Bledisloe Cup**	5	4	1	–	151	94
	World Cup	7	7	–	–	290	97
2016	**Wales** in **New Zealand**	3	3	-	-	121	49
	Rugby Championship and **Bledisloe Cup**	7	7	-	-	299	94
	In **USA, Italy, Ireland** and **France**	4	3	1	-	142	78
2017	**Samoa, Lions** in **New Zealand**	4	2	1	1	144	54
	Rugby Championship and **Bledisloe Cup**	7	6	1	–	264	142
	In **England, France, Scotland** and **Wales**	5	5	–	–	152	98
2018	**France** in **New Zealand**	3	3	–	–	127	38
	Rugby Championship and **Bledisloe Cup**	7	6	1	–	262	152
	In **Japan, England, Ireland** and **Italy**	4	3	1	–	160	65
2019	**Tonga** in New Zealand	1	1	–	–	92	7
	Rugby Championship and **Bledisloe Cup**	4	2	1	1	98	79
	World Cup	6	5	1	–	250	72
	TOTALS	*1316*	*1110*	*166*	*40*	*36,210*	*13,067*

¹non Tri Nations

SURVIVING NEW ZEALAND
REPRESENTATIVES

(over the age of 71 years as at 31 December, 2019)

	Born	Represented New Zealand
R.A. Roper	11 August, 1923	1949-50
J.M. Tanner	11 January, 1927	1950-51-53-54
W.A. McCaw	26 August, 1927	1951-53-54
M.S. Cockerill	8 December, 1928	1951
L.B. Steele	19 January, 1929	1951
K.F. Meates	20 February, 1930	1952
D. Young	1 April, 1930	1956-57-58-60-61-62-63-64
E.S. Diack	22 July, 1930	1959
S.G. Bremner	2 August, 1930	1952-56-60
D.L. Ashby	15 February, 1931	1958
C.J. Loader	10 March, 1931	1953-54
D.N. McIntosh	1 April, 1931	1956-57
B.P.J. Molloy	12 August, 1931	1957
W.S.S. Freebairn	12 January, 1932	1953-54
L.J. Townsend	3 March, 1934	1955
I.N. MacEwan	1 May, 1934	1956-57-58-59-60-61-62
F.S. McAtamney	15 May, 1934	1956-57
W.D. Gillespie	6 August, 1934	1957-58-60
K.F. Laidlaw	9 August, 1934	1960
R.J. Boon	23 February, 1935	1960
R.J. Conway	22 April, 1935	1959-60-65
D.M. Connor	9 September, 1935	1961-62-63-64
J.R. Watt	29 December, 1935	1957-58-60-61-62
T.R. Lineen	5 January, 1936	1957-58-59-60
S.R. Nesbit	13 February, 1936	1960
J.F. McCullough	8 August, 1936	1959
A.J. Soper	7 September, 1936	1957
R.W. Caulton	10 January, 1937	1959-60-61-63-64
B.E. McPhail	26 January, 1937	1959
J.N. Creighton	10 March, 1937	1962
D.W. McKay	7 August, 1937	1961-62-63
A.H. Clarke	23 February, 1938	1958-59-60
S.T. Meads	12 July, 1938	1961-62-63-64-65-66
D.H. Cameron	17 November, 1938	1960
K.A. Nelson	26 November, 1938	1962-63-64
B.A. Watt	12 March, 1939	1962-63-64
N.W. Thimbleby	19 June, 1939	1970
W.M. Birtwistle	4 July, 1939	1965-67
E.W. Kirton	29 December, 1939	1963-64-67-68-69-70
D.W. Clark	22 February, 1940	1964
A.G.T. Jennings	15 June, 1940	1967
W.J. Nathan	8 July, 1940	1962-63-64-66-67
J. Major	8 August, 1940	1963-64-67
A.J. Stewart	11 October, 1940	1963-64
M.J. Dick	3 January, 1941	1963-64-65-66-67-69-70
D.A. Arnold	10 January, 1941	1963-64
J.F. Burns	17 February, 1941	1970
R.A. Guy	6 April, 1941	1971-72

M.C. Wills	11 October, 1941	1967
T.N. Wolfe	20 October, 1941	1961-62-63-68
T.J. Morris	3 January, 1942	1972-73
P.H. Clarke	23 January, 1942	1967
R.W. Norton	30 March, 1942	1971-72-73-74-75-76-77
A.E. Smith	10 December, 1942	1967-69-70
W.L. Davis	15 December, 1942	1963-64-67-68-69-70
I.R. MacRae	6 April, 1943	1963-64-66-67-68-69-70
S.M. Going	19 August, 1943	1967-68-69-70-71-72-73-74-75-76-77
C.R. Laidlaw	16 November, 1943	1963-64-65-66-67-68-70
A.R. Sutherland	4 January, 1944	1968-70-71-72-73-76
R.A. Urlich	8 February, 1944	1970-72-73
P.A. Johns	16 March, 1944	1968
L.A. Clark	1 May, 1944	1972-73
W.D.R. Currey	2 June, 1944	1968
A.J. Wyllie	31 August, 1944	1970-71-72-73
A.R. Leslie	10 November, 1944	1974-75-76
R.J. Barber	14 January, 1945	1974
B.D.M. Furlong	10 March, 1945	1970
A.J. Kreft	27 March, 1945	1968
K.J. Tanner	25 April, 1945	1974-75-76
M.O. Knight	20 May, 1945	1968
G.F. Kember	15 November, 1945	1967-70
G.M. Crossman	30 November, 1945	1974-76
P.C. Harris	11 January, 1946	1976
L.W. Mains	16 February, 1946	1971-76
G.S. Thorne	25 February, 1946	1967-68-69-70
B. Holmes	7 April, 1946	1970-72-73
M.W. O'Callaghan	27 April, 1946	1968
I.A. Kirkpatrick	24 May, 1946	1967-68-69-70-71-72-73-74-75-76-77
G.J. Whiting	4 June, 1946	1972-73
S.E.G. Cron	7 July, 1946	1976
P.J. Whiting	6 August, 1946	1971-72-73-74-76
A.J. Gardiner	10 December, 1946	1974
O.G. Stephens	9 January, 1947	1968
H.H. Macdonald	11 January, 1947	1972-73-74-75-76
D.J. Robertson	6 February, 1947	1974-75-76-77
M. Sayers	1 May, 1947	1972-73
O.D. Bruce	23 May, 1947	1974-76-77-78
A.M. McNaughton	5 July, 1947	1971-72
J.E. Spiers	4 August, 1947	1976-79-80-81
M.G. Duncan	8 August, 1947	1971
K.A. Eveleigh	8 November, 1947	1974-76-77
D.A. Hales	22 November, 1947	1972-73
G.D. Rowlands	10 December, 1947	1976
R.L. Stuart	9 January, 1948	1977
G.R. Skudder	10 February, 1948	1969-72-73
R.N. Lendrum	22 March, 1948	1973
J.D. Matheson	30 March, 1948	1972
I.N. Stevens	13 April, 1948	1972-73-74-76
P.H. Sloane	10 September, 1948	1973-76-79
A.I. Scown	21 October, 1948	1972-73
V.E. Stewart	28 October, 1948	1976-79

NEW ZEALAND REPRESENTATIVES

1884–2019

Union affiliations are shown in parentheses, preceded by date of birth and, where applicable, date of death. A few of these dates have proved impossible to be traced and these are indicated with a question mark. War casualties are denoted by an asterisk. The numbers that follow each entry show the number of games played for New Zealand. These are followed in parentheses by the number of appearances in test matches, which are included in the total. Franchise team rather than Provincial teams have been used from 2013.

Name	B&D	Representative Team	Games	Tests
Abbott H.L.	1882-1971	(Taranaki) 1905-06	11	(1)
Adkins G.T.A.	1910-1976	(South Canterbury) 1935-36	10	(–)
Afeaki B.T.P.	1988-	(Chiefs) 2013	1	(1)
Afoa I.F.	1983-	(Auckland) 2005-06-08-09-10-11	38	(36)
Aitken G.G.	1898-1952	(Wellington) 1921	2	(2)
Alatini P.F.	1976-	(Otago) 1999-2001	20	(17)
Algar B.	1894-1989	(Wellington) 1920-21	6	(–)
Allan J.	1860-1934	(Otago) 1884	8	(–)
Allen F.R.	1920-2012	(Auckland) 1946-47-49	21	(6)
Allen L.	1870-1932	(Taranaki) 1896-97-1901	13	(–)
Allen M.R.	1967-	(Taranaki) 1993-95-96; (Manawatu) 1997	27	(8)
Allen N.H.	1958-1984	(Counties) 1980	9	(2)
Alley G.T.	1903-1986	(Southland) 1926; (Canterbury) 1928	19	(3)
Anderson A.	1961-	(Canterbury) 1983-84-85-87-88	25	(6)
Anderson B.L.	1960-	(Wairarapa Bush) 1986-87	3	(1)
Anderson E.J.	1931-2014	(Bay of Plenty) 1960	10	(–)
Anesi S.R.	1981-	(Waikato) 2005	1	(1)
Archer J.A.	1900-1979	(Southland) 1925	2	(–)
Archer W.R.	1930-2018	(Otago) 1955; (Southland) 1956-57	13	(4)
Argus W.G.	1921-2016	(Canterbury) 1946-47	10	(4)
Armit A.M.	1874-1899	(Otago) 1897	9	(–)
Armstrong A.L.	1878-1959	(Wairarapa) 1903	5	(–)
Arnold D.A.	1941-	(Canterbury) 1963-64	15	(4)
Arnold K.D.	1920-2006	(Waikato) 1947	8	(2)
Ashby D.L.	1931-	(Southland) 1958	1	(1)
Asher A.A.	1879-1965	(Auckland) 1903	11	(1)
Ashworth B.G.	1949-	(Auckland) 1978	7	(2)
Ashworth J.C.	1949-	(Canterbury) 1977-78-79-80-81-82-83-84; (Hawke's Bay) 1985	52	(24)
Atiga B.A.C.	1983-	(Auckland) 2003	1	(1)
Atkinson H.J.	1888-1949	(West Coast) 1913	10	(1)
Aumua A.J.	1997-	(Wellington) 2017	2	(–)
Avery H.E.	1885-1961	(Wellington) 1910	6	(3)
Bachop G.T.M.	1967-	(Canterbury) 1987-88-89-90-91-92-94-95	54	(31)
Bachop S.J.	1966-	(Otago) 1992-93-94	18	(5)
Badeley C.E.O.	1896-1986	(Auckland) 1920-21-24	15	(2)
Badeley V.I.R.	1898-1971	(Auckland) 1922	5	(–)
Bagley K.P.	1931-1999	(Manawatu) 1953-54	20	(–)
Baird D.L.	1894-1943	(Southland) 1920	9	(–)
Baird J.A.S.*	1893-1917	(Otago) 1913	1	(1)
Balch W.	1871-1949	(Canterbury) 1894	1	(–)
Ball N.	1908-1986	(Wellington) 1931-32-35-36	22	(5)
Barber R.J.	1945-	(Southland) 1974	6	(–)
Barrell C.K.	1967-	(Canterbury) 1996-97	4	(–)
Barrett B.J.	1991-	(Taranaki) 2012; (Hurricanes) 2013-14-15-16-17-18-19	84	(83)

Name	B&D	Representative Team	Games	Tests
Barrett J.	1888-1971	(Auckland) 1913-14	3	(2)
Barrett J.M.	1997	(Hurricanes) 2017-18-19	17	(17)
Barrett S.K.	1993-	(Crusaders) 2016-17-18-19	38	(36)
Barry E.F.	1905-1993	(Wellington) 1932-34	10	(1)
Barry K.E.	1936-2014	(Thames Valley) 1962-63-64	23	(–)
Barry L.J.	1971-	(North Harbour) 1993-95	10	(1)
Bates S.P.	1980-	(Waikato) 2004	2	(1)
Batty G.B.	1951-	(Wellington) 1972-73-74-75; (Bay of Plenty) 1976-77	56	(15)
Batty W.	1905-1979	(Auckland) 1928-30-31	6	(4)
Bayly A.	1866-1907	(Taranaki) 1893-94-97	20	(–)
Bayly W.	1869-1950	(Taranaki) 1894	1	(–)
Beatty G.E.	1925-2004	(Taranaki) 1950	1	(1)
Bell J.R.	1900-1963	(Southland) 1923	1	(–)
Bell R.C.	1893-1960	(Otago) 1922	8	(–)
Bell R.H.	1925-2016	(Otago) 1951-52	9	(3)
Belliss E.A.	1894-1974	(Wanganui) 1920-21-22-23	20	(3)
Bennet R.	1879-1962	(Otago) 1905	1	(1)
Berghan T.	1914-1998	(Otago) 1938	6	(3)
Berry M.J.	1966-	(Wairarapa Bush) 1986; (Wellington) 1993	10	(1)
Berryman N.R.	1973-2015	(Northland) 1998	1	(1)
Best J.J.	1914-1994	(Marlborough) 1935-36	6	(–)
Bevan V.D.	1921-1996	(Wellington) 1947-49-50-53-54	25	(6)
Bird D.J.	1991-	(Crusaders) 2013-14; (Chiefs) 2017	3	(2)
Birtwistle W.M.	1939-	(Canterbury) 1965; (Waikato) 1967	12	(7)
Black J.E.	1951-	(Canterbury) 1976-77-78-79-80	26	(3)
Black N.W.	1925-2016	(Auckland) 1949	11	(1)
Black R.S.*	1893-1916	(Otago) 1914	6	(1)
Blackadder T.J.	1971-	(Canterbury) 1995-96-97-98-99-2000	25	(12)
Blair B.A.	1979-	(Canterbury) 2001-02	6	(4)
Blair J.A.	1872-1911	(Wanganui) 1897	9	(–)
Blake A.W.	1922-2010	(Wairarapa) 1949	1	(1)
Blake J.M.	1902-1988	(Hawke's Bay) 1925-26	13	(–)
Bligh S.	1887-1955	(West Coast) 1910	5	(–)
Blowers A.F.	1975-	(Auckland) 1996-97-99	18	(11)
Bloxham K.C.	1954-2000	(Otago) 1980	2	(–)
Boe J.W.	1955-	(Waikato) 1981	2	(–)
Boggs E.G.	1922-2004	(Auckland) 1946-49	9	(2)
Bond J.G.P.	1920-1999	(Canterbury) 1949	1	(1)
Boon R.J.	1935-	(Taranaki) 1960	6	(–)
Booth E.E.	1876-1935	(Otago) 1905-06-07	24	(3)
Boric A.F.	1983-	(North Harbour) 2008-09-10-11	25	(24)
Boroevich K.G.	1960-	(King Country) 1983-84; (Wellington) 1986; (North Harbour) 1988	26	(3)
Botica F.M.	1963-	(North Harbour) 1986-87-88-89	27	(7)
Botting I.J.	1922-1980	(Otago) 1949	9	(–)
Bowden N.J.G.	1926-2009	(Taranaki) 1952	1	(1)
Bowers R.G.	1932-2000	(Wellington) 1953-54	15	(2)
Bowman A.W.	1915-1992	(Hawke's Bay) 1938	6	(3)
Bradanovich N.M.	1907-1961	(Otago) 1928	2	(–)
Braddon H.Y.	1863-1955	(Otago) 1884	7	(–)
Braid D.J.	1981-	(Auckland) 2002-03-08-10	6	(6)
Braid G.J.	1960-	(Bay of Plenty) 1983-84	13	(2)
Brake L.J.	1952-	(Bay of Plenty) 1976	5	(–)
Bremner S.G.	1930-	(Auckland) 1952; (Canterbury) 1956-60	18	(2)
Brewer M.R.	1964-	(Otago) 1986-87-88-89-90-91-92; (Canterbury) 1993-94-95	61	(32)

Name	B&D	Representative Team	Games	Tests
Bridge G.C.	1995-	(Crusaders) 2018-19	9	(9)
Briscoe K.C.	1936-2009	(Taranaki) 1959-60-62-63-64	43	(9)
Broadhurst J.P.	1987-	(Hurricanes) 2015-1	(1)	
Brooke R.M.	1966-	(Auckland) 1992-93-94-95-96-97-98-99	69	(62)
Brooke Z.V.	1965-	(Auckland) 1987-88-89-90-91-92-93-94-95-96-97	100	(58)
Brooke-Cowden M.	1963-	(Auckland) 1986-87	6	(3)
Brooker F.J.	1876-1939	(Canterbury) 1897	4	(–)
Broomhall S.R.	1976-	(Canterbury) 2002	4	(4)
Brown C.	1887-1966	(Taranaki) 1913-20	11	(2)
Brown H.M.	1910-1965	(Auckland) 1935-36	8	(–)
Brown H.W.	1904-1973	(Taranaki) 1924-25-26	20	(–)
Brown O.M.	1967-	(Auckland) 1990-92-93-94-95-96-97-98	69	(56)
Brown R.H.	1934-2014	(Taranaki) 1955-56-57-58-59-61-62	25	(16)
Brown T.E.	1975-	(Otago) 1999-2000-01	19	(18)
Brownlie C.J.	1895-1954	(Hawke's Bay) 1924-25-26-28	31	(3)
Brownlie J.L.	1899-1972	(Hawke's Bay) 1921	1	(–)
Brownlie M.J.	1896-1957	(Hawke's Bay) 1922-23-24-25-26-28	61	(8)
Bruce J.A.	1887-1970	(Auckland) 1913-14	10	(2)
Bruce O.D.	1947-	(Canterbury) 1974-76-77-78	41	(14)
Bryers R.F.	1919-1987	(King Country) 1949	1	(1)
Buchan J.A.S.	1961-	(Canterbury) 1987	2	(–)
Budd A.	1880-1962	(South Canterbury) 1910	3	(–)
Budd T.A.	1922-1989	(Southland) 1946-49	2	(2)
Bullock-Douglas G.A.H.	1911-1958	(Wanganui) 1932-34	15	(5)
Bunce F.E.	1962-	(North Harbour) 1992-93-94-95-96-97	69	(55)
Burgess G.A.J.	1954-	(Auckland) 1980-81	2	(1)
Burgess G.F.	1883-1961	(Southland) 1905	1	(1)
Burgess R.E.	1949-	(Manawatu) 1971-72-73	30	(7)
Burgoyne M.M.	1951-2016	(North Auckland) 1979	6	(–)
Burke P.S.	1927-2017	(Taranaki) 1951-55-57	12	(3)
Burns J.F.	1941-	(Canterbury)1970	9	(–)
Burns P.J.	1881-1943	(Canterbury) 1908-10-13	9	(5)
Burrows J.T.	1904-1991	(Canterbury) 1928	9	(–)
Burry H.C.	1930-2013	(Canterbury) 1960	11	(–)
Burt J.R.	1874-1933	(Otago) 1901	1	(–)
Bush R.G.	1909-96	(Otago) 1931	1	(1)
Bush W.K. TeP.	1949-	(Canterbury) 1974-75-76-77-78-79	37	(12)
Butland H.	1872-1956	(West Coast) 1893-94	9	(–)
Butler V.C.	1907-1971	(Auckland) 1928	1	(–)
Buxton J.B.	1933-2007	(Canterbury) 1955-56	2	(2)
Cabot P.S. deQ.	1900-1998	(Otago) 1921	1	(–)
Cain M.J.	1885-1951	(Taranaki) 1913-14	24	(4)
Calcinai U.P.	1892-1963	(Wellington) 1922	5	(–)
Callesen J.A.	1950-	(Manawatu) 1974-75-76	18	(4)
Calnan J.J.	1876-1947	(Wellington) 1897	9	(–)
Cameron B.D.	1996	(Crusaders) 2018	1	(1)
Cameron D.	1887-1947	(Taranaki) 1908	3	(3)
Cameron D.H.	1938-	(Mid Canterbury) 1960	8	(–)
Cameron L.M.	1959-	(Manawatu) 1979-80-81	17	(5)
Cane S.J.	1992-	(Bay of Plenty) 2012; (Chiefs) 2013-14-15-16-17-18-19	69	(68)
Carleton S.R.	1904-1973	(Canterbury) 1928-29	21	(6)
Carrington K.R.	1950-	(Auckland) 1971-72	9	(3)
Carroll A.J.	1895-1974	(Manawatu) 1920-21	8	(–)
Carson W.N.*	1916-1944	(Auckland) 1938	3	(–)

Name	B&D	Representative Team	Games	Tests
Carter D.W.	1982-	(Canterbury) 2003-04-05-06-07-08-09-10-11-12; (Crusaders) 2013-14-15	112	(112)
Carter G.	1854-1922	(Auckland) 1884	7	(–)
Carter M.P.	1968-	(Auckland) 1991-97-98	10	(7)
Cartwright S.C.	1954-	(Canterbury) 1976	7	(–)
Casey S.T.	1882-1960	(Otago) 1905-06-07-08	38	(8)
Cashmore A.R.	1973	(Auckland) 1996-97	2	(2)
Catley E.H.	1915-1975	(Waikato) 1946-47-49	21	(7)
Caughey T.H.C.	1911-1993	(Auckland) 1932-34-35-36-37	39	(9)
Caulton R.W.	1937-	(Wellington) 1959-60-61-63-64	50	(16)
Cherrington N.P.	1924-1979	(North Auckland) 1950-51	7	(1)
Christian D.L.	1923-1977	(Auckland) 1949	11	(1)
Clamp M.	1961-	(Wellington) 1984-85	15	(2)
Clark D.W.	1940-	(Otago) 1964	2	(2)
Clark F.L.	1902-1972	(Canterbury) 1928	4	(–)
Clark L.A.	1944-	(Otago) 1972-73	7	(–)
Clark W.H.	1929-2010	(Wellington) 1953-54-55-56	24	(9)
Clarke A.H.	1938-	(Auckland) 1958-59-60	14	(3)
Clarke D.B.	1933-2002	(Waikato) 1956-57-58-59-60-61-62-63-64	89	(31)
Clarke E.	1968-	(Auckland) 1992-93-98	24	(10)
Clarke I.J.	1931-1997	(Waikato) 1953-54-55-56-57-58-59-60-61-62-63-64	83	(24)
Clarke P.H.	1942-	(Marlborough) 1967	4	(–)
Clarke R.L.	1909-1972	(Taranaki) 1932	9	(2)
Cobden D.G.*	1914-1940	(Canterbury) 1937	1	(1)
Cockerill M.S.	1928-	(Taranaki) 1951	11	(3)
Cockroft E.A.P.	1890-1973	(South Canterbury) 1913-14	7	(3)
Cockroft S.G.	1864-1955	(Manawatu) 1893; (Hawke's Bay) 1894	12	(–)
Codlin B.W.	1956-	(Counties) 1980	13	(3)
Coffin P.H.	1964-	(King Country) 1996	3	(–)
Coles D.S.	1986-	(Wellington) 2012; (Hurricanes) 2013-14-15-16-17-18-19	69	(69)
Colling G.L.	1946-2003	(Otago) 1972-73	21	(–)
Collins A.H.	1906-1988	(Taranaki) 1932-34	15	(3)
Collins J.	1980-2015	(Wellington) 2001-03-04-05-06-07	50	(48)
Collins J.L.	1939-2007	(Poverty Bay) 1964-65	3	(3)
Collins W.R.	1910-1993	(Hawke's Bay) 1935	7	(–)
Colman J.T.H.	1887-1965	(Taranaki) 1907-08	6	(4)
Coltman L.J.	1990-	(Highlanders) 2016-18-19	8	(8)
Conn S.B.	1953-	(Auckland) 1976-80	6	(–)
Connolly L.S.	1921-2005	(Southland) 1947	5	(–)
Connor D.M.	1935-	(Auckland) 1961-62-63-64	15	(12)
Conrad W.J.M.	1925-1972	(Waikato) 1949	10	(–)
Conway R.J.	1935-	(Otago) 1959-60; (Bay of Plenty) 1965	25	(10)
Cooke A.E.	1901-1977	(Auckland) 1924-25; (Hawke's Bay) 1926; (Wairarapa) 1928; (Wellington) 1930	44	(8)
Cooke A.E.	1870-1900	(Canterbury) 1894	1	(–)
Cooke R.J.	1880-1940	(Canterbury) 1903	10	(1)
Cooksley M.S.B.	1971-	(Counties) 1992-93; (Waikato) 1994-95-97-2001	23	(11)
Cooper G.J.L.	1965-	(Auckland) 1986; (Otago) 1992	7	(7)
Cooper M.J.A.	1966-	(Hawke's Bay) 1987; (Waikato) 1992-93-94-96	26	(8)
Corbett J.	1880-1945	(West Coast) 1905	16	(–)
Corkill T.G.	1901-1966	(Hawke's Bay) 1925	4	(–)
Corner M.M.N.	1908-1992	(Auckland) 1930-31-32-34-35-36	25	(6)
Cossey R.R.	1935-1986	(Counties) 1958	1	(1)
Cottrell A.I.	1907-1988	(Canterbury) 1929-30-31-32	22	(11)
Cottrell W.D.	1943-2013	(Canterbury) 1967-68-70-71	37	(9)

Name	B&D	Representative Team	Games	Tests
Couch M.B.R.	1925-1996	(Wairarapa) 1947-49	7	(3)
Coughlan T.D.	1934-2017	(South Canterbury) 1958	1	(1)
Cowan Q.J.	1982-	(Southland) 2004-05-06-08-09-10-11	53	(51)
Creighton J.N.	1937-	(Canterbury) 1962	6	(1)
Cribb R.T.	1976-	(North Harbour) 2000-01	15	(15)
Crichton S.	1954-	(Wellington) 1983-84-85	7	(2)
Crockett W.W.V.	1983-	(Canterbury) 2009-11-12; (Crusaders) 2013-14-15-16-17	72	(71)
Cron S.E.G.	1946-	(Canterbury) 1976	6	(−)
Cross T.	1876-1930	(Canterbury) 1901; (Wellington) 1904-05	3	(2)
Crossman G.M.	1945-	(Bay of Plenty) 1974-76	19	(−)
Crotty R.J.	1988-	(Crusaders) 2013-14-15-16-18-19	48	(48)
Crowley K.J.	1961-	(Taranaki) 1983-84-85-86-87-90-91	35	(19)
Crowley P.J.B.	1923-1981	(Auckland) 1949-50	21	(6)
Cruden A.W.	1989-	(Manawatu) 2010-11-12; (Chiefs) 2013-14-16-17	50	(50)
Culhane S.D.	1968-	(Southland) 1995-96	9	(6)
Cullen C.M.	1976-	(Manawatu) 1996-97; (Wellington) 1998-99-2000-01-02	60	(58)
Cummings W.	1889-1955	(Canterbury) 1913-21	3	(2)
Cundy R.T.	1901-1955	(Wairarapa) 1929	6	(1)
Cunningham G.R.	1955-	(Auckland) 1979-80	17	(5)
Cunningham W.	1874-1927	(Auckland) 1901-05-06-07-08	39	(9)
Cupples L.F.	1898-1972	(Bay of Plenty) 1922-23-24-25	29	(2)
Currey W.D.R.	1944-	(Taranaki) 1968	7	(−)
Currie C.J.	1955-	(Canterbury) 1978	4	(2)
Cuthill J.E.	1892-1970	(Otago) 1913	16	(2)
Dagg I.J.A.	1988-	(Hawke's Bay) 2010-11-12; (Crusaders) 2013-14-15-16-17	66	(66)
Dalley W.C.	1901-1989	(Canterbury) 1924-25-26-28-29	35	(5)
Dalton A.G.	1951-	(Counties) 1977-78-79-80-81-82-83-84-85	58	(35)
Dalton D.	1913-1995	(Hawke's Bay) 1935-36-37-38	21	(9)
Dalton R.A.	1919-1997	(Wellington) 1947; (Otago) 1949	20	(2)
Dalzell G.N.	1921-1989	(Canterbury) 1953-54	22	(5)
D'Arcy A.E.	1870-1919	(Wairarapa) 1893-94	7	(−)
Davie M.G.	1955-	(Canterbury) 1983	5	(1)
Davies W.A.	1939-2008	(Auckland) 1960; (Otago) 1962	17	(3)
Davis C.S.	1975-	(Manawatu) 1996	2	(−)
Davis K.	1930-2019	(Auckland) 1952-53-54-55-58	25	(10)
Davis L.J.	1943-2008	(Canterbury) 1976-77	16	(3)
Davis W.L.	1942-	(Hawke's Bay) 1963-64-67-68-69-70	53	(11)
Davy E.	1850-1935	(Wellington) 1884	3	(−)
Deans I.B.	1960-2019	(Canterbury) 1987-88-89	23	(10)
Deans R.G.	1884-1908	(Canterbury) 1905-06-08	24	(5)
Deans R.M.	1959-	(Canterbury) 1983-84-85	19	(5)
Delamore G.W.	1920-2008	(Wellington) 1949	9	(1)
Delany M.P.	1982-	(Bay of Plenty) 2009	2	(1)
de Malmanche A.P.	1984-	(Waikato) 2009-10	5	(5)
Dermody C.	1980-	(Southland) 2006	3	(3)
Devine S.J.	1976-	(Auckland) 2002-03	10	(10)
Dewar H.*	1883-1915	(Taranaki) 1913	16	(2)
Diack E.S.	1930-	(Otago) 1959	1	(1)
Dick J.	1912-2002	(Auckland) 1937-38	5	(3)
Dick M.J.	1941-	(Auckland) 1963-64-65-66-67-69-70	55	(15)
Dickinson G.R.	1903-1978	(Otago) 1922	5	(−)
Dickson D.McK.	1900-1978	(Otago) 1925	7	(−)
Dixon E.C.	1989-	(Highlanders) 2016	3	(3)
Dixon M.J.	1929-2004	(Canterbury) 1953-54-56-57	28	(10)

Name	B&D	Representative Team	Games	Tests
Dobson R.L.	1923-1994	(Auckland) 1949	1	(1)
Dodd E.H.*	1880-1918	(Wellington) 1901-05	3	(1)
Donald A.J.	1957-	(Wanganui) 1981-83-84	20	(7)
Donald J.G.	1898-1981	(Wairarapa) 1920-21-22-25	22	(2)
Donald Q.	1900-1965	(Wairarapa) 1923-24-25	23	(4)
Donald S.R.	1983-	(Waikato) 2008-09-10-11	25	(23)
Donaldson M.W.	1955-	(Manawatu) 1977-78-79-80-81	35	(13)
Donnelly T.J.S.	1981-	(Otago) 2009-10	15	(15)
Dougan J.P.	1946-2006	(Wellington) 1972-73	12	(2)
Douglas J.B.	1890-1964	(Otago) 1913	9	(−)
Dowd C.W.	1969-	(Auckland) 1993-94-95-96-97-98-99-2000	67	(60)
Dowd G.W.	1963-	(North Harbour) 1992	8	(1)
Downing A.J.*	1886-1915	(Auckland) 1913-14	26	(5)
Drake J.A.	1959-2008	(Auckland) 1985-86-87	12	(8)
Drake W.A.	1879-1941	(Canterbury) 1901	1	(−)
Drummond M.D.	1994-	(Crusaders) 2017-18	2	(1)
Duff R.H.	1925-2006	(Canterbury) 1951-52-55-56	18	(11)
Duffie M.D.	1990	(Blues) 2017	2	(−)
Duggan R.J.L.	1972-	(Waikato) 1999	1	(1)
Dumbell J.T.	1859-1936	(Wellington) 1884	5	(−)
Duncan J.	1869-1953	(Otago) 1897-1901-03	10	(1)
Duncan M.G.	1947-	(Hawke's Bay) 1971	2	(2)
Duncan W.D.	1892-1961	(Otago) 1920-21	11	(3)
Dunn E.J.	1955-	(North Auckland) 1978-79-81	20	(2)
Dunn I.T.W.	1960-	(North Auckland) 1983-84	13	(3)
Dunn J.M.	1918-2003	(Auckland) 1946	1	(1)
Earl A.T.	1961-	(Canterbury) 1986-87-88-89-91-92	45	(14)
Eastgate B.P.	1927-2007	(Canterbury) 1952-53-54	17	(3)
Eaton J.J.	1982-	(Taranaki) 2005-06-08-09	17	(15)
Eckhold A.G.	1885-1931	(Otago) 1907	3	(−)
Eliason I.M.	1945-2019	(Taranaki) 1972-73	19	(−)
Elliot H.T.P.	1986-	(Hawke's Bay) 2008-10,12; (Chiefs) 2015	5	(4)
Elliott K.G.	1922-2006	(Wellington) 1946	2	(2)
Ellis A.M.	1984-	(Canterbury) 2006-07-08-09-10-11; (Crusaders) 2015	28	(28)
Ellis M.C.G.	1971-	(Otago) 1992-93-95	21	(8)
Ellison T.E.	1983-	(Wellington) 2009; (Otago) 2012	5	(4)
Ellison T.R.	1867-1904	(Wellington) 1893	7	(−)
Elsom A.E.G.	1925-2010	(Canterbury) 1952-53-54-55	22	(6)
Elvidge R.R.	1923-2019	(Otago) 1946-49-50	19	(9)
Elvy W.L.	1901-1977	(Canterbury) 1925-26	12	(−)
Ennor, B.M.	1997-	(Crusaders) 2019	1	(1)
Erceg C.P.	1928-2019	(Auckland) 1951-52	9	(4)
Evans B.R.	1984-	(Hawke's Bay) 2009	2	(2)
Evans C.E.	1896-1975	(Canterbury) 1921	1	(−)
Evans D.A.	1886-1940	(Hawke's Bay) 1910	4	(1)
Evans G.O.	1991-	(Hurricanes) 2018	1	(1)
Evans N.J.	1980-	(North Harbour) 2004; (Otago) 2005-06-07	16	(16)
Eveleigh K.A.	1947-	(Manawatu) 1974-76-77	30	(4)
Fanning A.H.N.	1890-1963	(Canterbury) 1913	1	(1)
Fanning B.J.	1874-1946	(Canterbury) 1903-04	9	(2)
Farrell C.P.	1956-	(Auckland) 1977	2	(2)
Faumuina C.C.	1986-	(Auckland) 2012; (Blues) 2013-14-15-16-17	50	(50)
Fawcett C.L.	1954-	(Auckland) 1976	13	(2)
Fea W.R.	1898-1988	(Otago) 1921	1	(1)

Name	B&D	Representative Team	Games	Tests
Feek G.E.	1975-	(Canterbury) 1999-2000-01	10	(10)
Fekitoa M.F.	1992-	(Highlanders) 2014-15-16-17	24	(24)
Fifita V.T.L.	1992-	(Hurricanes) 2017-18-19	12	(11)
Filipo R.A.	1979-	(Wellington) 2007-08	5	(4)
Finlay B.E.L.	1927-1982	(Manawatu) 1959	1	(1)
Finlay J.	1916-2001	(Manawatu) 1946	1	(1)
Finlay M.C.	1963-	(Manawatu) 1984	2	(–)
Finlayson I.	1899-1980	(North Auckland) 1925-26-28-30	36	(6)
Fisher T.	1891-1968	(Buller) 1914	5	(–)
Fitzgerald C.J.	1899-1961	(Marlborough) 1922	5	(–)
Fitzgerald J.T.	1928-1993	(Wellington) 1952-53-54	17	(1)
Fitzpatrick B.B.J.	1931-2006	(Poverty Bay) 1951; (Wellington) 1953-54	22	(3)
Fitzpatrick S.B.T.	1963-	(Auckland) 1986-87-88-89-90-91-92-93-94-95-96-97	128	(92)
Flavell T.V.	1976-	(North Harbour) 2000-01; (Auckland) 2006-07	22	(22)
Fleming J.K.	1953-	(Wellington) 1978-79-80	35	(5)
Fletcher C.J.C.	1894-1973	(North Auckland) 1921	2	(1)
Flynn C.R.	1981-	(Canterbury) 2003-04-08-09-10-11	17	(15)
Fogarty R.	1891-1980	(Taranaki) 1921	2	(2)
Ford B.R.	1951-	(Marlborough) 1977-78-79	20	(4)
Ford W.A.	1895-1959	(Canterbury) 1921-22-23	9	(–)
Forster S.T.	1969-	(Otago) 1993-94-95	12	(6)
Fox G.J.	1962-	(Auckland) 1984-85-86-87-88-89-90-91-92-93	78	(46)
Francis A.R.H.	1882-1957	(Auckland) 1905-07-08-10	18	(10)
Francis W.C.	1894-1981	(Wellington) 1913-14	12	(5)
Franks B.J.	1984-	(Tasman) 2008-10-11-12; (Hurricanes) 2013-14-15	48	(47)
Franks O.T.	1987-	(Canterbury) 2009-10-11-12; (Crusaders) 2013-14-15-16-17-18-19	108	(108)
Fraser B.G.	1953-	(Wellington) 1979-80-81-82-83-84	55	(23)
Frazer H.F.	1915-2003	(Hawke's Bay) 1946-47-49	15	(5)
Freebairn W.S.S.	1932-	(Manawatu) 1953-54	14	(–)
Freitas D.F.E.	1901-1968	(West Coast) 1928	4	(–)
Frizell S.M.	1994-	(Highlanders) 2018-19	9	(9)
Fromont R.T.	1969-	(Auckland) 1993-95	10	(–)
Frost H.	1869-1954	(Canterbury) 1896	1	(–)
Fryer F.C.	1886-1958	(Canterbury) 1907-08	9	(4)
Fuller W.B.	1883-1957	(Canterbury) 1910	6	(2)
Furlong B.D.M.	1945-	(Hawke's Bay) 1970	11	(1)
Gage D.R.	1868-1916	(Wellington) 1893-96	8	(–)
Gallagher J.A.	1964-	(Wellington) 1986-87-88-89	41	(18)
Gallaher D.*	1873-1917	(Auckland) 1903-04-05-06	36	(6)
Gard P.C.	1947-1990	(North Otago) 1971-72	7	(1)
Gardiner A.J.	1946-	(Taranaki) 1974	11	(1)
Gardner J.H.	1870-1909	(South Canterbury) 1893	4	(–)
Gatland W.D.	1963-	(Waikato) 1988-89-90-91	17	(–)
Gear H.E.	1984-	(Wellington) 2008-10-11-12	15	(14)
Gear R.L.	1978-	(North Harbour) 2004; (Nelson Bays) 2005; (Tasman) 2006; (Canterbury) 2007	20	(19)
Geddes J.H.	1907-1990	(Southland) 1929	6	(1)
Geddes W.McK.	1893-1950	(Auckland) 1913	1	(1)
Gemmell B.McL.	1950-	(Auckland) 1974	6	(2)
Gemmell S.W.	1896-1970	(Hawke's Bay) 1923	1	(–)
George V.L.	1908-1996	(Southland) 1938	7	(3)
Gibbes J.B.	1977-	(Waikato) 2004-05	8	(8)
Gibson D.P.E.	1975-	(Canterbury) 1999-2000-02	19	(19)
Gilbert G.D.M.	1911-2002	(West Coast) 1935-36	27	(4)

Name	B&D	Representative Team	Games	Tests
Gillespie C.T.	1883-1964	(Wellington) 1913	1	(1)
Gillespie W.D.	1934-	(Otago) 1957-58-60	23	(1)
Gillett G.A.	1877-1956	(Canterbury) 1905-06; (Auckland) 1907-08	38	(8)
Gillies C.C.	1912-1996	(Otago) 1936	2	(1)
Gilray C.M.	1885-1974	(Otago) 1905	1	(1)
Given F.J.	1876-1921	(Otago) 1903	9	(–)
Glasgow F.T.	1880-1939	(Taranaki) 1905-06; (Southland) 1908	35	(6)
Glenn W.S.	1877-1953	(Taranaki) 1904-05-06	19	(2)
Glennie E.	1870-1908	(Canterbury) 1897	6	(–)
Goddard J.W.	1920-1996	(South Canterbury) 1949	8	(–)
Goddard M.P.	1921-1974	(South Canterbury) 1946-47-49	20	(5)
Going K.T.	1942-2008	(North Auckland) 1974	3	(–)
Going S.M.	1943-	(North Auckland) 1967-68-69-70-71-72-73-74-75-76-77	86	(29)
Goldsmith J.A.	1969-	(Waikato) 1988	8	(–)
Good A.	1867-1938	(Taranaki) 1893	4	(–)
Good H.M.	1871-1941	(Taranaki) 1894	1	(–)
Goodhue E.J.	1995-	(Crusaders) 2017-18-19	14	(13)
Gordon S.B.	1967-	(Waikato) 1989-90-91-93	19	(2)
Gordon W.R.	1965-	(Waikato) 1990	3	(–)
Graham D.J.	1935-2017	(Canterbury) 1958-60-61-62-63-64	53	(22)
Graham J.B.	1884-1941	(Otago) 1913-14	19	(3)
Graham M.G.	1931-2015	(New South Wales) 1960	1	(–)
Graham W.G.	1957-	(Otago) 1978-79	8	(1)
Granger K.W.	1951-	(Manawatu) 1976	6	(–)
Grant L.A.	1923-2002	(South Canterbury) 1947-49-51	23	(4)
Gray G.D.	1880-1961	(Canterbury) 1908-13	14	(3)
Gray K.F.	1938-1992	(Wellington) 1963-64-65-66-67-68-69	50	(24)
Gray R.	1870-1951	(Wairarapa) 1893	2	(–)
Gray W.N.	1932-1993	(Bay of Plenty) 1955-56-57	11	(6)
Green C.I.	1961-	(Canterbury) 1983-84-85-86-87	39	(20)
Greene K.M.	1949-	(Waikato) 1976-77	8	(–)
Grenside B.A.	1899-1989	(Hawke's Bay) 1928-29	21	(6)
Griffiths J.L.	1912-2001	(Wellington) 1934-35-36-38	30	(7)
Gudsell K.E.	1924-2007	(Wanganui) 1949	6	(–)
Guildford Z.R.	1989-	(Hawke's Bay) 2009-10-11-12	10	(10)
Guy R.A.	1941-	(North Auckland) 1971-72	9	(4)
Haden A.M.	1950-	(Auckland) 1972-73-76-77-78-79-80-81-82-83-84-85	117	(41)
Hadley S.	1904-1970	(Auckland) 1928	11	(4)
Hadley W.E.	1910-1992	(Auckland) 1934-35-36	25	(8)
Haig J.S.	1924-1996	(Otago) 1946	2	(2)
Haig L.S.	1922-1992	(Otago) 1950-51-53-54	29	(9)
Halai F.	1988-	(Blues) 2013	1	(1)
Hales D.A.	1947-	(Canterbury) 1972-73	27	(4)
Hames K.S.	1988-	(Chiefs) 2016-17	10	(9)
Hamilton D.C.	1883-1925	(Southland) 1908	1	(1)
Hamilton S.E.	1980-	(Canterbury) 2006	2	(2)
Hammett M.G.	1972-	(Canterbury) 1999-2000-01-02-03	30	(29)
Hammond I.A.	1925-1998	(Marlborough) 1951-52	8	(1)
Handcock R.A.	1874-1956	(Auckland) 1897	8	(–)
Hardcastle W.R.	1874-1944	(Wellington) 1897	7	(–)
Harding S.	1980-	(Otago) 2002	1	(1)
Harper E.T.*	1877-1918	(Canterbury) 1904-05-06	11	(2)
Harper G.	1867-1937	(Nelson) 1893	3	(–)
Harris J.H.*	1903-1944	(Canterbury) 1925	8	(–)
Harris N.P.	1992-	(Chiefs) 2014-16-17-18	22	(20)

Name	B&D	Representative Team	Games	Tests
Harris P.C.	1946-	(Manawatu) 1976	4	(1)
Harris W.A.	1876-1950	(Otago) 1897	9	(–)
Hart A.H.	1897-1965	(Taranaki) 1924-25	17	(1)
Hart G.F.*	1909-1944	(Canterbury) 1930-31-32-34-35-36	35	(11)
Harvey B.A.	1959-	(Wairarapa Bush) 1986	1	(1)
Harvey I.H.	1903-1966	(Wairarapa) 1924-25-26-28	18	(1)
Harvey L.R.	1919-1993	(Otago) 1949-50	22	(8)
Harvey P.	1880-1949	(Canterbury) 1904	1	(1)
Hasell E.W.	1889-1966	(Canterbury) 1913-20	7	(2)
Havili D.K.	1994-	(Crusaders) 2017	5	(3)
Hay-MacKenzie W.E.	1874-1946	(Auckland) 1901	2	(–)
Hayman C.J.	1979-	(Otago) 2001-02-04-05-06-07	46	(45)
Hayward H.O.	1883-1970	(Auckland) 1908	1	(1)
Hazlett E.J.	1938-2014	(Southland) 1966-67	12	(6)
Hazlett W.E.	1905-1978	(Southland) 1926-28-30	26	(8)
Heeps T.R.	1938-2002	(Wellington) 1962	10	(5)
Heke W.R. (played as W. Rika)	1894-1989	(North Auckland) 1929	6	(3)
Helmore G.H.N.	1862-1922	(Canterbury) 1884	7	(–)
Hemara B.S.	1957-	(Manawatu) 1985	3	(–)
Hemi R.C.	1933-2000	(Waikato) 1953-54-55-56-57-59-60	46	(16)
Hemopo J.N.	1993-	(Highlanders) 2018-19	5	(5)
Henderson P.	1926-2014	(Wanganui) 1949-50	19	(7)
Henderson P.W.	1964-	(Otago) 1989-90-91; (Southland) 1992-93-95	25	(7)
Hendrie J.M.	1951-	(Western Australia) 1970	1	(–)
Herewini M.A.	1940-2014	(Auckland) 1962-63-64-65-66-67	32	(10)
Herrold M.	1869-1949	(Auckland) 1893	2	(–)
Hewett D.N.	1971-	(Canterbury) 2001-02-03	24	(22)
Hewett J.A.	1968-	(Auckland) 1991	1	(1)
Hewitt N.J.	1968-	(Hawke's Bay) 1993; (Southland) 1995-96-97-98	23	(9)
Hewson A.R.	1954-	(Wellington) 1979-81-82-83-84	34	(19)
Hickey P.H.	1899-1942	(Taranaki) 1922	2	(–)
Higginson G.	1954-	(Canterbury) 1980-81; (Hawke's Bay) 1982-83	20	(6)
Hill D.W.	1978-	(Waikato) 2001-06	3	(1)
Hill S.F.	1927-2019	(Canterbury) 1955-56-57-58-59	19	(11)
Hines G.R.	1960-	(Waikato) 1980	12	(1)
Hobbs F.G.	1920-1985	(Canterbury) 1947	6	(–)
Hobbs M.J.B.	1960-2012	(Canterbury) 1983-84-85-86	39	(21)
Hoeata J.M.R.A.	1982-	(Taranaki) 2011	3	(3)
Hoeft C.H.	1974-	(Otago) 1998-99-2000-01-03	31	(30)
Hogan J.	1881-1945	(Wanganui) 1907	2	(–)
Holah M.R.	1976-	(Waikato) 2001-02-03-04-05-06	39	(36)
Holden A.W.	1907-1970	(Otago) 1928	3	(–)
Holder E.C.	1908-1974	(Buller) 1932-34	10	(1)
Holmes B.	1946-	(North Auckland) 1970-72-73	31	(–)
Hook L.S.	1905-1979	(Auckland) 1928-29	12	(3)
Hooper J.A.	1913-1976	(Canterbury) 1937-38	7	(3)
Hopa A.R.	1971-1998	(Waikato) 1997	4	(–)
Hopkinson A.E.	1941-1999	(Canterbury) 1967-68-69-70	35	(9)
Hore A.K.	1978-	(Taranaki) 2002-04-05-06-07-08-09-10-11-12; (Highlanders) 2013	83	(83)
Hore J.	1907-1979	(Otago) 1928-30-32-34-35-36	45	(10)
Horsley R.H.	1932-2007	(Wellington) 1960; (Manawatu) 1963	31	(3)
Hotop J.	1929-2015	(Canterbury) 1952-55	3	(3)

Name	B&D	Representative Team	Games	Tests
Howarth S.P.	1968-	(Auckland) 1993-94	10	(4)
Howden J.	1900-1978	(Southland) 1928	1	(–)
Howlett D.C.	1978-	(Auckland) 2000-01-02-03-04-05-06-07	63	(62)
Hughes A.M.	1924-2005	(Auckland) 1947-49-50	7	(6)
Hughes D.J.	1869-1951	(Taranaki) 1894	1	(–)
Hughes E.	1881-1928	(Southland) 1907-08; (Wellington) 1921	9	(6)
Hullena L.C.	1965-	(Wellington) 1990-91	9	(–)
Humphreys G.W.	1870-1933	(Canterbury) 1894	1	(–)
Humphries A.L.	1874-1953	(Taranaki) 1897-1901-03	15	(–)
Hunt D.	1995-	(Highlanders) 2017-18	2	(1)
Hunter B.A.	1950-	(Otago) 1970-71	10	(3)
Hunter J.	1879-1962	(Taranaki) 1905-06-07-08	36	(11)
Hurst I.A.	1951-	(Canterbury) 1972-73-74	32	(5)
Ieremia A.	1970-	(Wellington) 1994-95-96-97-99-2000	40	(30)
Ifwersen K.D.	1893-1967	(Auckland) 1921	1	(1)
Innes C.R.	1969-	(Auckland) 1989-90-91	30	(17)
Innes G.D.	1910-1992	(Canterbury) 1932	7	(1)
Ioane A.L.	1995-	(Blues) 2017	1	(–)
Ioane, J.	1995-	(Highlanders) 2019	1	(1)
Ioane R.E.	1997-	(Blues) 2016-17-18-19	29	(29)
Irvine I.B.	1929-2013	(North Auckland) 1952	1	(1)
Irvine J.G.	1888-1939	(Otago) 1914	10	(3)
Irvine W.R.	1898-1952	(Hawke's Bay) 1923-24-25-26; (Wairarapa) 1930	41	(5)
Irwin M.W.	1935-2018	(Otago) 1955-56-58-59-60	25	(7)
Ivimey F.E.B.	1880-1961	(Otago) 1910	1	(–)
Jack C.R.	1978-	(Canterbury) 2001-02-03-04-05; (Tasman) 2006-07	68	(67)
Jackson E.S.	1914-1975	(Hawke's Bay) 1936-37-38	11	(6)
Jacob H.	1894-1955	(Horowhenua) 1920	8	(–)
Jacob J.P. LeG.	1877-1909	(Southland) 1901	2	(–)
Jacobson, L.B.	1997-	(Chiefs) 2019	2	(2)
Jaffray J.L.	1950-	(Otago) 1972-75-76-77-78; (South Canterbury) 1979	23	(7)
Jaffray M.W.R.	1949-	(Otago) 1976	4	(–)
Jane C.S.	1983-	(Wellington) 2008-09-10-11-12; (Hurricanes) 2013-14	55	(53)
Jarden R.A.	1929-1977	(Wellington) 1951-52-53-54-55-56	37	(16)
Jefferd A.C.R.	1953-	(East Coast) 1980-81	5	(3)
Jennings A.G.T.	1940-	(Bay of Plenty) 1967	6	(–)
Jervis F.M.	1870-1952	(Auckland) 1893	10	(–)
Jessep E.M.	1904-1983	(Wellington) 1931-32	8	(2)
Johns P.A.	1944-	(Wanganui) 1968	6	(–)
Johnson L.M.	1897-1983	(Wellington) 1925-28-30	25	(4)
Johnston D.	1903-1938	(Taranaki) 1925	2	(–)
Johnston W.	1881-1951	(Otago) 1905-07	27	(3)
Johnstone B.R.	1950-	(Auckland) 1976-77-78-79-80	45	(13)
Johnstone C.R.	1980-	(Canterbury) 2005	3	(3)
Johnstone P.	1922-1997	(Otago) 1949-50-51	26	(9)
Jones I.D.	1967-	(North Auckland) 1989-90-91-92-93; (North Harbour) 1994-95-96-97-98-99	105	(79)
Jones M.G.	1942-1975	(North Auckland) 1973	5	(1)
Jones M.N.	1965-	(Auckland) 1987-88-89-90-91-92-93-94-95-96-97-98	74	(55)
Jones P.F.H.	1932-1994	(North Auckland) 1953-54-55-56-58-59-60	37	(11)
Joseph H.T.	1949-	(Canterbury) 1971	2	(2)
Joseph J.W.	1969-	(Otago) 1992-93-94-95	30	(20)
Kahui R.D.	1985-	(Waikato) 2008-10-11	18	(17)

Name	B&D	Representative Team	Games	Tests
Kaino J.	1983-	(Auckland) 2004-06-08-09-10-11; (Blues) 2014-15-16-17	83	(81)
Kane G.N.	1952-	(Waikato) 1974	7	(–)
Karam J.F.	1951-	(Wellington) 1972-73-74; (Horowhenua) 1975	42	(10)
Katene T.	1929-1992	(Wellington) 1955	1	(1)
Keane K.J.	1953-	(Canterbury) 1979	6	(–)
Kearney J.C.	1920-1998	(Otago) 1947-49	22	(4)
Kelleher B.T.	1976-	(Otago) 1999-2000-01-02-03-04; (Waikato) 2004-05-06-07	58	(57)
Kelly J.W.	1926-2002	(Auckland) 1949-53-54	16	(2)
Kember G.F.	1945-	(Wellington) 1967-70	19	(1)
Kenny D.J.	1961-	(Otago) 1986	3	(–)
Kerr A.	1871-1936	(Canterbury) 1896	1	(–)
Kerr-Barlow T.N.J.	1990-	(Waikato) 2012; (Chiefs) 2013-14-15-16-17	29	(27)
Ketels R.C.	1954-	(Counties) 1979-80-81	16	(5)
Kiernan H.A.D.	1876-1947	(Auckland) 1903	8	(1)
Kilby F.D.	1906-1985	(Wellington) 1928-32-34	18	(4)
Killeen B.A.	1911-1993	(Auckland) 1936	2	(1)
King R.M.	1980-	(Waikato) 2002	1	(1)
King R.R.	1909-1988	(West Coast) 1934-35-36-37-38	42	(13)
Kingstone C.N.	1895-1960	(Taranaki) 1921	3	(3)
Kirk D.E.	1961-	(Otago) 1983-84; (Auckland) 1985-86-87	34	(17)
Kirkpatrick A.	1898-1971	(Hawke's Bay) 1925-26	12	(–)
Kirkpatrick I.A.	1946-	(Canterbury) 1967-68-69; (Poverty Bay) 1970-71-72-73-74-75-76-77	113	(39)
Kirton E.W.	1939-	(Otago) 1963-64-67-68-69-70	49	(13)
Kirwan J.J.	1964-	(Auckland) 1984-85-86-87-88-89-90-91-92-93-94	96	(63)
Kivell A.L.	1897-1988	(Taranaki) 1929	5	(2)
Knight A.	1906-1990	(Auckland) 1926-28-34	14	(1)
Knight G.A.	1951-	(Manawatu) 1977-78-79-80-81-82-83-84-85-86	66	(36)
Knight L.A.G.	1901-1973	(Auckland) 1925	5	(–)
Knight L.G.	1949-	(Auckland) 1974; (Poverty Bay) 1976-77	35	(6)
Knight M.O.	1945-	(Counties) 1968	8	(–)
Koteka T.T.	1956-	(Waikato) 1981-82	6	(2)
Kreft A.J.	1945-	(Otago) 1968	4	(1)
Kronfeld J.A.	1971-	(Otago) 1995-96-97-98-99-2000	56	(54)
Kururangi R.	1957-	(Counties) 1978	8	(–)
Laidlaw C.R.	1943-	(Otago) 1963-64-65-66-67; (Canterbury) 1968; (Otago) 1970	57	(20)
Laidlaw K.F.	1934-	(Southland) 1960	17	(3)
Lam P.R.	1968-	(Auckland) 1992	1	(–)
Lambert K.K.	1952-	(Manawatu) 1972-73-74-76-77	40	(11)
Lambie J.T.	1870-1905	(Taranaki) 1893-94	12	(–)
Lambourn A.	1910-1999	(Wellington) 1934-35-36-37-38	40	(10)
Larsen B.P.	1969-	(North Harbour) 1992-93-94-95-96	40	(17)
Latimer T.D.	1986-	(Bay of Plenty) 2009	6	(5)
Laulala C.D.E.	1982-	(Canterbury) 2004-06	3	(2)
Laulala N.E.	1991-	(Crusaders) 2015-17-18 (Chiefs) 2019	26	(26)
Laumape K.H.	1993-	(Hurricanes) 2017-18-19	15	(13)
Lauaki S.T.	1981-2017	(Waikato) 2005-07-08	17	(17)
Law A.D.	1904-1961	(Manawatu) 1925	4	(–)
Lawson G.P.	1899-1985	(South Canterbury) 1925	2	(–)
Lecky J.G.	1863-1917	(Auckland) 1884	7	(–)
Lee D.D.	1976-	(Otago) 2002	2	(2)
Leeson J.	1909-1960	(Waikato) 1934	5	(–)

Name	B&D	Representative Team	Games	Tests
LeLievre J.M.	1933-2016	(Canterbury) 1962-63-64	25	(1)
Lendrum R.N.	1948-	(Counties) 1973	3	(1)
Leonard B.G.	1985-	(Waikato) 2007-09	14	(13)
Leslie A.R.	1944-	(Wellington) 1974-75-76	34	(10)
Levien H.J.	1935-2008	(Otago) 1957	8	(–)
Leys E.T.	1907-1989	(Wellington) 1929	5	(1)
Lienert-Brown A.R.	1995-	(Chiefs) 2016-17-18-19	44	(43)
Lilburne H.T.	1908-1976	(Canterbury) 1928-29-30; (Wellington) 1931-32-34	40	(10)
Lindsay D.F.	1906-1978	(Otago) 1928	14	(3)
Lindsay W.G.	1879-1965	(Southland) 1914	4	(–)
Lineen T.R.	1936-	(Auckland) 1957-58-59-60	35	(12)
Lister T.N.	1943-2017	(South Canterbury) 1968-69-70-71	26	(8)
Little P.F.	1934-1993	(Auckland) 1961-62-63-64	29	(10)
Little W.K.	1969-	(North Harbour) 1989-90-91-92-93-94-95-96-97-98	75	(50)
Loader C.J.	1931-	(Wellington) 1953-54	16	(4)
Lochore B.J.	1940-2019	(Wairarapa) 1963-64-65-66-67-68-69-70; (Wairarapa Bush) 1971	68	(25)
Lockington T.M.	1913-2001	(Auckland) 1936	1	(–)
Loe R.W.	1960-	(Waikato) 1986-87-88-89-90-91-92; (Canterbury) 1994-95	78	(49)
Lomas A.R.	1894-1975	(Auckland) 1925-26	15	(–)
Lomax T.S.	1996-	(Highlanders) 2018	1	(1)
Lomu J.T.	1975-2015	(Counties Manukau) 1994-95-96-97-98-99; (Wellington) 2000-01-02	73	(63)
Long A.T.	1879-1960	(Auckland) 1903	10	(1)
Loveday J.K.	1949-	(Manawatu) 1978	7	(–)
Loveridge D.S.	1952-	(Taranaki) 1978-79-80-81-82-83-85	54	(24)
Loveridge G.	1890-1970	(Taranaki) 1913-14	11	(–)
Lowen K.R.	1976-	(Waikato) 2002	1	(1)
Luatua D.S.	1991	(Blues) 2013-14-16	15	(15)
Lucas F.W.	1902-1957	(Auckland) 1923-24-25-28-30	41	(7)
Lunn W.A.	1926-1996	(Otago) 1949	2	(2)
Lynch T.W.	1892-1950	(South Canterbury) 1913-14	23	(4)
Lynch T.W.	1927-2006	(Canterbury) 1951	10	(3)
Maber G.	1869-1894	(Wellington) 1894	1	(–)
McAlister C.L.	1983-	(North Harbour) 2005-06-07-09	31	(30)
McAtamney F.S.	1934-	(Otago) 1956-57	9	(1)
McCahill B.J.	1964-	(Auckland) 1987-88-89-90-91	32	(10)
McCarthy P.	1893-1976	(Canterbury) 1923	1	(–)
McCashin T.M.	1944-2017	(Wellington) 1968	7	(–)
McCaw R.H.	1980-	(Canterbury) 2001-02-03-04-05-06-07-08-09-10-11-12; (Crusaders) 2013-14-15	149	(148)
McCaw W.A.	1927-	(Southland) 1951-53-54	32	(5)
McCleary B.V.	1897-1978	(Canterbury) 1924-25	12	(–)
McClymont W.G.	1905-1970	(Otago) 1928	3	(–)
McCool M.J.	1951-	(Wairarapa Bush) 1979	2	(1)
McCormick A.G.	1899-1969	(Canterbury) 1925	1	(–)
McCormick J.	1923-2006	(Hawke's Bay) 1947	3	(–)
McCormick W.F.	1939-2018	(Canterbury) 1965-67-68-69-70-71	44	(16)
McCullough J.F.	1936-	(Taranaki) 1959	3	(3)
McDonald A.	1883-1967	(Otago) 1905-06-07-08-13	41	(8)
Macdonald A.J.	1981-	(Auckland) 2005	2	(2)
Macdonald H.H.	1947-	(Canterbury) 1972-73-74; (North Auckland) 1975-76	48	(12)
MacDonald L.R.	1977-	(Canterbury) 2000-01-02-03-05-06-07-08	56	(56)

Name	B&D	Representative Team	Games	Tests
McDonnell P.	1874-1950	(Wanganui) 1896	1	(–)
McDonnell J.M.	1973-	(Otago) 2002	8	(8)
McDowall S.C.	1961-	(Auckland) 1985-86-87-88; (Bay of Plenty) 1989; (Auckland) 1989-90-91-92	81	(46)
McEldowney J.T.	1947-2012	(Taranaki) 1976-77	10	(2)
MacEwan I.N.	1934-	(Wellington) 1956-57-58-59-60-61-62	52	(20)
McGahan P.W.	1964-	(North Harbour) 1990-91	6	(–)
McGrattan B.	1959-	(Wellington) 1983-84-85-86	23	(6)
McGregor A.A.	1953-	(Southland) 1978	3	(–)
McGregor A.J.	1889-1963	(Auckland) 1913	11	(2)
McGregor D.	1881-1947	(Canterbury) 1903; (Wellington) 1904-05-06	31	(4)
McGregor N.P.	1901-1973	(Canterbury) 1924-25-28	27	(2)
McGregor R.W.	1874-1925	(Auckland) 1901-03-04	10	(2)
McHugh M.J.	1917-2010	(Auckland) 1946-49	14	(3)
MacIntosh C.N.	1869-1918	(South Canterbury) 1893	4	(–)
McIntosh D.N.	1931-	(Wellington) 1956-57	13	(4)
McKay D.W.	1937-	(Auckland) 1961-62-63	12	(5)
Mackay J.D.	1905-1985	(Wellington) 1928	2	(–)
McKechnie B.J.	1953-	(Southland) 1977-78-79-81	26	(10)
McKellar G.F.	1884-1960	(Wellington) 1910	5	(3)
McKenzie D.S.	1995-	(Chiefs) 2016-17-18	23	(23)
MacKenzie R.H.	1869-1940	(Auckland) 1893	2	(–)
MacKenzie R.H.C.	1904-1993	(Wellington) 1928	2	(–)
McKenzie R.J.	1892-1968	(Wellington) 1913; (Auckland) 1914	20	(4)
MacKenzie R.M.	1909-2000	(Manawatu) 1934-35-36-37-38	35	(9)
McKenzie W.	1871-1943	(Wairarapa) 1893; (Wellington) 1894-96-97	20	(–)
Mackintosh J.L.	1985-	(Southland) 2008	2	(1)
Mackrell W.H.C.	1881-1917	(Auckland) 1905-06	7	(1)
Macky J.V.	1887-1951	(Auckland) 1913	1	(1)
McLachlan J.S.	1949-	(Auckland) 1974	8	(1)
McLaren H.C.	1926-1992	(Waikato) 1952	1	(1)
McLean A.L.	1898-1964	(Bay of Plenty) 1921-23	3	(2)
McLean C.	1892-1965	(Buller) 1920	5	(–)
McLean H.F.	1907-1997	(Wellington) 1930-32; (Auckland) 1934-35-36	29	(9)
McLean J.K.	1923-2005	(King Country) 1947; (Auckland) 1949	5	(2)
McLean R.J.	1960-	(Wairarapa Bush) 1987	2	(–)
McLeod B.E.	1940-1996	(Counties) 1964-65-66-67-68-69-70	46	(24)
McLeod S.J.	1973-	(Waikato) 1996-97-98	17	(10)
McMeeking D.T.M.	1896-1976	(Otago) 1923	2	(–)
McMinn A.F.	1880-1919	(Wairarapa) 1903; (Manawatu) 1905	10	(2)
McMinn F.A.	1874-1947	(Manawatu) 1904	1	(1)
McMullen R.F.	1933-2004	(Auckland) 1957-58-59-60	29	(11)
McNab J.A.	1895-1979	(Hawke's Bay) 1925	1	(–)
McNab J.R.	1924-2009	(Otago) 1949-50	17	(6)
McNaughton A.M.	1947-	(Bay of Plenty) 1971-72	9	(3)
McNeece J.*	1885-1917	(Southland) 1913-14	11	(5)
McNicol A.L.R.	1944-2017	(Wanganui) 1973	5	(–)
McPhail B.E.	1937-	(Canterbury) 1959	2	(2)
MacPherson D.G.	1882-1956	(Otago) 1905	1	(1)
Macpherson G.	1962-	(Otago) 1986	1	(1)
MacRae I.R.	1943-	(Hawke's Bay) 1963-64-66-67-68-69-70	45	(17)
McRae J.A.	1914-1977	(Southland) 1946	2	(2)
McRobie N.	1873-1929	(Southland) 1896	1	(–)
McWilliams R.G.	1901-1984	(Auckland) 1928-29-30	27	(10)
Maguire J.R.	1886-1966	(Auckland) 1910	6	(3)
Mahoney A.	1908-1979	(Bush) 1929-34-35-36	26	(4)

Name	B&D	Representative Team	Games	Tests
Mains L.W.	1946-	(Otago) 1971-76	15	(4)
Major J.	1940-	(Taranaki) 1963-64-67	24	(1)
Maka I.	1975-	(Otago) 1998	4	(4)
Maling T.S.	1975-	(Otago) 2001-02-04	13	(11)
Manchester J.E.	1908-1983	(Canterbury) 1932-34-35-36	36	(9)
Mannix S.J.	1971-	(Wellington) 1990-91-94	9	(1)
Markham P.F.	1891-1953	(Wellington) 1921	1	(–)
Marshall J.W.	1973-	(Canterbury) 1995-96-97-98-99-2000-01-02-03-04-05	88	(81)
Masaga L.T.C.	1986-	(Counties Manukau) 2009	1	(1)
Masoe M.C.	1979-	(Taranaki) 2005; (Wellington) 2006-07	20	(20)
Mason D.F.	1923-1981	(Wellington) 1947	6	(1)
Masters F.H.	1893-1980	(Taranaki) 1922	4	(–)
Masters R.R.	1900-1967	(Canterbury) 1923-24-25	31	(4)
Mataira H.K.	1910-1979	(Hawke's Bay) 1934	5	(1)
Matheson J.D.	1948-	(Otago) 1972	13	(5)
Mathewson A.S.	1985-	(Wellington) 2008-10	5	(4)
Mathieson R.G.	1899-1966	(Otago) 1922	4	(–)
Matson J.T.F.	1973	(Canterbury) 1995-96	5	(–)
Mattson H.A.	1900-1980	(Auckland) 1925	6	(–)
Mauger A.J.D.	1980-	(Canterbury) 2001-02-03-04-05-06-07	46	(45)
Mauger N.K.	1978-	(Canterbury) 2001	2	(–)
Max D.S.	1906-1972	(Nelson) 1931-32-34	8	(3)
Maxwell N.M.C.	1976-	(Canterbury) 1999-2000-01-02-04	36	(36)
Mayerhofler M.A.	1972-	(Canterbury) 1998	6	(6)
Meads C.E.	1936-2017	(King Country) 1957-58-59-60-61-62-63-64-65-66-67-68-69-70-71	133	(55)
Meads S.T.	1938-	(King Country) 1961-62-63-64-65-66	30	(15)
Mealamu K.F.	1979-	(Auckland) 2002-03-04-05-06-07-08-09-10-11-12; (Blues) 2013-14-15	133	(132)
Meates K.F.	1930-	(Canterbury) 1952	2	(2)
Meates W.A.	1923-2003	(Otago) 1949-50	20	(7)
Meeuws K.J.	1974-	(Otago) 1998-99-2000-01-02-04; (Auckland) 2003	45	(42)
Mehrtens A.P.	1973-	(Canterbury) 1995-96-97-98-99-2000-01-02-04	72	(70)
Mehrtens G.M.	1907-1954	(Canterbury) 1928	3	(–)
Messam L.J.	1984-	(Waikato) 2008-09-10-11-12; (Chiefs) 2013-14-15	45	(43)
Metcalfe T.C.	1909-1969	(Southland) 1931-32	7	(2)
Mexted G.G.	1927-2009	(Wellington) 1950-51	5	(1)
Mexted M.G.	1953-	(Wellington) 1979-80-81-82-83-84-85	72	(34)
Mika B.M.	1981-	(Auckland) 2002	3	(3)
Mika D.G.	1972-2018	(Auckland) 1999	8	(7)
Mill J.J.	1899-1950	(Hawke's Bay) 1923-24-25-26; (Wairarapa) 1930	33	(4)
Miller P.C.	1975-	(Otago) 2001	2	(–)
Miller T.J.	1974-	(Waikato) 1997	4	(–)
Milliken H.M.	1914-1993	(Canterbury) 1938	7	(3)
Mills H.P.	1873-1905	(Taranaki) 1897	8	(–)
Mills J.G.	1960-	(Auckland) 1984	2	(–)
Millton E.B.	1861-1942	(Canterbury) 1884	7	(–)
Millton W.V.	1858-1887	(Canterbury) 1884	8	(–)
Milner H.P.	1946-1996	(Wanganui) 1970	16	(1)
Milner-Skudder N.R.	1990-	(Hurricanes) 2015,17-18	13	(13)
Mitchell J.E.P.	1964-	(Waikato) 1993	6	(–)
Mitchell N.A.	1913-1981	(Southland) 1935-36-37; (Otago) 1938	32	(8)
Mitchell T.W.	1950-	(Canterbury) 1974-76	17	(1)
Mitchell W.J.	1890-1959	(Canterbury) 1910	5	(2)
Mitchinson F.E.	1884-1978	(Wellington) 1907-08-10-13	31	(11)
Moala G.	1990	(Blues) 2015-16	4	(4)

Name	B&D	Representative Team	Games	Tests
Moffitt J.E.	1889-1964	(Wellington) 1920-21	12	(3)
Moli A.	1995-	(Chiefs) 2017-19	5	(4)
Molloy B.P.J.	1931-	(Canterbury) 1957	5	(–)
Moody J.P.T.	1988-	(Crusaders) 2014-15-16-17-18-19	46	(46)
Moore G.J.T.	1923-1991	(Otago) 1949	1	(1)
Moreton R.C.	1942-2016	(Canterbury) 1962-64-65	12	(7)
Morgan H.D.	1902-1969	(Otago) 1923	1	(–)
Morgan J.E.	1945-2002	(North Auckland) 1974-76	22	(5)
Morris T.J.	1942-	(Nelson Bays) 1972-73	23	(3)
Morrison T.C.	1913-1985	(South Canterbury) 1938	5	(3)
Morrison T.G.	1951-	(Otago) 1973	5	(1)
Morrissey B.L.	1952-	(Waikato) 1981	3	(–)
Morrissey P.J.	1939-2013	(Canterbury) 1962	3	(3)
Mourie G.N.K.	1952-	(Taranaki) 1976-77-78-79-80-81-82	61	(21)
Mo'unga R.	1994-	(Crusaders) 2017-18-19	18	(17)
Mowlem J.	1870-1951	(Manawatu) 1893	4	(–)
Muliaina J.M.	1980-	(Auckland) 2003-04-05; (Waikato) 2006-07-08-09-10-11	102	(100)
Muller B.L.	1942-2019	(Taranaki) 1967-68-69-70-71	35	(14)
Mumm W.J.	1922-1993	(Buller) 1949	1	(1)
Munro H.G.	1896-1974	(Otago) 1924-25	9	(–)
Murdoch K.	1943-2018	(Otago) 1970-72	27	(3)
Murdoch P.H.	1941-1995	(Auckland) 1964-65	5	(5)
Murray F.S.M.	1871-1952	(Auckland) 1893-97	20	(–)
Murray H.V.	1888-1971	(Canterbury) 1913-14	22	(4)
Murray P.C.	1884-1968	(Wanganui) 1908	1	(1)
Myers R.G.	1950-	(Waikato) 1977-78	5	(1)
Mynott H.J.	1876-1924	(Taranaki) 1905-06-07-10	39	(8)
Naholo W.R.	1991	(Highlanders) 2015-16-17-18	27	(26)
Nathan W.J.	1940-	(Auckland) 1962-63-64-66-67	37	(14)
Nelson K.A.	1938-	(Otago) 1962-63-64	18	(2)
Nepia G.	1905-1986	(Hawke's Bay) 1924-25; (East Coast) 1929-30	46	(9)
Nesbit S.R.	1936-	(Auckland) 1960	13	(2)
Neville W.R.	1954-	(North Auckland) 1981	4	(–)
Newby C.A.	1979-	(North Harbour) 2004-06	3	(3)
Newton F.	1881-1955	(Canterbury) 1905-06	19	(3)
Ngatai C.J.	1990-	(Chiefs) 2015	1	(1)
Nicholls H.E.	1900-1978	(Wellington) 1921-22-23	7	(1)
Nicholls H.G.	1897-1977	(Wellington) 1923	1	(–)
Nicholls M.F.	1901-1972	(Wellington) 1921-22-24-25-26-28-30	51	(10)
Nicholson G.W.	1878-1968	(Auckland) 1903-04-05-06-07	39	(4)
Nonu M.A.	1982-	(Wellington) 2003-04-05-06-07-08-09-10-11-12; (Highlanders) 2013; (Blues) 2014; (Hurricanes) 2015	104	(103)
Norton R.W.	1942-	(Canterbury) 1971-72-73-74-75-76-77	61	(27)
O'Brien A.J.	1897-1969	(Auckland) 1922	3	(–)
O'Brien J.	1871-1946	(Wellington) 1901	1	(–)
O'Brien J.G.	1889-1958	(Auckland) 1914-20	12	(1)
O'Callaghan M.W.	1946-	(Manawatu) 1968	3	(3)
O'Callaghan T.R.	1925-2004	(Wellington) 1949	1	(1)
O'Connor T.B.	1860-1936	(Auckland) 1884	7	(–)
O'Dea R.J.	1930-1986	(Thames Valley) 1953-54	5	(–)
O'Donnell D.H.	1921-1992	(Wellington) 1949	1	(1)
O'Donnell J.M.	1860-1942	(Otago) 1884	7	(–)
O'Dowda B.C.	1874-1954	(Taranaki) 1901	2	(–)
O'Halloran J.D.	1972-	(Wellington) 2000	1	(1)

Name	B&D	Representative Team	Games	Tests
O'Leary M.J.	1883-1963	(Auckland) 1910-13	8	(4)
O'Neill K.J.	1982-	(Waikato) 2008	1	(1)
Old G.H.	1956-	(Manawatu) 1980-81-82-83	17	(3)
Oliphant R.	1870-1956	(Wellington) 1893; (Auckland) 1896	3	(–)
Oliver A.D.	1975-	(Otago) 1996-97-98-99-2000-01-03-04-05-06-07	67	(59)
Oliver C.J.	1905-1977	(Canterbury) 1928-29-34-35-36	33	(7)
Oliver D.J.	1907-1990	(Wellington) 1930	3	(2)
Oliver D.O.	1930-1997	(Otago) 1953-54	20	(2)
Oliver F.J.	1948-2014	(Southland) 1976-77; (Otago) 1978-79; (Manawatu) 1980-81	43	(17)
Orchard S.A.	1875-1947	(Canterbury) 1896-97	8	(–)
Ormond J.	1891-1970	(Hawke's Bay) 1923	1	(–)
Orr R.W.	1923-2011	(Otago) 1949	1	(1)
Osborne G.M.	1971-	(North Harbour) 1995-96-97-99	29	(19)
Osborne W.M.	1955-	(Wanganui) 1975-76-77-78-80-82	48	(16)
O'Sullivan J.M.	1883-1960	(Taranaki) 1905-07	29	(5)
O'Sullivan T.P.A.	1936-1997	(Taranaki) 1960-61-62	16	(4)
Paewai L.	1906-1970	(Hawke's Bay) 1923-24	8	(–)
Page J.R.	1908-1985	(Wellington) 1931-32-34-35	18	(6)
Page M.L.	1902-1987	(Canterbury) 1928	1	(–)
Palmer B.P.	1901-1932	(Auckland) 1928-29-32	18	(3)
Papali'i D.R.	1997	(Blues) 2018-19	3	(3)
Parker J.H.	1897-1980	(Canterbury) 1924-25	21	(3)
Parkhill A.A.	1912-1986	(Otago) 1937-38	10	(6)
Parkinson R.M.	1948-2009	(Poverty Bay) 1972-73	20	(7)
Parsons J.W.	1986-	(Blues) 2014-16	2	(2)
Paterson A.M.	1885-1933	(Otago) 1908-10	9	(5)
Paton H.	1881-1964	(Otago) 1907-10	8	(2)
Pauling T.G.	1873-1927	(Wellington) 1896-97	9	(–)
Pene A.R.B.	1967-	(Otago) 1992-93-94	26	(15)
Pepper C.S.*	1911-1943	(Auckland) 1935-36	17	(–)
Perenara T.T.R.	1992-	(Hurricanes) 2014-15-16-17-18-19	65	(64)
Perry A.	1899-1977	(Otago) 1923	1	(–)
Perry R.G.	1953-	(Mid Canterbury) 1980	1	(–)
Perry T.G.	1988-	(Crusaders) 2017-18	8	(6)
Petersen L.C.	1897-1961	(Canterbury) 1921-22-23	8	(–)
Phillips W.J.	1914-1982	(King Country) 1937-38	7	(3)
Philpott S.	1965-	(Canterbury) 1988-90-91	14	(2)
Pickering E.A.R.	1936-2016	(Waikato) 1957-58-59-60	21	(3)
Pierce M.J.	1957-	(Wellington) 1984-85-86-87-88-89-90	54	(26)
Piutau S.T.	1991-	(Blues) 2013-14-15	17	(17)
Pokere S.T.	1958-	(Southland) 1981-82-83; (Auckland) 1984-85	39	(18)
Pollock H.R.	1909-1984	(Wellington) 1932-36	8	(5)
Porteous H.G.	1875-1951	(Otago) 1903	3	(–)
Porter C.G.	1899-1976	(Wellington) 1923-24-25-26-28-29-30	41	(7)
Potaka W.P.	ca 1903-1967	(Wanganui) 1923	2	(–)
Preston J.P.	1967-	(Canterbury) 1991-92; (Wellington) 1993-96-97	27	(10)
Pringle A.	1899-1973	(Wellington) 1923	1	(–)
Pringle W.P.	1869-1945	(Wellington) 1893	5	(–)
Procter A.C.	1906-1989	(Otago) 1932	4	(1)
Proctor M.P.	1992-	(Hurricanes) 2018	1	(1)
Pulu A.W.	1990-	(Chiefs) 2014	2	(2)
Purdue C.A.	1874-1941	(Southland) 1901-05	3	(1)
Purdue E.	1879-1939	(Southland) 1905	1	(1)

Name	B&D	Representative Team	Games	Tests
Purdue G.B.	1909-1981	(Southland) 1931-32	7	(4)
Purvis G.H.	1960-	(Waikato) 1989-90-91-92-93	28	(2)
Purvis N.A.	1953-2008	(Otago) 1976	12	(1)
Quaid C.E.	1908-1984	(Otago) 1938	4	(2)
Ralph C.S.	1977-	(Auckland) 1998; (Canterbury) 2001-02-03	16	(14)
Ranby R.M.	1977-	(Waikato) 2001	1	(1)
Randell T.C.	1974-	(Otago) 1995-96-97-98-99-2000-01-02	61	(51)
Randle R.Q.	1974-	(Waikato) 2001	2	(–)
Ranger R.M.N.	1986-	(Northland) 2010; (Blues) 2013	6	(6)
Rangi R.E.	1941-1988	(Auckland) 1964-65-66	10	(10)
Rankin J.G.	1914-1989	(Canterbury) 1936-37	4	(3)
Rawlinson G.P.	1978-	(North Harbour) 2006-07	4	(4)
Read K.J.	1985-	(Canterbury) 2008-09-10-11-12; (Crusaders) 2013-14-15-16-17-18-19	128	(127)
Reece, S.L.	1997-	(Crusaders) 2019	7	(7)
Reedy W.J.	1880-1939	(Wellington) 1908	2	(2)
Reid A.R.	1929-1994	(Waikato) 1951-52-56-57	17	(5)
Reid H.R.	1958-	(Bay of Plenty) 1980-81-83-84-85-86	40	(9)
Reid K.H.	1904-1972	(Wairarapa) 1929	5	(2)
Reid S.T.	1912-2003	(Hawke's Bay) 1935-36-37	27	(9)
Reihana B.T.	1976-	(Waikato) 2000	2	(2)
Reside W.B.	1905-1985	(Wairarapa) 1929	6	(1)
Retallick B.A.	1991-	(Hawke's Bay/Bay of Plenty) 2012; (Chiefs) 2013-14-15-16-17-18-19	81	(81)
Rhind P.K.	1915-1996	(Canterbury) 1946	2	(2)
Richardson J.	1899-1994	(Otago) 1921-22; (Southland) 1923-24-25	42	(7)
Rickit H.A.	1951-	(Waikato) 1981	2	(2)
Ridge M.J.	1969-	(Auckland) 1989	6	(–)
Ridland A.J.*	1882-1918	(Southland) 1910	6	(3)
Riechelmann C.C.	1972-	(Auckland) 1997	10	(6)
Righton L.S.	1898-1972	(Auckland) 1923-25	9	(–)
Roberts E.J.	1891-1972	(Wellington) 1913-14-20-21	26	(5)
Roberts F.	1882-1956	(Wellington) 1905-06-07-08-10	52	(12)
Roberts H.	1862-1949	(Wellington) 1884	7	(–)
Roberts R.W.	1889-1973	(Taranaki) 1913-14	23	(5)
Roberts W.	1871-1937	(Wellington) 1896-97	8	(–)
Robertson B.J.	1952-	(Counties) 1972-73-74-76-77-78-79-80-81	102	(34)
Robertson D.J.	1947-	(Otago) 1974-75-76-77	30	(10)
Robertson G.S.	1859-1920	(Otago) 1884	8	(–)
Robertson S.M.	1974-	(Canterbury) 1998-99-2000-01-02	23	(23)
Robilliard A.C.C.	1903-1990	(Canterbury) 1924-25-26-28	27	(4)
Robins B.G.	1958-	(Taranaki) 1985	4	(–)
Robinson A.G.	1956-	(North Auckland) 1983	4	(–)
Robinson C.E.	1927-1983	(Southland) 1951-52	11	(5)
Robinson J.T.	1906-1968	(Canterbury) 1928	3	(–)
Robinson K.J.	1976-	(Waikato) 2002-04-06-07	12	(12)
Robinson M.D.	1975-	(North Harbour) 1997-98-2001	8	(3)
Robinson M.P.	1974-	(Canterbury) 2000-02	9	(9)
Rokocoko J.T.	1983-	(Auckland) 2003-04-05-06-07-08-09-10	69	(68)
Rollerson D.L.	1953-2017	(Manawatu) 1976-80-81	24	(8)
Romano L.	1986-	(Canterbury) 2012; (Crusaders) 2013-14-15-16-17	32	(31)
Roper R.A.	1923-	(Taranaki) 1949-50	5	(5)
Ross I.B.	1984-	(Canterbury) 2009	8	(8)
Ross J.C.	1949-	(Mid Canterbury) 1981	5	(–)

Name	B&D	Representative Team	Games	Tests
Rowlands G.D.	1947-	(Bay of Plenty) 1976	4	(–)
Rowley H.C.B.	1924-1956	(Wanganui) 1949	1	(1)
Rush E.J.	1965-	(North Harbour) 1992-93-95-96	29	(9)
Rush X.J.	1977-	(Auckland) 1998-2004	8	(8)
Rushbrook C.A.	1907-1987	(Wellington) 1928	10	(–)
Rutledge L.M.	1952-	(Southland) 1978-79-80	31	(13)
Ryan E.	1891-1965	(Wellington) 1921	1	(–)
Ryan J.	1887-1957	(Wellington) 1910-14	15	(4)
Ryan J.A.C.	1983-	(Otago) 2005-06	9	(9)
Ryan P.J.	1950-1985	(Hawke's Bay) 1976	5	(–)
Ryan T.	1863-1927	(Auckland) 1884	9	(-)
Sadler B.S.	1914-2007	(Wellington) 1935-36	19	(5)
Saili F.	1991-	(Blues) 2013	2	(2)
Salmon J.L.B.	1959-	(Wellington) 1980-81	7	(3)
Sapsford H.P.	1949-2009	(Otago) 1976	7	(–)
Savage L.T.	1928-2013	(Canterbury) 1949	12	(3)
Savea A.S.	1993-	(Hurricanes) 2016-17-18-19	46	(44)
Savea S.J.	1990-	(Wellington) 2012; (Hurricanes) 2013-14-15-16-17	54	(54)
Saxton C.K.	1913-2001	(South Canterbury) 1938	7	(3)
Sayers M.	1947-	(Wellington) 1972-73	15	(–)
Schuler K.J.	1967-	(Manawatu) 1989-90; (North Harbour) 1992-95	13	(4)
Schuster N.J.	1964-	(Wellington) 1987-88-89	26	(10)
Schwalger J.E.	1983-	(Wellington) 2007-08	2	(2)
Scott R.W.H.	1921-2012	(Auckland) 1946-47-49-50-53-54	52	(17)
Scott S.J.	1955-1994	(Canterbury) 1980	4	(–)
Scown A.I.	1948-	(Taranaki) 1972-73	17	(5)
Scrimshaw G.	1902-1971	(Canterbury) 1928	11	(1)
Seear G.A.	1952-2018	(Otago) 1976-77-78-79	34	(12)
Seeling C.E.	1883-1956	(Auckland) 1904-05-06-07-08	39	(11)
Sellars G.M.V.*	1886-1917	(Auckland) 1913	15	(2)
Senio K.	1978-	(Bay of Plenty) 2005	1	(1)
Seymour D.J.	1967-	(Canterbury) 1992	3	(–)
Shannon H.G.	1869-1912	(Manawatu) 1893	6	(–)
Shaw M.W.	1956-	(Manawatu) 1980-81-82-83-84-85; (Hawke's Bay) 1986	69	(30)
Shearer J.D.	1896-1963	(Wellington) 1920	5	(–)
Shearer S.D.	1890-1973	(Wellington) 1921-22	8	(–)
Sheen T.R.	1905-1979	(Auckland) 1926-28	8	(–)
Shelford F.N.K.	1955-	(Bay of Plenty) 1981-84-85; (Hawke's Bay) 1983	22	(4)
Shelford W.T.	1957-	(North Harbour) 1985-86-87-88-89-90	48	(22)
Sherlock K.	1961-	(Auckland) 1985	3	(–)
Siddells S.K.	1897-1979	(Wellington) 1921	1	(1)
Simon H.J.	1911-1936	(Otago) 1937	3	(3)
Simonsson P.L.J.	1967-	(Wellington) 1987	2	(–)
Simpson J.G.	1922-2010	(Auckland) 1947-49-50	30	(9)
Simpson V.L.J.	1960-	(Canterbury) 1985	4	(2)
Sims G.S.	1951-	(Otago) 1972	1	(1)
Sinclair R.G.B.	1896-1932	(Otago) 1923	2	(–)
Sivivatu S.W.	1982-	(Waikato) 2005-06-07-08-09-11	46	(45)
Skeen J.R.	1928-2001	(Auckland) 1952	1	(1)
Skinner K.L.	1927-2014	(Otago) 1949-50-51-52-53-54; (Counties) 1956	63	(20)
Skudder G.R.	1948-	(Waikato) 1969-72-73	14	(1)
Slade C.R.	1987-	(Canterbury) 2010-11; (Highlanders) 2013; (Crusaders) 2014-15	21	(21)
Slater G.L.	1971-	(Taranaki) 1997-2000	6	(3)
Sloane P.H.	1948-	(North Auckland) 1973-76-79	16	(1)

Name	B&D	Representative Team	Games	Tests
Smith A.E.	1942-	(Taranaki) 1967-69-70	18	(3)
Smith A.L.	1998-	(Manawatu) 2012; (Highlanders) 2013-14-15-16-17-18-19	92	(92)
Smith B.R.	1986-	(Otago) 2009-11-12; (Highlanders) 2013-14-15-16-17-18-19	85	(84)
Smith B.W.	1959-	(Waikato) 1983-84	10	(3)
Smith C.G.	1981-	(Wellington) 2004-05-06-07-08-09-10-11-12; (Hurricanes) 2013-14-15	94	(94)
Smith C.H.	1909-1976	(Otago) 1934	2	(–)
Smith G.W.	1874-1954	(Auckland) 1897-1901-05	39	(2)
Smith I.S.T.	1941-2017	(Otago) 1963-64; (North Otago) 1965-66	24	(9)
Smith J.B.	1922-1974	(North Auckland) 1946-47-49	9	(4)
Smith P.	1924-1954	(North Auckland) 1947	3	(–)
Smith R.M.	1929-2002	(Canterbury) 1955	1	(1)
Smith W.E.	1881-1945	(Nelson) 1905	1	(1)
Smith W.R.	1957-	(Canterbury) 1980-82-83-84-85	35	(17)
Smyth B.F.	1891-1972	(Canterbury) 1922	3	(–)
Snodgrass W.F.	1898-1976	(Nelson) 1923-28	3	(–)
Snow E.M.	1898-1974	(Nelson) 1928-29	16	(3)
Solomon D.	1913-1997	(Auckland) 1935-36	8	(–)
Solomon F.	1906-1991	(Auckland) 1931-32	9	(3)
Somerville G.M.	1977-	(Canterbury) 2000-01-02-03-04-05-06-07-08	67	(66)
Sonntag W.T.C.	1894-1988	(Otago) 1929	8	(3)
So'oialo, R.	1979-	(Wellington) 2002-03-04-05-06-07-08-09	63	(62)
Soper A.J.	1936-	(Southland) 1957	8	(–)
Sopoaga L.Z.	1991	(Highlanders) 2015-16-17	18	(16)
Souter R.	1905-1976	(Otago) 1929	4	(–)
Speight C.R.B.	1870-1935	(Auckland) 1893	7	(–)
Speight M.W.	1962-	(North Auckland) 1986	5	(1)
Spencer C.J.	1975-	(Auckland) 1995-96-97-98-2000-02-03-04	44	(35)
Spencer G.	1878-1950	(Wellington) 1907	5	(–)
Spencer J.C.	1880-1936	(Wellington) 1903-05-07	6	(2)
Spiers J.E.	1947-	(Counties) 1976-79-80-81	28	(5)
Spillane A.P.	1888-1974	(South Canterbury) 1913	2	(2)
Squire L.I.J.	1991-	(Highlanders) 2016-17-18	24	(23)
Stalker J.	1881-1931	(Otago) 1903	6	(–)
Stanley B.J.	1984-	(Auckland) 2010	3	(3)
Stanley J.C.	1975-	(Auckland) 1997	3	(–)
Stanley J.T.	1957-	(Auckland) 1986-87-88-89-90-91	49	(27)
Stapleton E.T.	1930-2005	(New South Wales) 1960	1	(–)
Stead J.W.	1877-1958	(Southland) 1903-04-05-06-08	42	(7)
Steel A.G.	1941-2018	(Canterbury) 1966-67-68	23	(9)
Steel J.	1898-1941	(West Coast) 1920-21-22-23-24-25	38	(6)
Steele L.B.	1929-	(Wellington) 1951	9	(3)
Steere E.R.G.	1908-1967	(Hawke's Bay) 1928-29-30-31-32	21	(6)
Steinmetz P.C.	1977-	(Wellington) 2002	1	(1)
Stensness L.	1970-	(Auckland) 1993-97	14	(8)
Stephens O.G.	1947-	(Wellington) 1968	1	(1)
Stevens I.N.	1948-	(Wellington) 1972-73-74-76	33	(3)
Stevenson D.R.L.	1903-1962	(Otago) 1926	4	(–)
Stewart A.J.	1940-	(Canterbury) 1963; (South Canterbury) 1964	26	(8)
Stewart D.T.	1872-1931	(South Canterbury) 1894	1	(–)
Stewart E.B.	1901-1979	(Otago) 1923	1	(–)
Stewart J.D.	1889-1973	(Auckland) 1913	2	(2)
Stewart K.W.	1953-	(Southland) 1972-73-74-75-76-79-81	55	(13)

Name	B&D	Representative Team	Games	Tests
Stewart R.T.	1904-1982	(South Canterbury) 1923-24-25-26-28;	39	(5)
		(Canterbury) 1930		
Stewart V.E.	1948-	(Canterbury) 1976-79	12	(–)
Stohr L.	1889-1973	(Taranaki) 1910-13	15	(3)
Stokes E.J.T.	1950-	(Bay of Plenty) 1976	5	(–)
Stone A.M.	1960-	(Waikato) 1981-83-84; (Bay of Plenty) 1986	23	(9)
Storey P.W.	1897-1975	(South Canterbury) 1920-21	12	(2)
Strachan A.D.	1966-	(Auckland) 1992; (North Harbour) 1993-95	17	(11)
Strahan S.C.	1944-2019	(Manawatu) 1967-68-70-72-73	45	(17)
Strang W.A.	1906-1989	(South Canterbury) 1928-30-31	17	(5)
Stringfellow J.C.	1905-1959	(Wairarapa) 1929	7	(2)
Stuart A.J.	1858-1923	(Wellington) 1893	7	(–)
Stuart K.C.	1928-2005	(Canterbury) 1955	1	(1)
Stuart R.C.	1920-2005	(Canterbury) 1949-53-54	27	(7)
Stuart R.L.	1948-	(Hawke's Bay) 1977	6	(1)
Sullivan J.L.	1915-1990	(Taranaki) 1936-37-38	9	(6)
Surman J.F.	1866-1925	(Auckland) 1896	1	(–)
Surridge S.D.	1970-	(Canterbury) 1997	3	(–)
Sutherland A.R.	1944-	(Marlborough) 1968-70-71-72-73-76	64	(10)
Svenson K.S.	1898-1955	(Buller) 1922; (Wellington) 1924-25-26	34	(4)
Swain J.P.	1902-1960	(Hawke's Bay) 1928	16	(4)
Swindley J.T.	1876-1918	(Wellington) 1894	1	(–)
Ta'avao–Matau A.W.F.	1990	(Chiefs) 2018-19	14	(14)
Tahuriorangi T.T.H.	1995	(Chiefs) 2018	3	(3)
Taiaroa J.G.	1862-1907	(Otago) 1884	9	(–)
Taituha P.	1901-1958	(Wanganui) 1923	2	(–)
Tamanivalu S.	1992-	(Chiefs) 2016-17	5	(3)
Tanner J.M.	1927-	(Auckland) 1950-51-53-54	24	(5)
Tanner K.J.	1945-	(Canterbury) 1974-75-76	27	(7)
Taumoepeau S.	1979-	(Auckland) 2004-05	4	(3)
Taylor C.J.	1991-	(Crusaders) 2015-16-17-18-19	50	(50)
Taylor G.L.	1970-	(North Auckland) 1992-96	6	(1)
Taylor H.M.	1889-1955	(Canterbury) 1913-14	23	(5)
Taylor J.M.	1913-1979	(Otago) 1937-38	9	(6)
Taylor K.J.	1957-	(Hawke's Bay) 1980	1	(–)
Taylor M.B.	1956-	(Waikato) 1976-79-80	30	(7)
Taylor N.M.	1951-	(Bay of Plenty) 1976-77-78; (Hawke's Bay) 1982	27	(9)
Taylor R.*	1889-1917	(Taranaki) 1913	2	(2)
Taylor T.J.	1989-	(Crusaders) 2013	3	(3)
Taylor W.T.	1960-	(Canterbury) 1983-84-85-86-87-88	40	(24)
Tetzlaff P.L.	1920-2009	(Auckland) 1947	7	(2)
Thimbleby N.W.	1939-	(Hawke's Bay) 1970	13	(1)
Thomas B.T.	1937- 2018	(Auckland) 1962; (Wellington) 1964	4	(4)
Thomas L.A.	1897-1971	(Wellington) 1925	3	(–)
Thompson B.A.	1947-2006	(Canterbury) 1979	8	(–)
Thomson A.J.	1982-	(Otago) 2008-09-10-11-12	31	(29)
Thomson H.D.	1881-1939	(Wanganui) 1905-06; (Wellington) 1908	15	(1)
Thorn B.C.	1975-	(Canterbury) 2003-09-10-11; (Tasman) 2008	60	(59)
Thorne G.S.	1946-	(Auckland) 1967-68-69-70	39	(10)
Thorne R.D.	1975-	(Canterbury) 1999-2000-01-02-03-04-06-07	51	(50)
Thornton N.H.	1918-1998	(Auckland) 1947-49	19	(3)
Thrush J.I.	1985-	(Hurricanes) 2013-14-15	12	(12)
Tialata N.S.	1982-	(Wellington) 2005-06-07-08-09-10	44	(43)
Tiatia F.I.	1971-	(Wellington) 2000	2	(2)

Name	B&D	Representative Team	Games	Tests
Tilyard F.J.	1896-1954	(Wellington) 1923	1	(–)
Tilyard J.T.	1889-1966	(Wellington) 1913-20	10	(1)
Timu J.K.R.	1969-	(Otago) 1989-90-91-92-93-94	50	(26)
Tindill E.W.T.	1910-2010	(Wellington) 1935-36-38	17	(1)
Tiopira H.	1871-1930	(Hawke's Bay) 1893	8	(–)
Todd M.B.	1988-	(Crusaders) 2013,15-16-17-18-19	25	(25)
Toeava I.	1986-	(Auckland) 2005-06-07-08-09-10-11	37	(36)
Tonu'u O.F.J.	1970-	(Auckland) 1996-97-98	8	(5)
To'omaga–Allen J.L.	1990-	(Hurricanes) 2013-17	3	(1)
Townsend L.J.	1934-	(Otago) 1955	2	(2)
Tregaskis C.D.	1965-	(Wellington) 1991	4	(–)
Tremain K.R.	1938-1992	(Canterbury) 1959; (Auckland) 1960; (Canterbury) 1961; (Hawke's Bay) 1962-63-64-65-66-67-68	86	(38)
Trevathan D.	1912-1986	(Otago) 1937	3	(3)
Tuck J.M.	1907-1967	(Waikato) 1929	6	(3)
Tuiali'i M.M.	1981-	(Auckland) 2004-05-06	10	(9)
Tuigamala V.L.	1969-	(Auckland) 1989-90-91-92-93	39	(19)
Tu'inukuafe G.Z.K.	1993	(Chiefs) 2018	13	(13)
Tuipulotu P.T.	1993-	(Blues) 2014-16-17-18-19	32	(30)
Tuitavake A.S.M.	1982-	(North Harbour) 2008	7	(6)
Tuitupou S.	1982-	(Auckland) 2004-06	9	(9)
Tunnicliff R.G.	1894-1973	(Buller) 1923	1	(–)
Turnbull J.S.	1898-1947	(Otago) 1921	1	(–)
Turner R.S.	1968-	(North Harbour) 1992	2	(2)
Turtill H.S.*	1880-1918	(Canterbury) 1905	1	(1)
Tu'ungafasi A.O.H.M.	1992-	(Blues) 2016-17-18-19	37	(35)
Twigden T.M.	1952-	(Auckland) 1979-80	15	(2)
Tyler G.A.	1879-1942	(Auckland) 1903-04-05-06	36	(7)
Udy D.K.	1874-1935	(Wairarapa) 1901-03	9	(1)
Udy H.	1860-1933	(Wellington) 1884	8	(–)
Umaga J.F.	1973-	(Wellington) 1997-99-2000-01-02-03-04-05	79	(74)
Urbahn R.J.	1934-1984	(Taranaki) 1959-60	15	(3)
Urlich R.A.	1944-	(Auckland) 1970-72-73	35	(2)
Uttley I.N.	1941-2015	(Wellington) 1963	2	(2)
Valli G.T.	1954-	(Southland) 1980	1	(–)
Vanisi O.K.	1972-	(Wellington) 1999	1	(–)
Vidiri J.	1973-	(Counties Manukau) 1998	2	(2)
Vincent P.B.	1926-1983	(Canterbury) 1956	2	(2)
Vito V.V.J.	1987-	(Wellington) 2010-11-12; (Hurricanes) 2013-14-15	33	(33)
Vodanovich I.M.H.	1930-1995	(Wellington) 1955	3	(3)
Vorrath F.H.	1908-1972	(Otago) 1935-36	12	(–)
Waldrom S.L.	1980-	(Taranaki) 2008	1	(–)
Wallace W.J.	1878-1972	(Wellington) 1903-04-05-06-07-08	51	(11)
Waller D.A.G.	1974-	(Wellington) 2001	3	(1)
Walsh P.T.	1936-2007	(Counties) 1955-56-57-58-59-63-64	27	(13)
Walter J.	1904-1966	(Taranaki) 1925	7	(–)
Warbrick J.A.	1862-1903	(Auckland) 1884	7	(–)
Ward E.P.	1899-1958	(Taranaki) 1928	10	(–)
Ward F.G.	1900-1990	(Otago) 1921	1	(–)
Ward R.H.	1915-2000	(Southland) 1936-37	4	(3)
Waterman A.C.	1903-1997	(North Auckland) 1929	7	(2)
Watkins E.L.	1880-1949	(Wellington) 1905	1	(1)

Name	B&D	Representative Team	Games	Tests
Watson J.D.	1872-1958	(Taranaki) 1896	1	(–)
Watson W.D.	1869-1953	(Wairarapa) 1893-96	3	(–)
Watt B.A.	1939-	(Canterbury) 1962-63-64	29	(8)
Watt J.M.	1914-1988	(Otago) 1936	2	(2)
Watt J.R.	1935-	(Southland) 1957; (Wellington) 1958-60-61-62	42	(9)
Watts M.G.	1955-	(Taranaki) 1979-80	13	(5)
Webb D.S.	1934-1987	(North Auckland) 1959	1	(1)
Webb P.P.	1854-1920	(Wellington) 1884	8	(–)
Weber B.M.	1991-	(Chiefs) 2015-19	5	(5)
Webster T.R.D.	1920-1972	(Southland) 1947	4	(–)
Weepu P.A.T.	1983-	(Wellington) 2004-05-06-07-08-09-10-11-12; (Blues) 2013	73	(71)
Wells J.	1908-1994	(Wellington) 1936	3	(2)
Wells W.J.G.	1867-1911	(Taranaki) 1897	7	(–)
Wesney A.W.*	1915-1941	(Southland) 1938	3	(–)
West A.H.	1893-1934	(Taranaki) 1920-21-23-24-25	24	(2)
Weston L.H.	1892-1963	(Auckland) 1914	1	(–)
Whetton A.J.	1959-	(Auckland) 1984-85-86-87-88-89-90-91	65	(35)
Whetton G.W.	1959-	(Auckland) 1981-82-83-84-85-86-87-88-89-90-91	101	(58)
Whineray W.J.	1935-2012	(Canterbury) 1957; (Waikato) 1958; (Auckland) 1959-60-61-62-63-64-65	77	(32)
White A.	1894-1968	(Southland) 1921-22-23-24-25	38	(4)
White H.L.	1929-2016	(Auckland) 1953-54-55	16	(4)
White R.A.	1925-2012	(Poverty Bay) 1949-50-51-52-53-54-55-56	55	(23)
White R.M.	1917-1980	(Wellington) 1946-47	10	(4)
Whitelock G.B.	1986-	(Canterbury) 2009	1	(1)
Whitelock L.C.	1991-	(Crusaders) 2013-17-18	8	(7)
Whitelock S.L.	1988-	(Canterbury) 2010-11-12; (Crusaders) 2013-14-15-16-17-18-19	117	(117)
Whiting G.J.	1946-	(King Country) 1972-73	31	(6)
Whiting P.J.	1946-	(Auckland) 1971-72-73-74-76	56	(20)
Wickes C.D.	1962-	(Manawatu) 1980	1	(–)
Wightman D.R.	1929-2012	(Auckland) 1951	4	(–)
Williams A.J.	1981-	(Auckland) 2002-03-04-05-06-07-08-11-12	78	(77)
Williams A.L.	1898-1972	(Otago) 1922-23	9	(–)
Williams B.G.	1950-	(Auckland) 1970-71-72-73-74-75-76-77-78	113	(38)
Williams C.W.	1916-1998	(Canterbury) 1938	4	(–)
Williams G.C.	1945-2018	(Wellington) 1967-68	18	(5)
Williams P.	1884-1976	(Otago) 1913	9	(1)
Williams R.N.	1909-2001	(Hawke's Bay) 1932	1	(–)
Williams R.O.	1963-	(North Harbour) 1988-89	10	(–)
Williams S.	1985-	(Canterbury) 2010-1-12; (Chiefs) 2014-15; (Blues) 2017-18-19	58	(58)
Williment M.	1940-1994	(Wellington) 1964-65-66-67	9	(9)
Willis R.K.	1975-	(Waikato) 1998-99-2002	12	(12)
Willis T.E.	1979-	(Otago) 2001-02	7	(5)
Willocks C.	1919-1991	(Otago) 1946-47-49	22	(5)
Willoughby S. de L.P.	1904-1985	(Wairarapa) 1928	4	(–)
Wills M.C.	1941-	(Taranaki) 1967	5	(–)
Wilson A.	1874-1932	(Auckland) 1897	8	(–)
Wilson A.L.	1927-2009	(Southland) 1951	7	(–)
Wilson B.W.	1956-	(Otago) 1977-78-79	12	(8)
Wilson D.D.	1931-2019	(Canterbury) 1953-54	14	(2)
Wilson F.R.*	1885-1916	(Auckland) 1910	2	(–)
Wilson H.B.	1957-	(Counties) 1983	3	(–)

Name	B&D	Representative Team	Games	Tests
Wilson H.C.	1868-1945	(Wellington) 1893	7	(–)
Wilson H.W.	1924-2004	(Otago) 1949-50-51	13	(5)
Wilson J.W.	1973-	(Otago) 1993-94-95-96-97-98-99-2001	71	(60)
Wilson N.A.	1886-1953	(Wellington) 1908-10-13-14	21	(10)
Wilson N.L.	1922-2001	(Otago) 1949-51	20	(3)
Wilson R.G.	1953-	(Canterbury) 1976-78-79-80	25	(2)
Wilson R.J.	1861-1944	(Canterbury) 1884	6	(–)
Wilson S.S.	1954-	(Wellington) 1976-77-78-79-80-81-82-83	85	(34)
Wilson V.W.	1899-1978	(Auckland) 1920	7	(–)
Wise G.D.	1904-1971	(Otago) 1925	7	(–)
Witcombe D.J.C.	1978-	(Auckland) 2005	5	(5)
Wolfe T.N.	1941-	(Wellington) 1961-62; (Taranaki) 1963-68	14	(6)
Wood M.E.	1876-1956	(Wellington) 1901; (Canterbury) 1903; (Auckland) 1904	12	(2)
Woodcock T.D.	1981-	(North Harbour) 2002-04-05-06-07-08-09-10-11-12; (Highlanders) 2013; (Blues) 2014-15	118	(118)
Woodman F.A.	1958-	(North Auckland) 1980-81	14	(3)
Woodman T.B.K.	1960-	(North Auckland) 1984	6	(–)
Woods C.A.	1929-	(Southland) 1953-54	14	(–)
Wright A.H.	1914-1990	(Wellington) 1938	4	(–)
Wright D.H.	1902-1966	(Auckland) 1925	7	(–)
Wright T.J.	1963-	(Auckland) 1986-87-88-89-90-91-92	64	(30)
Wright W.A.	1905-1971	(Auckland) 1926	1	(–)
Wrigley E.	1886-1958	(Wairarapa) 1905	1	(1)
Wulf R.N.	1984-	(North Harbour) 2008	4	(4)
Wylie J.T.	1887-1956	(Auckland) 1913	12	(2)
Wyllie A.J.	1944-	(Canterbury) 1970-71-72-73	40	(11)
Wyllie T.	1954-	(Wellington) 1980	1	(–)
Wynyard J.G.*	1914-1942	(Waikato) 1935-36-38	13	(–)
Wynyard W.T.	1867-1938	(Wellington) 1893	7	(–)
Yates V.M.	1939-2008	(North Auckland) 1961-62	9	(3)
Young D.	1930-	(Canterbury) 1956-57-58-60-61-62-63-64	61	(22)
	1874-1946	(Wellington) 1896	1	(–)

NZR ANNUAL AWARDS

Since 1994 the NZRU has hosted, at the end of each year, an annual awards function to honour players, personalities and teams. With the exception of the Tom French Cup all trophies were new. The Tom French Cup had been presented in 1949 by Mr J. Morris of Sydney, following the New Zealand Maori tour of Australia, in honour of the team's coach Mr T.A. French. The trophy has been awarded to the outstanding Maori player each season.

PLAYER OF THE YEAR
Kelvin Tremain Memorial Trophy

1994	Zinzan Brooke (*Auckland*)
1995	Jonah Lomu (*Counties*)
1996	Sean Fitzpatrick (*Auckland*)
1997	Jeff Wilson (*Otago*)
1998	Josh Kronfeld (*Otago*)
1999	Andrew Mehrtens (*Canterbury*)
2000	Tana Umaga (*Wellington*)
2001	Todd Blackadder (*Canterbury*)
2002	Chris Jack (*Canterbury*)
2003	Richard McCaw (*Canterbury*)
2004	Daniel Carter (*Canterbury*)
2005	Daniel Carter (*Canterbury*)
2006	Richard McCaw (*Canterbury*)
2007	Daniel Braid (*Auckland*)
2008	Andrew Hore (*Taranaki*)
2009	Richard McCaw (*Canterbury*)
2010	Kieran Read (*Canterbury*)
2011	Jerome Kaino (*Auckland*)
2012	Richie McCaw (*Canterbury*)
2013	Kieran Read (*Canterbury*)
2014	Brodie Retallick (*Waikato*)
2015	Ma'a Nonu (*Wellington*)
2016	Beauden Barrett (*Taranaki*)
2017	Samuel Whitelock (*Canterbury*)
2018	Kendra Cocksedge (*Canterbury*)
2019	Ardie Savea (*Wellington*)

ALL BLACKS PLAYER OF THE YEAR

2019	Ardie Savea (*Hurricanes*)

SUPER RUGBY PLAYER OF THE YEAR

1996	Joeli Vidiri (*Blues*)
1997	Christian Cullen (*Hurricanes*)
1998	Andrew Mehrtens (*Crusaders*)
1999	Byron Kelleher (*Highlanders*)
2000	Scott Robertson (*Crusaders*)
2001	Deon Muir (*Chiefs*)
2002	Chris Jack (*Crusaders*)
2003	Carlos Spencer (*Blues*)
2004	Daniel Carter (*Crusaders*)
2005	Rico Gear (*Crusaders*)

2006	Daniel Carter (*Crusaders*)
2007	James Cowan (*Highlanders*)
2008	Andrew Hore (*Hurricanes*)
2009	Mils Muliaina (*Chiefs*)
2010	Alby Mathewson (*Blues*)
2011	Wyatt Crockett (*Crusaders*)
2012	Conrad Smith (*Hurricanes*)
2013	Ben Smith (*Highlanders*)
2014	Jerome Kaino (*Blues*)
2015	Lima Sopoaga (*Highlanders*)
2016	Beauden Barrett (*Hurricanes*)
2017	Samuel Whitelock (*Crusaders*)
2018	Richie Mo'unga (*Crusaders*)
2019	Ardie Savea (*Hurricanes*)

TEAM OF THE YEAR

2000	New Zealand Under 21
2001	Canterbury
2002	New Zealand Sevens
2003	All Blacks
2004	Canterbury
2005	All Blacks
2006	All Blacks
2007	Auckland
2008	All Blacks
2009	Canterbury
2010	Black Ferns
2011	All Blacks
2012	All Blacks
2013	All Blacks
2014	All Blacks
2015	All Blacks
2016	All Blacks
2017	Black Ferns

NEW ZEALAND TEAM OF THE YEAR

2018	Black Ferns Sevens
2019	Black Ferns Sevens

NATIONAL TEAM OF THE YEAR

2018	Crusaders
2019	Crusaders

PREMIER DIVISION
PLAYER OF THE YEAR
Duane Monkley Medal
from 2017

2006	Richard Kahui (*Waikato*)
2007	Isa Nacewa (*Auckland*)
2008	Jamie Mackintosh (*Southland*)
2009	Mike Delany (*Bay of Plenty*)
2010	Robbie Fruean (*Canterbury*)
2011	Aaron Cruden (*Manawatu*)
2012	Robbie Fruean (*Canterbury*)
2013	Andy Ellis (*Canterbury*)
2014	Seta Tamanivalu (*Taranaki*)
2015	George Moala (*Auckland*)
2016	Jordie Barrett (*Canterbury*)
2017	Jack Goodhue (*Northland*)
2018	Luke Romano (*Canterbury*)
2019	Chase Tiatia (*Bay of Plenty*)

HEARTLAND
CHAMPIONSHIP
PLAYER OF THE YEAR

2006	Scott Leighton (*Poverty Bay*)
2007	Ross Hay (*North Otago*)
2008	Cameron Crowley (*Wanganui*)
2009	Asaeli Tikoirotuma (*Wanganui*)
2010	Peter Rowe (*Wanganui*)
2011	Jon Smyth (*Wanganui*)
2012	Peter Rowe (*Wanganui*)
2013	Jon Dampney (*Mid Canterbury*)
2014	James Lash (*Buller*)
2015	Lindsay Horrocks (*Wanganui*)
2016	Te Rangatira Waitokia (*Wanganui*)
2017	Scott Cameron (*Horowhenua Kapiti*)
2018	Brett Ranga (*Thames Valley*)
2019	Josh Clark (*North Otago*)

MAORI
PLAYER OF THE YEAR
Tom French Cup

1949	Johnny Smith (*North Auckland*)
1950	Manahi Paewai (*North Auckland*)
1951	Percy Erceg (*Auckland*)
1952	Keith Davis (*Auckland*)
1953	Keith Davis (*Auckland*)
1954	Keith Davis (*Auckland*)
1955	Pat Walsh (*South Auckland*)
1956	Bill Gray (*Bay of Plenty*)
1957	Muru Walters (*North Auckland*)
1958	Pat Walsh (*Counties*)
1959	Bill Wordley (*King Country*)
1960	Mac Herewini (*Auckland*)
1961	Victor Yates (*North Auckland*)
1962	Waka Nathan (*Auckland*)

1963	Mac Herewini (*Auckland*)
1964	Ron Rangi (*Auckland*)
1965	Ron Rangi (*Auckland*)
1966	Waka Nathan (*Auckland*)
1967	Sid Going (*North Auckland*)
1968	Sid Going (*North Auckland*)
1969	Sid Going (*North Auckland*)
1970	Sid Going (*North Auckland*)
1971	Sid Going (*North Auckland*)
1972	Sid Going (*North Auckland*)
1973	Tane Norton (*Canterbury*)
1974	Tane Norton (*Canterbury*)
1975	Bill Bush (*Canterbury*)
1976	Kent Lambert (*Manawatu*)
1977	Bill Osborne (*Wanganui*)
1978	Eddie Dunn (*North Auckland*)
1979	Vance Stewart (*Canterbury*)
1980	Hika Reid (*Bay of Plenty*)
1981	Frank Shelford (*Bay of Plenty*)
1982	Steven Pokere (*Southland*)
1983	Hika Reid (*Bay of Plenty*)
1984	Michael Clamp (*Wellington*)
1985	Wayne Shelford (*North Harbour*)
1986	Frano Botica (*North Harbour*)
1987	Wayne Shelford (*North Harbour*)
1988	Wayne Shelford (*North Harbour*)
1989	Wayne Shelford (*North Harbour*)
1990	Steve McDowell (*Auckland*)
1991	John Timu (*Otago*)
1992	Zinzan Brooke (*Auckland*)
1993	Arran Pene (*Otago*)
1994	Zinzan Brooke (*Auckland*)
1995	Robin Brooke (*Auckland*)
1996	Errol Brain (*Counties Manukau*)
1997	Mark Mayerhofler (*Canterbury*)
1998	Tony Brown (*Otago*)
1999	Norman Maxwell (*Canterbury*)
2000	Daryl Gibson (*Canterbury*)
2001	Caleb Ralph (*Canterbury*)
2002	Carlos Spencer (*Auckland*)
2003	Carlos Spencer (*Auckland*)
2004	Carl Hayman (*Otago*)
2005	Rico Gear (*Nelson Bays*)
2006	Carl Hayman (*Otago*)
2007	Daniel Braid (*Auckland*)
2008	Piri Weepu (*Wellington*)
2009	Zac Guildford (*Hawke's Bay*)
2010	Hosea Gear (*Wellington*)
2011	Piri Weepu (*Wellington*)
2012	Liam Messam (*Waikato*)
2013	Liam Messam (*Waikato*)
2014	Aaron Smith (*Manawatu*)
2015	Nehe Milner-Skudder (*Manawatu*)
2016	Dane Coles (*Wellington*)

2017	Rieko Ioane (*Auckland*)
2018	Codie Taylor (*Canterbury*)
2019	Sarah Hirini (*Manawatu*)

NZ RUGBY PLAYERS' ASSN
KIRK AWARD

2016	Justin Collins (*Northland*)
2017	DJ Forbes (*Counties Manukau*)
2018	Fiao'o Faamausili (*Auckland*)
	Keven Mealamu (*Auckland*)
2019	Josh Blackie, Seilala Mapusua
	& Hale T-Pole

AGE GRADE
PLAYER OF THE YEAR

1994	Taine Randell (*Otago*)
1995	Anton Oliver (*Otago*)
1996	Andrew Blowers (*Auckland*)
1997	Norman Maxwell (*Northland*)
1998	Doug Howlett (*Auckland*)
1999	Samiu Vahafolau (*Auckland*)
2000	Ben Blair (*Canterbury*)
2001	*Under 21*
	Richard McCaw (*Canterbury*)
	Under 19
	Sam Tuitupou (*Auckland*)
2002	Luke McAlister (*North Harbour*)
2003	Ben Atiga (*Auckland*)
2004	Jerome Kaino (*Auckland*)
2005	Isaia Toeava (*Auckland*)
2006	Michael Paterson (*Canterbury*)
2007	Zac Guildford (*Hawke's Bay*)
2008	Zac Guildford (*Hawke's Bay*)
2009	Aaron Cruden (*Manawatu*)
2010	Liaki Moli (*Auckland*)
2011	Sam Cane (*Bay of Plenty*)
2012	Jason Emery (*Manawatu*)
2013	Ardie Savea (*Wellington*)
2014	Damian McKenzie (*Waikato*)
2015	Akira Ioane (*Auckland*)
2016	Jordie Barrett (*Canterbury*)
2017	Asafo Aumua (*Wellington*)
2018	Tom Christie (*Canterbury*)
2019	Fletcher Newell (*Canterbury*)

SEVENS
PLAYER OF THE YEAR
Richard Crawshaw Memorial Trophy
from 1998

1994	Eric Rush (*North Harbour*)
1995	Jonah Lomu (*Counties*)
1996	Christian Cullen (*Manawatu*)
1997	Caleb Ralph (*Bay of Plenty*)
1998	Rico Gear (*Auckland*)
1999	Orene Ai'i (*Auckland*)
2000	Karl Te Nana (*North Harbour*)
2001	Karl Te Nana (*North Harbour*)
2002	Chris Masoe (*Taranaki*)
2003	Eric Rush (*North Harbour*)
2004	Liam Messam (*Waikato*)
2005	Amasio Valence (*Hawke's Bay*)
2006	Tafai Ioasa (*Hawke's Bay*)
2007	D.J. Forbes (*Auckland*)
2008	D.J. Forbes (*Counties Manukau*)
2009	Zar Lawrence (*Bay of Plenty*)
2010	Kurt Baker (*Taranaki*)
2011	Tim Mikkelson (*Waikato*)
2012	Tomasi Cama (*Manawatu*)
2013	Kurt Baker (*Taranaki*)
2014	DJ Forbes (*Counties Manukau*)
2015	Scott Curry (*Bay of Plenty*)
2016	Rieko Ioane (*Auckland*)
2017	DJ Forbes (*Counties Manukau*)
2018	Scott Curry (*Bay of Plenty*)
2019	Tone Ng Shiu (*Tasman*)

WOMEN'S
PLAYER OF THE YEAR

1994	Anna Richards (*Auckland*)
1995	Rochelle Martin (*Wellington*)
1996	Vanessa Cootes (*Waikato*)
1997	Louisa Wall (*Auckland*)
1998	Farah Palmer (*Otago*)
1999	Suzanne Shortland (*Auckland*)
2000	Fiona King (*Otago*)
2001	Annaleah Rush (*Auckland*)
2002	Monique Hirovanaa (*Auckland*)
2003	Monalisa Codling (*Auckland*)
2004	Stephanie Mortimer (*Canterbury*)
2005	Melissa Ruscoe (*Canterbury*)
2006	Amiria Marsh (*Canterbury*)
2007	Victoria Heighway (*Auckland*)
2008	Victoria Grant (*Auckland*)
2009	Victoria Heighway (*Auckland*)
2010	Carla Hohepa (*Otago*)
2011	Fiao'o Faamausili (*Auckland*)
2012	Rawinia Everitt (*Auckland*)
2013	Kelly Brazier (*Otago*)
2014	Rawinia Everitt (*Counties Manukau*)
2015	Kendra Cocksedge (*Canterbury*)
2016	Selica Winiata (*Manawatu*)
2017	Sarah Goss (*Manawatu*)
2018	Kendra Cocksedge (*Canterbury*)

BLACK FERNS PLAYER OF THE YEAR

2019   Charmaine McMenamin *(Auckland)*

FARAH PALMER CUP PLAYER OF THE YEAR
Fiao'o Faamausili Medal

2017   Hazel Tubic *(Counties Manukau)*
2018   Kendra Cocksedge *(Canterbury)*
2019   Chelsea Bremner *(Canterbury)*

WOMEN'S SEVENS PLAYER OF THE YEAR

2013   Portia Woodman *(Auckland)*
2014   Sarah Goss *(Manawatu)*
2015   Tyla Nathan-Wong *(Auckland)*
2016   Sarah Goss *(Manawatu)*
2017   Ruby Tui *(Canterbury)*
2018   Michaela Blyde *(Bay of Plenty)*
2019   Tyla Nathan-Wong *(Auckland)*

COACH OF THE YEAR

1994   Brad Meurant *(North Harbour)*
1995   Graham Henry *(Auckland)*
1996   John Hart *(All Blacks)*
2001   Colin Cooper *(New Zealand Under 21)*
2002   Robbie Deans *(Crusaders)*
2003   Wayne Pivac *(Auckland)*
2004   Vern Cotter *(Bay of Plenty)*
2005   Graham Henry *(All Blacks)*
2006   Graham Henry *(All Blacks)*
2007   Peter Russell *(Hawke's Bay)*
2008   Graham Henry *(All Blacks)*
2009   Dave Rennie *(New Zealand Under 20)*
2010   Gordon Tietjens *(New Zealand Sevens)*
2011   Graham Henry *(All Blacks)*
2012   Steve Hansen *(All Blacks)*
2013   Steve Hansen *(All Blacks)*
2014   Steve Hansen *(All Blacks)*
2015   Steve Hansen *(All Blacks)*
2016   Steve Hansen *(All Blacks)*
2017   Glenn Moore *(Black Ferns)*

NEW ZEALAND COACH OF THE YEAR

2018   Clark Laidlaw *(All Blacks Sevens)*
2019   Corey Sweeney & Allan Bunting *(Black Ferns Sevens)*

NATIONAL COACH OF THE YEAR

2018   Alama Ieremia *(Auckland)*
2019   Scott Robertson *(Crusaders)*

REFEREE OF THE YEAR

1994   Colin Hawke *(South Canterbury)*
1995   Paddy O'Brien *(Southland)*
1996   Paddy O'Brien *(Southland)*
1997   Steve Walsh jnr *(North Harbour)**
1998   Paddy O'Brien *(Southland)*
1999   Colin Hawke *(South Canterbury)*
2000   Colin Hawke *(South Canterbury)*
2001   Kelvin Deaker *(Hawke's Bay)*
2002   Paddy O'Brien *(Southland)*
2003   Paddy O'Brien *(Southland)*
2004   Paddy O'Brien *(Southland)*
2005   Paul Honiss *(Waikato)*
2006   Paul Honiss *(Waikato)*
2007   Steve Walsh *(North Harbour)*
2008   Bryce Lawrence *(Bay of Plenty)*
2009   Bryce Lawrence *(Bay of Plenty)*
2010   Bryce Lawrence *(Bay of Plenty)*
2011   Bryce Lawrence *(Bay of Plenty)*
2012   Glen Jackson *(Bay of Plenty)*
2013   Chris Pollock *(Hawke's Bay)*
2014   Glen Jackson *(Bay of Plenty)*
2015   Glen Jackson *(Bay of Plenty)*
2016   Glen Jackson *(Bay of Plenty)*
2017   Ben O'Keeffe *(Wellington)*
2018   Glen Jackson *(Bay of Plenty)*
2019   Paul Williams *(Taranaki)*

* for the Outstanding Referee Performance (Canterbury v Auckland round robin match)

STEINLAGER SALVER
For outstanding service to rugby

1999	Colin Meads
2000	Zinzan Brooke*
2001	Sir Terry McLean
2002	Fred Allen
2003	Sir Brian Lochore
2004	Peter Bush
2005	Richie Guy
2006	Stan Hill
2007	Ron Don
2008	Tane Norton
2009	John Graham
2010	Keith Quinn
2011	Jock Hobbs
2012	Ray Harper
2013	Graham Mourie
2014	Dick Littlejohn
2015	Mike Eagle
2016	Gavin Service
2017	Wayne Smith
2018	Waka Nathan
2019	Steve Tew

* celebrating 25 years of the NPC

VOLUNTEER OF THE YEAR
Charles Monro Memorial Trophy
from 2009

2002	John George (*Taranaki*)
2003	Ru Rangi (*Wellington*)
2004	Adelle Wakely (*Hawke's Bay*)
2005	Daphne Boden (*Hawke's Bay*)
2006	Jason Martin (*Otago*)
2007	Robbie Ball (*Northland*)
2008	Ken Swain (*Horowhenua Kapiti*)
2009	Blair Crawford (*Otago*)
2010	Hilton Williams (*Horowhenua Kapiti*)
2011	Andy MacDonald (*Canterbury*)
2012	Ray Watson (*Bay of Plenty*)
2013	Rob Jones (*Manawatu*)
2014	Dean File (*Horowhenua Kapiti*)
2015	Tania Karaitiana and Vio Ugone (*Wellington*)
2016	Gary Donovan (*Auckland*)
2017	Sid Tatana (*Wairarapa Bush*)
2018	Irene Eruera-Taiapa (*Horowhenua Kapiti*)
2019	Ian Spraggon (*Bay of Plenty*)

SKY FANS TRY OF THE YEAR

2013	Selica Winiata (*Black Ferns*)
2014	Malakai Fekitoa (*Highlanders*)
2015	Samu Kubunavanua (*Wanganui*)
2016	Isaiah Punivai (*Christ's College*)
2017	Portia Woodman (*Black Ferns*)
2018	Chris Hala'ufia (*St Peter's College*)
2019	TJ Perenara (*All Blacks*)

471

OBITUARIES

NEW ZEALAND REPRESENTATIVES

Keith Davis (*Auckland*) was a splendid halfback who for much of the 1950s gave loyal and exemplary service to Auckland, New Zealand Maori and in 10 of the 30 tests played in that decade for the All Blacks. Small, but chunkily built, Davis hailed from the Bay of Plenty and came to rugby prominence as a boarder at one of the game's noted schoolboy nurseries, Auckland's Sacred Heart College.

Not long out of the school, he played for Auckland B from the Marist club in 1951 and in his first representative A season in 1952 so impressed he won the first of his many NZ Maori selections and aged only 22 made his All Blacks debut in the second test at Athletic Park against the touring Wallabies. He was chosen for the 1953/54 tour of Britain, France and North America and was preferred for all five internationals and the prestige match against the Barbarians ahead of his older relative, the more experienced Vince Bevan, who in 1950 had played all four tests against the British Lions.

A swift passer and capable of making telling blindside breaks, Davis, after such a successful tour, might have expected a lengthy run as a regular test selection. Journalist Terry McLean, who covered the 1953/54 tour, described him as the "new Jimmy Mill", another fine Maori halfback who had been a star of the 1924/25 "Invincibles". But in common with his inside back contemporaries he was a victim of the inconsistent and somewhat illogical selection policies which prevailed in the 1950s.

Though there were only 30 tests in the entire decade no fewer than eight different halfbacks were used. Davis played only the third test against the 1955 touring Wallabies and then waited another three years before being recalled for the three tests against the Wallabies in 1958. He was a reserve to Ponty Reid for the last two tests against the 1956 Springboks, yet the following year was overlooked as Reid's deputy for the tour of Australia and despite captaining one of the final trial teams to an easy win.

He thus made only one tour with the All Blacks, though twice he toured with Maori sides, as captain in 1954 on matches in New Zealand and Fiji and in 1958 to Australia, where three unofficial tests were played against fully fledged Wallaby sides. Davis, with another Sacred Heart product, Pat Walsh, and Bay of Plenty midfield back Bill Gray were the foremost Maori players of the 1950s, with Davis winning the Tom French Cup for the season's outstanding Maori player in 1952–53–54.

If he was ever embittered by the cavalier way he was treated by national selectors, Davis never showed it. He retained a life-long passion for the game, and his contribution as a coach and administrator to his Auckland Marist club saw him made a life member. He also served as a New Zealand Maori selector and was an active member of the Barbarians. His interest in the game's grassroots continued into his latter years and, as a resident on the North Shore's East Coast Bays, he was a faithful supporter of the North Harbour Marist club when it started in the late 1980s. (*Obituary contributed by Lindsay Knight*).

Keith Davis' first-class record:

For	Matches	Tries	PG	Points
Auckland (Marist) 1952(8), 1953(4), 1954(7), 1955(8), 1956(11), 1957(11), 1958(5)	54	9	–	27
Auckland B 1951(4), 1952, 1959	6	1	–	3
Barbarians Club 1954(3), 1955(2)	5	–	–	0
Spartans Club 1954	1	–	–	0
Tai Tokerau 1954, 1956, 1957, 1959	4	1	–	3
New Zealand Maori Trials 1958(2), 1959(2)	4	1	–	3
North Island Maori 1955	1	–	–	0
Maori XV 1958	1	–	–	0
New Zealand Maori 1952(5), 1954(7), 1955(2), 1956(2), 1958(8), 1959(3)	27	1	1	6
North Island 1954, 1955, 1958	3	–	–	0
New Zealand Trials 1953(3), 1957(2), 1958	6	1	–	3
New Zealand Touring Team 1954	1	–	–	0
NEW ZEALAND 1952, 1953/54(20), 1955, 1958(3)	25	4	–	12
TOTALS	**138**	**18**	**1**	**57**

At Auckland, March 2, 2019, aged 88.

Ian Bruce Deans (*Canterbury*) gained selection in the 1987 World Cup squad following strong performances for his union over preceding seasons and a good game in the final trial match of 1987. However, the halfback did not get a run during any of the six cup games as first-choice halfback David Kirk was promoted to captain following Andy Dalton's injury before the first game. First five-eighth Frano Botica was the other squad member not to get on the field during the tournament.

Late in 1987 Deans and Graeme Bachop were the halfbacks on the five-match tour to Japan, Deans playing in both unofficial tests against Japan, scoring on debut in the first test and a further three tries in the second. During 1988, with Kirk having gone to Oxford University, Deans became the established first-choice halfback and played in all five tests, two against Wales (scoring a try in each), and three tests on the tour of Australia. In 1989 Deans played in all five home tests, against France (two), Argentina (two) and Australia. On the end of year tour to Wales and Ireland Deans played six games but Bachop was preferred for the two tests. During his three-year All Blacks career Deans scored a remarkable 14 tries in 23 games, six being scored during his 10 tests.

Born at Cheviot on November 25, 1960 Bruce Deans attended Cheviot School, Waihi Preparatory School and Christ's College where he was in the first XV 1974–78 and a talented cricketer. After studying at Lincoln College, he returned home to the farm in 1982 and played for Glenmark club. He joined his brother Robbie in the Canterbury squad and soon displaced Steve Scott as the preferred halfback. Later in the 1982 season he was in the team that won the Ranfurly Shield off Wellington and was in involved in all 25 successful defences of the shield until it was lost to Auckland in 1985. Consistent fine form for Canterbury earned Deans a place in the 1985 South Island team and the NZ Emerging Players team. Early in 1987 Deans travelled to Britain with the NZ Barbarians side captained by David Kirk.

1990 was to be Bruce Deans' last season in New Zealand. Two early season games for

Canterbury, an All Blacks trial and a first-class game for Canterbury Country completed his playing career. By now Graeme Bachop had become the leading halfback for both Canterbury and New Zealand. Deans headed to USA and then Ireland to play and coach before returning home to the family farm in 1995.

Bruce Deans' first-class record:

For	Matches	Tries	Con	PG	Points
Canterbury (Glenmark) 1982(12), 1983(17), 1984(15), 1985(16), 1986(15), 1987(17), 1988(14), 1989(8), 1990(2)	116	31	3	1	133
Canterbury B (Lincoln) 1981	2	1	–	–	4
Canterbury Country 1982, 1983(2), 1984(2), 1985, 1990	7	3	–	–	12
New Zealand Barbarians Club 1987	2	–	–	–	0
South Zone 1987(2), 1988, 1989	4	2	–	–	8
New Zealand Emerging Players 1985	2	–	–	–	0
South Island 1985, 1986	2	–	–	–	0
New Zealand Trials 1987, 1989, 1990	3	2	–	–	8
NEW ZEALAND 1987(3), 1988(9), 1989(11)	23	14	–	–	56
TOTALS	*161*	*53*	*3*	*1*	*221*

At Christchurch, August 16, 2019, aged 58.

Ian Matheson "Legs" Eliason (*Taranaki*) holds a record that may never be bettered in New Zealand rugby. His 222 first-class appearances for Taranaki, over a period of 18 seasons, is the most by a player for any team. Fergie McCormick played 220 for Canterbury and Wyatt Crockett 203 for the Crusaders. During the 16 seasons 1966–1981 he missed only 18 games, no fewer than eight being due to commitments to North Island, NZ Juniors or national trial teams. His only serious injury was a broken leg suffered against Southland in 1969 which forced him to miss the final four games of the season. He was a legend of Taranaki rugby and later served his union as president (2012–13), made a life member and, at the time of his death, was patron.

Before retiring from his dairy farm and moving into New Plymouth, Ian Eliason lived all his life near Kaponga where he was born and educated prior to attending Opunake High School for a little over two years, leaving in June 1960 one day before his fifteenth birthday to commence work on the family farm. All his club rugby was for the Kaponga club.

By today's standards Eliason was not a big lock forward (1.90m, 100kg), but he was very effective in the lineout and tight play. After several appearances in All Blacks trial matches, his first being in 1966, he finally won selection in May 1972 when, aged 26, he was a member of the team which, after playing NZ Juniors, toured the provinces playing a heavy schedule of eight games in 19 days. Eliason wasn't an original selection, being brought in when Sam Strahan withdrew with injury. The durable Eliason played the full 80 minutes of each provincial game, as did the captain Ian Kirkpatrick. Eliason's form improved as the tour progressed and he scored tries in each of the final two games, against Wairarapa Bush and Manawatu.

Taller locks Sam Strahan and Peter Whiting were preferred for the test series against the visiting Wallabies, but Eliason was included in the squad to tour Britain and France later in the year. Eliason played in 11 of the 32 tour games but did not appear in any of the five internationals. Peter Whiting and Hamish Macdonald were the test locking pair while Eliason and a promising young Andy Haden were regular midweek players. Although not as big and effective as the other three locks, Eliason gave his best with each appearance and was a popular tourist.

Ian Eliason's rugby career is best remembered for his sterling service to Taranaki, commencing in 1964, five days before his nineteenth birthday, and concluding in 1981 at the age of 36. His final first-class game was in March 1982 and played on his home ground at Kaponga, Victoria Park. The Kaponga club, celebrating its 75th jubilee, staged a festival game against a Taranaki XV. With Eliason in the Kaponga Invitation team were All Blacks forwards Graham Mourie (capt.), Andy Haden, Gary Knight, Mark Shaw, Geoff Old and in the backs Dave Loveridge, Bill Osborne, Murray Watts and Kieran Crowley. Eliason contributed a try to his team's 40–24 win

Ian Eliason's first-class record:

For	Matches	Tries	Points
Taranaki (Kaponga) 1964(2), 1965(6), 1966(13), 1967(11), 1968(12), 1969(9), 1970(14), 1971(12), 1972(13), 1973(13), 1974(15), 1975(13), 1976(12), 1977(16), 1978(14), 1979(21), 1980(13), 1981(13)	222	16	58
Vikings Club 1978	1	–	0
Kaponga Invitation XV 1982	1	1	4
New Zealand Juniors Trial 1967	1	–	0
New Zealand Juniors (Under 23) 1966, 1968	2	–	0
North Island 1970, 1971, 1972	3	–	0
New Zealand Trials 1966, 1967, 1970(2), 1971, 1972, 1973, 1974, 1976, 1977	10	–	0
NEW ZEALAND 1972/73	19	2	8
TOTALS	**259**	**19**	**70**

At New Plymouth, February 24, 2019, aged 73.

Ronald Rutherford Elvidge (*Otago*), who was the oldest living All Black, aged 96, at the time of his death, had long been a legendary figure because of his heroics while captaining the All Blacks in the third test of the 1950 series against the touring British and Irish Lions. Injured severely just before halftime with a damaged collarbone and a facial gash which required stitches, Elvidge resumed playing, acting in a roving role in the backline. The need for him to continue playing had been caused by the fact the All Blacks would have been down to 13 men, had he stayed off the field, because of an earlier serious knee injury to prop Johnny Simpson.

Despite his handicap, Elvidge in the second spell, when the All Blacks were trailing 3–0, loomed up on the outside of a backline attack to crash over for a try, which eventually led to the All Blacks snatching a 6–3 win, and clinching the series. Earlier in the first test at Dunedin's Carisbrook Elvidge had also barged over for a late try which enabled the All Blacks to draw 9-all.

Elvidge captained the All Blacks in the first three tests in 1950, reluctantly assuming a leadership role on the 1949 tour of South Africa. With Fred Allen standing himself down after the first two tests, and the appointed vice-captain Ray Dalton unable to win a position ahead of the preferred props Simpson and Kevin Skinner, Elvidge became captain for the third and fourth tests.

A hard-running and strong tackling midfield back, Elvidge emerged in the 1940s as one of the mainstays of the great Otago sides of that decade when under the inspired coaching of Vic Cavanagh junior there was a memorable Ranfurly Shield reign. Elvidge, as captain, quickly became one of Cavanagh's chief lieutenants and with his powerful physique was a tactical factor in setting up the second-phase rucks, on which so much of Otago's success was derived.

And even in the staid social environment of the 1940s Elvidge, who had grown up in Dunedin and had attended John McGlashan College before studying medicine at Otago University, became something of a cult hero among the rugby-loving public. One correspondent to a Dunedin newspaper claimed he was even more popular than the famous American crooner and film star of that time, Bing Crosby.

Elvidge himself was always modest about his own exploits. But in 1979–80, while compiling a history of the Ranfurly Shield, Shield Fever, this writer had cause to be grateful for the considerable help his research received from Elvidge, particularly his assessment of Cavanagh.

Elvidge became an All Black in the first post-Second World War tests, against the touring Wallabies in 1946. He partnered in the midfield the champion Kiwi army centre Johnny Smith in the 31–8 first test win at Carisbrook and with Smith injured South Canterbury's Morrie Goddard in the second at Eden Park. Elvidge scored the first of his four test tries to give the All Blacks a 14–10 win at Eden Park. He was unavailable for the following year's tour of Australia.

After his 1950 injury against the Lions Elvidge dropped out of rugby to further his medical career, becoming one of Auckland's leading gynaecologists. Elvidge never sought the limelight but because of his own experience and his medical knowledge he became a trenchant critic of rugby's international rules not allowing injury replacements. That was especially so after the New Zealand Universities' being reduced to 12 players against the touring Springboks in 1965. (*Obituary contributed by Lindsay Knight*).

Ron Elvidge's first-class record:

For	Matches	Tries	Points
Otago (Univ) 1942(3), 1943(4), 1944(2), 1945(3), 1946(3), 1947(5), 1948(8) (Union) 1950(2)	30	15	45
Otago XV 1947	1	1	3
Otago Military District 1942	1	–	0
South Island Universities 1944, 1945, 1946, 1947	4	1	3
New Zealand Universities 1945, 1946	2	2	6
South Island 1943, 1945, 1946, 1947, 1948	5	3	9
New Zealand Trials 1948(3), 1950	4	6	18
NEW ZEALAND 1946(2), 1949(14), 1950(3)	19	5	15
TOTALS	**66**	**33**	**99**

At Auckland, March 30, 2019, aged 96.

Charles Percy Erceg (*North Auckland and Auckland*) played on the wing in all three tests during the 1951 unbeaten tour of Australia. The following year, after playing in the 14–9 loss to Australia at Christchurch, he was replaced for the second test and never given a further trial for All Blacks honours. A determined runner, he was in the NZ Maori team for three years, scoring eight tries in seven games.

Percy "Sonny" Erceg was born at Waipapakauri in Northland on November 28, 1928, the son of one of the many immigrants from Dalmatia who settled in Northland. He was educated at Paparore School before attending Sacred Heart College in Auckland 1944–47. Returning home, he joined New Zealand's most northern rugby club Aupouri and the 19-year-old gained selection, at centre, for North Auckland's first game of 1948, against NZ Maori at Whangarei, and he celebrated with a try. He played three games in 1948, the Almanack noting him as "fast and clever", but the long drive of over three hours to Whangarei would restrict his availability and he chose to venture down to Auckland to further his career.

In Auckland Erceg joined Grafton club and his form as a wing soon attracted notice. He qualified, through his mother, for Maori teams and played for Tai Hauauru in its win over Tai Tokerau in the 1950 Prince of Wales Cup fixture at Whangarei. Following this game, he appeared for NZ Maori against the touring Lions and scored a try. During September he played for Auckland B in four first-class games.

Early in 1951 he was promoted to the Auckland A side and scored a try in his first game, against North Auckland. Four days later he scored in the North Island trial for All Blacks selection and, three days later, a try for North Island in the annual inter-island game. After this game the 22-year-old's name was included in the All Blacks team to tour Australia. A newspaper commented on his trial form: "Most play went to North's left winger, P. Erceg, who revealed the Maori characteristic of nimbleness but fumbled a shade too much for one in the top class. His greatest attribute is his ability to make play for himself."

After a seven-hour flight by flying boat from Wellington to Sydney the All Blacks' first game was against Newcastle. Erceg was given the honour of leading the haka and within three minutes of the game commencing, he scored a try in the corner. He made an excellent debut but his only tries in his other tour games were at Melbourne where he crossed the line twice. The team won all its games including a difficult encounter against Auckland which was played just a few hours following a long overnight flight, again by flying boat, from Brisbane.

The 1951 tourists had been issued boots with aluminium sprigs but the manager, in his report to the NZRFU, was not impressed, saying they "were not as good or safe as leather sprigs. He had never known players to be so cut about the legs and thighs, and their socks were torn to pieces. Some of the sprigs were not of regulation size, and unless they were, he was strongly opposed to their use."

After the tour Erceg enjoyed a full season with Auckland and had two games for NZ Maori, scoring two tries against Fiji. At the end of the season he was awarded the Tom French Cup for Maori player of the year. But his form appeared to slip during the latter part of 1952 and in 1953 he played only five games for Auckland. He returned to North Auckland and gave his home union two full seasons during 1955 and 1956. He was made a life member of the Mangonui sub-union in 1976.

Percy Erceg was a NZ Maori selector 1972–83 and coached the team on its 1979 tour to Australia and Pacific Islands and the 1982 tour to Wales and Spain. In 2016 he was made a life member of the Maori Rugby Board.

Percy Erceg's first-class record:

For	Matches	Tries	Points
North Auckland (Aupouri) 1948(3) (Awanui) 1954(2), 1955(11), (Kaitaia Pirates) 1956(9)	25	5	15
Auckland (Grafton) 1951(11), 1952(10), 1953(5)	26	11	33
Auckland B 1950	4	2	6
Vikings Club 1957	1	–	0
Tai Hauauru 1950, 1951	2	1	3
Tai Tokerau 1954	1	–	0
New Zealand Maori Trial 1956	1	–	0
New Zealand Maori 1950, 1951(2), 1952(4)	7	8	24
North Island 1951	1	1	3
New Zealand Trial 1951	1	1	3
NEW ZEALAND 1951(8), 1952	9	3	9
TOTALS	**78**	**32**	**96**

At Kaitaia, May 26, 2019, aged 90.

Stanley Frank "Tiny" Hill (*Canterbury and Counties*), who was always known by his nickname "Tiny", was a tough-minded, aggressive second-row forward of the 1950s and early 60s who became a fabled figure in New Zealand rugby despite, by today's standards, a relatively short span in the All Blacks. Hill, between 1955 and 1959, played only 11 tests and made only one All Blacks tour, to Australia in 1957. But his durability and uncompromising toughness were stamped indelibly on his younger, and later distinguished, contemporaries like Colin Meads, Wilson Whineray and Kel Tremain.

Though Hill has become synonymous with Canterbury, like many who have played with distinction for that union, he was originally from the North Island, growing up in coastal Taranaki at Okato. He moved to Canterbury as an army serviceman in the late 1940s after having been in the Japan occupation forces. It was there he started to develop his rugby, playing with another soldier who later became a noted All Black, Poverty Bay's Richard White. They also shared the same nickname, "Tiny", bestowed on them because they were in stature the very opposite, both being 6 feet 3 inches or, in modern measurements, 190cm. In 1956 both would be together in the powerful All Blacks pack which helped win an epic series against the Springboks.

Partly because of his army service, Hill made a late entry into provincial rugby, playing for Canterbury aged 24 firstly in 1951. He quickly became one of the mainstays of the usually strong sides fielded by that union, notably its 1953–56 shield reign, which also included a win over the Springboks. He played the last of his 88 matches for Canterbury in 1960 and captained the side in 1959 to a win over the Lions. His last game for Canterbury was a memorable shield challenge against Auckland which was lost in the last minute 19–18. In this match he enhanced his place in shield folklore when he and Tremain, who had played under him in 1959, had an altercation. After Tremain had called him "Grandad", he soon found himself prone on the ground and having to be assisted from the field.

When Canterbury took the shield from Wellington in 1953 Hill was one of the influential figures, hassling Wellington's inside backs when playing as a breakaway. Hill had not featured in calculations for the upcoming 1953/54 All Blacks tour of Britain and France, but that performance projected him into national reckoning in the next few seasons. In 1954 he made the South Island team for the first time and the Rest for a festival match against the All Blacks from the 1953/54 tour. He also was outstanding in Canterbury's shield defences, especially his role in securing the final try for a last-minute draw against Otago.

He made his All Blacks debut in 1955 in the third test against the touring Wallabies, played three tests against the Springboks in 1956, toured Australia as vice-captain in 1957, played another test against the Wallabies in 1958, then four against the 1959 Lions. In 1957 he led the All Blacks in a couple of midweek matches, thus winning inclusion among the many All Blacks captains from the Christchurch club.

His career concluded with three more domestic seasons, with Canterbury in 1960 and then, after having been transferred to the Papakura Military Camp, with Counties for 20 matches in 1961–62. A flanker for much of the first half of his career, he played most of his second half as a lock. In his era he was always seen as a giant, an impression enhanced because like Meads he always seemed to play with a scowl. But by today's standards his height and physique would not have been exceptional, a point emphasised when in a Christchurch newspaper photograph in the 1970s he was dwarfed by his basketball-playing sons, Stan and John, both of whom were Tall Blacks.

Hill's contribution to rugby continued almost to the end. He was a Canterbury selector-coach in 1975–79, then a national selector in 1981–86, president of the Canterbury union in 1996–97 and in 2006 he was awarded the Steinlager Salver for his service to the game. At the time of his death he was patron of his local Rolleston club. (*Obituary contributed by Lindsay Knight*).

Stan Hill's first-class record:

For	Matches	Tries	Con	Points
Canterbury (Christchurch) 1951(12), 1952(5), 1953(6), 1958(12), 1959(8), 1960(10), (Burnham Army) 1954(11), 1955(7), 1956(7), 1957(10)	88	2	–	6
Counties (Army) 1961(11), 1962(9)	20	1	–	3
Centurions Club 1954, 1961	2	–	–	0
New Zealand Army 1949(2), 1950(2), 1952(2), 1953(2), 1954(2)	10	–	–	0
New Zealand Services 1952(6), 1953(2), 1955(2), 1956, 1957(2), 1959(2), 1960(3), 1961(4)	22	4	–	12
New Zealand Maori 1956	2	–	–	0
South Island 1954, 1956, 1957, 1958, 1959, 1960	6	–	–	0
New Zealand Trials 1953, 1956, 1957, 1958, 1959(2)	6	–	–	0
Black XV 1957	1	–	–	0
Rest of New Zealand 1954	1	–	–	0
New Zealand XV 1956	3	–	–	0
NEW ZEALAND 1955, 1956(3), 1957(10), 1958, 1959(4)	19	–	1	2
TOTALS	*180*	*7*	*1*	*23*

At Christchurch, October 2, 2019, aged 92.

Brian James Lochore (*Wairarapa and Wairarapa Bush*) made a huge contribution to New Zealand rugby in various roles over a long period, a contribution that has rarely, if ever, been equalled. He was a splendid player, the first in the now distinguished line of All Black No 8 specialists. He was a fine captain and later a successful coach, selector and mentor.

But his most invaluable service to the game's well-being arguably came in 1995, soon after returning from that year's World Cup when he had been the All Blacks' campaign manager. With Jock Hobbs he played a pivotal role in persuading the country's leading players not to join the rebel World Rugby Corporation. The efforts of Hobbs and Lochore helped save rugby from what might have been a cataclysmic split as damaging at that of the league breakaway a century before.

Lochore, like his friend Colin Meads, achieved rugby fame playing for a small rural union. He never lost his natural humility and, like Meads, he remained true to his origins and even when the game had become professional continued to exemplify its best values.

Only a year or two out of Wairarapa College, aged just 18, he made the Wairarapa representatives in 1959, playing his first major game as a flanker for the combined Wairarapa-Bush team against the touring British Lions. He had his first All Blacks trial in 1961 but did not come under the national focus until two years later at the 1963 trials. Lochore by then had developed into a rangy, promising forward, but in case anyone missed his playing ability an Athletic Park spectator ensured that would be recognised. Whenever there was a lull in play the spectator's loud voice reverberated around the park: "Come on Lochore."

Lochore duly made the All Blacks team captained by Wilson Whineray for the 1963/64 tour of Britain and France. Until then all Lochore's rugby had been as a flanker or lock. But on tour he began to specialise at No 8, a position to which he was suited because of his height at the rear of lineouts, his deceptive speed and his cover defending skill known then as "corner flagging". Lochore was the first All Black to really define the No 8's specialist role. Since the switch to a 3-4-1 scrum formation in the 1930s the back-row position in All Blacks sides was never properly settled. It was interchanged among the loose forwards and often locks, including Meads, or even props, Ian Clarke against the 1955 Wallabies for instance, were placed there.

Despite his All Blacks elevation Lochore took some time before establishing himself. In the first part of the 1963/64 tour he was very much a midweek fringer, being chosen for only five of the first 15 matches. Lochore later admitted to feelings of frustration eased only by the wise counsel to be patient from a senior player, John Graham. Lochore played the internationals against England and Scotland but only because of injuries to Stan Meads and Waka Nathan and in New Zealand the following winter in 1964 he was overlooked for the series against the touring Wallabies.

He became a regular test selection in the 1965 series against the touring Springboks and from then until his retirement after the 1970 tour of South Africa he had an automatic place at No 8, his sequence broken only by injuries which ruled him out of two tests in 1968, against Australia and France.

Lochore became the All Blacks captain for the 1966 series against the Lions, when coach Fred Allen surprisingly chose him ahead of many who seemed better qualified, including Meads and another of Lochore's friends, Kel Tremain. It was an inspired move which vividly illustrated Allen's shrewd judgement and its wisdom was underlined by the readiness with which senior players accepted Lochore's leadership.

The crowning glory of the Lochore-Allen All Blacks tenure came in 1967 on the tour of Britain and France. Apart from a midweek draw in Wales all matches were won and the chance of a "Grand Slam" of four international wins on a British and Irish tour was lost only because the team could not play Ireland due to a foot and mouth disease outbreak. The 1967 team is still revered as one of the best of all time.

Lochore retired after the 1970 tour of South Africa which, even though every provincial match was won, was disappointing because the test series was lost. However, in dramatic circumstances he was recalled for the 1971 third test against the touring Lions, Lochore reluctantly agreeing to play at lock when the All Blacks had an injury crisis. That, of course, was far from the end of Lochore's rugby involvement.

After coaching his Masterton club, he moved to the Wairarapa Bush representative team, famously winning promotion to the provincial championship first division in 1982. He then joined the national selection panel and enjoyed notable triumphs as the All Blacks coach, including the win of the depleted "Baby Blacks" over France in 1986 and at the 1987 World Cup. He returned to the All Blacks as the 1995 World Cup campaign manager and in 2004–07 was again a national selector and mentor to both players and team management.

Honours galore came his way, including New Zealand union life membership and in 1999 a knighthood, though to his many friends rather than Sir Brian he remained "BJ". The knighthood was as much for his services to the community, to the farming industry in which he was also a leader and to conservation as chairman of the Queen Elizabeth II National Trust. His sporting interests were never insular. In his youth he had been an excellent tennis player and for some years he chaired the sports funding agency then known as the Hillary Commission. Truly, he was, in the words of Almanack co-editor Clive Akers "one of New Zealand's most highly regarded citizens". (*Obituary contributed by Lindsay Knight*).

Brian Lochore's first-class record:

For	Matches	Tries	Points
Wairarapa (Masterton) 1959(9), 1960(8), 1961(8), 1962(9), 1963(10), 1964(13), 1965(8), 1966(9), 1967(11), 1968(2), 1969(10), 1970(3)	100	15	45
Wairarapa Bush 1959, 1963, 1965, 1966, 1971	5	–	0
WJ Whineray's XV 1966	1	–	0
Centurions Club 1970	1	–	0
NZRFU President's XV 1973 (v All Blacks)	1	–	0
NZRFU Invitation XV 1973 (v All Blacks)	1	–	0
President's Overseas XV 1971 (in England)	4	–	0
North Island 1964, 1965, 1966, 1967, 1968, 1969	6	1	3
New Zealand Trials 1961, 1963(4), 1965, 1966, 1967(2), 1968, 1969, 1970(2)	13	1	3
New Zealand XV 1965, 1966	2	–	0
NEW ZEALAND 1963/64(16), 1965(4), 1966(4), 1967(15), 1968(9), 1969(2), 1970(17), 1971	68	7	21
TOTALS	*202*	*24*	*72*

At Masterton, August 3, 2019, aged 78.

 **Brian Leo "Jazz" Muller** (*Taranaki*) was one of the heaviest forwards of his era, a tighthead prop (1.85m, 114kg) and was a regular in All Blacks teams from 1967 until 1971. He made his debut in 1967 against Australia when Ken Gray was unavailable then toured Britain and France, appearing in the tests against England, Wales and France. Injury restricted his appearances on the 1968 tour of Australia, but he played in the first test. He also played in the first test against France, at Christchurch, and the following year the first test against Wales, also at Christchurch, but after selection for the second test was forced to withdraw with injury. In South Africa in 1970 Muller played in the first, second and fourth tests. He also played in all four tests of the 1971 series against the touring Lions. He played a total of 14 tests.

Muller disliked training runs, none more so than early on the South African tour when his weight rose to 120kg and coach Ivan Vodanovich ran him hard to lose weight. Yet the big man was immensely strong, often ripping the ball from opponents' clutches. He was also deceptively fast across the field; in 1967 he ran 100 yards in 11.6 seconds. He was a popular tourist, a man of few words, but had a tremendous sense of humour and enjoyed playing practical jokes on teammates and management with his array of gadgets, exploding cigarettes, wigs and masks.

Muller was born into a large family in 1942 at Eltham, being the youngest of 10 boys with three — John, Albert and Mick — representing Taranaki during the late 1940s and early 50s. The family also included three girls and their parents had immigrated from Switzerland. It was the older brothers who gave young Brian the "Jazz" name and he was to outlive all his 12 siblings. Jazz was raised on a farm and attended St Joseph's Convent School in Eltham. He worked in a cheese factory before spending 24 years at the Eltham meat works. He joined Eltham club, commencing in the fourth grade for two years, one year in junior grade, then stepped up to the seniors when aged 18.

In 1963 he made his debut for Taranaki, appearing at lock, but it wasn't until 1966 that he gained a regular place in the team. It was in June 1967 that Muller attracted national attention. Wellington visited Hawera and Muller gave All Black prop Ken Gray a torrid time in the scrums. North Island selection followed and then All Blacks honours. When free from injury he was in grand form through until 1971 when his form fell away in a long season. After three games for Taranaki early in 1972 he retired, with high blood pressure being a factor in his decision.

In later years Jazz Muller suffered from arthritis and became a self-imposed hermit, living alone in Eltham with no telephone or television and he seldom ventured into town. His home was decorated with all his rugby memorabilia. There was considerable media attention when he revealed having trimmed his hedge with a Masport lawnmower. As a result of the publicity Masport gave him a new mower. He was immensely proud of being an All Black and will be fondly remembered as one of the real characters of the amateur era.

Jazz Muller's first-class career:

For	Matches	Tries	Points
Taranaki (Eltham) 1963, 1965(2), 1966(11), 1967(11), 1968(11), 1969(9), 1970(3), 1971(13), 1972(3)	64	3	9
Taranaki Colts 1965	1	1	3
North Island 1967, 1968, 1969	3	–	0
New Zealand Trials 1967(2), 1968, 1969, 1970(2), 1971(2)	8	2	6
NEW ZEALAND 1967(10), 1968(6), 1969, 1970(14), 1971(4)	35	3	9
TOTALS	**111**	**9**	**27**

At New Plymouth, December 12, 2019, aged 77.

Samuel Cuningham Strahan (*Manawatu*) played his best rugby during three tours commencing in 1967 as 22-year-old locking partner with Colin Meads in Britain and France followed by the 1968 tour to Australia and the 1970 tour to South Africa. In addition, he joined Meads in home tests against Australia (1967) and against France (1968). The experienced gained playing alongside Meads in 11 tests and 11 tour games saw Strahan regarded as the outstanding lock in the country during the early 1970s. In the days before lifting in lineouts was allowed, the tall Strahan had the agility to leap above opposing forwards to take clean two-handed ball from the thrower. His experience was missed during 1971 when he made himself available only for his Oroua club. In 1972 injury after selection prevented him playing on the All Blacks' internal tour, but he partnered Peter Whiting in the three-test series against Australia and he would have been a valuable asset to the All Blacks on the end-of-year tour to Britain and France. However, as in 1971, Strahan was unavailable, placing family and farm commitments ahead of a long four-month overseas tour. In 1973 he played in each of the four games of the internal tour and the test against England. He played a total of 17 tests, and the 1.91m, 101kg lock developed into an outstanding lineout ball-winner, several critics rating him the best seen in over a decade. When he retired in 1974 the Almanack commented: "The retirement of Strahan meant the loss of the outstanding lock in the country."

Born on Christmas Day 1944, Sam Strahan joined Oroua club in 1962 following his education at Apiti School, Huntley Preparatory School and Wanganui Collegiate. He was a Manawatu third grade rep in 1962 and junior grade rep the following year. He travelled to Britain and watched some of the 1963/64 All Blacks' tour games without imagining that, three years later, he would be joining Colin Meads and other tourists on a similar tour. After three senior club games in 1965, Strahan, aged 20, made his debut for Manawatu. The next year he played for NZ Juniors against the Lions.

Following the retirement of Stan Meads, the search was on in 1967 for someone to partner his brother. Strahan attracted attention with his excellent lineout work during Manawatu's Ranfurly Shield challenge against Hawke's Bay. His performance earned him a place alongside Colin Meads in the North Island forward pack in which only Strahan and Jazz Muller were not All Blacks. Two weeks later this same forward pack, with the exception of Ken Gray (injured and replaced by Jack Hazlett), played Australia in the Jubilee test at Wellington. Two months later Strahan was off to Britain with the All Blacks, establishing himself as a test lock.

In 1969 Taranaki's Alan Smith was preferred by the new selectors for the series against Wales, but Strahan returned for the South African tour the next year where he played the best rugby of his career, particularly during Colin Meads' absence due to a broken arm. Strahan scored tries in successive games, against South West Africa and Transvaal.

Manawatu challenged North Auckland for the Ranfurly Shield in 1972, a game drawn 4–4, despite Strahan and locking partner John Callesen winning the lineouts 35–9. Strahan continued to represent Manawatu until 1974 when he retired after failing to regain All Blacks selection. He continued to play for his club and made the occasional appearance for Manawatu when in time of need, most notably in 1976 when John Callesen was injured, Strahan played the last four games of the season, the first two being the first defences of the recently won Ranfurly Shield.

Strahan later coached Oroua club and was made a life member in 2002. He was president of Manawatu union 2003–06 and made a life member in 2007. Four days before his 75th birthday Sam Strahan died suddenly, in his sleep, at his home at Kiwitea. Only four days prior to his death Strahan, the last surviving member of 10 forwards who played in the 1967 tests against England, Wales and Scotland, had travelled to Taranaki to deliver the eulogy at teammate Jazz Muller's funeral.

Sam Strahan's first-class career:

For	Matches	Tries	Points
Manawatu (Oroua) 1965(3), 1966(10), 1967(10), 1968(7), 1969(12), 1970(2), 1972(9), 1973(11), 1974, 1975, 1976(4)	70	2	6
Manawatu-Horowhenua 1966	1	–	0
Evergreens Club 1974	1	–	0
New Zealand Barbarians Club 1977	1	–	0
New Zealand Juniors 1966	2	–	0
North Island 1967, 1968, 1969	3	–	0
New Zealand Trials 1967(2), 1968, 1969, 1970(2), 1974	7	–	0
NEW ZEALAND 1967(12), 1968(11), 1970(14), 1972(3), 1973(5)	45	3	10
TOTALS	**130**	**5**	**16**

At Kiwitea, December 21, 2019, aged 74.

Douglas Dawson Wilson (*Canterbury and Wellington*) was one of the earliest of what has become a long line of All Black five-eighths who have been produced by Christchurch's Boys' High School. But unlike many of those who have followed him, the likes of Andrew Mehrtens, Aaron Mauger and Dan Carter, his tenure in All Blacks sides was brief. He was taken on the tour of the British Isles and France in 1953/54, but while he played the internationals against Scotland and England, he was limited to just 14 of the tour's 36 matches. And while his slim build probably best suited him to the first-five position, he had only two matches there, all of the others being in the midfield.

In the early 1950s Wilson played in some strong High School Old Boys club sides and first made the Canterbury representative side in 1952, playing mainly at second-five outside another All Black, John Hotop. However, an injury to Hotop midway through the 1953 season meant more chances for Wilson at first-five and a series of impressive performances, in which his speed in broken play and flair for blindside attacks were evident, took him into the All Blacks touring team. Those performances included three tries in one of the early trial matches, a try for the South Island, and being in the Canterbury team which spectacularly took the Ranfurly Shield from Wellington.

He was again at first-five in the 1954 inter-island match and for most of Canterbury's shield defences that season. A transfer in 1955 took him to Wellington where he was again used more in the midfield, including scoring a try in a failed shield challenge against his old union.

Wilson received only sporadic chances with Wellington in the next few seasons and was not included in any of the national trials held to select the All Blacks for the 1956 test series against the touring Springboks. But in 1957 his career had a brief revival when he was placed on the wing for much of Wellington's season, and his pace and try-scoring knack were well exploited. He scored two tries in the shield defence against Wanganui and another when the shield was lost to Otago. He finished the season with 10 tries in all in his nine appearances, including four against Southland and two against Taranaki.

Once again, he was little used in the 1958 season, ending his first-class career, where it had begun, in Canterbury when in a fund-raising fixture he played for the Cantabrians against Canterbury. He showed he retained his try-scoring penchant by scoring two in the Cantabrians' win.

Wilson was not the only young back taken on the 1953/54 tour to be quickly discarded. Others in their early twenties like wing Stuart Freebairn, midfield backs Colin Loader, Brian Fitzpatrick,

Jim Fitzgerald and first five-eighths Guy Bowers also never played for the All Blacks again. Clearly developing players for the future was not a priority in the planning of the then national selectors. (*Obituary contributed by Lindsay Knight*).

Doug Wilson's first-class record:

For	Matches	Tries	Con	PG	Points
Canterbury (HSOB) 1952(10), 1953(6), 1954(10	26	9	–	–	27
Wellington (Oriental) 1955(9), 1956(2), 1957(9), 1958(2)	22	17	–	1	54
Wellington XV 1958	1	–	–	–	0
Wellington B 1955, 1956(2)	3	–	–	–	0
Centurions Club 1955(2), 1957	3	4	1	–	14
Cantabrians Club 1958	1	2	–	–	6
South Island 1953, 1954	2	1	–	–	3
New Zealand Trials 1953	3	3	–	–	9
New Zealand Touring Team 1954	1	–	–	–	0
NEW ZEALAND 1953/54	14	5	–	1	18
TOTALS	*76*	*41*	*1*	*2*	*131*

At Wanganui, May 18, 2019, aged 88.

PROVINCIAL REPRESENTATIVES

Anthony Westray "Tony" Aston (*New Zealand Universities*) toured Australia with the 1960 team but did not play in either of the two 'tests' against Australia Universities, his appearances being in the six minor fixtures. In 1962 the speedy wing represented NZ Universities against Canterbury. A noted athlete he ran against Peter Snell on many occasions. At Auckland, January 19, 2020, aged 81.

Francis William "Frank" Baigent (*Golden Bay-Motueka*) appeared at fullback in 1946 for a combined Nelson-Marlborough-Golden Bay-Motueka against West Coast-Buller before making his solitary appearance for his union the next season. He had served in New Caledonia during the war. At Nelson, October 26, 2019, aged 97.

Graeme Reid Bassett (*Otago*) played for games on the wing in 1958 and in 1959 scored three tries for Otago B against North Otago. His rugby career has often been confused with his identical twin brother Ian who also played on the wing with Graeme for both Otago University and Otago. At Palmerston North, August 9, 2019, aged 81.

Leslie John Bradley (*North Auckland*) was a wing in 56 games for his union, scoring 31 tries. He had a national trial in 1971. At Whangarei, October 22, 2019, aged 70.

Brian Peter Brown (*Manawatu and Taranaki*) made seven appearances for Manawatu 1957–58 before moving to Taranaki where he played once in 1961 and two further appearances in 1964. He was a prop forward. At New Plymouth, August 23, 2019, aged 81.

Arnold Max Bryant (*Manawatu*) was a No 8, and later prop, in 42 games 1958–63. In addition to scoring five tries he kicked 27 conversions and 17 penalty goals. Later worked at Ruakura Research Centre. Member of the NZ Order of Merit (*MNZM*) 2010 for services to the dairy industry. At Hamilton, October 2, 2019, aged 82.

Owen Neville "Rusty" Campbell (*Counties*) played 55 games 1960–66 and represented the Counties-Thames Valley combined side against 1966 touring Lions. At Papakura, November 1, 2019, aged 80.

Peter James Carde (*Wellington*) made four appearances during 1957 as well as appearing for the B team 1957–58. He was later a Catholic priest in Fiji for 30 years. At Havelock North, March 3, 2019, aged 82.

Ian Edward "Hoagey" Carmichael (*NZ Services*) was a policeman in Wellington when playing for Combined Services against West Coast in 1969. At Wellington, March 11, 2019, aged 72.

Gary Haswell Catley (*Waikato and Wellington*) was a five-eighth playing 51 games for Waikato 1962–65, 67, 69. He was in Wellington 1966 and represented that union in 12 games. A son of All Black Has Catley, Gary had a national trial in 1966. At Hamilton, October 27, 2019, aged 77.

George Law Cawkwell (*Auckland*) played three games for Auckland in 1941 and games for army teams in 1942. He became a Rhodes Scholar and played for Oxford University 1946–47, Barbarians Club and was selected for Scotland for one international in 1947, against France. At Oxford, England, February 18, 2019, aged 99.

Paul Anthony Cowan (*Poverty Bay and Manawatu*) was a fullback for Poverty Bay in 21 games 1956–59 and for Manawatu in five games in 1961. He scored 99 points in first-class rugby. At Havelock North, April 6, 2019, aged 81.

Edward Arthur "Artie" Cumpstone (*King Country*) was a midfield back making one appearance in 1949 and three the next year. Brothers Fred, John and Laurie also represented the union. At Te Kuiti, January 26, 2020, aged 91.

Laurence George 'Hoot' Cumpstone (*King Country*) was halfback in 43 games 1955–62 and appeared for the combined Wanganui-King Country side in 1956. At Otorohanga, November 10, 2019, aged 86.

Peter William Danks (*Hawke's Bay*) was a pupil at Napier High School in 1944 when selected to play on the wing against Wairarapa. At Hastings, April 13, 2019, aged 93.

James Norman Darling (*Otago and North Otago*) was a fullback playing 14 games for Otago 1957–58 and 13 games for North Otago 1962–63. He also appeared in first-class games for Otago B 1955 and 1965 and for Otago Country in 1967. At Dunedin, April 1, 2019, aged 83.

James Benney "Jim" Darrah (*Thames Valley*) played 57 games 1956–64 and had a national trial in 1957. At Hamilton, July 31, 2019, aged 87.

Stuart James Dermody (*Southland*) played four games in 1970 from Tokanui club. At Christchurch, May 26, 2019, aged 68.

John Gray "Jack" Dougan (*Wellington*) was a five-eighth playing 67 games 1947–57 scoring 11 tries and 12 dropped goals. He received a national trial in 1957 and his first-class career of 91 games included appearances for Wellington B and Colts teams, Centurions club and Olympians club. At Masterton, November 8, 2019, aged 93.

Greenwood George "Jim" Duncan (*Poverty Bay*) was a halfback playing 53 games 1950–56 and for Poverty Bay-East Coast 1955–56. He played in a national trial in 1953. He later served on Poverty Bay RU management committee and was chairman 1979–83. At Maroochydore, Queensland, August 2019, aged 89.

Norman Eathorne (*Bay of Plenty*) made one appearance, against North Auckland, in 1953. At Napier, July 17, 2019, aged 91.

Ronald Albert Eaton (*Manawatu*) made one appearance, against Royal NZ Navy, in 1948. At Feilding, November 28, 2019, aged 95.

Matthew John Farrell (*Hawke's Bay*) played three games in 1954 from the Napier Marist club. At Napier, August 24, 2019, aged 86.

Morris Robert 'Morrie' Geenty (*Bay of Plenty*) was halfback in five games during 1960. He was from Kaingaroa Forest club. At Rotorua, August 18, 2019, aged 83.

Owen Bertram Gibbons (*Golden Bay-Motueka*) was one of few deaf players to play provincial rugby, appearing at prop or lock in each of his union's seven games of 1955. At Auckland, May 9, 2019, aged 90.

Roger Bernard William Gill (*Wellington*) made seven appearances for his union in 1968 and a further two in 1970. At Picton, September 26, 2019, aged 76.

Owen William Gleeson (*Manawatu*) was a loose forward who, after serving in the Korean War, played in 24 games 1954–55 and 1957. Later, he followed his brother Jack as Manawatu sole selector-coach 1970–74. He was president of Manawatu union 1980 and 1986 and made a life member in 1987. At Palmerston North, December 28, 2019, aged 89.

Paul John Goldsworthy (*Bush and Hawke's Bay*) played 16 games for Bush 1968-69, kicking 86 points. In 1971 the loose forward played four games for Hawke's Bay. At Woodville, January 7, 2020, aged 70.

Melville Walter Gudgeon (*Counties and Hawke's Bay*) was a flanker appearing in 28 games for Counties 1968–70 and twice for Hawke's Bay in 1977. At Hastings, April 11, 2019, aged 70.

Denis Astley Harding (*Otago*) was a medical student playing at halfback in seven games during 1958. The same year he also appeared in a national trial and for South Island Universities. At Auckland, March 7, 2019, aged 83.

Robin Melville Harris (*Auckland*) was a five-eighth in 14 games 1952–53, represented NZ Universities in 1953 and took part in three of the trials for selection for the 1953/54 All Blacks tour to Britain. At Auckland, April 17, 2019, aged 86.

Harold Bert 'Harry' Hayward (*Manawatu*) was halfback in three games during 1941 prior to serving overseas as a pilot in the RNZAF. In 1947 he made one further appearance for his union. MBE (Mil) 1962 for services in the training and education of airmen cadets joining RNZAF. At Lower Hutt, September 16, 2019, aged 101.

Robert Luke "Bob" Hooper (*Bay of Plenty*) was a halfback from Rotorua club playing in the union's sole fixture of 1943. Then in 1946, now with Kahukura club, he played in all three fixtures. At Te Puke, December 14, 2018, aged 95.

Desmond Milton Hughes (*Nelson and Wellington B*) generally played at No 8, playing 22 games for Nelson 1957–59 followed by 17 first-class games for Wellington B 1960–67. At Auckland, July 9, 2019.

Donald Keith Hunt (*Taranaki*) played five games in 1962, one game in 1964 and two games in 1965. At New Plymouth, February 14, 2019.

John Barrie Skilbeck Hutchinson (*Wellington and Auckland*) played 88 first-class games 1949–59 including 13 for NZ Universities 1950–59 and All Blacks trials 1957–59. He moved many times between Auckland and Victoria universities, being at Auckland 1949–50, Victoria 1951–52, back to Auckland 1954–55, Victoria 1956–58, and finally back at Auckland 1958–59. He represented Auckland in 21 games and Wellington in 32 games. At Auckland, February 14, 2019, aged 92.

Winston George "Win" Jones (*Manawatu and Hawke's Bay*) played five games for Manawatu in 1956 followed by 17 for Hawke's Bay 1957-58, 60, 62. At Christchurch, January 29, 2020, aged 83.

Bruce Charles Kirkland (*Golden Bay-Motueka*) made one appearance, against Nelson, in 1968. At Auckland, July 12, 2018.

Rodericke Charles Garrick Leonard (*Bay of Plenty*) was a wing appearing once in 1958 with a further five games in 1959. At Tauranga, April 25, 2019, aged 80.

Horace Lewis (*Poverty Bay, North Harbour, Otago, Hawke's Bay, Central Vikings and East Coast*) appeared for six provincial teams commencing with Poverty Bay in 1987. He was with North Harbour 1991–92, Otago 1993, back with North Harbour 1995, Hawke's Bay 1996, 98, Central Vikings 1997, back to North Harbour 1999 from where he became a loan player to East Coast that year before settling to wear the Coast jersey for the next 11 seasons to 2009. His 23 years of first-class rugby totalled 129 games, mostly for East Coast (*87 games*), North Harbour (*12*) and Hawke's Bay (*14*). In 1992 the loose forward made one appearance for NZ Maori when he was a replacement during a tour of Pacific Islands. At Ruatoria, April 12, 2019, aged 50.

Wesley Owen "Bud" Lisle (*South Island Railways*) had his sole first-class appearance in rugby union in the 1954 inter-island fixture played by employees of NZ Railways. Played at Rugby Park, Christchurch, Lisle scored a try on the wing for his team. Strangely, in the days when a union player switching to league was banned from any return to union, Lisle was a regular Wellington league representative 1953–63. Yet he was not spotted by union officials. In 1957 he established a club league competition in Manawatu, was a life member of St George club (*Wellington*), Manawatu league and NZ Universities league. In 2002 he was made a Member of the NZ Order of Merit (*MNZM*) for services to rugby league. At Papakura, June 30, 2019, aged 88.

Victor Allan McCollum (*Thames Valley*) was halfback for one game in 1947, against Bay of Plenty. At Paeroa, October 7, 2019, aged 94.

Roderick Bruce McDonald (*Thames Valley*) played three games for his union in 1965, twice at fullback and once at centre. At Thames, June 29, 2019, aged 78.

Robert Morton "Bob" McGill (*Manawatu*) was hooker in 1953 for one game, against a Wellington XV. At Palmerston North, April 7, 2019, aged 86.

Robert Ian "Bob" McHardy (*Thames Valley*) was a lock in 10 games for his union 1954–56. At Thames, July 16, 2019, aged 87.

Douglas Grant "Chum" McLeay (*Auckland*) played once for the A team, in 1972 and also three first-class appearances for Auckland B, two in 1970 and one in 1972. At Auckland, August 18, 2019, aged 73.

Noel Robert McMillan (*West Coast*) played at prop in 13 games 1963–65, one appearance in 1967, then 12 further games 1970–71. At Greymouth, June 25, 2019, aged 82.

Eric McQueen (*Manawatu*) played four games for his union 1947–48 and returned in 1951 for one more appearance. At Palmerston North, May 29, 2019, aged 92.

Hupa James "Jim" Maniapoto (*Auckland, Bay of Plenty and Thames Valley*) enjoyed a long career of 188 first-class games commencing with 25 for Auckland 1962–64. Generally playing at lock, he had 105 games for Bay of Plenty 1965–75 and three games for Thames Valley 1977. He was a regular in NZ Maori teams, 29 games 1964–73, toured Australia with the 1964 NZ Colts team, was in the NZ Juniors team that met the 1965 Springboks, and represented North Island in 1971. One honour that eluded him was an All Blacks trial. At Tauranga Taupo, Lake Taupo, June 16, 2019, aged 76.

Kenneth Alan Mansfield (*Nelson Bays*) made one appearance in 1980, at prop, but it wasn't until 1988 that he returned for three more games. At Nelson, May 23, 2019.

Campbell Laird Mitchell (*Manawatu and King Country*) played four games for Manawatu in 1959 and for the combined Manawatu-Horowhenua side against the Lions. He moved from Massey College to Lincoln College in 1960. The wing was a regular NZ Universities representative 1959–62 and included a major tour of California and British Columbia. In 1962 he played four games for King Country, scoring three tries. In total, he scored 16 tries in his 30 first-class games. At Auckland, May 25, 2019, aged 80.

Warren Moran (*Auckland*) played four games in 1958 and 10 in 1960, the wing scoring 10 tries. At Auckland, August 13, 2019, aged 82.

Barry Nichols (*Wellington B*) appeared in eight first-class games for Wellington B 1965–67. He represented NZ at softball 1968–72. At Wellington, September 24, 2019, aged 77.

Robin Gerard "Bob" O'Neill (*Manawatu and Waikato*) was a loose forward in 55 games for Manawatu 1961–65, captaining the Manawatu-Horowhenua combined side against the 1965 Springboks. In 1967 he played six games for Waikato. At Christchurch, September 11, 2019, aged 82.

Richard Ambrose "Dick" O'Sullivan (*Auckland B*) was a forward playing three first-class games for Auckland B in 1969 during its tour to Wanganui, Horowhenua and Wairarapa. At Auckland, July 20, 2019.

John Hayes Perkins (*Wairarapa*) was hooker in 15 games for Wairarapa 1960–63. At Palmerston North, January 21, 2019, aged 82.

Richard John "Dick" Phelan (*Canterbury*) was a three-quarter who played once in 1962, nine games in 1966 and one in 1967. He also appeared in 13 first-class games for Canterbury B and Country teams. At Auckland, June 20, 2019, aged 79.

George Ned Pivac (*North Auckland*) was a forward from Kaitaia club in five games between 1958 and 1961. He was the father of Wayne. At North Shore, June 7, 2019, aged 86.

Kingi Michael Porima (*Bay of Plenty*) made one appearance in 1966 and two the following year. At Rotorua, July 29, 2019, aged 82.

Bruce James Read (*Hawke's Bay*) made one appearance at five-eighth, against Bay of Plenty, in 1953. At Hastings, February 19, 2019, aged 86.

Donald John Riesterer (*Otago, Bay of Plenty, Taranaki and Wellington*) was a loose forward who commenced his first-class career with Otago 1950–51 (*3 games*), then two games for Bay of Plenty 1952, 18 for Taranaki 1954–55 and, finally, four games for Wellington 1956–57. He was later mayor of Opotiki 1989–2001. At Whakatane, February 27, 2019, aged 88.

Robert Gerard Henry "Bob" Rogers (*Manawatu*) was a wing appearing in six games in 1963, two in 1965 and two in 1967. He represented NZ Universities in 1963. At Browns Bay, North Shore, October 11, 2019, aged 76.

Roy Robert Shanks (*Golden Bay-Motueka*) was a three-quarter playing in two games 1950 and all three of his union's games of 1951. At Auckland, March 4, 2019, aged 92.

William Anthony "Tony" Short (*Manawatu*) was a three-quarter in 33 games 1957–60 and returned in 1963 for one further game. At Palmerston North, September 6, 2019, aged 81.

Alan James Sissons (*Horowhenua*) was a flanker playing 38 games for his union 1959-64. At Levin, January 21, 2020, aged 81.

Frank Graham Soper (*Golden Bay-Motueka*) played nine games 1947–49 appearing at halfback, five-eighth and wing. At Takaka, November 20, 2018, aged 94.

Alan William Stevens (*Otago*) was halfback in 13 games 1958–59. Later Otago coach during 1978–79. At Dunedin, March 21, 2019, aged 85.

Michael Tamoaieta (*North Harbour*) appeared in 18 games for his union 2017–18 and 10 games as a prop for the Blues 2018. At Auckland, March 1, 2019, aged 23.

Ernest James "Pat" Thomas (*Golden Bay-Motueka*) played in four games in 1956 with one further appearance in 1959. As a referee he controlled one first-class game in 1967, between Golden Bay-Motueka and Taranaki Colts. At Westport, August 18, 2019, aged 89.

Garry Thompson (*Poverty Bay*) played 73 games for his union 1961–71, captaining the team 1966–68. A loose forward, he was in the Poverty Bay-East Coast combined sides which met the 1965 Springboks and 1966 Lions. At Gisborne, December 10, 2019, aged 80.

Robert Stewart "Bob" Turner (*Hawke's Bay*) played on the wing in nine games 1974–75. At Hastings, August 20, 2019, aged 69.

Maurice Anthony "Tony" Waldin (*Hawke's Bay*) appeared in three games 1965–66. At Hastings, March 28, 2019, aged 76.

Edward George "Ned" Wilson (*Marlborough*) played in the forwards in eight games during 1954. At Greymouth, May 24, 2019, aged 89.

Frederick Charles Wilson (*Manawatu and Taranaki*) made his debut for Manawatu in 1953, then eight games in 1954 and three in 1957. A loose forward, he played two games for Taranaki in 1958. At Timaru, October 3, 2019, aged 85.

Francis Patrick "Frank" Woods (*Bay of Plenty*) made one appearance in 1956, nine during 1960 and one in 1961. Died July 20, 2018, aged 81.

Rhodes Moorhouse "Rod" Yates (*North Auckland*) was a three-quarter playing in 60 games from 1956 until 1964. He represented NZ Maori in 1961. Died December 7, 2019, aged 85.

DISTINGUISHED OPPONENTS

Johannes Theodorus Claassen (*South Africa*) was well-known to New Zealanders during his involvement in five tests series between the two countries. As a tall lineout forward, he was lock in 28 tests 1955–62 appearing in the 1956 series in New Zealand and the 1960 series in South Africa. He was then Springbok coach during the 1970 and 1976 series. Finally, he was manager of the 1981 Springboks in New Zealand. At Pretoria, January 6, 2019, aged 89.

Michel Celaya (*France*) played in 11 of the 13 games on the 1961 tour of New Zealand including all three tests. On tour he generally appeared at the back of the scrum but also at lock and flanker. He played 50 tests between 1953 and 1961. At Biarritz, January 1, 2020, aged 89.

Michel Crauste (*France*) was a loose forward playing 63 tests 1957–66, captaining France during the 1961 tour of New Zealand. He also played in the 1964 test against Whineray's team. At Pau, France, May 2, 2019, aged 84.

Lloyd Clive McDermott (*Australia*) played on the wing for Queensland against the 1962 All Blacks and in the two tests that followed. At Sydney, April 6, 2019, aged 79.

Bruce Elias Malouf (*Australia*) played only one test, being hooker at Christchurch in 1982. Playing for New South Wales against the 1980 touring All Blacks he suffered a broken jaw. At Gold Coast, November 14, 2019, aged 63.

Wilfred Rosenberg (*South Africa*) toured New Zealand in 1956 but injuries restricted his appearances to only five games. He did, however, play at centre in the third test, at Christchurch, scoring a try. He made his Springboks debut during the 1955 series against the touring Lions and after playing against France in 1958 he had a successful league career with Leeds and Hull clubs. At Herzliya, Israel, January 14, 2019, aged 84.

James Terence Small (*South Africa*) was a wing in 47 tests 1992–97, nine being against the All Blacks including the 1995 Rugby World Cup final. At Johannesburg, July 10, 2019, aged 50.

John Edward Thornett (*Australia*) was a grand forward who did much to raise the standard of Australian rugby. He played 37 tests 1955–67, 12 being against New Zealand. He played at flanker, lock and later prop and was Wallabies captain from 1962. At Bateman's Bay, January 4, 2019, aged 83.

Chester Mornay Williams (*South Africa*) was a wing in 27 tests 1993–2000, six being against the All Blacks including the 1995 Rugby World Cup final. At Cape Town, September 6, 2019, aged 49.

FIRST-CLASS REFEREES

Rodney Hill (*North Harbour and Wellington*) commenced his first-class career with North Harbour in 1985 (*two games*) before moving to Wellington where he controlled 53 games 1987–1996. From 2011 until 2017 he was NZ Rugby's high-performance referee manager. At Wellington, June 16, 2019, aged 67.

Robert Leslie "Bob" Hines (*Thames Valley*) controlled 20 games 1957–65 including two Ranfurly Shield fixtures and five provincial games against Wallabies and British Lions. At Te Aroha, June 29, 2019, aged 85.

Ian Donald Lobb (*Taranaki*) controlled 11 games between 1970 and 1977. At New Plymouth, January 13, 2019, aged 79.

Mervyn Robert Williamson (*King Country*) controlled two home games 1973–74. He was King Country RU president 1989–90. Died in a car accident near Cambridge, April 25, 2019, aged 86.

ADMINISTRATOR

Raymond Aubrey Ian Harper (*Southland*) gave excellent service as a player, coach-selector, administrator and benefactor, to rugby and sport in general, especially in Southland. As a centre Harper played 44 times for Southland 1948–54, including wins over the Wallabies in 1949 and 1952 and over the British Lions in 1950. He was a Southland selector-coach 1961–67 and on the union management committee 1965–86. He served on the New Zealand council 1975–86 and managed the All Blacks on two 1980 tours, to Australia and Fiji and then to North America and Wales. A master builder, Harper was a huge and practical contributor to the Southland community and his chairmanship of the local licensing trust coincided with significant funding for a range of sports and facilities, notably the ILT indoor stadium. This was the venue for his funeral service which was attended by 600. In his honour the stadium for the day was renamed the Ray Harper Stadium. He was awarded the QSM in 1991 and for his services to rugby the Steinlager Salver in 2012. Noted rugby writer Bob Howitt was his son-in-law. At Invercargill, April 4, 2019, aged 91. (*Obituary contributed by Lindsay Knight*)

AMENDMENTS

to 2019 edition

Page 25	Scott Gregory's middle name is John, not William.
Page 34	Referee v Argentina (at Buenos Aires) was M. Raynal (France).
Page 52	Game was played at Invercargill, not Dunedin.
Page 64	Opposition scored 8 conversions, 86 points.
Page 66	Total points against is 129. Game v Japan was played at Narbonne, the score 67–0. Score v France 7–16. Score v South Africa 30–42.
Page 201	Lavaka, not Lavalea, scored against East Coast. Kelly, not Winter, was referee v Thames Valley.
Page 210	N. Briant was referee v Counties Manukau. Score v Waikato was 19–33.
Page 220	R. Kelly was referee v South Canterbury (October 12).
Page 257	S.J. Savea played 212 games.
Page 260	G. Jackson. Add July 28 SR s-f Lions v Waratahs at Johannesburg.
Page 261	M. Lash. Delete Oct 10 Southland v Auckland.
	D. Macpherson. Add June 2 East Coast v Poverty Bay at Tolaga Bay.
	J. Nutbrown. Add April 27 SR Hurricanes v Sunwolves at Wellington.
Page 263	B. Pickerill. Add Sept 29 HC Wairarapa Bush v South Canterbury at Masterton.
	N. Webster. Delete Nov 1 NZ Heartland v Vanua XV at Taupo.
	M. Winter. Add Nov 1 NZ Heartland v Vanua XV at Taupo.
Page 264	P. Williams. Delete March 31 Brumbies v Waratahs. Delete Sept 29 Wairarapa Bush v South Canterbury.
Page 300	New Zealand Barbarians Schools. Patrick Teddy (Napier BHS) was omitted from the listed squad.
Page 324	Second semi-final of Premiership. Counties Manukau 24 Waikato 14 at Hamilton.
	Premiership final. Canterbury 52 Counties Manukau 29 at Christchurch.
Page 370	Wellington's 2018 status was Championship, not Premiership.
Page 400	September 19. 1.3 million euros should read 11.3 million euros

to 1984 edition

Page 114	Pita Coffin played against Counties only. Hutana Coffin played in the last four games.